Drama, Theatre, and Identity in the American New Republic

Drama, Theatre, and Identity in the American New Republic investigates the way in which theatre both reflects and shapes the question of identity in post-Revolutionary American culture. Richards examines a variety of phenomena connected to the stage, including closet Revolutionary political plays, British drama on American boards, American-authored stage plays, and poetry and fiction by early republican writers. American theatre is viewed by Richards as a transatlantic hybrid in which British theatrical traditions in writing and acting provide material and templates by which Americans see and express themselves and their relationship to others. Through intensive analyses of plays both inside and outside of the early American "canon," this book confronts matters of political, ethnic, and cultural identity by moving from play text to theatrical context and from historical event to audience demographic.

JEFFREY H. RICHARDS is the author of *Theater Enough: American Culture and the Metaphor of the World Stage, 1607–1789* (1991), and *Mercy Otis Warren* (1995), and has edited three other books. He has published articles in *Early American Literature, William and Mary Quarterly*, and other journals and collections. He has taught at the University of North Carolina, Duke University, and is currently Professor of English at Old Dominion University.

CAMBRIDGE STUDIES IN AMERICAN THEATRE AND DRAMA

General editor
Don B. Wilmeth, *Brown University*

Advisory board
C. W. E. Bigsby, *University of East Anglia*
C. Lee Jenner, *Independent critic and dramaturge*
Bruce A. McConachie, *University of Pittsburgh*
Brenda Murphy, *University of Connecticut*
Laurence Senelick, *Tufts University*

The American theatre and its literature are attracting, after long neglect, the crucial attention of historians, theoreticians, and critics of the arts. Long a field for isolated research yet too frequently marginalized in the academy, the American theatre has always been a sensitive gauge of social pressures and public issues. Investigations into its myriad of shapes and manifestations are relevant to students of drama, theatre, literature, cultural experience, and political development.

The primary intent of this series is to set up a forum of important and original scholarship in and criticism of American theatre and drama in a cultural and social context. Inclusive by design, the series accommodates leading work in areas ranging from the study of drama as literature to theatre histories, theoretical explorations, production histories, and readings of more popular or para-theatrical forms. While maintaining a specific emphasis on theatre in the United States, the series welcomes work grounded broadly in cultural studies and narratives with interdisciplinary reach. Cambridge Studies in American Theatre and Drama thus provides a crossroads where historical, theoretical, literary, and biographical approaches meet and combine, promoting imaginative research in theatre and drama from a variety of new perspectives.

BOOKS IN THE SERIES

1. Samuel Hay, *African American Theatre*
2. Marc Robinson, *The Other American Drama*
3. Amy Green, *The Revisionist Stage: American Directors Re-Invent the Classics*
4. Jared Brown, *The Theatre in America during the Revolution*
5. Susan Harris Smith, *American Drama: The Bastard Art*
6. Mark Fearnow, *The American Stage and the Great Depression*

7. Rosemarie K. Bank, *Theatre Culture in America, 1825–1860*
8. Dale Cockrell, *Demons of Disorder: Early Blackface Minstrels and Their World*
9. Stephen J. Bottoms, *The Theatre of Sam Shepard*
10. Michael A. Morrison, *John Barrymore: Shakespearean Actor*
11. Brenda Murphy, *Congressional Theatre: Dramatizing McCarthyism on Stage, Film, and Television*
12. Jorge Huerta, *Chicano Drama: Performance, Society and Myth*
13. Roger A. Hall, *Performing the American Frontier, 1870–1906*
14. Brooks McNamara, *The New York Concert Saloon: The Devil's Own Nights*
15. S. E. Wilmer, *Theatre, Society and the Nation: Staging American Identities*
16. John H. Houchin, *Censorship of the American Theatre in the Twentieth Century*
17. John W. Frick, *Theatre, Culture and Temperance Reform in Nineteenth-Century America*
18. Errol G. Hill, James V. Hatch, *A History of African American Theatre*
19. Heather S. Nathans, *Early American Theatre from the Revolution to Thomas Jefferson*
20. Barry B. Witham, *The Federal Theatre Project*
21. Julia A. Walker, *Expressionism and Modernism in the American Theatre: Bodies, Voices, Words*
22. Jeffrey H. Richards, *Drama, Theatre, and Identity in the American New Republic*

Drama, Theatre, and Identity in the American New Republic

JEFFREY H. RICHARDS

CAMBRIDGE UNIVERSITY PRESS
Cambridge, New York, Melbourne, Madrid, Cape Town, Singapore, São Paulo

CAMBRIDGE UNIVERSITY PRESS
The Edinburgh Building, Cambridge, CB2 2RU, UK

Published in the United States of America by Cambridge University Press, New York

www.cambridge.org
Information on this title: www.cambridge.org/9780521847469

© Jeffrey H. Richards 2005

This book is in copyright. Subject to statutory exception
and to the provisions of relevant collective licensing agreements,
no reproduction of any part may take place without
the written permission of Cambridge University Press.

First published 2005

Printed in the United Kingdom at the University Press, Cambridge

A catalogue record for this book is available from the British Library

ISBN-13 978-0-521-84746-9 hardback
ISBN-10 0-521-84746-x hardback

Cambridge University Press has no responsibility for
the persistence or accuracy of URLs for external or
third-party internet websites referred to in this book,
and does not guarantee that any content on such
websites is, or will remain, accurate or appropriate.

For Elizabeth Quantz Richards,
who endured

Contents

Acknowledgements		xi
	Introduction	1
1	American identities and the transatlantic stage	17
PART I	Staging revolution at the margins of celebration	35
2	Revolution and unnatural identity in Crèvecoeur's "Landscapes"	37
3	British author, American text: *The Poor Soldier* in the new republic	60
4	American author, British source: writing revolution in Murray's *Traveller Returned*	85
5	Patriotic interrogations: committees of safety in early American drama	105
6	Dunlap's queer *André*: versions of revolution and manhood	124
PART II	Coloring identities: race, religion, and the exotic	141
7	Susanna Rowson and the dramatized Muslim	143
8	James Nelson Barker and the stage American Native	166
9	American stage Irish in the early republic	188
10	Black theatre, white theatre, and the stage African	211
PART III	Theatre, culture, and reflected identity	239
11	Tales of the Philadelphia Theatre: *Ormond*, national performance, and supranational identity	241

12 A British or an American tar? Play, player, and spectator in Norfolk, 1797–1800   259
13 After *The Contrast*: Tyler, civic virtue, and the Boston stage   296

Notes   316
Bibliography   362
Index   384

Acknowledgements

FOUR CHAPTERS HERE (2, 4, 9, AND 10) APPEAR IN ALTERED AND expanded form from their original publication in *William and Mary Quarterly* 55 (1998), 281–96; *Early American Literature* 33 (1998), 277–90; *New Hibernia Review* 3.3 (1999), 47–64, and *Comparative Drama* 34 (2000), 33–51, respectively. I wish to thank the editors of those journals for permission to reprint unchanged portions of the original articles. I direct continuing appreciation to the librarians at Old Dominion University, especially those in Cataloguing and Special Collections, and Mona Farrow in Microforms, Beverly Barco in Interlibrary Loan, and the acquisitions librarian, Pamela Morgan, for their unflagging help in locating or procuring materials. The rare book and manuscript department of the Swem Library at the College of William and Mary has been gracious in assisting me with St. George Tucker materials. I also thank the Clement Library at the University of Michigan for permission to cite a manuscript letter in their possession. A number of colleagues have suggested works to read or angles of attack to employ or provided encouragement: Imtiaz Habib, Jane Merritt, Mike McGiffert, Sandra Gustafson, John Saillant, Heather Nathans, Tom Kitts, Dennis Moore, and the anonymous reviewers of the manuscript, as well as two whose passing I still lament, Everett Emerson and Norman Grabo. To each I am indebted. I greatly appreciate the efforts and support of Don Wilmeth and Victoria Cooper in seeing this project to publication. I am also grateful to students in several graduate seminars at Old Dominion University where a few of these ideas were tested out. As always, my real inspiration comes from those closest to home: Stephanie Sugioka, Sarah Richards, and Aaron Richards. With them, my gratitude carries with it no confusion.

Introduction

ALTHOUGH THE OUTLINE HISTORY OF DRAMA AND THEATRE IN early America has been told before, with the exception of Royall Tyler's *The Contrast*, relatively little has been said *in detail* about the particular plays or performances that graced – or disgraced – the stages and pages of American theatres and notebooks in the early republic. It might be a stretch to call the citizenry of the incipient United States a theatre-going nation in 1775; it would be considerably less difficult to say so in 1825. Yet in either case, plays and stage performances seemed to occupy some part of the consciousness of many men and women, certainly the seaboard elite, but additionally a number of people not restricted to the wealthy and educated. The Continental Congress during the Revolution thought it best to proscribe theatrical amusements, but the British military on American soil asserted the opposite, launching seasons in New York, Boston, and Philadelphia when they occupied those cities. After the war, debates ensued in many areas about the appropriateness of resuming stage entertainments in a republic – were they not the delight of the late oppressors of the land? But except in Boston, the forces for restoring theatre prevailed in relatively short order. By 1790, nearly every coastal city of size, as well as many smaller towns and such inland locales as Richmond, had some professional or semi-professional theatrical troupe performing in public venues. By 1800, a number of these cities had built or were building new theatres to replace the smaller pre-Revolutionary or converted structures put to use in the immediate aftermath of the war. And by 1825, larger theatres than these were being constructed or contemplated to meet the increased demand by a more accepting and diverse populace.[1]

Although most histories of American drama and theatre stress native authorship, the fact remains that actual spectators at American early republican theatres saw very few plays written by persons resident in the new United States or acted by persons born in North America. Given the rapid rise of theatre as a widely subscribed entertainment, one might inquire as to what exactly Americans were seeing and how this fare influenced both American writers and spectators as they tried to establish themselves as selves in the former colonies. Whether before the war or after, English-language Americans almost exclusively encountered playbills promising British fare. In cities or towns with German- or French-speaking populations, one might find occasional performances in those languages; but the vast majority of plays and performances in the early United States were English-language of British provenance. The few American dramas in English that did make it to theatres all show the marked use of British templates in their construction, even if the matter and setting appear to be "native" to American locations and situations. As will be discussed in a subsequent chapter, Philadelphians between May 1792 and July 1794 would have been exposed to over 160 evenings of professional theatre in their city, but only on two of those, only slightly more than one percent of the total, would they have witnessed a main play written by someone living in the United States. Some of the others might have been inspired by French or German dramatists, but the overwhelming majority were written by British playwrights for British stages. To speak of "American" drama or theatre is necessarily to confront "British" texts and practices, even to the point where one might plausibly insist that the theatre of the newly independent nation was in reality simply a provincial stage of the British empire.[2]

Nevertheless, as I will argue in some specific cases, these plays from London or Dublin were not always enacted or printed or read or seen without some local American factors altering the context in which they would be perceived. It has been long understood, for instance, that Tyler's *The Contrast*, the best-known play by an American from before 1800, bears the signs of two plays being performed in New York while Tyler was there: Richard Brinsley Sheridan's comedy of manners *The School for Scandal* and John O'Keeffe's operetta *The Poor Soldier*. But what does it mean that *The Poor Soldier* – a rather feeble play with a great many engaging songs – was the most popular afterpiece on American stages before 1815? To what extent did American audiences nationalize O'Keeffe's comic rendering of Irish soldiers home from fighting for the British army in America? Did they see this as a "British" play, or was it to some extent their own, converted either by acting or staging or by projection on the part of the audience into something approximating an

"American" amusement? Such are the kinds of questions the chapters in this volume seek to address.

At the same time, when Americans do pen their own plays, they must choose the particular British texts on which to model their own. One overwhelming factor in American playwright choice of template is certainly popularity. Tyler knew that to refer to *The Poor Soldier* in the dialogue of *The Contrast*, which he does explicitly, would be to evoke an immediate and knowing response; by April 1787, the month *The Contrast* premiered in New York, O'Keeffe's musical had already entered into the playgoing vocabulary of theatrically minded Americans, and the Irish character Darby, to whom Tyler's Yankee Jonathan directly alludes, had become nearly a household name, at least in New York. But for a playwright like Judith Sargent Murray, mere reference to a well-known British comedy would not be enough; as she cast about, perhaps, for something familiar on which to ground her attempt to construct a native play, she decided to borrow heavily from a text that itself portrayed a transatlantic situation, Richard Cumberland's *The West Indian*. As a sentimental comedy, *The West Indian* had few rivals on American stages; most of the comedic writing then in vogue was sharply satiric and distinctly anti-sentimental. Cumberland, however, found a ready audience in the American colonies, then later, in the new United States. For her play of the American Revolution, *The Traveller Returned*, Murray could borrow character types and plot situations from *The West Indian* without making any direct allusions in the way Tyler does to O'Keeffe. Not only could she provide her audience with that air of familiarity that theatre managers thought the spectators required, but she also could demonstrate the differences between a play that valorizes London versus one that affirms Boston – to the favor of the latter.

The matter of influence may or may not have produced anxiety among playwrights, but it became an inescapable fact of the literary and cultural life of the new republic. Tyler and Murray are but two of the American writers who look at what their contemporaries are paying money to see in order to construct their texts. For a playwright like William Dunlap, the early republic's most prolific professional dramatic author, both British and German plays provide models or sources for direct translation; he makes, in essence, no particular claim to originality or American genius. Despite his attempt to find the right formula that would produce a paying script – Dunlap was a manager during much of the 1790s and had to worry about receipts – he rarely created a vehicle that lasted more than a handful of performances. His most popular play was probably his translation of Kotzebue's *The Stranger*, a perennial favorite in American theatres, but never billed as Dunlap's. One of those that were performed, only that usual handful, his relatively original tragedy *André*, is known today as a play about the Revolution; but as I seek to demonstrate below, that play is so implicated in Dunlap's understanding of his *ur*-text, Thomas Otway's *Venice Preserved*, as to cause us to inquire whether nationality is even an appropriate rubric for a drama that makes a virtual hero of an enemy spy. The same might be said for a less audacious and ambitious play than Dunlap's, the comedy *Independence* by the young South Carolina writer William Ioor. Despite its title, nothing in Ioor's play speaks directly to the American strand. It is based on an English novel, is set in England, and contains only English characters. No one gives a Huzza! for George Washington or speaks in reverent tones of Yorktown or Bunker Hill, as other more overtly patriotic plays do in the 1790s and early 1800s. Rather, the test of its Americanness seems to be simply its authorship; the audiences in Charleston that witnessed the premiere would have known who wrote it, and the printed version proudly announced his even more local origins as a son of the then-deserted town of Dorchester, South Carolina. But again, one wants to ask what people saw: a reminder of their vaunted British heritage, now that the bloodshed of the Revolution was being forgotten? Or did they patriotically convert the English pastoral scene to an equally pastoral South Carolina one – devoid of slaves – and take pride in the title word more than the literal setting? Ioor was fully aware of the power of patriotic appeal; his other play overtly depicts a famous battle of the Revolution, Eutaw Springs. Even in that play, however, he equivocates to some degree on national identity, mixing his sympathies among American and British combatants, as if such a thing as nationality were so "fluid," in Heather Nathans's phrasing, as to be always negotiable in the world of capital T Theatre. In other words, when Americans thought of or participated in the theatre, they entered into a cultural space that was transatlantic and without fixed national borders, even though the content may have appeared nationalistic and local.³

Most studies of early American drama take the emerging or incipient nationalism of the colonies or early United States as the chief point of such plays, their ostensible lack of literary merit often excused in order to get to the "rise" of American drama – a rise that cannot be too quickly brought to the twentieth century. To be sure, much can be learned from this perspective. What I argue here, however, is that *identity* is a complex and often paradoxical matter, especially when rendered through drama and theatre. It is not restricted to nationality, even if from American stages one could have heard appeals to a developing ideology of nationalism. Although the early republican American stage was occasionally a testing-ground for questions of nationality, more often the issues it evoked or represented were ones that might have seemed more immediate than the often vague and not entirely coherent notions of citizenship and allegiance then circulating. Susanna Rowson's *Slaves in Algiers* has been read in recent times as an appeal to American liberties in the context of the Barbary captivity crisis, in which American sailors had been captured on the high seas by North African corsairs, but the play invokes a myriad of ethnic and other identities, many with complex genetic histories. Certainly the figure of Ben Hassan brings forward a British tradition of unpleasant Jewish stereotypes, while Muley Moloc is the oddly familiar and flat stage Muslim. But when looked at theatrically, Rowson's Algerian dey, in particular, rides a peculiar stage history into the Anglo-American playwright's text, most of which has nothing to do with contemporary politics or Barbary corsairs. Theatregoers in 1794–1796, the years of greatest popularity for *Slaves in Algiers*, would have recognized the stage Muslim tyrant as a type from a variety of earlier plays, some of which are clearly reflected in Rowson's Moloc. Negotiating religion and ethnicity in the context of contemporary events and stages past and present creates interpretive difficulties for a play that appeals to desires for strong female characters or a triumphing American ideology of human rights.[4]

Reading the writing and performance of *Slaves in Algiers* illustrates much of what I intend to pursue. Essentially, this book puts forward three interrelated problems: the significant un-Americanness of the American theatre and what that means for the identity of the institution of the stage; the recognition that most American plays, like most British dramatic texts, are influenced primarily by other plays more than by current events; and the ways in which American spectators might have seen themselves in the drama and performances of that theatre, particularly as the plays reflected and shaped a host of identities, many of them having little directly to do with the political re-creation of the colonies as a distinct "nation." To be sure, Americans were busy with a variety of rituals that expressed some understanding of an "imagined" national "community," in the terms of Benedict Anderson. As David Waldstreicher describes, publicized toasts, street rituals, parades, and other gatherings helped groups make claims for national identity that were often at odds with those of other groups. But the very rivalry in the streets between Federalists and Democratic-Republicans, or whites and blacks, to name but two types of difference, indicates the volatility of identity during the formative years of the early republic. In addition, because nationality was in a fluid stage, people in the United States would have found themselves allied to or rejected from a variety of communities, some based on "objective" registers of difference – dialect, perceived skin color, or sex – some on proximity – "from" Savannah or Newburyport. Curiously, the theatre, staffed often by itinerant actors or troupes, created a community as well, the community of theatregoers, who shared in the perception of a common set of stage practices, actors, and repertoire. Therefore, in a world of reconsidered communal identities, the stage functioned as a supra-community, whose traditions in some ways superseded those of the culture immediately outside its doors, even as they acknowledged them, in the syntax and diction of the theatre.[5]

Even the term *identity* is problematic for this period. Identity is only meaningful when placed in opposition to something else. An early seventeenth-century Nansemond man living along the river in Virginia that still carries that name might have considered himself distinct in part from members of the other tribes in the Powhatan confederation, but he would have shared with tribes to the east and north a common language, Algonkian. However, he probably never imagined himself an "Indian" and thus forcibly connected to people he considered as his hereditary enemies to the west and south until the Englishman Captain Smith and cohorts called such a distinction to his attention. An eighteenth-century British American woman faced with the fact of "independence" would have had to learn a new distinction, too, perhaps not so different from the Nansemond to other Algonkians; yet at the same time, she would also have to negotiate new uncertainties in her position as woman, as white, as not French in 1793 or not Irish in 1798 (years of sudden and large migration from St. Domingue and Ireland), as New Englander or Carolinian, as once Anglican now Episcopal, in addition to not British but then again not entirely not-British either. Not surprisingly, persons resident in the newly declared United States would have been somewhat uncertain about what exactly made up "identity." The confusions could come from a variety of markers: class, religion, race and ethnicity, gender, region or locale, as well as nationality. As Waldstreicher remarks, "In the late eighteenth century, identity itself had become increasingly unstable. Highly mobile young people, particularly young men in cities, found that they could make and remake themselves by manipulating appearances." Beyond the kind of social masking that a Benjamin Franklin or his con-man alter ego Stephen Burroughs entertains, the theatre, of course, is that cultural space where the making and remaking of appearances occurs nightly, where identities are roles and roles change as plays change. What I entertain in these pages is the interpretive problem of how to read plays and performances in terms of a world where identity is volatile and where the oppositions that create identity themselves often shift or mushroom or wither in a relatively short time. The meeting of audience and stage on the level of identity is a constant negotiation, inflected by social and political conditions on the one hand, but given shape by long-standing dramatic and theatrical practice on the other. What makes the theatre even more complex to discern as a register of American identities is the explicit foreignness of it.[6]

One measure of foreignness centers on the very nature of theatre itself in a land that prides itself on natural virtue. Colonial Americans used theatrical tropes for a variety of contexts, including politics, but they did so from a position of some skepticism about literal theatre. There was a big difference between the providential "theatre of God's judgments," whereby individuals played out parts true to themselves and assigned by the divine (settling New England or fighting the Revolution, for instance), and the small stage theatre of deliberate falsification, much abhorred by Puritans, Quakers, and others, including radical American whigs.[7] As John Howe remarks of the tension between figural and literal theatre:

> Though the metaphor of politics as theatre could provide insight into the revolution's gleaming place on the stage of history, the theater, with its calculated distinction between appearance and reality, offered a deeply troubling referent for civic affairs, especially in a republican culture suffused with worry over hidden conspiracies and thus sensitive to the public dangers that arose when appearance and reality diverged. The theatrical transaction between actors and audience was both complicated and ambiguous. While actors concealed their true identities behind the characters they created on stage, speech, action, and scenery combined to transport audiences into far realms of imagination. Such a complex, calculated, and constantly shifting process of discursive negotiation seemed altogether unsuited to the honest conduct of republican politics.[8]

To bring theatre to British America meant some kind of negotiation, whether between communities and theatre managers to have it at all, or between spectators and players, in terms of what people would see and how they would see it. As a British institution on republican soil and as a presentation of shifting, unstable identities, theatre could irritate or please, depending on the degree of willingness of republican audiences to accept the playacting of identities as a dimension of American culture, British plays as the primary repertoire, and their own power to transform productions when occasion suited.

Another aspect of the theatre that brought foreignness to North America was a specialty of the eighteenth-century British stage, ethnic typing, a specialty reiterated and transmuted in the American theatre. Rowson's "American" play parades a variety of such types – Jew, Muslim, Spanish, as well as English and Anglo-American – in a style familiar to aficionados of British drama. To see an Irish character on stage, in another instance of ethnic typing, was in the 1790s or early 1800s to be linked to a long, and largely derogatory, history of representation in English drama of the people of Eire. In the 1790s, however, an Irishman on stage was not always simply a laughable Paddy but might have reminded Americans of the Irish rebellion, an event that brought a vocal, liberty-seeking set of individuals to the United States in search of a sympathetic, anti-British population that would harbor them. What tensions in American theatres were created by 1798, the year the uprising in Ireland was put down by British troops, between the desire to laugh at a dialect-speaking fool and the feelings of sympathy or antipathy real Irish political exiles produced in English-majority American cities? Quite possibly none at all, given the political battles of that year occasioned by the XYZ Affair and the Alien and Sedition Acts, yet the surviving texts of American plays with Irish characters show a particular interest in staging and restaging Irish characters as divergent variants of a type. Indeed, Irishness becomes peculiarly implicated in Americanness in the post-Revolutionary period, a trope for sympathy or mockery or both. Because Irish people were in the early republic a small minority, their presence on stage signals another history, a complex one of representation and evocation within the theatre itself.

Other ethnic groups with loaded histories also show up on American boards, including Native and African Americans. In many ways, the ethnic distinction between these two groups is elided in the theatre. In George Colman, Jr.'s *Inkle and Yarico*, a popular British production that had surprising vitality on American stages, the identity of Yarico as Indian overlaps her cultural position as African, one that Colman confuses by speaking of the color of Indians as both tawny and black. But the issue raised by the play – amidst songs and comedy – is miscegenation and the loyalty of an Englishman, Inkle, to a woman of color, Yarico. To sell her into slavery, Inkle's choice, seems entirely consonant with American practice; to be forced to relent and declare for her as an equal, the play's conclusion, would appear to raise disquieting questions about race relations and market forces. Nevertheless, if the play ever did tweak any conscience in America, that tweaking did not stop it from being produced in many cities over two decades, including theatre centers in the South.

Less affirmative about ethnic integrity are such American plays of the early nineteenth century as James Nelson Barker's *The Indian Princess* and Samuel Woodworth's *The Forest Rose*. Both musicals, like *Inkle and Yarico*, they can hardly be held to too strict an accounting of reality; still, they build on popular assumptions about what constitutes race, or race as a represented state. Barker is the first American playwright to deal fully with the Pocahontas myth, but his understanding of the Rolfe–Princess relationship takes some of its shape from lines explored by Colman's English comedy. Ethnicity comes to be a markedly theatrical concept; the labels Islamic or Irish or Indian or African have little to do with the living beings who claim those identities and more with previous and necessarily distorted representations on stage. Despite the literal presence of Native peoples in playhouses, such as the Cherokee chiefs who both sat in the boxes and performed on the stage of the new John Street Theatre in New York in 1767, the "Natives" in dramas more often resembled "natives" from other plays – plays originally written by London playwrights – rather than the hungry, besieged, persecuted, and embattled nations who lived on the American frontier.[9]

Anglo-American stages offer a distinctive set of African types. Even a closet dramatist like St. Jean de Crèvecoeur makes use of a crude dialect to portray his servants of loyalists and patriots in the Revolutionary War play, "Landscapes." Blacks often become registers of other issues, as they do for Crèvecoeur, reflecting the virtues or vices of their respective masters. But again, certain British plays often shape Americans' rendering of their characters. One of the most influential plays on the depiction of blacks in American theatre is Isaac Bickerstaff's 1768 *The Padlock*. His comically abused character Mungo, as played in the colonies and United States by Lewis Hallam, Jr., was much applauded and served as a direct influence on a character created by Royall Tyler in his now-mostly-lost comedy, *May Day in Town* (Jarvis, "Royall Tyler's Lyrics"). Both

Crèvecoeur and Tyler generate sympathy for their Africanized characters through speeches on abuse, but both authors equally avoid looking at the causes with too keen an eye. Several decades after those two writers, the dramatist Samuel Woodworth cares nothing for sympathy; his figure of Rose is simply a comic butt, abused, yes, but never allowed to assert any form of subjectivity. She suffers particularly at the hands of the stage Yankee, that figure made popular in Tyler's *The Contrast* as a lovable naif, but by Woodworth's time, a type that in at least one of its manifestations lacks any sympathy for others – especially blacks. Benevolence and paternalism have been succeeded by naked cruelty, all in the name of humor, all sung to fetching music for the delight of the heterogeneous American audience.

If the Indian question or the African question gets peculiar theatrical answers, so does the history question. How does one make American history something entertaining? Dunlap tried it with *André*, failed, he thought, then bowdlerized his own text to produce a chronically popular July Fourth vehicle, *The Glory of Columbia, Her Yeomanry!* Sack the tragedy, praise the farmer captors of the English spy, sing and dance. Some early writers on the Revolution – Mercy Otis Warren and Hugh Henry Brackenridge, for instance – took a tragic tone, even when the action was not classically tragic in scope, for the purpose of elevation and education of a population in need of lessons on civic virtue. Later writers, however, found that sermons on stoicism did not match the mood of the rising generation. Indeed, the Revolution itself did not always translate well to the stage. With just one relatively minor motif – the portrayal of committees of safety – one can see the fireworks and flag-waving that became the signs of the Independence spectacle were often less on playwrights' minds than the doubts about democracy that adhere to the committee trope. It is not as if any American playwright fully understood the dramatic significance of the committees, those patriot inquisitorial bodies that became the arbiters of political correctness during the early Revolutionary period, but writers such as Crèvecoeur, Robert Munford, and Murray comprehended readily enough that when the loyalty of citizens is put on trial by other citizens, matters of innocence and guilt can become woefully muddied in short order. Thus the kind of stereotyping that the stage indulges in ethnic characterization can yield to more subtle, politically tinged discourse and plot devices and allow the plays to speak as registers of different kinds of anxieties from those represented by race alone.

INTRODUCTION   11

How much actors and managers thought of the *problems* of ethnic representation can only be guessed at, at least until some economic circumstance called their attention to them; more likely, their minds were on seasons, those periods spent in particular cities, as well as tickets and what plays could be enacted with the particular actors in the company. By the early nineteenth century, the large urban theatres had their own house casts; seasons ran from fall through spring. In those days before the long single run, managers had to provide an ever-shifting variety of plays: *Merchant of Venice* on Wednesday, the musical *Robin Hood* on Friday, an Elizabeth Inchbald comedy on Saturday. Much can be learned about cultural practices and theatrical tastes from analyzing a season. For example, a novel such as Charles Brockden Brown's *Ormond* makes occasional but telling references to the Philadelphia theatre. The novel takes place during the yellow fever epidemic of 1793, but other action occurs just before and just after. Given the kinds of disguises donned by characters in that novel of shifting identities, what might the theatre have to say about the way the novel portrays the instability of nationality? If one looks at the plays offered in Philadelphia at the time of the novel, one finds dimensions of Brown's often elusive text that can be exposed more fully insofar as they resonate with something being performed on the boards of the old, then the new theatres in town. By the same token, a smaller venue, Norfolk, about which no contemporary novel offers much insight, may serve in miniature to represent the problematic nature of identity and spectatorship in late eighteenth-century United States theatres. For instance, in 1798 that city witnessed one of the rare representations of Dunlap's *André* outside New York. What else did the managers of the main southern traveling company have to offer the citizens of a slaveholding seaport town only lately come to the sophistication of supporting an active theatre? What does it mean that the most popular play in Norfolk between 1797 and 1800 was John C. Cross's *The Purse*? To what extent was the repertoire adjusted or altered to meet local conditions? Such questions force us to see drama not as a fixed text but as a fluid set of changeable signs whereby something British becomes something American without being, exactly, either one.

Up the James River from Norfolk, at his home in Williamsburg, a lawyer named St. George Tucker turned away from his legal papers from time to time to keep active a creative streak. Tucker had supported the Revolution, participated in it as a soldier, and emerged as an important interpreter of law in the new republic. On occasion he wrote poems, including a published work on liberty, but he also wrote plays. Despite his efforts to interest managers, particularly in Philadelphia, Tucker never had the pleasure (or agony) of seeing one of his texts converted into an acted drama; but that did not stop him from using drama to render contemporary affairs. From near the end of the Revolution to the end of the War of 1812, Tucker wrote a number of topical and other dramas that indicate how potent the medium was for him. A vigorous Jeffersonian by political creed, unlike such more theatrically successful playwrights as Tyler, Murray, and Dunlap, the Virginian reflected a more Francophile political line than was popular among the elite after the Jacobin terror. Tucker, indeed, remained hostile to Britain and British interests, later excoriating the Federalist foot-dragging, even downright secessionist sentiment, in the Anglophile fear to confront British depredations on American shipping. His two War of 1812 plays are often pulled right from the newspapers – a technique that as Ginger Strand has observed had been employed by Revolutionary-era playwrights to rouse interest in the patriot cause. Tucker sent his plays to friends, but it seems that the circulation world of these efforts was not large. His fame came as a lawyer, but he desired expression as an American playwright. His opposition to British foreign policy perhaps lay behind his writing, for it was the theatres' British-only policy on the boards – with a few, occasional exceptions – that prevented any class of American playwrights from developing. Sometimes, a self-taught writer like the Philadelphian John Murdock grabbed the attention of managers long enough to earn a performance or two and publication of his plays, but it was never for long, and best to have a day job on top. For every nominally successful Murdock, how many Tuckers were there in early republican America, writing plays, finding no stage that would take them, then consigning their efforts to some trunk that would be emptied and its contents discarded by descendants more in search of redeemable notes than grandpa's or grandma's old plays? Tucker's plays were saved because Tucker was at his death a famous man, even if for other reasons than playwriting. Others, perhaps, were not as fortunate.[10]

Far from being a theatrical history wasteland, the period under review here, 1775–1825, contains an extraordinary wealth of cultural artifacts that even such a study as this only barely exposes. A play is an artifact, insofar as it leaves a trace: a published text, a manuscript, a notice in the newspaper, a reaction in a diary. It is not merely a good play or bad, theatrically successful or not, even American or not, but a hieroglyph whose meanings

INTRODUCTION 13

are layers and threads of history, cultural practice, spectator point of view, location of production or publication. Held simply in the light of traditional dramatic history, an early American play looks "bad." Examined under the microscope of theatrical history, an early American play is "rare." But examined under a variety of lights and lenses, an American play leads to a British play or a tradition or a local circumstance or a personality or a coded reference to an unseen but present servant in the gallery or on stage as he moves the scenery. Each turn of the artifact reveals something else: a worn patch, a heretofore unseen thread, a fragment of something older and more distant. *The Contrast* is not the only such American artifact; so is John O'Keeffe's *The Highland Reel*, performed in Norfolk in June 1797 and April 1800 with different casts and altered characters, not only from the London original but from each other. There is a whole world of practices and assumptions contained in the staging of an Irish playwright's Scottish fantasy in slaveholding Virginia beyond the cold fact of its having been performed.

To return to a moment to grandma's old plays – at least some that were saved – the career of Mercy Otis Warren deserves some mention in this context of identities. Like Tucker in her choice of form, and preceding him, Warren turned to drama to frame her responses to the growing crises of pre-Revolutionary Massachusetts. The daughter of a merchant, sister to a lawyer, wife to a farmer and Plymouth public servant, and mother of five sons, Warren declared her own identity outside such traditional demarcations for a woman by writing poems that she often shared with friends and relatives, then, in 1772, by writing and publishing a play critical of policies maintained by the royal governor of Massachusetts, Thomas Hutchinson. Warren wrote a total of five plays, all published; so notorious was her career – the political woman of the 1770s and 1780s who demanded the public eye through her dramas – that plays not by her, including the anonymous *The Blockheads*, *The Motley Assembly*, and *Sans Souci*, were often attributed to her by contemporaries and continued to be so by later historians. In her early career as dramatist, Warren had political goals, to strike points against tories and for whigs; but her consciousness of being a woman who wrote satire, and her later turn to tragic verse drama in the English tradition, suggests that she never lost sight of the particular problems raised by dramatic form. For her, a woman writing a play and a woman in a play evoked such a complex of feelings and considerations that her allusion-thick dramas make for difficult reading. A woman could be something like Liberty, as in the enigmatic figure who appears at the end of *The Group*; or she could be a Spanish historical character made to voice American republican sentiments, as Donna Maria does in her verse drama *The Ladies of Castile*. But a woman could also be a playwright who, unlike Tucker, had few, or possibly no, opportunities to see a produced play. Warren thought of herself as a patriotic American, a thorough republican, a whig, a Democrat of the Jeffersonian stripe, but she never abandoned her identities as mother, daughter, sister, wife, or friend – in short, her sense of self as woman. Her plays are not just about women and in fact make few assertions about their being by a woman, but they serve as a register for the often insoluble contradictions of how a woman in America is represented in dramatic, or even theatrical, form. Although she never had a play staged, Warren inspired other American women, most certainly Judith Sargent Murray, who did. Yet at one time, in the late 1780s, she hoped to have her verse dramas performed – on the London stage. That did not happen – but what does it mean for an American female republican playwright to seek fame at Drury Lane? Warren's identities, like those of other women represented on American stages, are not easy to sort out.[11]

The book ends not with a triumph but with another playwright's struggle to deal with the institution that ironically would give him his only lasting fame. Royall Tyler, no longer the young playwright in New York but a jurist in Vermont, never quite forgot the professional theatre, even though he stopped writing for it. In a number of poems, he recurs to the stage but in ways that show his own confusion about the cultural location of the commercial stage. Tyler's memories of his own early essays upon the stage, as a college student in a renegade production of *Cato*, become intertwined with a conservative, religiously inspired morality that makes the presence of professional theatre in his America something not to celebrate but regret. Tyler was not the voice of the future, but of the past – yet that did not stop him from prophesying. His poetic cautions about the stage suggest that at least for the generation of Warren, Tucker, and Tyler, theatre could never be taken as a neutral cultural commonplace, accepted by tradition, but had to be reevaluated in the context of a continuing memory of a past tied to Addison and London, via Washington and the memories of a virtuous Revolution.

The purpose of this book is to investigate some of the ways the American theatre and a few playwrights struggled with the bold outlines and curious details of national, cultural, and ethnic representation to American audiences. There is not really a master narrative; the book

INTRODUCTION

follows a roughly chronological progression but deliberately brings back plays discussed previously for second and sometimes third looks, each time taking a different angle on the text or its performance. At the same time, the chapters below make no claim to be comprehensive; instead, they represent attempts to probe particulars, investigate phenomena that, like the announced subjects of Washington Irving's *Sketch-book* or Nathaniel Hawthorne's *Twice-Told Tales*, are oftentimes more out of the way than in the broad avenue; in other words, they are not always the stops that the tourist bus of early American culture normally makes. As a consequence, I do not have a chapter on *The Contrast*, although Tyler's famous comedy may be the most referred-to play in the book; nor do I have chapters that reaffirm developing American nationalism, as if that were the only point of the drama. Rather, I seek to complicate the whole matter of American identities during this period, especially as the drama takes them up or throws them back to audiences that may not know themselves quite exactly, in the wake of the Revolution, who they really are.

The themes discussed above run through more than one chapter; and the amalgamation will present a more thickly detailed vision of early American drama and theatre than that provided by the survey histories. Chapter 12, on the Norfolk theatre, brings together many of the plays and ideas discussed earlier into the context of theatrical seasons in a single location, but each chapter is intended to interlock with and complicate the matter in the others. One of this book's implicit arguments is that knowledge – the more the better – of what Americans saw on stage and what and how they tried to write for the theatre has the potential of deepening or even changing our views of what life in the early republic was like. But the nature of that knowledge – the particular plays appearing in particular cities at particular times – makes the difference between a set of amusing items and the discovery of new rooms or the opening of long shut windows in the rambling hodge-podge of a house that is Revolutionary and post-Revolutionary American culture.

The more explicit argument rests on the confusions in identity raised by the transatlantic nature of the theatrical and dramatic enterprise in America. In that sense, the book represents a challenge to historicist and cultural critical methodologies, although without discarding them entirely. For the confusions of identity registered by stage plays in early republican America come not simply from external political and social conditions in the United States, but also from internal theatrical ones based on an Anglo-American understanding of what theatre is supposed to be. In other words, generic and institutional conventions, shaped by centuries of practice in the British Isles, resist local American cultures, even as they bend or twist to absorb them. These confusions can be illustrated as well in the work of Mercy Warren, who sits at the beginning of a nationally conscious drama. Warren was a fifth-generation *Mayflower* descendant – indeed, so was her husband, James – a famous whig, a well-known anti-federalist, an ardent revolutionary, but even she could not imagine her dramatic enterprise without some consideration of the British tradition of playwriting and performance. If a Warren, who may never have actually seen either an amateur or a professional production of a play, felt her understanding of dramatic identity tied to London, how much more so the committed theatre people – the British-born actors on American stages, for example, or the American playwrights (and spectators) who had read and seen nothing but British plays? This is not to reduce American drama to a mere subspecies of British, but to suggest that Americanized identities on stage often begin in forms familiar in a British package. The chapters here, therefore, query the degree to which American drama is American – or is something more transnational, a quality constantly negotiated in a play space governed by rules imported during the colonial era. It is not Jonathan's Yankeeness that is so much at stake here, as his, well, English Irishness or Yorkshireness, that is, his role on stage as a dialect-speaking peasant. Indeed, theatrical identity is confusing, heterogeneous, not always contained by clear markers of gender, race, class, ethnicity. Even plays whose narratives contain no surprises may surprise when taken from Covent Garden and plunked down in New York or Norfolk, all while doing their darnedest to resist surprise altogether.

I

American identities and the transatlantic stage

IN MANY WAYS, IDENTITY IS BOTH THE OLDEST AND THE NEWEST theme for American writing and culture. Who are we? asked residents of the new United States as they faced the fact of war with the once-parent country. Who are we? they asked again, when peace was declared and something had to be made of independence. Who are we? Americans still ask after more than two centuries of "freedom," decades of identity politics, the retreat of former great powers before the overwhelming military and economic power of the United States, and the dynamic of a population influenced by immigration from lands hardly imagined by men and women in the early republic. It is the inevitable result of the question in a pluralistic society that "we" are perhaps no nearer to an answer now than were the founders.

One of the registers and molders of public understandings of Revolutionary American identity was the theatre. From its humble origins in the colonial period to the all-pervasiveness of the stage in the mid-nineteenth century, the American theatre displayed before its citizens a variety of depictions of characters and types that gave back clues about the ways in which residents of the United States imagined who they were – or were not. Even though most of the plays that eighteenth- and early nineteenth-century Americans encountered were of British authorship and purported to take place in locations other than North America, the popularity of some dramas offers insight as to what mirror was being held to the audiences. Occasionally, an American-authored text would get its night or two of professional production, providing spectators with a rare, immediate glimpse of how one of its own citizens viewed dramatic writing and performance. At the same time, a number of Americans wrote plays that never appeared on a playhouse stage; these plays, usually but not always political in nature, dealt often with more controversial material than the theatre felt it could support and were sometimes more directly revealing of national identity issues than those presented on the boards. Taken altogether, the largely British fare presented in American theatres, the few plays written by Americans that were staged professionally, and the closet plays of Revolutionary and post-Revolutionary culture suggest a number of ways in which the world of acting or imagined performance gave Americans opportunities in the first fifty years of the republic to test out costumes of identity.

The term *identity* is, as suggested above, a slippery one. Colonial Americans made certain assumptions that attempted to negate any particular ambiguity about such a word: English were English, Indians Indians, men men, women women. But a seventeenth-century text like Mary Rowlandson's narrative might have brought forth a number of anxieties about identity.[1] Indians are "hellhounds" but treat her with a certain care; she is English, reads her Bible, yet adapts rather quickly to a Native economy. As a woman, she seems vulnerable to unspoken but imagined violations; yet the character of Mary shows herself fully capable of gritty survival, without the protection of her husband. The story ends before the real trials of identity begin – where captivity becomes lengthened, old language and religion slip away, resistance becomes adoption, and the seemingly fixed categories of English Protestant Christian woman begin to slide into some hybrid or lose their force altogether. Nevertheless, Rowlandson demonstrates all too closely the possibilities in colonial America for identity markers to erode, alter, and create confusion.[2] The decade of the mid-1760s to mid-1770s must also have created similar anxieties. The pride of being British – for those who were – at the end of the Seven Years' War began to give way to complaints that as British Americans, colonials were no longer quite British enough to enjoy the privileges of the so-called British constitution. Of course, the matter of political independence had its own identity moment, but the more compelling social and cultural question is the degree to which the military and political upheavals that became the War for Independence unsettled previous patterns of identity formation among Euro-American residents. Rather than belabor the point, suffice it to say that for the purposes of this study, identity begins in those ways in which persons might label themselves or others rather than in the psychological phenomenon of the integrated or fractured self: Indian or English, whig or tory. I presume, too, that identity is never singular nor inchoate, but even in its most emphatic forms is permeable at the margins and subject to mutation.

I take as a point of departure that there is no monolithic "American" identity to which all residents of the United States subscribe – only a changeable cluster of identities that individuals or groups might recognize as pertaining to them. Nor is this to say that "Irish" or "Negro" or even "woman" is a fixed, predetermined category, even for the eighteenth or early nineteenth century – only a marker whose mass understanding is always challenged by local and individual circumstances.

For pre-Revolutionary Americans, the theatre posed identity dilemmas that victory at Yorktown could not readily solve. Most notably, a general resistance to the living stage coexisted with an appreciation for dramatic form. Variants of dramatic writing had served a number of authors well, even those with a marked antipathy to the playhouse. Writers as antitheatrically orthodox as Michael Wigglesworth and Edward Taylor had, in different ways, made use of conversational exchanges in their various poetic renditions of Calvinist doctrine: Wigglesworth in the trial transcript of final judgment in *The Day of Doom*, Taylor in such speech and response poems as those of Christ and the Soul in *God's Determinations*.[3] Even so, the number of residents in the mainland colonies who resorted to play form in their writing appears to be quite small. In other words, although drama *per se* was never proscribed – only performances – there is very little belletristic dramatic authorship and just a scattering of political and other plays (mostly in the form of dialogues) published before 1765.[4] Therefore, it appears that colonists, insofar as they thought of themselves as having any particular identity associated with life in the New World, did not often imagine their lives as convertible to boards-and-curtain stage drama, dramatic though life on the frontier or even in the coastal cities could be.

Part of the problem of thinking of American identity in stage-related terms obviously has to do with early prohibitions on theatrical performances. Most theatre histories note the various attempts to suppress theatre, even in the larger cities, before and during the Revolution. Not until Boston lifted its ban in the early 1790s could professional theatre be said to have established itself on a permanent footing in the United States. As Peter Davis observes, the anti-theatrical legislation by Congress in 1774 and 1778 had its origins in a long history of suspicion of the stage as a threat to economic development; by 1774, with various local efforts to resist British imports in effect, the theatre became one more commodity to be resisted and thus an economic liability for those who offered it. This would suggest that the restoration of theatre was for economic as well as cultural reasons: imported British plays were now viable as desired goods.[5] Still, theatre was never absent entirely from British North America, as one can perceive from the history of Virginia alone: from Captain John Smith's depiction of a Virginia masquerade among the Powhatans in 1608 to the tavern production of *The Bear and the Cub* in 1665 to the collegiate dialogues at William and Mary at the end of the century or William Byrd's oral readings of plays at the beginning of the next to various amateur and semi-professional acting troupes that appear in Williamsburg and elsewhere before 1750, some people at all periods of colonization from the time of the earliest permanent English settlements forward remained conscious of theatre as a desired or recognized form of culture, art, or entertainment.[6] Nevertheless, given the extent of British American territory by 1700 and the rapidity of settlement to the Appalachians, theatre as an institution rather than as isolated occurrences had virtually no standing until the David Douglass–Lewis Hallam company began its tours and playhouse construction program in the 1750s and 1760s. Metaphoric stages aside – and there were plenty of those, as Nathaniel Hawthorne knew well when he wrote *The Scarlet Letter* – few platforms adorned the landscape whose purpose was to support playacting, not just punishment or politics.

The residents of the mainland colonies, then, while not without some interest in literary drama, especially Shakespeare, and its political satiric closet cousin, and not entirely devoid of theatrical experiences, would have had relatively few opportunities to imagine themselves from the point of view of a playhouse stage that they could actually attend. Some Americans did resort to theatrical metaphors, but unless the writers or speakers had been to England and attended the stage there, they would have formed their tropes from other, nontheatrical sources: from John Calvin, for example, or even John Foxe.[7] Despite a rich figurative tradition of *theatrum mundi* and other tropes of the stage in American rhetoric, the absence of literal theatres might be one of the reasons why, after the war, with the growing popularity of theatre and the new interest in playwriting by Americans, there are only a modest number of plays before 1800 or even 1825 that represent life in the United States. That relative scarcity of dramas with American content serves, however, to intensify the interest in those that do portray life as lived, as well as call attention to those British plays that proved popular on American boards. How does drama serve as a vehicle for identity formation or reflection in a society where its popularity as a genre for homegrown writers is very recent in its own history?

For one thing, the transition from British American creole to plain American is not made all at once – if at all. As Washington Irving slyly observes in "Rip Van Winkle" (*Sketch-Book*, pp. 33–49), the difference in the title character's village from before the war to after is little more than a new vocabulary (federal and democrat) and a slight alteration on the tavern sign, exchanging the referent George III for George Washington without repainting the king's face. With the wartime and republican theatres playing almost nothing but British plays and with private American libraries reflecting an interest primarily in the published versions of London productions, it is not surprising to see that American writers cling rather tightly to the coattails and dress hems of the playwrights whose works had become familiar. Many an American play, even about life in the United States, begins life as a British one on whose plot or character type or dialogic peccadillos the American writer builds and alters her or his text. American identities are rendered as variants of British; subtle changes grow large by comparison, particularly from the pens of amateur dramatists who fear that to create something too new would only alienate an audience raised upon a diet of Rowe, Farquhar, and Centlivre. Occasionally, something original breaks forth, as in the various attempts to capture the Yankee type. But even the characters most peculiar to its regions – Native Americans first, Africans in America next – had been anticipated by British playwrights before any British American dramatic author conceived them. This is not to say that anyone would have granted British writers any large degree of accuracy of portrayal, based on living contact with the subject; only that, by priority of conception and the plays' likely appearance at Smock Alley, Covent Garden, Haymarket, or Drury Lane, the writers on the eastern side of the Atlantic forced those on the western to shape their own observations of native, slave, or even white life into molds not immediately of American design.

For another thing, then, one must turn to those moments of originality or semi-originality to find where the gap occurs between British the adjective and American the noun. To be sure, this precursory writing by British authors functions as an omnipresent lens through which American writers view their own identities as Americans. Despite this, critics would be mistaken either in dismissing early American drama as imitative only or in ignoring that it is imitative. That is, its imitativeness has to be taken into account in comprehending the rendering of things and people American; but its variations also must be considered, along with the specific qualities being imitated, in order for one to understand the subtleties of American dramatic self-representation. Susanna Rowson nods to Aaron Hill's *Zara* for her play *Slaves in Algiers*, for instance, a fact that informs her text in significant ways; and while she has other things in mind than simply imitating an English forebear's translation of a French play, many of them having to do with the Philadelphia of 1794, rather than the London of 1736, she cannot avoid the overdetermination wrought by the institution of the theatre on even the most topical subject matter. Rowson is herself the space or hyphen between the two English-speaking cultures. Born in colonial America of English parents, come to adulthood in England, then returned to a republican United States as a mature, married woman, this not-quite-Rip brought her British vision to the heterogeneous population of her adopted country and attempted to guide its sense of itself through a stage play that reminded the audience of something old even as it spoke of events that seemed quite new.[8] Rowson could no more discard the British dramatic tradition than fly to India in a balloon (the subject of Elizabeth Inchbald's *The Mogul Tale*, a mildly popular British farce in the new republic), but she understood through her brief experience of acting in Philadelphia that performance on an American stage altered to some degree the reception of the words and story from its British original.

One of the issues raised by Rowson's play, slavery, would have had a variety of implications for playgoers in 1794. A comedy about persons of multiple nationalities, albeit in North Africa, *Slaves in Algiers* hints at the less comic dimensions of ethnic identity in the United States. A researcher looks largely in vain to discover such words as "diversity" or "multiculturalism" in the writings of the new nation, but the early American theatre certainly registered anxiety and amusement over heterogeneity. We are white and English, Americans through law and custom seemed to be saying, but a number of plays that were written by citizens of the United States or performed on American stages make it clear that "we" were also many other things, even if not necessarily what the plays depicted. To attend the theatre in one of the larger cities of the 1790s was to encounter representations of many nationalities: Irish, Jewish, Dutch, Spanish, and French to be sure, African most certainly, with Scythian, Persian, Lydian, Arabic, Native American, South Asian, and Turkish likely to appear before chronic readers and spectators of the drama. What did this frequent recourse to ethnic representation, to cite only one type of identity marker, mean to consumers of culture in the newly independent nation? What did it have to do with "us"?

One thing that spectators had to have assumed, in common with audiences in Great Britain and elsewhere, was that ethnicity could be performed. The actor (in this case, John William Green in Philadelphia) who in the afterpiece might represent the English character Young Wilding in Arthur Murphy's comedy, *The Citizen*, could in the main play perform the Algerian dey Muley Moloc in Rowson's *Slaves in Algiers*. All in the Philadelphia audience that night (June 30, 1794) would recognize Green from performances in other plays on the nights previous as one of the Thomas Wignell company's mid-level and mediocre players, relatively new to the city and a migrant from England. In the four months prior to the evening alluded to, Green had performed roles as a Spaniard, Irishman, Englishman, Frenchman; a Scottish lord, an English colonel, an Italian, a Greek; more Scots, English, French, Irish, Spanish, and Italian characters; a Danish king, a Swede, and a harlequin character. Given the frequency of his appearance, his performance in supporting roles, and his reputation as one of the least of the company's actors (one local critic rated him a 5 on a 15-point high scale), audiences would have seen him, at least in part, as "Green" again, a speaker of lines in shifting accents and costumes, whose presence as actor – one who more likely swells a progress than dominates a scene – reminds audiences more of his native Englishness (and therefore his suitability for the acting profession) than his representation of a particular, non-English, ethnically inscribed character.[9]

Nevertheless, the career of Green suggests how often Philadelphia and other American spectators encountered performed "others." It is also clear that some others were more other than other others. Green as Duncan, the soon-to-be-slain Scottish king in Shakespeare's *Macbeth*, or as Hamlet the elder, the already slain Danish king in the bard's tragedy, would hardly raise a ripple of difference because the plays were by Shakespeare, whose familiarity to American readers and playgoers alike was so great as to absorb him into the national consciousness, understood simply as a name widely recognized. Universal Shakespeare trumps English Will, and his characters lose their ethnicity in the trick – unless, of course, one of his characters is Othello. Green never rose to star status during his early Philadelphia period, never seems to have played the Moor there, but he does play a Moor-like character in Rowson's topical drama of 1794. Muley Moloc is a character more drawn from farce than even main-play comedy, but because the captivity of Americans by Algerians at the time was news, and the Islamic nations of North Africa were perceived as the enemy, Green could have done just about anything with the character to mark Muley Moloc as "Algerian," and it probably would have worked with an audience unused in the streets of Philadelphia to such a specific Islamic designation. As long as he was not "Negro" or "Irish" – that is, a type with demonstrable stage traits – Green could have given the dey any manner of accent or tic and gotten away with gross inaccuracies, measured against a flesh-and-blood Algerian. Enough that the audience witnessed a non-European, probably turbaned figure, speaking in an accent, that Green be accepted as a foreign and piratical ruler, easily reviled; but since Muley is also a coward and capitulates quickly to the slave revolt at the end, the man Green portrays could easily be overlooked as a character whose ethnicity means very little on its surface and nothing very much to American playgoers except comic enemy, the quickly dismissed theatrical other.

But if ethnicity is a performance, even by a second-tier player like Green, then the more radical social dimension of such a statement is itself disguised in the actor-centered criticism of stage plays performed in the early republic. Prior to the reopening of theatres in the post-war period, the majority of plays written in America were not performed on professional stages; consequently, such closet dramas, when they address the question of ethnic identity, say, only suggest the enacting of roles. They may borrow tropes and dialectal practices from produced plays, but without a Green or anyone else to whom to assign a role, these closet texts have a different kind of life that creates friction with the imagined life of staged drama. In one of the first American-authored plays to feature an African American character, *The Downfall of Justice* (1777), the anonymous author satirizes the actions of wealthy farmers during a time – the Revolution – of food scarcity.[10] Whereas the farmer justifies the high prices he demands for his crops, as well as his withholding foodstuffs from market to drive up the price, regardless of the suffering of people in town, his servant or slave, Jack, expresses sympathy for the plight of the poor.[11] The farmer's daughter, Sarah, remarks that the townsfolk will soon approach the family as paupers: "I expect some of them along to-morrow or next day begging as the Indians us'd to do the day after thanksgiving. I can't but laugh to see how foolish they'l [*sic*] look – He! he! he!" The farmer and his wife have a laugh over that prospect, but Jack refuses to join in the merriment. He speaks in the stock stage Negro dialect of the day but seizes the moral high ground from the caricature of rural greed: "Well Masser, I don't tink 'tis fair ting when poor folk he canno get no noting in he belly ... Masser got

rye enuf, wheat enuf, cyder enuf, ebery ting enuf . . . Jack pitty poor folk."
For this remark, Jack draws the scorn of the farmer and his family; he
becomes "you black Bastard" (*DJ* 7) and told to "mind his own business"
(8). Yet the irony seems clear enough; the author supports Jack's sympathetic posture, and thus he or she plays the "black" role in the "comedy."
Without the image of an actor interfering, without the literal presence of a
blackface white drawing attention to his performance, Jack speaks as the
voice of the good American, the moral center of the play, a person abused,
marginalized, discarded as "trash," and never in the text centered as heroic.
The author makes the logical leap that a person who suffers, even when he
has "victuals" enough "to stop your mouth," can best appreciate the
suffering of others – Natives once, now townspeople denominated without reference to ethnic origin but presumed to be white. In a simple speech
of common charity, Jack creates an identity problem for readers and
playwright alike. Best to bring the family on at the end for a good old
rousing song, as the anonymous playwright does, and sweep Jack's challenge both to white authority and white identity out the back door.
Otherwise, the question of agricultural pricing would be lost in the
more destabilizing issue of black is right and white is not.

Curiously, the author of this Revolutionary-era piece chose to address
the problem of hoarding and price-gouging in the form of a play that she
or he knew would never be performed on any literal stage. The author was
well aware that in the rhetorical politics of the 1770s satiric drama served
as a frequently used vehicle for political statements. Mercy Warren's three
plays on the administration of Thomas Hutchinson in Massachusetts or
John Leacock's satire against the administration of Lord North in *The Fall
of British Tyranny* or the various tory mockings of patriot views and
military prowess, as in the anonymous *The Battle of Brooklyn* and Jonathan
Sewall's *Cure for the Spleen*, all appeared in the space of about three or four
years, all addressing the crisis of the moment, even if localized.[12] *The
Downfall of Justice* rarely gets a mention in the company of these other,
better known political plays, yet it contains complexities of identity that
make it worth considering in the development of a theatricalized concept
of American types and characters. From whence does Jack arise?

From life, perhaps; but to some degree, too, from genre. By 1777 there
already exists an agreed upon way of rendering African American dialect
in printed speech; and while the dialect as printed may resemble in some
measure certain linguistic features of African American vernacular as
spoken in the eighteenth century, it is just as likely to come from the

drama itself, whether performed or read. Not only does Jack's dialect resemble that of other stage African characters on the British stage, but also his particular character – simple, humble, but grounded in a clear Christian morality – may itself be a trope of the stage. Many Americans by 1777 were familiar with Isaac Bickerstaff's comic opera, *The Padlock*, adapted from a story by Miguel de Cervantes.[13] In it, a black slave to the Spanish master Don Diego is abused and resents the abuse, and, to be sure, Mungo hardly seems to deserve the beatings he receives. Nothing in the plot of *The Padlock* suggests a direct influence on *The Downfall of Justice*, but it is possible that the character of Mungo, a sympathetically portrayed slave who speaks in a theatrically acceptable dialect ("Me wish to de Lord me was dead"), casts a histrionic shadow over the conception of a Connecticut servant trying desperately to keep his dignity before a Yankee master (*Padlock* 11). In other words, the distinction between Jack as a character in an American play about an American situation and Mungo as a figure in a British play about a Spanish situation is hard to maintain. Jack is "black" but disconcertingly reflects moral problems in white behavior; Mungo, a blackface character played by a white actor, shapes a type, the comic, abused, even sympathetic slave, but exists in the play largely to entertain. The presence of an Africanized character in an American play may suggest a variety of things, some directly related to the racial culture of the United States, some more to the theatre itself than to the life experienced by real people. Yet one of the advantages of using drama as a genre, even if with nary a thought to the text's enactment on a stage, is this startling fluidity of identity. The simplicity of Who are we? collapses under the complexity of sorting out one theatre from another, playhouse from farm house, default white from at-fault white, stage slave from rural servant. If "we" pity the poor in the Connecticut food crisis, even as "we" catch the echoes in Jack of that entertaining Mungo, "we" are all a little black, it seems, and "we" do not even know it.

In post-war society, the degree of sympathy a white reader might have maintained for a represented moral black was threatened, however, by a rise in black self-assertion and African Americans' own claims to nationality and national pride. From stirrings of community identity in the 1790s to the black nationalist parade on July 5, 1800, in New York, and subsequent celebrations of the type, African Americans sought to move beyond being objects either of abuse or sympathy and claim some other identity based on rights they observed among whites. But in many respects the white stage moved in an opposite direction. The more blacks attempted to take control of their streets, their economic welfare, and their sense of justice, the more brutal the mockery, whether in counter demonstrations in public, satires in print, or one-dimensional characterizations in the theatre. Violence against black parades was one thing, but the scathing ridicule to which abolitionist blacks were subject in the so-called "Bobalition" broadsides from 1816 onward drew on the same use of dialect, exaggerated by malapropisms and distortions, that one would have found on American and British stages for decades. Compared to the portrayal of Lid Rose in Samuel Woodworth's 1825 *The Forest Rose*, the end product of Bobalition scorn, Jack in *Downfall* is a paragon of subtlety, complexity, and sympathetic black subjectivity.[14]

If one pursues this matter of ethnicity further as an example of many registers of identity, *The Downfall of Justice* refers to another other, Native Americans, as a category to be included under those to be scorned. In Sarah's speech, written a century after Mary Rowlandson's New England captivity, the farmer's daughter raises the specter of hungry indigenous people seeking to share in the plenty of the Anglo harvest, in imitation of the fabled first thanksgiving of Wampanoags and English Separatists. Readers cannot know directly how the farm family treated those beggars, but those of the time no doubt assumed, by the threats to refuse agricultural bounty to any townsperson coming to the farm without coin, that "Indians" would have stared at the windows without success, a show for the family, a rural theatre of suffering and high humor. Such a scene is not represented in the play, only spoken about; and in subsequent variations of the Indian theme in American drama, Natives as contemporary, hungry people (rather than as historical types) are routinely elided from the stage. But such hunger was real in Connecticut and elsewhere and did not disappear. When my grandfather was 100, he shared with me a story of his grandmother on the Minnesota frontier, terrified as a girl when hungry Natives came to her window in the nineteenth-century reenactment of the eighteenth-century story told by Sarah. More than any stories of his own life, this one he did not experience directly, a story told to him of a family member's frightened encounter with starving others, was the one on his mind that December day. It was the last story he ever shared with me in his life. I mention this as a gloss to the dramatized tale of Connecticut greed – how one line in a pamphlet play reveals the author's understanding that those people needing food, consigned to their hunger by their nativity, live in the imagined memory of the farmer's daughter in an obscure play. Had Sarah absorbed those faces in the window? Would she, if a reader were to project her life beyond the play, be telling that story to her grandchildren decades later? Then she, like my German American grandfather, would find herself some part Indian, the very representation of her rejection of a despised other. L'indien, c'est moi.

One might aver, then, that the depiction or performance of racial marginality is in itself a challenge to American identity, in that the existence of theatre makes all identities interchangeable through the real or imagined figure of the actor. For readers and spectators of the time, however, the practices of stagecraft and dramatic authorship put presumed limits on the shapes that Proteus might take. After all, if one restricted the physical appearance of actors on stage to whites, even as portrayers of Natives, Africans, or Algerians, then one might assume that mimicry goes one way. The genius of the Euro-American, in the Anglo-American eye, is the ability to transform to non-European, or really, non-English types. Of course, one might have found any number of condescending portrayals by contemporary Natives or Africans who imitated white rituals and behavior, but in the absence (largely) of literal ethnic others appearing on the traditional (and not metaphoric) stage, the knowledge that Africans or Natives might enact whites is muted to a degree that the average audience member would not likely consider such mimicry to be theatre in the limited sense.

If non-white staging of white identity is put aside for the moment, one finds other issues concerning white adaptation of roles that cause some consternation in American playwrights. The prologue to the opening performance of Royall Tyler's *The Contrast*, the first comedy written by a permanent resident of the United States to be mounted by a professional company, directs the playgoers' attention to the habit of young New Yorkers to indulge their "imitative sense" in the pursuit of foreign fashions.[15] As critics have noted, *The Contrast* is very much about identity, with the foppish Anglophile Billy Dimple expelled from the stage by the stoical Revolutionary officer Colonel Manly.[16] Nevertheless, the play's self-consciousness about its place in the theatre and the nuances of character that Tyler incorporates make an easy assignment of traits to English and American more difficult than it might seem initially. Jonathan, the colonel's Yankee servant, appears to be quintessentially native, the Vermont villager without a clue about how to interpret the Europeanized cityscape of New York, but he enacts an absurdist naiveté that shifts the ideological burden of identity to Manly. That latter, the "unpolished, untraveled American," in Dimple's attempt at a damningly denominative phrase, has considerably more polish than Jonathan, knows eighteenth-century European political thought and history well enough to reflect on his country's future in their terms, conducts himself with more decorum at the theatre than the well-traveled Dimple, and evinces all the sympathetic reticence of a well-known British comedic hero type – some combination of, say, Charles Dudley in Richard Cumberland's *The West Indian* (1771) and Mr. Belville in Frances Brooke's *Rosina* (1782). In short, Manly conducts himself in the name of the American patriot in terms disarmingly conformable to English theatrical precursors. If Dimple and Charlotte are the rampant imitators of overseas fashion, and Jonathan the bumbling, bundling, and low comically likable, home-grown original, then Manly is American by residence, his regimental coat, and his love for his country – and not much more.

Tyler's breakthrough at the John Street Theatre exposes the limits that eighteenth-century performance clamps on artistic renderings of identity formation. The theatre during the early republic has a deeply conservative foundation: do the new only when it reminds of the old. Whatever cultural changes were occurring more broadly in the United States after the war, the theatre itself could render directly only those that met with audience appreciation – or so the managers presumed. This propensity suggests another level at which identity can be read: in the negative. With theatrical companies thinking *new* meant latest hit on the London stage, audiences expected and even demanded British dramas well into the nineteenth century. As late as 1845, Anna Cora Mowatt was having to justify the writing of an American play when she first launched *Fashion* – a work that seems as much like *The Contrast* as that latter comedy resembles Sheridan's *School for Scandal*.[17] Yet Mowatt knew, as did Tyler, that American audiences, whatever their love for Frederick Reynolds or Henry Bulwer, had certain experiences of living in the United States that made their viewing of those foreign vehicles something against which they could test their own identity. In that sense, there are two American dramatic cultures: that of the stage, with its British-play orientation, and that of the closet, with its more free-wheeling depiction of American themes, language, and situations. As Thoreau would say of body and soul, a reader of culture must reverence both.[18]

Of course, many Americans chose to ignore both drama and theatre, or else had no exposure to organized theatrical experiences. The religious objection to the stage lasted well into the nineteenth century. Jonathan in his famous scene in Tyler's *The Contrast* is surprised to learn he has been at the theatre, which he believes to be "the devil's drawing room," based no doubt on Calvinist sermons he has absorbed in rural Vermont (*TC* 33). Mowatt recalls in her autobiography that in her early years in the Episcopal church, she heard a number of sermons denouncing the theatre and, on account of those religious strictures, almost refused to go with the family in 1831 to see Fanny Kemble act.[19] Even past mid-century, Moncure Conway, while serving as a Unitarian minister in Cincinnati in 1857, discovered a great deal of suspicion and criticism directed at him for writing affirmatively of the theatre in that city.[20] Rather than follow Colonel Manly into Stoic appreciation of playhouse drama, many Americans observed religious dictates that kept them from enjoying the increasingly popular theatrical amusements of the new republic. For those citizens, nothing could more deleteriously define American identity than the stage.

During the nineteenth century, however, the tide of cultural history went against such precise determinations of the theatre's moral failings. To be sure, managers were often careful not to offend local sensibilities overmuch. As the early Christian theologian John Chrysostom observed centuries before, the theatre and the church often find themselves competing at the level of entertainment for the attention of the population;[21] at the same time, the stage sometimes serves as a kind of secular church, one that validates a popular conception of moral goodness but which avoids any sectarian specificity. In the 1840s, stage morality manifested itself in the well-known image of the self-sacrificing woman, such as the character Mary Middleton in W. H. Smith's *The Drunkard* (1844), who upholds her alcoholic husband until he reforms.[22] Before that, however, there is a kind of civil religion established by plays that shapes a good bit of what constitutes proper American identity. In John Beete's *The Man of the Times* (1797), Charles rejects his father's usurious ways in order to marry the virtuous Lydia.[23] He has been schooled in England, but returns home to a better situation in America where, as his future father-in-law Major Upright, declares, "Republicans can only be properly instructed in republican governments" (*Man* 2). Such declarations on the part of Upright are not unlike ministerial admonitions; as another character says of him later, he's "so sententious, 'tis as good as a sermon to hear him" (33). Like Colonel Manly, whose utterances his Chesterfieldian sister Charlotte claims "made me as melancholy as if I had been at church" (*TC* 20), Upright fosters a stage morality based on American citizenship and virtuous character. By ultimately encouraging Charles to renounce his father, and thus his Old World business practices, the major establishes a specifically republican code of behavior that is "as good as a sermon" without being one. Therefore, while the theatre may have seen itself at odds with the church based on denunciations from the latter, it sought to palliate its audiences with depictions of goodness that run the line from Stoic to sentimental Christian.

Still, most playgoers probably did not confuse the playhouse with God's house, nor did they worry overmuch about it. The evangelical Christian author Harriet Beecher Stowe may have famously watched a dramatized version of *Uncle Tom's Cabin* from the wings because she did not wish to be seen in a theatre (she thought that "bad" plays outnumbered good ones at a ratio of five to one), but the act of going to the play was not necessarily something that would occasion a spiritual or moral crisis.[24] The diary of Elihu Hubbard Smith details his frequent attendance at New York stage plays in the 1790s, but this friend of William Dunlap, despite his Calvinist upbringing, rarely talks about plays and theatre in anything but their own terms.[25] For the post-Revolutionary stage, one goal must have been to de-demonize the institution, make potential patrons see it as a common, expected, and desired part of social activities. This meant that American authorship often included some manner of justification for the enterprise of playwriting and theatre attendance in a republic. To be American and attend the theatre generated an identity that had, in essence, to be created on stage and reflected back to the spectators in order to validate the very action of watching. Tyler's prologue to *The Contrast* negotiates between a perceived culture imported from "foreign climes" and the author's desire to discourse on "native themes," to the prejudice of the latter, but it also recognizes that in a Franklinesque world of "imitation" one can affirm the imitative art, drama, without mimicking (to a fault) the behaviors of its old country origin (*TC* 7).

Of course, Tyler chose to write about a situation that would be recognized as American, and thus offers Manly and Maria as national types, fit to be imitated by "modern youths, with imitative sense" (7). For other playwrights, the staging of an American scene was not necessary to a play's claim on the nationalist identities of its audience. Mrs. Marriott's *The Chimera* (1795) is a farce set in England with the usual Lord Aberfords and Sir Lamberts, but her prologue effervesces with Revolutionary sentiments. She begins with a paean to George Washington and the heroes of the late war, then extends the discussion to those who support drama:

> And, O America! these sons are thine,
> These luminaries that will ever shine,
> In many a future age and foreign clime,
> Their names immortal thro' revolving time.
> Ye kind supporters of the drooping muse,
> Whose smiles to genius are nectareous dews,
> Cheering each bud that else would fade and die,
> From every clime to you she loves to fly.[26]

Marriott envisions American drama not just as an import adapted to local situations but as a future export product back to those same "foreign climes" that Tyler tacitly denounces. The United States now becomes the prop of drama itself, the place where smiles encourage genius and where the stage can find its fit home. With this strategy, Marriott makes content of the play functionally irrelevant. American identity rests on playgoing and support, not necessarily citizens' seeing themselves reflected in theatre's local mirror. Through such competing claims on an audience's sympathies as those of Tyler and Marriott, the relationship of stage to identity allows for no large-scale affirmation of a peculiarly American dramatic aesthetic. Most playgoers, then, probably resorted to the theatre because it was entertaining and had an increasingly negotiable social cachet, not because they expected or demanded a new art for a new republic. Following Mrs. Marriott's line of argument, spectators may have felt that it was patriotic simply to show up at the theatre and applaud. Somehow, by a prodigious logical leap, one can affirm Washington, liberty, and the frothy betrothal of Rupert and Matilda, Marriott's stage lovers, all at once without having an American identity crisis.

Yet it should be added that *The Chimera* did not, any more than most other productions written in the United States before 1800, become a repertory staple. Its single New York performance (it had played once before in Philadelphia) was greeted by this comment in *The New York Magazine*: 'A farce from the lady's own pen – a farce certainly unequalled by any thing except its own prologue; a prologue unrivalled by any thing but its own farce.'[27] An Edinburgh native, Mrs. Marriott played but one long theatrical year in the United States (1794–95) before dying in Norfolk, neither her acting, her prologue, nor her farce creating any particular long-lasting interest among the republican spectators.[28] Although it is tempting to see Marriott's stunted career as an emblem of what happens to a theatrical personage from a "foreign clime," that conclusion would hardly accord with the fact that most professional actors in America before 1800 were

British-born. Thus even in the premiere of *The Contrast*, the actors playing the small-*n* native American types Manly and Jonathan, Lewis Hallam, Jr., and Thomas Wignell, were both natives of England. When an 'American' appears on stage, that 'character' is enacted in accordance with the players' own British training and sensibility. To be sure, these same British actors could adapt quite readily to American conditions and expectations. Susanna Rowson, the daughter of a British military officer, made herself over into a patriotic American much more convincingly than Mrs. Marriott, stayed around, and lived out her days in her adopted nation as a republican actress, playwright, novelist, and school teacher. Nevertheless, on stage there is no American without British. The stage Yankee and the stage Yorkshireman, a familiar London comic type who is himself related to the stage Irishman, are kith if not exactly close kin, second cousins, perhaps, at the nearest relation, and each performed as the whim of the public suits. That by 1825 American audiences were showing a decided preference for the Yankee over his north-of-England stage colleague had less to do with the distinctiveness of the type than the politics of the representation.

If for the most part the actors in the main theatres were constant and predictable – degree of preparation for any given role aside – the roles they assumed, their theatrical identities, underwent nearly nightly shifting in the era before the long stage run. Amidst a swirl of nationalities and ethnic types, represented by persons often costumed without much regard to historical accuracy or consistency,[29] American audiences would have seen identities so recognizable as to be unquestioned – the foppish Frenchman, the innocent country lass – and yet so many identities coming from many more influences, that they may be pardoned if they left the theatre with an aftertaste of confusion about who they had just seen – or even who they were themselves. If anything, what follows in this study works in opposite directions: these chapters argue, on the one hand, the deep dependence on a foreign dramatic literature that dominated the American stage throughout the period, while on the other, they maintain that the nearly single-minded obsession with London favorites came to represent both gross and subtle reflections of a multiplicity of identities quite other than "British." In other words, the drama appearing in the early republican United States belonged to a theatre that satiated the taste for the predictable even as it resisted its own sameness.

Part I

Staging revolution at the margins of celebration

THE FIVE CHAPTERS IN THIS FIRST SECTION EXAMINE PLAYS THAT have something to do with the American Revolution, but none of the focus plays truly celebrates a thorough-going nationalism, the sort of thing one might have encountered in a July 4 parade. Even plays that basically affirm the Revolution encode some doubt about what precisely is to be the character of the American people either during the conflict or when the war is over. With the exception of William Dunlap's *André*, the plays discussed below for the most part have not been examined in detail by scholars of the drama, yet each one presents a document saturated with matters of identity. From Crèvecoeur's and Munford's closet plays to Murray's stage comedy and Dunlap's acted tragedy to the British musical by O'Keeffe, the Revolution gets sometimes a nod, sometimes a straight look, but rarely would a reader or spectator be left with much in the way of glory or the illusion of political consensus in the United States. From the 1770s through the 1790s, identity in these plays cannot be separated from the anxiety of separation generated by independence. For not only does one nation split from another, but the drama itself threatens to fracture, as authors attempt to bridge the gap between a once unified, if contentious, space, the pre-war British American stage, and the new incarnation of two separate national theatres, as writers and audiences encounter the uncertainties of form and substance the Revolution inevitably provokes.

2

Revolution and unnatural identity in Crèvecoeur's "Landscapes"

THE AMERICAN REVOLUTION PROMPTED A NUMBER OF PUTATIVE American playwrights to adopt dramatic form in order to translate the swirl of political, economic, and military upheavals in their midst. The majority of these plays stake out ideological positions that leave little doubt of their intention. Mercy Warren's three political satires, *The Adulateur*, *The Defeat*, and *The Group*, resolutely stick Massachusetts royal governor Thomas Hutchinson and his followers on her well-hoisted poniard in the service of whig politics. For his part, Hugh Henry Brackenridge turns the Quebec expedition of December 1775, with its fallen hero, General Richard Montgomery, and the Bunker Hill battle of the following spring into heroic tragedies, while John Leacock pillories the British government and celebrates early American successes in his *Fall of British Tyranny*. On the tory side, there are fewer examples of closet political plays that have survived, but *The Battle of Brooklyn*, for one, mocks the incompetence of Washington and his army in the New York campaign of 1776.[1] Given the polarizing atmosphere of the 1774–1776 period in particular, such clear denomination of party and cause is not surprising. For these playwrights, the markers "British" and "American" take on new meaning; new identities are quickly forged in the world of these plays, patriot and loyalist, rebels and tyrants. Such plays serve to rally or mock, stir or propagandize. This is not to say that each play does not have its subtleties. Warren in *The Group*, for instance, certainly allows her most venal tory characters to incriminate themselves by speeches of rank self-interest, but she also generates complications in the voices of mandamus councillors, those appointed by the king to carry on royal government in Massachusetts against popular wishes, who have not always stood in the breadline of royal preferment. Additionally, in her portrayal of General Gage she shows the playwright's latent hope that an enlightened

British administrator will be able to sort out the treachery of American tories from principles shared by both British and American patriots. Nevertheless, it, like the others, establishes an identity politics of pure motive, asking its readers to affirm or deny but stand no middle ground. Reading behind such politics allows us to see that even a staunch whig like Warren still held out hope as late as 1775 that "British" and "American" would still eventually be complementary labels.

One play of this type that stands out for its richness of texture even in the service of a particular politics is Crèvecoeur's "Landscapes," a text not published in English during the author's lifetime. Few Revolutionary-era writers defy categorization as resolutely as Michel Guillaume Jean-de-Crèvecoeur, or, as he was known to British America, J. Hector St. John. Best recognized for his book *Letters from an American Farmer* (1782),[2] Crèvecoeur wrote several other essays, sketches, and other short works that, in their English originals, remained in manuscript until 1925 or, in a few cases, until 1995. One of those fugitive pieces, a collection of dramatic scenes, is "Landscapes" (1777?), a bitter, deeply ironic denunciation of the Revolution that not only raises critical questions about the idealized America depicted in the famous Letter III, "What is an American?" but goes so far as to claim that the Revolution will destroy all recognized forms of social identity in that country.[3] Although there is very little scholarship on "Landscapes" – indeed, on most of the originally unpublished short works – the play engages a number of significant themes raised in different contexts by *Letters*.[4] For Crèvecoeur, the Revolution proved, at least in its early stages, to be a deeply disappointing, even horrifying, event. In "Landscapes" the collapse of whig ideals, the perversion of local control over public affairs, and most especially the dangers for domestic life in a world torn by political tumult reflect darkly the more buoyant depiction of American life in the first half of *Letters*.

Most teachers of the author's American classic are well aware of the contradictions within that text. In Letter III, Farmer James, the politically neutral narrator (or so he appears), seeks or promotes conditions that ensure the happiness of the individual family in an overall atmosphere of liberty and social contentment.[5] Generations of writers and instructors have mined that letter for definitions of what it means to be American, especially its (qualified) melting pot notion of the "new race of men" who have left behind European "voluntary idleness, servile dependence, penury, and useless labor" for "ample subsistence" grounded in a labor based on "self-interest" (*L* 70). In later letters, notably IX and XII, the depiction of slavery in South Carolina in the one and the expression of fear by Farmer James at what the new violence will bring in the other demand that readers ask questions about the values asserted in III. As David Carlson reminds us, contrary to the traditional anthologists' treatment of the text, "Crèvecoeur's book does *not* leave its readers ebulliently optimistic about the future of the nation."[6] Still, within the overall frame of *Letters*, the antiphonal responses to the clarion trumpet of III tend to be muted or somewhat obliquely related to the main anthem. "Landscapes," by contrast, shows a world where whig cruelty destroys the hopes of neutrals and loyalists to recreate anything like home again, giving it a political bite that is not as immediately detectable in *Letters*. Privacy, domestic tranquility, individual religious liberty, freedom of political opinion, even master–slave relations, as they define the American of Letter III, all become casualties of a revolution that in Crèvecoeur's drama has no moral purpose – at least one that Farmer James would recognize. Paradoxically, 'Landscapes' portrays the War for Independence as a war for identity but the very thing that denies to Americans any identity worth saving. In the end, the play casts serious doubt on the ability or desire of a new republican regime to continue the policy of prosperity and tolerance to which Farmer James pays eloquent homage in *Letters* and, by extension, on the meaning of "American" that James so joyfully touts in the first three letters. Indeed, conventional markers of identity, including gender and social class, become distorted in the craven new world of whiggish egalitarianism.

The basic narrative of "Landscapes" features as main character the chairman of a patriot committee of safety, Deacon Beatus, who, in an unnamed location but one with characteristics of both New York and Pennsylvania, oversees the wartime interrogation of suspected tories and the confiscation of their properties. Other characters include Beatus's wife, Eltha; Potter, a tavern keeper, who is being put out of business by the strife; various citizens and partisans; two slaves; and loyalist victims of the purge. The play contains an introduction; some stage directions; six interconnected scenes, each a numbered "landscape"; and a description at the end of four "plates" (not pictured in the manuscript) that may have been intended to serve as illustrations for the scenes. Although not unique among his works in having dialogue, "Landscapes" is the only piece Crèvecoeur constructed entirely as a drama.

While Crèvecoeur might have had some familiarity with the stage, either from his youth in France or occasional attendance at the New York theatre, his play shows relatively little influence of the sort of dramas then popular. "Landscapes" lacks a single tragic figure whose story holds the whole together, like Calista in Nicholas Rowe's *The Fair Penitent* or Beverley in Edward Moore's *The Gamester*, nor does it have the usual plot trajectory of rise-reversal–fall, except on the scenic level. Still, in the patriot characters especially are echoes of anti-whig Restoration comedies, like those of Aphra Behn, and anti-fool or anti-hypocrite satiric plays, such as those by Samuel Foote. Further, Crèvecoeur participates in the eighteenth-century closet political play tradition by creating stark contrasts between sides, leaving one with all the moral weight and the other, as with Warren's Massachusetts tories, to serve as the embodiment of wickedness and cruelty. Indeed, 'Landscapes' resembles the newspaper-type plays of the time, like Leacock's *Fall of British Tyranny*, at least in its effort to acquaint potential readers with abuses exacted in the name of current policy. Because, too, speakers in a play can articulate positions in such a way as to allow the audience the illusion it is deciding on its own volition with whom to sympathize, Crèvecoeur may have found that for this particular situation, where loyalists must meet certain tests to retain their property or face confiscation and banishment, that merely dramatizing the conflict between victim and victimizer would more compactly and immediately illustrate his point of view than a series of sentimental anecdotes.

The matter of voice is a complex one in Crèvecoeur and not easily resolved. As with British plays of an earlier era, the author begins with an introductory essay that recognizes the point of view intended in the drama. However, the very format of a play makes determination of a 'voice' in a deliberately multivocal performance problematic. Crèvecoeur includes an introduction to the play that, as will be noted, casts a grim look at the American scene. While this voice is not entirely consistent with the more naive-sounding James of *Letters*, a theme of declension pervades both *Letters* and the play. The introduction argues that the Revolution is "unnatural," that citizens have been "allured" by "poisons and subtle sophisms" to cast off every "ancient prejudice" or allegiance.[7] The narrator's purpose, then, is to show scenes that are "genuine copies of originals" that he has witnessed, and he asks to be judged by their fidelity to truth (*L* 426, 427). In the first 'landscape,' the deacon, his wife, and their son Eliphalet discuss the previous night's harassment of local tories by another son, Anthony.[8] The family is suddenly visited by Squire Rearman, a suspected loyalist who has just been released from prison. Rearman complains of the treatment he received for his alleged political leanings, his separation from his family, and the general terror instituted by the committee of safety. After Rearman leaves, Eltha announces that despite the Sabbath, she and her husband will visit the condemned estate of a loyalist fugitive (Francis Marston) to get an early look at the household goods to be auctioned. Of Mrs. Marston, Eltha remarks, 'I want to see how the woman looks with all her little Tory bastards about her" (438). The next, brief scene shows Eltha and Beatus on the road as they converse with a militia officer who has tried unsuccessfully to catch Marston.

The third and fourth landscapes take place in a tavern owned by Potter, "a landlord." The chairman and "chairwoman" have stopped off on their way to Marston's and try to convince Potter that life is better under the whigs. The landlord speaks of his obedience to the new regime while indicating that his sentiments lie with the monarchical governance and Anglican worship that he associates with the region's one-time prosperity. After the couple leave, others arrive in the long fourth scene to debate the issues of the day. Some, like Colonel Tempelman and Aaron Blue-Skin (whose last name is a slang term for a rigid Calvinist), are warm patriots; others, like Ecclestone and the foreigner, Iwan, cast doubts on the nobility of the whig cause. The climactic moment occurs when Captain Shoreditch, a committee militia officer, brings in three Quakers as enemies of the people. That such peaceable folk have become anathema provides Crèvecoeur with a powerful illustration of the reversal of order that is the "unnatural" dimension of the Revolution.

Scenes five and six show martyred loyalists. In five, Beatus and Eltha examine Mrs. Marston on the whereabouts of her husband, while she takes a principled stand against the destruction of her family and civil order. In six, the committee officers meet a person on the road denominated "The Woman in Despair," Martha Corwin. With her child dead and herself homeless, this victim of patriot justice gives a final voice to the suffering of innocent families caused by what she sees as committee persecutions.

Consistent with *Letters*, "Landscapes" rarely refers in specific terms either to the military conflict or the philosophical struggles about governance of the 1770s. Rather, it focuses almost entirely on the consequences of a hostile invasion of the private domain by an anarchic instrument of terror, the committee of safety. The play's power derives from the contrast of the woeful present with the idyllic past, which Crèvecoeur had framed in *Letters* as a vision of *felicity*. This type of happiness depends on the skill of the farmer's hands, the richness of his soil, and the "mild bands" of a government whose chief purpose, it appears, is to protect the intimate space of individual families from intrusion. This happiness is grounded in domesticity. The metamorphosis of the European peasant into the American farmer culminates at the happy hearth; the chief emblem of this classic transformation is the picture in Letter II of the farmer at home:

> When I contemplate my wife, by my fireside, while she either spins, knits, darns, or suckles our child, I cannot describe the various emotions of love, of gratitude, of conscious pride, which thrill in my heart and often overflow in involuntary tears. I feel the necessity, the sweet pleasure, of acting my part, the part of an husband and father, with an attention and propriety which may entitle me to my good fortune. (53)

Thus the end of the American experiment, at least in the early portion of *Letters*, is the farmer's tender contemplation of the domestic scene that is the result of his material success – and his leisure, won by agricultural labor, to write about it.[9] Implicit in this scene, however, is the farmer's complete control over the identities of all he surveys: quiet, maternal wife, performing traditional gendered roles; suckling, dependent child; and himself, "acting my part," performing as well the roles of "husband and father" that leave little doubt about who controls the domestic comedy before his gaze.

If in *Letters* the ideal American man is free to form a vision of domestic bliss, where a life taming nature is "natural" and unobtrusive, the view from Crèvecoeur's drama renders that possibility of hearthside happiness virtually unattainable. For its part, "Landscapes" portrays the collapse of domestic identities by skewering patriot laws, heroes, and politics with an irony that rivals Jonathan Swift's in intensity and loyalist propagandists such as Jonathan Sewall in antagonism to a popular regime. It is a long distance from the elegiac yet modestly hopeful tone of Letter XII to the enmity for the Revolution and the satiric vitriol contained in "Landscapes."[10] As probably one of the last pieces written by Crèvecoeur before he fled to New York (or perhaps even written partly while there), "Landscapes" reveals the wider implications of the vision of America that precedes it.[11] Gone is any overt reference to the process of personal transformation that Farmer James describes in Letter II: "the progressive steps of a poor man, advancing from indigence to ease, from oppression to freedom" through good habits and "emigration" to English America (90).[12] Instead, we have episodes of hypocrisy, cruelty, and shocking violence in the farmer's home region, the likes of which are matched in *Letters* only by the horrific image of the slave dying in the cage in Letter IX – a scene that itself raises deep questions about identity and its relationship to slavery.

Letters offers a picture of the good life, grounded in liberty and individual autonomy, where personal and familial independence are maintained by honest labor, property ownership, civil rights, mutual respect, peace, and the institution of marriage. Farmer James equates this American package of English liberties with domestic tranquility, rendered as home and polity, yet he refuses to engage in any partisan political rendering of the life he depicts. In "Landscapes" each of the interlocking components of civil and personal felicity breaks apart in the Revolution. The enemies are not outsiders but neighbors – the very whigs whose political doctrine embraces the liberties that James non-dogmatically affirms. For Crèvecoeur, whig practices defeat whig principles. In the name of peace, the partisans conduct terror; for domestic bliss, the patriots substitute political success. The author "repeatedly affirmed, albeit with bias, that tyranny, lust for power, greed, and other corruptions – in the guise of policy, justice, patriotism, liberty, self-defense, constitutional reason, and other honorable garments –" were the underlying causes of the Revolution.[13] No invader could more resolutely destroy whig principles than the whigs themselves. Letter XII, in which the narrator speculates on life among the Indians, in flight from the Revolution, shows a world tilted; "Landscapes" pictures that world upside down.

The depiction of committee terror in "Landscapes," discussed in more detail in Chapter 5, shows this reversal immediately. Beatus, called variously Deacon, the Chairman, and Colonel, emerges as a Presbyterian hypocrite whose intrusive execution of laws enacted by the Continental Congress ruins the lives of the innocent. Victims of Beatus's intimidation – Squire Rearman, Landlord Potter, and Mrs. Marston – decry the loss of property that gave them some measure of happiness in the past. If there is to be politics at all, Crèvecoeur suggests, then government ought to maintain the rights of citizens to live without intrusion in domestic tranquility. The true commonwealth is in the home, with the gender and social roles of patriarchy maintained. Unfortunately, the play argues, the relative absence of government in America, caused by a doctrine of personal autonomy and distant central authority, makes domesticity the first target when local politicians step into the vacuum.

By marking his objects of satire as both Presbyterians and whigs, Crèvecoeur shows his awareness of identity politics in upstate New York, where the author lived, and in Pennsylvania, where he sets the scene of *Letters*. Manorial landlords controlled much of the land in upstate New York, renting to tenants, but also exacting a certain loyalty to the owner's politics. When the war broke out, the tenant populace tended largely to side with the manor's owner; if a whig, so were they, if tory, then likewise.[14] The world that Crèvecoeur seems to have reverenced, at least in "Landscapes," is one in which an artisan-farmer class – that is, those who do manual labor – pays deference to a manorial lord, has no interest in partisan politics for its own sake, and cares mostly about the continuation of domestic happiness within the confines of the property the worker controls without having to worry about grand debates about independence or liberty or party. Such a view places the burden of responsibility on the owner of the estate; disrupting that system decapitates the population at large, who lose all direction without the wise head of the landlord in charge. The landlord's domestic tranquility and security, or lack thereof, affect those dependent on him. To have underlings, as the patriots are in "Landscapes," seize control of the political discourse – without their having been bred to it – suggests in the play a loss of stability for all concerned. Despite the rhetoric in *Letters* that affirms the ability of former peasants to rise in station in America, that in "Landscapes" reinforces a more rigid class hierarchy.

In Pennsylvania, the polarizing atmosphere of the Revolution brought out sharp divisions based on ethnicity and religious orientation. As Owen Ireland has observed, party affiliations and loyalties broke sharply at the fault line of Scots-Irish Presbyterian on one side, and Quakers, Anglicans, and Lutherans on the other. The Ulster folk, having already migrated to Pennsylvania because of poor treatment at the hands of absentee English landlords back home, formed a militant community of anti-British partisans who rigorously supported the use of loyalty oaths and other such tests in the United States for patriotic purity. Although something like a coalition mentality held in the immediate pre-war years, with cooperation possible among Calvinists and non-Calvinists, the outbreak of violence changed things radically: "When a majority of Quakers opted for neutrality and a minority of Anglicans remained loyal to the crown, they left their coreligionists enfeebled *vis-à-vis* the Presbyterians, who sprang with near unanimity to the Revolutionary cause and, in a dramatic reversal, broke the long established Quaker-Anglican political hegemony."[15]

Crèvecoeur's depiction of committee zealots and Quaker victims draws, it appears, on his knowledge of these local political factors.

In "Landscapes," the nature of authority, particularly in the application of domestic models to the political sphere, is clearly construed. In the introduction, Crèvecoeur's narrator invokes analogies to painting to describe what he is about to portray in dramatic terms. Crèvecoeur pictorially sketched his own farm in 1778; in doing so, he probably had some awareness of European art traditions.[16] The textual scene that shows Farmer James gazing contentedly on his wife and infant by the fire is cast in a pose very reminiscent of the French rural domestic scenes painted by Greuze, Chardin, and others that fix, in the manner of a stage tableau, an intensely sentimentalized bond among the family members depicted.[17] The narrator calls his readers' attention to subjects and textures that would escape those who would gaze on "the pompous, the captious, the popular, the ostensible, the brilliant part of these American affairs" (424). In a revealing shift of metaphor, the narrator remarks, "'Tis not the soaring eagle, rivaling the clouds in height and swiftness, I mean to show you; 'tis only the insignificant egg from which it is hatched" (424). It is not the magnificent bird, and of course the symbol of the patriots, that he wishes to limn, but the egg and, as he adds later, "the nest in which it was hatched" (425) – that is to say, the originating domicile.[18]

But painting may not be adequate as a medium to portray all the shades of contrast between eagle and egg. To capture the desired landscape – a word that can mean "faint or shadowy representation" or "the depiction or description of something in words" (*OED*) as well as scenic picture – the narrator turns to drama. Reflecting the analogies drawn by Denis Diderot in the 1750s between art and the theatre, and anticipating the general thrust of stage entertainments in the nineteenth century, the prospective painter becomes distressed dramatist, who turns to a genre more fully suited to represent the scenes he claims to have witnessed. In his own Letters II and III, as in French paintings of humble interiors, the domestic scene is rendered as a sentimental moment, a congeries of emotions, satisfactions, even wonders that, in Michael Fried's term, leads to a powerful "absorption" – in the case of Farmer James, the result of contemplating his own home-centered bliss. Crèvecoeur's earlier writing anticipates the predominating doctrine that motivates the French origination of melodrama: the establishment of a cohesive set of values rooted in home and hearth whose potential or actual disruption creates highly charged images of the ruin of virtue.[19] In other words, the American, as

Farmer James would have it, is identified thoroughly with the domestic sphere, extended to the fields that surround his house. Crèvecoeur is not a melodramatist, precisely, but he anticipates the domestic dramas of the next century by centering the American in the small space of the hearth rather than the amphitheatre of world history.

The implications of this choice can be seen in the way Crèvecoeur represents domestic life and the effects of political and religious identity on gender construction within the domestic framework. Where *Letters* focuses largely on the farmer himself as proud husband and father, "Landscapes" makes much of women as emblems for the presence or absence of home-centered virtue. As Dennis Moore rightly affirms, the primary female figures in "Landscapes" are "among Crèvecoeur's most vivid creations."[20] In fact, unlike the wife of Farmer James, a woman usually seen through the filtering gaze of the farmer himself, the women in the scenes speak in their own voices, offering themselves as subjects. This direct speaking is the great advantage of drama as a literary form, but given the title of his play, the author forces us to consider that speaking in the context of distinct visual images. Crèvecoeur was certainly aware that the depiction of the female in popular art of the time – notably the political cartoon – amounted frequently to iconographic transferral: the body of the woman was the body of the state – and thus too a symbol of the domestic sphere or, as Judith Sargent Murray called the family, "a well regulated Commonwealth." Since women are focal for the drama, their characterization especially reflects Crèvecoeur's conception of domestic values in the farming region.[21]

The principal female character is Eltha, the wife of the chairman and a prototype of the vindictive Jacobin woman most notably rendered in the figure of Charles Dickens's Madame Defarge in *A Tale of Two Cities*. Eltha's behavior is consistent throughout the scenes; she is venal, political, calculating, and finally ruthless, and does not fit one scholar's characterization of "Crèvecoeur's women [as] stereotypes of domestic enterprise but frailty under stress."[22] As the woman without feeling, she represents the implications of a world without unquestioned masculine and paternal authority. Without a compassionating center – figured in the later ideology of republican motherhood as the woman of both reason and feeling – the family becomes a potentially dangerous force, whose unrestrained desires find power in the politically destabilized world outside the home. Whereas the chairman falsely claims to be above the cupidity of the arch-partisans, Eltha makes no such assertions and, indeed, no apologies for her persecutions of loyalists. Crèvecoeur offers, then, a powerful counter to the identity of the American patriot woman sketched by Warren in *The Group*, where females are portrayed as victims of tory brutality and as the voices of political idealism. In his play, the republican woman is a monster.

Indeed, of all the identities questioned in the play, that of what constitutes an American woman is the most powerfully and controversially portrayed. For Crèvecoeur, whiggish republicanism destroys the home and robs its inhabitants of the apolitical bliss of pre-war private life. With the sentimental centrality of the female as an icon for domestic tranquility, any alteration in the image of a woman carries symbolic weight. The woman who, through a vacuum created by the expulsion of the benevolent squirarchy, abandons sentimental attachment to home for Machiavellian maneuvering comes to represent dramatically the dark side of Lockean authority in a landscape of revolution. Unlike the loyalist women figured later in the play, Eltha appears as a perversion of female power under the old system; she trades her normal sphere, the care of those in her household, for another, the reordering, without care, of others' homes. Her character is not so much the cause of the Revolutionary attack on privacy as a reflection of it.

In the first landscape, Eltha, Beatus, and one son, Eliphalet, appear as they gather for Sunday morning prayer. When Beatus asks after another son, Anthony, Eltha excuses him by claiming, 'He was all night a-Tory-hunting and did not go home till 'most break of day' (428). Eltha seems to play a sentimental role, as one who excuses her children's lapses to the punishing father; however, because the son has been busy abusing the innocent, Eltha's advocacy for Anthony reveals the decay of familial values in the radical whig home. Shortly after this conversation, Squire Rearman enters, freed from a patriot jail through the protective intervention of an unnamed citizen. When Rearman criticizes the arbitrary power of the committees, Eltha urges the squire to court popularity by relinquishing such protection. Should the protector himself become a political liability, then Rearman will be more exposed to arbitrary justice: "The chairman, to be sure, has got power, but he can't always do as he pleases. I'd have you, good sir, take notice of that. My husband is too good, and were he to follow my advice, some people would not have to reproach him, as they do, with tenderness of heart" (433). Thus even if Beatus were to show such tenderness – not likely in Crèvecoeur's satire – he would find no reinforcement for it from the mother of his children. Again, as with her son, she plays what seems to be a mediating role: defending her husband against criticism from the outside world. Nevertheless, she insists that whatever indulgence he grants his son for hunting tories not be turned toward the enemies of the state. In Crèvecoeur's vision of a whig world gone mad, domestic tenderness, figured in the woman, has no place in political relations.

In a later scene, Eltha confronts the woman whose wealthy husband has been pursued by the whigs but has escaped into British-controlled territory. As a victim of the charges against her husband, Mrs. Marston fears to lose her lands and home. Eltha does not sympathize with a woman who defends her husband's honor and her children's interests – what she herself has done in the first landscape – if the cause be wrong, but beats her down with argument after argument, all the while picking out choice Marston family items for herself. Where the ideal whig, in the stoic language of Revolutionary rhetoric, sacrifices self-interest to providential cause, Eltha inverts the formula, to suggest that self-interest and cause are one and the same. All of this is highly ironic, given Farmer James's touting of self-interest as the stimulant to productivity in the New World. The Mandevillean cynicism of the play grates against the more traditional patriotic claim, Crèvecoeur seems to assert, if the cynic is a patriot woman. When a mother gives in to an appetite for personal wealth, her inability to identify with the interests of others represents how far domestic tranquility has been perverted. Eltha's claims to represent her own family's interests become, instead, a source for fresh brutality – ironically, against the domestic world of the other – not the rightful desires of an American household. This is also the theme of another play written at the same time, the previously mentioned *Downfall of Justice*, whereby familial greed, including that of mother and daughter, becomes a virtual attack against the society at large, but in 'Landscapes,' the focus on the woman's venality is starker and more unsettling.

In wartime, only the example of the widowed or violently estranged woman trying desperately to protect her brood has the possibility – such as it is – of sparking the humanity that once flourished in the countryside. In another Crèvecoeur sketch, "The History of Mrs. B.," a tory fighter recounts to the narrator the haunting story of a patriot woman with two nursing children whose heroic acceptance of her fate causes him some pangs. More famously, the image of the butchered domestic woman coalesced in the story of Jane McCrea some months after Crèvecoeur wrote "Landscapes."[23] This situation likewise prefigures how the supplicating woman will be used in nineteenth-century melodrama to evoke feeling from blunt male characters but be unable herself to right wrongs. In "Landscapes," the heroic widow is Mrs. Marston. Eltha attacks her for being "too high," that is, arrogant and unrepentant before the committee. Mrs. Marston replies, "Oppression rather inflates me; misfortunes animate me. How else should I bear their weight? What precaution have I need to take?" (*L* 472). Mrs. Marston has heretofore regulated her home to the benefit of all, under the benign authority of her husband and, more distantly, the king. Eltha, by contrast, has not run her home with the same care, but in fact, if the actions of her sons be the proof, has shown herself to be arbitrary in use of authority. When misused domestic power spreads into the political vacuum created with the loss of the monarch, the result is tyranny.

Domestic life suffers further in revolution when black servants and slaves find themselves with corrupt white masters. In this regard, Crèvecoeur's play parallels its contemporary, *The Downfall of Justice*, yet further. In "Landscapes," as with the *Downfall* author and the portrayal of Jack, Crèvecoeur shows some daring as one of the first American writers to include African American characters in a play.[24] We know already from *Letters* that race is problematic in Crèvecoeur's rural space. As Doreen Saar notes, in *Letters* both Africans and Native Americans "have been covertly excluded from the process of Americanization; they remain outside the melting pot process open to the English and the Europeans."[25] In the early pieces, Farmer James, both in his own voice and that of his wife, comments on his fat, happy slaves (49, 53). In Letter IX, James cries out against the cruelties of southern slavery, which he lays at the feet of the planter class, who parade their wealth among the *beau monde* of the corrupt urban landscape. Most notable is the end of that letter, when James, visiting friends in South Carolina, comes across a black man in a cage, being punished for wrongdoing. The man's eyes are pecked out by birds, he is desperately thirsty, and after getting water from James, he asks, in dialect, that he be poisoned and put out of his pain. James cannot oblige that last desire; instead, he must go to dinner with the slave's executioners. Symbolically, the exile and treatment of the slave can be traced in part to moral rot at the domestic core of the white household. In Letter XI, Farmer James ventriloquizes a traveler, Iwan, who listens with approval as the botanist Bartram describes how he has freed slaves and admitted them to his table as freemen. Thus Crèvecoeur dodges the question of equality by reincorporating former slaves into the domestic space ruled over by a benevolent, home-centered landholder. Since he uses an Iwan in "Landscapes," Crèvecoeur may also be saying that this foreign visitor can see the problems of race in America more clearly than an Anglo-American.[26]

In "Landscapes," blacks appear as characters or in references on several occasions but always in connection with a white household. Crèvecoeur complicates the issue of black loyalty by showing what happens to a domestically stable slave system under a whig regime. In Leacock's play, the blacks in Virginia identify their interests as allied to Lord Dunmore's forces and thus are seen in the whig politics of *The Fall of British Tyranny* as enemies of American "freedom."[27] The first African character in "Landscapes" who enters is Tom, slave to the deacon's family.[28] At the end of the first landscape, Eltha charges Tom to ready the horses for the ride she and Beatus will take to interrogate tories. Her way of encouraging his execution of the task is to offer him whiskey on Sunday morning, to which he replies, "Tanky you Missy. Wisky is good these cold weather for Negro" (439). Tom speaks in a dialect that differs somewhat from stage African English, perhaps inflected by the Dutch that many slaves in New York colony and state learned; in any regard, his speech marks him as dependent on a master with greater facility in English for direction. Thus by giving him alcohol, Eltha disrupts the pattern of dependence by violating the trust he would have to put in her. Not only does Eltha's action add to the picture of her as a religious hypocrite, but it also shows that black loyalty to patriot families must be bought through the corruption of the slave's otherwise loyal and good nature. Eltha's offering Tom alcohol shows she does not have the moral authority, grounded in her role as sentimental center of the household, to urge his natural compliance.

By contrast, the slave of Mrs. Marston, Nero, remains at his post for better reasons than Tom. Eltha asks Nero if he would come live with her son, the tory-hunter, Anthony: "They say you are a good fellow, only a little Toryfied, like most of your colour" (472). Here, Crèvecoeur demonstrates his understanding of the appeal of tory and British administrators to slaves of patriots to find freedom by deserting the whig cause, but he frames the matter as a choice between right- and wrong-thinking masters. Nero, unlike the already corrupted Tom, rejects the bribe: "no Missy, me stay and help Massa children. What do here without Nero, you been by, take all meat, all bread, all clothes?" When Eltha counters that he must be sold and might as well live with Anthony as anyone, Nero again refuses on moral grounds: "me never live with a white man who shot my master."

Responds Eltha, "You are a liar, you black dog, and I'll soon make [you] sing a new song" (472). Like Jack in *Downfall*, Nero stands for moral rectitude against white vice, but in "Landscapes," the slave has backing in the form of his tragically elevated mistress. Crèvecoeur's awareness of color as a sign can be seen later. Mrs. Marston, in a long speech denouncing the overturning of all previously revered order, remarks, "Everything is strangely perverted; black is become white, and white is become black" (479). For her, racial black means happiness in the home of the white squire and family; for Eltha, black is nothing more than an extension of white vice, venal and corrupt. In both cases, black character is shaped by white owner.

This linkage of black identity with loyalty, in its several senses, is maintained even at the very end, after all the African characters have departed from the scene. Eltha blisters Martha Corwin for her charges against whigs: "These Tories are just like the Negroes: Give them an inch, they will take an ell" (487–88). Blacks are "Toryfied," tories are like blacks, but both are loyal – a loyalty that is fatal when domestic identities are destroyed in the name of liberty. Thus the final marginalization of tories is to think of them in racial terms, and vice versa: the alliance between blacks and tories is one of apparent natural loyalty (and natural class distinction) and, from the point of view of Crèvecoeur's patriots, must be suppressed through the destruction of the loyalist home. Like revolutionaries in more recent times, the whigs here see elimination of "natural" forms of relationship, including loyal black slave to "kind" master, as key to the success of their rebellion.[29] The linchpin to what is natural in class, race, and political participation is the identity of the woman. When she takes upon herself "unnatural" powers or attitudes, the rest of society suffers. Given the usual run of female characters in eighteenth-century British drama, the presence "on stage" of a woman who remains, essentially, unpunished for her disruptions of domestic order is a startling one.

Slaves may have suffered greatly from whig attitudes, and in particular, the loss of firm patriarchal control in the family, but they were not alone. Certainly, the play details cruelties that are intended to make its readers revile the perpetrators. The most pathetic victims are those who have children and the children themselves. Like melodramatists a half-century later, Crèvecoeur maximizes the distress created by violence against the family by surrounding the moaning adults with suffering innocents. In the sixth landscape, the Deacon and Eltha come upon Martha Corwin, the widow of a man hanged by "Lord Sterling," the patriot commander.[30]

She is mad, or so the others interpret her raving speech, but she has clearly been driven to distraction by the loss of her husband and her world. She reproves the hypocrites, as she calls them, for persecuting the defenseless and allowing her child to die, while it now lies unburied. Her last speech, the penultimate one in the play, serves as a remonstrance against the rapine spawned from seeking violent change: "Great God, give me strength and patience to wait with resignation for the day when the restoration of government shall restore to us some degree of peace and security" (488). This plea resonates with Crèvecoeur's position on government: only distant and established authority, not local and upstart power, can ensure the tranquility necessary for families to live in peace. At the same time, Martha's speech serves as a strategic piece of theatre that reinforces all that is wrong when one woman cannot respond to the domestic agony of another.

Behind the violence that leaves the innocent dead is another casualty of war, religious toleration. Crèvecoeur, whose Farmer James all along has been suspicious of state religion, sees America as that place where one is free not only to profess but from profession. He identifies his villains in the play as Presbyterians with a marked taste for George Whitefield's sermons. Although Whitefield was an Anglican with Methodist leanings, the play voices the fear, grounded in a generic distrust of New Light enthusiasm, that an ideologically rigid Calvinism will be imposed as a state doctrine – and thus become an unwarranted intrusion on the private choices made by the family. This accords with the historical partisanship of Ulster-originated Calvinists in eastern Pennsylvania. The object of the author's satire is clear from the first scene. After the deacon's sons have returned home from tory hunting and Eliphalet has regaled the family with Anthony's adventures in persecution, Beatus offers up thanks: "(*Here he fetches a deep sigh and with a quivering voice*, [thus] *goes on.*) Gracious God, pour Thy blessings on Thy favourite people. Make [us thy] chosen race to increase and prosper by the influence of Thy heavenly showers –" (429).[31] The play identifies the American Calvinist rhetoric of the chosen people as a source of Revolutionary violence, for it justifies acts against helpless and innocent civilians. As Squire Rearman declares, in a speech that might serve as a motto for all of Crèvecoeur's wartime essays, "Common mercy is departed" (431).

In essence, then, Crèvecoeur privileges no sect, although he clearly excoriates the Presbyterians. Rather, religion serves its role in society only insofar as it encourages a form of social interaction that relies on mercy, tolerance, and deference. The author scorns the notion that Americans are an elect, or more precisely, that Calvinist Americans are such. The deacon cannot recognize that, as the squire chides him, "Tories are men as well as yourself" (432); at the same time, judicial proceedings conducted under the Deacon's authority as chairman of the committee of safety are without "the least show of humanity or even reason" (433). Beatus and Eltha play right into those charges in a following scene, when Eltha prophesies the new Jerusalem and the Deacon claims, "God is good; God is great; His mercy is immense. If we serve Him faithfully, I am sure, He tells my heart, that He will reward us with the spoil of our enemies" (441). These "pretended saints, veteran Puritans," as another character, Ecclestone, calls them, are in fact inadequate interpreters of truth. Acting from passions, and not from reason, ill-educated religious fanatics force a narrow Calvinism upon society, destroying, in the name of God's mercy, the sustaining doctrine of family life – common mercy.[32]

If Crèvecoeur rejects the limitation of an American identity as Calvinist only, he does so in a form, the drama, that promises a nonsectarian affirmation of traditional moral values. In the way that the stage resisted a too-close identity with any religious creed, as discussed earlier, so the author of this closet play argues against any religion dominating American life to the point where others are directly harmed by it. He goes further by demonstrating that in fact it is virtually un-American to follow the blueskin tenets of the Presbyterians. The hypocrisy of the Revolutionaries and their self-justifying faith appears most tellingly in the long fourth landscape at the tavern. Although colonial inns sometimes had reputations for disorder, the tavern in 'Landscapes' makes another house, a refuge whose internal order has been violated by the imposition of arbitrary laws of condemnation and confiscation. Once the symbol of a rightly ordered society – a place of tolerance for a variety of backgrounds and beliefs – Landlord Potter's establishment now becomes an emblem, indeed the gathering point, for clashing voices and irreconcilable attitudes, much as the pre-war coalitions of ethnically and religiously diverse Pennsylvanians fractured into vicious opposition with the onset of war. One visitor, a committee of safety member, Aaron Blue-Skin, enters to denounce tories and praise God. After he leaves, Iwan, a foreign visitor, takes his measure:

> This is a curious fellow, admirably well-fitted for the time. No wonder he stands so high in the estimation of the people. Profligate yet apparently religious, conceited and stubborn, he can do mischief with all the

placidity of a good man and carefully avoid the ostensible parts of the sinner. (459)

In "Landscapes," the show of religion is more important than the actuality; it impresses the mob, gathers power to the impersonator. Another example of religious division in the tavern scene occurs at the entrance of Captain Shoreditch, his militiamen, and the three Quakers, the latter tied up and under arrest for noncompliance with the laws of military support and service. Their peaceable manners and courtesy contrast with the patriot Colonel Tempelman's hot-headed denunciations of their creed; indeed, Tempelman, like the Deacon and his wife and like Aaron Blue-Skin, speaks a policy of political-sectarian cleansing. We will have an orderly society, he says, as soon as these "plaguey Tories" and "dangerous" Quakers are expelled. Says the colonel, set up New Pennsylvania – a social experiment based on peace and tolerance – on the moon.

The relationship of the Society of Friends to an American identity had long been problematic by the time of "Landscapes," but as mentioned above, became more so once the Revolution began. If during the Seven Years' War, Pennsylvania Quakers could be publicly secure in their refusal to support the war effort, even if privately desirous to help the military cause, the Revolution posed higher stakes. In attempting to remain neutral, many Quakers were suspected of loyalism while others were more confirmed in their allegiance to the crown. As Crèvecoeur shows, there is a price to be paid for practicing a religion other than the tacit state faith, depicted in the play as Presbyterianism. While the bound Quakers argue for something like Farmer James's earlier ideal of a polity in which all sects are encouraged – perhaps as checks to each other – "under the benign shadow of a just and upright government" (*L* 464), the text promises affliction for the advocates of peace. The upshot of a world in which law sanctions religiously inspired violence and directs it primarily against the family is a choice between death or exile. Thus the very differences between neighbors celebrated in Letters II and III as elements of a peaceful society based on mutual respect now become intolerable forms of persecution. Landlord Potter, whose establishment has mimicked the domestic in accommodating those harmless little quarrels that occur in all households, can only give away his wares and look to expulsion from his own tavern. Public spaces, once mirrors of the domestic situation of the American farmer, now become sites of the counter-domestic in which loyalty is political, not familial, and tolerance a sign of weakness, not the precondition to human metamorphosis. Given a Quaker-like refusal to join in intolerance, characters are left with flight or death as the last principled options for those who believe in common mercy as signal to American identity.

It is not much of a choice. Throughout "Landscapes," the language of exile makes itself felt. Mrs. Marston claims to the committee leaders that her husband has done what he can to protect his family and home, but with whig patrols out hunting and threatening to kill him, he has no choice but to flee. Perhaps laying the groundwork for his own flight from spouse and farm, Crèvecoeur portrays Francis Marston as a man of deep suffering, who must abandon those he loves to give them any chance at peace. Yet the whole effort proves futile. Mrs. Marston argues with Beatus and Eltha that forcing her husband to decide among hateful alternatives makes a mockery of his supposed free will:

> They sent word that if he did not quit in three hours, the whole should be in flames. He roused himself up once more and with streaming eyes and a bleeding heart he bade me farewell. Yet this is the man you proclaim a traitor. He would have been a traitor to himself had he stayed any longer. 'Tis for my sake and that of his children, 'tis to preserve these buildings and what they contain, that he quitted. Can you in the face of that pure sun, can you say he went away out of choice? (480)

Mrs. Marston's cry reflects Crèvecoeur's locus philosophy, delineated in such sunny fashion only a few years before. Where once voluntary flight from Europe led the wanderer to the welcoming farmland of the transforming American landscape – that "asylum," as Farmer James calls it – now that ground is itself spoiled, and those who remain risk treachery to themselves. The domestic refuge cannot survive in a corrupted world.

In *Letters from an American Farmer*, James ends by planning to flee his farm for the frontier. Although in Letter III he has criticized frontiersmen as depraved, by Letter IX, he has declared that in terms of comparative corruption, cities are worse than the backwoods. Thus in Letter XII, "Distresses of a Frontier Man," he imagines taking his family to live with the Indians, not without regret, but as a measure that will allow him some freedom to hold the hearts and minds of his children to some part of civility, even in the heart of the forest. In "Landscapes," no such option exists. By the time he writes the play, Crèvecoeur knows that the backwoods now are full of renegade tories and Indians – the very people who attack his own home when he flees to New York City. For the exiles in the drama, wandering is all that is left.

This fate is most ruefully depicted in the sixth and final landscape, which features Martha Corwin. Her husband hanged, a child recently dead and unburied, Martha wanders the roads, a person whose sufferings ought to spur the conscience of any feeling human being. In prophetic language, Crèvecoeur puts in her mouth the most powerful accusations of the play. Responding to the cruelty of Beatus and Eltha, she cries, "Gracious God, why dost Thou suffer these rulers to plunder the widows and their children and call their rags their country's inheritance – a miserable one, which, to feed and pamper a few, leaves hundreds desolate, a prey to death and despair? And you are the chairman!" The Deacon's only response is to deny her authority: "You are mad" (486).

But madness is relative. After all, the stage is full of famous madmen and madwomen whose distraction is sometimes temporary or put on, sometimes permanent and pathetic. When Eltha later repeats the charge of "mad" against Martha, the victim shows she is mad with grief, but clear-eyed about its cause. She regales her antagonist with the crux of Crèvecoeur's complaint against the Revolution, the despoliation of the domestic realm. In an ironic reversal of Letter II, which shows Farmer James admiring his wife as she nurses their child, Martha cries out to her calumniators that her milk has gone, "and my poor baby, by still suckling the dregs, fed awhile on the dregs of sorrow." She turns on Eltha, who, in a world where domestic bliss feeds on the cosy sentiments of the heart, should be sympathetic to a suffering woman:

> Aye, ma'am, that's spoken like yourself. Mingle religion with obduracy of heart, softness of speech with that unfeeling disposition which fits you well for a chairman's wife. Despise the poor, reject the complaints of the oppressed; crush those whom your husband oversets; and our gazettes shall resound with your praise. Mad woman! Yes, I am mad to see ingratitude and hypocrisy on horse-back, virtue and honesty low in the dirt. (486–87)

Once political power produces hardness of heart, then children may be starved, widows condemned, and all justice overturned. It is a bleak ending, promising not a good thrashing of the whigs as a pro-British play, *The Battle of Brooklyn*, does, but only foreseeing a long continuation of conflict, bigotry, and the destruction of domestic peace in the agricultural district. In its anticipation of the melodramatic situation – the threat to domestic expressions of sentiment by implacable enemies to feeling – "Landscapes" serves as a forerunner of the plays that would hold

American dramatic audiences until nearly the twentieth century. Yet unlike those plays – such Anglo-American vehicles of middle-class domestic value as Douglass Jerrold's *Black-Ey'd Susan*, George Aiken's version of *Uncle Tom's Cabin*, or Augustin Daly's *Under the Gaslight* – where salvation comes at the last minute, Crèvecoeur's play offers little hope that threats to hearth and home will, by a timely entrance, be overcome in favor of middling manners.[33]

Still, Crèvecoeur cannot resist one parting shot. After the last scene, he adds four numbered paragraphs, three of which augment or repeat what has been dramatized in the landscapes. The first paragraph describes "a copper plate" that shows two chained men on horseback, falling after being shot, perhaps suggesting the kind of violence perpetrated by the Deacon's son Anthony. The second illustrates the persecution of the tied Quakers by Captain Shoreditch and the militiamen. The third portrays Martha Corwin leaning against a tree, talking with Eltha and Beatus. The fourth, which may or not have been intended for an unwritten scene,[34] reads thus: "A stallion rushing from the woods and covering the mare on which Eltha rides; she stoops on the neck; her husband [behind whipping] the horse, but in vain" (489).[35] This symbolic rape of Eltha by the backwoods stallion is the only indication of some kind of justice in the play; as such, it is crude and perplexing. The writer's vengeance on the Revolution is to imagine the bestial humiliation of the woman, Eltha, whose corruption personifies the destruction of domestic stability. As with cartoons that displayed Britannia or America being raped or poked by leering representatives of contending countries, Crèvecoeur here makes the rape of the female emblematic of historical retribution. Omitting the scene as part of his dramatic text, he renders it at the last as a landscape of perverse violence. In this form, Crèvecoeur offers a picture of the anti-Columbia, the republican mother punishable for crimes against society. Inverting the rape–mutilation cartoons, this final picture leaves a reader with no sympathy for the new victim, Eltha – and no hope for the restoration of the domestic ideal short of the violent return of the old order. It is as if, after the main play, the author has conjured up as an afterpiece a crude pantomime or dumb show to serve for a dark comic commentary on the serious matter of the six scenes.

Unlike *Letters*, where Farmer James posits at least the possibility of a reconstructed domestic space among the denizens of the frontier, the voice of "Landscapes" offers a pessimistic rejection of the idea that a system of independent, well-regulated households can ensure an ordered society. Once household identities become corrupted and break out of the limits of the home, the identities of all are threatened by the resulting moral infection. In its protest, and perhaps contrary to the author's intention, the play reveals the fundamental error behind a vision of society that relies on domestic tranquility as the end of political life. One lesson of "Landscapes," then, is this: No society constructed on the belief that venality will be tempered by a commodious farm and fertile soil can resist the implacable surge of human passions. In other words, prosperity alone cannot combat the appeal to power fostered by revolutions. The man who gave Americans for many generations the picture of themselves they most wanted to see – the tolerant, prosperous, landholding, peaceable, and domestic people outlined in Letter III by the naively optimistic (or deeply satiric) Farmer James – also gave them in "Landscapes" the image of its opposite, a nightmare of popular cruelty and personal despair.

Through irony and bitter satire, Crèvecoeur leaves the afterimage of identities lost to the Revolution: men who establish firm household control over wives and dependants, including slaves; women who remain content with fostering the virtue of the home; religious people who keep their faith to themselves; rude mechanicals who know they are lost without the direction of the local squire; and bound Africans who model their loyalty on that established by the benevolent manorial lord. Whereas his play serves as a corrective to whig celebrations of a cause supported through intimidation and violence, it also expresses desires for a set of identities that cannot be maintained in a revolutionary age. Far from the voice of progressive transformation of the constricted European peasant, the Crèvecoeur of "Landscapes" shows himself a deep reactionary whose skill emerges in the portraits of loss and despair caused by wartime zealotry.

In the small flurry of plays written in the early Revolutionary era, Crèvecoeur's stands out for its complexity of treatment of current events. Beneath the high rhetoric of independence and liberty in the Boston Massacre orations, on the margins of guerrilla and battlefield warfare, the linked scenes of "Landscapes" dramatize in colloquial and domestic terms a whole variety of identities and postures: tory and whig, black and white, victim and victimizer, domestic angel and heartless virago, religious neutral and Calvinist tyrant. Play form allows the author to explore the voices of arrogance and despair through the experiences felt by individual citizens rather than cast the thousands of small conflicts of the people's war as one totalizing and abstract cause. Warren and

Brackenridge imagine their playscapes as declamatory stages; Crèvecoeur, like his contemporary, the *Downfall of Justice* author, uses the form to better advantage, coaxing even from closet drama the intimacies only possible in imagined domestic spaces. The irony of patriotic attainment of liberty is that once the war is over, the new political landscape makes it difficult to mount plays that are seriously critical of the Revolution. Crèvecoeur's landscapes of unnatural identity, acted as he thought in the real homes and taverns of his time, could not be shown, either in 1777 or even years later, on any literal American stage.

3

British author, American text: The Poor Soldier *in the new republic*

Crèvecoeur's manuscript scenes notwithstanding, the majority of American-authored texts published as plays during the Revolution, all intended for the closet, supported the patriot side or took no direct stand against the whigs or the war. Except for the possibility of private readings or as yet unknown or unconfirmed amateur productions, these plays were not performed as scripts for the stage.[1] They enacted their roles in the ideological and propaganda battles fought in print, have their place in American drama history, but made little immediate contribution to the theatre of the new republic. During the war, of course, few patriots had contact with the stage, unless they happened to be in British-occupied cities; Washington's famous production of *Cato* at Valley Forge is only the exception that proves the general case. This is not to say that such a production is unimportant; as Randall Fuller has shown, the Valley Forge *Cato* plays against the Philadelphia spectacle mounted by the British military, the *Meschianza*, in a number of symbolic ways.[2] But in large measure, when whigs concerned themselves with theatre, it had more to do with vehicle than tenor, the figure than the literal boards. Once the war was over, the more radical whigs sought to limit theatre altogether, but for others, there was the sympathetic question: What would be shown?[3] The answer came quickly enough. When the theatres reopened to the American public in the mid-1780s, the companies produced what their British-born actors knew: the old favorites from the pre-war repertory and the new things from London yet to be shown in North America. How, then, might one establish matters of American identity in a theatrical diet surfeited with English and Irish plays?

Because the early American theatre had virtually no native playwrights writing for the stage until Royall Tyler's *The Contrast* opened at the John

Street Theatre in New York in April of 1787, American playgoers in that city and elsewhere contented themselves, usually quite happily, with what they took as the standard fare imported from London: Shakespeare, the odd Restoration tragedy, and eighteenth-century comedies, pantomimes, proto-melodramas (*George Barnwell, The Gamester*), musical dramas, and farces of all sorts. One of the plays that Tyler saw in New York in March during his visit there was John O'Keeffe's *The Poor Soldier* (1783), a two-act comic opera well spiced with songs and airs, the music for which was provided by William Shield or borrowed from popular tunes of the day. O'Keeffe, an Irish-born playwright, specialized in musical comedies that he turned out in abundance and with great popularity for stages in London. Playgoers in the United States may not have seen an O'Keeffe before the war (he gained popularity in England only after 1780), but they might have known his songs, which were often published separately from the libretto; consequently, theatre managers could anticipate that their audiences would want to see the work of a playwright well-renowned in Britain, who would not give direct offense to Americans. During its performance by Lewis Hallam the Younger's Old American Company, the recently renamed American Company of Comedians, *The Poor Soldier* featured several of the troupe's mainstay actors, including John Henry as Patrick and Thomas Wignell as Darby.[4] The latter fact is repeated humorously in *The Contrast* when Colonel Manly's waiter, Jonathan, also played by Wignell, describes his unwitting visit to the theatre the night before and mixes together character name with actor: "Darby Wag-all."[5] Well after Tyler's play had faded from memory, O'Keeffe's comedy remained vigorously upon the stage for decades.

The plot, if one wants to call it that, involves the return of Irish-born British soldiers to rural Ireland after their participation in the American war. One, an officer and man of the city named Fitzroy, sees a local beauty, Norah, and decides to stay in the village in which he has stopped to secure his catch. Another, a foot soldier named Patrick, has come home and looks up his girlfriend – this same Norah – from before he went to war. Meanwhile, two other local swains, Darby and Dermot, vie for the affections of another Irish lass, Kathleen. Two lesser characters, Fitzroy's servant Bagatelle, a self-styled Frenchman whose home is this very village, and the local priest, Father Luke, who is either guardian or uncle of the two young women, make their complicating appearances at various points. In the end, Patrick gets his girl and Dermot his, while Darby, having lost out to Dermot, contemplates joining the military in order to get the acclaim that Patrick earns. The play ends with a song in which all the major characters have parts.

The Poor Soldier premiered in Dublin on March 28, 1783, then opened at Covent Garden on November 4. Its sprightly music and comic Irishman Darby made it a quick favorite as an afterpiece on British stages, one of several O'Keeffe productions to reach broad popularity. By 1800, *The Poor Soldier* had been performed 170 times in London alone, making it the fifth most popular musical drama (newly written) in the last quarter of the eighteenth century.[6] Appearing for its first American production in New York on December 2, 1785, the play found the same kind of success in the United States as it had in Britain, becoming a repertory standard in several cities. In Philadelphia, then under antitheatrical laws, *Poor Soldier* was performed first as a puppet show, then advertised as a "musical entertainment," under which guise it was given half a dozen times in the first two months of 1787.[7] By the time Tyler saw it at the John Street Theatre in March 1787, the Old American Company had put it on at least twenty times in New York alone.[8] Given the response of the Virginia jurist St. George Tucker to the July 21, 1786 performance in New York – "I never saw a better representation – the Characters were all well filled & well supported"[9] – the company must have realized that they had as close to a sure thing as any play they enacted. What is most remarkable about *The Poor Soldier* is its overwhelming and continuing popularity in American theatres. Between 1785 and 1815, O'Keeffe's musical comedy was the most popular such amusement in the entire country, playing in the five major theatre centers – Boston, New York, Philadelphia, Baltimore, and Charleston – 233 times in that period.[10] In addition to the major cities, *Poor Soldier* appeared before 1800 in many smaller venues with limited seasons, including Alexandria, Petersburg, Norfolk, and Richmond, Virginia; Salem, Massachusetts; Newport and Providence, Rhode Island; and Hartford, Connecticut. This kind of widespread production suggests that very many, if not most, English-speaking Americans had relatively easy access to seeing the O'Keeffe–Shield comic opera. Even afterwards, it continued to be trotted out before audiences in cities like Cincinnati and New Orleans as well as frontier venues[11] and could be found in New York as late as 1849. So much did the comic opera become part of the entertainment consciousness of the new republic that it might fairly be called an American play.

The Poor Soldier is one of many British plays of the period that become appropriated via the American stage to perform the cultural work of the

United States. The circulation of plays and players, like that of fashions and trade goods, becomes part of a transatlantic, or circum-Atlantic (to use Joseph Roach's term), movement of entertainment across newly created national boundaries.[12] Dramas, particularly comedies, comic operas, and farces, could often be altered in the theatre to meet local circumstances or potential objections, thereby allowing for a kind of Americanization (or even Philadelphia-ization) of a British-authored text. In addition to clamors over the degree of mockery in Bagatelle's French impersonation, productions of *The Poor Soldier*, for instance, sometimes featured breeches performers on American stages or involved substitutions of ethnicity for Bagatelle. John Durang found it to be a sufficiently malleable vehicle in translation to take to German-speaking audiences in Pennsylvania and Maryland.[13] It directly provoked the American playwright William Dunlap to write a sequel, *Darby's Return*, as an appeal to republican audiences. And in *The Contrast*, Tyler alludes to the play in such a way as to assume that the audience is completely familiar not only with *The Poor Soldier* itself but also its application to an American scene.

It should be acknowledged that the play's popularity rests at least in part on its broad humor and engaging songs, many based on folk tunes, in the English ballad opera tradition, whether played in London or New York or Philadelphia.[14] Musical comedies proved to be box-office money-makers on both sides of the Atlantic, and the simple love plot would hardly be remarkable in any European-derived dramatic form. But where others of O'Keeffe's comic operas, such as *The Son-in-Law, The Agreeable Surprise*, and *Peeping Tom of Coventry*, were roughly equal successes to *The Poor Soldier* in English theatres,[15] the story of Darby and Patrick was considerably more often played in the new republic than other O'Keeffe offerings.[16] If one adds to those performances the various productions of O'Keeffe's sequel, *Patrick in Prussia; or, Love in a Camp* (1786), which premiered in New York one week before *The Contrast*, then the Darby–Patrick duo gains further popularity. American audiences must have felt engaged with the story of soldiers returning from the Revolution, while finding in the clownish lover Darby a character at whose naiveté they could laugh sympathetically.

In the Prologue to *The Contrast*, Tyler remarks that his play will celebrate "native themes," meaning the plainness of address in America and "the homespun habits" that constitute the essential American character (*TC* 7). And while the main plot of his comedy centers on elite figures, the three most identifiably "American" characters, Manly, Maria, and Jonathan, all give voice to a simplicity and integrity of values that has the potential, at least, to cut across class lines. Although *The Contrast* is set in New York, Jonathan refers frequently to his home village; and while his naivete is exceptional, his essential loyalty and honesty mark him in stage terms as fully in the American grain. But given Tyler's homework – his attendance at the John Street Theatre – that American stamp to Jonathan's character owes more than a little to O'Keeffe's comic opera. In *The Poor Soldier*, O'Keeffe keeps all his action in an Irish village, identified in his autobiography as "Carton, the seat of the Duke of Leinster, a few miles from Dublin," but in the Dublin edition of 1786 and the Philadelphia edition of 1787 as simply "A Country Village."[17] For American spectators, this setting has two implications. One is that village life as such, whether in Ireland or Vermont, is pretty much the same. The happiest and healthiest characters are those who speak honestly, from the heart, and who display the kind of loyalty to home and friends that we see in Jonathan. Anticipating later Yankee plays, where the small town or rural scene becomes the setting into which a wily, conniving man of the city enters for spoil, O'Keeffe's comedy rewards the integrity of Patrick, the eponymous character, when Fitzroy, whose life Patrick has saved during a Revolutionary War battle in America, recognizes the simple man's village traits as those of common decency. The city-bred officer is thus reformed by learning magnanimously to cede his interest in Norah to the more deserving poor soldier.

On a symbolic level, then, *The Poor Soldier* offers a comforting, mildly whiggish view of the late unpleasantness. Insofar as American audiences might identify with the village as a site of innocence and virtue, they find in the theatre that just about any village will do, Irish or otherwise, if the villagers are given some basic integrity. Patrick is the selfless patriot, village-born and to the village returned. He has seen a great war, performed nobly in rescuing his superior officer, and now desires nothing more than to marry his girl and settle back from whence he came. Patrick desires what Crèvecoeur in "Landscapes" intimates as ideal, a hearth-and-home society in which little people, farmers and foot soldiers, retreat from the great affairs of the world and lose themselves in domestic routine. By carefully eliding anything in the story that might create a partisan identification, O'Keeffe prevents his text from being claimed as simply a justification by the British for their conduct of the war. Rather, Patrick's challenge is to win Norah from the urbane Fitzroy, who is unaware at first who Patrick is, but who might represent to American audiences the British themselves, figured as from the metropolis. In Fitzroy's recognition of Patrick's just claim to Norah – the land itself – American spectators might find validation for their village-innocent assertion of their legitimate rights. Thus the urban man's acknowledgment of the villager's just deserts makes possible the kind of reconciliation that theatre managers desire: the war's over, let's all be friends and remember our common ties. In the play, the common tie is Ireland, but only noted by a few local place names and a reference to potatoes; for American audiences, the associative substitution of known villages in the United States would have been a relatively easy one to make. Shorn of any of the bitterness of Crèvecoeur's closet drama, O'Keeffe's comedy creates a desire for a humble, pre-war life in which the simplicity of the village dominates the world view of citizens.

If one aspect of its popularity rests on the setting's universality, another centers on its Irishness. For a century, British playwrights had made considerable comic hay from Irish characters, using a variety of types from the crude shillelagh-bearing brute to the more recent sentimental brogue figure dreaming of hearth and potatoes. A frequent source of amusement for London audiences was the use of the bull, a confused expression on the part of the Irish character that showed his benighted status and allowed the normative English characters to establish their own linguistic or social superiority by contrast. As will be discussed in another chapter, the reception of Irish characters on American stages is connected in some degree to the immigration patterns of Irish in America; people of Irish background, the majority Protestant, could be found in most cities along the coast during the late eighteenth century. With the Irish rebellion of 1798, new immigrants arrived that in the first wave of sympathy inspired a number of parallels to be drawn between the Irish fight for independence and the recent American struggle. Therefore, in the late 1790s and early 1800s, Irish characters might generate positive fellow feeling from republican audiences. O'Keeffe, himself Irish, depicts his village folk without the heavy hand of English satire and typing, keeping the brogue light and the stock English elite out of the picture altogether, allowing playgoers to see the Irish villagers as the norm and the one urban character, Fitzroy, as out of step. In the usual formula, the stage Irishman is the odd man out in London, made to look the fool against English dominant manners. For American audiences, then, the combination of a positive portrayal of Irish people in a village setting would have disposed them favorably to *The Poor Soldier*.

Curiously, O'Keeffe criticism has tended to minimize the Irish dimension of his plays; as Karen Harvey and Kevin Pry have stated, this overlooking of O'Keeffe's references to his homeland prevents contemporary readers from seeing what spectators of the time might have observed. Heinz Kosok, for instance, argues that O'Keeffe's participation in English theatrical traditions, despite his Irish birth, makes the business of Irishness inconclusive.[18] In any event, what Irish tint there is to *The Poor Soldier* can be achieved as much by actor inflection as anything one reads directly in the text. If, on the one hand, the Irishness is present but somewhat muted, on the other there is nothing in the play to incite hostility to Ireland or to make Irish characters or manners the butt of satire or heavy-handed ethnic jokes. Consequently, references to Ireland can easily be appropriated to affirm the sort of country values that Tyler sought to incorporate in *The Contrast* but without too much of the benighted dialect humor struck from the Irish equivalent of Jonathan.

O'Keeffe also connects with American audiences through references to the Revolutionary War and to soldiering itself. Strategically acute, the playwright nationalizes the war only slightly, thereby making adaptation in America relatively easy. He may have learned a lesson from a play that he wrote just before this one, a now lost text called "A Definitive Treaty." Rejected by Thomas Harris, manager at Covent Garden, as too political, this play, according to O'Keeffe, would have run the table on global politics:

> I personified the respective wrangling nations of the world, belligerent and neutral, (but indeed none were suffered to be the latter,) by characters as assembled by chance at a table-d'hôte at Spa; and produced incidents very exactly similar to the original causes and progress of the wars that were at this time terminated:– showing the part each nation took, what they gained, and what they lost. All this, each in the single character representing his particular nation – a Dutchman, a Frenchman, a German, a Swiss, an Italian, a Spaniard, a Portuguese, a Swede, a Dane, a Russian, a Prussian, a Turk, an American, an Englishman, a Scotchman, and two Irishmen; and afterwards the manner how all was made up and peace concluded:– the complete affair in the shape of a tavern party, squabbling over the bottle, with skirmishes of bloodshed and battery, kicked shins, broken heads, and tattered garments; when, good-humour reviving, a general shake hands concluded the piece, leaving some of them with black eyes and broken noses: and showing how some *paid* their bill, and others *bilked* the house.[19]

For O'Keeffe, the spa tavern functions as that space where differences flare up, but where amity finally reigns – the quality that was lost from the public house, in Crèvecoeur's vision, in the American Revolution. Although O'Keeffe in his autobiography gives no indication of who paid and who bilked, he depicts here a general desire to see harmony among nations, even after war has separated them. Most likely, his view of the Revolutionary War was that of kicked shins, and therefore, after the shaking of peaceful hands, there would be no good served by rehashing the causes in future plays. Beyond that, though, O'Keeffe, himself an Irish transplant to London, recognizes the implicit transnationality of the theatre as itself another version of the table-d'hôte or tavern. In the way in which he figures in a play the mutual shaking of hands of a list of national types, so the theatre is that space in which one person may play many parts – "a Dutchman, a Frenchman, a Swede" – as John William Green does in Philadelphia, or any other regular player on either side of the Atlantic. By understanding the relative absurdity of national identification through the trope of the costume, O'Keeffe can visualize a stage world in which such identity is transformed into a broader human comedy.

In his next play, O'Keeffe drops all but the most casual reference to global politics. We learn that Patrick has been wounded – which wound frightens Darby for a while out of enlisting – and that in a battle in "Carolina" he had dragged Fitzroy to safety. In one of dozens of slight to substantive differences among texts (English, Irish, and American), the battle that O'Keeffe had specifically in mind was at Beattie's Ford, named as such in the London edition, but a place-name changed in the Dublin text to the generic-sounding "Johnston's Ford" and in the Philadelphia printing to "Johnson's Ford" (*PS* 19).[20] Why the author chose that as the single site to be named is not clear. Beattie's Ford was a main crossing point on the Catawba River in Piedmont North Carolina and in late January 1781 was defended by men from the militia led by Daniel Morgan, whose main body of troops was retreating from Cornwallis after defeating Tarleton at Cowpens in extreme northern South Carolina. In the early morning of February 1, Cornwallis ordered a feint at Beattie's but crossed the bulk of his forces at a nearby private ford, Cowan's, which while guarded had insufficient troops to halt the British advance. There were modest casualties on both sides, and British forces were able to rendezvous at Beattie's once the American militia fled the scene. The skirmish was a relatively minor one compared to the two major battles that bracketed Beattie's Ford, Cowpens, and Guilford Court House. Although the battle allowed Cornwallis to continue his campaign through North Carolina, nothing of great significance was determined there.[21] That may have been the point: to give the play authenticity by mention of a real battle but to suppress its significance for a British public ready to put the war behind them. In the London version, O'Keeffe includes more specific references, including to Patrick's being wounded by "an American grenadier" and his participating in the victory at Guilford.[22] In the American versions, the managers remove the offending comments, being sure that neither dialogue nor songs ever name(s) British or American sides as such or speak of victory or loss. An American could watch *The Poor Soldier* and feel sympathy for Patrick as a soldier who took a wound in battle without having that feeling confused by the play's trumpeting British nationalistic sentiments or remembering the battle as one of humiliation or bitterness.[23]

At the same time, in the only song whose lyrics were not composed by O'Keeffe himself, Patrick touts the soldiering life, where poverty has no dominion – "How happy the soldier who lives on his pay,/and spends half a crown out of six-pence a day/Yet fears neither justices, warrants, or bums,/But pays all his debts with the roll of the drums" – but notes that on return, he has little in the way of worldly goods.[24] As Tyler observes in *The Contrast*, American audiences in the 1780s would have been aware of the general problem of Revolutionary soldiers without money, particularly those trying to claim their proper pensions. Tyler, of course, takes up their cause through Colonel Manly; in O'Keeffe, the issue presents itself more generally, without the specific political implications of funding pensions for American veterans. On its surface, the opera honors the soldiering life as service, a safe position for a play to take on either side of the Atlantic. Patrick's description to Darby of his injury could apply to any loyal soldier in any national army: "Only a wound I got in battle, in endeavouring to save my Captain's life. – I was left for dead in the field of battle, bleeding in my country's cause – there was glory for you" (*PS* 11–12). Thus theatre managers in the United States, eager to keep the pipeline to London open but also desirous of satisfying patriotic sentiments among their clientele, could mount *The Poor Soldier* in relative safety, generating a variety of sympathies that paralleled American issues or values without producing any controversy that one or another more American-specific allusion might create.

These explanations for its popularity ironically serve to underscore why *The Poor Soldier* often stirred controversy, nonetheless. After it opened in New York in December 1785 on a bill with Edward Moore's *The Gamester*, it quickly became an afterpiece staple with the Old American Company, being acted by them for the sixteenth time in seven months on June 26, 1786. The company played a brief Philadelphia season in early 1787, shortly after the passage of antitheatrical laws in that city. Beginning on January 22, the play was advertised as "a musical entertainment; called 'Darby & Patrick'; with (by particular desire) the OVERTURE to the Poor Soldier." This ruse of its being advertised as musical only would probably have allowed it to be performed in full. This same kind of imposture was used in antitheatrical Boston in 1792, in which songs from *The Poor Soldier* were linked to a "moral lecture" in the form of lines from John Home's *Douglas*. Even in cities where theatre was proscribed or limited, companies took the risk of mounting the afterpiece, clearly anticipating a profit.[25]

But this emphasis on music over text was the least of the changes seen in early republican theatres. Other alterations had more to do with politics and identity, notably with the otherwise minor character Bagatelle. In O'Keeffe's original, Fitzroy's servant is an Irishman from the same village as Patrick and Darby (although unaccountably not recognized by any of the locals) who has adopted a French accent and metropolitan mannerisms as a way of distancing himself from the rustics. This latter aspect may have at least partly inspired Tyler in his character of Jessamy, the Chesterfield-spouting servant to Billy Dimple. When Hallam and Henry brought *The Poor Soldier* back to New York from Philadelphia in February and March of 1787, they trimmed the character of Bagatelle considerably in a deliberate attempt to ameliorate criticism from Francophiles who thought the servant's portrayal a slur on the late allies of the country. As the managers announced to the public on March 21, "it is both their duty and invariable study to please, not to offend, as a proof of which, they respectfully inform the public, they have made such alterations in the part alluded to [Bagatelle] as they trust will do away with every shadow of offence."[26] This attempt to placate in turn ignited a letter war in the New York press, with several writers questioning this policy and asking whether this would lead to the elimination of all ethnic humor and national types from the stage – an early attack on what was seen as political correctness by the managers of the John Street Theatre. The criticism of the managers reached its satiric peak with a letter in the *Daily Advertiser* on April 4, from a reader who offered lessons in how to cut plays. "I shall continue my strictures 'till the English comedy is reduced to the insipidity of a Presbyterian sermon, and hope to see the church vestry and the corporation of all the others, in the Pit, when the *Hypocrite* is acted, and *Fool's Mirror* the entertainment.'"[27] In other words, to cut is to butcher, and to bow to political expediency is to turn the playhouse into a meetinghouse — a poor choice from the perspective of those in the audience who wanted a quick reconciliation with Britain and whose identity was still tied up in English values and mores.

This tempest over Bagatelle — one that replayed itself in several cities, including sparking a riot in Boston in 1796 — reveals the degree to which audiences could react to something as seemingly insignificant as cutting the lines of a secondary character in a two-act comic opera.[28] In other words, despite the satire in *The Contrast* of audience inattention to plays, where Charlotte lists all the things spectators do besides watch the stage, New York and other audiences at least took to the lists to defend certain beliefs relative to what theatre means. Several writers resented the limitation on ethnic humor, foreseeing a curbing of Scots, Irish, and even English characters, all in the name of fearing to offend. One should expect to see types in the theatre, the argument ran; without stereotyping, the theatre ceases to be — it is no better than a church, where moralizing and monotony replace satire and entertainment. But beyond that, the newspaper quarrel shows how much Americans had taken *Poor Soldier* as their own. There is virtually no equivalent stir made about an American play before 1800; indeed, it was as if O'Keeffe's play was already an American one, a defensible and sacred text to which only certain amendments would be allowed.[29]

One other strategy to avoid the Bagatelle problem was recorded at the Boston Federal Street Theatre. In order to avert the criticism of Francophiles and a repetition of the riot that occurred as a result of hostility between Jacobin and Federalist over this minor character,[30] the managers converted the character to a black servant named Domingo and therefore employed a type that would only offend the group least able to affect the economics of the theatre.[31] The name Domingo evokes both the well-known character Mungo from Bickerstaff's *The Padlock* (played as an afterpiece early in the history of professional theatre in Boston), and Santo Domingo, the name for Hispaniola, the island nation whose western portion would be claimed from the French by the black revolutionaries as Haiti. Such a change would not affect the plot significantly, but it would the cultural message being sent. Substitution of a stage African for a stage Irishman is not simply replacement of one ethnic type for another but an acknowledgment that however white Americans might feel about

Irish or French, they would certainly be unanimous in recognizing the African as someone to laugh at. In one scene, Fitzroy beats Bagatelle; and while physical abuse was frequently enacted on the English stage, it has special poignancy in *The Padlock*, where Mungo often complains of rough treatment. As suggested in the discussion of *The Downfall of Justice* and "Landscapes," the abused African servant/slave was rapidly becoming a common motif in American drama and theatre; after all, Royall Tyler had created such an abused black character in *May Day in Town* (1787). To beat a black would then be assumed acceptable to urban American audiences, who had their own social history of abusing African ancestored people. Ironically, O'Keeffe himself was against the slave trade and in another play, *The Basket Maker* (1790), had included in the last song the lines, "Hail fellow! black, yellow/Souls are all of one colour." In *The Young Quaker* (1783) his title character, Reuben Sadboy, who comes into possessions of American tobacco plantations, declares near the end of the play, "while Liberty is the boast of Englishmen, why should we still make a sordid traffic of our fellow creatures? – No, my good Sir! on my return to America, every slave of mine shall be as free as the air he breathes."[32] Thus to convert an Irish character in masquerade as a Frenchman to a black bondman was to adapt to local conditions but diverge from the author's beliefs as expressed elsewhere; Americans were authoring the Irish Londoner's play in ways he could neither foresee nor approve.

If blacking a character is one thing, having all the characters played by African Americans is another. Perhaps it is no real surprise to discover that one of the plays in the repertory of New York's African Theatre was also *The Poor Soldier*. By 1825, African Americans had been involved with theatrical activities for many years in New York, including as actors in their own productions and as stage hands at the Park Theatre, but the best known of the early troupes was a corps of black actors, variously called, who began seasons in earnest in 1821. As George Thompson and Shane White have made abundantly clear, blacks in New York fought prejudice, fire, white violence, and poverty to put on plays, even build a theatre, in order to perform for audiences of both blacks and whites. Despite the scanty records and generally poor newspaper coverage of their activities, surviving documents show that the African Theatre corps mounted *The Poor Soldier* at least twice, once in company with Carlo Delpini's pantomime *Don Juan* and shortly thereafter with *Othello*. Discerning precisely how the African Theatre actors performed O'Keeffe's comic opera is difficult to judge, given that the sole surviving observations come from white spectators with demonstrable racial biases. Still, it is worth investigating to what extent *The Poor Soldier* underwent transformation in the hands of African American professionals in a city that still held slaves.[33]

Of the second known performance by the troupe, the pseudonymous observer only says that the actors used the same barrel-hoop scimitars, costumes, and scenery as in *Othello* and that it was "very little better performed" than the main play.[34] Because properties had been damaged in a concerted act of hooliganism by whites, Simon Snipe's criticism hardly gives anything to go on except, perhaps, that the company was determined and resourceful in the face of adversity.[35] The principal document on performance of *The Poor Soldier* comes from a writer who signed himself Twaites, possibly after the comedian William Twaits, who was popular in the American theatre earlier in the century. For the August 9, 1822 opening of the new theatre building on Mercer Street, the leading actor, James Hewlett, played Patrick, while the two female roles of Norah and Kathleen were realized by Mrs. Williams and Miss Dixon respectively. No other major characters appear to have been used by the small corps – at least no others are listed in a newspaper ad – and in the pantomime, only three characters are named as well, two of them repeats from *Poor Soldier*.[36] Given the limited personnel and resources, the company chose, interestingly, to eliminate Darby, the most popular character among white audiences; Dermot and Fitzroy, the lovers in rivalry with Darby and Patrick; and Bagatelle, the most theatrically controversial figure in the United States performances. According to Twaites, the August 9 show began with an unnamed African American who enacted a servant – or so Twaites describes his appearance. What the satirist may have intended was to mock an authentic servant who had come upon the stage in the function of a stage hand, although the writer indicates that his performance was a "pantomime." In whatever capacity, "He wandered about the stage with just such a vacant air as a negro boy would carry, who had cleaned his knives, and had nothing to do until the hour arrived for filling his tea-kettle." Whether Twaites signaled respect in the authenticity of representation or meant to suggest that the individual on stage was perfectly fit to be a servant by virtue of his race, the text does not indicate. In any event, Hewlett's entrance as Patrick must have been genuinely impressive, for Twaites remarks, with little hint of irony, that he was a "fine dashing fellow," an appearance that contemporary accounts of other roles by Hewlett reinforce. Twaites next describes some apparent coaxing by Hewlett, delivered as a prompt to the actress playing Norah, which brought out Mrs. Williams to sing what was probably Air VI ("The meadows look chearful, the birds sweetly sing") in her first appearance at the window. Once again, Twaites plays to what he presumes will be agreement in his audience about race and humor – that her singing is "*fine*," with italics, and her lips "pouting," as if there were nothing she could do to please *him*, exactly, even though she may well have been quite excellent.[37]

For most of the rest of the account, Twaites signifies that he could not anticipate how the action would transpire; the playing involved different actors with some memory of the lines in a particular scene speaking ahead of the others, while the rest essentially caught up: "with all my ingenuity, I found it impossible to tell what would come next." Shane White interprets this passage as (unintentionally) ascribing agency to the actors for playing the scenes backwards, as a kind of inspired improvisation. One might equally interpret the remarks as describing actors with more verve than preparation returning to correct pronunciations or using clever on-stage prompts when lines were seemingly forgotten. Twaites suggests as much by praising the African players against those at the elite Park Theatre for coming on in their errors/improvisations more boldly than the equally forgetful but more timid white actors. In any event, and however much obtuseness one wishes to assign to the writer for his not giving proper credit to the actors on racial grounds, Twaites's document provides evidence that the African Company found in the vehicle of *The Poor Soldier* an opportunity to stage professionally some pantomime, song, love badinage, and at worst, creative extraction from difficult circumstances. Whatever else he may have intended by his commentary, Twaites was not bored: "I do not know that I have ever witnessed this familiar play with more interest since I first saw it represented." Despite that by 1822, *Poor Soldier* was considered by most critics a tired piece of theatre, the African Company seems to have made it truly theirs, an expression of black artistic desires and theatrical methods.[38] The plasticity of the play, the company's removal of all traditional political bellwether characters, and their boldness in playing it without regard to white audience expectations indicate that *The Poor Soldier* belonged to them as much as it did to the actors and audiences at the white-owned Park Theatre – no blackface Bagatelles needed.

Even more, the African Company made *The Poor Soldier* a dangerous play. Without Darby and the comforting humor of a restored village society, the actors shaped a performance around the "dashing" figure of the soldier in the body of the handsome and (likely) sword-carrying James Hewlett. Hewlett, whose most famous role was Richard III, may have played Patrick with something of Captain Fitzroy's officer assuredness, combining in one soldier the successful lover with martial bearing and command. Given the backlash against black success in New York with the impending end to slavery (in 1827), Hewlett and the African Theatre dared to represent kings, princes, and officers upon the stage, post bills in public streets, and demand payment to see them perform. White writers attempted to minimize the power of these performances through belittling remarks, as Shane White has copiously illustrated, and as one can glean from the remarks of Twaites and Simon Snipe; but the very presence on stage of a poor soldier whose heroic blackness overwhelms the character's ostensible humble Irishness shows dramatically how O'Keeffe's musical served as an appealing shell to be stuffed with a full variety of American identities.[39]

Another strategy used by managers to create interest in what quickly became a staple of the American theatre was to have actresses play some of the male parts, most notably Patrick, the poor soldier himself. Although breeches parts were not new – indeed, they were *de rigueur* for such boy roles as Little Pickle in *The Spoiled Child* – the use of female performers for the role was not standard in the new republic. The Old American Company stuck to its traditional staging, with John Henry as Patrick, but other groups took their cue from the first Covent Garden performance and played a woman in soldier's garb. In Philadelphia in 1791 (Mrs. Kenna) and 1796 (Mrs. Warrell) and Boston in 1796 (Mrs. Williamson) and 1808 (Mrs. Woodham), different actresses performed Patrick, while in a performance in the former city on February 10, 1792, both Patrick (Mrs. Kenna) and Bagatelle (Mrs. Bradshaw) were enacted by women.[40] For the most part, such gender switches appear to have been more for novelty purposes than permanent arrangements. Mrs. Kenna's May 4, 1796 Philadelphia performance was billed as for that night only. The only switch the other way that I am aware of occurred in a pantomimic ballet version of *The Poor Soldier*, entitled *Dermot and Kathleen*, that was mounted in Philadelphia in December 1796, when William Francis performed a character not in the original, Mother Kathleen.

Although the reasons for the breeches roles may have been seen as theatrical, such substitutions create interesting identity problems for audiences. Unlike boy roles such as Little Pickle, that of the poor soldier is a grown man and war veteran. True, Patrick is a sentimental character, and in keeping with the gender codes of sentimental literature of the period, managers might have thought he could be more effectively portrayed as such by an actress. But Patrick is also a soldier, and though there is also a tradition of the sentimental soldier – most notably, the Irish Captain O'Flaherty in Richard Cumberland's *The West Indian* – managers may have been at least half-conscious of the signs sent to the audience through gender casting and preferred, in light of the recent war, to stress his bravery. At the same time, though, given Susanna Rowson's *Slaves in Algiers*, a play that features several characters who cross-dress within the performance and which premiered in Philadelphia in 1794, and the numerous British plays with cross-dressed women or breeches roles, there may have also been local circumstances that would give warrant to playing Patrick as a breeches role. Although much has rightly been made of Deborah Sampson Gannett's groundbreaking appearance on American stages in 1802, exhibiting herself as the now revealed but once disguised Continental soldier of the Revolution, the way may have been smoothed by audience experiences of breeches Patricks (and other female soldier figures) on American stages.[41] To play Patrick thus fit the model of the Covent Garden original, but deciding how to cast the character brought to the fore both stage and cultural considerations of box-office and personnel on one side, notions of masculinity and femininity on the other. Casting Patrick as female may have appealed to women, a population whose presence or absence in a theatre often meant the difference between financial success or failure for managers. But it also indicates that Patrick's identity as the poor soldier could be so sentimentalized (or sensationalized) as to put the character out of the immediate experience and identification of urban playgoers. Audiences could feel sympathy for Patrick, but worry less over a switch in the actor's gender than they would over a change in Bagatelle's ethnic identity.

Yet for women in the audience, such cross-dressing Patricks might have played to a number of desires. Women in uniform have occasionally been popular in British drama, Mrs. Gripe in Thomas Shadwell's *The Woman Captain* (1679) and the Widow Ranter in the play of that name (1689) by Aphra Behn being but two such roles; but in the United States, given the attempts by at least some women to seize greater participation in public affairs, female audience members might have gotten some satisfaction from the portrayal of a war hero who underneath his uniform was a woman. That appeal to the martial spirit of the republican woman may have inspired John Daly Burk's play for American stages on Joan of Arc,

Female Patriotism, where the wearing of armor becomes the point on which the English execution of their enemy turns.[42] Such expansion of the usual roles played by women would have validated to some degree the visibility of women in public arenas, including the stage.[43] Women could embody various abstractions, like Liberty, but those were traditional, given iconographic practices in the eighteenth century; to cross-dress for the entirety of a performance – no revelation scenes as in *As You Like It* – and to woo a woman successfully into the bargain would display for female spectators the possibility of a greater range of powers, including sexual, than might otherwise be imagined. As with the African Theatre productions, cross-dressed plays nearly always featured Patrick, not Darby, as the key figure, giving to the player the dignity of a theme role in an otherwise light comedy. No one is seriously threatened in identity by the gender shift in *Poor Soldier*, at least not to the degree for whites of Hewlett's presence in the role, but at the same time, such occasional transformations kept the performance of a well-known vehicle edgy and suggestive and gave to women an image of themselves more in line with that usually reserved on stage for men.

Whatever the appeal, whether through songs or the novelties of black actors or cross-dressed actresses, *The Poor Soldier* proved to be as close to a guaranteed draw in the afterpiece as anything else put on in the first fifty years of the United States. Not only was it the kind of play that actors liked for their benefit nights, when they received the proceeds of the house, but it was useful for charity benefits, as in Philadelphia in 1794 when it appeared on a bill entitled "Benefit of American Citizens, Captives in Algiers."[44] In addition to the irony of the theatre's staging two British plays (the other was Elizabeth Inchbald, *Every One Has His Fault*) as a benefit for American captives, there is perhaps another in O'Keeffe's having encountered American prisoners of war during the Revolution before he cobbled together *The Poor Soldier*. In Portsmouth, England, the playwright observed both Americans and French who were imprisoned, and noted the differences in demeanor: "the Americans walked about either alone, or in melancholy, silent, or low-speaking groups, while the French, with vivacity, danced and sung and paid compliments, and through the palisades held conversation with females and others who were outside."[45] Although Patrick is a man of feeling, there is nothing in *Poor Soldier* to suggest melancholy; in the stage terms of the eighteenth century, it is hard to imagine a melancholic Irish village. Whether or not the managers in Philadelphia assumed that captive

Americans would be wandering about Algiers in morose, low-speaking groups, they clearly understood that a comedy and a comic opera from England would be the best combination to attract an audience large enough to cover their expenses and leave a few dollars over for the prisoners. In other words, managers saw no irony in staging well-worn British plays to inspire American patriotic identity.

As *The Poor Soldier* changed to meet the times and local conditions in the United States, it also became absorbed into other plays written by Americans. Most well-known is Tyler's *Contrast*, which takes its audience with Jonathan to the very theatre in which they saw Thomas Wignell, the Jonathan of Tyler's comedy, as Darby in O'Keeffe's. Tyler scores comic points through the connections between Jonathan and Darby – they are both unlucky in love, both are fooled by pretentious servants, and both have a provincial outlook based on simplicity of mind and a resolutely rural perspective on the world. Beyond that and other ties already mentioned, though, Tyler puts some distance between his play and O'Keeffe's. In a comic vein, Jonathan offers a criticism of his Irish counterpart, all while not realizing that what he has seen is a play: "he is a cute fellow. But there was one thing I didn't like in that Mr. Darby; and that was he was afraid of some of them 'ere shooting irons, such as your troopers wear on training days. Now, I'm a true born Yankee American son of liberty, and I never was afraid of a gun yet in all my life" (*TC* 35). Although this speech ignores that Darby eventually becomes a soldier in Europe, as audiences would have seen the week before in the New York premiere of *Patrick in Prussia*,[46] it is true of Darby in both, since the Irish character in the sequel is seen as a shirker rather than a true follower of Patrick in bravery. In any event, Tyler makes the point that Jonathan, while like Darby, is not Darby, even if played by the same actor.

More tellingly, the American hero, Manly, is an elite not a poor villager. Like Patrick, he is proud to have served without any more honor than the service itself, but he comes to the city as an officer looking after his men and someone with sufficient private wealth not to have to cash in his commutation notes before they are due. Patrick is a villager, down to his last sixpence, and in the noncommissioned ranks. True enough, he earns an officer's epaulet at the end, courtesy of the grateful Captain Fitzroy, and his bearing is remarked upon by the captain as praiseworthy – that is, as un-village-like, if Darby and Dermot are the points of comparison. But Tyler's Manly has read in classical history and modern political philosophy, as his Act IV disquisition on luxury indicates, even while his wooing of Maria is accidental and lacks the polish of O'Keeffe's captain or Patrick's more heartfelt expressions. If anything, Manly is something of a hybrid: he has Fitzroy's elite and urban background with Patrick's natural nobility and self-effacement. To that extent, Tyler may be suggesting that *The Poor Soldier*, as popular as it is, must be altered in significant ways to translate fully into American terms.

Although Tyler was a Federalist and a long-time associate of the cultural conservative Joseph Dennie, he makes another important shift by having his faux characters be English rather than French. O'Keeffe's Bagatelle becomes an object of ridicule at the end; Fitzroy beats him for his deceptions in the servant's own attempt to secure Norah and consigns him to peasantry for the rest of his days: "You had better stick to your spade than meddle with sword and pistol" (*PS* 28). In Tyler, Dimple and Jessamy enact virtual self-absorbed Englishmen, and while Dimple is expelled by Manly in Act V, he gets to call his colonel opponent an "unpolished, untravelled American" before stalking off the stage, even though by play's end we are asked to admire that provincial more than the Chesterfield-bred pseudo-sophisticate (*TC* 56). While, on the one hand, Tyler marks out imitation of London rather than Paris as the more dangerous path for republican youth, on the other he withholds the objects of satire from ridicule, much as Manly has declared as the proper attitude for an American theatre to take. Here Tyler, like O'Keeffe but in a different way, walks a fine line between criticizing British urban mores and rejecting them altogether. Fitzroy might powder his hair, which in Carton seems like an enormous affectation, but he never stoops to outright deception, like Bagatelle, and indeed, is big enough to step aside from his romancing of Norah for the more deserving Patrick. Dimple does deceive the three women with whom he is involved and has contracted significant debt, but Tyler does not rub his nose in his defeat, perhaps suggesting that once affectations are put aside, British and American culture can join in the affirmation of "probity, virtue, honour" (*TC* 57) as proclaimed from an Anglo-American stage. By refraining from French jokes and reconstructing his elite in village terms, Tyler corrects his London model to meet American cultural conditions.

For his part, William Dunlap also saw *The Poor Soldier* as a ticket to entering the stage world as an American playwright. Dunlap's first acted play was *The Father, or American Shandyism*, which appeared four times in September 1789 as acted by the Old American Company at the John Street Theatre. His next to appear was *Darby's Return*, a sequel to both O'Keeffe plays, and performed before an audience that included the President of the United States on November 24. Once again, Thomas Wignell played Darby, and this being his benefit night, he perhaps played it with more relish than his usual stint in O'Keeffe's comic opera. Dunlap draws entirely on the audience's knowledge of the two Darby plays to construct this "comic sketch." Darby has come back to Carton, explicitly cited as the scene of action. To music from Shield's score for *Poor Soldier*, Darby tells the assembled villagers that he has not only been to Prussia but also to the United States and has returned to tell the villagers what he's found.[47] Many of his first speeches rehearse what we learn of Darby's adventures just prior to and during *Patrick in Prussia*, but Dunlap adds a postscript of Darby's leaving the German wars for those in central Europe against the Ottoman army:

> the curst Turks, those whisker'd, sabred dogs,
> Man-eating Hannibals, with hearts like logs,
> Made war upon us; then I thought 'twas best,
> To seek an army that was more at rest;
> Not that I minded fighting: Not a button!
> ... But being taught by *Father Luke*,
> That Turks are heretics, I wisely took
> Precautions not to have my morals hurt,
> By an intercourse with such vile dirt.[48]

This extraneous piece of autobiography, between Darby's departure from Silesia and his arrival in America, adds to the comic portrayal of Darby as coward, the very aspect of him that Tyler's Jonathan recoils against. At the same time it adds something not in O'Keeffe, Darby as a religious bigot, albeit spoken of in mock-crusader tones. The Irish playwright, after writing a play ("A Definitive Treaty") that included the wars against the Turks as part of the mix, largely refused thereafter to evoke international affairs (the slave trade excepted) in his plays, other than in the way of minor details, as with the conflict at Beattie's Ford; even *Patrick in Prussia* is more about love affairs than European military politics. Dunlap, however, conjures up the crudest of stereotypical images for the generic stage Muslim, the big whiskers and threatening scimitar, even though the point of the speech goes more to establish Darby's fear of fighting than condemnation of Turks. Still, it is a somewhat discordant image, whatever laughs it evoked from an audience already used to anti-Islamic dramatic situations, and marks a distinct alteration from O'Keeffe's original.

Of more immediate moment for the New York spectators would have been Darby's recital of his disembarking in their city and his immediate love of all he saw. Conveniently, Darby misses the Revolution; unlike Patrick, he will not bear a wound from battle back to Carton. Instead, he observes the New York parade celebrating the adoption of the Constitution in 1788 as an event that he thinks is the result of:

> A revolution without blood or blows;
> For as I understood the cunning elves,
> The people all revolted from themselves;
> Then after joining in a kind confession,
> They all agreed to walk in a procession;
> So turners, taylors, tinkers, tavern-keepers,
> With parsons, blacksmiths, lawyers, chimney sweepers,
> All neatly dress'd, and all in order fair,
> Nice painted standards, waving in the air,
> March'd thro' the town – ate beef – and drank strong beer. (*DR* 11)

Dunlap presents this procession as the beginning of a transforming experience for Darby. This mixture of social types in orderly agreement, the image if not the reality of democracy, coupled with their dieting on British staples, gives Darby a new vision of society in the context of one that he already knows. To this allegory of economic opportunity Dunlap adds Washington's inauguration, "another show," all in celebration of a man, who:

> *Like me* had left his *farm* a *soldiering* to go;
> But having gain'd his point, he had, *like me*,
> Return'd his own *potato ground* to see;
> But there he coldn't [*sic*] rest.

With the help of Dermot, Darby enlarges the comparison between Washington and a poor Irish farmer by noting how the poor in America "love him, just as he was poor!/They love him like a father or brother," to which Dermot adds, "As we poor Irishmen love one another" (*DR* 11). The combination of the constitutional spectacle and the presidential inauguration fixes Darby in his determination to return to the United States after his Carton visit and become an American citizen. Now a poor soldier as well as a poor farmer himself, Darby realizes that he can never thrive in Ireland. Dunlap sees in O'Keeffe's Darby saga the general hopelessness of the rustic's situation; a failure in love, a failure as a soldier (he is punished in the second play for things like falling asleep at sentry duty), and with his farm already sold, the Irish Darby has no future. In Dunlap's revision to the sketch, Darby can find new incentive to reconceive his identity as that of an American workingman. That play, of the transformed Darby as productive citizen, the disenfranchised laborer become self-interested worker, we can only imagine, not see.

For Dunlap, Darby's identification with Washington suggests an appeal of America over Europe, and thus a return to Ireland: a perceived equality of the lowly and the high-born. But of course that is not precisely what is going on. In his *History*, the American playwright recalls that during the premiere of *Darby's Return*, all eyes were on one member of the audience, especially during Wignell's voicing of Darby's lines about the President. At first smiling, then growing serious as he prepared for an embarrassing barrage of compliments, the First Spectator of the land and object of Darby's praise gave "a hearty laugh" once he knew Darby was not going to lather it on too thickly.[49] But of course, Darby's equality with even a fictional Washington was a joke. As with Jonathan in *The Contrast*, Darby here can fantasize all he wants about the advantages of American simplicity of ceremony, but neither play offers any real hope that such characters can, or should, achieve anything that would put them in positions of prestige or power. American equality a la Darby is a comedy, something to speak, but also something to laugh at. No wonder audiences loved Darby – his naivete, his cowardice, his general bungling threaten no one. He will serve his new country with, at best, menial labor – one of those who, like the reformed Bagatelle, is better off with a spade in his hand than a sword.

The political editing that accompanied *Poor Soldier* to New York in 1787 and Boston in the 1790s clipped away at Dunlap's play, too, leaving some lines written but unspoken in 1789. In the original *Darby's Return*, Dunlap includes one more adventure for Darby between the United States and his return to Ireland, a visit to France at the start of the revolution there. Again, one assumes the deletion of Darby's account of the fall of the Bastille (which had occurred only four months previous to the performance of the play), executions, and a more sanguinary demonstration than he had witnessed in New York had much to do with Hallam's and Henry's not wishing to offend Francophiles in the audience. At the same, however, the lines indicate Dunlap's desire to contrast, although not harshly, the two revolutions, one orderly, one "in a nice commotion." Darby chooses to leave France quickly; equality there means "the *liberty* to plunder others" (*DR* 12) rather than the right to march in straight rows and dine on beef and beer. Given Darby's fear of conflict and the unlikelihood of his succeeding anywhere else, his choice, via Dunlap, to recreate himself in New York as an American has a distinctly Anglophile twist.

Dunlap's play is only the most overt of the appropriations made of *Poor Soldier* by Americans for the theatres of that country. Yet it suggests something about audience reception that such variations as gender and ethnicity do not: the most important role for masculine white audiences is not Patrick, the original poor soldier, but Darby. In contrast to the later African Theatre staging of *Poor Soldier*, Dunlap includes in his sketch most of the original villagers but not Patrick nor his lover turned wife, Norah. Some of this choice no doubt has to do with the actor playing Darby; the play was written for Wignell's benefit, after all, and there was no point in creating a character to divert attention from Darby. On the surface, the choice of centering Darby would seem to reinforce what Tyler learned two and a half years before: that while Manly was a good theme character, the audience wanted to see Jonathan. Nevertheless, for Dunlap, such a choice created identity problems for what or who would represent America on the stage. In his history of the American theatre, Dunlap has harsh words for Tyler's Yankee on this score: "Tyler, in his *Contrast* and some later writers for the stage, seems to have thought that a Yankee character, a Jonathan, stamped the piece as American, forgetting that a clown is not the type of the nation he belongs to." By "clown," Dunlap means rustic, but the tone suggests something more, a sneer of contempt for the comic naif. If Jonathan is a clown and "not the type" of the United States, then what is Darby? Dunlap's puzzling remark about Tyler comes in his history right after his discussion of the premiere of *Darby's Return*, a play he includes among others as having "local" interest.[50] Putting aside that after forty years Dunlap might still harbor jealousy for his late dramatic colleague for having created a more lasting character than anything the historian had, one realizes the Darby–Jonathan contrast is also a clue to Dunlap's larger concerns about what constitutes an American drama.

For Dunlap, a "national drama, distinct from that of our English forefathers," was not a consummation devoutly to be wished. Shakespeare and later dramatists "are ours, as much ours, being the descendants of Englishmen, as if our fathers had never left the country in which they were written." Such a statement leaves little doubt about what Dunlap imagines as the proper material for a writer and an audience to admire: "Old English literature, as well as that of remote antiquity on which it is founded, is the basis on which we build, and is an integral part of our mental existence.' Indeed, he also means very recent English literature, including such lightweight stuff as O'Keeffe's comic operas. The limits of Dunlap's originality in depicting a previously executed character are far greater than those of Tyler in his conversion of O'Keeffe, but they are justified by the historian as the limits that connect American drama to British as of one indissoluble tradition. Having Darby declare himself a potential emigrant to the United States is as far as Dunlap is willing to go (in 1789) in declaring independence from British drama; in essence, there is no such independence, he argues. The only distinctions possible are those that amend the tradition in light of American government: 'Inasmuch as we may hereafter deviate from the models left us by our ancestors, it will only be, as we hope, in a more severe and manly character, induced by our republican institutions, and approaching the high tone of the Greek drama.'[51] No one would confuse *Darby's Return* with Greek drama or Darby with a manly character – Tyler's play comes closer than Dunlap's to creating both – but a reader or spectator might be forgiven for taking the author's sketch as a feeble imitation of a British afterpiece, slightly Americanized. If we trust Dunlap's latter-day beliefs about nationalism and theatre, that is all he intended. Somehow, then, an Irish clown on the American stage was to be preferred to an American one on that same stage, as the one more properly in the Anglo-American dramatic tradition.

Dunlap's virtual self-damnation indicates that *Darby's Return* has less merit in its own right than as a gloss on O'Keeffe and the American reading of it. Neither *The Contrast* nor the more evanescent sketch by Dunlap could compete in longevity and repeat performances with the original, although in modern times Tyler's play commands vastly more attention than either *Poor Soldier* or *Darby's Return*. At the same time, its frequency of appearance and the dependence that early American playwrights show on O'Keeffe's comic opera suggest that the influence of *The Poor Soldier* was far more pervasive than a quick reading of the text would prompt. Giving opportunities for adjustment to American mores and political conditions, *The Poor Soldier* was a malleable vehicle for the shifting currents of American culture in the 1790s and early 1800s. Although its familiarity worked against commentary – Elihu Hubbard Smith, an inveterate theatregoer, can only muster "pretty well performed" for the one production he bothers to mention in his diary – and the critics may have tired of it – Joseph Dennie's *Port Folio* complains in 1801 it is "worn to rags, to very tatters" – managers and actors clung to it like a rag doll, refusing to let go of something that made American audiences feel good about coming to the theatre.[52] Written by an Irishman for London audiences, *The Poor Soldier* reflected back to American spectators portrayals of themselves that reinforced a convenient fiction of republicans as innocent villagers, undermined the very notion of American identity as distinct from British, and yet provoked spectators into startling awareness of politics, gender, or ethnicity. Imitated, absorbed, scorned, loved, *The Poor Soldier* was one of the most American of plays in the early republic.

4

American author, British source: writing revolution in Murray's Traveller Returned

ASIDE FROM THE POLITICAL PLAYS WRITTEN IN THE EARLY TO mid-1770s and various pageants and ephemeral patriotic productions in the immediate post-war years, American writers of the new republic penned relatively few full-length plays about the Revolution that made it to the stage. Although the stage entertainments about the war might be held to be "commemorations" in the same vein as speeches, parades, and other forms of Revolutionary remembrance,[1] they also have another history, the determining shape of British theatre. For early republican British Americans, this meant that reading the Revolution in the theatre often depended on spectator and manager response to British-authored plays, including John O'Keeffe's *The Poor Soldier*, a text that unusually alludes to the war but for the most part steers clear of direct statements about the politics behind the conflict. Even so, a few plays that directly confront the Revolutionary United States did make it to American stages. Royall Tyler's *The Contrast* remains the best-known such drama, but it sets the scene in post-war society and refers to the conflict itself largely through Colonel Manly's praising of Washington and Lafayette. Among plays that actually portray wartime America, John Daly Burk's *Bunker-Hill, or The Death of General Warren* (1797) stands out as a spectacle of battle, declamation, and pyrotechnics, one that William Dunlap loathed but that audiences embraced, at least enough for most of the major theatres to support multiple productions.[2] Burk, an Irish republican émigré from the political struggles between his home isle and England, naturally found in the Revolution a subject matter with which he could readily identify. Full of fustian and the dramatically artificial tragedy of love between an American woman and a British soldier, *Bunker-Hill* validates American bravery in the identity politics of the early Revolution. General Joseph Warren and his colleagues are noble Romans, and the identity of the American cause is fixed on republican Rome. Speeches evoke Brutus, Cassius, Cincinnatus, and others of that stripe in nearly every act, but Warren most often appears to himself and his fellow officers as another Cato. The British support a lost, despotic regime; the American patriots uphold a doctrine of stoical sacrifice. Burk's Warren deliberately puts himself in harm's way as the British charge the hill and takes his bullet with almost the same force of choice as Addison's rebel against Caesar turns the blade upon himself. The consequences of British war-making, then, are the deaths of Warren, the character loudest in speech for principle (and who, as the historical person, once wore a toga when delivering the annual Boston Massacre oration),[3] and the unhappy lover, Abercrombie, who is forced by duty to stay with his regiment, even though he knows, as he tells Elvira, that he has been "Sent here, to rob thy country of its rights" (*BH* 74). Such clearcut sides, coupled with the use of cannons and burning buildings on stage, made *Bunker-Hill* an easily absorbed vehicle that, despite his muttering, gave Dunlap a number of well-paying nights to support his often financially sagging theatrical enterprise.

Whatever the agonies suffered by Dunlap at Burk's dialogue, the drama was a *coup de théâtre*, the sort of thing managers might mount to assuage vocal critics of an apolitical or Federalist-leaning stage. It features a principled woman, Elvira, who makes the choice of love of country over love of British officer in remaining loyal to the patriot side rather than accept Abercrombie's affections, and it recreates a wartime patriotism that prompts anti-British sentiments at a time when the Federalist government was largely pro-British in policy.[4] In Boston, *Bunker-Hill* became emblematic of a split in loyalties to the theatre as well. It opened on February 17, 1797 at the Haymarket, the newly built Democratic–Republican playhouse, and thus served as a riposte to the fare at the Federal Street Theatre, a Federalist-dominated stage.[5] In short, it displayed its nationalism and partisanship openly, creating clear lines of identification for the audience.[6]

A more complex and earlier treatment of identity in the war, and not nearly as remunerative to its producers, was Judith Sargent Murray's stage play, *The Traveller Returned* (1796).[7] Murray, primarily known as an essayist, was long attracted to the stage; she was an early supporter of a professional Boston playhouse, wrote favorably about actresses and other American playwrights, and once even risked the displeasure of her Universalist coreligionists to attend a performance in disguise.[8] She had written an earlier play, *The Medium; or Happy Tea Party*, a comedy that was mounted on the Boston stage on March 2, 1795 and later printed under the title *Virtue Triumphant*.[9] In the manner of *The Contrast*, that first drama looks at social life in the post-war period and makes a few allusions to the Revolution, notably in celebration of Washington. Borrowing from Sheridan, Farquhar, Garrick, and other eighteenth-century playwrights, Murray outdoes Tyler in minimizing overt statements of nationalism for the sake of virtue and worth. One of her female characters, Augusta, learns from Matronia, the wise mature woman, to honor her 'husband's wishes' in order to find happiness (*VT* 77); another, Eliza, discovers a British colonel is her uncle. The play affirms women's rational choices, stoic values, and other, more dramatically conventional, comic virtues but makes relatively little (in the form of direct speeches on the subject) of its being set in America as the source of those virtues. If anything, the plot reinforces the Federalist program of reconciliation with Britain, but does so in the context of a typical manners comedy, with all the usual familial identities exposed. A pastiche of English dramatic forms, *Virtue Triumphant* Americanizes its content only enough to establish location, then suppresses any significant linkage between scene and theme except that of minimizing differences between what is British and what is American.[10]

Murray's second comedy takes more interest in questions of American situations and identity and as such complicates understandings of who will succeed in a post-colonial republic. As with Tyler, Murray could not hope to create a new drama from whole cloth and have it appear on an American stage. Despite the presence of nationalist sentiment in playhouse audiences, spectators demanded new British plays or recent favorites as the main repertoire of companies, even if slightly amended or cut so as not to offend republican sentiments.[11] Like her predecessor, she, too, had to cast about for models of plays successful in theatres in the United States – plays inevitably written by British authors. Whereas in her first play, which lasted in the theatre but a single performance, she had borrowed from *School for Scandal* here, or *The Beaux' Stratagem* there, Murray may have felt the need to find a single source on which to construct a drama and therefore free her, in some degree, for a more thorough opportunity to establish its American particularities. There are no overt allusions to O'Keeffe's still popular *The Poor Soldier* in *Traveller Returned* in the way that Tyler and Dunlap evoke the Irish writer's comic opera, but in some ways, her choice of model leaves her with more options for variation, at least compared to *Darby's Return*. She certainly knew *The*

Contrast, having witnessed a performance in Philadelphia in 1790 and contributed an epilogue to a 1794 production in her home town of Gloucester, and some of the sentiments reflect Tyler's overall views on patriotism and virtue.[12] But as relatively popular as *The Contrast* was, Murray recognized that her affirmation of Washington and duty, like Tyler's, required as prototype a more proven theatrical success than her countryman's had been.

Traveller Returned is set in an American coastal city (read Boston) in the last year of the Revolutionary War.[13] It features a pseudonymous American, Rambleton, whose return to his native country from England causes suspicion; a young officer, Camden, whose unawareness of his parentage nearly leads him into an incestuous relationship with his sister, Harriot Montague; a theft of Rambleton's valuables by his landlords, the Vansittarts; an inquisition by the local Committee of Safety; and a happy conclusion in which Rambleton is reunited with his son, daughter, and estranged wife, the thieves are caught, and the young couples properly matched. As one of the few plays by an American before 1800 to reach an American stage, *The Traveller Returned* has until recently mostly been taken as a good effort by an earnest writer and not much more.[14] A quick-paced and multi-dimensional play by one of the early republic's most talented writers, it raises questions about gender, ethnicity, and class as sources of American identity and takes a more complex view on the Revolution itself than her contemporary Burk. In its own time, however, it met with critical scorn and a fatal single run. In a series of responses to the play and to its defenders in the *Federal Orrery*, Boston writer Robert Treat Paine criticized *Traveller* for its "tedium of uninteresting solemnity" and its overuse of "patriot sentiments." In addition to the evident misogyny of his critique, an important factor in the history of play reception in the 1790s, Paine based his standards on admiration for recognized British comedies, since he complains that the author substitutes "broad humor for wit, and dulness for pathos." Murray's attempt to construct an American play that promises some kind of Anglo-American reconciliation failed to satisfy Paine's belief that in the theatre world, at least, one could not be British enough. The play was not revived after 1796, and after her final play *The African* failed on stage, Murray effectively stopped writing her own works for publication and performance.[15]

What Paine failed to observe, however, is just how "British" Murray's "American" play is. When the American writer looked for models, she decided to borrow heavily from one of the most popular British comedies on American stages, Richard Cumberland's *The West Indian* (1771).[16] Although not nearly as well known now as he was in his own time, Cumberland was a skillful writer of social comedies whose plays long held the boards in England, the United States, and Jamaica. Despite the satiric portrayal of him in Sheridan's *The Critic* (1779) as Sir Fretful Plagiary, Cumberland had sufficient reputation in the 1780s that John Adams, during one of his post-war diplomatic missions, sought him out (along with Arthur Murphy) on behalf of American playwright Mercy Otis Warren.[17] It is not surprising that Murray, an admirer of Warren's plays and correspondent with her, and a political supporter of Adams (to whom she dedicated her collection of essays, plays, and fiction, *The Gleaner*), should herself turn to Cumberland's work as a model for her own.

The West Indian was first produced by David Garrick in January 1771 at Drury Lane, with American productions opening in Williamsburg, Virginia, by late October of that year and in Annapolis a year later. Reprinting in America quickly followed; a Philadelphia edition appeared in 1772 coincidentally with its first production in that city on November 9. On April 13, 1773, the play was performed by students at Yale, and, as part of the American Company repertory, *The West Indian* was mounted professionally at least ten times by May 1774. The British military enacted Cumberland's comedy several times, including three performances in New York in January and February 1778, three more in 1780, and one each in 1781 and 1782, while the first professional company to start up after hostilities ceased, the Wall–Ryan troupe, put it on in Baltimore and Annapolis five times between 1782 and 1783. It also continued to serve as a stock item with Lewis Hallam's Old American Company, who performed the play during the war years in Jamaica, then in their inaugural return season in New York in 1785–1786.[18] According to Dunlap, Hallam as the protagonist Belcour and John Henry as the significant minor character O'Flaherty "made this play as popular in America as in England."[19] Significantly for the connection to Murray, it played at the Federal Street Theatre in Boston in 1794 and was published in that city at about the same time; it also appeared that same year in Mathew Carey's collection, *The American Theatre*, an anthology that lacks a single American-authored text.[20] In addition to Baltimore, Annapolis, Philadelphia, New York, and Boston, *The West Indian* played in Charleston, Richmond, Norfolk, and other cities for the rest of the century and into the first decade, at least, of the next. In short, it was a play that would have been well known to most American theatregoers, including Judith Sargent Murray, by 1796.

The West Indian introduces an English native of the islands, Belcour, who has come to London with slaves, ostensibly to see an interested correspondent, Stockwell, and the sights. A passionate and impetuous fellow, Belcour impresses the locals with both his naivete and rashness, qualities which lead him into love for the beautiful but poor Louisa Dudley and nearly a duel with her brother, Charles.[21] Meanwhile, a conniving pair, the Fulmers, make off with jewels that Stockwell has entrusted to the keeping of Belcour; complications concerning an inheritance ensue; and the chastened but still passionate Belcour is brought to the altar after all. There is the revelation that Stockwell is in fact Belcour's father; the Fulmers are caught; Charles Dudley gets his love, cousin Charlotte; and Captain Dudley, the poor but honest soldier, turns out to be the inheritor of a large estate in favor of the odious Lady Rusport. It is a clever sentimental comedy with typical Georgian elements in terms of plot and theme.

The West Indian, however, does make central a New World man, Belcour, trying to negotiate Old World ways, an important element for its adaptation to an American setting. The play validates the essential honesty of the West Indian in a somewhat corrupt urban world but at the same time establishes differences between forms of British culture on each side of the Atlantic. For that reason, the play may have appealed to Murray. After all, Americans in the post-war era found themselves in an awkward position *vis-à-vis* the theatre.[22] Proscribed from producing plays by congressional acts in 1774 and 1778, patriotic Americans in the more open cultural environment of the 1780s and 1790s had little in the way of a local tradition of writing for the stage to draw upon. As has been noted, pre-war British favorites proved to be popular after the Revolution as well, and companies quickly learned that London hits could be New York or Philadelphia hits in a short time. In order to create plays that reflected both the American situation and contemporary theatrical taste, American authors had little choice but to craft their work upon London models. Murray, then, turned to a popular play that attempted to deal with transatlantic distinctions at a time when Americans were self-consciously trying to negotiate their way to understanding what their own culture would be.

Murray herself contributed to the debate over the place of drama in the new republic. In *Gleaner* XXIV, she uses the conflict in Boston that led to a repeal of the ban on theatre (1792) to argue that "in the present enlightened era and administration of liberty, the citizen would hardly consent to an abridgment of those amusements" (*G* 2:225). For her, the natural desire of the country is "that none but a *virtuous and well regulated theatre* will be tolerated" (227). Indeed, from a theatre that is "chaste," citizens will have models of rectitude, and youth "will learn to think, speak, and act, with propriety" (230). Yet she recognizes that Americans will come to support a formerly banned institution only with time. During the 1790s, cultural enthusiasts believed that France and England governed taste, although individuals could be partisans of one or the other. In *Gleaner* XCVI, she sees that "those who rally round the standard of America are reduced to a very inconsiderable party" (3:260). And because the stage is a form of civic education, she asks, "Is it not then of importance to supply the American stage with American scenes?" (262). Without encouragement, she admonishes, few writers will step forward. Those who do – and Murray specifically cites Royall Tyler and Mercy Warren – receive no patronage. If the situation were to change and American dramatists were to be given support, "Is it not possible . . . that under the fostering smiles of a liberal and enlightened public, Columbian Shakespeares may yet elevate and adorn humanity?" (264). Thus, while acknowledging the brilliance of the British stage, Murray in turn asserts the need to convert that tradition to a distinctly American vision. In that regard, she declares herself willing to go further toward a theatrical nationalism than William Dunlap but without alienating those who cannot conceive of a theatre at all without its grounding in British drama.

Two processes are at work in borrowing a play from a former colonizer and wartime enemy who is also of one's race and speaks one's language: imitation and resistance. In the case of the first, Murray structures her play very much along plot lines established by Cumberland. In the matter of the second, Murray writes against Cumberland, situating the text of her drama in a different cultural landscape from the London of *The West Indian* and altering characters and situations just enough to put some stamp of originality (and American nationality) on her creation. Part of what follows traces some of the parallels in order to demonstrate that *The West Indian* is, in fact, a significant source for *The Traveller Returned*. The rest of the chapter pursues Murray's method of distinguishing her play from Cumberland's,[23] examining Murray's points of resistance to the British play and noting her own contributions to a number of features that in time become identified as distinctive of American drama. The object here is to clarify what choices were available to an American playwright in the 1790s and to investigate how one talented author attempted to negotiate those choices in an American setting. In other words, how could Murray, with a British comedy as model, write an American play about its key historical moment, the Revolution? The answers have a great deal to say about her consequent understanding of American identities.

Among the plot and character parallels, four have importance. First, of course, a long-separated father–son pair reunite through a transatlantic voyage by one of the men. Standing on the American side of the ocean, Murray switches the traveler and the provenance. In Cumberland, the son comes to England, not knowing that his friend Stockwell is in fact his father. While Stockwell reveals the fact immediately to the audience, Belcour does not find this out until the final scene. In Murray, the father travels from England to America. He had fled his home country years before over suspicion that his wife no longer loved him, but now has returned under an assumed name to learn about the fate of his wife and children. His son at his parting direction years before has been raised by friends in Virginia. When Rambleton (his real name is Edward Montague) meets Major Camden very early in Act I, he expresses delight with the officer's patriotism and rectitude but waits to be sure before he can be open about being Camden's father. In both plays, the young man must pass a test established by the father but not shared with the son until the end. Belcour, like Camden, at first pleases, then gives offense. In both as well, all grows clear by the end; new perceptions correct errors from old ones; and fathers publicly reveal their parentage as part of the final scene.

Second, both plays also show two pairs of young lovers who struggle to get connected. In *The West Indian* Charles Dudley loves his cousin Charlotte Rusport, but his poverty prevents him from declaring his sentiments. Belcour, meanwhile, falls madly in love with Louisa Dudley, the sister of Charles, but is led by Mrs. Fulmer into thinking that "sister" in England means "mistress." That does not change Belcour's ardor, but it does affect his tactics, which lead to the charge of insult to virtue and the near duel with Charles. In *The Traveller Returned* Harriot Montague, like Charlotte, is a light-hearted young woman who prefers a young spark named Stanhope to her mother's choice, the upright Camden. In her household resides a poor cousin, Emily Lovegrove, like Louisa Dudley (and like Maria in *The Contrast*), a serious, self-sacrificing woman of complete virtue. Where Cumberland darkens the plot with the imputation of Louisa as sexual adventurer and matches couples by opposites in personality, Murray's play substitutes the twist of near-incest and lines the lovers up by type: a stoic with a stoic, one bon vivant with another. This suppression of sexual impropriety, even an unfounded accusation of it, meets Murray's own stated criteria in *The Gleaner* for a "chaste" stage.

A third parallel occurs in the use of Irish characters. For Cumberland, Major O'Flaherty has become the escort of Lady Rusport, but he is also friend to the Dudleys, having special respect for the father, Captain Dudley, with whom he has served in the military. While O'Flaherty speaks in a slight dialect and is an important minor comic character, Cumberland restrains the portrayal and avoids the usual jokes aimed at the major's Irishness. This writing against stereotype was deliberate, for in his *Memoirs* (1806), Cumberland reveals that "the art, as I conceive it, of finding language for the Irish character on the stage consists not in making him foolish, vulgar, or absurd, but, on the contrary, whilst you furnish him with expressions, that excite laughter, you must graft them upon sentiments, that deserve applause."[24] Even so, the Irish character, played by John Moody in 1771, was one of the reasons for the play's early stage success.[25] To some extent, O'Keeffe's self-denying Patrick in *Poor Soldier* draws upon Cumberland's alteration of the buffoon to the more noble, self-sacrificing O'Flaherty.

For her part, Murray equips Rambleton with an Irish servant, Patrick O'Neal. Very much the stage Irishman as the type was usually figured in British comedies, Patrick represents one of the first such characters in American drama. He speaks in a broad stage brogue and provides much of the humor in *Traveller*. In her use and development of the lower-class Irishman, Murray anticipates the great success on the American stage of the type. Given more depth later by Dion Boucicault in the mid-nineteenth century, the stage Irishman in Murray's version – a lazy, "tipsy," self-deluding, but lovable rascal – would hold American public attention in performing media well into the 1900s. Despite the differences in Irish types and Murray's deliberate choice to reject Cumberland's portrayal, both plays feature an Irishman as a figure around whom a certain amount of humorous business circulates.[26]

A fourth parallel arises in the use to which each playwright puts a scheming, thieving couple, below the main characters in class. In *The West Indian* the Fulmers are an unhappy and technically unmarried pair whose fortunes are on the wane. As Catholics, they find themselves out of the mainstream, but Mrs. Fulmer accuses her husband of ruining her peace by bringing her to England from Bologna, where she had been living. He has tried everything, he says, legal or not, including treason, to get his fortune but has failed. The bookseller's shop he maintains and the room he lets to Captain Dudley provide him with insufficient income to satisfy his wife. Mrs. Fulmer is clearly the ambitious one of the two. A plotter and grasper, she proposes to make use of Dudley's beautiful daughter as a commodity and browbeats her partner into pursuing this course. Similarly, in *Traveller*, the Vansittarts are landlords who find themselves in debt. Like the Fulmers, the wife is the prime mover, the husband a timid, small-visioned man who accedes to his comically Lady Macbeth-like spouse. Again, in keeping with her suppression of stage sexuality, Murray keeps her couple, the husband of whom speaks what passes as Dutch dialect, out of the flesh market, but like the Fulmers, the Vansittarts steal valuables belonging to one of the principals and attempt to get away from creditors and all through flight. Both Fulmers and Vansittarts are caught, their lower-class strivings thwarted, and their foreignness implicated in their crime.

Of course it is likely that Murray had other plays in mind besides Cumberland. As Elizabeth Yearling notes, there are some plot similarities among *The West Indian*, Oliver Goldsmith's *The Good-Natured Man* (1768), and Sheridan's *School for Scandal*: "All three plays have a flawed but generous hero, an older relation whose presence ensures that the hero will not ultimately suffer, a heroine prepared to overlook his faults."[27] In Act Four, scene 4, Harriot chides Emily for being tight-lipped by saying, "you still remain as profound as a pedant who studies obscurity, or as close as Olivia in the Good natured Man" (*TR* 139). There is one other connection to Goldsmith's play in Murray's inclusion of a seeming incest situation.[28] Nevertheless, the specific parallels between Cumberland and Murray are significantly greater than connections between Murray and either Goldsmith or Sheridan. There are also similarities to Cumberland of a minor nature, as well. In both plays, soldiering makes up much of the discussion, though in Murray's play it is complicated by the Revolution. In both, the traveler must make his way through a city whose mores differ significantly from what he is used to: Belcour, accustomed to slavery, finds the numerous lower-rung officials through whom he must pass on his way from the dock to his lodging an annoyance. Rambleton must deal with a committee of safety, who inquire into his motives and patriotism.

Although the parallels to *West Indian* are many – enough to establish Murray's use of Cumberland as a source – the true significance of her turning to *The West Indian* as a model remains to be explored. While no doubt attempting to duplicate the popularity of Cumberland's play, Murray made changes that effectively comment on the similarities through the exploitation of the novelty of difference. Indeed, what we see at work is not simply an adaptation but a reconstruction, in which a highly sentimental and successful British play provides a template whose outline is only partly recognizable in the finished American work. For Murray, determining identity on the stage raises any number of possible confusions when "British" vehicle and "American" setting merge.

For example, as noted above, both plays suggest differences between old world and new, although the contrast is more overt in *The West Indian*. Speaking in a language that sounds much like that used later by Crèvecoeur in *Letters from an American Farmer*, Stockwell says of Belcour, "he comes amongst you a new character, an inhabitant of a new world" (*WI* 69). In Murray, Camden tells Rambleton in Act I of the many merits of Washington and "FREE AMERICANS" without making direct contrasts with the British invader (*TR* 112). Each play, on the score of transatlantic differences, ameliorates them and provides room for accommodation, although Murray goes much further in suppressing such differences. In Cumberland, the reconciliation of the colonial son with the imperial father argues an essentially conservative British theme, that is, that the colonial rashness of the son can be contained by the forbearance and fortune of the parent.[29] In Murray, the affirmation by Rambleton of American mores, figured in his approval of Camden, validates the Revolution and the breaking of imperial bonds; in other words, the son has already achieved his manhood without the present agency of the biological father (although Washington serves as the worthy proxy who has done his work before the play begins), and therefore the duty lies with the father to accept the reality of the son's adult identity as an American patriot. For Cumberland, an American identity, with a little metropolitan trimming, can be absorbed back into Greater Britishness (one can observe a similar process in Frederick Pilon's *The Fair American*). For Murray, American identity draws upon a British tradition of liberty and virtue, but for the sake of the principles, not the originating nation. If there is any trimming, it will come at the expense of Rambleton and his reabsorption into American life as Edward Montague.

Murray's play, however, refuses to make a theatrical conflict over American versus British nationality. Because the idea of post-war reconciliation with England was a strong one among Federalists, there was no point, she might have thought, in exaggerating character and cultural differences between Britain and the United States in the post-colonial era. In *Virtue Triumphant*, Murray acknowledges the post-war antagonism to Britain but symbolically overcomes it in the revelation of Colonel Mellfont's relationship to Eliza. In *Traveller*, she emphasizes the distinctiveness of American liberty without probing for behavioral contrasts between American and British sensibilities. Cumberland's title alone marks difference – that is, how will a "West Indian" fit in English society? Murray's title is neutral as to character. The traveler, Rambleton, knows England and knows America. He returns to his native country and finds it strong, but if he makes comparisons, as he does in viewing American troops, it is to see them as doing "honour" to those in Europe (*TR* 125). Murray's play serves to put the United States on equal footing with Britain to disavow both dependency and continued antagonism to the former parent country. That country's dramatic types can also be ours, she seems to say, but with our own particular stamp. In this, she may be contrasted to Dunlap, as both offer ideas about what an American theatre must be. Like Dunlap, who in his *History* cannot imagine a separate United States dramatic tradition, Murray implicitly rejects the creation of a radically distinctive American drama in favor of a modified British one with American features, but against her fellow commentator, she insists, as in *Gleaner* XCVI, upon a greater degree of Americanization, enough to establish a clear enough difference without sacrificing ancient ties.

Another difference between Murray and Cumberland centers on the overall conception of female characters. Although there are several analogous pairs (Harriot–Charlotte, Emily–Louisa, and Mrs. Montague–Lady Rusport), the contrast between the latter two illustrates a broader split in the plays. Cumberland's females follow stock eighteenth-century types – the sportive, but finally innocent woman (Charlotte); the poor but resolutely virtuous female (Louisa); and the older, calculating woman whose wealth makes her arrogant and whose reversal cuts her down to size (Lady Rusport). While on the surface Harriot and Emily closely approximate the types, Mrs. Montague, a once-proud woman now reduced by experience, is a different sort from her Cumberland counterpart. When we meet her, she reads inveterately, and not romances or sentimental novels, but science and philosophy. As Sharon Harris points out, this image of a woman using her intellect on stage runs against the grain of eighteenth-century stage practice.[30] Writing for the American stage just before Murray, Susanna Rowson puts a book in the hand of her heroic matron, Rebecca, in *Slaves in Algiers* (1794) as that character in North African captivity tries to preserve that "intellectual heavenly fire" that lets her escape material circumstances.³¹ Although Murray may not have known a play that appeared only a few scattered times in Philadelphia, New York, and Baltimore, she, like Rowson two years before, seeks to equate mature woman with some intellectual endeavor.³² Mrs. Montague's reunion with her estranged husband forces her to apologize for the affair that sent him packing, but he too apologizes, showing that Murray intends to allow her shamed character to keep her dignity and thus resist providing the audience with an easy moral about overreaching women.

In Cumberland's comedy, it is enough only to give Lady Rusport her comeuppance. Early and throughout *The West Indian*, Lady Rusport scorns the Dudleys, to the point where even the daughter is disgusted with her mother's behavior. She has inherited money by mistake – money that is rightly the Dudleys – and thus much of the momentum of the play is directed at the last act revelation that she has no inheritance and no position from which to mock others. The comic turn in *The West Indian* rewards virtue and loyalty and punishes the most egregious expressions of self-interest. For her part, Murray complicates the landscape. By reading science, Mrs. Montague has redirected her self-interest into intellectual pursuits and made herself into the post-Revolutionary equivalent of a nun. She denies herself pleasures – those having gotten her into trouble – but she does not die, either, the favored dramaturgical solution along with comic humiliation for dispensing with females who err.³³ Murray suggests that the American woman has a mind; she can use it and raise two young women in the process, even though her reading to excess takes her attention away from Harriot's love life. She does not seek her husband, but when presented with him, admits simply and with grace her part in the events that led to their estrangement. Honesty, intellect, and self-control will serve the American woman if indulgent self-interest (as opposed to virtuous concern for one's well-being) and error temporarily cloud her judgment. She need not go into decline or be the butt of satire, but she can turn her life around. Not as powerfully rendered on stage as the routing of a hated character, Murray's showing the self-recovery of a woman who has been chastened by experience but who can also grow through admission of error nevertheless works thematic territory left largely unexplored by British male playwrights in the 1770s. In restoring her equilibrium through the reunion with her husband, a reconciliation in which she functions as equal partner, Louisa may now recover some balance in her studies and greater attentiveness to her monitory role. This is not simply the figure of the Republican Mother but of the woman as professional being and a further claim for the maturity of the United States to raise creative progeny, literally or in public culture.[34]

The male characters also divide just where they conjoin. Stockwell and Rambleton are cut from the same cloth. Both have committed errors or indiscretions in their earlier manhood – Stockwell has an affair that produces the child Belcour while Rambleton lets his suspicions of his wife send him into exile abandoning her and his daughter. Both men have learned from their experience and now devote their energies largely to observing and fostering their sons' success. Except for one being stationary and one a traveler, little significant difference remains between the characters of the fathers. However, Murray adds a plot element not present in Cumberland. Stockwell's wife (he secretly marries the daughter of his employer, old Belcour) has died long before the play begins; the Englishman's attentions are solely focused now on the son. Rambleton's wife, he learns, is very much alive. She also has a name, Louisa – perhaps borrowed from the upright Louisa Dudley of *The West Indian*. Murray's traveler splits his actions between reconciliation with his spouse and revelation of his parentage to his son and daughter. Avoiding the convenience of a dead wife, Murray instead forces all parties to face up to their errors and to find strength and happiness in the reconstituted family in which everyone has achieved a measure of independence.

The sons differ from each other more significantly than the fathers. Whereas Camden recalls Colonel Manly of *The Contrast* – upright, respectful of women to the point of self-abnegation, and patriotic – Belcour is the Creole: hot-tempered, passionate, determined to get a woman. Although Belcour shows himself to be disinterestedly benevolent on occasion, Murray realizes how dangerous such a character would be in the figure of an American, especially in the lover's lead. Whereas Cumberland, as well as those presumed enemies of sentimentalism, Goldsmith and Sheridan, all subscribe in some form to Shaftesburian notions of virtue found in the generous, if flawed, man, Murray suppresses the sentimental reversal of character for a more Calvinist consistency of character. Camden is virtuous throughout – he is only perceived differently by Rambleton.[35] Knowing full well that post-Revolutionary young men have been criticized for aping European fashion and displaying all the signs of effeminizing corruption – what Manly in *The Contrast* denounces as "luxury" – Murray must be careful not to have the young male lover motivated only or even primarily by sex. Unlike Belcour, Camden shows himself capable of the supreme sublimation, in which his romantic confusions of being forced into marriage with Harriot but drawn to Emily are converted into a larger, more abstract love. Of his heart conflict, Camden soliloquizes:

> Indeed, these struggles do not well suit with my profession! America, now weeping over her desolated plains and warriors slain in battle, should be my sovereign lady. It is not thus her heroes – it is not thus that WASHINGTON inglorious wastes his hours! (*TR* 123)

Marry first the country before the woman: that strategy makes possible the father's approval, which leads to the revelation of parentage, breaks the ill-advised incestuous match, and frees him to declare to Emily. *The West Indian* allows Belcour to draw upon his natural good feeling, once he knows the truth about Louisa; *Traveller*, meanwhile, advises self-control, patriotic redirection of eros, and a respect for woman that is consonant with respect for country. For Murray, a woman is more than an object of desire: she represents the ideal nation for whom men seek larger, loftier goals than the satisfaction of passion.

Although the supporting male, Charles, to some extent plays the role of the rectitudinous young man in *The West Indian*, his parallel in *Traveller*, Stanhope, ends up with the features of the man about town. Despite his name, an echo of Lord Chesterfield's given name, Philip Stanhope, Murray's friend to the hero plays only a minor role and that as one only slightly deviant from the patriotic, stoic norm. Stanhope and Camden are never at serious odds, as Belcour and Charles are over the imputation that Louisa Dudley is a kept woman, and Stanhope comes to Camden's aid in freeing Rambleton from the inquisition at the committee of safety. But Murray makes her point that the pursuit of pleasure is a minor not a major trait, not bad when held in bounds but not to be rewarded with center stage either. American manhood of whatever stripe is loyal to friends, respectful of women, and honors the father in a forceful but restrained – not extravagantly sentimental – way.

In *Traveller*, the honor of the father is deflected from the disguised Rambleton to the offstage Washington. In Act III, Camden leads the troops, and as he speaks to them, his father swells with pride. Camden's oration in celebration of Washington, Liberty, and the Rights of Man cites the American general as another Cincinnatus, but unlike Burk's chronic Romanizing of American figures, Murray restricts hers to a few lines. Rambleton values his son for the latter's praise of the national father and his submission to a larger cause than himself. Cumberland's Stockwell only hopes that Belcour's character is not "unprincipled" (*WI* 5). Thus while both fathers want their sons to prove to be admirable figures, for the British play it is enough that social character be affirmed; for the American play, social behavior – held to a stricter standard – must also be buttressed by stoic dedication to the national cause. Curiously, Rambleton tests Camden's commitment by bringing up the most problematic affair in Washington's generalship, the hanging of John André, and the report that some people "question his sensibility." Camden's rejoinder reveals his loyalty to his father's satisfaction: "Question his sensibility, Sir! he deeply laments the casualties of war! and, while his soul bleeds for his country, the delicacy of his feelings acknowledges a suitable sympathy with the unfortunate of every description" (*TR* 111). To serve her thematic end, that an American play affirms the peculiar politics of the new republic, Murray sacrifices the more satisfying stage character of the impetuous and extravagant Belcour for the irreproachable and preachy Camden. The latter is more admirable by principle than Belcour, but not nearly as interesting on stage. A major component of the American play, then, is elimination of bawdiness (or imputation of same) in the main characters for the affirmation of ideological themes linked to Revolutionary stoicism and republican virtue. While this choice declares American patriotic identities to be grounded in values beyond mere nationalism, it also limits the appeal of the play to an audience used to a more risque stage practice through British comedic drama.

This is not to say that Murray avoids entertainment. On the contrary, her decision to concentrate the comedy in the servant-class characters represents a significant shift from the equivalent roles in *The West Indian*.[36] Both plays include servants, although *The West Indian* includes one set omitted by Murray – African slaves. In Patrick O'Neal, Murray provides the Irish figure with a class-designated role that makes him more of a broadly comic character than Cumberland's Major O'Flaherty. For instance, when his employer asks him about the house they are to stay in and the day, Patrick answers in accents that would become quite familiar to American theatregoers in coming decades:

> Ow, as to the day, I don't *bodder* myself about that, at all, at all; for, d'ye see, I don't matter time three skips of a grasshopper; but, as for the house,

Ow, if I was in my own sweet Killmallock, in the county of Limerick, in dear Ireland *itshelf*, my own born mother could not be better to me; why, they have already given me *three breakfasts*, and as many dinners; and, as to drink, my dear honey, ow, let me alone for that, Master. (134)[37]

Whereas main character Belcour generates most of the humor in the main plot of *The West Indian*, minor character Patrick provides a good deal in *Traveller* in his attachment to Rambleton. The latter, then, can retain his own 'dignified mien and prepossessing aspect,' as Camden calls it (*TR* 106), while his man makes outlandish remarks and gets drunk, moony, and disputatious in his defense and service. This division of humor between monied and serving classes Americanizes comedy toward an ethnically or class-inscribed comedy of types that fit the demographics but remain outside the 'national character': Anglo-American, educated, and economically advantaged.

Significantly, Murray also provides what Cumberland most certainly does not: a Yankee. No doubt taken with the comic success of Jonathan in Tyler's *The Contrast*, Murray features Obadiah, a servant whose small-town limitations have not been transcended by time spent in a seaboard city. Cumberland's servants are perfunctory, with no other names and definition than their occupation and their subordination to the main characters; Murray's Obadiah, along with Patrick, is particularized through dialect and mannerism to give flavor to the comedy. As servant to the Montagues, the Yankee is attached to an otherwise largely somber family unit of Louisa, Emily, and the fortunately more carefree Harriot. Obadiah first enters "*making a clamourous out-cry*" in company with Bridget, the straight maid to his clown role:

OB: Ouns! blood and thunder! what will become of poor Obadiah!
BRIDGET: What's the matter, Obadiah?
OB: Oh! the maple log, the maple log was in me! Oh, oh, oh! what shall I do! what shall I do?
BRIDGET: What is the matter, I say, Obadiah!
OB: Oh! tarnation, tarnation, tarnation! ... I have broke – I have broke th-th-the – what d'ye call it – I have broke th-th-the – what d'ye call it.
BRIDGET: Th-th-the – what d'ye call it – Now what the plague do you mean, Obadiah?
OB: Why that there glass thing, Bridget, by which folks finds out *when we should be cold and when we should be warm*.
BRIDGET: I'll be hang'd Obadiah, if you don't mean the thermometer.
OB: Yes Bridget, it is the *mormeter*. (*TR* 117)

Murray's use of New England dialect is even more pronounced than Tyler's in *The Contrast*, and Obadiah's slapstick – he jumps around on stage, swears, fears, and serves himself more than Jonathan – pushes the Yankee toward what he would become later: a single-dimensional character designed to be the primary generator of comedy in American plays. In Cumberland, servants never seize the action from the main characters; in Murray, servants provide nearly the entire comic interest. Thus, one can see the logic of her omitting slaves from the play – their presence as bondmen in a comedy about American liberty would be problematic and distracting – although later American playwrights would have no trouble incorporating them, too, into the comic mix.[38]

In summarizing the British playwright's career, Richard Dircks remarks that "Cumberland did not establish a new school of writers, nor is there evidence that any important dramatic writer attempted to emulate him."[39] Although that may be technically true for the English stage, the fact remains that something of *The West Indian* survived in Murray's *The Traveller Returned*. Even so, the alterations to the basic outline provided by Cumberland show that Murray had different ends in mind from the popular London comic author. For one thing, she had to write for a theatre that was not yet established, especially in Boston where the professional stage had only begun in 1793. Without surety of an established theatrical tradition behind her, the American may have sought to spread the appeal of her play among a broad socioeconomic range of spectators.[40] Not only does she give servants more life and action, but Murray also reserves for Obadiah her single reference in the play to things theatrical. When the Yankee earns some money from Harriot for keeping a secret, he exults, and says, "*I'll zee the Panorama, and the lion*, and all the wild *beastes – ay, and I'll zee a play*" (*TR* 126). Through this line, Murray acknowledges the role of the serving class as audience members at the theatre and argues at the same time for the legitimacy of other forms of theatrical entertainment. At the same time, however, she suggests that class does play a part, and that while the Obadiahs of Boston need their panoramas and animal exhibitions, the regulars at the Federal Street Theatre will want plays of substance and principle. In Cumberland's London, no such necessity to increase the franchise or to worry about popular attitudes toward the stage existed.

For another thing, however, Murray removes much of the sentimentality from her *West Indian* prototype. True, Rambleton and Louisa show themselves as characters of strong feeling, and Camden discourses warmly about Washington and Liberty, but throughout, the people whose unthinking feelings dominate their actions – the Vansittarts, Patrick – expose their characters as comic villains or buffoons. Writing against Cumberland, resisting his influence as popular British playwright, Murray recurs to a theme that has long preoccupied her, the necessity of reason in one's ability to "reverence" the self. Harry Camden comes by it through education and upbringing in a republican household, but for the women, as Murray had argued for years, such unsentimentalized self-assessments were impossible without the kind of care in education that elite young men received. Something of this concern lies behind the American playwright's own construction of her comedy, as if to write it all, and to begin with the frame provided by a well-known theatrical preceptor, were to face the necessity of self-reverencing in authorship and national identity. In a manuscript draft of an essay called "Reverence Thy Self," one that evolved into the now widely read piece, "Desultory Thoughts upon the Utility of encouraging a degree of Self-Complacency, especially in Female Bosoms" (1784), Murray declares the dual need to imitate and strike out on one's own:

> In the various systems of education, which have come under my observation, I hardly know an axiom, which I would not more readily surrender, than that which enforces the necessity of exciting, under proper reputations, in the bosom of the young proficient, a spirit of Emulation and Enterprize. Many a desirable, many a laudable achievement, is lost, from want of confidence, and kind of timidity, which persuades us that our abilities are inadequate to any considerable attainment. Ambition is a noble principle, and if its energies are judiciously directed, its results may be truly valuable.[41]

Her focus, as in 'Desultory Thoughts,' is primarily on female education; and to be sure, she knew that, as an American woman, writing a play for the Boston stage would generate opposition. Rather than construct a play on some starry-eyed desire for flattery, what Murray underscores in her essays as the sort of thing that unsettles young women who have not been raised properly to expect it, the author argues for 'Emulation and Enterprize,' imitation and originality. To Cumberland, she owes a debt in terms of plot construction, character types, and other tricks of the stage; but to herself as an American woman she owes another debt, one that allows her to separate from the master without repudiating him, to establish herself and her play with 'spirit' and not 'timidity.' In *Traveller*, excessive feelings undermine the marriage of the Montagues, but love shaped by reason and long periods of self-dependence bring them together again. By the same token, slavish imitation of British drama will never evidence the kind of "Ambition" necessary for American playwrights to reverence their own observations and experiences sufficiently to write plays that challenge the critics.

Murray's play, like many early American dramatic efforts, justifies itself as a vehicle for patriotic sentiments and reinforcement of a cultural ideology (fashioned on classical republicanism) based on virtue. Drama emerges as a discourse of national formation, a genre that, as sermons did in the past, offers stories of submersion of self-interest for some greater good. At the same time, Murray's variations on Cumberland reorient the theme and situation of his play to her own time and place, anticipate the further use of ethnic types and the Yankee, offer female characters who run against type, and argue for an American authorship willing to take risks through a dual strategy of "Emulation and Enterprize." In the heady days of the 1790s, a theatre that appealed to the mind and to political identity, that sought to incorporate a number of socioeconomic strata, and that attempted to place drama from the United States on the same stage as that from Britain seemed a formula for American success. Unfortunately for Murray, the play that continued to hold the boards in American playhouses after 1796 was *The West Indian*. Despite demands from audiences in various cities for patriotic songs, increased working-class membership in theatre audiences, and at least some acknowledgment from managers that a dose of American nationalism in the repertoire was necessary for good business, Murray faced the chronic problem of establishing a transatlantic identity that was not mere imitation by one nation's playwrights of another's. She discovered that audiences, managers, and actors preferred a British playbill to an American one, unless the American play – preferably a smoke-and-noise spectacle like Burk's – would generate significant box-office receipts. Thus the production of a slightly Americanized *West Indian* was more likely to remunerate theatre owners than a new play based on Cumberland's comedy, regardless of its politics and its literary merit. One wonders if, in Boston at least, Americans feared to see themselves on stage, preferring comedies of predictable others instead.

5

Patriotic interrogations: committees of safety in early American drama

Although American theatrical managers preferred to stage such demonstrable British favorites as *The Poor Soldier* and *The West Indian* to anything by an American author, playwrights in the United States recognized more readily than their transatlantic counterparts the dramatic potential of Revolutionary life. Either because of personal suffering or an acute eye for the marked change in social interactions as a result of the polarizing politics from 1775 onward, a few writers offered much darker assessments of republican life than, say, Royall Tyler in his generally affirmative *The Contrast*, assessments that asked serious questions about precisely who had control not only over social and political structures but also over personal life. As has been observed above, both Michel de Crèvecoeur and Judith Sargent Murray examine fractured domestic relationships brought about by the politics of separation, with one seeing only ruin, the other positing reconciliation as the outcome of a completed war. Yet in both plays, the writers leave a number of questions unanswered, especially about the larger implications of reconceived patterns of patriarchy, deference, and participation of previously subordinated or marginalized groups.

One of the questions the plays pose has to do with the legitimacy of popular, rather than elite, authority to prosecute public affairs. When the Continental Congress convened in 1774, it established the Continental Association, an agreement among the colonies not to import British goods. To enforce the policies of the Association, local bodies were formed called Committees of Safety. While resembling to some extent the previously created Committees of Correspondence, by which Samuel Adams and other patriots maintained a cadre of radical support in the pre-war years, the new bodies quickly spread to all parts of the colonies. By the time military hostilities broke out between Congressional and British troops, the committee meetings exceeded their original authority on enforcing nonimportation and became sites of interrogation, where members would hold hearings on ideological purity and assert their right to arrest, detain, try, convict, and confiscate the property of suspected tories or overt British sympathizers.[1] Although not as notorious as their French counterparts a half generation later, these committees invariably took liberties with what we would call today civil rights, and their actions most probably contributed to inhibiting a full reconciliation after the war between patriots and loyalists. Not all committees acted as inquisition courts, but enough did to prompt a variety of complaints from those caught up in its system.[2] Most tellingly, many committee members came from previously uninvolved groups outside the social and political elite; their inquisitions amounted not merely to hunts for political allegiance but also to inquiries into the lives of individuals toward whom committee members had been wont to defer by virtue of their wealth or class position.

Three playwrights found such committees dramatically compelling and incorporated interrogation scenes into their plays: Crèvecoeur in "Landscapes"; Robert Munford in *The Patriots*; and Murray in *The Traveller Returned*. Although the theatrical potential of committee interrogations might seem obvious, relatively few literary works of the Revolutionary and post-war period mention the committees at all. Indeed, this reluctance to discuss the committees extends to modern historians, who often gloss over them in histories of the Revolution.[3] Perhaps the committees were something of an embarrassment to contemporaries and remain so to latter-day, patriotic historians. Mercy Otis Warren, in her 1805 history of the war, mentions a committee only once, and that favorably, in the Maryland Council of Safety's intervention to protect the royal governor, Sir Robert Eden, from arrest.[4] More recent historians have followed suit, with a mention here or there in the secondary literature but with little direct attention to the committees for their own sake. Whatever the reasons then or now to shy away from the committees as an object of dramatic or historical presentation, the presence of committee scenes in these plays takes on special importance for their rarity.

In "Landscapes," the upstate New York author Crèvecoeur targets the head of a committee, Deacon Beatus, and his wife, Eltha, as types of patriotic hypocrite whose interrogations of loyalists lead to the latter's suffering or martyrdom. Although, as discussed above, Crèvecoeur for the most part avoids participating in ideological battles over the cause and conduct of the Revolution, this set of dramatic scenes is especially hostile to partisans on the patriot side. Committee members are portrayed as venal, duplicitous, crude, and destructive of order in a mannered, hierarchical society. Omitted from his English version of *Letters from an American Farmer* in 1782, "Landscapes" presents a blistering denunciation of whiggish assertions of popular governance over tory claims to private opinion and property. For Crèvecoeur, the committees amount to destructively reconstituted family units in which the squire or manor lord loses control as patriarch of the community and is replaced by subordinates who lack both perspective and compassion for those they simultaneously prosecute and persecute.

At nearly the same time in Virginia, Mecklenburg County landowner Robert Munford was also writing a closet drama in the same vein. Munford had earlier written a play, very much in the Farquhar–Foote style, called *The Candidates*, which portrayed local elections in Virginia as contests of drunkenness and vote-buying, all to the satire of popular sovereignty and the continued need for an enlightened squirarchy to maintain order. In *The Patriots* (1777?), Munford portrays two gentlemen, Trueman and Meanwell, who, among other things, get caught up in the machinery of a county committee.[5] Used to their station as masters and respected men, they find themselves suddenly labeled as tories and no longer secure in the deference they feel should be rightly paid them by craftsmen, tradespeople, and other dependents in a patriarchal plantation system. As with committee victims in Crèvecoeur, although in a different vein, the two men appear before the committee, but thanks to the rank hypocrisy of a true tory who has masqueraded as a fiery patriot, Tackabout, Meanwell and Trueman escape proscription. The play ends with their reincorporation, but without clarity as to what manner of society will eventually come to rule in a post-war Virginia.

Writing after the war, Gloucester, Massachusetts native Murray in *Traveller Returned* depicts a committee that interrogates the disguised patriotic protagonist, Rambleton. Unlike Munford's closet drama, which was only published after his death, and Crèvecoeur's, which remained out of sight of American readers until the twentieth century, Murray's appeared on stage, at the Federal Street Theatre, for three performances in 1796. Rambleton has returned during the Revolution from a period abroad, including residency in England, to reclaim his familial attachments. Accused to the local committee of being a British spy, he is cleared of suspicion when evidence of crimes by the accusers, his landlords, ends the questioning. Only present as a body for one scene, the committee of safety is essentially exculpated by the happy ending to the plot.

Nevertheless, *Traveller*, along with "Landscapes" and *The Patriots*, demonstrates that the "people" – taken as those whose caste is below that of a moneyed, educated elite – cannot be trusted to judge their "betters" without presence of a head – king, squire, or paternal President – to check their desires for destruction of the pre-war social order.

The committees in drama provide an intersection of two media for identity formation and interrogation. On the one hand, the radical nature of committees and the overthrow of traditional lines of authority create conditions whereby Americans imagine themselves in ways quite different from older models of deference and hierarchy. On the other, drama itself enters culture as a means of transmission of values, but an often regressive one, even in the service of remembering or idealizing the Revolution. As with the war itself, the committees have their own history and therefore have generated certain patterns of memory to which dramatists of the period are privy. The plays, then, enact or depict in a public way the small-room proceedings of those charged with enforcing patriotic ideology, sharing in the construction of memory and reconstituting the reality of committee work along literary or entertainment lines. If there is a history to depiction of popular sovereignty in British drama, that picture is almost always negative. Thus the "reality" plays of the Revolution and after structure committee scenes in familiar dramatic terms, to the criticism of committees.

The term "committee of safety" does not always signify quite what it seems to mean on the surface. The Boston committee in 1775 had a great deal to do with literal safety in its sponsorship of the Minutemen and its role in the Lexington, Concord, and Bunker Hill battles. But the committees generated by the law that created the Continental Association were clearly meant to monitor citizen behavior in support of, or in opposition to, the constriction of intercourse between British merchants and American consumers on the one hand, and tory support for British royal government and American whig institutions and control on the other. Congress declared in 1774:

> that a committee be chosen in every county, city, and town ... to observe the conduct of all persons touching this association; and when it shall be made to appear, to the satisfaction of a majority of any such committee, that any person within the limits of their appointment has violated this association, that such majority do forthwith cause the truth of the case to be published in the gazette; to the end, that all such foes to the rights of British-America may be publicly known, and universally contemned as the enemies of American liberty.[6]

Formed in late 1774 or early 1775, the committees had as one of their tasks, then, the public exposure of private opinions, forcing those whose politics had been assumed to declare themselves in language in consonance or opposition to the people. As such, they had their most important life through 1776; thereafter, in many areas, wartime regulations and more formal courts superseded the rules on committees. This period, 1774–1776, was one where allegiances were shifting, the direction of events uncertain, and loyalties most violently put to the test. In some counties, committees seemed to respond to a genuine sense of physical threat to their lives; in others, the committees took a preemptive stance, stopping loyalist sedition, as they saw it, before it could infect the populace overall. What emerges from a perusal of the minutes of some of the committees, however, is both a multiplicity of perspectives and stories – alternating identities of criminal and victim – and a certain sameness to procedures despite local and regional differences among the thirteen colonies. Crèvecoeur, Munford, and Murray, writing in differing circumstances, all recognize the importance of perspective in the miniature dramas that the committee interrogations in essence became.

One of the important tasks of committees was the declaration of individuals to be "inimical" to patriot interests, largely based on reported speech, especially in questioning either the cause or the authority of committees. A typical judgment in committee minutes was for the offender "to be publicly advertised as a person inimical to American liberty."[7] In Tryon County, New York, scene ultimately of some of the most brutal events of the war and north of Crèvecoeur's Orange County farm, the committee during hearings in 1775 took affidavits that implicated citizens in anti-patriot remarks or activities. Several quoted the deposed sheriff, Alexander White, as saying:

> that he would fight for his King and Country with his association and the party on the King's Side like a brave Man, and swore to be Sure, that they would conquer, but the party on the Country's side do fight with the halters on their Necks ... [and] that he hopes to have the pleasure of hanging a good Many yet for their Resistance against the Acts of Parliament.[8]

Although such statements of belief seem like so much blustering, other patriots alleged more sinister remarks from White, as Jacob Seeber claims to have been told by the sheriff: "You d–d Rebell, if you say one Word more, I'll blow your Brains out" (*MB* 57). In Tryon, acts of speaking became weapons of war, and the committee's own status took on a sacrosanct quality that turned condemnation into 'villain' language. As the minutes of committee meetings clearly indicate, there was no free speech in the Revolutionary United States; while threats are one thing and understandably prone to be brought before a court, declarations of political allegiance are another. The minutes remind readers that the legal principle of free speech that was later incorporated in the first amendment was not accepted as legitimate among those under the control of committees.

The matter of speech and language underlies many of the committee investigations. In Westmoreland County, Virginia, one David Wardrobe was charged by the local committee in late 1774 for publishing a letter in the *Glasgow Journal* inimical to patriot interests. The action of the committee was swift. For his letter, Wardrobe would be barred from keeping his school in a county church; the committee would urge parents not to send their children to his school; and in addition to appearing in court, he would be required to issue a retraction. Eventually fearful of losing his livelihood and becoming a pariah, Wardrobe, after a short period of resistance, issued a letter of contrition.[9] Indeed, as Robert Calhoon observes, fear of "estrangement from the community" motivated a number of persons accused of the language of loyalty to retract. Richard Reed of Marblehead, Massachusetts, was another such as Wardrobe, who expressed regret for signing a declaration of approval for Governor Thomas Hutchinson, saying, "I do now publicly declare that I had no such design and therefore renounce the said address in every respect and am heartily sorry that I ever signed it and hope to be forgiven by my town and my countrymen."[10] Another case in Virginia, this one in Fincastle County, June 1776, shows the local committee charging John McCartey as follows: "that he has often discovered an unfriendly Disposition to the American Cause & has often attempted to degrade the Characters of Many Members of this Committee, that he has said that he keeps a particular account of the men who he knows to be in favour of the Country, & of all their Transactions, & expects One Day or other to appe[ar] as a Witness against them." Another Fincastle resident, Shadrick Morris, was complained against in these terms: "That the s[ai]d Morris had declared openly that he would Join the Kings Troops, that he was a Kings man and would not deny."[11] The implication of these hearings is clear: repent and be readmitted to the company of acceptable citizens or defy the committee and be branded as anathema to the county's and country's interests.

If in the beginning the committees were created with the purpose of using nonviolent intimidation against suspected tories, it was perhaps inevitable that some people amidst the anti-tory campaign would find violence a more direct means of harassing the enemies to the whig cause. Sometimes the committees would take more drastic action than demanding retractions, even to the point of condoning vigilante behavior. Peter Oliver, a long-time associate of Thomas Hutchinson, describes the actions in Connecticut in February 1775 against Abner Beebe, a physician who affirmed tory sentiments:

> he was assaulted by a Mob, stripped naked, & hot Pitch was poured upon him, which blistered his Skin ... They threw the Hog's Dung in his Face, & rammed some of it down his Throat; & in that Condition exposed to a Company of Women. His House was attacked, his Windows broke, when one of his Children was sick, & a Child of his went into Distraction upon this Treatment. His Gristmill was broke, & Persons prevented from grinding at it, & from having any Connections with him.[12]

Oliver does not specifically identify this violence as committee-inspired, but it does indicate the "tory view" of how loyalists were viewed by patriot authorities, whose tacit approval Oliver assumes. Oliver mentions another persecution that in his telling takes on a similar tone to that in Crèvecoeur: 'a Loyalist, but an inoffensive one in his behavior ... had an amiable Wife & several amiable Children; the Rebel Cart, in Imitation of the Inquisition Coach, called at his Door in the Morning, & they ordered him into the Cart, not suffering him to take his Hat with him; his Wife, at the same Time, begging on her Knees, to spare Husband; & his Daughters crying, with Intreaties.'[13] The aggrieved loyalist position, then, is one of victimization and violence against the family as a trope for disruption of traditional order in the state. For many others, tarring and feathering or other extralegal means were used to compel obedience to the patriot regime. Anthony Warwick in Isle of Wight County, Virginia, found himself the victim of this cruelty "after being called to account by the local committee."[14] As Richard Maxwell Brown argues throughout his essay on whig violence, while for patriots, the committees reflected a doctrine of popular sovereignty, for tories or noncommittal victims of committee interrogation, they were something else, a kind of democratic menace that could quickly metamorphose into the great fear of the eighteenth century, mob rule. Whether by speech, action, or passive noncompliance, a number of American residents were the objects of inquiry by committees of safety, and many were treated with rough justice.[15]

As the committee minutes indicate, free and loyal expressions of speech, even toasts, were subject to suspicion, inquiry, or punishment. For Crèvecoeur, this restriction on speech was only one of several complaints made in his play against whig committees. Perhaps his biggest charge in 'Landscapes' against the chairman of the committee and his wife is that they have become inured to the cruelty they exact in the name of the whig cause. When in the first landscape the family of Deacon Beatus and Eltha gather to talk approvingly of their elder son's late-night escapades (in which he has terrorized and harassed suspected loyalists), they pray to a Calvinist God who will "enable us to find out and punish those traitors to our cause ... who put on the appearance of Whigs and thereby deceive the vigilance of our committees."[16] This kind of heavy-handed irony, in which the hypocrisy of churchgoing persecutors is made all too apparent, dominates the tone of the play. For the author, the natural order of a civil society has been disrupted not only by war itself but by the complete overturning of civil behavior. The dramatized victims of committee terror are people of means, or those who once had prosperity but now are being or have been stripped of their worldly goods. The play implies that without the stability provided by paternalistic landowners, American society collapses on itself in a frenzy of acquisition and domination that has no end other than autocracy or anarchy.

With committees auctioning tory estates or forcing them from their owners at low prices, and by late 1777 with Congress urging the confiscation of loyalist property, it is not surprising that Crèvecoeur should center such acts of dispossession in his play. The primary victims in 'Landscapes' are the Marston family. Francis Marston, a landowner and prominent figure in the county, is being pursued by vigilantes. Mrs. Marston must endure the visits of Beatus and Eltha as they interrogate her and arrange for the auction of her property. The dramatist casts her passive resistance in the high style of the wronged citizen:

> You have insulted and treated my husband worse than a slave these six months. You have hired myrmidons to hunt him, to kill him if possible; if not, to threaten setting fire to his house that he might fly to save it, and that, by flying, his extensive estate might become a sweet offering to the rulers of this county. Now you are going to strip me and his children of all we possessed, and pray, what can you do more? (*L* 472)

In the context of the play, committee action reaches beyond the accused male to his family and his entire circle of acquaintance. Not only is

Marston proscribed, but his wife and children are about to be 'stripped' – a word that shows up frequently in the accounts of tory victimization.[17] In a sense, Crèvecoeur suggests that tories cease to exist as human beings in the minds of whigs. Without a social context for identity, without the property that is the emblem of identity, Mrs. Marston becomes a virtually disembodied voice, and truly so as the unenacted role of a closet drama.

Whatever the specific source of Crèvecoeur's wronged family, he apparently had any number of alleged victims in New York to choose from. The story of Sir John Johnson bears some resemblance to that of Marston. A member of the ruling elite in Tryon County and a vocal tory with his own guard, Johnson was arrested and paroled for his views. Fearing for his life, he fled to Canada, leaving his wife, Mary Watts Johnson, in charge of the family estate. The Albany committee then ordered her arrest, which, according to the loyalist memoir by Thomas Jones, led to the ransacking of her home. Jones's account, as with Crèvecoeur's of Mrs. Marston, makes clear the class dimensions to the event:

> The farm in Sir John's own occupation was robbed of his cattle, his negroes, his horses, hogs, sheep, and utensils of husbandry ... This done, Lady Johnson was escorted under a guard to Albany, a lady of great beauty, of the most amiable disposition, and composed of materials of the most soft and delicate kind. Besides this, she was more than seven months advanced in her pregnancy. She was suffered to go to Albany in her own carriage driven by a servant of her own. But in order to add insult to insult, she was obliged to take the Lieutenant who commanded the detachment into the carriage with her, who was now converted from a mender of shoes in Connecticut into an officer holding a commission under the honourable the Continental Congress. Thus was Lady Johnson conducted from Sir John's seat to Albany, guarded by a parcel of half-clothed dirty Yankees and squired by a New England officer, by trade a cobbler, as dirty as themselves, until he had decorated himself with a suit of Sir John's clothes, and a clean shirt, and pair of stockings, stolen at the Hall ... And yet these were the people who during the whole war boasted of their humane, generous, behaviour, and taxed the British and Loyalists as butchers, cut-throats and barbarians.[18]

This is a remarkable passage for all it reveals of the aggrieved tory perspective, its assumptions about class, and its portrait of the high-born woman wronged, all of which Crèvecoeur incorporates into his play. Mrs. Marston objects to the naked use of power against her, while her husband is in flight from prosecution, but she also objects to Eltha as a woman of a class well below her and therefore unfit to be making decisions about disposition of her property. To be sure, the author makes Eltha a corrupt, conniving woman, unsympathetic in almost any light, but the terms of Mrs. Marston's complaint resemble the direction of Jones's account of the Johnsons. Mrs. Johnson is a proper woman, truly feminine; those who arrest her are cobblers with officers' garb, impostors, 'dirty' at the core. In 'Landscapes,' the committee leaders cannot appreciate the heroic and tragic nature of her womanhood; Mrs. Marston speaks to a deaf audience within the play, but ostensibly to one attuned to suffering outside it. When the low are raised and the high fall, then identity is all playacting, the wearing of a uniform by Crèvecoeur's booby committee member, Aaron Blue-Skin, for example, or the grasping of power by an Eltha. In a proper tory world, natural forms of deference would prevent such precipitate elevation, but in a committee world, all verities collapse in a radical reordering of the interrogator and the interrogated.

Even more than Letter XII of *Letters from an American Farmer*, in which Farmer James contemplates flight to the wilderness to escape the oncoming war, "Landscapes" conducts its own interrogation into the ideological formation of the emerging republic. In other scenes, for instance, a landlord at an inn must suppress his own views and essentially give away his liquor to visiting patriots and hotheads. Later, three Quakers who refuse to pledge allegiance to the whig forces are tied up and humiliated by committee renegades. In the final scene, a widowed mother holds her dead infant and lashes out at the heartlessness of Beatus and Eltha, as well as committee violence, while the chairman and his wife show no compassion or possibility of seeing the destructiveness of their path. In the end, the woman, Martha Corwin, stands as a lament for the loss of a hierarchy that keeps in check the brutal instincts of those who have nothing but who desire to possess the property and power of those who have. Crèvecoeur might well have agreed with one real-life citizen of Pennsylvania who was cited by his local committee for saying of Congress and the Revolution that "the whole was nothing but a scheme of a parcel of hot-headed Presbyterians."[19] But to have said that was to be hauled before the committee. It is not surprising, perhaps, that Crèvecoeur fled to British-occupied New York in 1778; although a professed neutral, he must have known that he would have had to face committee inquisition from some shoemaker, perhaps, who resented his marrying into tory wealth and position.

Munford betrays many of the same anxieties in Virginia as his contemporary does in New York. Although in pre-war Virginia the writer had achieved a certain local prestige in the usual fashion, having been appointed magistrate in the newly formed county of Mecklenburg and elected a burgess, by early 1777 his reputation had taken a few blows.[20] Like "Landscapes," *The Patriots* portrays a world in which traditional forms of deference have been erased, a ludic world of Plautine reversals where the lower class rule and the masters must dance to their tune. Whereas Crèvecoeur's play is a cry of rage and despair over the unfairness of patriot hegemony, Munford's is something different, a squeaky wheel on a cart without an apparent horse, headed slowly downhill, but without enough friction to completely retard the cart's progress. Although it shares a common set of conservative concerns with the other plays over the social ramifications of committees, *The Patriots* also displays some local circumstances that establish it as a Tidewater story.[21] The committee, composed of such men as Thunderbolt, Squib, Colonel Strut, Mr. Summons, Brazen, and Skip, betray their "natural" station by their names, all derivatives of Restoration and early eighteenth-century low comic character types. Their main order of business early in the play is to proscribe Scots, men of which nationality occupied key positions in the economy of the Tidewater, either as factors or as tradesmen in shipping towns, like Norfolk at the mouth of the James River and Chesapeake Bay. As with Crèvecoeur's three Quakers, whose pacifism is assumed to be loyalism, Munford has his three Scots brought before the committee essentially to be tried for being Scottish born. Munford does not help their case by naming them M'Flint, M'Squeeze, and M'Gripe – although he had family ties to Scots, one suspects Munford had his own suspicions or difficulties with Scottish factors – but the playwright does satirize the absurdity of condemning a man merely because of his birth. To escape prosecution, one of the accused, M'Flint, says that while he was Scottish "bred" he was not Caledonian "born" – a patent lie, but good enough for the committee.[22] The other two refuse to deny their birth, and as their arrest is ordered, M'Squeeze defies taking an oath of allegiance while M'Gripe shouts his loyalty to the king. Thus, while the men are not entirely innocent of being loyalist sympathizers, Munford suggests that their loyalty cannot be ascribed purely to birth – that such prosecutions show a contemptible ignorance on the part of the committee. This is made clear in an exchange between the two central male characters, Trueman and Meanwell:

> TRUE: In the catalogue of sins, I never found it one before to be born on the north of the Tweed. (*aside to Mean.*)

MEAN: In nature's lowest works, I never saw before such base stupidity. (*aside to True.*) (*TP* 461)

In essence, the Scots, despite their overt loyalty to the crown at the end of the scene, are made martyrs to whig justice; Munford turns the tables on the patriots, interrogating his own side for its zeal and the absurd basis of prosecution.[23]

As with Murray, Munford does not make the committee investigations the primary focus of the play, but he cannot leave them alone either. In many ways, the declared stupidity of the Scots interrogations might be overlooked in the rest of the plotting, but Munford clearly has a complaint to register that ultimately reflects a much deeper anxiety about the meaning of the committees than such buffoonery with the Scots would suggest. The primary love plot is that of Trueman for Mira, but that is complicated by Munford's making her father, Brazen, a rough-spoken country gentleman of the Restoration type, be the most influential figure on the county committee. Meanwell and Trueman look at Brazen as little different from the others, and in dramatic terms, he is a typical senex (the elder who interferes with young lovers) and a throwback to various gulled squires who run afoul of Cavalier rakes from the city in Restoration comedies. Trueman says of him in the opening scene, 'Her father is a violent patriot without knowing the meaning of the word. He understands little or nothing beyond a dice-box and race-field, but thinks he knows every thing; and woe be to him that contradicts him! His political notions are a system of perfect anarchy, but he reigns in his own family with perfect despotism' (*TP* 449). Despite this withering assessment by Munford's protagonist, Brazen cannot be easily dismissed. He becomes the instrument for exposing Captain Flash, a character who, like David Garrick's of the same name in *Miss in Her Teens*, is all talk, no action; and when he finally bestows Mira on Trueman, Brazen does so not as a fool but as a victor.[24] That is, in many ways, this old-style dramatic character and frequent butt of urban humor becomes in this committee play suddenly a vision of a future that Munford does not like but cannot prevent.

In Revolutionary Virginia, the power structure of traditional elites was seriously challenged from a variety of previously marginalized groups, affecting not only who were elected as representatives or to county offices but also forcing gentry to adjust their conservative positions toward more radical whig calls for full independence.[25] This is apparent in the scene in

Act IV by which Trueman and Meanwell are finally tried for associating with Scots and failing to declare themselves as warm whigs. To some extent, Munford has prepared us for this moment by the dialogue between the two men in Act I, scene 1. Trueman criticizes his potential father-in-law for believing in a "state of nature and liberty without restraint" (449). For Meanwell, this indicates "that all heads are not capable of receiving the benign influence of the principles of liberty" (450); a few, like him and Trueman, are quietly warmed by "the rays of the sun of freedom," but the majority display their "zeal" by "bawling against" tyranny. Trueman echoes these sentiments, and notes that "many temporary evils must be supported with patience" before that end is reached (451). The most pressing "temporary" evil is their appearance before the committee as the accused. Trueman, who "hates these little democracies," must with his cohort in patrician forbearance put up with the humiliation of being queried by those whose highest aspirations seem to be winning at cards or, like Colonel Strut, collecting from the public treasury without actually having to do something as onerous as military service. Trueman refuses to commit to a political identity, decrying the use of such inflammatory terms as *tory* and *whig*; but as in Murray's play, a plot device allows Trueman and Meanwell to escape the justice of the committee. Before the hearing takes place, they confront privately their accuser, Tackabout, and force him to reveal his true tory identity. When the committee finally hears of Tackabout's perfidy, Brazen quickly denounces the accuser and pronounces Trueman a good man. Although Meanwell and his partner condemn Tackabout as a hypocrite rather than as a tory, it is his toryism that damns him and saves the others. Munford reluctantly acknowledges that in the seemingly crude justice of the committee, there is justice, even if not observed with paternalistic forms. In this regard, then, *The Patriots* equivocates on the committees it has set out to condemn; Munford's muse is confused, indeed.

Although the committees are an American phenomenon and therefore would seem to provide the playwrights with unique, homegrown material, as in Murray's ways of distinguishing her play from *The West Indian*, Munford clearly borrows from a number of Restoration and eighteenth-century plays, including the Duke of Buckingham's *The Rehearsal* (the play explicitly likens Captain Flash to Drawcansir, a comical *miles gloriosus* type), George Farquhar's *Recruiting Officer* (Munford's Flash is a recruiter),[26] and the aforesaid Garrick play. Beyond those obvious debts – and he might have seen both latter plays in Williamsburg[27] – Munford's satire nevertheless bears an uncanny resemblance to a British play from the previous century, Aphra Behn's *The Widow Ranter*. I say uncanny because the arch-royalist Behn was hardly known in American theatrical circles. While her play about Bacon's Rebellion is now read in American literature classes,[28] it had only a brief run in late 1689 in London and was never acted in the colonies; the most comprehensive listing of colonial productions records not a single performance of any Behn play – not even the popular *The Rover* – in British America before 1775.[29] Still, a few parallels are striking.[30] In *The Widow Ranter*, Virginia is governed by a council of locals, whose names, as in Munford, expose their inadequacy for the task: Dullman, Timorous, Whiff, Whimsey. Munford's committee and Behn's council shift opinions with each new piece of evidence; in Behn, the rebel Bacon is either hero or enemy, depending on the whim of the mob, and the council follows popular opinion. Behn uses the council to satirize democratic rule, and at the end, replaces the low-born tradesmen with gentlemen of the stripe Munford creates in Trueman and Meanwell. In both plays, the central figure on the council or committee displays some integrity: Wellman in Behn, Brazen in Munford. Both plays have a female virago figure who displays more courage and true martial bravado than the men on the council or committee. In Behn, the sword-wielding woman is the Widow Ranter herself, a smoking, drinking, swearing but still attractive woman who decides on a man and does anything, including cross-dress and enter battle, to get him. In Munford, Isabella leaves off such Restoration boldness as the swearing and drinking, but she demands of Colonel Strut that he put on the reality of a soldier, and in Strut's confrontation with the equally cowardly Captain Flash, the only one willing to enter the fray is Isabella. In her case, however, she gives up her man when he proves to be a rank coward.[31] There are other ties, but the point is that Behn and Munford – despite the unlikelihood of Munford's owning a copy of Behn's play or ever seeing it performed – make the same critique about popular rule: democracy does no favors for Virginia, and putting power into the hands of cobblers and farriers makes a mockery of rule based on social codes of submission to "natural" forms of patriarchal leadership. Even so, Munford's play shows much less confidence than Behn's about the likely outcome of conflict. Whereas *The Widow Ranter* ends with the low-born councilmen retreating to their original occupations and the well-born gentleman combatants moving in to take their place, *The Patriots* ends with Brazen still in charge of the unchanged committee and the gentlemen to some extent still dependent on his favor for their position. Cavalier cockiness has been supplanted by Revolutionary anxiety – an anxiety not able to be dispelled by plot alone.[32]

Although she could not have known Munford's or Crèvecoeur's unpublished dramas, Murray seems aware of the ideological problems posed by staging committee scenes in an otherwise patriotic play and tries to avoid some of the searing criticism of Revolutionary rhetoric in which her predecessors indulge. In Murray's comedy, the committee functions as a complication in the Rambleton plot. In the late years of the war, Rambleton/Montague has returned to Massachusetts on a British-owned ship at his private expense to see if there is any hope of reconciling with his estranged wife, Louisa. Naturally, this act incites suspicions of his origins and motives. At the beginning of Act III, Rambleton goes with Harry Camden, a young American officer – and the unrecognized Montague's son – to review the troops. The scene, although brief, is filled with patriotic sloganeering, cheers for Washington, the glorious cause, and the Rights of Man. Rambleton, still disguised, beams with pride in the soldiers, in his son, and in the hopes that his "inquiries" into Louisa's situation are going well. Thus, while the personal and familial take precedence in the play over the political, Murray offers a new order, one in which a renewed squirarchy will take its place under the leadership of a recognized member of the elite and patriot hero, Washington.

Meanwhile, the keepers of the inn where Rambleton is staying, the Vansittarts, plot to get Rambleton's money. She's a scheming malapropist; he is a dialect-speaking Dutchman and a coward. Both desire quick wealth and an escape from creditors; although not exactly equivalent, they function in *Traveller Returned* somewhat like Beatus and Eltha do in 'Landscapes.' Mrs. Vansittart, struck by the quality of her guest's possessions, tells her husband that Rambleton is a "*spyington* from the British." She further identifies Camden as her lodger's "accomplishment" – *accomplice* and a clever play by the author – and, drawing the analogy to André and Arnold, concludes, "It would be doing a *jonteel* thing, and a *patrolitical* thing, to inform against them to the Committee of Safety."[33] The advantage, she explains to her slow-witted spouse, is that Rambleton's appearance before the committee will give the Vansittarts time to rifle through his things, take the valuables, and abscond, without being detected. We will have "served ourselves," she says, "at the expense of *abomination* tories," and as "the goods of a Tory are free plunder!" therefore their theft will be patriotic and justifiable (*TR* 127).

Given the rhetoric in Crèvecoeur, one can see even in the comic interchange between the Vansittarts a suspicion in Murray of the value of the committees. The Vansittarts, like Beatus and Eltha, are motivated by greed and justify by sophistry. There is a further parallel to Munford's Tackabout; that character does not make his accusations so much for money as to protect his own position as closet tory. Although his ideological position seemingly differentiates him from Beatus and Eltha or the Vansittarts, he, like the others, is self-serving and uses the committee as a convenient platform by which to ruin others in pursuit of hypocritical, antisocial ends. Crèvecoeur stages the committee in "Landscapes" to reject the entire premise of the Revolution; their rising from the lower class, their failure to defer to the landed gentry, and their religious hypocrisy all mark them as unsuitable to take positions of power in society. Munford is unsure, but finally decides that the Revolution will get a lukewarm affirmation by his isolating the villain as shape-shifting tory. Murray for her part intends that the Revolution be validated. As a consequence, the complication of the committee must serve to darken the prospects of Rambleton without casting too heavy a shadow on the ideology of republican liberty. By suppressing criticism of the committee *per se* and by identifying the troublemakers as ethnically inscribed others, rather than by class, the postwar playwright attempts to find her way out of the *impasse* a committee scene poses.

The confrontation in *Traveller* comes in Act IV. Rambleton is ordered by an officer of the committee to appear before it, on charges of spying. Rambleton calls it "officious interference" – echoing the critiques in Crèvecoeur and Munford, as if this will be one more innocent man forced to suffer under the suspicions of people below him in degree. He speaks aside his worst fear – that the complaint was lodged by Harry Camden – but when assured by the officer that he will "receive every indulgence, that the nature of the case, and the circumstances of our country will admit" (*TR* 135), Rambleton agrees to go. Such committee politeness – absent in Crèvecoeur and Munford – further mitigates the sting of being called, but Murray rightly understands that she could not let Rambleton come to town from England without his allegiance being a point of contention. In Act V, scene 3, we enter on an interrogation that has been going on "for many hours," but the accused insists to the committee on his right not to reveal his "private reasons for wishing to remain concealed at present" (146) – the very justification used by Meanwell and Trueman in *The Patriots* and repeated in actual committee minutes by passively obedient loyalists. Rambleton's attachment to Harry Camden causes one on the committee to suspect the young officer as himself involved in a plot; a second and third member bring forward Arnold's treachery as the source of their having to be *vigilant* – the name, in fact, of the committee's secretary. When Camden suddenly announces that Rambleton has been robbed by the Vansittarts, who brought the complaint, the suspected tory reveals his identity and is released from custody and suspicion. The plot then quickly resolves itself in the arrest of the thieves and the matchmaking of lovers.

Murray's play hints, then, at the conflict in the republic between private and public. Most of the scenes have to do with personal matters; while set during the Revolution, the play is only secondarily about the war. Nevertheless, Murray interrogates the nature of revolutionary interrogations. What right does any agency have to inquire into the personal circumstances of individuals? When Murray wrote her drama, the French Revolution was providing the Americans with examples of committees of safety run amok. A Federalist, Murray would have shared the suspicions of citizens' councils held by such people as John Adams, whose long-running argument with his estranged friend Mercy Otis Warren on the nature of a republic showed his own distrust of democracy and the crossing of class lines.[34] Ironically, it was Adams who supported the restrictions on free speech and expression contained within the Alien and Sedition Acts of 1798, the very sort of thing Warren feared. This episode suggests that Murray did not fear constriction of liberty *per se* as the issue, but rather the questioning of someone whose education and fortune should entitle him to deferential treatment from those without either.

Traveller never resolves the issues ideologically. The drama follows the stock formula of disguise, that is, that merit will out. Rambleton's patient endurance of his interrogation validates the intent of the process, while the outcome justifies his private reasons for keeping his identity obscure. Without the *deus ex machina* of Camden's entrance during his father's hearing, however, the play suggests that the deep suspicions of the committee, their seeing the object of interrogation as another Arnold or André, would have led to a darker, if not finally fatal, resolution. With the grasping strivers, the Vansittarts, under arrest, and the drunken Irish servant, Patrick, shown to have been a cause of the problem by ignoring Rambleton's request to watch over his valuables, *Traveller* finally affirms a conservative Revolution whose instrumentalities – the committees – have no further place in a society where class provides the order absent in wartime upheavals. The real problems are ethnic characters, unassimilated members of the lower orders, not English ancestored characters who speak like the elites they represent.

In the end, all three plays ask significant questions about democracy and the limits of popular sovereignty and republican governance. Despite their different conclusions – one tragic, two comic – Crèvecoeur, Munford, and Murray put real-life conflicts in dramatic form in order to demonstrate the impact of revolutionary ardor on noncombatants and the higher ranks of society. To varying degrees, each play centers one or two natural noblemen whose intentions are misunderstood and satirizes the persecuting or prosecuting partisans for their hypocrisy of motive. To follow David Shields's analysis of early republican culture,[35] one might say that these plays reject incivility and affirm a society constructed most firmly in the protection of polite – that is, elite – discourse. Murray's post-war perspective allows her to wave the flag of patriotic victory while signaling caution for future experiments in democracy. Crèvecoeur's early war view imagines only chaos or democratic tyranny, where merit, station, and decorum are swallowed by majoritarian venality, while Munford tepidly supports whig goals even as he forswears their methods. It is as if popular sovereignty is only an unfortunate, even hateful, consequence of the separation from Britain – not a principle worth the suffering the playwrights suggest it might have caused.

All three writers, however, affirm drama as a genre appropriate for rendering and critiquing this ritual of dark interrogation whereby public display of private lives is seen to lead to a perversion of class-influenced social relations. Is the United States a country that allows its citizens to overthrow not only a system of government but also a longstanding pattern of acknowledgment of social superiority? For these playwrights, civility, order, and class position – values affirmed in the British dramatic tradition – override the rights of citizens to form committees for the purpose of determining ideological purity in the name of national security. Drama in America, insofar as it retains the class assumptions of eighteenth-century British drama, resists making heroic the most radical dimensions of the Revolution. Crèvecoeur rejects the Revolution as an act entirely; Munford and Murray affirm the act but reject the consequences of pursuing anything other than a military solution to a political problem. Each one borrows a literary form that inscribes satire against the lower class and acceptance of elite rights and claims on loyalty as an assumption of the form.

In many ways, each of these plays, through the trope of the committee, qualifies the affirmations each author ostensibly makes about his or her country. "Landscapes" plays against Crèvecoeur's assertions of social mobility in *Letters from an American Farmer* by showing that the social upheavals caused by committee interrogations so disrupt the constitution of ordinary society as to render life functionally meaningless. For its part, *The Patriots* tries desperately to find a place within the whig Revolution for cautious, private gentlemen, and while it fits them in marginally at the conclusion, the rhetoric of the play essentially defeats Munford's purpose. Unless elites are willing to recognize that the franchise has grown much broader very rapidly and is not likely to reverse, they threaten to become the new others as the others pass them by. And in a strange way, *Traveller Returned* is an important gloss to a modern-day reading of Murray's essays that argue for a new understanding of women in culture. For Murray, feminism (taken here to mean in her terms a consciousness of the *human* equality of men and women), while it can alter perceptions of women as intellectual beings or as souls or change modes of female education, cannot significantly reconfigure women's civil or social position. To do so, by analogy to the committee disruptions, would endanger other kinds of order brought about by class position. The failure of the committee to prove anything against Rambleton allows him to reunite with his wife, correcting her error of long ago in showing interest in another man and restoring her to the wholeness of a full marital relation rather than confirming her in her singleness. In the larger sense, Murray demonstrates that such committees have no purpose beyond the war, once the elite patriotic cream rises to the surface; class supersedes democracy, gender equality taken as rights, or any other threat to maintenance of assumedly natural class position. All three playwrights ask troubling questions about the nature of interrogation and so leave their audiences, imagined or real, with doubts about whether some new system of personal relations, whereby traditional class structures are rearranged, can ever properly replace what has gone before. Their answer, emphatic in Crèvecoeur, more subtle in Murray and Munford, is no.

6

Dunlap's queer André: versions of revolution and manhood

THE THREE COMMITTEE PLAYS SUGGEST HOW DRAMA CAPTURES the ambiguities of the Revolution and the uncertainties of Anglo-American identity in the wake of separation from Britain. All three plays lack a demonstrable on-stage hero, and while Harry Camden presents himself as an admirable patriot, the only personage with sufficient stature to fill the hero's role, Washington, never appears in *Traveller Returned* except as a spoken object of admiration. Of course, earlier closet plays had attempted to generate American heroes as warriors for liberty: Joseph Warren in Burk's *Bunker-Hill*, for instance, or Richard Montgomery in Brackenridge's *The Death of Montgomery*. In Mercy Warren's *The Group*, Liberty herself seems to stand out from among the ill-intentioned mandamus council members as an emblem of purpose. After the war, however, once the immediate need for patriotic propaganda had been removed, playwrights were faced with difficult choices in terms of how precisely to honor the Revolution without simply betraying political positions on post-war allegiance with France or Britain. Among early republican dramatic attempts to portray American history on stage without reference to the committees, William Dunlap's *André* (1798) displays some of the problems of identification in recalling a war whose stings had not entirely been forgotten. Dunlap's tragedy stands out for its problematic portrayals of Major John André, the British spy offered up as the titular hero, and George Washington, the unnamed "General" whose decision to execute André nearly remakes the patriotic icon into a vulnerable and fallible cruel father.[1] The plot is simple: having been captured by patriot militia after arranging the betrayal of Benedict Arnold, André is sentenced to death. The key issue in Dunlap's play is whether he will be hanged or shot, although the audience knows full well, in the manner of a Greek spectator at a tragedy, that history dictates what the outcome will be. Taking up André's cause is an American officer, Bland, who was once helped by André when Bland was held captive in a British prison ship. With the General's insisting that André hang as a spy rather than be shot as a military prisoner of war, the play ends with his offstage execution. By eliding Arnold from the play, Dunlap leaves his audience to choose among André, the General, Bland, or two other patriot officers, the isolationist Seward or the rational internationalist M'Donald, as figures worthy to be incorporated into national identity. As his contemporaries must have recognized, Dunlap complicates considerably the question of finding a nationalist signifying character.

In its first New York performance, the play was hissed by some "veterans" in the audience when Bland, a man of feeling, threw down his cockade (confused also by some in the audience with an emblem for New York Federalists) in disgust at the impending fate of the popular and otherwise virtuous British major, a situation that forced Dunlap to rewrite a later scene to restore Bland to patriotic good graces.[2] Yet surely, that little episode, made much of in commentary on the play and by Dunlap himself, had little to do with the play's relative lack of popularity. Elihu Hubbard Smith, a fellow member of the Friendly Club, who saw Dunlap daily and assisted him during the proofreading process of the play, notes simply that the first performance was "most wretchedly played" and that the actor playing Bland was "miserably deficient." By the third night, however, things had improved: "It was pretty well performed, & recd.," even if the attendance had dropped from opening night.[3] Although *André* was withdrawn from the Old American Company's repertoire after its three New York performances, traces of it resurfaced in Dunlap's more overtly pro-American vehicle, *The Glory of Columbia*, in 1803, a July Fourth play that enjoyed a long history on American stages.[4] Nevertheless, the original tragedy challenges the nature of national identity in more disconcerting ways than the popular version of five years later.

Commentators have long noticed the demands Dunlap's drama puts on an audience and readers. By 1798, well-used to celebrations on stage that included the reading of patriotic poems or acting in ephemeral pantomimes to Liberty and Columbia, American audiences accepted that their former president was only to be spoken of respectfully on the boards. The anti-patriarchal elements of the play, observed by Robert Canary and Jay Fliegelman, create a strong dissonance in the portrayal of someone Americans would expect to be the hero.[5] Nevertheless, those same audiences were also used to a steady diet of British plays, from Shakespeare and Sheridan to forgettable drivel, often at the expense of local playwrights, and thus making London the city that determined acceptable American stage fare. Royall Tyler's *The Contrast* notwithstanding, many of the American efforts to receive more than a token night or two in theatres were translations of German or French plays; and Dunlap, of course, was the chief promulgator in the United States of the plays of August von Kotzebue.[6] English-born actors formed the core of all American professional companies, and British drama the vast bulk of the repertoire. As Gary Richardson has observed, "the English flavor of the company meant that after the Revolution they suffered ... from the abiding suspicion that they were in effect, if not by design, part of a British cultural conspiracy to subvert republican virtue."[7] At the same time, however, American spectators expected British plays and measured acting by standards imported with the players. While, on the one hand, Dunlap attempted to meet a large gap in the repertoire by staging a play with more overt American content than his earlier *Darby's Return*, on the other he had to face the problematic demands of a theatre he now managed (the Park) and whose taste was largely met with a European bill.[8]

Still, to stage a play about the American Revolution and make a popular British military thespian, John André, the tragic hero was risky business, as Dunlap acknowledged many years later. After all, André, in arranging the betrayal of Arnold and the British seizure of the fort at West Point, was caught by American militia while he was dressed in nonmilitary garb and therefore considered, by the military codes of the time, a spy.[9] As with Murray's comic *Traveller Returned*, Dunlap's blank-verse tragedy suggests to audiences a complexity of sympathies, as is perhaps evident by more recent commentaries.[10] Within the framework of an ultimate affirmation of the Revolution, Dunlap calls on a tradition of English tragedy to make a noble character of a British enemy to the fledgling United States. In essence, *André* forces its viewers to hold in balance multiple allegiances, to the new republic and to the old theatre, to sons as well as fathers, at a time, 1798, when Francophile Democratic Republicans and Anglophile Federalists contended for the political soul of the nation.

It might be argued, as Richardson has done, that Dunlap uses the opportunity to advance a progressive politics in the context of his belief in the public value of a virtuous theatre: "*André* provides Dunlap the opportunity to articulate the young nation's republican ideology," he claims, "to contrast its values with antecedent social codes, to provide a living embodiment for the audience's continued emulation, and to argue that history has both claimed and freed the young nation to pursue its destiny."[11] But what exactly constitutes such an ideology? Dunlap himself was a progressive social thinker, for instance, and took an early and consistently principled stand against slavery long before there was an organized abolition movement. Yet the play also speaks to the hold those "antecedent social codes" have over Americans in the context of a theatre whose bread is often buttered by pre-Revolutionary British plays that gain their meaning from such codes.

In that sense, the history of *André* is one not only linked to an episode of the Revolution, but also to that of English political drama, particularly that shown on American stages. As a play about the Revolution, but as more than a nod to British drama, *André* shows itself to its audiences, readers and spectators alike, in a variety of versions, or "acts of turning," to recall the medieval Latin *versio*. Turned one way, the play looks thoroughly American; turned another, it looks remarkably British; turned still another, Dunlap's tragedy reveals previously unseen facets of private or subjective identities that do not fit comfortably at all in a nationalist setting. In one version, then, *André* is a *reversion* to the heroic dramas written a century before but still alive in the late eighteenth-century theatre.[12] Addison's *Cato* is the most famous of these, as both text and acted drama, a play known intimately by the Revolutionary generation. Whether Dunlap had *Cato* in mind in writing *André* is not entirely clear (although it is hard to imagine how anyone of Dunlap's generation with a modicum of literacy and theatrical spectatorship could not have lines from Addison's tragedy roiling in his or her head); however, it is quite certain that he knew another play from the period of the Popish Plot, Thomas Otway's 1682 tragedy, *Venice Preserved, or A Plot Discovered*. As other critics have noticed, in Act V, Bland remembers as a boy his own playing of Pierre in Otway's play.[13] Now he says André is Pierre, condemned to die, and he will be Jaffeir, the friend who dispatches the condemned compatriot before the state can exhibit his executed body for the rabble to see. André stops Bland from killing him with his sword, thereby from preempting the shame of execution, and says he will accommodate himself to hanging; but the overt reference to Otway makes clear that *Venice Preserved* informs Dunlap in ways that go beyond a parallel moment in the plays' respective plots.

Venice Preserved is the story of a rebellion, in this case against the corrupt (and republican) leadership of Venice. Here, however, there is no clear standard of virtue, at least in the political realm. Unlike an earlier play of rebellion, Nathaniel Lee's *Lucius Junius Brutus* (1680), which proved too controversial to be acted after the first year, Otway's tragedy held the boards in Britain for well over a century after its initial run. In the colonies and in the new republic, *Venice Preserved* was one of the most popular such plays, appearing first as early as 1752 in New York and in multiple performances there and in other cities in every decade thereafter to 1820 and beyond. It was especially well received in Philadelphia in the 1790s, with ten performances from 1790 to 1797, but it also played in New York in the post-war period, including at least one performance each in 1785, 1793, 1794, 1797, 1798, and three more in 1799. It was also a staple of the British military theatre in occupied New York, offered at least seven times by the "gentlemen of the Army and Navy" during 1777–1783.[14] Dunlap, as a resident at various times of British-occupied New York, London, then republican New York, would have had ample opportunity to see *Venice Preserved* on several occasions. In fact, it may have been his favorite play. At a testimonial for Dunlap in 1833, long after he had retired from stage life, the drama performed in his honor was *Venice Preserved*.[15]

Like other American playwrights, Dunlap knew or thought he knew that to create an effective American play he would need to adapt some successful English models. Another American, William Hill Brown, had already applied Otway to the Arnold treachery in a drama called *West Point Preserved* that played in Boston April 17, 1797, but whose text has not survived.[16] *André* is not a rewrite of Otway, but it borrows both meaning and motifs from its predecessor, leaving readers and viewers with a great deal of uncertainty about its message. Dunlap's play appeared during a time with analogies to the political conditions posited in the Restoration tragedy. In 1798, the country was riven by political controversy. Whereas 1680s England swirled with rumors and accusations of Catholic plots against the state and counter-measures against the accusers, the late 1790s United States worried about incendiaries in their midst that might spring upon the state a French-style revolution. Stung by hostility to the Jay Treaty, Federalists positioned themselves firmly against the French, whose designs and threats they took to be a kind of conspiracy against the nation's freedom to sign treaties with whomever it wished – in this case, England. The storm that led to the Alien and Sedition Acts carried with it overtones of conspiracy and plots against the nation, with the Federalists targeting Democratic–Republican newspapers and individuals as undermining the state.[17] Matters of loyalty were much in the air, as they distinctly are in *Venice Preserved*. Dunlap's version of revolutionary history carries with it an assertion of the personal against the political, as Otway's play does, leaving the political darkly figured, even if it acknowledges a grim justice in the execution of André and the outcome of the war.

Another version of *André*, then, is the *conversion* of an English model to an American setting. Reading *André* through Otway, one can observe that the ostensible politics of the playwright – royalist for Otway, noncommittal for Dunlap – lie intermingled with theatrical values in such a way as to prevent their overt and one-dimensional detection. Many early American plays, particularly those written in direct response to the patriot cause, make much of virtue as the source of the United States' strength; Brackenridge, Warren, Tyler, and John Parke, author of *Virginia*, are but a few who choose this route.[18] In *Venice Preserved*, Pierre is the idealist who, although motivated in part by self-interest – one of the corrupt senators has purchased time with his lady love, the courtesan Aquilina, and Pierre wants revenge – stoically manages to assert principle above individual concern. He is passionate, but not intemperate; his error in the play is to allow himself to be led by Renault, a French incendiary with a taste for blood.

When Bland assigns the role of Pierre to André, he provides us with a window into Dunlap's thinking about his tragic character. The playwright suggests we read or see his play with Otway in mind; André the character has links to Pierre in that he could be seen as the dupe of Arnold/Renault, while the connection of Bland to Jaffeir, the tortured friend who at first betrays, then proves his friendship, can be quickly made. The André of Dunlap's drama gains performative stature from the fact that casting for *Venice Preserved* almost always put the leading tragedian in the role of Pierre. In the two New York performances that immediately preceded the premiere of *André*, those of August 23, 1797 and January 5, 1798, Pierre was played by Thomas Abthorpe Cooper, a young but already very talented English-born actor who would become a major figure in New York, Philadelphia, and Boston.[19] In the 1798 production, Jaffeir was played by the co-manager of the theatre with Dunlap, John Hodgkinson, who replaced the earlier actor opposite Cooper, John Pollard Moreton.[20] For *André*, Cooper wanted the title role, the natural tie to his two Otway productions in the months previous, but Hodgkinson, who had control of the production, cast him as the hotheaded American, Bland, here the functional Jaffeir. Angry over the snub, Cooper learned his lines but poorly, contributing to the less than delirious reception the play had.[21] Nevertheless, the first performance of *André* created a strange intertextual commentary, whereby the audience was essentially asked to see the Cooper who played Pierre in the actor – Hodgkinson – who played André, all while hearing Cooper as Bland naming as an appropriate Pierre an actor who had just played Jaffeir less than three months before. Fearing, possibly, to be detected as a plagiarist, Dunlap's conversion included a theatrical *inversion* that may, for its first audience, have deflected some of the correspondence between the two texts – or merely complicated it.

Further, the friendship between André and Bland resembles the exceptional homosocial relations that mark many Restoration and Augustan tragedies. Consistent with such theatrical homosociality, the greatest passions expressed by anyone in Dunlap's play are those of Bland for André. Something like this situation is found in Otway as well. For Jaffeir, the principle of liberty takes second place to the gut feeling of revenge; but perhaps the strongest motivation he has to participate in the conspiracy against the senators is his love for his friend. Two remarks by Jaffeir will show this dimension. He suffers in his poverty for himself and his wife, Belvidera, and as he proclaims this to Pierre, he says, "Bear my weakness,/If throwing thus my arms about thy neck,/I play the boy, and blubber in thy bosom."[22] Later, in Act II, after Pierre tells his friend not to see Belvidera anymore, lest it undermine his courage, Jaffeir exclaims, "O Pierre, wert thou but she,/How I could pull thee down into my heart," wishing his friend were his wife, that he might express in more passionate tones the agony he feels (*VP* 344).

Because both Jaffeir and Pierre have attachments to women, and the women play prominent roles from the beginning, especially Belvidera, *Venice Preserved* asserts a hetero-normative sexuality, despite the fact that the most morally repugnant characters, Renault and Antonio, both slaver after young women and would have sex with any female their power or money would enable them to. Nevertheless, despite the offsetting character of Belvidera, the play makes much of the Jaffeir–Pierre friendship. In Dunlap, the action is considerably simplified, but the reading of the Bland–André relationship is complicated by the functional elimination of women from the central plot. Without a Belvidera, the exalted friendship shown in Otway becomes intensified in Dunlap to the point of distortion, at least in traditional stage economy. Young Bland has a good reputation as a soldier. When he learns that a spy has been caught, he shares the same feelings of patriotic satisfaction as the other officers, until he learns the captive is André. In the play, Bland, who is not a historical figure, credits the British captive in tones of tender affection with ministering to him while he was a prisoner of the British:

> This gallant youth, then favor'd, high in power,
> Sought out the pit obscene of foul disease,
> Where I, and many a suffering soldier lay,
> And, like an angel, seeking good for man,
> Restor'd us light, and partial liberty.
> Me he mark'd out his own. He nurst and cur'd,
> He lov'd and made his friend. I liv'd by him,
> And in my heart he liv'd, till, when exchang'd,
> Duty and honor call'd me from my friend –
> Judge how my heart is tortur'd (*A* 72).

André plays the role of nursemaid in this scene, with, in Bland's telling, a distinctly unmasculine attentiveness normally assigned to the selfless woman. Whereas Jaffeir also has such lines of love for Pierre, he speaks affectionately, as well as perversely, to Belvidera, who keeps his loyalties divided. Bland, despite expressions of caring for his father and his mother, has no other focus for his erotic energies than André.

When Bland first encounters the imprisoned André, they embrace and express affections for each other. André then explains his side of the story, properly, for a tragic hero, admitting his own mistakes in the Arnold affair. The sticking point for him is the hanging as a spy, rather than being shot as a respected enemy soldier. Deeply affected by André's concern, Bland exclaims:

> I will forswear my country and her service:
> I'll hie me to the Briton, and with fire,
> And sword, and every instrument of death
> Or devastation, join in the work of war! (*A* 80).

That is, he will, like Arnold – whose name by 1798 was anathema – abjure his loyalty to country for the sake of his friend. When M'Donald, the rationalist officer who attempts to cool Bland's petulant heat, says his friendship has carried him so far that it has become a "Perversion monstrous of man's moral sense!" Bland lashes out:

> Rather perversion monstrous of all good,
> Is thy accurs'd, detestable opinion.

> Cold-blooded reasoners, such as thee, would blast
> All warm affection; asunder sever
> Every social tie of humanized man.
> Curst be thy sophisms! (94)

As in the tradition of "ambivalent masculinities" identified by Julie Ellison, figured in the men on stage who weep the tears of sensibility in eighteenth-century tragedies, Bland demands that his theatre of suffering and weeping supersede the tearless, stoical posture of the contemporary rationalist.[23] While most commentators on *André* suggest that Bland's hysterics are overridden in the play by M'Donald, the General, and historical necessity, the echoes of *Venice Preserved* question the degree to which Dunlap denies feeling as a necessary aspect of masculine character. Although the play pits Bland's reckless youth against the more sober experience of the senior officers, his passion cannot be ignored entirely as merely youth's indiscretion. Because there is no other love affair of sufficient dramatic weight to offset Bland's desires for André, the play forces an audience to take his passion as honorable for its sincerity and sympathy.

Thus, Dunlap encodes another version of Otway, the *perversion* monstrous, from M'Donald's point of view, of a homo-normative bond that, untempered by stoical restraint – Shaftesbury's clubbical *sensus communis* – carries him past duty into the moral turpitude of betrayal.[24] The entire play spins not so much on André's fate, which is QED, but on Bland's incipient rebellion against his fathers – especially the symbolic ones of the General and M'Donald – and his becoming the monster pervert of traitor. Curiously, Bland's monstrous affection for André shrinks to more patriotic shape once André's mistress, Honora, makes her sudden appearance on the scene. There is little preparation for her arrival; in fact, she does not even appear on stage until Act IV, scene 2, and even then has little more function than to be one additional pleader for André's life before the General, and to shriek and faint a little, before she is led off at the time of execution. Once a woman interrupts the homosocial bond, then her presence suspends the spell of wild love between the two men. Bland first asks his absent, imprisoned father for forgiveness for putting his memory in "second place" to his "wildering passion" for André, then apologizes to M'Donald for his intemperance. In the hasty revision written by Dunlap after the first night, Bland restores his cockade to his hat after previously throwing it down at the General's feet in anger, as if to depoliticize his act; but what remains is Bland's intensity of feeling for his friend that Dunlap portrays as a passion far deeper than that expressed by the screeching, fainting Honora.

Bland has one more scene with André before the execution, a last moment that makes us wonder further about the "perversion monstrous." There, he offers, in memory of the Otway play, to run his sword through his friend. But when André, unlike Pierre, refuses the gesture, Bland recovers himself quickly: 'I was again the sport of erring passion' (*A* 105). Even so, his love for the spy persists past the execution; once the 'signal of death' has been given of the offstage hanging, Bland bids him 'farewell' and in the stage direction 'throws himself on the earth' (107) – the very posture in which Jaffeir lies at the slain body of Pierre. Unlike Otway's ending, however, whereby the several deaths of Jaffeir, Pierre, then Belvidera, leave the state of Venice intact and perhaps chastened enough to reform itself, Dunlap's, driven by the history of a successful Revolution, allows no clear *status quo ante* to return. Having suggested the supplantation of the new American republic with the restoration of British tyranny through André's foolishness and Arnold's and Bland's real or potential treachery to the patriot cause, Dunlap offers another version of the new order: one in which men give their all for other men, not in war, the traditional situation for literary homosociality, but in a republic of the personal. Following the death of André and Bland's lament in the dust, M'Donald's benediction is a dark look at the necessities of the Revolution, a never-to-be-repeated act of founding that future generations may not understand or even condone. In that new republic, says M'Donald, will 'Stand men who challenge love or detestation/But from their proper, individual deeds' (*A* 108). How Bland will behave in a private character once the wound of André's death and his own public service are past cannot be determined; we last see him, not accepting the inevitable and learning a lesson about self-control, as we at first suspect will occur, nor dead as in Otway, but in the dirt, pining for the beautiful British major, his friend. Bland's last act of disloyalty to country, in the form of attachment to male lover, links treacherous denial of stoical cause and homosocial coupling of enemy combatants together, the twin perversions monstrous, without a clear moral that condemns either one.

In his book *American Sympathy*, Caleb Crain attends to the complex of homosocial, homoerotic forms of expression among men in Dunlap's circle, particularly those associated with the Friendly Club. Although he notes Bland's love for André, Crain dismisses the play from his discussion by claiming that "Dunlap did not engage the central ambiguity in the nature of sympathy."[25] I would suggest the play, through its echoes of

Otway, says otherwise. For Dunlap, any version of American history on stage must be rendered in large measure by the theatrical shape provided by a European model. If *André*, like *Venice Preserved*, argues for no alteration of macro-political history, it also, like its predecessor, makes a thing of beauty out of a politically forbidden relationship between two young men. What *André* does differently, however, is to suppress the overt figuration of a vibrant, sexual woman or the exhibition of any act that might be construed as evil.[26] There is no Belvidera or Aquilina – only Bland's mother and the bland Honora; no Renault or Antonio – only scant mention of Arnold. Instead, Dunlap offers up an American history without female sexuality or any bad deed – only the passionate, unfulfilled love of an American officer for a British one.

Identity in this play rests in not simply the representation of some ideal or a type, a noble Washington or comical Yankee, but a series of unsettling questions about history, memory, and republican manhood. One might ask, for instance, to what degree the homosocial sentiments of *Venice Preserved* can be allowed to affect an American play. This aspect of influence posed a serious problem for Dunlap. On the one hand, feeling obliged to turn to foreign models by virtue of "our infancy as a people" and his concern that American material circumstances had "suppressed the exercise of talents to any extensive degree in the dramatic line," the playwright believed he had little other choice than to borrow, if not exactly steal, from European traditions. But to do so carried with it the risk that something false would be passed on as having American content:

> As our literary pursuits, therefore, are of the robust kind, and we are obliged to resort to the foreign source for the delicate productions of genius, which serve to amuse our leisure hours, and soften for a time the cares of real life, we cannot too severely reprehend the mean and unmanly spirit which would supply, by a pitiful alteration of names, to the people of America, those sentiments of national compliments which were originally devoted to the service of another.

Curiously, Dunlap connects authorship with manliness; to present a foreign play as anything other than foreign, and thus "delicate," would be to subvert a robust and masculine spirit that should be part of a vigorous American stage tradition. Further, he says, "The American dramatist, who steals the whole or part of an English play, cannot escape detection."[27] Yet, to a remarkable degree, Dunlap himself has escaped notice on the score of influence of *Venice Preserved*, a play that infuses the self-same "delicate" feelings that complicate the manliness which Dunlap feels obliged many years later to acknowledge. Even a committed patriot like M'Donald recognizes, contra Seward (another officer in Washington's army), that the United States should appropriate hard-won European knowledge, "Striving thus to leap from that simplicity,/With ignorance curst to that simplicity,/By knowledge blest; unknown the gulf between" (*A* 82).[28] Still, this is risky business. If the play rejects absolute isolation, as in Seward's cynical, anti-European views, there is cultural danger, at least, in embracing a tradition that has become, over time, foreign. In Dunlap's formulation, American manhood threatens to come undone, at least at the theatre, when the sentiments suitable for one nation are passed off as another; not only is virtue potentially compromised, but so is the vigor of national character.

For one critic, Dunlap demonstrates in his plays a "manly" ideal, a term she equates with "virtuous" rather than something specifically gendered. In the context of the Alien and Sedition Acts, she argues that Bland's fulminations to M'Donald and the General, themselves nearly traitorous, are allowed to go forward as free speech because "to legislate, to enforce appropriate expression and behavior by law, only keeps the citizen in perpetual rebellious youth, ever proclaiming, but never exercising, never realizing, his manly virtue."[29] For all the virtue of such a reading and its rescue of Dunlap from the charge that he's a solid Federalist, this very openness to free speech in language of male-to-male affection means that the play cannot escape a gendered reading of manliness. To a large extent, *André* is a play about negotiating manhood and nationhood as linked states, whereby the play allows a variety of masculine performances in an ambiguous political context.[30] If Bland is in political error for his overly warm affections for the British spy, he expresses himself in the "manly" terms of British Restoration drama, at once a violation of Dunlap's own strictures against passing off something English as American, and at the same time an affirmation that British and American are all one tradition. In addition, Bland's Restoration-style outbursts are a queer language for an American to be using in a historical drama about the recent past in the United States. One might argue that of all periods of pre-twentieth-century British drama, the Restoration offers plays with the broadest spectrum of male emotive behavior and therefore ones more susceptible to queer readings of texts.[31] Recent critics have exposed the homonormative discourse of members of the Friendly Club and their expressions of relational sympathy, although predominantly from the viewpoint of the novelist Charles Brockden Brown, a close friend to both Dunlap and Elihu Smith.[32] How much Dunlap might have been affected by the speech of his friend is not clear; Dunlap, unlike either Brown or Smith during this period, was married. But it seems as if more than a little of the passion of Jaffeir for Pierre makes its way into the body of the *André* text.

In Rinehart's reading, Bland and André both give vent to errors that need correction; the latter for hypocrisy, in his "condemnation of disguise" when the historical André was known as a man of the theatre; and the former in losing his "manly calmness" (*A* 107), as the conscience character, M'Donald, remarks.[33] Yet the problem that Otway creates in his play, the sympathy for enemies of the state that nearly overwhelms any ideological rejection of rebellion, remains in *André*. Bland's passion may be read as excessive, André's duplicity as justly punished, but the energy of the play forces us to consider that the General's correct behavior and M'Donald's reasonable mode of being in wartime cannot hold up to the rush of sympathy generated by the condemned spy and his lamenting lover at play's end. For Bland, the manly thing is a gush of feeling, whose power is acknowledged at the end in M'Donald's condemnation of the war and its effects on youth. Manhood is a divided realm: between different versions of the expression of sympathy, between sexual identities, between nationalities. Whatever Dunlap the historian had to say about the baneful effects of insinuating foreign drama into American packaging, the playwright of 1798 gave voice to a passionate need to cling to the neck of British drama, to sob piteously at its potential execution, and in short to sweep into the cloak of American manliness a range of feeling far beyond that limited by the nation's commercial necessities. After all, Dunlap is the same writer who also claimed that the drama of Shakespeare and Otway was in fact "our" own. Whatever virtues were inculcated through Dunlap's "manly exercises," the narrative logic of *André* is one that was likely, by Dunlap's own latter-day analysis, to unman its early republican audience.

Yet, in some ways, the play also "unwomans" female spectators looking for republican models. With only two adult female characters, both with minor roles, *André* leaves only the image of women impotently pleading, one for the fate of her husband, Bland's father, in a British prison if André is hanged, the other for the condemned spy. Whereas Dunlap gives Bland scope to vent his passion and make his mistakes, he only allows Mrs. Bland to appear maternal, without agency, as she, then Honora, takes her concerns about a spouse to the General. As the commander denies either woman any action that will alleviate their real or feared suffering, Mrs. Bland at least gains some small stature for standing firm as a mother and accepting what providence, or fate, has in store. For her part, Honora simply fills a space. Compared to her passionate male counterpart on stage, Honora largely vocalizes whereas Bland emotes. Facing the reality of André's execution, Bland throws himself in the dust; Honora faints. The play promises no special role for women; if anything, it appears to retreat to pre-republican female anonymity, at least compared to the more substantial theme roles played by female characters in the other plays under consideration. For Dunlap, history relegates the female to subordination, both in prominence during war and in passion amidst love. Such subordination thus highlights male appropriation of female tenderness and passion in the main plot.

Although the play contains a good republican mother in Mrs. Bland, it is Honora who creates the problem in the text, one of masculinity and its performance. For all the political issues raised by *André*, they cannot be separated entirely from the matter of manly behavior, one that depends in large measure on Honora's disordered state. Not only does the play encode conflicts between fathers and sons, but also among men in what Dana Nelson refers to as a "confraternity" in the early republic, the model of the Sons of Liberty that does not enfranchise the Daughters of same.[34] This attempt both to display and control the hysterical female in the play resembles very much the real-life struggle in the New York theatre to control another wild woman, Mrs. Hallam. As chronicled by Dunlap's former theatrical managing partner, John Hodgkinson, all the problems of the theatre could be largely contained in the figure of the alcoholic, vitriolic, uncivil, uncontrollable Mrs. Hallam, who the third partner, her husband Lewis Hallam, Jr., insisted perform, despite her appearance on stage in what Hodgkinson and Dunlap saw as a disgraceful condition.[35] The homosocial world of theatrical management and republican political organization depends upon a space in which the feminine is controlled or expelled; when it is not, masculine identities enter a state of crisis – one that correlates with the political crisis ensconced in *André*.

No wonder, then, that the Old American Company went back to multiple presentations of *Venice Preserved*. In struggling to create a new dramatic version of American history, Dunlap figured his effort in terms of conflicted masculinity, one colored additionally by an anxiety of influence that someone like Judith Sargent Murray neatly avoids; and in terms of suppressed femininity, whereby women on stage fill traditional spaces but themselves contain little of their own, the playwright having emptied them to fill the men further. By attempting to capture one of the most dramatically powerful of all Revolutionary scenes, Washington's agonized decision to hang André, Dunlap wrote against culture by removing from the mix the tragic treachery of Arnold and incorporating the more pathetic and ambiguous relationship of a patriot officer who nearly turns traitor out of love for a man in a red coat. More than nodding to Otway, Dunlap leaves his audiences with a confusion of passion and manly calmness, Englishness and not-Englishness, republican motherhood and purposeless fretting, free expression of forbidden love and the need to restore order after a one-man rebellion in the ranks of the revolutionaries. Rather than asserting some particular lesson about government – for instance, that Dunlap has a "democratically didactic purpose [and] validates the wisdom of M'Donald's position"[36] – *André* dramatizes the impossibility of any clear statement of national identity at a time when free speech is legally proscribed and international friends become enemies seemingly overnight. Such a lesson about lessons lacks clarity for an audience looking for definition. When he revised *André* as the spectacle *Glory of Columbia*, the author knew enough about popularity to signal his messages loud and clear. As Dunlap discovered through observing the bad acting and dwindling audiences that doomed his play to the library shelf, there was, ironically, a plot against him: that actors and audiences would rebel if Restoration-style passion suddenly put on the guise of the American.

The drama of the American Revolution sent a variety of messages to its spectators. Once the obvious politics are weeded from the mix – patriot v. loyalist, American v. British – the plays of the period speak to dislocation, anxiety, and uncertainty among those charged with creating a new American drama. While demanding new productions that spoke to American audiences, the dramatic public showed by their feet that they preferred *The Poor Soldier* or *Venice Preserved* to any homegrown vehicle of any substance. As Crèvecoeur, Murray, and Dunlap all suggest, loyalty in dramatic terms cannot be neatly substituted from one entity to another without cost. To be an American, these plays tell us, is to be divided, confused, even, in a way, dispossessed. If the Revolution brings independence, it also brings interrogation, confiscation, expulsion; if it fosters a sober manliness of the Colonel Manly or Harry Camden type, it also generates a more emotive one. If it presents to us images of stoical republican mothers, in the figure of Louisa Montague or the mother of Bland, it also presents women wronged and women wrong, not to mention the overwhelming agony of a Martha Corwin at one end, the artificial agony of an Honora at the other. Once the spectacle of celebration is set aside, or the heroic tableau of a dying Joseph Warren on Bunker Hill, the residue of Revolution in early republican drama offers a diminished legacy for patriotic affirmation. These plays figure this essential moment in American history as troubled and troubling for those paying close attention to the words of the national writers and the echoes of their foreign prototypes.

Part II

Coloring identities: race, religion, and the exotic

IF PLAYS ABOUT THE REVOLUTION APPEAR TO CONCERN themselves primarily with issues of nationality, drama in the new republic also presents race, ethnicity, and religion in terms familiar to an Anglo-American stage even as they complicate the question of American identities. While many of the Revolution plays tend to suppress this aspect in order to emphasize the more conventional, if conflicted, battles between British and loyalist, American and patriot, others, as in Crèvecoeur with his portrayal of Presbyterians and African slaves or Murray with her inclusion of ethnic characters, create more heterogeneous worlds. In Chapter 7, Susanna Rowson's *Slaves in Algiers* serves as but one play in a long tradition of British and American drama that portrays Islamic characters before the largely Christian audiences of early modern and eighteenth-century Britain and America. One point made here is that all American portrayals of ethnic characters, whether they reflect the demographics of the United States or not, grow out of earlier and contemporary representations of religion and ethnicity in British theatre. This is not to deny contributions by American writers to the traditions of such representation, but to acknowledge the difficulty for American authors of escaping the long shadow cast by London on New York or Savannah. Even, as in Chapter 8, when one takes up the matter of portraying Native Americans, playwrights such as James Nelson Baker often turn to a vocabulary established by the British stage, even in analogies between one race and another. Two other ethnicities, Irish and African, form the subjects of Chapters 9 and 10, not only in the works of the title playwrights but in a variety of others that act in concert to establish what parameters a particular stage type will carry forward. With both Irish and African, socioeconomic conditions in the United States play crucial roles in the politics of representation, but in both as well, the prominence or subordination of a character, the dialect or claimed terms of identity as racial or ethnic, all emerge out of language circulated on the transatlantic stage first. In the cases of all these topics, the establishment of ethnic others defines majoritarian culture as well – white and Protestant Christian, the theatre's default racial and religious identification.

7

Susanna Rowson and the dramatized Muslim

SUSANNA ROWSON, THE ENGLISH NOVELIST TURNED AMERICAN actress, was, like her fellow United States playwrights, a tyro, but she had the advantage, if one wants to speak in those terms, of having lived in England during the Revolution and the decade after and therefore having opportunity to attend London and provincial theatres during a time when the American stage was either moribund or in transition to its post-war revival. Her first successful effort as a dramatist was *Slaves in Algiers*, a comedy of Barbary captivity that had a modest run in Philadelphia and other cities.[1] With its topical subject of Americans being held for ransom in North Africa and its portrayal of liberty-seeking women, the play has attracted some recent attention on both those scores.[2] But in many ways, *Slaves in Algiers* is more dependent on earlier plays with Islamic characters than it is on current events. For all of Rowson's contributions to a feminist and a republican drama, the text of her play owes a considerable debt to at least one well-known tragedy of Christian captivity and to a character tradition that spanned two centuries. Her portrayal of an Algerian court is a musical comedy version of other such courts, often developed as more threatening than that of the dey in her play, Muley Moloc. By 1794, the bewhiskered, beturbaned Muslim tyrant had already become a well-worn stereotype that Rowson exploits for topical value; at the same time, she draws upon a long and complex history of rendering Islamic characters that informs her text in both overt and covert ways.[3] Even her American characters owe a great deal to analogous figures in earlier plays about captivity in Muslim nations. In determining the degree to which Rowson infuses *Slaves in Algiers* with 1790s republican sentiments, it is important first to sort out the dramatic precursors and the implied values they bring to her drama. Rowson's republican women define their political philosophy in a context of Algerian slavery, one controlled by Islamic men whom contemporary audiences would have recognized immediately as familiar and formulaic.

Of course, the history of American captives in Barbary states is relevant to a full understanding of *Slaves in Algiers*. However, throughout this book, I assert that what influences playwrights in their dramatic choices most is other plays rather than current events. In making this argument with regard to *Slaves in Algiers*, for example, I rely on the fact that Rowson shows knowledge of drama long off the stage. Her *The Female Patriot*, for instance, was advertised as being based on Philip Massinger's *The Bondman*, a political satire from 1623 which, as far as I know, had never been acted by a professional American company.[4] In the critical concern over political and social context, we can easily ignore the intratextual world of the theatre, which is often the rhetorical framework in which most of the plays under discussion here first appear. Rowson would have been exposed to any number of plays with Islamic subjects or settings, far more than can be recognized in this chapter, but any or all of which might have inspired choices, either in imitation or resistance, to what she wrote. In considering *Slaves* as an "American" play, critics and historians may want to remember that the entrance of a Muslim character on stage would have prompted a set of already established expectations in theatrical audiences. Although written after Rowson's play, the comments of Washington Irving's Jonathan Oldstyle on Islamic characters on stage in 1802 bear attention for his belief that such representations already had a long and tired history. In reviewing a play in New York called *The Tripolitan Prize*, Oldstyle writes of expectations thwarted:

> Presently I head a rustling behind the scenes – here thought I comes a fierce band of Tripolitans with whiskers as long as my arm. – No such thing ... Scene pass'd after scene. In vain I strained my eyes to catch a glimpse of a Mahometan phiz. I once heard a great bellowing behind the scenes, and expected to see a strapping Musselman come bouncing in; but was miserably disappointed, on distinguishing his voice, to find out by his *swearing*, that he was only a *Christian*.[5]

While a playwright could excite the promise of something new and topical by including in the title place-names from the gazettes, such as Algiers or Tripoli, most dramas with Islamic characters drew from each other rather than from fresh material or firsthand observation. As Irving wryly notes, managers felt little impulse to characterize Muslims with authentic details – a beard, the tried and blissfully false "phiz" were all that was needed, even if discriminating observers like Jonathan Oldstyle could see through the charade. The appearance of actual Muslims in the audience, as happened when Turkish prisoners from the Tripolitan war were brought to the Park Theatre to watch *Blue Beard*, a stage Muslim drama, in 1805, probably had little effect on the staging of Islamist characters in the American theatre – even if their announced appearance drew crowds of curious spectators.[6]

Slaves in Algiers takes place entirely at the court of Muley Moloc, the dey or ruler.[7] Among his Christian captives are Olivia, an American young woman whom the dey has placed in his seraglio and intends to wed; a young man named Augustus, who we learn later is Olivia's brother; and the parents to both, Rebecca and Constant. The plot involves the potential rescue of the Anglo-American captives by young American men; a slave revolt inspired by rebellion of women, including an Islamic convert to republicanism, Fetnah; the threat to Olivia if she does not submit to Muley Moloc; the realization of relationship among long separated family members; and a final confrontation between the Muslim tyrant and republican Christians. Except for its locale, the plot to *Slaves* is cobbled together from stock elements inherited from British drama. More compelling than the plot, which serves its theme reasonably well, the characters in *Slaves* form what seem like an unusual mix – there are certainly no British plays before Rowson's with Americans in North Africa. Nevertheless, the playwright's text is filled with echoes of similar characters from earlier drama.

Rowson's Olivia, for example, owes much of her depiction to a popular tragedy written some sixty years before. Among the many British plays to be performed in the North America of the eighteenth century, and one certainly known to Rowson either in the United States or more likely in England, Aaron Hill's *Zara* provides both a prototype (one of many) for Rowson of a play with a Christian–Muslim conflict at the heart and something of a test case of how different audiences might respond to the theme of Islamic captivity. Hill wrote his play as a translation of Voltaire's *Zaïre* in 1733; Drury Lane finally admitted *Zara* to its boards in January 1736 where it ran fourteen consecutive nights.[8] *Zara* would become a staple of the British stage, performed off and on through the rest of the century.[9] Consequently, it was a natural choice for the repertoire of early theatre companies in the American colonies. For Rowson, *Zara* offered a theme of liberty to inspire her own in *Slaves*, but at the same time it provided an opportunity to learn from previous attempts how in America a play that included a display of Christian characters among Muslim captors might be received.

Zara's relative popularity in North America over nearly thirty years gave Rowson a benchmark for testing how her themes might be read by American audiences. Set in the Jerusalem of the early Ottoman empire, *Zara*, like many plays of its time, offers a functional allegory of political issues that oppose absolutism to some other form of governance more attuned to the call of human freedom. Osman (the name of the Turk who historically founded the Ottoman dynasty *c.* 1300),[10] is in Hill the sultan of Jerusalem, a relatively enlightened man but still a ruler with complete individual power. Among his Christian captives are Lusignan, represented as the last surviving heir to the kingship of pre-Turkish Jerusalem; Zara, his daughter, one of the sultan's slaves and a love object; and two French officers, Nerestan and Chatillon. Despite the evocation of history, the playwrights take considerable liberties with the actual persons and events in the city at the heart of so many crusades. Lusignan was the name of the French noble family that served as dynastic kings of Jerusalem and Cyprus during the late twelfth and late thirteenth centuries, with Henri II defending Acre until it was lost to the Muslims in 1291 before finally returning to Cyprus. During the whole of that period, much of the land surrounding Jerusalem, if not the city itself, was under the control of other Muslim empires.[11] The Turks themselves, however, did not control the Holy Land until the sixteenth century; during most of the previous period, the Mamluks of Egypt had been the *de facto* rulers of the area. Therefore, one assumes that Voltaire and his translator had no particular interest in rendering the historical situation accurately; one need merely invoke the Turk with 'Osman,' the Christian rulers and their fallen glory with 'Lusignan,' and an eighteenth-century, predominantly anti-Islamic audience would have all that was needed to tell the story. At the time the play was first produced in England, London audiences were likely to see Islam and the historical Ottomans also as a figure for European governments with overweening power, most especially the Catholic monarchies and, in particular, France. Ever since Nicholas Rowe's *Tamerlane* (1702), the Grand Turk (in that play, Bajazet) had been understood as signifying the French monarch more immediately than the historical Bayezid I.[12] Nevertheless, imbedded in the text of *Zara* is a cultural history of representation of Islam that, in moments of crisis like that sparked by the Algerian captives in the 1780s and 1790s, would bring back the more literal meaning.

In brief, the plot of *Zara* revolves around the heroine's own identity as Muslim or Christian on the one hand and the sultan's desire for her and his subsequent jealousy of the French officer Nerestan, who tries to negotiate her release, on the other. At first Zara resigns herself to her fate to marry Osman. To her fellow slave Selima, who reminds her in Act I that she has Christian "blood," she responds with Voltairean logic that religion is an accident of birth that has nothing to do with love: "Born beyond *Ganges*, I had been a Pagan./In *France*, a Christian; – I am here, a *Saracen*."[13] Nerestan, meanwhile, has traveled to France and back to procure ransom money for his fellow captives and plans to return to captivity as a bond. Osman, in an act of generous despotism, tells Nerestan he and as many as one hundred Christians are free to go, and to take gifts besides. However, he blocks any attempt to secure either Zara or Lusignan. Nerestan then remains to see what he can do. In the meantime, the audience gradually learns that Nerestan grew up in slavery in Syria; escaped; then went to France to become a soldier for "warlike *Lewis*" (Z 20).[14] For his part, Lusignan reveals that his family had been killed by Osman's father, and his son and daughter taken. Through his story and the presence of a hidden cross around Zara's neck, Voltaire and Hill reveal the relationship between Zara and Lusignan, but with the effect that the former king pressures Zara to resist giving in to her prospective Islamicization. Osman, meanwhile, catching Zara and Nerestan in conversation and other suspected communication, assumes, Othello-like, that the Frenchman is her secret lover; he eventually stabs her when she resists the wedding, learning only at the end that Nerestan is her brother. Osman kills himself, and the play ends, unrelieved by a single humorous line or moment, with the liberty of the Christians but the death of the play's eponymous character.

The play appeals to the eighteenth century on a number of levels: the plot is relatively simple and contains exotic elements; the tragedy is unalloyed by comedy, important in the reaction against Restoration tragicomedy; and the conflict that Zara faces between love and religion makes a genuinely unresolvable one for the period, and thus provides good matter for tragedy. The high emotional pitch that Hill conveys both through his translation and slight alterations from Voltaire creates an intense piece of theatre, something likely to please a relatively broad audience in England, particularly one increasingly accustomed to the pathetic tragic tradition stimulated by Rowe. Most especially, perhaps, it makes liberal use of the word 'liberty' in a generic way and associates it with basic English values, regardless of political party. The play remained in print into the mid-nineteenth century, with London editions in 1736, 1752, 1763, 1778, 1791, and 1803; additional Dublin editions; and British anthologies such as *Bell's British Theatre* keeping the play constantly available to reading audiences in the British Isles and, through imports, British America.[15]

The first known professional production of *Zara* in the mainland American colonies occurred in Philadelphia by the American Company of Comedians on December 26, 1768, with the role of Osman played by Lewis Hallam, Jr; Lusignan by his stepfather, David Douglass; and Zara by Margaret Cheer. The same company took the play to New York to the John Street Theatre and performed it there on January 30, 1769.[16] How successful those performances were is hard to judge, absent any printed commentary; however, that the American Company did not revive the play before its departure in the wake of the ban on plays by the Continental Congress in 1774 suggests that it may have been the sort of thing to keep in repertory as an occasional item rather than as a regular feature. In addition, all non-Shakespearean tragedies played second to comedies during this period; thus any revival of a tragedy would have made a drama "popular" by comparison to many one-time performances of plays. At any rate, following the reopening of the John Street Theatre after the war, the now reconstituted Old American Company brought *Zara* back to New York in 1788, Philadelphia in 1790, and New York again in 1791 with Hallam, twenty years older, still playing Osman; his new partner, John Henry, as Lusignan; and Mrs. Henry (Ann Storer) as Zara. Two Philadelphia performances followed in 1796, but after this the play functionally disappears from the repertoire, with only an 1820 revival in New York to indicate that the actors and managers had not entirely forgotten it.

Yet this is not the entire story of American performance. The period of greatest popularity for *Zara* was in fact during the Revolution and just after. General John Burgoyne produced it with the military thespians in occupied Boston in 1775, and his counterparts in occupied New York enacted *Zara* four times in 1780 and 1781. In 1782, the Thomas Wall company, the first professional group to assemble after the end of Revolutionary hostilities, put on four additional performances of Hill's drama in Baltimore, three of them in April. Thus, at least nine nights of *Zara* graced stages in three cities during the war years and just after, more than the total number of performances known to occur in major cities in the rest of the period from 1768 to 1796.

How familiar Rowson was with the production history is not easily determined; however, as the daughter of an officer in the British military, she might have been aware of the play's popularity during the Revolution among the histrionic officers and their supporters. In the Boston of 1775, the British army maintained a significant presence following the battles in April and June at Concord and Bunker Hill. General Thomas Gage had replaced Thomas Hutchinson as governor,[17] and General John Burgoyne, himself a playwright, was a leading commander under General William Howe, the overall chief of military forces in Massachusetts. As was customary for the British, the performance of plays was seen as something to be expected, an outlet for the officers and men who had some acting ability, and the opportunity to appear civic minded, with proceeds going to charity – in this case, the "Widows and Children of the Soldiers."[18] To accompany the play, performed on December 2, 1775, Burgoyne composed a prologue and epilogue that were delivered by the then lieutenant Francis Lord Rawdon, later one of the scourges of the southern states. The prologue links politics and the stage in ways that recall the conflicts of the Restoration theatre, tying liberty to stage presentation. All this has a deliberate and ironical twist, of course, because Boston was the only major seaboard city in what is now the United States to prohibit theatre entirely before 1775 – and would be the last to permit its opening after the war was over. As the home of the Puritans, a fact that Burgoyne well knew, Boston made, in many ways, the ideal place to mount a play sprinkled with the word "liberty":

> In Britain once (it stains th' historic Page)
> Freedom was vital struck by Party Rage.
> Cromwell the Fever watch'd, the knife supplied,
> She[,] madden'd by Suicide[,] she died.
> Amidst her groans sunk every liberal art
> Which polish'd life or humanized the heart.
> Then sunk the Stage, quell'd by the Bigot roar,
> Truth fled with Sense & Shakespear charm'd no more.[19]

For Burgoyne, Zara is the stage itself, and her enemies, the antitheatrical zealots identified as the followers of Oliver Cromwell. Curiously, Burgoyne follows Restoration logic; one of the frequent targets of abuse for royalist playwrights was the Interregnum, indeed the entire civil war, with the date 1641 evoked as the year when all English culture went on the defensive. Plays such as Aphra Behn's *The Round-heads* (1682), set at the end of the protectorate, skewered the opponents of the theatre as witless hypocrites, leaving it clear that the real liberty was not the political enfranchisement of the common people but the liberty of the stage to determine norms of taste and political correctness as an adjunct to royal power.[20] In Boston, home to the descendants of Cromwellians, as he would have assumed, Burgoyne trots out the old argument over "Party Rage" as anticultural, it being a code phrase for "against the government" – at the time, the ministers led by Lord North.

The cure, then, for Party Rage is a play, in particular one that features beset virtue. Those in the city who object to the stage are nothing more than "Boston prudes" who reject "Form, Decorum, Piety" to speak slanderously of their theatrical adventure. "Behold the Test, see, at the Curtain's Rise," Burgoyne concludes, "How Malice shrinks abash'd from *Zara's* eyes."[21] Such language suggests the audience was directed to see the play as a blow for freedom against the Bostonian Ottomans, whose tyrannical sway over theatre has led to its virtual death. By bringing *Zara* in living form to the stage, not only does Burgoyne resist cultural tyranny, but he can then remind Boston of its fatal cruelty and invert occupation and liberation in their eyes. The true freedom fighters – the "Christians" – are the very British military men playing before the city (and the local women recruited to aid them in the production), not the soldiers of the Continental Congress gathered outside the city's boundaries. Ironically, such an allegory of captive drama can be seen in Rowson's play as well. Given the difficulty of getting locally written plays put on stage in the United States, the Islamic tyrant may more represent conservative theatre managers, holding American drama captive to reiterations of popular English vehicles. Despite the British army's use of *Zara* as an attack on American antitheatrical practices, it also informs Rowson's text as a critique of anti-American prejudices among Anglophilic theatre managers.

If one can assume a similar logic to the remaining wartime productions by the British military in New York – that is, Zara as the captive spirit of British America, awaiting liberation by the officers and gentlemen on stage – then one must shift perspective radically to meet the reception of the Thomas Wall Company performances in early 1782. Although some hostilities continued after the British defeat at Yorktown in October of 1781, the war, except for the evacuations of Charleston and New York, was over in the urban areas. Baltimore and Annapolis, the Wall Company's playing venues, were firmly under patriot control, and the audiences composed largely of persons interested in affirming the victory of the Continental troops. For them, *Zara* would have represented something other than a cultural victory over philistines; rather, the character Zara might have been linked to Lady Liberty herself, the icon of political theory, the emblem of resistance to tyranny and enslaving political (as opposed to cultural) oppression. Indeed, rituals of liberation – burning of Arnold effigies, patriotic ox roasts, and the like – were taking place throughout the states, and the putting on of theatrical plays would be seen in light of public celebrations.[22] The Turks in *Zara* are now the British occupiers, the Christians the American rightful heirs to the North American holy land. Lusignan is the arch-patriot father figure, a Washington; Osman, for his part, becomes the once 'indulgent' king, George III, turned ruthless, then repentant at his failed endeavor to conquer the spirits of his captives. In this reading, the death of Zara is not the end of liberty but the sacrifice involved in standing firm against a tyrant; Nerestan, as her brother, and the surviving captives will carry the torch for liberty in the new republic. As one additional nod to the war, the mounting of a play first written in French and featuring two heroic French officers who serve "warlike *Lewis*" would be a further acknowledgment of France's contribution to the American victory. For a moment, at least, the repetitions of *Zara* by Wall in Baltimore would seem to fit with the outburst of patriotic feeling in the immediate aftermath of the victory at Yorktown.

In both the British military and American post-war productions, Islam and the Turk would have been employed as stock tropes for repression, lust, and threat to the values of the producing side. Hill's *Zara* functioned as the perfect political drama, much like Joseph Addison's *Cato* in its early career, whereby the exotic setting and deflected identifications made the play suitable for opposing attitudes as to who was the tyrant (Boston whigs or British despot). With either version, the fact of Islam poses a problem for Christian characters, but its immediate linkage to actual Muslims and the occupation of the Holy Land would have seemed stock and somewhat remote to both Americans and Britons of the late eighteenth century. At best, one might assume, with Edward Said, a reception of orientalism, the cultural formation of the Islamic Turk as Other; but the political conditions of wartime suggest that Turks would hardly be looked at as Turks or Muslims in any meaningful sense.[23] War among Europeans and North Americans would have infused the immediate context.

That changed after the Treaty of Paris in 1783. Once the present exigency of political struggle and material hardship had passed – at least, for playgoing elites – the reception of *Zara* and its potential incorporation into an American drama would have shifted to new territory.

The March 7, 1788 return of *Zara* to New York by the Old American Company brought to a republican audience a drama that had last been played in that city seven years previous and then for spectators composed of British sympathizers and occupiers. Although Hallam's troupe continued to perform the sort of English favorites they played before the war, they were very conscious that appealing to American patriotism, at least some of the time, was good business. The year before, for instance, the company had premiered Royall Tyler's *The Contrast* and for other plays had often added patriotic songs or pantomimes to play between main drama and afterpiece. Therefore, they might have been partially aware that *Zara* could have continuing Revolutionary political implications in a New York that was in the midst of a ratification debate on the new constitution.

However, the post-war reception of *Zara*, as with the reception of plays during the highly partisan English Exclusion Crisis of the late 1670s and 1680s, would also have been linked to politics. In a closet comedy by the New Yorker Samuel Low, *The Politician Out-witted*, written at the same time as *Zara* was playing at the John Street Theatre, two characters refer directly to the Old American Company revival. Low used his play about young lovers to offer his own views on the ratification question through his acerbic Federalist schoolmaster, Trueman, while the author ridiculed opponents of the constitution in the figure of the foolish and lecherous old Anti-federalist, Loveyet. Early on, however, Trueman's daughter Harriet and her friend Maria attend the theatre, catching the performance of Hill's tragedy. Harriet argues that drama is a rational amusement, better read than seen, and that comedy, for example, is a good remedy for depression. Maria asks Harriet, "did you observe how much I was affected the other night at the tragedy of Zara?"[24] Harriet assumes she means tears, which she did not see but would like to have witnessed from her unsentimental friend, but Maria finally exposes the joke – that when the tragedy was over, she laughed, not at the play but at the sight of her jealous beau squirming in the box opposite at the sight of other beaux sitting near his lady love. The jealous Osman is now nothing more than a stage version of some callow New York youth, and Zara a mere performance with which to aggravate and tease him. Despite the cynical veneer, however, both women indicate that a tearful response to Zara's suffering is a sign of sentiment, and both agree that sentiment is a prerequisite for love. As Harriet starts to say, tragedy is the genre most conducive to "elegance of language, and refinement of sentiment" (*PO* 12); but in Low's partisan world, the sentiment inspired by Zara must be postponed for vigilance against lechers and political fools. In the end, however, Low suggests only a Federalist, a supporter of the new constitution, could appreciate *Zara*. In this perspective, Hill's translation is more viewed as a badge of elite culture than either as symbolizing current affairs or representing Oriental others.

A much less partisan but ironically more political reading of *Zara* is reflected in Rowson's *Slaves in Algiers*. The shape of the drama borrows considerably from Hill, whose play appeared in Philadelphia, Rowson's adopted home, in 1790. *Slaves in Algiers* features a number of parallels to *Zara*, most notably in the basic captive situation: the Islamic ruler, Muley Moloc, holds for ransom a dignified old Christian man, in this case the English officer, Constant, who serves as the Lusignan of the piece; his daughter, Olivia, the Zara of the play; and two young men, the Americans Frederic and Henry, the former of whom, like his French equivalent Nerestan, looks for ways to ransom the Christians. As with *Zara*, Rowson has a secondary female character named Selima and a right-hand man for the Muslim leader, in this case Mustapha, where Hill has Orasmin. As with Hill, Rowson makes much of absolute tyranny versus the freedom of English-speaking lands; but she differs in alluding more directly to modern Algiers (that is, to the contemporary issue of Christian captives by Barbary states) than Hill to the Holy Land of his own time and by having additional female characters, including Olivia's mother Rebecca, several of whom speak with passion about the political ideals of liberty. The captivity of Olivia inspires in her not passive acceptance but active plotting for escape; as with Zara by Osman, she has been marked by an Islamic ruler, here, the dey of Algiers, for his wife, and likewise offers to fulfill that role if it means freedom for the other captives. Rowson, however, is intent on comedy; no one will be stabbed or seriously threatened with rape. Rather, the Americans and their sympathizers succeed in mounting a revolt and converting Muley Moloc himself to a belief in republican-style liberty. On a basic level, both Christianity and Anglo-American liberty are seen as superior ideologies to Islam and Ottoman-inspired autocracy. For Rowson, *Zara* functions as a narrative and thematic template, but one that must be altered to meet the post-war affirmation of Revolutionary goals against continuing threats of absolutism from the Old World. It is not enough for a spectator to cry at the heroine's fate to show sensibility; instead, the American woman viewer must also see herself as an active participant in the scheme of the new political order, a champion of freedom on both individual and national levels. By echoing *Zara*, Rowson evokes the kind of sympathies for her heroine that Hill generates, but also claims differences by making Olivia, Rebecca, and Fetnah more politically astute and more active in determining their lives. *Slaves in Algiers*, on one level, is a commentary both on the power of *Zara* to shape an American drama and on the necessity to write over, in a palimpsest, the increasingly limited representational and allegorical value of the predecessor play for the American 1790s.

Nevertheless, with the Algerian captivities understood in America as an ongoing hostage crisis, Rowson recognized that she could manipulate the way in which audiences would perceive the Islamic characters. She also knew a more textured stage history than simple parallels to *Zara* indicate of how the Christian West had typed the Islamic East. One longstanding version of the Muslim tyrant was that of a voluptuary. From Shakespeare's *Titus Andronicus* forward, a play in which religion and race are bound together in the figure of the Moor, the elite Islamic male character threatens Christian female virtue simply by presence. As Anthony Barthelemy argues, the type becomes so standardized during Elizabethan drama that one cannot separate an Islamic ruler from his use of sexual desire as a weapon of state.[25] In a tragedy, such desire often has devastating consequences, whether or not the Christian object of desire is represented as having been forced literally into concubinage. In a comedy, however, the Muslim's desire is adumbrated by plot reversal, in which the Christian woman's virtue (or pluck) is shown to be a superior force, aided by timely interventions or other tricks of narrative, as in Isaac Bickerstaff's popular *The Sultan* (1775), a two-act afterpiece that premiered in Philadelphia on May 19, 1794, a few weeks before the first performance of *Slaves*.[26] Therefore, while the appetite of Osman for Zara plays to type and suits Rowson to a degree, the tragic plot does not. For her tyrant, Rowson created Muley Moloc, a paper oppressor whose bravado and licentiousness can easily be undone by clever Christian plotters against his unnatural authority. As with Murray in *Traveller Returned*, Rowson realizes that it will not do to represent rampant lust on an American stage in a play that portrays American characters; audiences and managers were not yet prepared to test the boundaries of taste in matters of sex. Rather than portray her dey as an omnipotent sultan, she chooses another path, related to the *Zara* type, but from a genetic history of representation of one single historical figure whose evocation in *Slaves* marks the way in which Islam would be rendered in an American context on the American stage.

"Muley Moloc" is but one variant spelling of a character who enters European history in the 1570s and English drama in the late 1580s, Mulai (that is, Prince or Lord) Abd el-Malik, King of Fez and Morocco from 1576 to 1578. As Mully Molocco and other such renderings, Abd underwent an extraordinary conversion in stage terms from a political (albeit secret) ally of Queen Elizabeth and near hero in George Peele's *The Battle of Alcazar* (*c.* 1589), to enemy of the hero in John Dryden's *Don Sebastian* (1689), to the comic fool in Rowson's play (1794). Whereas plays like *Zara* or James Miller's *Mahomet the Imposter* (1744), an adaptation from Voltaire's *Mahomet* (1741, sometimes titled *Le Fanatism ou Mahomet le Prophète*), are products of mid-eighteenth-century typing of Islam as the antirational enemy of Western reason, earlier views of Islamic characters cannot so easily be stamped.[27] In one recent formulation, the early modern relations between England and the Ottoman empire are marked by a higher degree of reciprocity and complexity than a scheme like Said's, which renders Islam universally in Other terms, would indicate. In this view, a play like Christopher Marlowe's *Tamburlaine*, Parts 1 and 2, never sinks to the kind of simple Christian v. Muslim typing of later literature, but instead views Turkish power as significant and Islam as something not necessarily at full odds with English Protestantism, most especially as both had a common enemy, Roman Catholicism, typified primarily by Philip II of Spain.[28] For Rowson to deploy a character name like Muley Moloc, then, is to register, perhaps even beyond her own intention to stereotype quite grossly, a history of a character for whom English-speaking audiences had not had a unitary reading.

Long before there was the swaggering buffoon of *Slaves in Algiers*, an actual member of the Saadian ruling family of Morocco had come to power in 1576 by overthrowing his nephew, Mohammed, and staking claim to both the kingdoms of Morocco, with its capital at Marrakech, and Fez, with its capital in that city. As brother to the ruler just previous to Mohammed, Abd el-Malik would have been the next in line, but once the old king named his son to power, Abd had to flee to Turkish-controlled North Africa to avoid being assassinated. With Turkish aid, Abd claimed the throne in a quick military action and, in alliance with his younger brother, Ahmed el-Mansur, drove Mohammed into the arms of Don Sebastian, the young king of Portugal. For the latter, North Africa was the place where the king's messianic zeal and desire to claim new territories for Christianity made him the deposed Mohammed's last-resort ally. In the famous battle of El-Ksar el-Kebir, or Alcazar as it was often referred to in Europe, the forces of Abd crushed the Mohammed loyalists and the Portuguese expeditionary army. Sebastian and Mohammed were killed, almost the entire Portuguese force either killed or captured for slavery or ransom, and the Saadian brotherly succession reconfirmed. On the day of the final battle, Abd also died, of disease rather than warfare, and was succeeded by his brother and ally Ahmed, who would rule from 1578 until his own death in 1603.[29]

There is not space here to trace the history of perceptions of the 'Moor' as a generic character or even of Abd el-Malik, but in brief, I want to follow the literary conversion of Abd in English drama before Rowson in order to interrogate her use of the descendent character in *Slaves in Algiers*.[30] Once Abd became ruler of Morocco and Fez, he entered into secret negotiations with Elizabeth's government for trade in munitions: in exchange for Moroccan saltpeter, a key ingredient in gunpowder, the English sent metals and firearms, including arquebuses, to their new Muslim ally.[31] As a consequence, writers in support of Elizabeth would have to be careful how they figured Islam, as Burton suggests, and any specific rulers with whom the English had negotiated treaties or trade arrangements. Given that history, then, it is not as surprising as it might seem to encounter in the first English dramatic rendering of El-Ksar, George Peele's *The Battle of Alcazar*, a positive portrayal of the Moroccan king, who in the play is called Abdelmelec. In the induction, a figure referred to as the Presenter intones the praises of Abdelmelec in his defeat of the "usurper," Muly Mahamet (Mulai Mohammed), and refers to the new king as "This brave Barbarian [that is, resident of the Barbary coast] Lord Muly Molocco."[32] When we first encounter him directly, he is giving praise to God and his men for the victory. A Turkish ally, representative from Amurath (Murad III), calls Abdelmelec 'Curteous and honourable' (*BA* 299). Although his brother accuses him of being too slow to punish Mahamet, the play validates Abdelmelec's restraint. Just before the final battle with Sebastian and his own death, the king affirms the resolution of his troops, then speaks a stoical line: 'Farewell vaine world for I have playd my parte' (*BA* 340). After the victory, his successor, Muly Mahamet Seth (Ahmed el-Mansur) calls their late leader that "cheerfull Sun-shine to his subjects all" (*BA* 345). Thus, while never quite achieving hero status, Abdelmelec emerges as a ruler with all the Christian virtues of honor, stoical resignation, restraint, patriotism, acknowledgment of God, and selfless devotion to cause by which British plays have denominated sympathetic figures. In short, with just a little tweaking and moved ahead two hundred years, Abdelmelec could be distant cousin to George Washington.

Where he next appears is not entirely clear. Philip Henslowe's diary notes a play *Muly Molocco*, for which no positive text can be identified.[33] Another play based on the same materials, *The Famous Historye of the life and death of Captaine Thomas Stukeley* (listed in the Stationers' Register in 1600), may be a survival of Henslowe's recorded *Muly Molocco*, for indeed, it does include that character.[34] Although the play centers the English Catholic adventurer Thomas Stukeley, it does include scenes from the battle of El-Ksar, at which Stukeley participated on the side of Sebastian and was killed. Similarly to Peele, the king is called Abdelmelek formally and referred to in conversation as Mullucco; as with Peele's king, he shows some restraint in dealing with Sebastian, offering him the opportunity to decline the fight.[35] Although again not fully heroic, the *Stukeley* author's ruler has dignity and shows courage when, raging with thirst from his illness, he still manages to rouse his troops to victory. Thus it seems that during the Elizabethan period, or late into it, there persisted a stage history that granted to the Moorish king a de-racialized nobility. Before Muley Moloc was a blundering and cowardly stage dey, he had been a figure inspiring respect in plays directly drawn from the El-Ksar imaginative history.

But it does not take long for the Elizabethan-era Moroccan ruler to slip in terms of integrity of character. Despite Abd el-Malik's positive portrayal in Peele, in a number of prose sources, and in the English translation of Montaigne's essay "Against Slothfulness," the English view of his brother, Ahmed el-Mansur, is already compromised by the end of Elizabeth's reign in the character of Mullisheg in Thomas Heywood's *Fair Maid of the West*, Part I.[36] Although by the conclusion of Part I the Moroccan king ratifies honor and virtue in his hosting of the marriage of the English protagonists, Bess and Spencer, both earlier, and in Part II, written considerably later, Mullisheg shows himself quite unlike Abdelmelec in lusting after Bess and willing to suppress honor for self-indulgent luxury.[37] Heywood abstracts Mullisheg to a cruder type than the more complimentary portrayals of Islamic rulers in Marlowe and Peele. By the final acts of both parts of Heywood, the Moor is brought back to English values, but something has been lost between his original in Abd el-Malik and the cultural representation of his literal and figurative heir, Mullisheg.

While it is not likely that Rowson knew the full history of sixteenth-century Moroccan kings on stage, it seems certain that she knew one other play about Abd el-Malik between Heywood and her own, namely Dryden's *Don Sebastian*.[38] With Peele and the *Stukeley* author, Dryden recurs to the

Battle of El-Ksar, but from an opposed perspective. Now the hero is the Portuguese king and the "good" Moor is Mohammed, while Abd el-Malik appears as Muley-Moluch, the enemy and villain. Muley-Moluch is extreme in both cruelty and lust, a dimension acknowledged by Dryden in his preface: "if I have allow'd him another day of life," Dryden says of his choice not to have Muley Moluch die before the final battle, "it was because I stood in need of so shining a Character of Brutality, as I have given him."[39] As with Heywood, Dryden has his Mulai lust after a virtuous woman, in this case Almeyda, a "captive queen of Barbary" and, as it turns out, a half-sister to Don Sebastian. In the interests of serving heroic love, the author depicts Almeyda as drawn to the European king (whose relationship to her she does not know), and repelled by the rampant desire of the Moor. Although the incest forces them apart at play's end – Dryden relies on legends that Sebastian did not die at El-Ksar – Sebastian has the satisfaction of seeing Muley-Moluch's head appear on a spear before he and Almeyda part separately for religious exile. Almeyda has been brought to Christianity and Sebastian, and though the love can be requited no further, their spiritual union accompanies the violent denigration and expulsion of Muley-Moluch. He has now become Moloch, not just friendly Molocco, the pagan figure of wrath and consumption, and no ally to the English.

Given her spelling of the name and the characterization, it appears likely that Rowson's Muley Moloc is based directly on Dryden's equivalent character; indeed, there are a number of plot and character parallels that establish the strong likelihood of her awareness of the play. *Don Sebastian* never appeared on a professional American stage before 1794, but it seems to have been well known in Britain,[40] where Rowson had spent her later childhood and early adulthood. John O'Keeffe in his memoirs sings the praises of Francis Aickin, the late eighteenth-century actor, for his rendering of Dryden's figure among other "tyrant" characters.[41] British editions of Dryden circulated widely and would have been easily available in Philadelphia, where Rowson wrote her play. Both her borrowings and her differences tell many tales, but whatever Rowson's knowledge of current events in Algiers – and one gathers from the play it must have been scant – the template she used, in addition to Hill's *Zara*, was provided by *Don Sebastian*.

As with Heywood's Mullisheg at the sight of Bess, so in Act I of *Don Sebastian*, Dryden's Muley-Moluch, after seeing the captive Almeyda (his niece, sister to Mahumet, the emperor's defeated enemy and nephew), has become enflamed with lust for her. At the beginning of Act II, he speaks to one of his advisers, a duplicitous Moor named Benducar, of his feelings for the new captive:

> A thousand things controul this Conqueror,
> My native pride to own th' unworthy passion,
> Hazard of Int'rest, and my Peoples love:
> To what a Storm of Fate am I expos'd!
> What if I had her murder'd? 'tis but what
> My subjects all expect, and she deserves.
> Wou'd not th' impossibility
> Of ever, ever seeing, or possessing,
> Calm all this rage, this Hurrican of Soul? (*DS* 102–3)

Whereas Heywood's Mullisheg expresses his desire for English Bess somewhat more temperately, Dryden's figure is overswept with low passion, to the point where it undermines his integrity as a royal personage and threatens to make him a slave to love. Muley-Moluch's passion is in part sparked by Almeyda's resistance in the first act to being unveiled by any hands than her own. Dryden portrays her as someone who chooses her own course, suffer how she will; she offers no violence in return, only character, which in *Don Sebastian* is sufficient to keep control of her body. Thus Dryden both inscribes a by-now (1689) stereotypical lust on his Moorish king and a degree of self-determination on his female protagonist that is somewhat rare in royalist Restoration tragedy.

In Rowson, the same desire for a captive appears, but not with such force or directness. Indeed, her Algerian Muley Moloc appears in relatively few scenes. Through other characters, notably the women, he is often more spoken of than speaking. At the beginning of *Slaves*, the English Jew Fetnah, ostensibly converted to Islam and purchased from her gold-loving parents, is one of Moloc's harem and a favorite. She recounts to Selima, one of the Moorish women and content with her lot as a concubine, how she told him directly that she does not love him:

> 'How!' cried he, starting from his seat, 'How, can't love me?' And he laid his hand upon his scimitar ...
> When I saw the scimitar half drawn, I caught hold of his arm. 'Oh, good my lord,' said I, 'Pray, do not kill a poor little girl like me ...'
> 'Take her away,' said he. 'She is beneath my anger.' (*SA* 60)

By Rowson's use of indirect discourse, the tyrant of Algiers loses most of his force; after all, Fetnah is alive and well in the telling and has survived to live another hour. For Rowson's purposes, this rejection of the dey's favor stimulates the next phase of Moloc's lust, by shifting his desire from the Jewish woman to the Christian, Olivia. This latter character, then, functions as Almeyda does in Dryden and more distantly as Bess in *Fair Maid*, the woman whose virtue instigates in tyrants the basest of desires. When he does speak, Rowson's dey cannot muster the darker power of other stage captors over enslaved Christian women. Whereas Mullisheg in Part 2 of Heywood's drama soliloquizes his way to attempting Bess's chastity a second time thus:

> Can a king swear against his own desires,
> Whose welfare is the sinews of the realm?
> I should commit high treason 'gainst myself
> Not to do that might give my soul content
> And satisfy my appetite with fulness (*FM* 2, 107)

Muley Moloc tells his adviser, Mustapha, "I cannot banish the beautiful Christian one moment from my thoughts. The women seem all determined to perplex me" (*SA* 74). Mullisheg has only to contend "with weak woman," while Moloc is perplexed by "all" women – a stark contrast in the implied threat of their respective characters. With his on-stage presence blunted, his objects of lust turned a unified band of woman warriors, and his appetites thwarted by characters bred on English virtue and American stoicism, Muley Moloc loses all potency by the end. He rather pathetically capitulates to the republican revolt of the slaves, and without forswearing Islam he bows to the superior power of American liberty. With his stage whiskers and Turkish-type costume, Rowson's Algerianized Moor is at best a second-rate Vice, loud for a while but well routed and made ridiculous by the end.

Muley Moloc is a long way from Abdelmelec; nevertheless, imbedded in the comic tyrant is the anxiety over a less comic, more heroic figure, whose ability to resist the siren call of republicanism would make him a more dangerous character in the flesh. In the tradition of representing historical Moroccan kings, both English and American drama show great ambiguity about the matter of Islam. Despite a prevailing cultural bias against the followers of Mohammed as pagans and enemies to reason and Christendom, not all Islamic rulers have been portrayed as inherently wicked in their faith. For Elizabethan England, European Roman Catholicism represented a far greater threat to national integrity than even Turkish imperial religion; thus in Peele and in the Stukeley play, the characters representing Abd el-Malik do not identify themselves as Muslim extremists but as rational men with a conscience, whose battles against the Catholic Christian Sebastian are engaged in reluctantly and only from a sense of duty and justice to their own nation's sovereignty. If in Dryden and Rowson, the Abd character turns blustering despot, the matter of Islam is still problematic. In *Don Sebastian*, the playwright must allow that at least some Muslims can be influenced by Christianity; otherwise, the alliance between the overthrown Mahumet (who never appears on stage in Dryden) and Sebastian is not credible. In *Slaves in Algiers*, Rowson types the dey as lascivious and makes his potential victim a virtuous Christian, but she alters the landscape to make republican virtue the ultimate ideology, not any of the recognized world religions. Under liberty's banner, Muslims, Jews, and Christians may join and therefore suppress, finally, the matter of religious difference. The message about Muley Moloc is thus multi-sided: he is a Muslim ruler and therefore acts to post-Elizabethan type, but faced with a political revolt, he can see reason in his self-interest, even as Heywood's Mullisheg can be shamed by English virtue, and accept a new political reality that supersedes religion, even if it does not overthrow it or replace it.

Importantly, Rowson has Olivia rewrite her Zara progenitress to suggest the power of women, especially American women, to reinscribe a victimized type in new potentialities. In Hill's drama, Zara is more or less isolated from creating any alliances that would allow her not only to resist but to triumph over her oppressor, Osman. Her death becomes foregone in the contest between Christian chastity and Islamic lust. In Rowson, Olivia, aided by her republican mother and Fetnah's quick conversion to American liberty, forms a network of women who become the most important agents for change in the play.[42] Even Zorina, Muley Moloc's daughter, becomes a "Christian in my heart" under Olivia's tutelage (*SA* 67). With the captive men serving largely as the physical force, Olivia, although willing, like Zara, to accept her death as the cost of freedom for others, has taken the actions necessary to make life and triumph possible. Whereas in *Fair Maid*, Bess's virtue requires also Spencer's absolute dedication to convince Mullisheg to relent, in *Slaves*, Olivia's virtue is spread out as a political belief, shared by many, whose numbers as well as force of will overturn the power relationship between captive and captor inherent in earlier dramas of Islamic bondage. In the end, if American women can de-fang the lusty Moor qua Algerine, then Islam *per se* is no particular threat to American national identity. Through the agency of the reinscribed woman, now a vocal proponent of liberty as the supreme form of virtue, chastity is no longer that which keeps a woman under lock and key in her own culture. Liberty applies to all, male and female, and its very spread curbs the libertine (whose creed is a perversion of liberty) from acting out of monarchical, absolute power against traditional Western virtues.

One other character type of interest relative to Rowson's *Slaves* is the renegade, the convert to Islam in service to the Turkish empire, who caused considerable cultural anxiety in England, particularly after the Elizabethan period. Such a character appears in a number of plays from the seventeenth and eighteenth centuries, Rowe's *Tamerlane* being just one. In Rowson, Fetnah, though raised in the "Moorish religion" retains "a natural antipathy to their manners" and thus resists at heart a conversion to a creed alien to her own English Jewishness (*SA* 61). Rather, Fetnah's father, Ben Hassan, functions as the true renegade, one who converts to serve himself and, to the Anglo-American world, turn his back on the shared values of Christian nations. As a frequently appearing figure in English drama about Islamic characters, the renegade, as Nabil Matar has maintained, is a very threatening type to English Christians, who feared, as Protestant Americans in captivity to Native Americans did, losing identity through a change in religion.[43] Although there is also a renegade Christian figure in Dryden, Rowson makes hers a Jew and therefore in stage terms a comic character whose switching of faiths is the most obvious sign of his self-interested duplicity. He serves Muley Moloc only as long as his personal wealth can be sustained or enhanced; later in the play, when the slaves revolt and his comfort is threatened, Ben Hassan goes so far as to dress as a woman to avoid punishment. He shows no loyalty to anyone but himself, not even to his daughter. For Rowson, both the renegade and the ruler deserve condemnation, the one for pursuing slavish self-aggrandizement at the expense of any personal loyalty, and the other for ruling without check to personal passions. Ben Hassan abandons his leader, but it is not the abandonment itself that the play critiques. In many ways, Rowson overlays the renegade with the stereotyped comic stage Jew – not the sympathetic one from Cumberland's *The Jew* (1794) but the older type, the one that informs Shylock.[44]

In Dryden, the renegade is Dorax, a one-time Christian who has become an adviser to the emperor. Despite his change of religion, Dorax retains a strong streak of honor; he refuses to participate in a revolt against Muley-Moluch, largely on the grounds the royalist Dryden uses in other plays for protecting the king, however bad – that all revolt against monarchy is damnable:

> But, while he trusts me, 'twere so base a part
> To fawn and yet betray, I shou'd be hiss'd
> And whoop'd in Hell for that Ingratitude. (*DS* 111)

Thus antimonarchical behavior, even against the worst of princes, brings such social disruption that no amount of justification can urge the royalist to act contrary to his king:

> Children may murder Parents, Wives their Husbands;
> All must be Rapine, Wars, and Desolation,
> When trust and gratitude no longer bind. (*DS* 111–12)

Rowson's renegade has no such scruples – after all, were he an unreconstructed royalist, he would be hissed from the Philadelphia stage – but neither is his religion finally of any true significance. To be sure, Rowson indulges in typing of the Jew character, a scheming, money-hungry, but ultimately fearful figure whose cross-dressing is the sign of his impotence. But when Fetnah remains behind to stay with her father, Rowson suggests not only good filial values in the daughter, but also that the only important conversion in the world of the play is to republican liberty. Dryden's renegade maintains a code of honor that he has retained from his Christian past; he is a good royalist, whose loyalty even to a bad king proves his nobility. For Rowson, however, it is better to condemn Ben Hassan's gross self-interest against Olivia's and Fetnah's more selfless ideals; therefore, her renegade Jew looks nothing like Dryden's renegade Christian. The message here, as with Olivia and Muley Moloc, is still the same: the religious renegade is less dangerous than the political one.[45]

A comedy of republican triumph, *Slaves in Algiers* both honors and alters a long tradition of representing conflicts between Muslims and Christians on English-speaking stages. The American contribution to the tradition is to allow the possibility of reformed types in which all the original codes are overcome by the superiority of a non-hierarchical, nonpatriarchal ideology that can be adopted by Christians, Jews, and Muslims, men and women, oppressors and oppressed.[46] At the end of *Slaves*, despite Rowson's use of "Christian" to signify the values affirmed by an American audience, Muley Moloc asks only that he be helped to be a better ruler, not a convert to the faith: "Teach me, then, you who so well know how to practice what is right, how to amend my faults" (*SA* 93). Like

Heywood's Mullisheg, Rowson's Muslim tyrant shows the capacity for conversion to a less self-interested form of kingship, whereby virtue replaces appetite as a reigning belief. In a way, Rowson points her reformed dey toward his earliest avatars in the drama, especially Peele's Abdelmelec, whose conduct in *The Battle of Alcazar* demonstrates a capacity for selflessness and honor the likes of which the English and American characters urge on Muley Moloc.

At the same time Rowson, through Olivia and the extended network of Rebecca, Fetnah, and Zorina, rewrites the history of Christian victimhood as represented by Zara and Almeyda. To be sure, Olivia has the capacity for sacrifice, something that unites her to Zara and her stage sisters, but even more radically than the cross-dressed active women in earlier drama, of the Bess type, she recognizes that wearing a sword and swaggering like a man does nothing to improve the general situation of captives everywhere. Thus Olivia, as a mouthpiece for liberty and the affirmation of subjecthood in one's own person, brings to American female identity on the stage much more than a role as suffering placeholder in dramas about Islamic cruelty. Olivia and her female circle – Christian mother, Jewish ally, and Muslim woman – offer the possibility of a new kind of "Algerian" drama, one in which political and social values can be affirmed in their capacity to change societies and individuals rather than as national characteristics that, in conflict, can only bring extremity of position and death to the opposition. Rather than fearing American renegades, Rowson suggests that the opposite is more likely to occur. Coming from a land where, as Rebecca has told Fetnah, "virtue in either sex is the only mark of superiority," American captives serve as *agents provocateurs*, seeking not to escape by any means nor masquerade in different sex, but to give full voice to a superior ideology that, in their view, has transformative power (*SA* 61). Especially through the medium of the philosophically assertive woman, Rowson maintains that republican values can overcome all obstacles of religion, geography, and social system.

Rowson's stage Muslims are finally not Satan's minions or mere pagans but characters that, in an offstage world, can adapt to new political philosophies. This statement does not excuse her from bias in the representation – after all, there is nothing particularly original in her initial images of the Muslim male characters – but to note that she has her place in a long history of representation, one that, at its outset, could honor an Islamic ruler in almost the same terms as a Christian king. While it is highly unlikely that the audience in Philadelphia in 1794 thought much about such things – as we know from more recent crises involving Islamic nations and people, Americans can quickly resort to demonized types for Muslim captors – Rowson herself castigated slavery in terms that would have forced anyone listening to apply the trope of the tyrant to their own shores. In her prologue, she announces forthrightly that the portrayed situation has universal applicability:

> What tyrant then the virtuous heart can bind?
> 'Tis vices only can enslave the mind.
> Who barters country, honor, faith, to save
> His life, tho' free in person, is a slave.
> While he, enchain'd, imprison'd tho' he be,
> Who lifts his arm for liberty, is free. (*SA* 58)

Wherever tyranny is found, it must be combated through a rigorous assertion of virtue. In the home, she tells the audience in her epilogue, women transform by humane governance: "Good humor makes a paradise at home," especially when men, as she says teasingly, "adore, be silent, and obey" them. At the same time, without naming any nation, she brings forward the "many a Christian . . . /In bondage languishing their lives away" and the joy felt by the "poor captive . . . freed from slavery's ignominious chain," whom she links by association to women under patriarchy and African American slaves as well as to Algerian captives (*SA* 94). The stage Muslim for Rowson, then, is not simply a marker for the Algerian other, but in its coarsest type the sign – and not the only one – of a tyrant, at home or abroad. In many ways, she distinguishes between individuals who identify as Muslim and the more abstract beliefs associated with Islam as a creed. That her Muslims may be reformed, not out of their Islam but out of their tyranny, says much about Rowson's commitment to republicanism and her reading of the dramatic tradition in which she so immersed herself in *Slaves in Algiers*.

8

James Nelson Barker and the stage American Native

In staging North Africans – undifferentiated "Moors" – Susanna Rowson became one of the first American playwrights to construct non-white, non-Christian characters for the stage, and she did so by beginning with types and situations with which transatlantic audiences were long familiar. Even in the decade or so after Rowson, there were relatively few enacted American plays with figures representing persons of color from outside of the world of Euro-American elites and their African American servants. Despite Natives' significance to American history and their place in such genres as the captivity narrative, Indian characters made virtually no appearances in stage plays by Americans before 1800; Ann Julia (Kemble) Hatton's 1794 *Tammany; or, The Indian Chief* is the rare exception, but its text has not survived. There were other outlets for depiction of Native peoples, including in such novels as Charles Brockden Brown's *Edgar Huntly* (1799) or Rowson's *Reuben and Rachel* (1798), and by the 1790s, most prose accounts of Indians depicted them as one-dimensional savages.[1] Of course, theatregoers in the new republic might have encountered stage Indians in dramas by Europeans; and in both the colonial and early national periods, Native chieftains sometimes attended the theatre when in New York, Philadelphia, or later in Washington on diplomatic business, giving local spectators opportunities to see them in person.[2] By 1850, that would change; attendants at the American stage would have been well used to Indian dramas, even surfeited by them; but in the early republic, the presentation of the Native figure created a number of problems and anxieties for playwrights and managers in terms of how a people, framed so frequently as the savage enemy, would be represented before post-Revolutionary audiences.

Curiously, one of the first American-authored plays to feature 'Indians' was David Humphreys's *The Widow of Malabar* (1790), a drama set in colonial South Asia and inspired by a play in French by A.-M. Le Mierre, *La veuve du Malabar* (produced 1779, printed 1780). Written in 1780, while the author was a resident at Washington's home in Mount Vernon, *Widow* opened in Philadelphia on May 7, 1790, and played in that city two more times through 1791; another version of the same source play, but by an English author, Mariana Starke, was performed on July 2, 1794, just two days after the premiere of *Slaves in Algiers*. Humphreys's version predates that of Starke, whose *Widow of Malabar*, produced at Covent Garden, first appeared in print in London, 1791, and was republished in Philadelphia in 1792. Like Humphreys's play, Starke's claims to be an "imitation" rather than a "translation," but one that eliminates the French characters from the mix and leaves only English and Indian. In the Philadelphia printing, Starke's version is presented as played by the Old American Company – which in 1792 was patently false – but the publisher gives away the ruse when he publishes the epilogue delivered by Mrs. Henry, with a name from Humphreys's, not Starke's play. However, Starke's version was played in Philadelphia later, a fact that seems to have escaped theatre historians.[3] In any event, the theatrical presentation of "Indians," whether in a Francophile or Anglophile package, was of great interest to Philadelphia managers.

Humphreys's play features the oft-condemned practice of *sati*, the ritual burning of a widow in Bengal, and uses the situation to argue for the relative rights of women in the West versus those in the "Asiatic" East. The drama fully participates in the demonization of the Brahmin priest, which post-colonial critics have identified as a salient feature of western literature about India, but it also focuses on the condition of the Indian woman, Lanissa, and her female confidante, Fatima, justifying her rescue by the French General, Montalban (who had known her before her marriage) and showing through the figure of the Young Brahmin that enlightenment may be brought to dark races in overcoming superstition and uncivilized brutality toward women.[4] The key elements, then, are the rescuing Europeans, with a strong leader; a virtuous Indian woman and her friend; the woman's rescue from the barbarity of her own people and customs; the expulsion of a malicious priest; the conversion of a young native man to European values; and concluding remarks, in the epilogue, that celebrate Columbian freedom from tyranny against women (including, presumably, Columbia herself): "For here, ye fair, no servile rites bear sway."[5] What Europeans bring is humanity and love; the General acts selflessly out of humanitarian regard (before he knows the intended victim is Lanissa) and then from the force of personal attachment. Thus one of the tropes that marks dramas of civilizing is that of romantic love as a humanizing force more powerful than sheer military might to overcome the presumed violence and ignorance of colonized non-Christians. Through erotic force, backed by martial competence, the doubly potent European defeats the doubly impotent "Indian," seizes the woman and the land, and expels the older, unchangeably "native" man, leaving only the younger Indian male on the colonized margin of the stage to wonder at the puissance of the western hero.

Although the link between South Asian Indians and North American ones may seem to be no more than a coincidence of word, the Anglo-American dramatic tradition often conjoins them, along with Turks and Moors (or generic North Africans, as in Rowson), in surprising and disturbing ways. The summary above of *The Widow of Malabar* could as easily be applied to any number of nineteenth-century American dramas that feature their own Indians. As Nabil Matar maintains, the English discovery of the New World and its early attempts at colonization occurred at the same time as Queen Elizabeth was reaching to Muslim nations and leaders for trade and political reciprocity.[6] For seventeenth-century Britons, seeing Turks (or South Asian Indians, for that matter) on the streets of London coincided with seeing such Native Americans in the city as Rebecca Rolfe, the former Mataoka of the Virginia Algonkians, who was known through Captain John Smith as Pocahontas. The latter's death in England in 1617 preceded by two years the first British importation of African slaves to its mainland American colonies. Further, the sudden swirl of nations and ethnicities from outside of Europe to which Britons were exposed in a relatively short period seemed to produce a palette of ethnic markers that mixed colors with races. *Moor* could mean *Negro*, *blackamoor*, or other terms that corresponded to shades, including *white*; *Turk* almost always signified something between white and black, although it too could take on a variety of hues. South Asian Indian as well could be expressed in color schemes that included the all-purpose "black." Thus the encounter with Native peoples in North America, another set of exotics, might inspire a range of color words, including "tawny," a term employed also for Moors and Turks. The world of stage drama often made no distinctions based on firsthand accounts or semi-scientific attempts to sort out often subtle, if existent, distinctions of skin shade. Whether tawny or black, the most pervasive color terms, the native peoples of North and South America, North Africa, sub-Saharan Africa, the Levant, Central Asia, and South Asia were often subjected to a universal colorizing/colonizing scheme that made it easy for actors in theatres to apply any shade of dark in order to represent the non-European other. That the early attempts by American writers to figure the First Nations fell prey to English color confusion indicates the degree to which those authors watched the stage more than their own backyards for clues on how to signify "Indians."

The first produced play explicitly about Pocahontas and the first staged play about Native Americans by an Anglo-American for which a complete text is extant, James Nelson Barker's *The Indian Princess* (1808), claims to be based upon Captain John Smith's *The Generall Historie of Virginia* (1624).[7] The play has songs and music by English-born composer John Bray, a contrived plot in the style of popular stage entertainments of the time, and a happy ending. Barker uses Smith's text freely, adds characters or changes their importance with only occasional fidelity to their original presentation.[8] The particular conversions he makes reflect not only dramaturgical preferences in the early nineteenth-century American theatre, but also the ways in which Barker reconstructs Smith's mythologies of colonization and national origin; radically alters his accounts of relations between whites and Natives and Natives with each other; and, especially, exposes the eroticizing of imperialist contact that Smith suggests but never develops – all in an attempt to convert history into a pleasing commodity for middling tastes. At the same time, Barker participates in stage traditions that create their own ideological world, well removed from the facts of colonization yet informing the ways in which a former "colonial" people imagined their role in colonizing to be.

Like many playwrights in the early period, Barker was not a full-time author. Born in Philadelphia in 1784, the son of the eventual mayor of the city, John Barker, and a political figure in his own right, James Nelson had his first significant stage success with his third play to be produced, *The Indian Princess*.[9] More than twenty years after the play's first production and publication, Barker wrote to William Dunlap that he had intended his play to be a serious drama,[10] but encouraged by the composer John Bray, who wrote the music, turned his text into what we might call now a light opera, and which Barker on the title page called "An Operatic Melo-Drame." Despite some problems with an unpopular actor in the first staging, *The Indian Princess* was mounted in Philadelphia, Charleston, Richmond, Baltimore, Norfolk, and New York in the years immediately following its premiere, and in London in 1820.[11] Its modest success likely inspired other dramatists to write Pocahontas and Indian plays, which appeared with some frequency in America for the next fifty years. Given the play's influence on later drama, it is worth probing Barker's choices as early attempts to find a formula for both popularity and substance in the rendering of Native characters, situations, and themes.

The criticism on the play largely looks at it in terms of the developing dramatic craft in America, literary nationalism – which Barker affirms – and the conflict between the "pastoral ideal" and the wilderness.[12] More recent treatments have given brief acknowledgment of its role in the Pocahontas myth or as an example of "Indian" drama.[13] In his book on the portrayals of Pocahontas – an important background study for any work about the "Indian princess" – Robert Tilton mentions Barker's play only briefly; however, given its historical importance as an inaugural drama in the nineteenth-century resurgence of the Pocahontas "narrative," as Tilton calls it, the "melo-drame" deserves a closer look than it has usually gotten.[14] Barker wrote at a time when interest in American history was enjoying a new popularity, especially as post-Revolutionary Americans searched the archives and their own memories for traces and traits that would foster some sense of national identity. Following Tilton's argument, one could assert that the popularity of John Davis's accounts, *Captain Smith and Princess Pocahontas* (1805) and the novel *The First Settlers of Virginia* (1805), most likely encouraged the playwright to imitate success in one genre with conversion to another. After all, it is Davis who provides the imaginative reconstruction of the Smith–Pocahontas relationship as that of lovers rather than adult male amused by child, as Smith himself sometimes frames it. But as Barker knew, even as he sought to capitalize on the cultural appeal a tacitly romantic relationship might have for audiences, turning fiction or history into drama was not simply a matter of rendering dialogue in place of exposition. The stage had its own rules, its own criteria for success, that depended on actors and audiences in confined public spaces more than literary taste or historical accuracy. Motivated at least in part by Davis's theory that Pocahontas's first love was John Smith, Barker would naturally claim to turn to an original account in order to appeal to authenticity.

On its surface, *The Indian Princess* dramatizes the successful establishment of an English colony on mainland North America, with all the advantages of hindsight and myth-making appropriate to a text written at the bicentennial of Jamestown's founding. Susan Scheckel examines the rhetoric of the play as part of the discourse of national founding and discerns in *The Indian Princess* a theme of domesticity along with the appropriation of Pocahontas to serve a number of ideological ends. The character of the princess is asked, says Scheckel, "to represent and legitimize American colonialist *and* nationalist projects; to serve both as the implicitly sexualized object of conquest and as the sanctified figure of the nation, the mother who unites all her citizens/children in a unified national 'family.'"[15] What she defines as 'domesticating' the drama is part of a complex response by the playwright to conditions both within and without the theatre of Barker's time – that is, the linkage of an initiating imperialist urge with aspects of nationalist and colonialist ideology as they emerge from a particularly theatrical inheritance.

The Advertisement for the play includes this comment: "The principal materials that form this dramatic trifle are extracted from the General History of Virginia, written by Captain Smith, and printed London, folio, 1624; and as close an adherence to historic truth has been preserved as dramatic rules would allow of."[16] This is true enough as far as it goes, particularly in light of Barker's qualification. The play loosely follows actions depicted in the Third Book of *The Generall Historie*, the one that covers Smith's personal involvement with Virginia, from his departure with the first colonists on December 19, 1606 (O.S.) to his return to England in the wake of a gunpowder explosion that injured him in the thigh – and possibly groin – in fall of 1609. Even so, differences between Barker's version and Smith's far outnumber similarities and reveal more about the state of American theatre than the simple fact of exhibiting an American subject on stage. If, as is likely, the novelistic accounts by John Davis are the means that bring Pocahontas back into cultural circulation, then the playwright's use of Smith must be read in the context of mediating arts, primarily the theatre, and the forms through which mythologies of colonization were practiced.[17]

One of the most striking divergences of the play from history is Barker's incorporation of women into his drama and the importance they have in the overall narrative.[18] Three white women, all lovers of white men, play prominent roles in the action of *The Indian Princess* – this despite the fact that Smith does not mention English women as among the company in the period of first settlement. In Smith's *Historie*, women occupy only a tiny fraction of the text, and English women almost nothing at all. For Smith, the imperial mission is a man's work, a homosocial enterprise of landing, taming, seizing, marking, and killing. Yet among Smith's adventures, women get some mention, nearly all as exotics. Therefore, while Barker's English women are either fabrications or functional anachronisms, it is less surprising to find Native women in the play, notably Pocahontas, who of course appears in Smith; but beyond his acknowledged source, the author of *Indian Princess* (like that of *Widow of Malabar*) adds a Native handmaiden to the female protagonist, Nima, who, like the Princess, also falls in love with a white man, the serving-class humor character, Robin.[19] Although the cultural implications of the dramatist's choice to stage white women alongside Native are profound, there are two practical reasons for the addition of such women to Smith's narrative: the economics of the early American theatre and sources for the play other than *The Generall Historie*. Both reasons play significant roles in creating the identity structures that the drama fosters.

In the case of the former, theatre managers in the first half of the nineteenth century had to rely on the broadest possible audience to survive. With the post-Revolutionary incorporation of literate women into the cultural life of the country, playwrights recognized that they had to construct vehicles for bringing middling and elite women as well as men of all classes into the theatre.[20] In the more established theatres of eastern seaboard cities, women – that is, respectable ones in the codes of the time – sat only in boxes, although in smaller theatres or those outside major urban areas, such as the Government Street Theatre in Mobile, men and women sometimes sat "promiscuously in the pit."[21] Nevertheless, with seat prices generally low, one dollar being a top rate for boxes in the antebellum period, managers depended on numbers in the house to make money.[22] As in the literary market, where publishers and authors increasingly recognized the purchasing power and presumed taste of women, so in the theatres: female customers often meant the difference between success and failure. Not only does Barker include female characters and love situations to make his appeal to that market, but, as will be explained further below, he also explicitly acknowledges women in the audience as the only hope his play has of continuing on stage. The point is, however, that the presentation of a truly "native" theme and the appeal to and incorporation of women go hand in glove.

The other reason, though, is connected to a problem whose solution was not fully realized by American playwrights until much later in the century: how to write a theatrically successful entertainment. As with American writers in nondramatic genres and such of his immediate forebears as Tyler, Dunlap, Rowson, and Murray, Barker and his fellow playwrights turned to the dramas that held the boards in their own country – British imports. In Barker's day, the plays best known to audiences were the staples of the late eighteenth-century stage – Shakespeare, comedies of manners, and musical productions – with the addition of the new melodramas. For a writer who wished to portray American-set material, as has been argued above, the essential problem of playwriting turned out to be how to graft that material onto a British vehicle. Although the functional narrative for *The Indian Princess* comes from Smith, and many motifs, such as cross-dressed "pages," come from Shakespeare, the use of songs and lovers could have been imitated from a number of plays, including any of John O'Keeffe's operas or Frances Brooke's perennial favorite, *Rosina* (1782).[23] Barker understood that for his play to have any chance at repeat performances, he needed to evoke those plays most repeated, insofar as they might suggest signs and structures by which his own play might be quickly comprehended.

One probable theatrical model for *Indian Princess* stands out. A favorite in America since 1789, George Colman, Jr.'s *Inkle and Yarico* (1787) had played in Philadelphia most recently in 1807, the year before *Indian Princess* took the stage.[24] Unusual (although, remembering Shakespeare's *The Tempest* and its Restoration revisions, Dryden's *The Indian Queen*, and Aphra Behn's *The Widow Ranter*, not unique) among British plays, its action takes place entirely in the New World.[25] With its songs and fanciful rendering of North America, with its sets of lovers, comedic ending, and most of all, its long-running success in theatres throughout the United States, Colman's play seemed a logical choice for Barker to adapt.[26] But to use *Inkle and Yarico* as a model of a longer musical romantic comedy set in North America, Barker also had to import that play's considerable cultural baggage and its own history of attitudes toward women, race, and colonization.

Although the plot of *Inkle and Yarico* bears only slight resemblance to that of *Indian Princess*, the situations within the play inform a number of scenes in Barker's play. Mr. Inkle and his man Trudge, on their way to Barbados, become marooned on the mainland of North America. While in this almost surreal landscape, populated by undifferentiated, racially inscribed others (described both as Blacks and Natives), the two men fear for their lives, until they stumble across a grotto with two Native women, Yarico and Wowski. Matching up by class, the princess-type Yarico falls in love with Inkle and the servant-type Wowski with Trudge. The men return the affections of the women, and all proceed to Barbados. Colman introduces complications when Inkle must face his scheduled marriage to Narcissa, the daughter of the island's governor, Sir Christopher Curry. Deciding between his economic self-interest and his heart, Inkle leans toward the former and nearly sells Yarico into slavery; Trudge, however, although previously affianced to the English woman Patty, stays loyal to the Native Wowski and upbraids his employer for not remaining fast to Yarico. Finally, through an accident of identification that allows Narcissa's lover, a sea captain named Campley, to marry Inkle's intended, Curry accepts the new son-in-law but blasts Inkle's perfidy. Inkle then turns back to Yarico, and the play ends with the three couples in happy relations.

As recent interest in the phenomenon has shown, the story of Inkle and Yarico has a long history before Colman's successful theatrical rendering. Originating as a brief narrative in Richard Ligon's seventeenth-century *A True and Exact History of the Island of Barbados*, resurfacing in a piece by Richard Steele in *The Spectator* in 1711, the story inspired a large number of poets, prose writers, and dramatists to give their versions of the narrative of the Christian man who, for personal gain, tried to sell his dark-skinned, pagan lover into slavery. One of the most popular motifs was that of letters, usually poetic, from Yarico to Inkle, in which the former expresses both love and despair for the cold-hearted mercantilist. Anonymous versions of this imagined epistolary lament appear in 1734, 1736, and 1738; rewritten texts of these plus slightly more original poems by John Winstanley and Edward Jerningham were published into the 1770s. Because of its central theme of a lover's duplicity and its evocation of the slavery question, the Inkle and Yarico plot appeared in a number of continental texts and performances, as well, almost all by French or German-speaking authors. Even Goethe intended to write a play, "Yncle et Jariko," in 1766, the year of Jerningham's poetic epistle. In the United States, the story inspired an anonymous poet in 1792 and Rufus Dawes in 1830 to offer versified forms. By the time Colman came to write his play, the phenomenon had reached its heyday of popularity; and while new versions of the story declined in number rapidly after the early 1800s, his own *Inkle and Yarico* kept the lovers before audiences into the second decade of the nineteenth century.[27]

As a musical play that deals with encounters between a representative of a colonizing power and a Native, Colman's version would seem a reasonable choice for emulation. Nevertheless, in a society as color-conscious as the new United States, *Inkle and Yarico* presents race problematically. While in

Barker the Native Americans are identified specifically with a history of the North American mainland and a people that spectators in 1808 would easily identify as Indian, Colman inherits and transmits a confused set of markers for his "native" heroine, Yarico. In Ligon, she appears to be a Native – "yellow" Carib, perhaps, but otherwise unspecified[28] – but in the 1734 poem, Yarico is called a "Negro virgin." This Africanizing of her occurs also in the play ascribed to Mrs. Weddell from 1742, and in Jerningham's poem, Yarico is a "Nubian." In the American poem of 1792, however, despite using the names Inkle and Yarico in the title, the scene shifts to India, and the characters are renamed Mercator and Barsina.[29] Perhaps under the influence of Humphreys's *Widow of Malabar* or Starke's play of the same title, the anonymous poet makes Yarico a South Asian Indian, further collapsing all non-Christian exotics into permeable categories of tawny and black.

In the first scene of Colman, in which Inkle, his uncle Medium, and servant Trudge are shipwrecked on what appears to be the American mainland, they see no sign of Europeans. Medium complains that the natives he has observed walk around "in the black buff" and that they are "as black as a peppercorn, but as hot into the bargain."[30] Compared to Threadneedle Street, London, Medium's medium of comparison, all things American are dark and threatening. He later is chased "by the Blacks" (*IY* 14), and Trudge laments to Inkle in the same vein, "But all my red ink will be spilt by an old black pin of a negro" (16). However, when the men encounter a sleeping Yarico in the cave, Inkle accounts her "beautiful as an angel" while Trudge qualifies the remark to "an angel of rather a darker sort" (19). In a telling sign of the imbrication of race and gender in Colman, whereas the male natives are spoken of in the most dismissive, derogatory terms as black, the women are referred to in a more heterogeneous set of color markers. "Rather darker" is quite different in tone and symbolic suggestion from "black as a peppercorn," for instance. After Inkle pairs up with Yarico in their love-at-first-sight encounter and Trudge with Yarico's maid, Wowski, Inkle's servant uses or hears language that identifies his lover as "Indian" (24, 37). In addition, Trudge (unlike Inkle) resists all efforts in Barbados to make him sell his mistress, even when scolded by a planter: "Why, sure friend, you wou'd not live here with a Black!" (37). Then again, when Trudge has to justify his keeping with Wowski to his former lady friend, Patty, he deflects the conversation to Inkle's lover. Trudge claims that Yarico is "of a good comely copper," to which Patty responds, "How! A Tawny?" (54).

TRUDGE: Yes; quite dark; but very elegant; like a Wedgewood tea-pot.
PATTY: Oh! the monster! the filthy fellow! Live with a black-a-moor! (55)[31]

Not only does Trudge realize he must be circumspect with Patty about his own mistress, but he also uses the occasion to crack a few stage jokes about complexions and those that 'rubb off.' If on the boards, color is a source of metatheatrical humor in its impermanence and transferability – there was always the danger that black face paint from a dark character could by proximity attach itself to a light one – on slaveholding Barbados, the represented colony, color is a medium of exchange, where for the planters all that is not white is black and all black a vendible commodity.[32] But in the world of the play, although the designating terms play against each other, the claim that Yarico is 'copper' signifies that while the other Natives, most particularly the males, may be cast as 'Negroes,' the two women are 'Indians' and therefore removed from the implied odium expressed by Medium for relations with a person of color. Women and men suffer somewhat different fates in dramatized colonialism: men are darkened beyond redemption, women lightened enough to kindle erotic interest in demonstrably white males.[33] *Inkle and Yarico* serves as the perfect register for the colonialist confusion of race first expressed, as Matar states, in the Elizabethan Age of Discovery.[34]

Unlike Smith's narrative history, Colman's opera gives women significant roles and makes love the major force in the men's lives. One key element is the vulnerability of the Native women to exploitation; like Pocahontas and Nima in *Indian Princess*, both Yarico and Wowski give themselves unreservedly to the white men, with the possibility of duplicity and betrayal on the part of Inkle held to be very real. For her part, Wowski answers Trudge's questions with the child/feminine 'iss' for 'yes,' but she also tells Trudge not to fear the cannibalism of her chief: "I fight for you!" (*IY* 23). For Trudge, this loyalty is enough for him to repudiate English women, who would fight 'with' rather than 'for.' But for Inkle, the complete affection of Yarico poses problems. He has sailed to America for the purpose of coming into his fortune through marrying Narcissa, and once in Barbados, he reorients himself from his grotto idyl to the business of life. Yarico senses Inkle's growing distance and sings to him of their time back on the mainland:

> For him by day with care conceal'd,
> To bring him food I climb'd the mountain;

> And when the night no form reveal'd,
>   Jocund we sought the bubbling fountain.
> Then, then wou'd joy my bosom fill;
>   Ah! think on this, and love me still. (*IY* 42)

Although seen in its time as sympathetic to dark-skinned races, *Inkle and Yarico* provided Barker with a theatrical model in which the possibility of exploitation and destruction is ineluctably stamped upon the radical, Rousseauvian innocence of the "belle sauvage."[35] In essence, the entire action of Colman's play is a tease because the sudden happy resolution in marriage for the quasi-Native Yarico only serves to mask the willingness of her lover to sell her into slavery and utter spoliation. Both the perfidious lover and the confused color labeling of Yarico pose difficulties for Barker, who needs heroic white male protagonists and a Princess whose color forms no barrier to assimilation, but neither can he entirely escape their influence.

In the Preface to his play, Barker draws analogies between a drama and an innocent being in a way that foreshadows his development of Native female characters who, like Colman's Americans, are open in their complete innocence to being treated as commodities. The author begins by speaking to the nationalist sympathies of his audience, but in terms that emphasize the vulnerability of an American text. By printing his play, Barker says:

> I am perfectly apprized of the probability that it goes only to add one more to the list of those unfortunate children of the American drama, who, in the brief space that lies between their birth and death, are doomed to wander, without house or home, unknown and unregarded, or who, if heeded at all, are only picked up by some critic beadle to receive the usual treatment of vagrants. (*IP* 115)

The child metaphor plays into his strategy of disarming criticism. As he remarks later, his desire in the Preface is "to deprecate the wrath of the critics, and arouse the sympathies of the ladies" (116). Whereas in Colman the sympathy of a female character reforms the corrupted Inkle (but only after he has been shamed by the governor and deprived of his fortune, vested in Narcissa), in Barker it is the collective sympathies of a female audience that will save his head, like that of his hero Smith, from the critical chopping block.

However, his practical concern about bringing women spectators into the theatre is complicated by ideological issues connected to the presentation of women on stage. To the male critics, Barker pleads, either "pat its cheek" and call the child-drama sensible, or if it is not, then let it go. "But do not, O goody critic, apply the birch" (*IP* 116). The play will best find its home not under the gaze of reproving men of the theatre but with women, whose maternal sympathies would presumably be engaged by the pathetic "urchin":

> To your bosoms, ladies, sweet ladies! the little stranger flies with confidence for protection; shield it, I pray you, from the iron rod of rigour, and scold it yourselves, as much as you will, for on your smooth and polished brows it can never read wrinkled cruelty ... and from you, dear ladies, correction would be as thrillingly sweet as that the little *Jean Jacques* received from the fair hand of Mademoiselle Lambercier. (116)

This allusion to Rousseau's *Confessions* suggests that female punishment is, in fact, erotic pleasure – and that that pleasure can be felt by the child as well as the adult.[36] Thus for the child-drama to flee to the bosoms of women in the audience suggests both intermediary protection from the threatening phallus, the iron rod of the critic, and an Oedipal delight in itself. In his prefatory remarks, Barker links commodity (his play) to market (audience), affirming that patriarchal rage threatens to sink his play's value while maternal succor, in the domesticated space of the theatre, has the power to contravene market forces and defuse that rage, through a discourse of Eros. As Bruce McConachie suggests, the "paternalistic theatre" of the post-war period is "waning," but as much for reasons of the appeal to women as the rise of nonelites in the audience.[37]

In the play, then, female characters provide points of identification for the women in the audience, and Barker delivers what he assumes they will want, love plots. Using well-worn techniques from *As You Like It* and other Elizabethan comedies, the American playwright brings two of his women to Virginia in disguise – Geraldine, in love with the gentleman, Percy; and her maid/boy, Kate, who is married to the Irishman, Larry. Another woman, Alice, loved by the adventurer Walter, rounds out the cast of saucy white women who will provide the heretofore deferred partnering for the males engaged in the business of nation-building. The European female characters come across as capable of scheming, restraint, and humor – and thus resist being read as eminently exploitable innocents. Nevertheless, those women all take a secondary position to the

Princess; they are, in a sense, an audience for the conversion of Pocahontas from tawny to pale. Their knowing competence and assertiveness have no place in the main plot relationship except as a protective cultural barrier to forecast more probably the Princess's happy union with the English. In Pocahontas, nativity and innocence conjoin; she knows nothing about European rituals of sexual attraction and functions as a blank slate on which the conquering Englishman can inscribe his own unedited text, but at the same time, she represents the stake Barker's female audience has in the outcome of the production. As Colman sent his *Yarico* into the market of theatrical consumption, to be sold one way or another by and to men without sentiment, so Barker sells his *Princess*, although in the American's case, to white women who symbolically blunt patriarchal rage for the purpose of absorption and diffusion of the play's Indianness into whiteness.

Although in *The Generall Historie* Smith the author mentions virtually nothing about European women in connection with the settling of Virginia, he does, through Native women, feminize the Virginia landscape. As John Seelye explains the implications of Smith's text, 'Pocahontas became the erotic incarnation of a fertile land, a friendly female presence, offering with open arms America's bountiful promise.'[38] The question is, however, whether it is Smith who makes Pocahontas thus or his interpreters. As a frequent go-between for Smith and her father, the leader of the Algonkian confederacy, Powhatan, Pocahontas is mentioned in several places in Smith's final version of events; but her most noteworthy appearance in the *Historie* is at Werowocomoco, where the captive Smith thinks his brains will be dashed: 'Pocahontas the Kings dearest daughter, when no intreaty could prevaile, got his head in her armes, and laid her owne upon his to save him from death.'[39] In Barker, the stage direction for the equivalent scene reads, "*the* PRINCESS, *shrieking, runs distractedly to the block, and presses* SMITH's *head to her bosom*" (*IP* 133). As an actual act of reclamation and transformation of Smith, as it may have been for the original performers of the ceremony in 1607/8,[40] the scene in Barker becomes something altogether different. At age 12, the Pocahontas of Smith's version offers head and arms to protect the captain from her father's wrath; the Princess in Barker is no child, but a woman with that protecting bosom. Indeed, as the illustrations in Tilton's book show, many of the nineteenth-century pictorial representations of the scene show a mature, bare-breasted Pocahontas shielding Smith in a way that emphasizes more *her* vulnerability than the white captive's. What Smith omits or barely hints at, Barker, under the influence of Colman's depiction of Yarico and the works by John Davis that inspired the Pocahontas craze, makes explicit, especially in the use of "bosom" language.[41] In this sense, though, Barker has more to fear for his *Indian Princess* than Colman his *Inkle*. The former's play must appear first in a country where theatre maintains as yet a somewhat tenuous hold, especially for the American writer; in essence, the drama is a Smith, the critic a savage Indian male, and the play's protectress not the Native girl alone but the company of adult women in the audience to whose bosoms it flies from hatchet-wielding commentators. Colman's play needs less protection, although it still appeals to women; it has the guarantee of a London audience as its register of legitimacy. In both plays, the authors make the exploitable innocence of the central female character the touchstone of resolution, but whereas Colman has behind his opera a long tradition of Yarico as a tragically sentimental subject and therefore must make exploitation the problem to be overcome, Barker makes Pocahontas's exploitation the very thing to be celebrated. Successful reception of American drama and of the British American colonialist project join in a dual theatrical mythology tied explicitly to female protection *and* erotic submission.

In Barker's text, the sense of erotic vulnerability is reinforced in the subsequent action, where the playwright clarifies the racial ideology at work. Telling Powhatan that she will "die with the white man," Pocahontas then "bows her head" to the chief's feet, engendering his "tenderness" and procuring the release of the captive. Smith, in blank verse, then proclaims:

> O woman! angel sex! where'er thou art,
> Still art thou heavenly. The rudest clime
> Robs not thy glowing bosom of its nature.
> Thrice blessed lady, take a captive's thanks! (*IP* 134)

As with Inkle's first depiction of Yarico, so Smith celestializes Pocahontas. Barker desires his child-drama, his "bantling," to reside in the bosom of female spectators; therefore, he places the head of his adult hero Smith in an eroticized zone, "glowing" yet safe – for him. Thus through the threatened head-bashing, Barker identifies male Indian blood-lust with the critic's rage; the Native female, like white women of his own time, acts by nature to protect the white man when circumstances force him to be as helpless as a child. For her part, however, protection produces pleasure. In the language of the stage directions, following

Smith's release, "*The PRINCESS shows the most extravagant emotions of rapture*" (134). In this virginal orgasm of beneficence, Pocahontas must be restrained – in this case by her father – from attending with her brother, Nantaquas, to learn the ways of the whites. Barker follows Humphreys in this regard, as well as other plays that feature non-Christian religions, particularly Islam, by placing the vulnerable female between two cultures, her own (one that will, through tradition, force her to submit) and the European (one that will, through love, more gently encourage her submission).

The central conflict in Barker's play turns out not to be what it is in Smith's text, the struggle between Powhatan and Smith for hegemony. Author Smith foregrounds their interactions in *The Generall Historie*, giving to each participant speeches that suggest historical significance, in which the Native chief speaks both cunningly and elegiacally to preserve his power and people, and Smith speaks practically and oracularly of the coming civilization. In the play, however, Powhatan, under the filial influence of the good daughter and the adaptable son – and under the additional female influence of his dead wife, whose memory Pocahontas often stirs – basically accepts the presence of whites. Although Barker wrote during a time when conflicts with Natives were still part of white American expansion, he "domesticates" the figure of the Native father and renders the chief's final acceptance of whites as a kind of impotence, putting Powhatan in a class that includes the pliably embracing Native women but with even less agency. As Jeffrey Mason observes about John Augustus Stone's play *Metamora* (1829), the construction of the Native man cannot be made realistic or even genuinely powerful because audiences would not countenance that kind of representation.[42] Thus Barker celebrates a colonizing white manhood built on the ascribed weaknesses and cruelties of the Native leaders.[43] Rather than have all his older traditional males be exposed for their errors, however, Barker allows Grimosco, the magus, and Miami, the savage suitor, to take the white heat and be expelled from the stage. As with Humphreys, the native son remains to admire the white "man of might," but in this case, Powhatan stays behind as an emasculated presence, soon to become, we assume, the drooling old man in the corner of his daughter's new home, a melodramatic precursor of the American stage's favorite daughter-dependent dad, Rip Van Winkle.

Not every Indian in Barker's play is so welcoming as Pocahontas. The resisters are Grimosco – again not a historical figure, although one could read some elements of Powhatan's brother Opechancanough in Barker's character – and Pocahontas's betrothed, a Susquehannock named Miami. In Smith's *Generall Historie*, the Susquehannocks lie outside the boundary of Powhatania, to the north, a large, fierce-looking people with whom Smith met briefly and cordially on his long trip up Chesapeake Bay. According to Smith, the Susquehannocks have little knowledge of Powhatan or his territories, and he makes no mention of any attempt to forge an alliance through marriage.[44] Barker, however, incorporates both recent and historical events as well as contemporary dramaturgy. In *Inkle and Yarico*, the stranded whites at the beginning encounter faceless "blacks" – Colman's all-purpose word for savages – who seek to murder and eat them. Needing a bloodthirsty enemy as foil to Powhatan, Barker appropriates "Susquehannock" from Smith simply to mean villain. The name Miami, not in Smith's text, would evoke for an 1808 audience the terrible defeat of an American military force in 1791 by the Miami and other Old Northwest Territory tribes.[45] In *The Indian Princess*, the dramatist makes the marriage between Miami and Pocahontas a political linkage; as the Princess drifts into the orbit of the white interlopers, Miami joins with Grimosco in fomenting a rebellion against Smith. Like Humphreys's Brahmin priest and like Muslim clerics in such plays as Rowe's *Tamerlane*, Grimosco represents all of the traits that mark the expungeable other: murderous intent, hostility to the desires of women, unchanging fidelity to a pagan creed, and implacable hatred for Europeans and their religion. Powhatan, swayed by Grimosco's rhetoric, buys into the plot briefly, but under the thoroughly whitened power of his daughter, accepts Smith's supremacy. While in *The Generall Historie*, Smith makes Powhatan's affection for Pocahontas apparent, the relationship between English captain and Algonkian supreme ruler never emerges as one of undissembled respect. Like Rowson's Muley Moloc, Barker's Powhatan has no real power to resist Euro-American hegemony, once his henchmen are neutralized. Rendered impotent by the implied potency of Anglo-Christian romantic love, Powhatan can only fall back on his domesticated role as toothless father of a headstrong daughter.

Having had her sensuality awakened by cradling Smith, Barker's Pocahontas transfers that desire to the character that history designates as her future husband, Rolfe (the playwright omitting, of course, her capture by whites in 1613, her tacit enslavement and at least semi-coerced conversion, and her role as a bargaining tool against Powhatan).[46] With the advent of the apparently younger man as admirer (although he did not arrive in Virginia historically until after Smith's return to England),

Barker's Smith converts the Princess into a child, much as the playwright has done for his play, telling Rolfe that she "as with cherub voice" pleaded for mercy for him. Rolfe exclaims over her "gentleness," "simplicity," and "angel softness," then "*goes to her. She timidly, but with evident pleasure, receives his attention*" (*IP* 137). She calls Smith "brother," but Rolfe teaches her to name her unnameable state toward himself as "lover" and, in the directions, "*Kisses her ardently*" (140). She tells him, "Lover, thou hast made my cheek to burn, and my heart to beat! Mark it." That last phrase is an invitation for Rolfe to put "his hand to her heart" – a gesture in this case with increasingly obvious erotic dimensions. Rolfe must explain her condition further: "Love: the noblest, the sweetest passion that could swell thy angel bosom" (140) – but before her swelling bosom carries her too far into indulgence, a timely call for Rolfe's military services (against the Powhatans) forces him to leave, and to remind the audience that what he has aroused in the young woman is "heavenly innocence" (141).

Pocahontas – whose name, as Seelye and Tilton remind us, means something like "Wantonness" – succeeds in inflaming Miami to a jealousy that hardens his hatred and leads not only to his attack later but eventually to his suicide. In the meantime, she runs to her father and threatens her own suicide if he forces her to marry the Susquehannock. Invoking the spirit of her mother, the Princess remarks, "her shade will pity her unhappy child, and I shall be at rest in her bosom" (*IP* 142). With the protecting maternal bosom not physically present, Powhatan, the doting father, cries, "Rest in my bosom, my child!" Barker succeeds for the moment, then, to restore to *bosom* its protective innocence – but only for a moment. An emissary from Miami brings a "red hatchet," with all its phallic implications of sanguinary violence: war and rape. Powhatan vows to protect his daughter; but when Pocahontas asks, "do I bring my father to the bloody war-path?" (143), Barker blames the red man for the red stain of forced embrace.

The future of the virgin land is enwrapped in the body of the virgin girl. In a virtual trope, reminiscent of the virgin-ravish language used by Smith's friend Samuel Purchas in 1625, Barker makes the well-being of the Native female the province of a gentlemanly white suitor, while all the threat of rape belongs to the bloodthirsty savage.[47] Indeed, all of Powhatan's attempts to quiet Pocahontas's fears prove fruitless until he says, "the brave English too will join us." "Ah!" exclaims the Princess, "then is thy safety and success certain" (143) – as of course in the play it proves to be. No Native male can act with certainty, the ideology suggests, without white guidance.[48]

Yet the action of the play suggests that no white male – with the possible exception of Captain Smith – can act at all without the promise of sex, including sex with Native women. In fact, desire is brought by whites, not expressed by Natives; in other words, Barker conflates sexual awakening with imperialist urge. Pocahontas has no name for her feelings toward Rolfe; in fact, Barker suggests that there seems to be nothing in Indian culture as a whole equivalent to Eros. Like Miranda in *The Tempest*, to which play Barker is also heavily indebted, and like Yarico in Colman's opera, the Princess sees the whites with a species of brave-new-world wonder. But if we observe the other characters, we see a world gone love-mad. Ridiculous transitions occur between sometimes clever, sometimes inane courtship talk of the other lovers, and the obligatory, plot-driven scenes of dark drama. With puns, cross-dressing jokes, and mooning love patter, Barker sugars Smith's no-nonsense rhetoric virtually beyond recognition, while at the same time he calls before the audience echoes of the pun-laden *Inkle and Yarico* as a superimposition on the dryness of *The Generall Historie*. After a scene of sexual assault (the page Robin on Walter's lover, Alice); Rolfe's expressed desire before he meets Pocahontas to "take a squaw o' the woods, and get papooses" (130); and Kate's teasing Larry – before revealing herself to him as female and his spouse – that she has slept with his wife, Barker seems bent on proving that the landscape is made erotic by Europeans. This last point is the theme of Annette Kolodny's study of early travel writing, *The Lay of the Land*, but in *The Indian Princess*, the landscape, shrunk to the world of the stage, becomes personalized in the figure of the Princess.[49]

Nevertheless, despite Barker's accretions, the author of *The Generall Historie* bears some responsibility for eroticizing Virginia. One might say that Smith inherited the sexualized trope; in other words, as Rebecca Faery remarks, "a great deal of ideological work prefaced that instance of appropriation [of Pocahontas as symbol of a colonized land] and made it possible, work that feminized and sexualized the 'new world' as the object of the masculine colonizer's desire."[50] In another famous scene in *The Generall Historie*, one that Leo Lemay calls "the most sensual exotic event narrated in seventeenth-century American literature,"[51] Smith describes what he calls a "Virginia Maske" – Pocahontas, coming to Smith with an "anticke": "thirtie young women came naked out of the woods," dancing and singing then offering ritual invitations, "Love you not me?"[52] This is as close as Smith gets in all of the Third Book to anything like a display of sexuality, and one gets the impression that he is glad to be done with the passage. Barker, however, reads into the scene what Smith will not say. Walter, claiming to have been with Smith, uses the "Virginia mascarado" to tease his lover Alice, stressing the women's nakedness, their state as "Madder than mad Bacchantes," and the "beauteous Wolf-head" who leads him to bed (*IP* 145, 146). The playwright then distinguishes between love play and animal need, where teasing, seduction, and postponed satisfaction mark a Euro-American erotics of control over Native customs and culture.

In their last encounter before the climax, Rolfe and Pocahontas, like Inkle and Yarico, play a little at Aeneas and Dido, as "honour" and "duty" call him from his lover.[53] She uses this departure to discourse on her fortunate fall, from "blood-stained and rude" "savage error" to western love. Barker buries religious doctrine in courtship language, where references to the "Holy One" become tantamount to allusions to Cupid. Thus Christianity too becomes implicated in the erotics of power that Barker celebrates. As Pocahontas proclaims her gratitude to Rolfe for releasing her from ignorance, she again sighs and phallicizes his teachings:

> what couldst thou more,
> Belov'd preceptor, but direct that ray,
> Which beams from Heaven to animate existence,
> And bid my swelling bosom beat with love!

Rolfe must declare for innocence and not let that ray penetrate too quickly. They "*embrace*," but he postpones their pleasure: he does not want "the face of morn [to] blush rosy red,/To see the dew besprent, cold virgin ground/Stain'd by licentious step" (*IP* 150). Alone, the Princess sings, impatient for day to come and their nuptials to be complete. She frets that "the tender flower droops till return of the light," but rejoices that with the sun comes tumescence: "Soon the flow'ret seeming dead/Raises up its blushing head,/Glows again the breast of love" (*IP* 151). Soon, too, the savages will be defeated, the Europeans and their Native adorers will triumph, and character Smith will pronounce nationalist themes of *translatio studii, translatio imperii*. But the political message has been subsumed in the erotic. Just as the sympathetic bosom of the female playgoer stands between the child-drama and the "iron rod" of the critic – with the implication that she stands ready to absorb its power – so too does the welcoming bosom of the Native Princess deflect the red hatchet of savage males and preserve the "blushing head" of her lover's rising flower for her future pleasure.

Although Rolfe succeeds Smith as Pocahontas's erotic partner, allowing the captain to play the role of imperial leader, Smith is not entirely divorced from the love proceedings and the figuration of the Native. In Act I, scene 4, Smith loses his way in a forest and fears that all his "golden dreams" of conquest and "laurel'd glory" will be lost. He quickly chastises himself for "these coward thoughts" and turns to "this trusty sword, /That made the Turk and the Tartar crouch beneath me" (*IP* 125). Thus before he (or the audience) ever encounters Native Americans, the character overlays their identity with those of non-Christian peoples he has ostensibly battled in his pre-Virginia life, peoples for whom there has already been a long tradition of stage representation. The historical Smith understood the difference between the Ottoman Turks, whom he fought and by whom he was captured; the Saadian rulers of Morocco (the brother and nephews of Abd el-Malik), whom he visited before leaving for Virginia,[54] and differing tribes of Native Americans, but in the play, all of Smith's experiences with Muslims are resolved into the all-purpose "Turks," all accounts with Natives turned to Indians, and distinctions between Turk and Native shrunk to infidels. As suggested earlier, defeat of Turks became standard fare for the British and American theatre, and Barker's evocation through Smith creates an expectation in the audience that another tawny race will meet with white suppression. Even before Smith's recollection, we have been prepared for the hero's personal history by Walter, who impresses the Irishman Larry with the captain's exploits: "O! 'twould have made your blood frisk in your veins to have seen him in Turkey and Tartary; when he made the clumsy infidels dance to the music of his broad sword!" (120). If it is Rolfe who most directly unveils the English phallus before the trembling Pocahontas, Smith has his own, that sword that tamed the Muslims of the Ottoman empire and the Caucasus. Taming Indians and taming Turks are the same act, Barker proclaims, but lest the play suggest a reading that Smith is not "man" enough in his defeat of a people reputed to be sodomites,[55] Walter's final song restores the mythology of Smith's conquering to the context of saving women. "Captain Smith is a man of might,/In Venus' soft wars or in Mars' bloody fight" (159). Walter retells Smith's ritual combat, described in the *True Travels*, of his killing of three Turks in Transylvania, followed by his winning the hearts of Tragibizandy, a Turkish woman, and Calamata, a woman in Russia. The song concludes with mention of the last of his three female rescuers, Pocahontas. Thus while we do not observe Smith on stage in love patter, we recognize that his military defeat of the Indians includes within it the captain's beheading of those other tawnies, the Turks, and a conquering of women whose reception of the European (and prospective American) replays the same story in theatrical Virginia. Fore-play and sword-play conquer copper-colored Others on stage, clearing the way for the play about those forms of play to triumph.

Barker's reading of Smith, filtered and transformed through Colman and innumerable other plays of whites conquering Asians, is that history is less war and negotiation and more sex and theatre, and that the representation of sex on stage, tied to the potential consumption of the Native virgin, should be both coy and conquering. As a performance before a flesh-and-blood audience that includes women and as a text that imagines those female spectators as so many Mademoiselle Lamberciers, *The Indian Princess* seeks to please the taste even as it provides a titillating vehicle for rendering history as popular culture. Despite the lightness of songs and scenes – qualities that Eugene Jones claims negate any seriousness to the entertainment – the message of the play is that the phallic permeates not only love and war, but theatre and imperialism as well.[56] Barker imagines women not as female warriors or militant republicans but as soothing saviors of both the national enterprise and his dramatic reputation, provided they offer their bodies, through the metonym of the glowing bosom, as vulnerable protectors of hero and play. At the same time, he conflates white woman and Native, a comic juncture that depends on the Native's conversion to the former. From the perspective of *The Indian Princess*, a drama about Native American history is nothing other than an elaborate fore-play, linking audience desire, authorial infantile sexuality, and imperial history in an endlessly repeated moment in which Native – and natal – innocence is teasingly consumed in an erotics of power. To this Barker owes more to the sexual themes of late eighteenth-century British plays like *Inkle and Yarico* and the theatrical characterization of Turks, Asians, and other people of color than he does to his putative source, Captain Smith's *Generall Historie* or to the actual lives of living Natives. Nevertheless, in a theatrical discourse that elides differences among Turks, Moors, Central Asians, Bengalis, and Native Americans, the playwright conveys to the American stage a political message that solidifies American identity as of overwhelming whiteness, capable of absorbing color without displaying any palpable mark of difference.

9

American stage Irish in the early republic

I F AT LEAST PARTLY INHABITED BY STAGE NORTH AFRICANS AND stage Natives, the early national American stage, like the late eighteenth-century London theatre, was home to Irish characters of all sorts. A few American playwrights before 1825 created Irish characters for their dramas, the subject of this chapter, but as with other ethnic types, the vast majority of plays featuring stage Irish figures were British (in the sense that they appeared in London before Philadelphia). Until the vogue for Irish stereotypes took control of the stage in the 1830s and 1840s, American playwrights were more likely to evoke other types first, notably the Yankee and the stage African, although in the English theatre, the man or woman of Ireland had been the comic foreigner of choice for a century.[1] By the mid-nineteenth century, home-grown Irish types proliferated in the American theatre and would continue in the playhouse and on the cinema screen for the next hundred years.[2] With Dion Boucicault, Irish comic characters on the American stage earned some measure of cultural stature and favorable critical commentary. Very little, though, has been said about the figuration of Irish types in American drama before the 1820s.[3] Even so, American playwrights in the early republic did employ Irish characters, and a few turned to the image of the brogue-speaking, moderately foolish type that was later absorbed into the more outrageous and coarsely delineated Paddy. Without the obvious kinds of external stimuli to provoke certain types, as the Americans captive in North Africa or the ongoing frontier wars with Indians might have prompted plays on those topics, the question raised by the appearance of stage brogue characters in American plays is the appeal such representations have for the American theatre. One of the peculiarities of Irish characters on stage, whether in Britain or the United States, centers on why such characters appear in contexts where situation logic would not call for them. As one scholar remarks of a play by George Colman the

Elder, one whose performance brought down catcalls of displeasure from Irish spectators and their English sympathizers, "Reading *The Oxonian in Town* today, it is difficult to see why Colman made [certain characters] Irish at all."[4] Something in theatrical logic called to playwrights in London to insert Irish characters, even at the risk of offending patrons. Given the power of London favorites in determining American tastes, it was inevitable that some American playwright, whatever the subject of the drama, would trot out a Patrick, if for no other reason than to test his efficacy before republican spectators.

As inherited from British drama, the Irish type covered a range of characters from the savage to the sentimental. Some of the earlier (late seventeenth- and early to mid-eighteenth-century) representations emphasized the crudeness of the Irish when placed next to the English. For Maurice Bourgeois, this type of stage Irish figure is one who:

> habitually bears the general name of Pat, Paddy or Teague. He has an atrocious Irish brogue, perpetual jokes, blunders and bulls in speaking and never fails to utter, by way of Hibernian seasoning, some wild screech or oath of Gaelic origin at every third word: he has an unsurpassable gift of blarney and cadges for tips and free drinks. His hair is of a fiery red: he is rosy-cheeked, massive, and whiskey loving. His face is one of simian bestiality with an expression of diabolical archness ... In his right hand he brandishes a stout blackthorn or a sprig of shillelagh, and threatens to belabour therewith the daring person who will tread on the tails of his coat.[5]

The more bestial type waxed and waned in both British and American theatres but was not the first choice of American playwrights in the new republic. Instead, authors in the United States tended to be attracted more to the clumsy speaker of accented English, the spouter of "bulls" or "blunders," whose "wild Irish" viciousness was fully curtailed or redirected into socially safe channels. By the 1780s and 1790s, when American playwrights first make substantial use of Irish characters, language functioned as the chief ethnic denominator on stage. For an Irish character, a *bull* is "a metaphorical statement stressing apparent connections which are not real" while a *blunder* is a "confusion of the Gaelic speaker who doesn't fully grasp the meaning of English words."[6] In either case, linguistic ineptitude marks the Irish character as a substandard speaker, different, an Other from the speakers of "proper" stage English. Related to the ways in which British playwrights created a "British" identity by marking off characters who sought entrance into the sphere of London Englishness but could not be fully absorbed, American playwrights must have found a similar attractiveness in Irish stereotypes for creating their own national identity.[7]

Several British plays with comic stage Irish figures made their way to American boards or American bookshelves in the late eighteenth century. Judith Sargent Murray, for example, might have seen Frances Brooke's comic opera *Rosina; or, Love in a Cottage* in Boston in 1794. That play features two Irish laborers who are accused of being lazy but who rescue the heroine, Rosina, from abduction. Other British dramas she and her contemporaries might have encountered from among the many that appeared in America, either on stage or in text, include Charles Macklin's *Love a-la-Mode* (1759) and *The True Born Irishman* (also called *The Irish Fine Lady*) (1762); David Garrick's *The Irish Widow* (1772); John O'Keeffe's popular *The Poor Soldier* and its sequel, *Patrick in Prussia*; and William Macready's *The Irishman in London* (1793).[8] In addition to plays, American playwrights probably heard any number of popular songs ('Paddy O'Blarney') or saw various skits or light entertainments ('Paddy Bull's Expedition') whose primary appeal was a comic Irish theme, motif, or character. Early republican playwrights could have encountered Irish stereotypes in almanacs, which in the early republic leavened their pages with comic Teagues and Paddys.[9] They probably also knew various expressions that made things labeled *Irish* a source of scorning amusement, most imported from British usage: "go to an Irish wedding" for empty a cesspool, or "Irish spoon" for shovel.[10] Whatever their own personal experience with Irish immigrants or persons of Irish descent – and there were modest but growing Irish populations already in Massachusetts, New York, and Pennsylvania – American dramatic authors would have come to associate things Irish *on stage* with comedy rooted in accent and language; alleged ethnic traits connected to crude desires and habits, homesickness and rusticity; and unthinking sentimentality.[11]

The Georgian theatre often served as a contested space for ethnic representation, particularly in identifying nationalities or ethnicities that were directly incorporated within the revived term *Britain*. As Michael Ragussis has observed, the contests over such depictions often provoked loud criticism, even near riots, when one group resented another's portrayal, or when spectator majorities – usually English – rose up and expelled ethnic others, including Jews and Scots, from their midst. But for Ragussis that same theatre also allowed for means to question the hardness of ethnic delineators, to create a space in which a play could, even in the guise of presenting an outrageous stereotype of Scot or Irish, resist the commonly held type or deconstruct it. One of the most popular plays in London and in colonial and early national theatres in America, Macklin's *Love a-la-Mode*, serves as a "paradigm" in which multiple ethnic characters, including an Irishman, a Jew, and a Scot, all confront the matter of their difference from London-defined Britishness. The Irish and Scottish characters "are neither fully assimilated as Englishmen nor fully at home in their native cultures"; they possess "a kind of double identity," at once seemingly comic, as brogue speakers fight over who speaks the best English, but destabilizing – the play was disliked by the German-speaking George II, perhaps on the grounds of its calling attention to the near impossibility of assimilation for anyone with an accent.[12] If Macklin, himself an Irish native who changed his name, his pronunciation, and his dress to be accepted in London, could at the same time raise questions about the cost of such transformation, he also must have seen the limits to stage resistance. As Paul Goring responds to Ragussis, the Georgian theatre "also had an immense capacity for counterresistance," muffling the very opportunities the theatre offered for querying the ways in which ethnic minorities could be incorporated into the trope of Great Britain.[13] Both resistance to the limitations imposed by theatrical types and counter-resistance to any changes to those types, then, migrate to the American strand and carry their potentialities to American theatres.

The first American-authored play written for the stage with Irish characters is Thomas Forrest's *The Disappointment* (1767), a ballad opera that was slated for production in Philadelphia but pulled by the producer, David Douglass, when the local objects of the play's satire objected to its performance. Published in 1767 under the pseudonym Andrew Barton and in a revised version in 1796, the play had no second chance and never reached the stage.[14] Among its variety of ethnic types appear three Irish characters: a cooper, Trushoop ("truss hoop"); his wife; and his servant, Terence. Trushoop is one of several dupes – the others include the Scottish tailor, McSnip, and compatriots, the ethnically inscribed but uncertain Raccoon and the ethnically undesignated barber, Washball – who fall for a plot to dig up Blackbeard's treasure.[15] In his construction of Trushoop, Forrest employs stock elements of Irishness borrowed from contemporary British plays. The barrel maker uses a stage brogue that marks him as a superstitious sentimentalist: "Arra, my dear"; "The devil doubt you, my dear honey"; "oh hon'acree"; "By my shoul!" (*TD* 57, 58). But he also shows traits of an older Irish stereotype, the wild man with a club, as he beats his own Irish servant: "By my showl, I'll give you shelaley, so I would." Terence, for his part in this latter scene, resorts to a familiar stage bull: "Master, dare, laave off, for shure I was aslape when I heard you call" (62). In the end, his cupidity and ignorance exposed by the characters who have played an elaborate jest on the treasure diggers, Trushoop turns matchmaker and successfully urges Washball to bless the marriage of the barber's daughter, Lucy, and the stock young man, Meanwell. Though his ignorance is fully apparent, in the end Trushoop's sentimentality furthers the positive outcome of the love plot. As David Mays rightly summarizes, "Trushoop is nothing more than one of a long line of 'Irishmen' who have amused English and American audiences for centuries, and who bear little resemblance to their ethnic prototypes" (18). As such, though, he is no more ethnically determined than any of Forrest's other characters, no more a dupe or fool, and allowed to participate positively in the comic outcome. If he is conventional, Trushoop nonetheless is not marked for special scorn or abuse, as Irish often are in eighteenth-century British plays; he is a type among types, part of Forrest's ethnic stew of dupes and dupers or what Ragussis refers to among British plays as a "multi-ethnic spectacle."[16] In other words, Irish is not English but is part of colonial America's colorful mixture of types.

In the case of Forrest, one answer to the question of why use an Irish character is simple. Like almost all American dramatists before 1825, he was an amateur playwright whose only models were plays he had read or seen performed; in Philadelphia Forrest could have seen productions put on by David Douglass and his troupe of traveling British actors. Just four weeks before *The Disappointment* was scheduled to be performed, for example, the American Company mounted Thomas Sheridan's *The Brave Irishman; or Captain O'Blunder*.[17] To be sure, Sheridan's play features a shillelagh-carrying, brogue-speaking Irishman, Captain O'Blunder, who is duped by Cheatwell; has his own Irish servant, Terence; but ends up winning the English girl, Lucy[18] – not a precise parallel to Trushoop but close enough in details to suggest an influence on Forrest. In comedies and in nameless afterpieces and farces, the laughable Irishman was a staple of the eighteenth-century stage. To be sure, some Irish immigrants lived in Pennsylvania in the 1760s; according to one documentary source, there was a real-life Irish cooper who served as the model for Trushoop (*TD* 5). But as in so many plays, the theatre is often a more potent influence than reality; the accents, the expressions, the bulls, the sighing, and shillelagh-wagging all come from a stage tradition that Forrest, as an Englishman in America, was trying to emulate.

Something of the same thing might be said of William Dunlap's *Darby's Return*. Based as it was on the musical play by John O'Keeffe, *The Poor Soldier*, Dunlap's comic sketch was short and aimed to capitalize on the immense popularity of its source. *Darby's Return* is a gently satiric look at a soldier who has traveled abroad, including in America right after the Revolution, and come back to his Irish village; it evokes a stereotype for popular effect, while at the same time it serves as a propaganda vehicle for the new republic of 1789. Dunlap also used Irish figures in *The Glory of Columbia: Her Yeomanry!* (1803); *Yankee Chronology* (1812); and *A Trip to Niagara* (1828). In *The Glory*, for instance, Dennis O'Bogg is a comic soldier in the British army who is captured by Americans, then turned into an American soldier at the siege of Yorktown. In this case, the Irish character plays the unassimilated newcomer, misguided at first by being in the conscripted British military, then redirected to new American values when he changes uniform. At the end of the sketch, he wears American patriotic garb, but he is still stage Irish, still speaking the language of the outsider. Dunlap's July Fourth vehicle – revived on holidays for fifty years – is a revision of his serious drama *André*, a play without any Irish character; O'Bogg speaks brogue and bulls and does his part to turn a tragedy into a comedy. Both Forrest and Dunlap were seeking for clues to theatrical success, and in observing what was popular with urban American audiences, both playwrights turned to Irish characters for instant comic effects. The American writers offered to readers and spectators the possibility for those laughable figures to be included in a national comic ending even as they held out little hope that Trushoop or O'Bogg will ever lose the linguistic marker of difference.[19]

Following Forrest's unproduced *The Disappointment* and Dunlap's staged comic opera interlude, other American playwrights imported Irish characters into their texts for the new national stage. One of the first full-length plays from this period to feature an Irish character is John Murdock's *The Triumphs of Love*, written in 1794 and first produced in Philadelphia in 1795 but removed from the Chestnut Street Theatre repertoire after one performance. As Heather Nathans has fully explained, Murdock came to the theatre with a background neither from the theatrical world nor from the cultural elite; he was a hairdresser by trade, a "mechanic," and represented a challenge to the Philadelphia elites who controlled the stage. Such a background gave the playwright a different perspective, since he may have associated with Irish workers in a greater degree of familiarity than other playwrights who came from employer-class backgrounds.[20] Murdock generates the bulk of his humor from a recently arrived servant to the United States, Patrick. His ineptitude leads his employer, Peevish, to call him a "blundering Irish fool" and "that Irish, buffleheaded blockhead"; indeed, Patrick's bulls and brogue mark him as fully within the stock type of British drama.[21] Murdock, however, exposes Peevish's peevishness as an employer and allows Patrick to defy type by being a notably sober Irishman; he even succeeds in marrying the Anglo-American servant girl, Jenny. As the angry Peevish is chastened in love and grows more civil toward his servant, Patrick rises in status. In the end, American democracy is touted as Peevish agrees to set up Patrick in the grocery business. Naturally, Patrick weeps with joy at the news and blurts to Mr. and Mrs. Peevish, "Blessings on both your swate shouls" (*TL* 78).

Although the play as much criticizes anti-Irish attitudes as it fosters a stage type and deserves credit for this small advance, Murdock points to a persistent problem with the portrayal of Irish characters: they are almost always in subordinate roles. As a consequence, Patrick's success, while significant, is muted by being set in a play largely about elites pursuing their love interests. The message of the social-climbing servant may have been lost on its audience – or, as in Nathans's view, seen as too democratic for a theatre audience largely used to a more complete subordination of Irish characters in British models.[22] It may be notable that Patrick operates in a milieu that includes an African American servant, Sambo, whose drunkenness engenders a kind of scorn that even the oft-abused Patrick rarely experiences. Patrick rises, in essence, at the expense of Sambo, and thus his ethnicity serves to mark him as below elite but absorbable in the larger republican world. For Sambo, no such absorption is predicted, even though his owner eventually frees him from slavery.

Murdock writes both in and against the Irish stereotype tradition, resisting and imitating. On the one hand, Patrick declares his station by his language; on the other, he achieves some modicum of freedom from bound labor, even if he must depend on his abusing employer to succeed. Murdock thus works in the paradigm evoked by Dunlap in *Darby's Return*: to establish in the context of a play to what extent an Irish serving-class character can see himself as an American. In other plays, including Judith Sargent Murray's *The Traveller Returned* (1796) and James Nelson Barker's *The Indian Princess* (1808), American writers shape their Irish characters as naifs, from whom a certain amount of humor may be struck.[23] Where the American play draws from a clear source text, dramatists often amend or add an Irish character who does not belong in the original. In the early republican plays, an off-the-boat Irish lower character – for example, Patrick O'Neal in *Traveller* and Larry in *Indian Princess* – conjures up the image of his home country as the land of potatoes and simplicity in contrast to the confusing but tempting America he finds himself in. A Patrick is a comic figure, a contrast to his serious betters; he gets into scrapes but comes out more or less unscathed at the end. Whether Patrick in these other plays, however, can become an American, as Murdock suggests can happen, remains to be seen.

Again, context creates possibilities or determines limitations. In Murdock, the presence of an Irish servant to an Anglo-American elite family in a social comedy would not be unusual, particularly one that emphasizes social mobility, but in *Traveller Returned* and *Indian Princess*, the contexts, while not completely unlikely, do not demand such a character as much as that in *Triumphs of Love*. Both Murray and Barker deal with American history and raise questions of national identity; therefore, even though Murray and Barker may be trying for popularity by evoking a stock comic type, the plays inevitably must include the Irish characters in their larger expositions on identity. In Murray's play, the return to America by Rambleton, his arrest, his appearance before a patriot committee of safety, and the revelations to his family of his true identity as Montague, described earlier, mark the main plot crisis. Patrick, the Irishman, enters the scene as Rambleton's serving man and plays his role largely in the low subplot. Beyond providing comic relief, Patrick's being Irish has no direct relevance to the workings of the main narrative, except to provide to an audience made up predominantly of Anglo-Americans an easily accepted excuse for the character's credulity.

Barker's Larry appears as one of the company of adventurers who have landed in Virginia to start that colony. Captain Smith is the theme hero, enunciating a theory of empire and remaining above the comic elements; Larry plays a small, supporting role in the business of nation-building but spends more time wishing he were with his love, Katy Maclure, and in the pastoral setting of the green isle. When Katy appears in Virginia, cross-dressed, the Irishman is first fooled, then delighted with this turn of affairs. As with Patrick's in *Traveller Returned*, Larry's Irishness has no direct bearing on anything having to do with the chief conflict in the play – in this case, between Natives and Europeans. He is there to add stage variety to what in the history of Jamestown is originally an ethnically homogeneous set of colonizers, whose chief distinctions (as presented in Smith's *Generall Historie*) are measured in strength of character and social class.

If, however, we consider the plays to be engaged with questions of national identity formation, then other attitudes than simply stage amusement must necessarily color an interpretation of Irish characters on the early American stage. For writers like Murray and Barker, the comic Irish figure serves as a laughable other, a not-quite-Anglo-American whose ties to the old country mark him as a new colonial.[24] In this sense, the Irishman is akin to Andrew the Hebridean, the provincial Scot whose first days in America are the source of some humor in Crèvecoeur's *Letters from an American Farmer*.[25] For Crèvecoeur, Andrew's peasant ways do not immediately translate to the American scene. After several comic episodes, including one in which he interprets some friendly Indian visitors as wild savages about to kill him, Andrew begins to shed his European narrowness for the expanded sensibility that Crèvecoeur identifies as American. He will eventually become one of those amalgamated Americans the author celebrates in the early letters, a transplanted being who learns the benefits of landholding and freedom. In the happy resolution of Andrew's immigration and settlement, Crèvecoeur implies that the Hebridean will accommodate to the new surroundings and enter a "new race of beings," the Americans.

Like the Scots, Irish immigrants, by virtue of English perception of their dialect, were seen as fair game for the amusement of Anglo-Americans. Even more than the Scots, though, Irish persons were depicted as victims of passion or poverty. Ireland had been colonized by the English for centuries, often by brutal means, and with the military defeat of Stuart sympathizers at the Battle of the Boyne in 1690, much of its population had been reduced to subsistence agriculture and grudging political acquiescence. For many Americans, memories of their own colonial experience and their successful throwing off the yoke were still fresh in 1796 and 1808. As William Williams remarks, "It is ironic, therefore, that Americans, who had freed themselves from British colonial rule, would have embraced so readily a stereotype of the Irish that had its roots in British imperialism and undemocratic concepts of class."[26] For Anglo-Americans, the Irishman may have been perceived to be to them as Yankee Doodle was to the pre-war colonizing English – a provincial whose narrow self-interest, colloquial speech, and overall ineptitude allow the dominant type to display cultural superiority through satire. In turn, this identification would have provided theatre-going Americans with a tacit, if not too overtly stated, alignment to English culture, allowing them, like their London cousins, to make the Teague a perpetual outsider, fit for service in a limited way, but certainly unfit to lead. American drama, then, would say to its audience: We as a rising people are not English, in the sense of corrupted European, but we can see ourselves as inheritors of English culture and thus superior to the still struggling Irish.

From her source text, Richard Cumberland's *The West Indian*, Murray might have gotten the idea to include an Irishman. Cumberland included one Irish character, Captain O'Flaherty, who in David Garrick's production at Drury Lane was played by John Moody, thought to be the leading actor of Irish roles in his day. Interestingly, despite the fact that the other major characters in Murray's play have analogues in Cumberland's, O'Flaherty bears little overt relation to Patrick. The captain has some humorous lines, but not the farcical Irish bulls, those often ludicrous contradictions that come to mark the type; he is a man of high moral purpose, bravery, and loyalty to his friends – in short, a gentleman and a soldier. As he explains in his *Memoirs*, Cumberland had made a point of resisting the broad stereotype of the Irishman so prevalent on the London stage in his time.[27] The playwright told his producer, Garrick, that he would use his real-life observations of Irish in Galway to flesh out O'Flaherty, with the implication that he would resist employing only previous stage characters as models.[28] This is not to deny stereotypical aspects to O'Flaherty or even to suggest that other British playwrights did not resist the type (Sir Callaghan O'Brallaghan in Macklin's earlier *Love a-la-Mode* is a tested soldier who speaks without heavy brogue, for instance, and even Captain O'Blunder wins his girl in Sheridan's *Brave Irishman*),[29] but only to note that Cumberland's character was created to stand out and to do so in such a way as not to threaten English audiences by this shift in expectation. Murray, in making changes to her model, must have been very conscious of the need to exploit a particular kind of Irishman in her play that would not allow the dignity Cumberland assigns to his captain.

Unlike O'Flaherty, Patrick is a servant, lazy, careless, and sentimental, never to be taken as a character with any more integrity or conscience than what he displays in his unthinking and clumsy loyalty to his master. His stage lineage may be the Teague, the Plautine tricky servant dressed in Irish clothes by English playwrights, but he lacks cunning or inclination to plot anything devious or mischievous.[30] By place references (the borough of Killmallock and the counties of Limerick and Cork) and calls to St. Patrick, he seems to be from southern Ireland and of Catholic origin. Given that most Irish in America in the mid-1790s were probably Protestant,[31] these details identify him as even more foreign than his dialect would reveal, although religion never enters overtly in the play as an issue. Because twice he expresses the wish that he had the 'white boys' with him, invoking the Irish peasant vigilantes who organized for violent opposition to the landlords, we can further assume his own humble origins. His name suggests the Patrick of *The Poor Soldier* and *Patrick in Prussia* and is a direct echo of Sir Patrick O'Neale, a brogue but dignified character in Garrick's *The Irish Widow*.[32] Yet none of these sources provide direct models for the hard-drinking, bull-spouting naif that the American author chooses to insert in her otherwise serious comedy. Indeed, Kent Gallagher notes that the American dramatic writers who follow Murray tend to reconstruct the British stage-Irish servant toward the type established here.[33]

Patrick appears in seven of the twenty-three scenes in Murray's five-act play, three each in the first and last acts. As with Murdock's Patrick, he shows up frequently enough to create comic interest, but never so much as to overwhelm the action. In Act I, scene 1,[34] he follows Rambleton with the sailors and trunks, and his first speech quickly reveals the type that Murray wants to portray: 'Ow, may I never see my own sweet country again, if I did not think this *land* of America had been all *salt water*, d'ye see, we were so long in finding it. Arrah now, *while we are standing here*, by my soul, we may as *well be looking after a place to rest our-shelves* in, so we may' (*TR* 105). Nostalgic, simple-minded, given to unintended contradictory remarks, and without motivation for labor, the dialect-speaking Irish servant reveals all his essential traits in one short speech. Unlike the Patrick in *Triumphs of Love*, this one shows no ambition nor attempts any significant action to establish himself on American soil. Except for the first, nostalgia, the other characteristics – simple-mindedness, verbal confusions, lassitude, and marked use of dialect – also distinguish another type, the stage African American servant. Take away one other, shiftlessness, and the remaining traits help identify a third type, the stage Yankee. Thus, we can begin to see a relationship implied among these three established theatrical figures – Irish, African, Yankee – as they bear the comic burden of American playwriting until the Civil War. To some extent, then, the inclusion of one or another of these types may only be convenience for a playwright looking for any stock comic figure to lighten a scene.[35] Nevertheless, because each of the types plays to a different sense of insider–outsider status, each has its own role to play in the declaration of identity.

Unlike her chief source, Cumberland, or her contemporary Murdock, Murray does not use black servant characters in her play. However, she does use a Yankee servant, Obadiah, of the Jonathan school,[36] whose misapprehensions and mispronunciations provide light moments during one scene. Obadiah is no more competent than Patrick, speaks English with difficulty, and appears largely for a gag. Of the serving-class characters, however, Patrick appears most often. He speaks a true Irish bull in the first scene. When told they are twelve miles from Rambleton's home, Patrick responds, "Ow then, that is but a trifle, my dear: It is only *six miles a-piece*, master" (*TR* 105). As if to complete the picture, Murray has Rambleton declare that it is not time to visit his family. For Patrick, this is an impossible thing to imagine: "Arrah, get out with that, now. If Patrick O'Neal was *three thousand miles separated* from his bit of an Irish girl, he shall swing his hammock *close along side of her for all that, Honey*" (106). For Rambleton, given the conflicted nature of his marriage – we later learn that he left America because of suspicions his wife was having an affair – the choice to go slowly is based on principle. For Patrick, there is no choice, only the instinct to be as close to a woman as distance will allow.

In Act IV, Patrick is present when Rambleton receives a summons to the committee of safety. He defends his master against the officer, offering to fight with "Mr. Tipstaff" and to be arrested with Rambleton that they might rescue themselves (*TR* 135). While his loyalty is dogged, Patrick and his burlesque logic undercut what for Murray is a sober theme of the relationship between popular sovereignty, figured in the threatening committee, and the nobility of elite individuals. After Rambleton leaves, consigning Patrick to remain at the inn, the servant replies, "Arrah, then I shall stay behind; for, he that is *willian* enough not to *plase* a man in distress, ought to have been *assassinated twenty years before he was born – so he had*" (136). Such bullmaking serves to signal to the audience that Rambleton's inquisition will finally not be such that his personal safety or integrity is seriously challenged. The Irishman, by his very presence, assures the audience of the success of the main characters by his own farcical failures to make rational sense of his American experience.

His alienation from a sober sense of duty and vigilance is reinforced in the last act when Patrick enters, drunk and singing. Since this is the act in which all plot complications must be resolved, the first scene sets the tone for how the strands will be woven together. In the text, largely because he has been absent for all but one scene in the middle three acts, Patrick's "tipsy" song and his later behavior provide some counterpoint and diversion for readers observing how the theme characters make their way to realization, but does not intrude overmuch. On stage, however, in the hands of a skilled and expressive actor, Patrick could quite steal the show, even to the point of submerging the Montague family reconciliation in the aftermath of his antic behavior. In scene 3, when Patrick awakens from his alcoholic stupor to discover that his master's trunks have been robbed, he "*raves and stamps about outrageously*," in the phrasing of the stage directions, and shouts out, "Oh! murder! robbery! bloodshed! fire and thunder!" (144, 145). The broad physical gestures complement the exaggerated diction, keeping the Irishman from ever being considered as a conscious subject except in a stance of nostalgia. Having failed Rambleton by giving in to drink, Patrick makes amends by helping to identify the criminals and the stolen goods. Murray has moved him conveniently away from the scenes of reconciliation and conclusion in order to restore order and dignity to the performance. Whereas Camden, Mrs. Montague, and Rambleton have all spoken philosophically in the play about their beliefs and concerns, the Irish servant speaks no other philosophy than instinct.

In Murray's hands, Irish identity is bound up not with political, philosophical, or moral principle, expressly stated, but with unthinking proximity to land, superstition, objects of desire, and a radical simplicity in which work plays no part. Antithetical to Murray's own Protestant/Universalist ethic of utility to society and to the literacy and sophistication of the major Anglo-American characters in *The Traveller Returned*, the Irishman exemplifies an earlier stage of human development, pre-Enlightenment, pre-Reformation, pre-capitalist. In an odd way, then, while her audience no doubt laughed at Patrick because of his difference from the sober and stoical Camden, Rambleton, and Mrs. Montague, they may also have looked at him with a twinge of envy at his Hibernian naivete. Since the rebellion of 1798 has not yet occurred, and the migration of Irish to America in the author's time has been modest and largely Protestant, Murray's majority Anglo-American audience would be free to enjoy Patrick's harmless thoughtlessness. In other words, Patrick is the simple peasant that English Americans never were, almost a kind of museum exhibition, an amusing curiosity, not a person with subjecthood to threaten Anglo-American elites or to be embraced as "one of us."

Thus for Murray, the Irish servant functions to lighten the seriousness of the play simply as another comic type; at the same time, however, he plays a more thematic role linked to national identity. A generator of disorder, this non-threatening layabout drinks, dreams, and bulls his way through life, protected from harm by a class structure based on genteel manners; proper, if unpretentious speech; and patriotism that is grounded, ironically, in an English tradition of rectitude and restraint. As long as Rambletons are revealed to be the defenders of their country's interest and Camdens are seen to be the leaders of the rising generation, then the Patricks can have their place in the lower orders of society. After all, in their rural simplicity, the Irish as portrayed in Murray's comedy are incapable of intrigue or treachery. This vision befits an essentially conservative understanding of the social order. For Murray, a Federalist, the satiric dimension to *The Traveller Returned* reinforces a union of English and American cultures, including an appropriation and alteration of some of the grounding types. For all of Richard Cumberland's efforts in *The West Indian* to liberate London audiences from the prison of Irish stereotyping, Murray in Boston restores it, extending the more limited, sharply delineated type into a culture looking for definition. In other words, in her resistance to being colonized by her imitation of Cumberland, Murray in essence colonizes the Irish for the sake of an Anglophilic American nationalism. Murdock, for his part, resists such counter-colonizing. Nevertheless, despite the differences between Murray's conventional servant and Murdock's newly made shopkeeper, each author's play suffered essentially the same theatrical fate; the audiences preferred their stage Irish in the context of British plays.[37]

Between Murray's play and Barker's, the Irish rebellion brought a new dimension to American politics, the émigré republican revolutionary. Indeed, the disturbances in Ireland provoked a significant increase in migration, with an estimated 60,000 or more Irish citizens coming to the United States in the 1790s, and perhaps as many as twenty percent of those Catholic.[38] One of the Irish revolutionaries, John Daly Burk, became himself an American playwright, penning his drama about the battle of Bunker Hill while on board ship for his new homeland. Burk is the first Irish American playwright, and though he did not create Irish characters for his dramas, *Bunker-Hill* was often restaged as a patriotic vehicle. For many of the émigrés, America served as a like-minded land of rebels against English authority; arriving during the period when Americans were drawing in upon themselves and the political world was deeply divided between Francophile Democratic Republicans and Anglophile Federalists. The new immigrants brought with them a fervent republicanism that may have tipped the balance toward the party of Jefferson. By 1808, the last full year of Jefferson's second term, Irish figures were well ensconced in politics and culture. In Philadelphia, the leading publisher was the Irish native Mathew Carey; in Petersburg, Virginia, the leading theatrical figure was John Daly Burk; and wherever the republicans had relocated, former members of the United Ireland movement took active roles in cultural and political debates, including concerns over drama. As David Wilson notes, "The Irish editors of *The American Patriot* in 1803 wanted state-run theaters that would 'promote charity, reform morals, foment patriotism and refine the taste and manners of the people.'"[39] In other words, United Irish political and cultural feelings were beginning to permeate American republican thinking, particularly with regard to culture. It may have been that the new citizens wanted theatres that would be liberated from the coarse stereotypes of Irish that promised little in the way of refinement of 'taste and manners.' And while Barker's play may reflect this implied interest in a new Irish immigrant character, *Traveller Returned* certainly does little to change elite prejudices about the natives of the other British isle. In short, the comic Irishman of the type exploited by Murray in 1796 could only have been remotely related (at best) to the flesh-and-blood Irish Americans who, as fervent republicans, hoped to shape the debate on what an American stage and American identity should be.

John Minshull's *Rural Felicity*, first printed in 1801 and eventually produced by Minshull at the Grove Theatre in New York on Bedlow Street in January 1805, reflects some of the new thinking brought about by Irish republican immigration. This Patrick is a laborer who brings with him loyalties both to Ireland and to the king, but his employer, Clover, makes no assertive counter-nationalist statements about either. He knows an Irishman – "Your national character is that of being refractory," he tells Patrick – but the combination of Clover's beneficent employment and Patrick's being in America will redirect those tendencies:

> You now are in my service, and, as long as you act consistent in our Republican Government, my house is your asylum; I have no objection to your singing songs in praise of your country ... Be assured if you act improperly, you'll be marked like a sheep, to share the just reward due to arrogant intruders.

Patrick defends himself and intends to prove "that an Irishman has a heart corresponding with a noble disposition."[40] The plot rewards him, not with marking, but a bride, a sign of his earning the trust of his master and community, an outcome not unlike Murdock's. Even so, Minshull puts into Patrick's mouth some of the most incomprehensible speeches in American drama, by way of making them seem colorful Irishisms, to the point where another laborer, Cockney, criticizes him for an Irish-poverty tendency to "run away with undigested ideas" (*RF* 55). Although Minshull, like Murdock before him, seems to affirm the possibility of an Irish immigrant entering the English-heritage society of the American republic, his point of view – an apparently Anglophilic one – makes it unclear how much we can expect Patrick to transform into anything but an honest Irish laborer in the United States rather than an "American." For Minshull, "republican" includes Anglo-American patronage and paternalism rather than a demonstrable Irish American independence and ability to contribute more than brawn to the national enterprise.

The Indian Princess, meanwhile, trots out an immigrant Irishman – and a lot more besides – not mentioned by the play's putative source, Smith's *Generall Historie*.[41] Larry is lovesick for Katy, nostalgic in most speeches, and while not a servant, clearly a more comic character compared to the figures of Smith, Powhatan, Pocahontas, and Rolfe. As with Murray's inclusion of Patrick, one might ask what Barker had in mind by introducing into the English–Indian conflict a sentimental Irishman who effects no other goal than to reunite with Kate. Like his predecessors, Barker may have decided that an Irish character makes good theatre, as defined by English models, and simply added a Larry for box-office purposes. If so, Barker alone – Dunlap and his *Glory of Columbia* excepted – among playwrights mentioned here was successful in creating an Irish-character play that lasted more than a short run. After its several American productions through 1810, *Indian Princess* was produced in London in 1820 where it became the first American play to be exported to a British stage after first opening in the United States.[42] But Larry may also be an unacknowledged nod to the United Irish republicans who had become amalgamated into the American political scene. Barker himself was a Jeffersonian politician – mayor of Philadelphia at one point – and he may have created the unhistorical Larry in order to recognize the new ranks of Irish supporters of his party. He may also have been influenced by Burk, whose plays he would have known and whose book on the founding of Virginia he may have read.[43] Therefore, while Larry does not correlate with any literal historical figure, his placement in a play about the founding of the nation may have been intended as a recognition that the Irish are in fact part of the post-Revolutionary landscape – fellow revolutionaries, in fact.[44]

Even so, the development of Larry as a character is problematic. Identified in the Dramatis Personae as one of the "Europeans," Larry's station in *The Indian Princess* is somewhat higher than that of any of the Patricks, and by reference to a place name, "Ballinamoné" (Ballymenone?), he appears to be from County Fermanagh in Ulster.[45] Like his counterpart in *Traveller Returned*, Larry invokes St. Patrick and cries "Arrah" now and then, but his being a soldier, not a serving man, and his identification of home as the north, not the south, suggests that he is meant to be perceived as Protestant. His stage lineage is the Plautine braggart soldier, the *miles gloriosus*, that marks an early development of the Irish character in English drama, but as Murray does with the servant, Barker softens the soldier, domesticates him, brings him into line with the values of a new republic whose manners have been shaped by European gentility. In some ways, Larry is closer to Cumberland's O'Flaherty and rather different from the Patricks. Larry is loyal to Captain Smith as well as to his memories of Ireland and Katy. He appears in a number of scenes, often to feed questions or lines to the young Englishman, Walter (whose wife, Alice, is also unhistorically at Jamestown), or simply to be a voice among many voices. His presence in the company gives the body of colonizers a variety on stage that a strict rendition of Smith's originating text would not have done. By orientation comic, although not ludicrous, the Jamestown Irishman provides some light moments in an overall blithe treatment of the military-erotic conquest of Virginia.

In two scenes, however, Larry has some prominence. In Act I, scene 2, he converses with Walter about Captain Smith, the consistent hero of the play. As a soldier, Larry might have been cast in an older model of the stage Irishman, as a warlike character who wears crude clothes and brandishes a shillelagh.[46] As has been shown above, traces of that type appear in Forrest's character Trushoop. The tough, stick-carrying Irishman survives into later eighteenth-century drama in such plays as Garrick's *The Jubilee* (1769),[47] a wildly successful musical afterpiece that played the major American cities beginning in the 1790s.[48] Cumberland's O'Flaherty, while more refined than that type, still projects a sturdy martial bearing, as does his predecessor Sir Callaghan O'Brallaghan. Yet already in Garrick, one can observe the combination of elements – primitive power and uncertainty in the city – that mark the transition to a more gently humorous, less threatening type.

Writing well after Macklin, Garrick, and Cumberland, Barker owes his version of the Irish soldier more to the image of sentimental peasant than fearsome fighter. Larry is in awe of Smith, and asks Walter to tell more of his exploits. The Englishman relates tales of Smith's European adventures (recounted first in Smith's *True Travels*), notably the captain's combat with and killing of three Turks, 'when he made the clumsy infidels dance to the music of his broad sword!' (*IP* 120). True to the emerging type, the Irishman is less martial than his English cohort: 'Troth now, the mussulmans may have been mightily amused by the caper; but for my part I should modestly prefer skipping to the simple jig of an Irish bag-pipe' (120). In fact, in the way that Patrick in Murdock's *Triumphs of Love* is measured against the African Sambo, so Larry plays against the Turks, who, while more warlike, come across in their stage absence as "infidel" fools for challenging the English (implied Christian) soldier Smith. At the same time, Turks also conflate with Natives, one other non-Christian ethnicity to be tamed by the sword – and to whom Larry rises superior. In this case, domestic pacifism and alignment with Smith make a more practical and sensible choice than fighting for infidel religion (Turk or Native) against the white colonizer. Although part of a military band, Larry thinks not of conquest but of rural pleasures recalled from his pastoral early life. Shortly, he will be remembering Kate, and how the 'constant creature [would] carol all day about, roving through the seas and over the woods' (121). Despite his differences from the Patricks, Larry, like that character in Murray, speaks not to duty but desire, the wish to put all that is threatening beyond and seek no more than the felicity of home and field.

Later in the scene, he talks with Rolfe's servant, Robin, about home: "didn't I leave as neat a black-ey'd girl, as pretty a prolific potato-patch all in tears –". Robin then puns: 'Your potato-patch in tears! that's a bull, master Larry –". And Larry returns a pun, "You're a calf, master Robin" (*IP* 122). Shortly, Larry will sing a nostalgic song of his departure from Katy Maclure, punctuated by Gaelic cries of 'Hubbaboo–Gramachree–Hone!' (123). Like Murray, Barker lays on the typing with a trowel, spreading nostalgia, desire, rusticity, and dialect thickly, then giving his construction a last comic dollop. After the song, Larry takes out a withered potato that he had dug up before he left Ireland, recalls the siblings of the decaying tuber, and laments: 'Och! my darling, if you had come hot from the hand of Katy, how my mouth would have watered at ye; now, you divil, you bring the water into my eyes' (123). Whatever conflicts may be ahead for the more valiant English, the sight of an Irishman sobbing over an old potato can only serve to remind the audience that no bad thing will happen to the protagonists.

Unlike O'Keeffe's farmer turned soldier Darby, however, Larry is not a coward. Barker includes him among those picked to rescue Smith from his famous capture by Powhatan's men. Rolfe calls him "brave Irishman" (*IP* 129); he is one of a group who sing "a lusty roundelay" after hard labor (131); he later chides Robin for fearfulness, which Larry calls "cowardly cookery" (136); he vows with Walter to pour cold water down the "silken sleeves" of the soft-handed gentlemen who complain about having to cut trees (147); and he is part of the troop in Act V that thwarts the Indian treachery and thus saves Jamestown from ruin. Although by dialect marked as different from the rest of the men (who in a stage direction are called "the ENGLISH"), Larry, unlike Murray's Patrick, is allowed to participate in the more important scenes of the main plot.

Even so, he more prominently appears in Act III, scene 3, when Kate appears and reveals herself. In the previous scene, Pocahontas has overheard a plot by Grimosco and Miami, two disaffected Natives, to "slaughter" the whites (*IP* 153). Scene 3 opens with Larry's observation of a large supply convoy arriving at Jamestown to reinforce the troops and give some sign that the colonists will be able to persist. Unaware of the previous plotting, Larry imagines only bliss with this English show of support. The newly arrived governor and men will "make this land flow with buttermilk like green Erin," he notes to a person he presumes to be a page; then he asks, "isn't this a nice neat patch to plant potatoes – I mean, to plant a nation in?" (154) This reinforced identification of Larry with potatoes establishes that he will have a difficult time making the transition to a new American character. That is, while Barker projects Larry's settling in Virginia, it is as an Irish farmer rather than a new being to match the new landscape. His rhapsody on the new nation is quickly cut short when the page – Kate in disguise – mentions Ireland as one nation better than that being planted. Before long, Larry is exclaiming, "Tinder hearts! Och, sweet Ireland!" (155).

Katy toys with Larry, telling him in song and jest – and still in the character of a male page – about her popularity back home and how she as page has slept with the object of his affections, lying together as "close as two twin potatoes" (*IP* 156). This toying naturally fires Larry with jealousy, but one never suspects violence from such a sentimentalist. When the game is exposed and Kate appears as herself, Larry is ecstatic, and by asking Kate for a kiss, becomes a vehicle for Barker to strike a joke from an allusion to Shakespeare's *Taming of the Shrew*. At this point in *The Indian Princess*, Larry becomes his most Irish, in the sense of using dialect and being linked to the peasant stereotype. Whatever valor might be imputed to him in a group of soldiers and whatever lip service he pays to founding a nation, Barker's seeming acknowledgment of Irish republicans in the audience, Larry quickly reverts to type in scenes where he is a principal figure. Barker means the Irishman as a contrast to Smith and the other English leaders; he's a follower for whom brogue and bog are nearly ineluctable signs of identity. The playwright tries to make Larry serve two competing ends: the "brave" Irish member of the American national founding and thus a good republican; and the comic stage Irishman, present in the play for laughs.

Unlike Larry, Kate does not speak with a brogue; rather, her language is gendered in a nineteenth-century sentimentalism that is meant to evoke sympathy, not laughs, from her audience. Katy reminds Larry that she stayed in Ireland to care for her sick mother, who has since died; and that she was finally able to come to America by caring for a lady (Geraldine, Percy's lover) whose carriage had broken down before her "humble cabin" and who needed a companion in her voyage to Virginia (*IP* 156). Barker clarifies one dimension of the type not dealt with by Murray: that the stage Irishman is a man only, and that like the Indian princess with her people, the Irish female character is closer at this point of stage development to English womanhood than to Irish maleness. One sees this strategy in *The Irish Widow*. Garrick has his Widow Brady speak brogue only as a strategy to discourage her old lover, whereas her father speaks a full brogue always. In Murdock, Patrick weds an English girl, Jenny, which, while a mark of assimilation, also indicates that love objects for Irish men are rarely themselves as Irish as they. As is Pocahontas for Indians and Europeans, the Irish female is seen in Barker's play as a mediating figure, bringing English domestic values to America to modify the exaggerated sensibility and naivete of the Irish male.

Therefore, at the end of the play, with the Indian rebellion against the whites suppressed, Powhatan neutered, and Pocahontas affianced to Rolfe, Larry and Katy join the company to sing the finale, "Freedom, on the western shore." Barker provides what must have looked like a vision of a pan-ethnic harmony, united under the banner of an Anglicized political culture and Americanized social values based on home and hearth.[49] Larry is allowed the last solo verse, calling to Katy to live "without formality" or what "in Irish" is named "Hospitality" (*IP* 165). Indeed, the theme of the play, figured in the marriage of Rolfe and Pocahontas, is the welcoming of the land, in the allegory of interracial marriage, for imperial conquest.

Lest that theme of *translatio imperii* be thought too heavy to sit upon the audience for long, Larry enunciates a simpler, more limited desire than the broad view spoken by Smith: to live with his love, without concern over the great issues of the day.

In *Triumphs of Love, Traveller Returned, Rural Felicity,* and *Indian Princess*, the Irishman provides a good deal of comedy, played off against the straighter, standard-English speaking sobriety of the main characters. Murdock, Murray, Minshull, and Barker make room for the Irishman in an American polity, but they also assert that the characteristics of male Irishness are not entirely consonant with the great themes of national independence, Anglo-American cultural hegemony, and the course of empire, even though Murdock, at least, tries to rewrite the themes. Although a British play like Macklin's *True-Born Irishman*, one that failed in London but had relative success in the United States, shows how one can keep dignity and Irishness by mocking the attempts of Mrs. Diggerty to become English, few American plays go quite as far in affirming Irish nationalism.[50] In essence, despite some tendencies in the opposite direction, American dramatists write against Crèvecoeur, hinting that the Irishman will never quite lose his peasant simplicity or his brogue even if, as in Murdock and Minshull, he gains some economic success. Rather, the nature of American republicanism, as depicted in these nationalist plays, almost demands a typecast underclass, in order to preserve something of a hierarchy in the American social experiment. The plays validate principle and conquest, while recognizing that the common people – depicted in the plays as Irish – will bow before that superiority in order to live their lives of quaint diction, tear-inducing potatoes, and simple desire for rustic pleasures near to hand. However, it should also be said that among the authors that employ the confining stereotype, Barker differs from Murray by providing a more positive model, a man capable of rising up at the right moment in a fight, even if he is not allowed to accept hero status. That no doubt reflects the political shift towards Jeffersonianism that has occurred in the dozen years that separate the two plays.

In essence, Barker and Murray, along with Murdock and Minshull, tame democracy for the elite, reminding the audience that the white-skinned Irish can safely be absorbed into the country because their mooning, apolitical ethnicity will keep them in their comic place.[51] Unlike Anglo-American stage Yankees, particularly those that come after Jonathan in Royall Tyler's *The Contrast*, who are often seen as cunning or sharp; unlike stage Indians, whose only hope for perpetuation is through absorption into a completely whitened identity (Pocahontas's marriage to Rolfe); and unlike stage Africans whose resolute otherness in color and speech draws mockery and abuse (as in Samuel Woodworth's 1825 *The Forest Rose*), the stage Irishman by 1808 has become "lovable" as a type because he also embraces qualities that make him pitiable, even as he resists normative values of hard work and Anglo-Saxon political philosophy. Audiences, eager for a comic character whom they can laugh at and feel sorry for at the same time, might have found the brogue Irishman an appealing spectacle in a play otherwise aimed at celebrating an emerging American identity. His presence allows room for theatrical spectators to feel pleased to welcome the immigrant who will not challenge the status quo or the elite privilege of established Americans.

But as history would prove, real Irish were not that tractable. The image of the uninvolved, brogue-speaking lover of potatoes and black-eyed girls, created by dramatists in the first decades of the republic, served for a century to reassure white elites that there was a comic ethnic buffer between themselves and darker, more threatening races in their midst. Murdock and Barker go further than Murray in recognizing the importance of Irish Americans to the development of a republican United States; their characters have more dignity and owe less to the well-worn stereotype used by the Boston writer. In the end, though, both Murdock and Barker succumb to stage tradition in the general delineation of the Irish immigrant to the new world. Few playwrights after Barker would resist the apparent demand for the stage Irish type, dressed in American garb; even Eugene O'Neill could not help but continue many of the characteristics assigned to Irish characters in early American plays. Nevertheless, the increased immigration, political involvement, and religious influence of later generations of Irish only served to show that the romanticized and domesticated theatrical type was nothing more than a trope of the stage. That trope, however, one forged in what Goring calls the "counterresistance" of theatre to alter a type, may have determined the course of a prejudice against the Irish in American society that lasted nearly as long as the stage Irishman in American theatres.

At the same time, these early attempts to translate British stereotypes into American characters show elements of resistance that complicate the matter of identities in America. If by virtue of British stage traditions, Irish as characters in American plays never quite escape the confinement of a comic type, they suggest that determining identity must take them into account. At the most simplistic level, English ancestored elites may simply see Irish on stage as representatives of a necessary laboring other, good for a laugh and the laundry, but figures whom one also incorporates into thinking about the perils of American democracy. At a more complex one, Irish as members of a founding national enterprise or Irish as free individuals capable of running their own shops or managing cultural affairs disturb the homogeneity of British American national construction. As with stage Africans, stage Irish prove ineradicable from the theatre, a necessary component for theatrical popularity in comedy and an increasingly significant dimension of American demographics. Persons of Irish descent no doubt grew tired of the drunken, bull-blathering fool in the theatre, but they also knew that his very presence on stage in even the most grotesque typing meant Irish Americans could not be ignored, either, in determining what exactly an American was.

10

Black theatre, white theatre, and the stage African

On March 4, 1801, Maria and Harriet Trumbull, the teenaged daughters of the Connecticut governor, were strolling about New York as part of their first extended visit to that city. They took in a variety of sights and experiences that day, including the inauguration celebration for Thomas Jefferson, which, as good Federalist girls, they were quick to deplore, but which, as country girls in the big city, they were sure to take in. At some point in their peregrinations, which included Chambers Street, where they stayed; Broadway, near the Park Theatre, where the inauguration procession traversed; and Vauxhall Gardens, just off Broadway, where the fireworks were launched, they noted in passing a curiosity to which they would have been unaccustomed in their home state: "they had a new play at the African Theatre."[1] What play? What theatre? On this, Maria's letter home is silent; after all, her parents held firmly to the antitheatrical sentiments of many in New England, despite the professional theatres in Boston and Hartford, and the girls were cautious when writing home in indicating their attendance at stage entertainments. But her one little clause tells us a great deal: Some time before March 4, 1801, a group of African Americans in New York City had banded together to put on plays, perhaps even "new" plays of their own devising, in a building that locals referred to as the "African Theatre." Such an enterprise must have been intended to provide several things: entertainment to the growing black population on Manhattan Island, an outlet for acting when African Americans were prohibited from the Park stage and other "white" theatres, and quite possibly a venue where the stereotypes of blacks, so prevalent in the British American playhouses of the day, might be overcome or made a point of amusement through metatheatrical mockery. Until new evidence about this theatre arises from the documentary record, we can only speculate. All we have from

211

Maria Trumbull is the subsequent comment, "what *silly* fools the new Yorkers are."

With recent research, however, we do know more about a later experiment, the African Theatre of 1821–1823, and its chief actor, James Hewlett.[2] Long considered to be the first black theatre in America, the African Theatre founded by William Alexander Brown cannot be regarded any longer as such, but the story is a compelling one nonetheless; if anything, the scant evidence of an earlier theatre suggests how persistent blacks' desires had been to act on stage and to create a theatrical experience that met the lives of black people in that city. In the later African Theatre, as has already been suggested above with *The Poor Soldier*, the company put on familiar plays in unfamiliar ways; in addition, they put on new plays, like *King Shotaway*, one that dealt with a Carib uprising on St. Vincent's island in the Caribbean, or plays in which slave selling or slave rebellion was featured, as in the Charleston market scene the company added to *Tom and Jerry* or the revolt of Jack against West Indian planters in *Obi, or Three-Fingered Jack*.[3] Hewlett himself studied the actors at the Park and billed himself as "Shakespeare's proud representative," playing Richard III and Hamlet.[4] As heroic as Hewlett's story is, however, he could resist but not stem the rising tide of racism that threatened so many attempts by blacks to assert themselves in the economy and culture of the new republic. Even Irish young men, themselves victims of ethnic prejudice, expressed their anger by "throwing stones at black churches and physically harassing black people on the city streets" as ways of affirming their "whiteness."[5]

Curiously, one of the spectators at a Hewlett performance was the English comedian Charles Mathews, who saw Hewlett's act as a source of new material. Hewlett had no doubt seen Mathews act as well, and used Mathews's "At Home" model himself, whereby the single actor would take on numerous characters. Back in London, Mathews revised his act to add American material gleaned from his tour, including that of a black actor playing Hamlet, whom he called "the Kentucky Roscius." When Hewlett heard of this theft, he protested, even traveling to England himself to confront Mathews on his own turf, but was unsuccessful in getting Mathews to acknowledge Hewlett as his source. When Hewlett returned to the United States, he continued the multiple impersonation program, putting on white actors like Edmund Kean, Thomas Abthorpe Cooper, and others, perhaps to out-Mathews the Mathews of the "At Home" persona.[6] In short, despite the obscurity under which the African Theatre lay until recently, its members were part of a transatlantic circulation of motifs, imitations, thefts, and distortions that at once provided an opportunity for blacks to seize control of the stage and offer their own versions of black identity in the theatre, but also left the African American actors struggling to maintain both theatre and dignity. It remained to whites to develop the anti-black abolition satires (Bobalition),[7] minstrel shows, and other blackface impersonations to make money from pretending to be black. By 1825, Hewlett was still making a go of his theatrical career and would continue to do so into the 1830s; but the African Theatre on Mercer Street as a distinct company of black actors was no longer viable. Spectators still came to see Hewlett when he was around, but for the most part they headed instead for the theatres in all cities where imitation black was featured over the presence of the real thing and where mockery of people of African ancestry was not only possible but encouraged.

One of the white entertainments of the time tells the tale of the appropriation of blackness in the Anglo-American theatre. Set in the Trumbull sisters' home state of Connecticut, Samuel Woodworth's musical play, *The Forest Rose* (1825), was one of the most successful American dramas on stage before *Uncle Tom's Cabin*, and, according to Richard Moody, the country's first "hit."[8] For at least forty years, *The Forest Rose* held the boards and provided a number of actors with a star vehicle for its Yankee part, Jonathan Ploughboy. So popular did it prove, in fact, that a run of over 100 performances in London was recorded with the famed American Yankee actor, Joshua Silsbee.[9] Based on a type exploited successfully by Royall Tyler in *The Contrast* and used in other works, and perhaps stimulated by the success of Mathews's Yankee imitations, Jonathan in Woodworth's play would seem to be constructed of the same elements that make Tyler's Jonathan a loveable character: naiveté, country dialect, ineptitude, and a good heart. The stage success of *The Forest Rose* helped revitalize the male Yankee type, and the play's continued appearance in theatres coincided with the reign of Yankee characters in England and the United States.[10]

In *The Contrast*, Jonathan identifies himself both by his outrageous misunderstandings of city life and by his difference from the corrupt sophisticate, Dimple. By the time of *The Forest Rose*, however, some changes have occurred in Yankee identity between Tyler and Woodworth – or some latent tendencies brought forward – that reorient the familiar features into a character far less naive than Colonel Manly's waiter. Jonathan Ploughboy is an inept lover, but he is also a shrewd shopkeeper;

a blunderer, yet a clever plotter. For David Grimsted, these post-*Contrast* developments of the type only confirm the Yankee's 'essential pure-heartedness and his innate good sense.'[11] Like later Yankees, Ploughboy escapes opprobrium on stage for his foibles by the "geniality" of his "calculating acquisitiveness."[12] Yet one development cannot be explained easily away in the notion of a simple, ultimately harmless, if "sharp" rustic. For above all, Woodworth's Jonathan – in contrast to Tyler's – is an out and out racist, whose signature comic line, 'I would not serve a negro so,' has grim consequences for the black character he does 'serve so,' Lid Rose. The fact that Mathews imitated both Yankees and Africans, and a Yankee slaveowner at that, is telling.[13] Woodworth's comedy of innocent rural lovers threatened by the schemes of a low-minded urban aristocrat is built on a racial conception that illustrates how, only a few years after its premiere, minstrel shows would find a welcome home on the American stage. What is significant, however, is not the fact of racism *per se*, but the way in which a stage African character functions to establish white identity, in the context of a particular tradition of representation. In other words, Woodworth's play contains within it a history of earlier representations of blacks that indicates the power of theatrical types to promulgate certain notions of identity construction even in the relatively new society of the United States.

Although minstrel shows have received significant scholarly attention,[14] the presence of stage African characters in other pre-twentieth-century American drama has not. When discussed at all, early drama is seen to exemplify some generic type, establish a character, or serve a national theme. The 'stage darky' is, of course, a recognized stereotype, but little has been done to examine the complexities of interaction the presence of such a character sometimes calls forth.[15] The problem is stated most eloquently by Toni Morrison in her by now often-cited *Playing in the Dark*. Not content simply to mark texts by white writers as racist, she queries the whole literary critical enterprise for the way it looks at – that is, does not see – what she calls 'Africanism' in American works. As she defines the term:

> Africanism is the vehicle by which the American self knows itself as not enslaved, but free; not repulsive, but desirable; not helpless, but licensed and powerful; not history-less, but historical; not damned, but innocent; not a blind accident of evolution, but a progressive fulfillment of destiny.[16]

In other words, Africanism, the marked but usually unnoted presence of a dark other, serves often to define whiteness in its desired characteristics.

At the same time, however, as Morrison shows with works such as Willa Cather's *Sapphira and the Slave Girl* and Ernest Hemingway's *To Have and Have Not*, the narrative attempt to elide or suppress black characters often has unintended and surprising consequences. As Mark Twain recounts the process of writing *Pudd'nhead Wilson*, another troubled book on race, the mulatto character Roxy, a minor presence in the extended joke tale, "Those Extraordinary Twins," forced her way into the story so far as to compel the author to start over with a "tragedy," *Pudd'nhead Wilson*.[17] Given Morrison's challenge, it seems well worth visiting a source of many Africanist characters, early American drama and theatre, in order to explore the interdependent formation of two key types, the stage Yankee and the stage African American.

The Forest Rose follows a pattern already familiar to playgoers raised on such popular British vehicles as Frances Brooke's *Rosina*. In Brooke's comic opera, a man of the city comes to the English countryside and finds what he thinks will be the easy plucking of an innocent rural flower, but as noted above, his plot is foiled, and virtue appears to triumph. Woodworth's musical comedy opens with sounds of a rural Connecticut dawn, followed by a somewhat mournful tune about a lost love sung by Lydia. A Londoner, Bellamy, enters the scene, exciting the interest of an innocent country girl, Harriet, who is loved by the rustic swain, William. Another well-dressed fellow, Blandford, also enters, looking, it turns out, for Lydia. Jonathan, meanwhile, woos Sally Forest, daughter of Deacon Forest, at whose home the "black" Lid Rose is a servant. The main plot revolves around William's attempt to get Harriet's affections back from Bellamy and expose the Englishman for the cad he is. At the end, a scheme that involves substituting a disguised Rose (who thinks she is being truly courted) for Harriet thwarts Bellamy and sends him fleeing back to England. The play ends with happy white lovers, a disconsolate black one, and a celebration of the virtues of the American countryside.[18]

To be sure, readers today expect to find African American characters in antebellum plays who are little more than crude stereotypes. What *The Forest Rose* brings to the type is the linkage of racist language and situation with the character seen as a true native type, the Yankee. As has been remarked upon in previous chapters, the early American stage inherited English dramatic styles, including comedies of manners, Elizabethan tragedies, and heroic tragedies, and a whole variety of light entertainments, farces, operas, musical dramas, and afterpieces. *The Contrast*, while it is set in New York and features only American characters, still contains sufficient echoes of two of its models, Sheridan's *School for Scandal* and O'Keeffe's *The Poor Soldier*, to keep its British-drama-fed audience in good humor. One of Tyler's relatively original touches is the character of Jonathan; in the way he centers the Yankee in the comic scenes and allows him to represent the uncorrupted, if humorously naive, American farmer, Tyler helps forge what would become a character thought on both sides of the Atlantic to represent the authentic American type. Woodworth's play as well makes much of the virtuous farmer (who also preexists the Yankee in British pastoral comedies) and concludes, as does *The Contrast*, with the successful expulsion of the vice-ridden urbanite from the scene. The enshrining of the yeoman farmer would become a staple of Jacksonian democratic ideology, and his appearance in *The Forest Rose* anticipates the appeal made from the theatre to an idealized folk in the coming decades.[19]

Nevertheless, Jonathan the generic character shows signs of corruption – if that is what it is – by 1825. His humor has gone from harmless misunderstandings in *The Contrast* (thinking the theatre is someone's living room, for instance) to cruel jokes and crude comments on allegedly offensive characteristics of black people in *The Forest Rose*. Jonathan Ploughboy may have gotten many laughs from his American and English audiences with his scene-ending, 'I would not serve a negro so,' but the humor now comes less at the Yankee's own expense than at the expense of someone else more vulnerable to scorn.[20] The jesting associated with Tyler's Jonathan – a post-Revolutionary Yankee buffoonery originating in pastoral purity – has given way to a race-determined comedy that requires the denigration of a scapegoat group to make its point. In Morrison's terms, the Yankee needs the Africanist target to make himself into the 'beloved' comic rendition of the idealized white rustic. Even further, *The Forest Rose* reflects a threatened and hostile white working/peasant class trying to claim status among higher classes by marginalizing African American servants and slaves. As George Schuyler observed satirically in 1927, American whites of the lowest classes have traditionally used blacks to give themselves feelings of superiority they would not otherwise have among other whites.[21] Woodworth shows that the process of shaping American identity on stage, forming an archetypal American, the Yankee, takes place simultaneously with the increased insistence that blacks are not 'Americans' – and that they deserve abuse.

Some of the problematic nature of Jonathan's portrayal is recognized by Francis Hodge in his groundbreaking study of the Yankee type. Hodge suggests some reasons for the "rude note" that has "crept into" *The Forest*

Rose from earlier Yankee types. 'Has his new position as a businessman created other problems? ... Buried in *The Forest Rose* were more inherent thoughts and feelings of Americans than had appeared in any of the play[s] with Yankees up to this time."[22] For Hodge, the Yankee is a vessel for actors and perceivers, not necessarily a fixed thing in himself. Woodworth's Jonathan is, indeed, a ruder version of Tyler's, traceable, as has been suggested, to the revival of Yankee types that began with Charles Mathews in his vehicle, *Jonathan in England* (1824). Although Hodge does not link Woodworth directly to Mathews, his depiction of Mathews's version of Jonathan – "uncouth, stupid, witless, dishonest, stubborn, easily insulted, unmannerly braggart, lost in a civilized society, a Negro beater, and mockery of true democracy"[23] – suggests some of the change in theatrical climate from Tyler's day. Mathews meant his portrayal to mock lower-class American mores; Woodworth seems to celebrate them, at least in part. Unfortunately, a long tradition of stage racialism underlies both versions.

Before 1825, American theatregoers would have likely seen African-origin characters represented on stage, but, with the exceptions of such Shakespearean figures as Othello or Aaron, almost never given centrality. Unless one went to the African Company productions of the early 1820s in New York, a spectator might never have seen an actual African American actor either.[24] Blacked-up characters appeared on American stages in such popular English vehicles as Isaac Bickerstaff's *The Padlock* (1768), whose Mungo was first put on to great effect in America by Lewis Hallam, Jr., the most prominent actor in the country before 1800; and Richard Cumberland's *The West Indian* (1771), where "negro servants" enter but do not speak. One of the most likely sources of black characters was in musical performances. Whether in independent songs or in lyrics connected to plays or operas, blackface characters appeared in comic or complaint roles.[25] Blacks were represented in such musicals as Richard Brinsley Sheridan, *Robinson Crusoe* (1781); Isaac Bickerstaff, *The Romp* (1786); George Colman, Jr., *Inkle and Yarico* (1787) and *The Africans* (1808); William Macready, *The Irishman in London; or Happy African* (1792); John Fawcett, *Obi, or Three Fingered Jack* (1800); and William Diamond, *The Aethiop* (1812).[26] Among American plays, black servants appear in J. Robinson, *The Yorker's Stratagem* (1792); John Murdock, *The Triumphs of Love; or, Happy Reconciliation* (1795) and *The Politicians; or, A State of Things* (1798); as well as another play by Samuel Woodworth, *The Widow's Son; or, Which is the Traitor?* (1825). Although there are variations and reversals of expectation in some of those plays, as will be discussed below, by 1825 white viewers or readers of plays would have come to expect that blacks would be treated humorously on stage, if at all, without any annoying subjective positions of sympathetic African American characters to complicate their reception.

One issue raised in the representation of African American characters is the degree to which white American identities in drama are molded by proximity to minority or foreign others. We have already seen this to some degree in the use of Islamic, Native American, and Irish characters in American plays, but the matter seems most acute with personae marked as black. To be African is to be represented as not quite – or not remotely – American in the context of the plays. Much of this is an inheritance from English and European drama, where to be a Moor or some surrogate stage nationality is always to be exotic or the minority of minorities.[27] But American playwrights pen on top of that tradition the more prevalent presence of blacks in the United States, even when the authors seem to resist the incorporation of racially marked others into the social worlds of American settings. In the anonymous *The Downfall of Justice*, one of the first American-authored plays to portray a black character with a significant role, Jack serves as an ironic moral yardstick for the farm family that withholds crops from market during a time of scarcity in order to drive up the price. As one who suffers the abuse of the family, Jack more quickly perceives community suffering than the rest and shows more sympathy with hungry whites than the white characters in the play. At the same time, he plays the Africanist counterpoint to Yankee rural identity, whereby the New England farmer is seen not as a benighted bumbler but a sharp-eyed marketeer, one who minds "the main chance," as Tyler's Van Rough often extols, regardless of social consequences. The *Downfall* author recognizes with his or her contemporary Crèvecoeur that the rural northerner has no particular allegiance to political or social ideals but only to self, figured in the 1777 play as the farmer's and his family's scorn for their unfortunate neighbors. *Downfall of Justice* marks the beginning of a tendency in American plays to identify slaves or black bound servants, whose characteristics are themselves bound to the identity of northern whites, with northern settings.

Ten years later, in *The Contrast*, no blackface actor appears on stage, but the white character Charlotte makes one reference to an offstage servant who is "black." Charlotte gossips with Letitia in the first scene, and to show her authority for the claim that their mutual acquaintance

Sally Bloomsbury is to be married, the former cites 'the best authority ... my aunt Wyerley's Hannah,' who hears from her presumably black brother who hears from the equally presumably black servant of Mrs. Catgut the milliner that a cap the milliner is making for Sally is allegedly a wedding cap. The scene establishes Charlotte's identity as a woman who enjoys gossip and social pleasure, but it curiously seems to require the figurative presence, through literal absence, of this chain of stage African characters to make the point. To what degree does Tyler rely for his humor upon social expectations in the audience concerning African American servants? In establishing her source's integrity, Charlotte feels obliged to qualify her to Letitia: "(You know Hannah; though a black, she is a wench that was never caught in a lie in her life)."[28] On the one hand, Charlotte trusts Hannah; on the other, Charlotte must distinguish Hannah from the rest of her kind in the understood premise that blacks as a rule have no claim to veracity. This has the effect of making Charlotte seem the more frivolous for her willingness to suspend her skepticism of the truthfulness of African American servants and thus prepare us for her eventual seduction by the false promises of Billy Dimple; at the same time, the brief piece of dialogue has the odd effect of leaving Hannah's ghostly presence on stage as a kind of afterimage, there but not there, referred to but not seen, perhaps an honest woman, but to the whites who occupy the stage still a 'wench,' a term derived from the slave market. Thus even characters relatively sympathetic to particular black persons require that certain boundaries be drawn to separate Hannah from Charlotte, boundaries that extend beyond mere class position to the often amorphous but to the audience very real distinctions by race. Imtiaz Habib points out regarding the 'early modern English black menial,' and in particular her representation as the blackamoor maid in drama of the period, 'As she does not exist in her colonizer's social grammar, so her oppressions do not appear in the narrative of his domestic life.'[29] Here Hannah is recovered briefly by two white female characters as part of the narrative of their elite domestic life, although remaining unseen and finally dispensable to both plot and audience, yet hauntingly present for all that.

Another play by Royall Tyler, *May Day in Town*, suggests a different part of the process of accommodation between stage representation and audience acceptance of black stereotypes. The play itself, produced a month after *The Contrast* in May 1787, is no longer extant, but the lyrics for this "comic opera" survive and tell of (if not show) situations in which a black servant in the north is treated harshly by whites. The story centers on the New York custom of marking May First as moving day and the experiences of the Surdus family as they undertake to change residences. The opening song forms an interesting contrast to the pastoralism of *The Forest Rose*, as one character intones, "No more sing the Beauties of rural May Day!/If Poets with Laurels their Temples would crown,/ Let them cull from their Stories the most rapturous lay,/To chant forth the Praises of May Day in Town."[30] Tyler of course is being satirical, for the 'fragrance' of the country is played against that of the city streets, and the satire continues by making the central character, Mrs. Surdus, a virago whose tongue lashes against family and servants alike.

While the husband suffers in silence – he pretends, it seems, to be deaf[31] – the black male servant, Pompey (played by Lewis Hallam, Jr., whose Mungo was much praised), sings on several occasions of the conditions he must endure. In his first song, Pompey, like Jack from *Downfall of Justice*, is motivated by compassion and in this case expresses sympathy with his master, whom he refers to as "poor Baccra," the Africanized word used by slaves for their white owners. Then Pompey looks at his own condition:

> But when my old Misse she rave, scol, and tomp,
> She lecture ole Massa, and fly at poor Pomp;
> When – 'tis Betty [another servant], you Slut!
> And Pompey, you dog!
> Go do this.[32]

Although later in the song he indicates he does not take it seriously, he still expresses the wish that "Misse were dumb." In short, by 1787 a northern audience was already conditioned to understand that (a) servants are the targets of considerable verbal abuse but (b) black servants, while they may complain, can absorb it without harm to their character. Again, as with the reference to Hannah in *The Contrast*, audience sympathy for the stage African figure is qualified by the assumption of attitudes in the audience that require black subordination and white ignorance of black subjectivity.

The second point is made in Act II, in another of Pompey's songs, but with additional information about how he is treated:

> When Massa cross and Misse glum
> And Misse ring her larum Tongue,
> See how Pompey drive of[f] Care,
> With ha, ha, ha! ha! ha! & c.
> Massa beat me black and blue,
> Misse plit my head in two
> With her tongue, and till she wou'd

> Say all Pompey for your good:
> Dus I tank her for her Care.
> Ha! ha! ha! ha! ha! ha!³³

Pompey laughs at the treatment he receives, but the catalogue of abuses – beatings and tongue lashings – seems funny only because the perpetrators are themselves objects of satire, and the victims are viewed as not harmed. Even in the finale, where the singers step out of the narrative proper and thus speak more as actors than characters, Pompey punningly reminds the audience, "Massa Cane and Misse Tongue,/Da always do keep moving."³⁴

If *Downfall* and *May Day* predict that the abused but sympathetic servant type will continue to be employed by American playwrights, two other plays that premiered on American stages illustrate some different possibilities in the practice of Africanist characterization. J. Robinson's *Yorker's Stratagem* first played in New York in April 1792, with at least one further performance in that city and one more in Philadelphia in June. Little is known about Robinson, but he must have had some direct experience in the West Indies, where the play is set. No American play before 1825 to my knowledge has as many black characters with speaking roles. The main character among the African islanders, Banana, occupies a position not unlike that of Mungo as a man somewhat at the whims of others. He loves a black woman, Priscilla, but is being thwarted in his pursuit of her by his mother, Mrs. Banana, herself a plantation owner, who wants Banana to marry a white girl, Louisa, daughter of the miser Fingercash, as part of her scheme to climb economically and socially. Interestingly, the play does not moralize on color, nor make the prospective marriage between Louisa and Banana an impossibility because of race – but of course Banana does not marry the white woman, at least not in New York and Philadelphia. Amidst all the plot complications in the comedy, though, a few moments remind the audience that color and starkness of condition are never far apart. Banana has a child, Quaka; Prissy tells her lover that if he marries the white lady, Quaka will die, perhaps because he would have to be abandoned. Ironically, Fingercash, who is happy to have Banana marry his daughter, claims that he lacks "education, and that bauble, sentiment,"³⁵ although Banana, like Jack and Pompey, on many occasions proclaims his concern for someone whose misfortune he takes as even worse than his own. The overt plot action generates some fun at the expense of Banana and his mother, but is much less dependent on clear-cut abuse than in Tyler's *May Day*.

In the end, both Mrs. Banana and Fingercash get their comeuppance for greedy schemes, through the agency of a pretend "Yankey clown," Amant, and the disguised white clerk Ledger who pretends for a while to be Banana. Playing at black and playing at Yankee remind the audience that 'black' and 'Yankee' are performances, both within and by implication without the theatre, but the two types part company on one point. Despite the almost complete suppression of overt racism in *Yorker's Stratagem*, the comedy concludes with a series of jokes based on color. Humor is struck by several characters from Fingercash's phrase "black plot" when the black-masked Ledger arrives in his Banana costume. Once more, even within the context of a sympathetic portrayal, the stage serves to mark characters by means of moral analogy: black is always the color of devious plots – this, despite the fact that white characters plot throughout the play without suffering any lingering suspicion about color. To his credit, Robinson gives Mrs. Banana, at least, the power to try to manipulate affairs and prevents any direct denigration of Banana in the way Hannah is, by implication, in *The Contrast*. Still, through the marked island creole the black characters speak, Robinson puts barriers between white audience and black character to prevent too close an identification between them. Even as the author imagines Africanist characters with some independence of means and motivation, he limits audience sympathies through distancing techniques that require recognition of otherness in order to establish the comic affirmation of Amant and Ledger.[36]

Another play to feature a slightly rounded African American character is John Murdock's *The Triumphs of Love*. To be sure, Sambo is a dialect-speaking slave, with all the attendant assumptions that go with it, but Murdock allows him a somewhat greater range, in the manner of Tyler's *May Day in Town*, from the stock serving character. Sambo thinks his owner, George Friendly, Jr., is a "drum rogue" – good fellow – and that he himself reflects a general tendency in the race: "we negro improbe berry much."[37] This sets up a situation analogous to that for Irish characters who come to the New World. The very contrast between his dialect and this statement undermines Sambo's otherwise sincere belief; the audience will no doubt snicker at the degree of "improvement" found in a character whose language marks him so distinctly as other. But Murdock is not content to leave Sambo so entirely exposed to ridicule. In a later scene, George disguises himself as a beggar in order to woo Betsey Peevish. Sambo appears at Peevish's house and does not recognize his master. When George appeals to Sambo and requests that he "do not be so hard on a poor unfortunate white man," Sambo, much like Jack in *Downfall*, takes pity upon the scene of misfortune and gives the beggar money – an extraordinary act of charity for a slave (*TL* 41). For that kindness, George gives him the qualified praise that he is "a good black" (42). For the first two acts of the comedy, then, Sambo plays a sympathetic supporting role, a testimony more to George's good nature than to his own subjective integrity. The traditional function of Africanist characters – to substantiate by contrast white identity – is essentially maintained.

This changes somewhat in Act III. Sambo enters a room, solus, looks in a mirror, and begins a soliloquy about his situation. While George observes unseen, the slave character reflects on his own person, abilities, and status as bondman. The speech is a relatively rare example of self-reflection accorded to a stage African character whose ostensible purpose is not to mock the character's self-perception as inflated or at odds, as in Act I, with his literal language and appearance:

> Sambo tink himself handsome. He berry complish'd to[o]; he sing well; he dance well; he play fiddle well. Can tink so, so, pretty well. He tink; he berry often tink why he slave to white man? Why black foke sold like cow or horse. He tink de great somebody above, no order tings so. – Sometime he tink dis way – he got bess massa in e world. He gib him fine clothes for dress – he gib him plenty money for pend; and for a little while, he tink himself berry happy.

But Sambo recognizes the limitations of this latter line of thought, the apologetic for slavery as a fair exchange of black labor for white benevolence. What if, he continues, "He pose massa George die; den he sold to some oder massa. May be he no use him well. When Sambo tink so, it most broke he heart" (*TL* 52). In order for the black character to be rendered sympathetic, he must first prove himself as a man of feeling. Having first applied his sympathies to George, he then applies them to himself, with the result that George's feelings are further engaged in a return act of sympathy. In a gesture nearly unmatched in American drama of the period, George frees Sambo from slavery on the spot and agrees to hire him for cash wages. Sambo is suitably grateful, as the language of benevolence demands, but he goes further in fixing his sights on socially worthy goals, contra expectations that freed blacks cannot think beyond their own primitive, physical needs when out of white ownership. His wages, he says, will be applied to the purchase of Sue, his lady love. He himself, in the most radical statement of all, will become, in the style of the French Revolution, "citizen Sambo" (53).

As if to emphasize the point, Murdock has Sambo slip from his pedestal as citizen by having him appear drunk later with two other freed slaves. George finds him and brings him home, occasioning a cynical remark by another white, Careless: 'So much for against [*sic*] liberating those people.' But George excuses the behavior on Lockean grounds. The drinking of a free man is no argument in favor of holding a whole people "in a state of slavery. Much is to be said in favour of them, for their want of education' (69).

In the end, Sambo's rise to citizen rests to a large degree on his having a sympathetic master rather than as part of a sustained critique on slavery. Still, Murdock's overall vocabulary in this play about liberty suggests, in the manner of Francophile republicans, that he does mean to condemn slavery and uphold the free humanity of African Americans.[38] In the context of a stage tradition of blackface figures, however, his plea is very much a minority voice swallowed by the popular expectations among audiences for something more predictable. Only lasting a single performance, *Triumphs of Love* marks the brief-candle moment of glory in the early republican white theatrical depiction of blacks in the United States. Despite his efforts in 1798 to continue with more fully realized African American characters – Cato, Pompey, Caesar, and Sambo in *The Politicians* all argue about politics and address each other as "citizen" – Murdock faced continuing rejection by the theatrical establishment.[39] His last effort at playwriting, *The Beau Metamorphized* (1800), omits black characters altogether. The problem faced by Murdock and other playwrights, insofar as they were conscious of it, was that the overwhelming force of stage practice reinforced a general bigotry in society as a whole that prevented blacks from ever appearing in their own bodies on stage or even in representation in anything approximating fully rounded characters. Even where audiences might be counted on for sympathy for black citizenship, spectators could not in a trice wipe away months or years of attendance upon plays whose stage African characters were walk-ons or buffoons. For instance, spectators at American theatres were certainly aware that blacks worked in various backstage capacities there, aiding their enjoyment of an evening at the play, but once the curtain went up, how they viewed those literal laborers became conditioned by theatrical practice. In his "comic prelude" to the opening of the Park Theatre in New York, William Milns portrays the flurry of getting a theatre ready for opening night; black workers are mentioned twice, although not shown, with one of the allusions to a "black wench" who steps on a not-yet-dry painted canvas.[40] It is not unimaginable that such an accident might occur, but Milns clearly intends to enhance the humor by making the offending worker black. Insofar as American playwrights would tackle the issues of race after 1800, they would need to do so in the face of a peculiar phenomenon: the increasing representational hostility to blacks as blacks in an era when northern states were passing laws abolishing slavery in their boundaries.

In an age when sympathy was much prized as a trait, Tyler, Robinson, and Murdock, even within a relatively limited scope, create the possibilities for audiences to respond to blackface characters in ways that highlight the spectator's own ability to feel, made the more self-congratulatory when the objects are those that society claims little deserve benevolence. Life in the north was hard for African Americans, particularly in cities, where mortality rates were far higher than those of whites.[41] The recent discovery of an eighteenth-century burial site for African Americans in New York and subsequent investigations by biological anthropologist Michael Blakey demonstrate forcibly that the sympathy was well placed, even if sympathy in general benefits the one who feels more than the one who suffers. The African Burial Ground in New York was the final resting place for thousands of black residents of the city. When the bodies were exhumed in the early 1990s, they were shown to have been malnourished, with evidence of untreated bone breaks, disease, and in general, physical abuse.[42] The suffering of the black in the north would have been nearly as desperate as that of the slave on the southern plantation. The literature of the time makes clear that abusive treatment of blacks was the expectation, or at least, would not have surprised northern playgoers. Here is a situation, then, where forensic anthropology augments the record of the texts, a kind of literary archaeology. With slavery dragging its way through the first quarter of the nineteenth century in the North (the last slaves in New York were not freed until 1827), restrictions on black franchise appearing even after the formal end to slavery, and court cases highlighting the abusiveness of employers toward their African American servants, few whites or blacks in the theatre would be surprised to see a servant of color abused.[43] Members of both groups were well aware, if in differing ways, of the lives northern blacks faced:

> Increasingly they were forced into appalling housing and segregated from all but the poorest whites. They were shunned in public and cordoned off, whether they wished it or not, into separate churches, separate schools ... They were condemned to scraping together a living in low-paying and menial occupations, cruelly caricatured in print, in paint, and on the stage, and denied the right to vote and even to walk

down the street without harassment. Not only that, but they, their lives, and their culture were appropriated by whites and packaged for entertainment and profit into something that could fuel the fantasies and longings of their oppressors.[44]

The question is, then, how far that mistreatment could be exhibited on stage before exciting more than casual sympathy from white viewers.

The Forest Rose gives us some idea. After the love complications are introduced in the first scene, we move to the secondary love interest with Jonathan and Sally. Jonathan is angry with Sally because she has allegedly kissed another man, Tom Clover. She pretends to make it up to the former by offering a kiss. Covering his eyes with her shawl to prevent his blushing, she says, Sally substitutes her servant girl, Rose. When Jonathan asks her (whom he takes to be Sally) if she loves him, Rose replies, "Yes Massa Jonathan, me lubber you berry bad."[45] Sally, in high spirits, asks, "is not that better than the samp-mortar," that is, than licking the bowl where corn is pounded. The following exchange sets the tone for the humor in the rest of the play:

> JONATHAN: Darnation! If I have not been bussing Lid Rose! Now, Sal Forest, that is too bad! I would not serve a negro so. [*Exit Sally*]
> ROSE: But you did serve poor negro so, and ax me to lubber you, and now you desert me. [*Exit*]
> JONATHAN: Be off with you, garlic chops ... Whew! how the wench smelt of onions. (*FR* 160)

Early in the play, then, Woodworth shows the many dimensions of Jonathan's trademark line. Meant to be a statement of his humanity – I would not treat a black, someone who is used to abuse, in the way you have treated me, a decent white person – Jonathan's self-defining rhetoric is turned against him by the physical presence of a literalized, but of course not a real, "negro," who in fact notes that he has served her ill. Rather than apologize, the Yankee acts to expel the departing woman by making her mouth odor into an inherent characteristic of her race. The audience must choose whether to condemn Jonathan's perfidy or laugh at the typing of blacks as having the repulsive smell of onions on their breath. Richard Moody, writing in 1955, simply says, without reference to the racialism in the play, that there is "less humor in Jonathan's colloquial speech than in that of his predecessors."[46] The problem of response can be seen as late as the 1970s, as Walter Meserve tries to balance what he rightly labels as Jonathan's "offensive attitude toward Negroes" with the description of the Yankee as "essentially a simple person."[47] The success of the play as a comedy makes clear where nineteenth-century audience sympathies lay.

For his stage abuse of the stage African, Woodworth may be drawing from two highly successful British musicals, Bickerstaff's *The Romp* and Macready's *The Irishman in London*. In the former, the character of Priscilla Tomboy – whose name may have suggested Jonathan Ploughboy – abuses her slave in ways not unlike the Yankee does Lid Rose; in the latter, the figure of Cubba, the West Indian slave woman in London, resembles to a degree Lid Rose, a benighted figure caught up in an unlikely love match with a white. Cubba is substituted for a white character at a wedding; that ruse is discovered, but Macready leaves open the possibility that she will wed the Irish servant, Murtock, in something like the linkage of Trudge and Wowski in *Inkle and Yarico*. Such stage prefigurations, however, are not the only contributors to Woodworth's using the kiss of a white man and black woman for racist humor. Contemporary almanacs made Pat the chronic Irish buffoon, but they also scored comic points off blacks. In an example reported by Shane White from the 1806 edition of *Hutchins Improved*, a black couple promise to pay a preacher to marry them only if he follows the white custom to the letter; agreeing, the preacher conducts the service, but is told by the new husband that he has failed to keep his bargain. What was omitted? "'Why,' answered the negro, 'you *forgot to salute the bride*.'"[48] In a later version of the same joke, the *Nantucket Inquirer* of August 12, 1822 presented a story called "Negro Politeness," in which a black couple comes to the altar before a white minister to be married. Commanded by the minister to kiss the bride, "Sambo" defers to the minister and says "after you sir." As John Saillant describes the joke, 'the minister, once faced with the prospect of kissing a black woman, always thereafter omitted that instruction from weddings."[49] The larger issue here is that Woodworth writes in a context where northern ears hear racist jokes, particularly those that involve the prospect of interracial sexuality, without offense. Woodworth and his managers must realize that the environment in 1825 is such that the mass of theatregoers could be entertained by objectifying, "love in the dark" humor.

Having made a grand joke of his apothegm, the Jonathan character is now free to exploit it whenever he sees an opening. In scene three of the first act, the romantic lead, Blandford, enters and encounters Jonathan, whom he takes to be some kind of rustic clown. When he accuses Jonathan of being a "*sharp*" shopkeeper, as Yankees are known to be, the latter replies, "I wouldn't serve a negro so." The conversation then moves to Blandford's quest for Lydia, whom Jonathan takes to mean Lid Rose. Again, he generates humor by an aside and another direct allusion to the smell of Rose's breath. When Blandford learns by one of Jonathan's remarks (that likens Rose to "the ace of spades") that the woman in question is not his lost love but "Lid Rose. Deacon Forest's negro wench," he curses Jonathan and laments the quick end to his sexual readiness: "The sweetest bud of hope has withered in a moment." "Bud of hope!" responds Jonathan. "Darn me, if I don't think she's more like a clove of garlic." Naturally, Woodworth gives Jonathan one more chance at scene's end to speak his signature. When Blandford asks the Yankee whether he can be trusted to give accurate directions, Jonathan asks in mock innocence, "Me!" and concludes with his trademark line (*FR* 161).

At the end of the first act, in scene 4, Jonathan gets another chance to measure his own importance against that of black servants. In a song, he complains of Sally's treatment of him, "*Wouldn't serve a negro so,*" before calling for "little Caesar with his fiddle." When Caesar enters, Jonathan calls him "my little blackey," whom he will accompany with a jew's harp. Thus in the three scenes of Act I in which he has been present, Jonathan has used his trademark line four times; referred derogatorily to Rose in two extended conversations and situations; and made one more minimizing remark to a black fiddle player. In short, the linchpin of his humor has been comic dismissals of black characters and consequent aggrandizement of his own importance.

On stage, it might be argued, such humor is harmless. After all, in nineteenth-century performances, the actress playing Rose would have been white, in dark makeup; the comedy is broad, playing on stereotypes all around, including the Yankee himself, the farmers, and the English city seducer; and no one is shown to be physically abused. Beyond that, one might say, *The Forest Rose* is just one more bad American play, doing nothing more than reflecting the prejudices of its time. After all, no one has seriously challenged what Oral Coad remarked in 1919, that Woodworth's plays "are almost devoid of literary excellence and beyond a certain amount of rather crude theatrical effectiveness their dramatic qualities are but mediocre."[50] The racism in *The Forest Rose* is foregone, the argument might conclude, and hardly worth the mention.

Unfortunately, perhaps because of that last-mentioned assumption, almost no one who has discussed the play, with the exception of Hodge and Meserve, has even noticed its racism, and the play itself has gotten only slight attention.[51] Indeed, its very theatrical success, on both sides of the Atlantic, and its position as the play chiefly responsible for reviving interest among American playwrights in the Yankee character would seem to make it a natural focus point for scholarly investigation. In discussions of Yankee literature and Yankee stage plays, however, allusions to race are often glossed over or ignored. Ironically, as a reviewer in the New York *Mirror* put it in 1835, the stage Yankee's 'idiom' is usually read as "unique, racy, and pungent,"[52] where "racy" meant "harmlessly violates good taste." Nevertheless, because race language plays a predominant role in Woodworth's drama, it seems now that "racy" means "insults other races with impunity." Clearly, few theatregoers were bothered by this language, for *The Forest Rose* was put on by professional companies in New York, Philadelphia, New Orleans, St. Louis, Mobile, Chicago, several California locations, and London.[53] Although Woodworth wrote the drama before the beginnings in America of the active abolitionist movement, the period of the play's greatest popularity was in the 1830s, 1840s, and 1850s, at the height of antislavery activity. Significantly, the play was chosen as a vehicle by actors who made careers as stage Yankees, including George Handel 'Yankee' Hill, Danforth Marble, and Joshua Silsbee. Since drama of the period was dependent on popularity – the mass audience had great power – then the persistence of such a play tells us something about evolving, or perhaps stagnating, cultural attitudes.

The storm of political rhetoric over slavery may have been raging outside the theatre, but inside, at least until George Aiken's version of *Uncle Tom's Cabin* in 1852, such issues as rights for blacks or concerns over their humanity could be conveniently, almost willfully, ignored on stage. Even with the dramatization of Harriet Beecher Stowe's novel, however, an audience would have seen black/white relations in the context of other staged performances of race, including *The Forest Rose*. As Jeffrey Mason, paralleling Morrison, observes, *Uncle Tom* "conveys a white vision of blackness, and a somewhat less self-conscious vision of whiteness";[54] but even further than its depiction of the politics of the 1850s, Aiken's play – with its own racist Yankee, Gumption Cute, seeking to make his place in the world by insulting the black character Topsy – is as much a construct of theatrical conventions as it is political history. That the acceptance of race as a source of humor was linked to the Yankee, a "native" character tied to American national identity, makes pursuit of the play's racial attitudes of more than casual interest.

In the second and concluding act of *The Forest Rose*, Jonathan continues to end scenes with "I wouldn't treat a negro so." However, the humor that has been largely restricted to him spreads to the rest of the characters, somewhat in the way that Robinson ends *The Yorker's Stratagem*. This can be observed most pointedly in scene 5. Harriet successfully brings together Lydia and Blandford and begins to see William's sincere devotion to her while grasping Bellamy's opportunism. She plans with Sally an elaborate plot that involves a presumed tryst between Bellamy and Harriet while the farmers are at a festival. Naturally, they plan to substitute Rose for Harriet. When the farmers and their families are summoned by Sally's cry of "Save Harriet Miller!" Harriet's father and William catch Bellamy at a presumed abduction and bring him up with the disguised Rose. Before the plot is revealed, Miller asks rhetorically, "What blacker crime is there in the whole catalogue of human depravity" than to ravish an innocent girl? Jonathan comments that it is a "very *black* affair." Then when Rose pulls aside her veil, and all shout with surprise, Blandford tweaks his friend, "Love in the *dark*! Hey Bellamy? Ha! ha! ha!"[55] Bellamy's response is on cue: "A damn black affair, sure enough." Then, as Bellamy threatens to return to England to write his indicting travelogue of America, William adds, "And don't forget to notice the beauty and fragrance of our black roses! Ha! ha! ha!" This leaves Bellamy to pronounce anathema, but in fact, what may be the play's message: "Fragrance, you creature! Strike me, exquisite, if all Roussell's perfume would annihilate the cloud of odours with which that caricature upon humanity has impregnated my glove" (*FR* 173).[56] Thus the plot and comedy of *The Forest Rose* come down to that conception of the black: a "caricature upon humanity." No one contradicts the defeated rake Bellamy because they all believe it. The revelation of the black Rose on stage and its consequent exposure of what Morrison has labeled Africanism is truly "playing in the dark."

Woodworth allows his play to look in several directions. In some ways, *The Forest Rose* both affirms a growing American pastoralism and spoofs it; as a consequence, one must be cautious in taking its morals too literally. On the one hand, the songs in the finale of Act II trot out the by-now familiar homespun images of rural virtue: "humblest ploughman's cot," "In nature's sweetest verdure drest," "honest breast," "some rustic chap, / A sheepish, awkward thing at best," all linked to the chorus of "For lords of the soil, and fed by our toil, /American farmers are blest, my boys, / American farmers are blest" (*FR* 173). On the other, those same songs make comic hay of the Jonathan figure. Earlier in the play, Bellamy gives

Jonathan money to help him snare Harriet. When he reveals this to Sally, she chides him for his making money by dishonesty. In the end, though, he justifies keeping the money by doing his part to help Bellamy, all while Sally is contriving the Rose affair. Jonathan's song, then, shows what happens to the image of the honest Yankee:

> By girls we may be thus cajoled,
> But not by any dandy blade:
> A Yankee's honour can't be sold,
> Whatever price be paid.
> But tempters are told, as we pocket the gold,
> 'Tis all in the way of trade, my boys
> 'Tis all in the way of trade. (*FR* 173–74)

Jonathan may be a fool with women, but he is a sharper in business who, in the name of "trade," will not let any excessive virtue cause him to return thirty-five dollars to a rake. Thus by play's end, an audience ought not to have any illusions that the Yankee is some naif whose occasional successes in love or business are no more than harmless accidents. He, like a substantial portion of the white, playgoing public, has his eye "on the main chance," as Van Rough in *The Contrast* would put it, and will not let honesty get in his way of improving his place in the world (*TC* 15).

The contemporary response and that of theatre historians thereafter has somehow overlooked the essential problem of Jonathan's lack of credibility. Portrayed as fundamentally honest and simple, he and his descendants have in fact been part of an elaborate confidence game, whereby a few choice country phrases translate into pastoral innocence. One of the better-known Yankee figures in nineteenth-century drama is Adam Trueman from Anna Cora Mowatt's *Fashion* (1845). Trueman is an example of the older, wiser Yankee type that developed after Woodworth's play. He enters the artificial world of the Tiffanys as a breath of fresh country air, calling a spade a spade and all to their duty. Uncomfortably for modern readers, however, Trueman has the habit of referring to the black servant, Zeke (rechristened Adolph by the social pretender, Mrs. Tiffany), as a "grinning nigger."[57] Indeed, Trueman only follows in the footsteps of other Yankees, such as Ebenezer Venture, from an 1841 play by that name, whose homespun diction finds "nigger" the word of choice for a black.[58] In *Fashion*, Trueman's language is part of his campaign to name a thing as what it is – as if to say a person of color, dressed in livery, or given a French name, is still only a "nigger" at the end. In Trueman's case, though, there is the added complication of his own deception, his unrevealed relationship to Gertrude, the young woman who lives with the Tiffanys but is in fact Trueman's granddaughter. Mowatt buries the implications of Trueman's deceit in the more obvious forms of social pretense engaged in by the urban characters. Even Mrs. Tiffany's ridiculous attempt to be fashionable and French somehow is made less a target for scorn than it might by its contrast to the verbal fumblings of the ethnically inscribed Zeke, who, unlike the white main characters, is reducible to a monochromatic race word not of his own choosing.[59]

Thus the distance from Tyler's Jonathan to Mowatt's Trueman, from a riotous naivete to a more serious knowledge of the world, is bridged by Jonathan Ploughboy, who identifies that his place in the world outside his home village is made at the expense of one more marginal than he, the black servant girl Rose. Zeke and Rose, both of whom, along with Tyler's Pompey, show awareness of their exploitation, are restricted by the playwrights from allowing that insight into their condition to rise to the level of explicitly stated injustice, largely through the comic interference of the Yankee. Even in Dion Boucicault's play about slavery, *The Octoroon* (1859), the "tragic octoroon," the marginally African Zoe, speaks only minimally to the injustice of the peculiar institution because the world view of the play has been enunciated by a Yankee. The "good" Yankee, Salem Scudder, who professes himself in love with Zoe, fixes his own social importance by speaking at length of the need for whites to exercise 'protection, forbearance, gentleness' in exchange for the historical necessity of forcing blacks, as well as Indians, to 'up sticks and stand around.'[60] Thus, their marginalization is ensured where white ineptitude and racial patronizing are allowed to continue past the time of the play, but the wrongs felt by blacks are not. Rose does not die for love, as Zoe does, but her love and her life are jokes, thanks to the Yankee. Rose in essence dies a death of humiliation, acceptable to audiences, apparently, now used to Africanist presence as a form of defining Yankee identity, but one that deprives spectators of any opportunity even to feel sympathy for her symbolic death.

As recent scholars have shown, New Englanders, however much their good intentions, their sympathy with plantation slaves, and their general shift toward abolitionism may have carried them, nevertheless retained a significant repulsion for blacks as people and as a presence in their increasingly provincial culture.[61] For every John Greenleaf Whittier or even William Lloyd Garrison – who, as his conflicts with Frederick Douglass indicate, had his own long education to undergo with regard to the beings he ostensibly fought for – there are many more "Yankees" without forceful interests in the welfare of African Americans, the Nathaniel Hawthornes, for instance, who virtually erase blacks from the written map of their reflected consciousness.[62] Even in the 1850s, the only represented blacks with any dignity on stage are mulattos, quadroons, octoroons, near-whites whose only tragedy is not being all white. In the midst of this northern social rejection of the African Americans – or rather, their Africanist caricatures – is the Yankee. The obvious distaste of the arch-Yankee spinster Miss Ophelia for Topsy in Aiken's play is just another reflection of the larger Yankee detestation of blacks in New England society. When Aiken's Ophelia says, "How shiftless!"[63] the third or fourth time, we are witnessing another generation of anti-black signature lines, made popular by Jonathan Ploughboy's "I would not serve a negro so." Ophelia's conversion to a more humane treatment of Topsy at the end cannot quite undo the general effect of striking comedy from abuse of a dark-faced character.

As if to ensure that his audience understands the significance of the racial humor in his play, Woodworth gives over the last two songs of the finale to the lover's deception from the climax. Rose sings to "city beaux" who may be attracted to "forest roses" to be sure that "there is no sable" in the girls of their eye, "Or you may rue the jest." She concludes enigmatically, "Our farmers all squint awhile at the tint,/Before it is placed in their breast, my dear,/Before it is placed in their breast," as if to say that love itself is colored and that one's heart grows "black" if one chooses a dark-skinned mate. After a chorus of "For lords of the soil," the play's city beau, Bellamy, warns prospective male lovers to "peep under her veil,/Before you make love in the dark, my boy,/Before you make love in the dark" (*FR* 174). Before the invention of the daguerreotype in 1839, the stage functioned as a *camera obscura*, highlighting darkness only long enough to ridicule its pretensions to light. In Woodworth's pun, love in the dark is playing in the dark, the exposure of whiteness to its assumed mirror, the audience of 1825. White villainy, whether Bellamy's, or more insidiously Jonathan's, is made to look like good humor in the Africanist glass of the blackened white actress playing Rose. Thus the good middling types in the audience are given leave to return home, guffawing all the way, if only to get one more laugh at the expense of their black servants: "Wouldn't serve a negro so." Ha! Ha!

Of course, *The Forest Rose* is not alone among American texts of the time that serve African Americans as objects of humorous dismissal. The point, though, is that racism on stage is so closely linked to the "true blue son of liberty," as Tyler's Jonathan labels himself, the Yankee.[64] Analogously, one finds in frontier humor, notably that of Davy Crockett, the same kind of typing from the margins, where the tall tale hero – himself, like the Yankee, an outsider to parlor culture – diminishes Mike Fink's prowess by saying he was only tough among "squaws, cat-fish, and big niggers" or refers to Natives as "red niggers,"[65] thereby lumping two races into one comic butt. By contrast, one can turn to Harriet Wilson's novel, *Our Nig; or Sketches from the Life of a Free Black* (1859), to find the perspective reversed, where Frado, the northern black forced into service, is seen in the suffering she endures from whites, without inciting laughter in readers. As the narrator of that book describes Frado's final trip into Massachusetts, the other Rose, the Africanist spirit beside the white foil, comes to view:

> Watched by kidnappers, maltreated by professed abolitionists, who didn't want slaves at the South, nor niggers in their own houses, North. Faugh! to lodge one; to eat with one; to admit one through the front door; to sit next one; awful![66]

The Bellmonts, Frado's northern employers, and their kind, while not *rural* Yankees, are depicted in the fullness of their bigotry for readers to see clearly. As Joanne Melish sees Wilson's novel, "Her blunt portrayal of the mechanics of 'racial' essentialism and its reproduction in white New England households ... dismantled the model of 'fire-side culture' that was the engine of its reproduction."[67] In other words, as Wilson and perhaps a minority of like-minded persons perceived, the whole construction of the genial, harmless Yankee is a fraud, self-perpetuated by northerners increasingly prone to see racial markers as absolutely marginalizing.

But on the American stage, such direct attacks on racism and Yankee false sympathy rarely appear. Nevertheless, if the cruelty of the Bellmonts toward Frado is more overtly and completely rendered than Jonathan Ploughboy's toward Rose, it is based on the same symbolic assumptions, whether they are called forbearance (Scudder), humor (Jonathan), indignation (Trueman), or prejudice (Bellmonts). Even if one tries to allow for the change of centuries and cultural commonplaces, it is hard for a modern reader to ignore that amidst the cleverness of Woodworth's hit – and it reads better than many another nineteenth-century play – is a structure of incident and language that necessitates the dehumanizing of Rose to assert the humanity of the rest. The stage Yankee, as well as his frontiersman cousin, for all his sendup of pretension, his metaphorically colorful colloquialisms, and his apparent democratic spirit, cannot abide to "sit next one" whose alienation from humane treatment threatens to expose the Yankee's contribution to racial contempt.

As for black characters themselves, even given their use to frame certain types of whites, it is nevertheless still possible to recover at least the hints of more subversive identities than the example of Lid Rose would seem to suggest. No American playwright from before 1825 – at least whose texts are currently available – created African American characters with any overt nobility or clearly marked traits of stoic virtue beyond what Murdock deploys with Sambo in *The Triumphs of Love*. On the other hand, a number of playwrights thought stage African characters worth at least the mention or actual portrayal, as if to recognize the inelidable reality of persons in American society whose origins are other than Europe. One can hardly talk about Tyler's Pompey or Murdock's Sambo as "representative" of persons of color in the social fabric of the new republic – better to speak of James Hewlett, "Shakespeare's proud representative" for that – but at the same time, one can construe the presence of blackface actors as at least acknowledging that an American play true to the fulness of that society should offer characters like those one might encounter on any busy street in an American city. After all, there had just recently been African theatres in New York, and there might be more coming. Even as figures who take abuse – and the suffering Uncle Tom on stage simply fulfills a long-standing theatrical tradition – black characters subvert the structures assumed to be the bedrock of Yankee and other white stage identity. Jonathans rise upon the presumed scars on the backs of the blacks they abuse – meaning of course that they can also fall when that abuse is either exposed as such or at the moment, unrealized on the late eighteenth- and early nineteenth-century white stage, when black characters would more overtly resist such treatment. Even in Tyler's *May Day* and Murdock's *Triumphs*, however, Pompey and Sambo articulate their treatment in such a way as to cast doubt on the efficacy of the slave system; and in the closet plays *Downfall* and Crèvecoeur's "Landscapes," the attacks are more direct, if not finally sufficient to move audiences to denounce slavery entirely. The drama of the new republic reflects many conflicting attitudes on the nature of republican society, including its own uncertainties about the legitimacy of owning and abusing persons and the possibility that abused slaves may be able to speak in voices that register the literal suffering encountered by real people in New England and elsewhere. At the same time, following their British counterparts, American dramas enacted in white theatres require the presence of mockable African others to make whiteness the acknowledged color of the staged nation.

American readers of plays and spectators at the theatre would have found themselves accosted by a variety of enacted ethnic and religious identities – far more than discussed in these chapters – that would have reflected back to them attitudes about race, nationality, and the self that both reinforced and destabilized the white Protestantism that most citizens considered to be normative. The Muslim tyrant, for example, made a seemingly easy target for vilification or comedic contrast, but based as it was on a long tradition of Islamic characters from the English theatre, the stage Muslim can be read as something more complex than the single-featured neo-Vice that seems to dominate new republican texts. American confusion meets British confusion on many points about representing ethnicity; Muslims, especially "Turks," meld into other identities – Native American, for instance. Even with indigenous peoples, race is often fluid; the Indian Princess becomes, in essence, white by the end of Barker's play, while Yarico, the "Indian" of Colman's opera, turns functionally black in the economy of the portrayed West Indies. Meanwhile, Irish characters abound in late eighteenth-century Anglo-American theatre – one can find them alongside Native Americans, Moors, and Africans, as well as English and Anglo-Americans – but beyond their being characters guaranteed to bring comic relief, or a further comic headache, they reflect a confusion about who exactly the Irish are. Are they primitives, European Indians or Africans, with their big sticks and clumsy creole? Or are they tacit Englishmen, who only need the polishing stone of civilization to take off the burr of brogue? They are that and more, it appears, barometers of tolerance and prejudice. Yet when Africans are rendered as such on stage, tolerance is often in short supply. African Americans in 1801 and 1821 created their own stages to ensure the sympathy not found at the Park Theatre in New York, but relatively few whites would have been affected by exposure to the African Theatres. Even the most sympathetic portrayals of the stage African character on white stages fall well short of granting even to objects of pity any hope of incorporation in the Anglicized societies to which they reluctantly belong. At the same time, however, blackface characters – played by whites, we must always remember – often expose the ugliest aspects of whiteness, if unwittingly. Audiences embraced the Jonathan Ploughboys of the time as Jacksonian emblems of American innocence and anti-European simplicity and honesty, but they also hugged to their spectators' bosoms a vicious racialism that clung to the Yankee like a dark, conjoined twin – the American Luigi from *Pudd'nhead Wilson* ineluctably attached to its Angelo. Whatever the politics of abolition or

Indian removal, of Irish acceptance or anti-Irish prejudice, of hostility to Algerians or celebrations of peace following the Tripolitan War, the theatre functioned as an uncertain register of contemporary social and cultural attitudes by forcing those American perspectives into long-standing structures of characterization that had belonged to the British stage for, in some cases, hundreds of years.

Part III

Theatre, culture, and reflected identity

As theatre grew in popularity during the Washington, Adams, and Jefferson administrations, it generated its own local theatre cultures in the expanding number of cities that engaged with professional companies. Those performance cultures in turn had their influence on other cultures, even among citizens who were not necessarily aficionados of the stage or only occasionally attended. Literate residents of any city of size would have encountered advertisements in newspapers when the companies were in town or playbills posted at various points in the city on the day of performance. Actors were well-known personages, even those who repeatedly appeared in subordinate roles, and individual players often generated a corps of followers or a band of detractors. Just the fact of theatre itself could create controversy, despite the removal of legal barriers to theatre construction or performance, as citizens chose to scorn the profession or the politics they thought they observed in the playhouse. Some Americans wanted to see themselves more clearly represented in their republican identity. As one writer to a newspaper complained in 1794 of the Charleston theatre and its British offerings:

> If on the American Stage we are to be entertained with dramatic productions exhibiting the theatrical foppery of passionate Kings, pouting Queens, rakish Princes, and flirting Princesses, knavish Ministers and peevish Secretaries, lamenting misfortunes in which the bulk of mankind are no way concerned; daggering, poisoning, or hanging themselves for grievances that are purely imaginary, better we were without them.[1]

Clearly, the Henry Jones drama, *The Tragedy of the Earl of Essex*, the opening play of the 1794 season, did not meet the American public in its immediate circumstances, but whether the theatre could respond to the letter-writer's challenge was, in the 1790s, uncertain.

The Philadelphia author Charles Brockden Brown, for example, did not write for the stage, but he was well aware of its presence; two of his closest New York friends, William Dunlap and Elihu Hubbard Smith, were in one case a theatre manager and playwright and in the other a chronic spectator and a playwright as well. At the same time, he also knew the history of the theatre in his home city of Philadelphia and allowed that history to infiltrate his novel *Ormond*, a text about disguise, imposture, and the difficulty of identifying an American at all. Meanwhile, for small cities like Norfolk, Virginia, theatre provided a welcome cultural space for citizens to gather when public entertainments other than hangings were otherwise few and scattered. One could attend the occasional concert or fireworks show in Norfolk, but when the actors were in town, not only could citizens see an enormous variety of plays, but the actors themselves sometimes participated in circuses, musical and dance concerts, and otherwise fostered related entertainments. Although little known to theatre history, Norfolk in fact forms an epitome for all theatres in America, small and large, north and south, with its citizens finding on its stages all manner of signs and characters that encouraged or provoked negotiations about identity. The chapter on Norfolk serves also to bring together elements from many of the earlier chapters in a concentrated period of time and in a single place, with its particular social structure, economy, and demographics. Finally, the section and the book close with the person often seen as at the beginning of an American drama and theatre, Royall Tyler, who in poems in his later life reflected on theatre, specifically that in Boston, and wondered whether the stage was a worthy vehicle at all for the shaping of identity. The stage itself was poised to seize the nation as the mass entertainment of choice in 1825 but found in one of its earliest supporters a resistance to its popularity that queried the relationship between theatre and nation.

11

Tales of the Philadelphia Theatre: Ormond, national performance, and supranational identity

AMERICAN DRAMA SITS AMIDST A VARIETY OF CONTEXTS outside of its own textuality, most especially those connected with the physical institution of the theatre. Unfortunately, in examining the theatre of the early national period, investigators find few material traces of the early stage; there are no eighteenth-century theatre buildings extant, for example, and even where the foundation of one can be located, as in Williamsburg, a systematic dig produces relatively few artifacts.[1] Yet we know from other sources that theatres were often well-placed in cities, and their size would have made them noticeable to all. Those who could not or would not have attended the Philadelphia theatre, for example, would certainly have known where the building was, and by reading advertisements on walls and in newspapers would have been aware of the evening's program. To those who supported theatres, the building itself might have served as a beacon of civility, an announcing light that my city, too, encourages the arts found in imperial capitals elsewhere.[2] To those who did not want theatrical performances, the literal stage may have seemed more like a blot on the landscape, a material reminder of the corruption of European vice that had invaded virtuous American space. For the rest, the theatre was simply a fact of urban life, a generator of interest and income, perhaps, and a place to be noted or ignored, but a spot in the eye nonetheless, present, even in its off-season silence. And when the season was running, playhouse, players, concession sellers, spectators, playbill distributors, prostitutes, pathogens, gawkers, carriages, horse manure, all would have assaulted body and senses and at least the casual interest of passersby, leaving their traces in the nostrils, blood, and consciousness of dwellers, denizens, and visitors in the growing cities of the United States.

One register of the impact of theatre on society is the novel; yet even there, the new republican theatre leaves more after-images than direct encounters. Few works of fiction make theatre central to their narratives; in the United States, one has to wait until late 1855 and the publication of three novellas by Anna Cora Mowatt under the collective title of *Mimic Life* to find the stage and those who work there the main focus.³ Still, allusions to dramas, theatres, actors appear throughout the period; one cannot grasp the full effect of Nathaniel Hawthorne's *The Scarlet Letter* (1850) or *The Blithedale Romance* (1852), for example, or Herman Melville's *Moby-Dick* (1851) or *The Confidence Man* (1858) without reference to theatrical practices and personalities of mid-century America.⁴ But even in earlier works, allusions to drama and theatre register various themes and tensions connected to questions of individual or national identity. Hannah Webster Foster's *The Coquette* (1797) invokes the theatre as an uncertain barometer of cultural attitudes not just to the theatre as an institution but to republican politics and the performance of roles, notably those of gender, on the stage of urban New England social life. For Foster, theatre projects itself onto cultural practice in highly complex ways, whereby one correspondent in the epistolary novel can condemn circuses for the display of the female body while the main character, Eliza Wharton, constantly evaluates her own performing before suitors, all while she and others take measure of her as a virtual allegorical character in the masque of the American republic.⁵

A novel contemporary to Foster's pursues the problem of both theatre and performance into even darker corners of the developing awareness of Americans of their Americanness. Charles Brockden Brown's *Ormond* (1799) is set largely in the years 1793 and 1794, a period in Philadelphia history marked by the yellow fever epidemic and the presence of the new government of the United States; by French emigration from Europe and St. Domingue and by racial tension between whites and the city's African American population; and by expansion of trade as well as the development of the city as a cultural center, including the building of a new theatre. As a city open to international trade and influences, it was susceptible to infection and destabilizing forces; Philadelphia became at once the capital of a new nation, the emblem of its embrace of the world, and the very sign of all that is dangerous about such openness.⁶ *Ormond* reflects these conflicting views, yet, in many ways, it is a curiously un-American novel; if anything, Brown's text sustains a critique of whether such a thing as America even exists as an independent cultural entity. A novel of disguises and impostures, *Ormond* suggests that Philadelphia, and hence the United States, is nothing more than a space on which international, even supranational, intrigues play themselves out while things American only serve as an unidentifiable mass that can be manipulated and exploited by forces whose center of power lies outside its national boundaries.[7] As will be seen below, Brown uses the theatre of his time to inflect the novel's uncertainty of location as an American text. In some ways, *Ormond* is no more American than *The Poor Soldier* is British or Irish, but unlike that very malleable play, the novel makes malleability and uncertainty its themes – themes tied to a society shaped by the stage.

For the young Brockden Brown, though, the stage could hardly have been as exciting, had his family been the least inclined to attend, as his own life. In Peter Kafer's telling, six-year-old Charles, child to Quaker parents, would have seen his father hauled off by Revolutionary authorities who branded him as "inimical" to patriot interests. Although the committees of safety had been supplanted by the time of Elijah Brown's arrest in September 1777, the Scots–Irish Presbyterians who formed the party loyal to the 1776 Pennsylvania Revolutionary constitution still used the committees' favorite denunciatory term and found ample opportunities to attack or intimidate neutral Quakers for their alleged sympathies with Britain. Suffering through the eight-month absence of his father, who was exiled to Virginia, and the sounds of harsh street mobs that shattered Quaker windows or ransacked homes,[8] Brown may have grown up with a deep suspicion of popular authority, much like expressed in Crèvecoeur, Munford, and Murray. Although there are virtually no direct allusions to the American Revolution in *Ormond*, the novel's failure to celebrate or affirm anything American may draw some of its negative energy from Brown's early experience at being an American whose family was denounced for not being American in the right way.

Ormond is set largely in Philadelphia and tells the story of Constantia Dudley, a virtuous young woman who must care for her father, Stephen Dudley, when he loses his business and his eyesight. Told through the narration of Sophia Westwyn Courtland, a woman who does not enter the tale in her own person until the plot is nearly complete, the novel introduces various unusual characters, including Craig, a New Englander who dupes Dudley, embezzles the assets of his business, and poses a continuing threat to both Dudley and Constantia; Ormond, a wealthy man with an exotic past that includes life among both Cossacks and Native Americans; and Martinette, Ormond's sister, herself unusual for her revolutionary activities and one-time sanguinary masquerade as a soldier. Both Ormond and Craig prove physically and psychologically threatening to Constantia, but she is rescued by Sophia and taken to Britain, where the latter has set up housekeeping with her husband.

There is hardly a single character in the novel who could be called "American" in the sense of having been born there and developed an identity grounded in values that are distinctive to the place. With the possible exception of such minor characters as Melbourne and Roseveldt, about whose backgrounds we know little, the one who comes closest, at least among the principals, is Constantia, but even she leaves the country at novel's end for England, presumably never to return. One has to ask, then, what Brown means by such denationalizing, especially in late 1798, the period when he was writing, or 1793–1794, the time of the text.[9] After all, the 1790s, as the first decade of government under the Constitution, mark a particularly self-conscious period of national identification by which allegiances to Britain and France are tested, argued over, and reversed; during this period too, one can detect the origins of American literary nationalism, the attempts by writers to create distinctive works or to argue against such distinctiveness. Brown certainly played his own role as the creator of a national literature, as his friend William Dunlap did in the theatre, but as Dunlap discovered in his own plays, Brown in *Ormond* especially saw the project of setting novels on his native soil did not in itself make them American. Brown again faced an analogous problem to that of his fellow citizens who wrote plays, the lack of local models and thus the seeming necessity to look abroad for clues to composition. William Godwin's *Caleb Williams* exerts a greater influence on *Ormond* than, say, *The Coquette* or William Hill Brown's *The Power of Sympathy* (1789), to name two earlier native-authored fictions set in the United States. As Bernard Rosenthal has pointed out, the early nineteenth-century British reviewers saw Brown as essentially an English novelist, with only the scene names in America distinguishing his works from those set in England, but Rosenthal ascribes this critical tendency to Brown's being primarily a "metaphysical" rather than a "geographical" writer.[10] Other critics have noted also about Brown's texts that identity is fluid in general, as if to say in each case that the author disavows anything specific in an American scene or character.[11] What I would suggest, however, is that Brown *is* conscious of geography,[12] but in a way that deliberately undermines clear national identity; in the way that Brown shows skepticism "toward self-determination, justice, truth, and providence," by following his European influences, so he does toward nationality.[13] In *Ormond* Brown creates pan- or supranational characters as a means of overwriting any pretensions to nationalism in the United States, as if to say the new republic exposes like no other place that nationality is always a performance, never an identity.

From the beginning, we encounter in *Ormond* a vagabondish population. Like the actors in contemporary theatre companies, most of whom were from someplace other than the United States, Brown's characters have a variety of origins that call into question their particular allegiances. Stephen Dudley has spent his young manhood abroad, studying art in Italy; after his numerous reverses, including the onset of blindness, he draws upon his international experience to instruct his daughter Constantia in politics and the languages of the countries he knew at firsthand. The one object in which he puts any store, the lute, was purchased in Italy; during his blindness especially, its tones bring comfort and solace. After his recovery of both fortune and sight, Dudley plans to go abroad for a prolonged period, a trip that is prevented by his murder by an unknown assailant, whom we learn later to be Craig. As far as Dudley is concerned, the United States is that country where his father, mother, and wife die, where he operates a business out of necessity, and where all his struggles occur. Europe, by contrast, is where he lived at ease and freedom, pursuing his dream career, painter. For practical reasons, if none other, Dudley can hardly imagine himself at his core to be anything but an internationalist whose years in America have been only so much suffering and compromise. Although Brown had not himself traveled outside the United States, his friend Dunlap had, in pursuit of a painting career; given that part of the novel is set in Perth Amboy, New Jersey, Dunlap's home, the novelist may be suggesting that, like his friend, Americans with artistic and intellectual interests need to imagine themselves part of a larger, transatlantic world of thought and culture in order to find fulfillment.

Dudley comes to ruin by the imposture of Thomas Craig, a would-be Yorkshireman, who works his way into Dudley's apothecary business through an assumed identity; he proves later to be a confidence man from New Hampshire – a Stephen Burroughs, perhaps, whose autobiographical narrative of his own impostures had just recently been published.[14] Although an American and possibly named Mansfield at birth, Craig determines to acquire his fortune through the costume of another nationality. Curiously, he chooses to be Yorkshire English, a geographical identity that allies him with one of the British stage types that contributes to the construction of the American stage Yankee.[15] When he completes his embezzlement of Dudley's business and departs New York, it is allegedly to Jamaica, then still a British colony and the theatrical center of the English-speaking West Indies as well as the one-time haven of British-born actors in the mainland colonies during the Revolution. Although later he dies on American soil, Craig, too, has forgone any particular identity tied to his upbringing. If the evidence of his mother's semi-literate letter is any indication, he has undertaken to transform himself, an imitator of Ben Franklin, by refashioning his national identity in international terms and henceforth seeing the United States as a stage on which to play whatever role suits his own acquisition of gain. In the cases of both Dudley and Craig, the characters acquire new names not only as disguises but also as strategies for the dissolution of identity; as Wil Verhoeven puts it, "in *Ormond* naming is not a means to establish identity, but to postpone identification indefinitely."[16] Most of the discussion of identity has to do with psychological forces brought on by a world without clear moral focus. As Steven Watts remarks about *Ormond*'s characters in general, "Stripped of family support, religious values, and community commitments, they struggled in vain to find solace in ideology or worldly achievement."[17] The attempt to deny nationality, change it, or supersede it can be explained as either coming from a world without commitments or in fact contributing to it. In any event, Brown's characters are all highly conscious of national identity, even if identity as a psychological or epistemological category defies Lockean sensationalism, except insofar as they *are* Americans – a peculiar state of affairs for a novel by an American written in and about the United States.

Although neither of these characters has the role-playing power of Ormond himself, their pairing is instructive for understanding the antinationalist terms of Brown's novel. Dudley, following his ruin in New York, moves to Philadelphia and assumes a new name, Acworth, thereby disguising his presence and fooling nearly everyone, including Craig, who also comes to Philadelphia and takes up a friendship with Ormond. Even a character whose faults are hardly deserving of his ill fate finds it necessary in his homeland to become something else, even as a thin mask of a name without trace. Not exactly an impostor, Dudley still changes his history – that of an elite with the wherewithal to have lived abroad for that of a poor man with a virtuous daughter and no outward pretensions to cosmopolitanism. Craig, meanwhile, native-born and bred, deliberately creates an overseas pedigree that, while out of the metropolis, still conveys to the Europeanized Dudley a kind of trustworthiness that perhaps saying one was from a semi-literate family in New Hampshire might not have created. Ironically, Brown suggests that in the world of the novel, an "honest Yorkshireman" – a term that formed the title of a comedy by Henry Carey that was performed in the colonial theatre – carried more likelihood of truth than "honest Yankee," as if he anticipated the dark side of the type as it developed in the later American theatre. In neither Craig's nor Dudley's case does the character link himself inextricably and honestly to his homeland.[18]

Among other characters, the ties to America seem tenuous at best. Constantia's rescuer from a group of leering thugs is one Balfour, a Scottish merchant, whose counting-house ways Constantia later finds repugnant. Scots played an equivocal social role in early national America as both British and not, American and not. During the Revolution, the Scottish Lord Bute was often pilloried or hanged in effigy for his allegedly evil advice on the American situation to King George, and a scotch bonnet became an American street protest symbol of British duplicity; both before and after the war, prejudice against Scots could be found in a number of colonies turned states.[19] As one patriot stated the case against Scottish merchants, they are "something like the stinking and troublesome weed we call in Virginia wild onion. Whenever *one* is permitted to fix [i.e., to root], the number soon increases so fast, that it is extremely difficult to eradicate them, and they poison the ground so, that no wholesome plant can thrive."[20] Scots appear in many British plays as Sawney, or variants of the type, tight-fisted, linguistically marked as not quite English – Archy Macsarcasm, for instance, in Charles Macklin's *Love a-la-Mode*. Among American playwrights, Thomas Forrest plays with the type in his character McSnip in the Philadelphia-set *The Disappointment*, while Robert Munford brings forward the proscribed Scots M'Flint, M'Gripe, and M'Squeeze in his Virginia closet play *The Patriots*. Thus whatever Constantia's sympathies or antipathies toward Balfour personally, he has no particular identity as an American, except insofar as Brown may be suggesting that the United States is nothing more than an amalgamation of dubious figures from other lands. These national characters do not, Crèvecoeur-like, melt away by achieving a new creolized identity in their new home but are stuck, as are theatrical Irish or Jews, in their assigned national or ethnic type. At the same time, however, Balfour has no real identity as a Scotsman either[21]; his originating characteristics lose their national flavor on American soil or only become a kind of bleak comic typing, shadows of the comedies on Philadelphia stages that enact typed European identities.

Or take another case, that of Baxter, the watchman who observes Martinette's burial of a shadowy man named Roselli and seems so badly to misinterpret what he sees. In her extended and exceptional analysis of that scene in terms of his role as spectator, Julia Stern claims that Baxter becomes a register of "nativist" sentiment, with the implication that *native* means American.[22] But Baxter's earlier career as a military man in the British army in the European theatre, and his subsequent hatred of the French, can only be interpreted here as a British nativist, not an American nativist posture, however much Brown may be evoking partisan politics in the United States. Baxter says nothing that identifies him specifically as an American national other than his suspicions of individuals he perceives to be foreigners, but suspicions whose origins lie well outside Philadelphia or the United States. Like the Anglocentric American theatre, Baxter imports his prejudices, and like Balfour, retains some putative national trait in a land that ostensibly does not recognize those traits as inherent in its own, but whether he is only a British native in Philadelphia or now an American native with British prejudices is difficult to distinguish.

The two characters most easily identified as supranational (that is, beyond nationality) are Ormond and his sister Martinette, siblings whose idealisms take one into support of popular and fully public political revolutions, the other into perverse and secret plots for social manipulation and control.[23] Like Constantia, Martinette lives in Philadelphia under an assumed name, Ursula Monrose, but has no particularly diabolical reasons for doing so – a convenience only, to prevent undue attention, no different from the Dudleys becoming Acworths. Martinette's saga of her childhood, and thus Ormond's, includes such a hodge-podge of backgrounds and experiences as to preclude for her any national claim. She speaks French and English with perfect clarity, but by her Greek Cypriot mother and Sicilian father, not to mention birth in Syria, she knows two languages of the ancient Christian church, Slavonic and Syriac, that in the eighteenth century would not have been spoken widely as indigenous tongues, as well as Greek and Arabic. One has to assume that she knows Italian (or Sicilian or both) as well, not only through her residence in Verona but also from her father and her guardian, even though it is unclear precisely as to the nationalities either of her father or Roselli, the latter only identified as a merchant of Marseilles with an Italian name. Indeed, she may also know German and Spanish from having lived in

Vienna with Lady D'Arcy's husband Antonio de Leyva for a time. Martinette functionally has no particular national origin nor does Sophia or Constantia condemn her for this frequent shifting of national guises. She accomplishes in the person of her character what an actor like Philadelphia's John William Green did on successive nights at the Philadelphia theatre in 1794: put on accents and identities without regard to coherence or consistency.

Ormond, for his part, shares a youth with Martinette, then a period of schooling in Switzerland before his years with the Cossacks in Russia and as an explorer of the trans-Mississippi West. Unlike Martinette, who from Constantia (or, indirectly, Sophia) keeps back no vital information, Ormond withholds his life story almost entirely. He maintains, it appears, some secret correspondence with a network of fellow totalitarian idealists, which most commentators have shown to be the Bavarian Illuminati, an international organization founded by a German.[24] He differs from Martinette primarily at the level of secrecy over publicity, which then manifests itself morally in his attempted rape of Constantia versus Martinette's often friendly intervention on her behalf, but both characters in effect enact nationalities that they do not intend to claim on a permanent basis. Indeed, Ormond is distinguished by Sophia for his ability to mimic others in public, putting on costumes of identity at complete odds with his own position as an elite, but strangely, the one role we witness – secretly, it seems – is his portrayal of a black chimney sweep. As Julia Stern suggests, "his expropriation of a bondsman's color, garb, and labor would seem to repeat in theatrical form the very dynamic of exploitation and commodification that marks slavery itself; the libertine clearly profits from assuming the (negative) power of blackness."[25] No doubt taking his cue from the enactment of the stage African in European and American theatres, Ormond, in effect, goes beyond the crude typing in the theatres to adopt a more insidious form of performance. He plays at race and occupation, knowing he need not genuinely suffer in the way African American chimney sweeps, who dominated the trade, did in their literal crawls through cramped, sooty chimneys.[26] This enactment has considerable resonance in terms of power relations, but in a peculiar way, the role is also as close to a "native" role as any that Ormond adopts while living in America. But we also know, from the experience of Philadelphia's African Americans, that blacks were typed to carry the dead in the yellow fever epidemic precisely for their foreignness, that is, their alleged racial ability to withstand the infection. A black chimney sweep is someone both American and not, seen and unseen, perfect for Ormond's cynical use of disguises but problematic in terms of national identity. Whereas in plays of the time the Africanist character plays against and defines white characters, in *Ormond* the title character incorporates the Africanist figure in his own person, a performance that outperforms what went on at the Southwark Theatre in its self-deconstruction. If a white can pantomime a black with authority, then in effect no national or ethnic identity can be presumed secure from being stolen and performed. "Black" is located not outside of white but within, while those in society marked as black are reminded daily of their being without.

Except for a few scenes whereby tradespeople enter or exit, as with the African American carters that Constantia meets during the height of the fever, "*Ormond* seems oddly empty of city activity ... it is peopled only with the few characters of major importance,"[27] not unlike a stage set and a drama. That so many characters function in effect as social actors is consistent with the fact that during the 1790s, Philadelphia vied with New York as the theatre center of the new republic. It cemented its reputation as a theatre city by hosting the two most important companies then in the United States: the Old American Company when it left New York and the Wignell–Reinagle troupe. The latter company played at the Southwark Theatre during the summer of 1793, but closed its season early with the sickness of some of its members and the onset of the yellow fever. For six months, there was no theatrical activity in the city. In February 1794, however, after the fever epidemic ended, as Sophia tells us, "Public entertainments were thronged with auditors. A new theatre had lately been constructed and a company of English comedians had arrived during the prevalence of the malady. They now began their exhibitions, and their audiences were overflowing."[28] The New Theatre on Chestnut Street gave those weary of worrying about infection something with which to forget its ravages, particularly among the white elite who had the wherewithal to remove from the city when the infection first arrived. This theatre background plays itself out in *Ormond* in a variety of ways: as the institution that gives rise to a series of metaphors employed by Sophia, such as the "theatre of calamity" or "theatre of suffering" (*O* 91, 175); as the cultural activity that provides public models of masking and disguise; and as the medium by which American spectators viewed entertainments that often maintained national characters quite other than those of the United States qua Anglo-America. It is this last dimension of theatre in Philadelphia that has most relevance for the supranationalism of Brown's novel.[29]

The degree of Brown's playgoing probably did not match that of his New York Friendly Club associates William Dunlap, the manager of the John Street and Park theatres, and Elihu Hubbard Smith, the physician, poet, playwright, and diarist, but he could not help being aware of the stage not only through them but also through simply living in Philadelphia and spending long periods in New York. For Brown and Smith, conversation with like-minded friends, male and female, was more likely to satisfy than a night at the theatre;[30] nevertheless, the very presence of theatres in New York and Philadelphia was enough to enter the cultural and discourse consciousness of any group of intellectuals and literati in those two cities. No scene in *Ormond* takes place at the theatre, but as above, Brown directly mentions the stage at its reopening, with more than a hint of scorn in Sophia's voice for the swelling crowds so soon on the eve of the fever's abatement. The same scorn for the literal theatre appears also in the description of Ormond's acting ability: "He blended in his own person the functions of poet and actor, and his dramas were not fictitious but real. The end that he proposed was not the amusement of a playhouse mob. His were scenes in which hope and fear exercised a genuine influence, and in which was maintained that resemblance to truth so audaciously and grossly violated on the stage" (*O* 130–31). The crowds who attend the Southwark or Chestnut Street stages are mobs – perhaps with a lust for spectacle like those patriot mobs that terrified Philadelphia Quakers during the war – and the actors violators of truth. Part of Brown's project is to say that social acting has far deeper and darker ramifications than that of the theatre, but to some degree, Brown is also commenting on the fare served up on American boards and the palpable falsehood of its character types. In either case, Brown affirms that theatre threatens structures of identity less than social theatricality, whose effectiveness presumes the belief that what one encounters outside the playhouse doors is true to itself.

If one surveys the offerings in Philadelphia from the start of the Old American Company's spring and summer season in 1792 through the conclusion of the Wignell and Reinagle season in July 1794, the approximate dates of the action in the novel, one finds only a handful of dramas or entertainments that could in the least be called American. Those include the debuts of J. Robinson's comedy, *The Yorker's Stratagem* in 1792 and Susanna Rowson's *Slaves in Algiers* in 1794, plays by writers who were adult immigrants to the United States. What appeared to be a revival of David Humphreys's *The Widow of Malabar* (previously performed three times in Philadelphia in 1790 and 1791) the night following Rowson's play (July 2) was in fact a new production of the "imitation" of Le Mierre's French original by English writer Mariana Starke – in itself a telling fact.[31] Two nights out of 162 performance days (1.23 percent) over the 26 months covered in the period were devoted to American productions – the rest were almost exclusively plays by British playwrights.[32] However, if we examine the two American plays, we discover that neither of them is "American" in the sense that either of them depicts life in the United States. *The Yorker's Stratagem* takes place in the British West Indies; and while two characters playact Yankees as dialect-speaking gulls, they only do so to catch the avarice of an island character. Rowson's *Slaves in Algiers* has American characters but is set in Algiers, with an international cast of enacted nationalities including English Protestants, English Jews, North African Arabs, and British Americans, with the odd Spaniard thrown in for good measure. (Even had Humphreys's *Widow* been performed, the former Revolutionary officer's play is about Hindu *sati*, with nary an American among the dramatis personae.) Among the British plays, two of note make some allusion to North America, Richard Cumberland's *The West Indian* and George Colman, Jr.'s *Inkle and Yarico*, but in both cases, as with Robinson's comedy, the connections are to the West Indies, not the mainland, a telling detail given Craig's reported period in the islands in *Ormond*. With the possible exception of a very occasional patriotic afterpiece or interlude, Philadelphians attending professional productions between May 1792 and July 1794 saw no full-length play by either a British or an American writer that depicted life in the United States.

Of the plays that were shown, the overwhelming majority were comedies, with such writers as Isaac Bickerstaff, Colley Cibber, George Colman, Sr., George Colman, Jr., Susanna Centlivre, Elizabeth Inchbald, Frederick Reynolds, and John O'Keeffe some of the authors with multiple plays in production. Among the few tragedies produced, the two companies put on the usual Shakespeares, including *Othello*, *Hamlet*, and *Macbeth*, with a scattering of tragic works by more contemporary authors such as Edward Moore's *The Gamester* and George Lillo's *The London Merchant*, or, as it was usually billed, *George Barnwell*. Of the other tragedies, though, there are a few worth noting in the context of Brown's novel. Among the artistic accomplishments of Ormond's mistress, Helena Cleves, is the ability to act with such feeling that "she appeared to have drank in the very soul of the dramatist" (141). Although Helena's acting is acclaimed as such – she does not try to disguise herself in society as Ormond does – that she does not appear on the professional stage may be Brown's further attempt to criticize the actors who are not attentive to the dramatist's "soul." One of her impersonations is that of Calista, the tragic heroine of Nicholas Rowe's *The Fair Penitent* and long considered to be a choice role for a leading actress in her prime. Calista has one "guilty night" with Lothario before her fiancé, Altamont, returns from the wars to wed her, which of course has tragic consequences.[33] Calista throws her feelings away on one undeserving of them, an action that fits well in Brown's scheme and suggests that he has both play and theatre in mind in creating Helena. To be sure, the Philadelphia companies offered those long popular works of Rowe, both *The Fair Penitent* and *Jane Shore*, with the two "she-tragedies" combining for four performances over two years.[34]

Of greatest interest, perhaps, are some isolated Philadelphia performances of three political tragedies: Thomas Otway's *Venice Preserved*, Joseph Addison's *Cato*, and Henry Brooke's *Gustavus Vasa*, all relatively popular on the colonial stage, the first two especially so, but all of which faded from the regular repertory by 1800. All three plays focus intensely on the matter of *liberty*, a word much invoked during the Revolutionary period but, during the 1790s, both at the time of the action in the novel and that of Brown's writing, one much feared or contentiously used in popular discourse and a word in *Ormond* that resonates with ambiguous determinations of virtue and vice. Brooke's play features a proscribed nationalist hero, Gustavus Vasa, who disguises himself as a stranger until such time as he rises up in his own person to lead the independence fighters for Sweden against the occupying Danes. In essence, Brooke legitimates the necessary disguise – a popular device in nineteenth-century drama as well – for the purposes of some greater good, in this case, liberty from an oppressive, tyrannical power whose yoke stifles exercise of freedom more than expression of nationalism. In that vein, Martinette de Beauvais, who disguises herself as a male warrior and participates in the fight for liberty both in the American and French Revolutions, would find justification in a play like Brooke's. For an author, Brooke's play has special significance; banned from the stage by means of the Licensing Act of 1736 for its alleged political relevance to Walpolean England, *Gustavus Vasa* only appeared in theatres in the New World. In that sense, it was a British play about a Swedish patriot that could only be enacted in North America – a drama that crossed and erased national lines and identities in the sense that liberty was not "Swedish" or

"British" but supranational, operative where it found a fit home, but was forced to flee again when the home to liberty turned tyrant against it.[35]

The history of *Cato* in America needs no explanation, but the context in post-Revolutionary America is worth a brief look. In many ways, Constantia derives a certain amount of her ability to weather the vicissitudes of poverty and yellow fever through what amounts to a stoical commitment to duty, even though Brown expresses it as a rational choice. Cato, of course, glorifies this stoical engagement with forces that may lead to death, in the name of greater goods to which one is providentially committed; in Addison, as in Brooke, the primary good is liberty. Beyond that, though, Cato, a Roman, is fighting in Africa against other Romans; among his allies is Juba, the African prince who possesses, as one of Cato's sons expresses it, a Roman soul. By *Roman*, Addison means something pan-national, or really supranational, a commitment to liberty that supersedes the nationalist agenda of an imperial power for a set of values that lies beyond any national denomination. Both Cato's suicide and Juba's survival serve as rejections of national commitment for the larger, nation-defying ideal of a free-floating doctrine of liberty.[36] The shadow of *Cato* behind the novel marks Martinette's commitment to liberty as selflessly "Roman," and Ormond's to libertinism as egregious self-interest.

The other non-Shakespearean tragedy of note to play during the period of action in the novel, Otway's *Venice Preserved*, was especially popular during the 1790s. In Philadelphia, professional productions were mounted twice each in 1792 and 1794 with one other performance in the plague year of 1793; additionally, it played four times in the city in 1797. In New York, as noted above in connection with Dunlap's *André*, Otway's drama appeared once each in 1793, 1794, 1797, 1798, and three times in 1799. Because of its frequency of performance and the fact it was his friend Dunlap's favorite play, *Venice Preserved* could hardly have been missed by Brown in either city. It too is a liberty play, but unlike Brooke and Addison, Otway complicates the political end by portraying the failure of liberty to last past the time of the play. The deaths of two of the conspirators, Jaffeir and Pierre, are nobly presented, but their international plot against the Venetian republic is fraught with corruption, and in the case of Jaffeir, betrayal. Full of metaphors of disease both for the existing state and the conspiracy against it, *Venice Preserved* has much of the kind of atmosphere Brown represents in feverish Philadelphia, not to mention a conspiracy leader – the putative Frenchman, Renault – whose overweening ambition, contempt for those outside the conspiracy, and attempted rape of the tragic female character, Belvidera, all remind one of Brown's eponymous character. By play's end, Renault has been arrested and executed, the conspiracy demonized and destroyed, Belvidera driven to distraction and death by events, and the most committed plotter for liberty, Pierre, killed. Liberty itself hardly stands a chance, even were it possible to assert it in a better guise. Yet what is also significant here is the way in which Otway implicates men of many nations in service to a supranational ideal, even if for nearly all the conspirators the motives for liberty – to Otway's tory sensibility – are corrupt.[37] Brown writes against Otway by introducing more forceful female characters, who work together enough to make it possible for Constantia to survive her ordeal, but like the British dramatist, he leaves readers without much hope that the general air of contagion and corruption that pervades Philadelphia will be dispelled simply by the deaths of Craig and Ormond.

The characters most associated with liberty in Brown's novel are Martinette and her English husband, Wentworth. Although we only meet Wentworth at second hand, he comes across in Sophia's narration as one of the most purely motivated characters in the novel, second only perhaps to the African American carters who assist Constantia during the fever epidemic. Despite the country of his birth, Wentworth defies the traditional nationalist obligation and travels to America to fight on the side of the patriot rebels against the British military. According to the story related to Constantia by Martinette, Wentworth arrives first in St. Domingue in 1777, makes it to Richmond, then joins Washington in time for the battle of Germantown in Pennsylvania (historically, on October 4), where he is wounded and made prisoner. Shipped back to England as an enemy to his home nation, Wentworth dies in prison, unremarked upon even by his own family. Martinette, however, gains currency in London as a noble wife, whose courageous behavior is attested to by returning officers from the war and who becomes almost literally a theatrical object, "exhibited at operas and masquerades" (203) among the pro-American set in England.

Wentworth's significance is not that he fought for American independence, and thus a nationalist cause, but that he committed himself to liberty, a supranational one. Indeed, he does not even die in the United States but abroad, thus depriving the land of a potential martyr. Thereafter, Martinette commits herself to liberty, fighting next in the French Revolution for that ineffable ideal, wielding a sword ruthlessly in its defense. News of the Revolution deeply influenced popular discourse in the 1790s, including that among women. As French women took action on behalf of various causes in France, so American women observed and in some cases imitated. Wearing French Revolutionary fashions or adopting French expressions ("citoyenne") served as a kind of street theatre for American women who saw the example of their French counterparts as an opportunity for greater participation in public affairs. Therefore, to introduce a female Revolutionary partisan accords with contemporary events and attitudes among women in Philadelphia and elsewhere.[38]

Brown's position on this, however, as with so much in the novel, is ambivalent. On the one hand, Constantia's new acquaintance claims to have become the devotee of liberty in her new role as revolutionary soldier for France, but on the other, this leads her to slaughter, including the killing of thirteen officers in one battle in 1792. At one point, she states that she was prepared to assassinate the Prussian general through a performance of national and political disguise, then kill herself in a principled act – reminiscent perhaps of Cato – and only the retreat of the Prussians prevented her from enacting that role. A nobler (though not necessarily more virtuous) figure than Constantia, particularly as the latter lapses into a near caricature of the sentimental heroine, Martinette, in her supranationality, violates all of Constantia's codes for civilized, rational behavior in the ready embrace of bloodletting for cause – an echo of what Otway ultimately critiques in *Venice Preserved*. Constantia kills to prevent rape, but Brown prevents that desperate act from being read as pure allegory. It is not an American nationalist victory over a foreign criminal nor a blow for any cause outside of personal safety, for she immediately departs with Sophia for England thereafter. Martinette, repudiating any lasting national identity or association, chooses to engage in world events that functionally require her to draw blood – a supranational version of the American martial heroine, Deborah Sampson Gannett, whose fictionalized biography had been published in 1797. Like Sampson Gannett for her biographer Herman Mann, Martinette creates potential anxieties for Brown as a woman in uniform, moving far from traditional female identities; but Brown attempts to solve the problem by having Martinette leave the action and restore to Constantia, who takes center stage in the last quarter of the text as a potential rape victim, the more traditional vulnerability of the woman as a reassurance to readers that the whole world is not topsy-turvy.[39]

Despite its American setting, *Ormond* displays its author's peculiar aversion to rendering his homeland as anything other than a stage for the playacting of identities that never last much longer than a single performance. At once scornful of the theatre as an institution suited to the mob and distortions of the truth, the novel, at least from Sophia's perspective, figures the world and life experience frequently in terms of the playhouse; at the same time, as it evokes a number of plays popular on American boards in the 1790s, *Ormond* portrays a culture of social and political disguise and imposture that has far more devastating and threatening effects on culture and individuals than anything the theatre itself can conjure.[40] Unlike such plays as *Cato* or *Gustavus Vasa* or Rowe's *Tamerlane* – an early favorite in colonial theatres – where supranationalism is presented as the *sine qua non* of achieving liberty, Brown's novel portrays the supranationalist character as both principled and a fraud, heroic and murderous, more powerful than local characters but also more insidious. At the same time, however, Brown never asserts anything like a nationalist ideal to counter the conspiratorial nature of nationalist disguise; indeed, there is virtually nothing that suggests that "American" as a category has any concrete existence except as a temporary geographical locator. As Stern remarks, the novel concludes with " a stunningly barren vision of the early national future."[41] In that sense, critics may wish to query what it means to call *Ormond* an American novel at all; or to ask whether Brown saw fiction as others saw liberty or the stage, as a cultural production unlocatable in the culture it purportedly reflects.

Ironically, however, the most "American" thing about *Ormond* may be its invocation of the Philadelphia theatre. A space where the American landscape was almost never represented, the stage referred to by Brown in his text played before citizens of the city a variety of identities whose multiplicity is mirrored in the figuration of identity in the novel itself. Without intending to do so directly, Brown exposes the instability of identity both on the stage and in the street, asking whether liberty or, for that matter, theatre, can be located in any national enterprise. But in some ways, it is the presence of theatre at all that allows Brown to define his native country by default as the land without fixed identities. Closed by fever and opened in its wake to help citizens forget all about its ravages, the Philadelphia stage conjured up by the novelist holds an uncertain mirror to nature, reflecting back to the capital of the new republic only the instability of performance and the evanescence of nationality. Brown's reference to seasons almost devoid of American dramatic authorship, his portrayal of characters whose social acting undercuts all certainty based on region and nationality, and his satiric remarks about Philadelphia spectators as a mob or as unfeeling consumers of pleasure, who flock back to the theatres over the backs of the yellow fever dead, all call into question the degree to which theatre has anything to say about identity in the United States as a distinct nationalism. Brown's view is not definitive, nor did it have any retarding effect on theatregoing in the United States, but *Ormond* exposes the continuing problem of determining identity in a world where both actors and citizens carry on imitations, try on disposable ethnicities, and resist being fixed by any unitary standard of Americanism.

12

A British or an American tar? Play, player, and spectator in Norfolk, 1797–1800

THE SKEPTICISM OF A BROCKDEN BROWN ABOUT THEATRE'S ability to render identity or the darkened mirror of racial, gender, ethnic, and class representations as contained in some of the plays discussed above could hardly stop the development and spread of theatre beyond the major sites of New York, Boston, Philadelphia, and Charleston. By 1790 the seaport town of Norfolk, Virginia, at the confluence of the James and Elizabeth Rivers and the entrance to the Chesapeake Bay, had risen from the ashes of the Revolution to become a bustling, growing, cosmopolitan city. Having been largely burned on January 1, 1776, by the departing royal governor of Virginia, Lord Dunmore, Norfolk had reconstructed its waterfront and downtown sufficiently to attract two traveling, professional theatre companies in 1790, that run by the Kennas and the new one formed by Thomas Wade West and his son-in-law partner, John Bignall. In the following year, Norfolk became a regular stop for West and Bignall on a circuit of Southern cities that included, in its heyday, Charleston, South Carolina, and five cities in Virginia: Richmond, Petersburg, Alexandria, Fredericksburg, and Norfolk. In 1792, West arranged the purchase of an L-shaped piece of property facing Fenchurch Street in Norfolk and over the next year constructed a new theatre building, relatively small in comparison to theatres built by West elsewhere, but made of brick and thought in its time to have fine appointments. By 1793, not only was West's company playing regular seasons in the New Theatre, but West and his wife, the actress Margaretta Sully West, had purchased an adjoining lot for their home at the corner of Fenchurch and Main, a few muddy blocks from the market center. Thus, even though West and company did not play Norfolk every year, the troupe, or at least its managers, viewed Norfolk as the home base, in the geographical center of the circuit, and therefore offered to the town the best of its repertoire.

Despite being virtually ignored by theatre historians, Norfolk provides a particular window through which to observe issues of stage and identity in the early years of the new republic. What Norfolk saw in the last seasons of the eighteenth century and how it observed the over one hundred plays produced by the company is the subject of this inquiry.[1] For Norfolk, as for other cities, the theatre involved a continuous negotiation among actors and managers, plays and histories of performance, and spectators and other residents in acting before the community what it thought its patrons wanted to see.

By 1797, Norfolk probably had something close to 6,000 permanent residents, including well over 2,000 African Americans.[2] Among its white population were persons from a variety of European backgrounds, including a substantial French population that arrived in the wake of the revolutions in France and St. Domingue. Not counted in the census figures were no doubt hundreds of sailors from many nations from some of the thousand or more ships that docked in Norfolk annually, men whose legendary rowdiness and visits to Bank Street and Little Water Street in search of drink and accommodating women gave the city a reputation for bawdiness that had not entirely disappeared in the late twentieth century. Factors for Tidewater planters, merchants, shipbuilders, and others engaged in trade made up Norfolk's elite, and provided the core of supporters for a theatre that must have served as a sign of the city's importance and its own cultural image. Nevertheless, audiences were probably well mixed, with sailors and prostitutes in attendance, slaves and free blacks, tradespeople, shopkeepers, and elite women and men, not to mention visitors to Norfolk or others passing through.[3] In short, Norfolk would have offered a diverse and representative cross-section of those who made up the population of American seaport cities, albeit shaped to Chesapeake plantation culture and on a smaller scale than places like Philadelphia and New York, each of which in 1800 had populations approximately ten times the size of Virginia's leading port. If the city differed beyond that from its larger northern cousins, it may have been in the lack of crippling party divisions that damaged the theatrical cultures in major ports; Norfolk was predominantly a Democratic–Republican town, even though the standard of criticism of the stage was often expressed in British terms.[4] Norfolk saw what New York, Boston, and Philadelphia saw – and in a few cases, plays that one or more of those cities did not see – and thus, for the most part, what London saw as well, a year or two or more later.

Examining the faded and often poorly photographed pages of the *Norfolk Herald*, virtually the only source of information on the seasons in Norfolk, one finds a typical mix of plays for the period: a large preponderance of comedies, mostly recent; a few Shakespeares; a few tragedies by other authors; and a number of musical performances, largely in the afterpiece, including grand pantomimes.[5] Many evenings featured entr'acte performances, usually dancing or singing, and similar entertainments as a bridge between the main play and the afterpiece. This meant that West's company had to maintain a sufficient corps of actors to accommodate a variety of play types; singers and dancers who could double as actors but whose merits in the other lines would have been sufficient to attract customers; and a small orchestra, including at least one person capable of writing arrangements or even composing new music.[6] In its prime, the company would have been as large, or nearly so, as the companies kept in New York and Philadelphia, the two most important theatre centers.

Thomas Wade West had extensive experience acting both in English provincial and London theatres by the time he arrived in the United States around 1790.[7] The core of his troupe included his wife, Margaretta, who played a full variety of roles but specialized in tragic female lead; his partner, John Bignall, who also had extensive experience in Britain and who often acted comic leads, including such singing roles as that of Shelty in John O'Keeffe's *The Highland Reel*; and his daughter, Ann West Bignall, who usually played comic female lead, and was thought by some to be the equal of any actress in her line working in the United States.[8] The other actors who comprised the Virginia and Charleston Company, and later the Virginia Company, often came immediately from other theatres in the United States, but nearly all of them were Irish-, English-, or Scottish-born, with some experience on British boards. Although for many actors there is not sufficient information to determine origins, on occasion one can discover Americans or surmise American beginnings. Still, as with New York and Philadelphia, Norfolk would have seen on its stage a preponderance of British native and trained actors who may or may not have been willing to adjust their styles of presentation to meet particular conditions found in individual American cities or the United States as corporate entity.[9]

Under examination here are three seasons played over four years, 1797–1800; the Virginia Company did not play in Norfolk at all during 1799. By 1797, the company had stopped playing in Charleston, its main venue from 1793 to 1796, for a variety of reasons, one being competition in that city, where theatre had a much longer and more extensive tradition than in any of the Virginia locations.[10] In 1794, John Bignall had died in Charleston, depriving the company of its co-manager and its best singing comic actor; Thomas Wade West then assumed sole managership until his death on July 28, 1799, from a fall at his Alexandria theatre.[11] Thereafter, until 1804, his widow, Margaretta, managed the company, until she relinquished day-to-day duties to John William Green.[12] Thus the 1800 season was under the control of Mrs. West, making her one of the most important theatre managers in the United States and the most successful female manager in the early republic;[13] of the three seasons being discussed, more information survives about 1800 than any other. Key members of the company for all three seasons include Green and his wife, Frances Willems Green; James West, an actor unrelated to the manager, and his wife, the widowed Ann West Bignall, who now acted under the name Mrs. J. West, and after her father's death, Mrs. West, junior; Isaac Bignall, probably the younger brother of the now-deceased John Bignall; Thomas Wade and Margaretta Sully West; and their son, Thomas C. West. Others appeared for a single season or two during the period, some remaining with the company into the first decade of the nineteenth century, others finishing contracts begun in earlier seasons, and many in and out in a space of one or two years. Given the volatility of the profession, managers had constantly to be on the alert for new talent, but the travel schedule of the Virginia Company made recruiting abroad difficult. The Philadelphia actor turned impresario Thomas Wignell could get backing in 1792–1793 to travel to England and assemble one of the most impressive companies in early America from scratch,[14] but West had to rely on contacts within the American theatrical world and his own trips north. The majority of players in Norfolk not originally with the West company or related to one of its original members, like Margaretta's brother Matthew Sully and his several theatrical children, came to it from engagements at other theatres in the United States rather than directly from Great Britain.

The travel schedule could be difficult. While they had the luxury of decent theatres in most of their venues and had more stability and notoriety than some of the smaller, more ephemeral groups touring the South, the West company could be uprooted often in order to catch cities at peak times – Petersburg for the horse races, for instance, or Richmond while the legislature was in session. For 1797 alone, the Virginia Company followed a schedule that included at least the following cities: Richmond, Petersburg, Norfolk, Petersburg, Norfolk, Fredericksburg, Petersburg, Richmond.[15] Even with this known itinerary, the troupe had to pack up seven times in a calendar year, taking scenery, costumes, instruments, personnel, and families with them. Such a travel schedule could affect the kinds of plays being offered. For a one-week Petersburg season, for example, the Wests may have decided to carry only their most portable scenery or properties, or only use what they had in storage, limiting the degree of spectacle. In longer seasons, they could mount more elaborate shows, such as John Daly Burk's *Bunker-Hill*, or perhaps take more risks with the bill. At any rate, we know relatively little about the full extent of the material world of eighteenth-century theatres; much more work needs to be done in order to ascertain the full relationship between property and play and the degree to which theatre space and available scenic artists, for example, might influence the type of shows being presented.[16]

Whatever might be the archaeology of a season, the company stayed busy when they came to town. In Norfolk, the Virginia Company usually performed four nights a week – Monday, Wednesday, Friday, and Saturday – often advertising daily either that night's or the next night's show. Rarely was the same play acted on two successive nights, and only about half the plays were performed twice or more during the four-year period. There were at least 113 different plays offered in Norfolk over the seasons of 1797, 1798, and 1800, including farces, significant pantomimes, and two- or three-act comic operas, but excluding various entr'acte entertainments: primarily monologues, dances, recitations, songs, instrumentals, and novelty acts. Something less than 20 percent of those plays would fall under the all-purpose heading of "serious drama": tragedies, history plays, or tragicomedies. The remaining plays were comic, including Shakespeare's *As You Like It* or David Garrick's revision of *Taming of the Shrew*, *Catherine and Petruchio*, but more often the comedies produced in Norfolk were the products of the moderns: Frederick Reynolds, Isaac Bickerstaff, and Thomas Morton, to name a few of the most popular playwrights in Norfolk. With the rest of the nation in the 1790s, Norfolk liked to laugh, to share in satire, to shed a few tears, as long as the outcome was a happy one. In addition to such fare as Richard Brinsley Sheridan's *School for Scandal* and *The Critic*, or the many Elizabeth Inchbald farces and comedies (six different ones played over three years), a large number of plays included songs, either by intention or by theatrical tradition. *Macbeth*, for instance, was often played as a singing drama, at least in part; but the more usual case was the burletta or comic opera, including such favorites as George Colman, Jr.'s *The Mountaineers* and John O'Keeffe's *The Poor Soldier* (performed three times each in the period), as well as Prince Hoare's *No Song, No Supper*, and O'Keeffe's *Highland Reel* (four times each), and the most popular play over the three seasons, John C. Cross's *The Purse: or Benevolent Tar* (five times), one of many nautical-character plays to be performed in this seaport city.[17]

In common with theatres in the rest of the United States, the overwhelming majority of plays shown in Norfolk were of British authorship. Excluding for a moment British plays that were altered to meet local conditions, there were only three plays with speaking texts and one pantomime (a few of the other pantomimes may have been conceived by choreographers in the United States) that can be called original American dramas: John Daly Burk's *Bunker-Hill*, William Dunlap's *André*, the pantomime *The Death of Major André*, and John Beete's *Man of the Times*.[18] Several plays were translations or thinly concealed adaptations. The acting text of Kotzebue's *The Stranger*, for one, was probably that written by Dunlap, who wrote several translations of the German's plays. Others, like Inchbald's *Animal Magnetism* or Samuel Foote's *The Lyar*,[19] have acknowledged French sources. Otherwise, for about 95 percent of the separate plays produced by West and company, the name on the title page of the printed play, if there was one, was English, Irish, or Scottish, regardless of originating idea or story line.

When the Wests came to town, Norfolk residents could be assured of seeing new plays, clever plays, lots of musicals, many comedies, and enough Shakespeare (nine of his plays were performed from 1797 to 1800, making him by number of distinct dramas performed the most popular playwright) to keep it all respectable. Except for the few occasions when American plays were performed – and the Wests had brought Tyler's *The Contrast* and Mrs. Marriott's *The Chimera* to town in a previous season – the basic question to be pursued is how audiences responded to seeing British-born actors putting on British-authored plays in a small but bustling port town in the United States.

Certainly, the theatre reflected back to its spectators the variety of ethnic types that had populated the stage in the eighteenth century, and it could sometimes do that with more than a touch of authenticity. Daniel M'Kenzie (or M'Kinzie), who had been with West before 1797, and who left the company in a huff during a dispute, returned to West and played several very full seasons in Norfolk starting in 1800. Said to have a completely convincing Scottish accent and probably Scottish-born, M'Kenzie would have been ideal for such roles as Glenalvon in *Douglas*, Charley in *Highland Reel*, and Malcolm in *Macbeth*, all of which he enacted in 1800.[20] But for the most part, actors played to their place in the company, not from their ethnic background. They were expected to attain to some stage version of Irish brogue, Africanized dialect, English rural speech, or Welsh inflection to convey the illusion that, in the context of the play, the ethnic identification could be maintained sufficiently to carry the production to its dramatic conclusion. Most of the West company actors were English-born, including Matthew Sully and his sister Margaretta West, but they were expected to adopt whatever nationality a play or their particular part in the company required.[21] Ethnicity was a theatrical trope, a special language maintained for the purpose of satisfying certain expectations about what one would see performed in an English-speaking playhouse in the 1790s. In that sense, Norfolk differed little from its East Coast neighbors in the extensive ethnic variety of its characters – or the lack of variety among its players.

Still, though, there were moments on the Norfolk stage when the homogeneity of players was sometimes turned heterogeneous without intention. As far as can be determined, no person of African descent played any role on stage in Norfolk during this period, even though a modest number of the plays enacted called for black characters – a not surprising fact in United States theatres overall. However, at least one of the stage crew in 1800 was African American, and his presence on stage during a scene change for *Richard III* occasioned a protest from the local critic: "The throne of state left in the open field was rather an eyesore, especially as the negro in an oznaburg jacket and trowsers who removed it did no credit to Richard as a *livery servant*."[22] The complaint was not simply that he was black and in the public eye, but that his clothes, the traditional cheap imported cloth jacket and pants given to slaves, did not make an appropriate costume in a play about monarchy. Regardless, a black male stepped out on the Norfolk stage before spectators on their benches and transgressed the boundary of back stage/front stage that the white newspaper critic expected. It was a surprise, or simply a violation of illusion, but in any case forced at least one spectator to reconsider Shakespeare in the light of a Norfolk reality.

Naturally, one of the promises of a theatre is that it will bring the exotic, the remote, the foreign before the eyes of audiences. The Virginia Company attempted to meet the demand for such entertainments with a variety of plays, many of which could be mounted without too much worry over historical accuracy or ethnographic correctness. It is doubtful that any one worried about pleasing or offending South Sea islanders, for instance, or seeking actors with that Hawaiian "look"; Norfolk, like other American cities, was probably happy to imagine the natives of the Pacific in whatever costumes the actors wore in Jean-François Arnould's and John C. Cross's grand historic pantomime *The Death of Captain Cook*, seen twice in 1798, rather than try to measure them against something more anthropologically precise. By the same token the India of Inchbald's *Mogul Tale* or the Poland of Thomas Morton's *Zorinski*, even the Italy of *Romeo and Juliet* or the Germany of *The Stranger*, could be created by almost any tricks of stagecraft or costume that would lead audiences out of the realm of the familiar London street or English village. What mattered was to create a sufficient illusion of the stage *in the terms of previous stage practice* such that members of the audience believed themselves to be somewhere other than Norfolk, Virginia, with its heat, its mud, its flies, its stenches.[23] Because the Wests put great store by their scenery and costumes, they probably succeeded in that limited goal, at least in part.

Of all the exotic types one would have found on the eighteenth-century stage, the stage Muslim character or situation figures prominently. Although there were no Algerian captivity dramas in Norfolk during the 1797, 1798, and 1800 seasons (John Brown's *Barbarossa; or, The Fall of the Tyrant of Algiers* had been performed in 1795), a small number of plays did deliver what was coming to be a common motif of pitting Islamist against Anglo-Christian characters in dramatic situations. The most popular stage Muslim drama in Norfolk was Colman's *The Mountaineers* (1793), a comic opera set in Spain during the occupation by the Moors. Its plot bears little immediate resemblance to Susanna Rowson's *Slaves in Algiers*, but it shares at least one common motif. Zorayda is the daughter of Bulcazin Muley, the governor, and the man charged with fighting the Christians; she claims to be a "Christian at heart,"[24] very much as the daughter of Muley Moloc is attracted to a Christian man and his ways. Zorayda has a Christian servant, Agnes, in whom she confides; Agnes tells Zorayda to follow her heart, disobey her father, and run away with Virolet, the Christian officer with whom she is in love. For her part, Agnes is beloved by Sadi, a Moor. Both couples flee the governor's castle and go through the mountains to the Christian lines. In the end, Sadi loses his Islamic prejudices, beginning with his fear to taste alcohol, while Zorayda, threatened with death by her father, triumphs in her love for the Christian. In the end, Bulcazin gives his permission for his daughter and Sadi to remain with the Christians, setting up the stock ending of Western Christian overcoming Oriental Muslim with romantic love, wine, and what the text takes for granted as superior ideology. The transposition of such a situation to an American setting – where Moors become Native Americans – might have been made by playwrights like James Nelson Barker, whose *Indian Princess* appeared in Norfolk in 1809; but it was also probably made by Norfolk audiences, for whom the generic superiority of English Christianity over any brand of heathen would be assumed.

In the other two main Islamist plays in Norfolk, Bickerstaff's *The Sultan* and Inchbald's *The Mogul Tale*, the resolution is similar. *The Sultan*, a longtime comic favorite in the afterpiece and played twice in Norfolk this period, features the spunky Christian slave, Roxalana, and her contentions with the sultan, Solyman. In the end, his love for her, as well as the unusual experience of her saucy resistance to his absolutism, leads him to marry her and make her his queen and equal. Although this is not a conversion play, it shows the Western woman as having the power to command entire nations, at least when they are not Great Britain or the United States. One can imagine that Susanna Rowson also had this play in mind when writing *Slaves of Algiers*. In *The Mogul Tale*, played one season under the name *The Norfolk Cobler* (discussed further below), the shoemaker and his wife, who find themselves captive to the Indian Muslim ruler, by dint of pluck and virtue – and a mogul with droll sense of play and irony – free themselves from captivity without violence. However, Inchbald manages to work in a critique of English prejudice against Islam. Johnny Atkins, the cobbler, speaks of the Indians in racially marked terms: 'blacky' and 'blackamoor'; meanwhile, the Mogul orders the deaths of Fanny and Johnny in such a way as to tell us he's kidding: "You are not now before the tribunal of an European, a man of your own color. I am an Indian, a Mahometan, my laws are cruel and my nature savage."[25] Even so, this play honors plain speaking and simple, Western ways, especially when Johnny praises his wife's beauty over that of the other women in the seraglio: 'one morsel of British beauty is worth a whole cargo of outlandish frippery' (*MT* 18). In the Norfolk production, 'British' was probably changed to 'American,' for reasons stated later, but the message is still clear: the Oriental, the Muslim, even if educated (the Mogul is never fooled by the English attempts to play to superstition), ironic, and humane, still suffers in comparison to the rough-speaking, bigoted, but 'lovable' English/American shoemaker.

The theatrical victory of English–Western–Christian over the stage Muslim tyrant would have met with few protests in Norfolk, with its reliance on the shipping trade and its natural concern about the safety of vessels from seizure by the Barbary states. Except for some slaves and the occasional visitor or sailor, there would have been few Muslims in the city to challenge accepted stage representation. It is possible, however, that some awareness of Norfolk's ethnic mix might have influenced the bill at the theatre. For one thing, there are almost no Jewish characters in the plays offered from 1797 to 1800. In 1795, the West company had mounted Richard Cumberland's *The Jew*, that writer's attempt to portray a stage Jew positively, as the subtitle, *The Benevolent Hebrew*, suggests. Otherwise, during the three years under review, a single performance of *Merchant of Venice* in 1797 and the Norfolk premiere in 1800 of Thomas John Dibdin's *The Jew and the Doctor*, an afterpiece, constituted the only plays with prominent Jewish characters. Given that the stage Jew was a well-worn stereotype by this time, and might have been exploited as well in Virginia as London, there may be reasons for West's restraint. To be sure, the repertory for American theatres elsewhere did not include many plays with Jewish characters, although the type was well-known, as Rowson demonstrated for the Philadelphia company in *Slaves in Algiers*. Beyond that, however, the manager (either Thomas or Margaretta) would have known, for instance, that among Norfolk ethnic identities, Jews were nearly if not in fact the smallest minority; before 1780, they were unknown to Norfolk as year-round residents. But in 1787, a Jewish couple, Moses and Eliza Judah Chapman Myers, moved to the city, becoming the first known Jews to live in Norfolk on a permanent basis, where they raised a large family.[26] Moses Myers maintained a fleet of ships and engaged in transatlantic trade; in 1792 he built a fine brick home north of downtown (which still stands) and soon became a prominent citizen including election to the Norfolk Common Council.[27] In 1795, Myers paid to West a sum of £200 to enlist as a subscriber to the theatre – in essence, to help Thomas West pay the loan on the theatre building he had constructed two years before.[28] Myers's patronage of the theatre and his generous assistance (only one man of the ten who enlisted as subscribers contributed more) may have determined West not to perform plays that diminished Jews. Indeed, it is possible that the performance of *The Benevolent Hebrew* in 1795 was directed at Myers in honor of his support for West and his company. Still, given the general eighteenth-century insensitivity to ethnic insult in the drama, Thomas or Margaretta's consciousness of plays as potential disparagements of a loyal friend of the theatre is hard to prove.

Dibdin's *The Jew and the Doctor* makes an interesting test for the stage portrayal of Jews in the late eighteenth century.²⁹ The moneylender Abednego cares for a Christian orphan, Emily. Like Cumberland's "benevolent" Jew, Dibdin's is sentimental and respectful, preserving Emily's religious identity as Christian without sacrificing his own as Jew.³⁰ Dibdin marks his speech with an accent that both minimizes Abednego – like the Irish, he is not quite "one of us" – and allows the audience to feel sympathy for him in its own benevolent, paternalistic way. He describes for his ward how he found her:

> So I took [the child] up, and ax'd all over de place whose little shild it vas – All de people he laugh at me, and said vat it vas my own, and I vanted to sheat 'em, and dat I vas Jew, and wou'd take in te devil; but I told dem I vould take in noting but de shild. So I took pity upon you, ma tear, for I remembered ven I vas a poor little poy myself, and sold rollers a top o' the street. (*JD* 9)

By accent, he is marked as other, but by sentiment, he shares in the values of the theatregoing public when he has to resist prejudice to maintain his basic good intentions and show he chooses humanity over lucre. While the stylized appearance, one assumes, and the stock dialect of the stage Jew may not have pleased the Myers family, who as their portraits in the Myers House indicate dressed in current Anglo-American fashions, Abednego's declarations for essential human values at the end and the affirmation of his goodness might have come as a welcome sign of changes possible in the English-language theatre in its portrayal of Jews. Nevertheless, despite the presence of a prominent Jewish family in Norfolk and the managers' care not to rely heavily on traditional stage Jew stereotypes, audiences still apparently took their cue for understanding ethnicity from the stage. After the Scottish-born Daniel M'Kenzie, whose Celtic inflection was much praised when he played Scots characters, played Cumberland's Sheva, a spectator "was heard to say, that he would be *circumcised* if Mr. McKenzie was not a *Jew* naturally."³¹

The same concern for ethnicity of audience might have influenced the Virginia Company's portrayal of stage African characters. The black population of Norfolk in the 1790s was substantial, over 40 percent of the permanent residents, mostly slaves but by 1800 over 300 free blacks,³² and the numbers were probably swelled on occasion by the arrival of African American sailors or of slaves who had come to town with planter masters, as well as the numbers of slaves arriving in port to be sold. It is likely that blacks made up at least a portion of any given night's audience; African American sailors, many free, would have been looking for entertainment after days, weeks, or months on the water, and probably came to the theatre as did their white fellow seamen.[33] Indeed, it is possible that blacks sat where they could afford rather than be restricted to a particular section, absent any public statements about racially divided seating until 1805.[34] Certainly, we know that late eighteenth- and early nineteenth-century African Americans took their entertainment seriously, and as most slaves had Saturday night off, they might well have been more in evidence on that night.[35] In any event, while African Americans were not subscribers nor courted openly by the management, their presence meant seats taken and house revenues increased. Even in the slaveholding South, blacks played a vital role in the maintenance of theatre, at least in the early republic, and managers would have had to walk a careful road not to offend their big contributors among whites while at the same time making sure that blacks felt comfortable enough to attend. Of course, the presence of African Americans in the house did not stop managers elsewhere from mounting productions with the most egregiously stereotyped black characters, and while the West company did not put on many plays in Norfolk between 1797 and 1800 that relied on African typed characters, it still performed them, often multiple times.

If comic stage Africans made up only a small portion of the company's repertoire, the character of the noble African was virtually absent. Although it had been performed by West in the past, both in Charleston and Norfolk in 1796, there was no *Othello* among the Virginia Company offerings, nor any *Cato*, nor any play with an African of the Juba type from 1797 to 1800. Since the Revolution, *Cato* had lost its popularity and no longer appeared regularly in repertory (although West and Bignall had produced it in Charleston in 1794), but *Othello* was always maintained as part of the stock Shakespearean offerings. Still, there was concern about putting *Othello* on in the South; there is no recorded performance of the tragedy in Richmond by any company until 1806,[36] and the West and Bignall production in Charleston was the first in that city since before the Revolution. One finds no plays with a "noble Moor" among the dramas performed in Norfolk for the seasons at the end of the century.

The stage African characters that do appear in those years are all in subordinate roles – there is not even a *Padlock* to provide a prominent, dialect-speaking Mungo, a character last offered to Norfolk in 1795. Slaves are represented in Colman's *Inkle and Yarico*, a comic opera performed twice during the 1800 season and a play replete with mixed messages on race in its conflation of Native American and African.[37] However, with Yarico and Narcissa played as nominal Indians, rather than Africans, the problematic love relations involving the Englishmen Inkle and Trudge might have been overlooked in slaveholding cities. Silent slaves appear also in Cumberland's *The West Indian*, carrying the baggage of the arriving planter, Belcour, and "black" servants attend the character Vortex in Thomas Morton's *A Cure for the Heart-Ache*.[38] For the four performances of that latter popular play during the period or *The West Indian's* two, white members of the audience might have only noted the presence of slave characters in passing, as in a scene common to their own lives, with all forms of hierarchy maintained.

More significantly, in *The Romp*, the truncated version of Isaac Bickerstaff's comic opera *Love in the City* and an often-used afterpiece in United States theatres (four times in Norfolk from 1797 to 1800), the main character, Priscilla Tomboy, has a black servant whom she abuses verbally on a number of occasions. She is in England and from "the plantations" of Jamaica; true to her slaveowning past, Priscilla threatens Quasheba with a horse-whipping "till there is not a bit of flesh left on your bones" if she reveals any of a conversation Priscilla has had with Penelope. The last expresses concern – "Oh, poor creature!" – while Priscilla retorts, "Psha! what is she but a neger? If she was at home in our plantations, she would find the difference; we make no account of them there at all: if I had a fancy for one of their skins, I should not think much of taking it."[39] Later, when she toys with Watty, her meek-hearted suitor, with going to Jamaica with her, she insists she can handle the business of correcting slaves: "it's only beating them well, giving them a few yams, and they'll do any thing you bid them" (*Romp* 24). All ends well for Priscilla, as she will marry the romantic lead, Captain Sightly; her island racism is more or less forgiven and never seriously challenged by the Londoners she is among. Despite the viciousness of her attitude toward slaves, the Tomboy character was much coveted by young lead comic actresses, the same ones who would have played Little Pickle in a play sometimes attributed to Bickerstaff, *The Spoiled Child*. In Norfolk, Priscilla was enacted by Ann West, the best comic actress in Norfolk, and thus the play was intended to be, perhaps, a signature afterpiece by the company. Through such plays as those just mentioned, black characters are barely seen, not often heard, yet their status as silent slaves or objects of contempt remains patent and visible, keeping African American audience members mindful of white attitudes, even on stage.

Otherwise, the only significant blackface characters in the 1797–1800 seasons are two found in plays set not in the Americas but in Great Britain. One is Benin, the oddly placed servant in the Scottish rural fantasy, *The Highland Reel*, a comic opera that has for its scene an obscure island, Coll – one of the last settings in which one might expect to find a creole-speaking, stage African character. As mentioned previously, the author of the libretto, John O'Keeffe, was an abolitionist and provided antislavery statements in the mouth of Reuben Sadboy, the title character in *The Young Quaker* – a play not shown in Norfolk in the seasons under discussion. The figure of Benin, however, is one that presents a deeply conflicted understanding of the Africanist character, at once sympathetic and yet playing to some of the worst aspects of black portrayal in the British theatre. He first appears in Act III, the final one, with a letter to Jenny, one of the two heroines, saying she has won a share of a lottery. Benin's main function in the play is to assist Moggy M'Gilpin, the functionally imprisoned daughter of the cheating steward of the island, in a plot to trick old M'Gilpin into believing in witchcraft and dropping his guard long enough for her to free herself and run off with her lover, Charley.

In the midst of this plotting, however, Benin gets himself into deep trouble when he interrupts M'Gilpin while his master is practicing a speech. As heard by Charley on stage, following Benin's offstage announcement that Shelty the piper has arrived, M'Gilpin threatens to beat Benin and by the cries from the latter, we assume that such a beating is taking place. Both characters come on stage, one 'in a rage,' the other 'crying.' Charley stands by and listens as M'Gilpin curses Benin as 'An impudent scoundrel!' 'You villain!' and 'This black dog.'[40] When Benin tries to justify himself – 'Why, Massa, I did taught –' – M'Gilpin unloads on his servant the following:

> You thought, you Canibal! – There had I got into my fine speech on the African slaves – painting the distresses of the poor blackamoors – (You damn'd dog, you shall live on bread and water for this.) I was describing, in the most pathetic – the most feeling manner, the cruelty of the planters to the unhappy Negroes – I had work'd myself up to such a pathos, that even recounting their sufferings brought tears in my eyes! – (I'll cut the flesh off your bones, you miscreant!) (*HR* 52–53)

The hypocrisy of this speech is patent, the professed abolitionist who beats his own black servant. In the plot, M'Gilpin is exposed for cheating his employer, the Laird of Coll, and he gets his comic comeuppance with Moggy's marrying Charley. However, even the sympathetic character Charley, who mildly intervenes on Benin's behalf, starts to laugh at Benin's plight, to which the servant retorts, "You may laugh – Massar never beats you – Oh, eh do! he did so tump a me –" (53). Charley, rather than apologizing, simply notes in an aside how this situation presents an opportunity to advance his "scheme" to marry Moggy. Therefore, while Benin is soon laughing himself later in the scene, the play isolates M'Gilpin as the offender, while Charley escapes without any chastisement for his self-interested enjoyment of Benin's suffering. The rebuke to slaveholding or to abuse based on race is light, although more pronounced than in most plays written before 1800.

Thomas Wade West and John Bignall were the first professionals to stage *The Highland Reel* in America, opening their 1793 Charleston season with it as the main play. Benin was played by Mr. Riffets (spelled variously), an actor of minor roles who performed with the Virginia and Charleston Company from 1791 to 1795. In its first New York production, January 20, 1794, Benin was played by John Durang of the Old American Company, while the white servant to the Laird of Raasay was played by James West, an actor from the theatre at Bath, who would eventually join the Thomas West Company as romantic comic lead actor and play Sandy, the disguised young laird. In Norfolk, 1797, Benin was played by Mr. Copeland, an actor who has left few traces beyond his two years with the Virginia Company; Copeland had played the same role also in 1796. By using Copeland, West essentially chose not to emphasize Benin's character.

But for some reason, Thomas West decided not to continue to play *Highland Reel* with Benin. One possibility is the manager's need to reduce the time of acting. In 1797 and in the first production from 1798 (for which no cast list survives), *Highland Reel* played as the main feature, presumably in its original three acts. In the second 1798 production, it was cut to two acts and moved to the afterpiece.[41] Such cutting occurred frequently in the early national theatre to meet the need to offer two plays with additional entertainments and get the audience out of the theatre at a decent hour[42]; it would be expected that one or more minor characters would be omitted. However, O'Keeffe's opera was back to main play status at its next run-through, on April 18, 1800, but nonetheless the cast list excluded Benin. It is unlikely that Copeland was such an indispensable Benin that the part went begging without him in the company. But it may have had more to do with the ostensible politics of the piece and the identity of the master as a hypocritical tyrant, as well as the portrait of the suffering and sympathetic servant, that Norfolk audiences detected. That is, rather than enact on a southern stage a situation where an abusive master in an unsympathetic character is exposed for beating a black servant, the Wests decided not to include the scene or the character at all.

The other stage African character of note found in the Norfolk theatre of this period is Cubba, the servant of Caroline in William Macready's *The Irishman in London; or, The Happy African*. A farce with some songs, Macready's two-act play became popular in many theatres in the afterpiece, and in Norfolk it was paired in both of its productions (1798, 1800) with *The Highland Reel*. Thus while the ostensible linkage between the two plays is Celtic comedy with music, the other, more haunting tie is that they were the only two plays in Norfolk at the time with important, speaking stage African characters. Although problematic for later readers, Cubba would have raised few white hackles in Norfolk. She enters the play as having come to London from Jamaica with Mr. Frost and his daughter Caroline – a situation that might have been duplicated in real-life Norfolk, a port open to Indies trade, and one that parallels that in *The Romp*. She is loyal to Caroline in a buffoonish, sentimental way, denying her own subjectivity for one based upon the subject position of the mistress. When Caroline complains of her love situation, Cubba responds, "Missa, you frettee so, you make a de rain come in poor Cubba's yies."[43] Later, Frost remarks that he had hoped Cubba would take her liberty in London, since legally that was now possible, but he remarks that her loyalty prevents her leaving – she "sticks like bird-lime" (*IL* 21). At the end of the play, her fate is uncertain; the plot links Cubba to the Irish servant, Murtock Delany, in a comic love interest, but there is no promise of marriage. It would be possible, through physical gestures, to indicate to an audience that such a match could never happen.[44]

In the only performance with a cast list, April 18, 1800, Cubba was played by Harriet West Bignall, the daughter of Margaretta West and the wife of Isaac Bignall, brother to one of the original managers of the Virginia Company. Given her importance to the troupe – she appeared twenty-six times each in the 1800 and 1801 seasons, including a reprise of Cubba in 1801 – the managers clearly saw no reason to delete such a role, for nothing on stage would have been seen as subversive of the racial politics of Norfolk, even though some aspects of Cubba – her unswerving loyalty to Caroline, for instance – would have been read as sympathetic by a white audience. How African Americans in the audience interpreted Cubba is not clear. Most likely, they would have seen Cubba's refusal to take advantage of an opportunity for liberty as unrealistic at best, a mere white fantasy based on master-class assumptions about the ostensible childlike nature of blacks. Yet the possibility of a cross-racial relationship, such as that suggested by Trudge and Wowski in *Inkle and Yarico*, may have supplied both white and black members of the audience with a titillating scenario, even if covered over by the outrageous comedy created by linking two potential grotesques, the stage Irishman and the stage African woman. The choosing of plays and how to play them required a constant negotiation in dealing with audience identities – mockery of blacks was acceptable, if not overdone, but satirizing cruel masters was not.

Among other ethnic or national identities portrayed by the West company, a spectator at the Norfolk Theatre might have seen a variety of Europeans. There are, for example, Italians in any of several Shakespeare plays or their adaptations (*Catherine and Petruchio*, *Romeo and Juliet*, *Merchant of Venice*) or in something like Otway's *Venice Preserved*, but more contemporaneously they appear in Sheridan's *The Critic*, a comedy offered in the afterpiece in 1797 and 1800. There, a group of Italians comes to the house of Dangle, a theatre critic; when his wife answers the door, she cannot understand them, and turns to a translator, who only speaks French, a language she does not understand either. With few Italians in Norfolk, except those who might have come as sailors on ships, there was no demand for entertainments featuring Italian figures – although Norfolk, as with most other large East Coast cities, was visited by Signior Falconi, the stage illusionist, puppeteer, and demonstrator of wonders, who may or may not have been of Italian origin.[45] As for the French, characters ostensibly of that nation appear also in Inchbald's *Animal Magnetism* (originally a French farce), Eyre's *The Maid of Normandy*, Arnould's pantomime *La Fôret Noire*, another pantomime called *The Siege of Quebec*, and *Jean de Saintré*, a play not performed in New York, Philadelphia, Richmond, Baltimore, or Charleston during this period, so far as I can determine. Because Norfolk did have a substantial French population, at least during the volatile 1790s, and some French-speaking actors had been involved with the West company starting in 1794, there was probably more demand or interest on the part of the managers to meet the French taste.[46] Plays that contained derogatory references to the French were probably altered to avoid the partisanship and insult such statements implied; in Philadelphia, for instance, Thomas Wignell and Alexander Reinagle removed a prejudicial line from Reynolds's *The Dramatist*,[47] a comedy that appeared three times in Norfolk during the period, and one assumes the Virginia Company followed suit. At any rate, while there are the usual references to French fashion and its comic potential in English settings, relatively few plays can be seen as especially insulting to French persons, at least in the way that *Irishman in London* is toward African Americans.

Like its transatlantic cousins, the Norfolk theatre featured stage Irish characters with which to entertain its patrons. Norfolk saw Darby and Patrick three times in the period, along with Garrick's *Irish Widow*, Cumberland's *West Indian*, Macklin's *Love a-la-Mode*, and Macready's *Irishman in London* twice each. Irish characters pop up elsewhere, too, as in Frances Brooke's comic opera *Rosina*, where two Irishmen become the instruments of salvation for the kidnapped heroine, and Colman's *The Mountaineers*, which, while taking place in Moor-occupied Spain, has its requisite Irishman in Killmallock. Together, those two operas accounted for four performances over the three seasons. With just these few plays alone, significant Irish characters appeared in fifteen separate productions, guaranteeing to Norfolk at least a few favorite Irish characters each season. As with the portrayal of Jews, the characterization of Irish on the Norfolk stage at century's end avoided for the most part the worst of the stereotyping found in eighteenth-century British drama. As noted in an earlier chapter, the characters from *The Poor Soldier*, for example, are only nominally Irish – few laughs are struck from such stock elements as the bull or potato worship. Nevertheless, Irish characters are invariably different from English, if often very like their predecessors on stage; playwrights can expand or shrink that difference as they wish, and actors playing Irishmen can often do the same, even when the text does not demand a heavy brogue.

As suggested in the chapter on Irish characters, such figures can serve as indirect registers of American identity. *The Irishman in London* illustrates this. The eponymous character is Colloony, a gentleman with a brogue with whom Frost has contracted (through his father) to marry Frost's daughter against her wishes. When Colloony arrives in London, he exclaims his joy at being there, and, throughout his endeavors to make the match, he constrains his Irishness, occasionally limiting his brogue and even going to the extreme of calling his Irish servant by the English name of Dill. The servant, however, whose real name is Murtock, will have nothing of this imposture. He speaks unashamedly in dialect, moons sentimentally for Erin, and reproves "Maister Pat" for his willingness to denigrate Ireland for the sake of trying to accommodate himself to English manners and prejudices. Indeed, Murtock's blunter, more traditional Irishness brings out Colloony's repressed brogue, especially as he gets angry, and all pretense at speaking in polite English evaporates. To American audiences, such a tension between the former colonial gentleman who tries still to curry favor with the colonizing elite and the rough-speaking native who abjures any pretense and identifies strongly with his native country would have sympathetic resonance, at least among those who were not extreme Anglophiles. Part of the popularity of Irish characters in Norfolk may have had to do with their standing as a kind of underclass who, as whites, could also attempt to command some respect from the English or Anglophilic elite. From the point of view of the elite, Irish were finally little threat, especially in cities where they constituted a small and mostly Protestant minority; their inability to disguise their ethnicity meant they were always under control – or at least, under surveillance.

At the same time, though, one should not minimize the likely possibility that Irish, of whom there were a modest number in Norfolk, were thought by the English-descended elite as naturally funny. The brogue humor of a Murtock or a Colloony, or that in Macklin's or Garrick's comedies, no doubt met the expectations of some of its audience for characters who would be automatically assumed to be humorous in the old ethnic-humor sense. A comment in the *Herald* from the unidentified local critic suggests at least one dimension of popular prejudice outside the immediate stage context:

> The Theatre on Tuesday evening, was a scene of order and quietness, notwithstanding its being crowded, excepting the trifling incident of a gentleman having a *voluntary* fit of *sneezing*, which being observed by a large raw-bon'd Irishman, *Pat* twisted it, (as he said) to prevent its *leaking*![48]

The Irish spectator is immediately Pat, his comment like those used by playwrights as a bull or blunder on stage. Thus when the critic gazes into the audience, he sees the Irishman of humorous intent from the stage of yore, a type from which even the most sympathetic portrayals could not escape. As suggested with *The Indian Princess*, a Larry may show all sorts of good traits suitable to becoming an American, but he carries with him always the baggage of past representations, whether a character on the stage or a spectator in the house.

For a theatre company, it was important to have one of the best actors play Irish characters. Because very often the heart of a comedy centered on an Irishman (almost never an Irishwoman, who rarely speaks brogue), even if the role was minor, managers depended on a strong figure in the Irish slot. For Thomas and Margaretta West, the choice for the seasons under review was Isaac Bignall. In his first two full seasons in Norfolk, Bignall did not play an Irish character. In *The West Indian* productions of 1795 and 1796, for example, he played Fulmer, the cowardly thief, rather than O'Flaherty, who in 1795 was played by the more experienced Marlborough Hamilton; the latter also played one of the Irishmen from *Rosina*, and in 1797 Killmallock in *Mountaineers*. With Hamilton gone temporarily in 1796, then for good after the 1797 season, the company could not sustain plays with Irish characters without an actor dedicated to serving in them. But starting in 1798, Bignall began to take over the major Irish roles, playing Colloony both that year and in 1800, and adding for that last season Sir Callaghan O'Brallaghan from *Love-a-la-Mode*, Father Luke from *Poor Soldier*, and Captain O'Flaherty from *West Indian*. He played all four roles again in 1801. Meeting the demand for Irish characters, which remained high in American theatres well into the nineteenth century, meant considering the practical matter of having someone who could play them effectively.

For the seasons beginning in 1798, Isaac Bignall met the requirements, which then allowed the company to offer more plays with Irish characters than they had been mounting. Even so, his benefit in 1800 (in Morton's saga of Polish liberty, *Zorinski*, along with the "Grand Serious Domestic Pantomime," *La Fôret Noire*, on July 2) only produced a "*thin house*," a fact noted by the *Herald* in a season in which benefits for others were well attended.[49] There were many reasons for poor attendance at benefits, outside of popular feelings for a player, but given the good showing for others, this fact suggests that Bignall was a competent, rather than an especially dynamic player; at least he is not listed among the people the critic for the *Herald* would like to see in his ideal production.[50] Perhaps the spectators were finally more diverted by the Pat in the house than by Pat on stage – or wanted more of an extreme type than Bignall was willing or able to deliver. At any rate, from the little criticism available for the 1800 season, Bignall was neither praised nor censured for any of his roles; perhaps stage Irishness was merely taken for granted, a routine so common as to be thought unworthy of special mention unless extraordinarily good or bad.

Of course, beyond the Irish, whom they could both sympathize with and laugh at, Norfolk audiences watched a full complement of British types over the three seasons: the usual English baronets and senex fathers; dutiful, distressed young English women, and their supposedly impoverished young English lovers; Gloucestershire farmers, Highland lasses, rural swains; sulky servants, and eager chambermaids. In Frederick Reynolds's *Fortune's Fool* they could laugh at the misadventures of the unlucky Welshman; in *Highland Reel* or Thomas Holcroft's *Deserted Daughter* or John Home's *Douglas*, concern themselves over various Scots. With English and Scottish comprising the ancestry of the bulk of the white population in Norfolk, the overall repertoire is not particularly surprising. For the most part, and most nights, theatregoers could observe types reinforced over several generations of comic vehicles, announcing not only the triumph of young love over heavy-handed patriarchy but also British values that limit the power of fashion, reward virtue, and keep class identities more or less fixed. At the same time, managers were probably careful not to let too many direct references to British government, class structure, or social practices remain in the spoken scripts. With the exception of Shakespeare, Massinger's *New Way to Pay Old Debts*, Garrick's revision of the Beaumont and Fletcher *Rule a Wife and Have a Wife*, and Otway's *Venice Preserved*, all the plays in Norfolk were products of the eighteenth century, with Cibber's *The Provoked Husband* and Farquhar's *Beaux' Stratagem* the only comedies with direct roots in the Restoration. This latter fact is important because it meant that many of the plays observed in the Virginia port city affirmed not urban values, as in Restoration comedies, but rural life, itself often pitted against a jaded, self-indulgent sensibility tied to urbanity.

Perhaps of all the motifs or settings from British drama that translated to some degree to an American environment, the rural comedy best fitted into a Jeffersonian understanding of popular identity in the United States. Comic operas like *Highland Reel* and *Poor Soldier*, ostensibly set in Scotland and Ireland, could easily be absorbed by a primarily rural state, Virginia, that perhaps prided itself on an orderly pastoral ideal as the backbone of society there. Bickerstaff's *Love in a Village* and *Thomas and Sally*, Brooke's *Rosina*, Prince Hoare's *No Song, No Supper*, and Morton's *A Cure for the Heart-Ache* are some of the comic operas and plays that affirmed rural settings and characters as places and people who maintained virtue in its purest simplicity. Other rural plays seen in Norfolk include O'Keeffe's *The Farmer*, Kemble's *The Farm House*, and Macready's *The Village Lawyer*, although the last-mentioned farce does not idealize the country in the way Brooke's opera does. In O'Keeffe's *The Farmer*, the simple and honest agriculturist, Farmer Blackberry, gets his reward for enduring the insults of the urbanized rake of a landlord by coming into the landlord's property. He goes to London, attains to his fortune, and in essence brings his pastoral values into the city, improving the latter.[51] Such a play might easily be appealing to Norfolk, a small city that often housed planters and farmers doing business at the port, for its affirmation of honesty in both urban and rural environments.

Rosina, the fifth most popular musical drama from the period 1785–1815 in the United States, is one of the most straightforward of these plays (and a model for O'Keeffe and others), opening on a "rural prospect" at sunrise.[52] The curtain reveals the three women in the opera all busy with farm-related labor. Dorcas and her granddaughter Phoebe are country people who understand the village life and are content; Rosina, we learn, is really an elite girl who has been orphaned and lives in the country, yet she too is happy with her life and is even willing to glean fields to have enough to eat. Brooke shows that the poverty of villagers makes them potential prey to those who would lure them into concupiscence with money, as the rake Captain Belville attempts to do with Rosina via Dorcas. While William and Phoebe go through their comic courtship, Rosina falls shyly in love with the local landowner, Mr. Belville, but his brother the captain – who fears to marry a "gleaner" because of the threat to his social status in the city – organizes her abduction to be his mistress when she refuses to consort with the Londoner. Two Irishmen, recently hired by Belville against the desires of his steward, Rustic, save Rosina from the thugs and Captain Belville's French (!) valet. In the end, Rosina accepts the love of Mr. Belville and forgives the rapist captain, provided he "retire" and correct his errors (*R* 44). The Irishmen prove themselves to be courageous, not merely "lazy" as Rustic thinks; in addition, the pastoral setting allows for virtuous love to prevail, as the two timid lovers, Mr. Belville and Rosina, are paired, and it provides the possibility of curing the rake of his vice. In this case, Irish are identified further with rural simplicity and loyalty, while the class distinctions – Rosina in fact does have an inheritance – are preserved in her marriage to the local elite landholder.

Whereas O'Keeffe would modify the formula in *The Farmer* to limit criticism of the city by staging the second act in London (or perhaps modified in production to an American city, even Norfolk), *Rosina* takes place entirely in the country, a place often seen as especially vulnerable to corruption, either in satiric comedy – the witless rustics who are easy marks for urban sophisticates – or in sentimental drama, whereby the plot affirms pastoral simplicity. In the Wignell–Reinagle promptbook for the Philadelphia performances of the comic opera, some of that vulnerability was reduced by the omission of lines that stress Rosina's potential openness to exploitation or that demonstrate Capt. Belville's knowledge of prostitutes as well as by cutting lines that emphasize English versions of class structure ('lords and squires').[53] If one assumes similar cuts in Norfolk, with perhaps some care in discussing the nationality of the valet, *Rosina* could easily be made into a vehicle in which planters and others dependent on an agricultural economy would see themselves reflected in the wholesomeness promised by Brooke's operatic countryside.

The same could be said for another popular comic opera, *No Song, No Supper*. Frederick is a young Cornish squire who has kept his landholding secret from the country girl he courts, Louisa. Her father, Crop, is a good-hearted soul, who has been partly corrupted by a lawyer, Endless, who in turn has instigated a number of lawsuits, largely to the ruin of many of the local people, including the lover of Margaretta, Robin. In the end, Margaretta exposes the lawyer in his attempt to gain sexual favors with Dorothy, Crop's second wife and Louisa's jealous stepmother; Crop and his wife, who have often quarreled, make up; Frederick and Louisa, Robin and Margaretta all unite; and the lawyer and his city values are expelled. In an earlier scene, Frederick provides the play's ideological motto. Fearful that Frederick, who has revealed his station, is now too upper-class for her, Louisa expresses her belief that their relationship is finished. "No, Louisa," Frederick answers, "thank Heaven, we live in a country that knows no distinction of persons, but in virtue."[54] Such a line would no doubt resonate as easily in Norfolk as in London – indeed, it is the sort of stage line that blurs the distinctions between English values and American, the Revolution notwithstanding. In many ways, the popularity of rural-setting comic operas reveals not merely an aspect of American identity tied up in agricultural life but also a longing for origins in the English countryside (without those being stated too overtly on-stage), where, despite a claim of equality in the denial of distinction, separation by class still persists, in a "natural" alignment of elite with elite, villager with villager, where all unite to expel the hypocritical lawyer or corrupted urbanite from the fantasy of pastoral harmony.

The values of patriarchy assert themselves most clearly in one other rural-set comedy, *A Cure for the Heart-Ache*, played twice each in 1798 and 1800 in Norfolk. In the way that Endless corrupts the locals in *No Song*, the new landowner in Gloucestershire, Vortex, does the same in Morton's play. Since he has moved into the newly named Bangalore Hall, Vortex, called by many 'the Nabob,' has expended what appears to be his colonial booty from India on purchasing lavish appointments and seducing the benighted farmers into parting with their cash at his gambling tables. One of these victims, Farmer Oatland, who when he first enters is *'dressed in a compound of rusticity and fashion*' (*CHA* 7) – a no doubt ludicrous costume – has gotten himself so far in arrears on his land rental to the old-family squire, Sir Hubert Stanley, that it threatens the baronet's own financial situation. This, of course, is all part of the Nabob's plan: to push Sir Hubert into financial exigency and being forced to sell or be dependent on him. Morton shows the two children of Oatland, Frank and Jessy, able to maintain their virtue against their father's ruinous pretensions – he sometimes tosses off Italian and French phrases, a sure sign of decadence – and their willingness to go into service in order to make money to keep their farm is the mark of their commitment to the land and to paying the debt they owe Sir Hubert. In the end, the Nabob's riches prove illusory, and Sir Hubert recovers his own holdings and his pride, while Oatland returns to his senses and his farm. Most importantly, Sir Hubert's paternalistic style of land ownership receives full affirmation. Early in the play, we learn that it is the baronet's practice to feed the poor and keep rents fixed, rather than exploit the locals in the way Vortex intends. Whereas Sir Hubert would rather not deal in money at all – seat the poor at his table rather than corrupt them with coin – Vortex, in a device picked up from *Rosina*, thinks nothing of dropping a purse of money in front of Frank to tempt him to steal it. The play then pits a system of benevolent dependency, under the headship of the resident patriarch, against new money and gross self-aggrandizement, operated by someone with no attachment to the land or its people.

This last dimension is made manifest in an extraordinary speech by Sir Hubert to his son Charles, the admiring romantic lead. More than one Virginia squire in the Norfolk audience might have nodded in agreement with the squire from Gloucestershire as he assessed the effect of the Nabob's presence in a community long used to different ways:

> You have heard how my father kept alive the benevolent hospitality that once distinguish'd old England, and I not finding in modern ethics aught likely to improve either the morals or happiness of mankind, determin'd

to persevere in the ways of my fathers. Soon after you went abroad the adjoining estate was purchas'd by an East Indian, groaning under wealth produc'd by groans. Like the viper, after collecting in the warm sunshine his bag of venom, he came to the abode of peace and innocence and disseminated his poison. (*CHA* 19–20)

In a sense, the values of Sir Hubert come closer to those asserted by the next generations of Virginia plantation owners, as the South becomes "Old" and the plantation system justified on the basis of its long continuance. Nevertheless, his vision of the benevolent, paternalistic ideal, ratified by the son who calls his father's principles "just and liberal" (20), formed the basis for an orderly plantation society in the Chesapeake, with one important variant: it was the Virginia laborers, the slaves, who "groaned" under the lash directed, if not physically wielded, by the patriarch. One wonders if anyone in Norfolk in 1800 caught the irony.

If plays with rural settings were one type of British drama that might have resonated with Norfolk theatregoers, then those with nautical themes and situations were another. In many ways, the two types are related and often intermixed. In a popular afterpiece, Bickerstaff's *Thomas and Sally*, many of the same issues surface as appear in *Rosina*, only the virtuous lover, Thomas, is a sailor lad, who rescues Sally from the clutches of the seducing squire. It is almost all songs, linking rural happiness, the vigors of the sea, service in the navy, and English patriotism in one tidy vehicle: "Ye British youths, be brave, you'll find,/The British virgins will be kind," the two lovers sing at the end.[55] Performed in Norfolk three times in the period, *Thomas and Sally* must have pleased the spectators, although as indication of the importance of the music to the piece, a local critic thought it would be "a better relish, if the Band was encreased in the Orchestra."[56] In *No Song, No Supper*, something of the same pastoral–nautical patriotism emerges through the figure of Robin. As the nautical subgenre develops, the character of the sailor becomes the sidekick to an elite, as Robin is to Frederick. Both men have been involved in a shipwreck off the Cornish coast, and Robin has saved Frederick's life. The former becomes the model for the archetypal "British sailor," who is fearless and loyal to "his king, his country, and his friend," (*NS* 4) and often speaks in nautical lingo. Again, given the pattern of cuts in Philadelphia and changes in subtitles in Norfolk, we can assume that deletions of overt references to British nationality and monarchy or changes of names and customs to American marked both plays. In *No Song*, Robin ends up being the main character, something in the way that

Shelty does in *Highland Reel*; he's not the romantic lead, but that character, Frederick, proves to be a theatrical nonentity, while Robin, like Shelty, gets many of the good lines. As with the American Yankee character, the sailor threatens always to take over a play, even in his position as second fiddle to the romantic male character's first violin. His humorous squeaks and comic notes prove more entertaining than the lead's smooth strains, and thus appeal to a working and nautical socioeconomic class in the audience.

In Norfolk, that class was likely substantial. We know from commentary in the newspaper in 1800 and 1801 that sailors attended the theatre and were heard by others to talk back to the stage.[57] In addition to *No Song* and *Thomas and Sally*, the men from the many ships in port might have enjoyed Charles Dibdin's *The Waterman*, and the main character Tom Tug, or Dibdin's *The Wapping Landlady*, subtitled *The Generous Tar*, in which a male performer (in Norfolk, Isaac Bignall) often played the landlady because of a demanding on-stage costume change, and that in Norfolk on both June 21 and June 25, 1800 included "The Sailor's escape by a Leap through a Window, followed by Tom Bowling, through a picture eight feet high."[58] No doubt the local tars – named so for their characteristic hats, tarpaulins – would have delighted in the athleticism of the Sully brothers, Matthew, Jr., and Chester, in that last scene, as both were also trained as circus performers and in fact, in company with their father, Matthew Sully, Sr. (also an actor in *Wapping Landlady*), held a circus in Norfolk during the 1800 season at Brigg's Point.[59] Nautical plays tended to be musical, affirm basic values such as bravery and loyalty, and occasionally demonstrate broad, physical humor or feats of daring on stage. The sailor is sturdy, sometimes indecorous, but always finds his place in the middle of the on-stage social hierarchy.

The most popular nautical drama and indeed overall during the period was Cross's *The Purse; or, Benevolent Tar*, the only play to be mounted as many as five times. The sailor, Will Steady, is a likable chap, whose chronic use of shipboard jargon in non-naval situations produces a good deal of the verbal humor. Curiously, *The Purse* unites both the nautical and the Gothic, another subgenre then currently in fashion. The Baron has been waiting at his castle for eight years for his son, Edmund, to return; in the meantime, Theodore, an unrelated young man living at the castle, has taken the son's place in the Baron's eye, but he is also embezzling. Naturally, Edmund returns in the company of Will, whose knowledge of the terrain helps the true heir find his way back to the Baron's;

they have been held captive since a shipwreck, presumably by the Algerians – one reason, perhaps, for the popularity of the play for American audiences, who were very conscious of their countrymen being held in North Africa. When Will meets a page and learns of the boy's poverty, he gives him a purse with all his money – yet another purse play, although this time, one given for good. Complications ensue when Theodore accuses the boy of embezzling and the Baron is about to banish him; but Will and Edmund enter, Will realizes the page is his son whom he has never met, the Baron and Edmund reunite, and Theodore's plot is exposed. Both the page and Will urge leniency for Theodore, in an ending that will become familiar in the melodrama, with Will's comment to the true embezzler being particularly piquant:

> Well, friend Down-in-the-mouth, you'll not be brought to a court-martial this bout; but take a tar's advice, use the rudder of honesty instead of deceit, and then you'll steer clear of the shoals of punishment and quicksands of disgrace.[60]

The music and songs, the happy reunions, and the shipboard slang of the good-hearted tar all unite in one crowd-pleasing vehicle in a maritime city.

In addition, there's a nationalistic element, which could easily have been changed to meet American audiences. As Will says of his captivity with Edmund, "a British sailor loves *native* freedom too well, even to willingly let a *foreigner* interfere with it" (*TP* 10). Given such overt nationalizing, managers in Norfolk and other cities faced a problem of how much to honor the original text or their understanding of audience expectations. In 1796 John Hodgkinson in Boston turned *The Purse* into a piece subtitled *American Tar* and was taken to task for it in the Anglophile *Federal Orrery*. Hodgkinson may have made substitutions similar to the way the line quoted above was played in New York, where "British" was replaced by "benevolent," "*native*" by "universal," and "*foreigner*" by "slaves."[61] Whether "American" replaced "British" in any of the Norfolk performances in 1797, 1798, or 1800, I do not know, but in 1796, the play was advertised with the subtitle *The American Tar*, as per Boston, suggesting that, at least on that occasion, the play was altered enough to make Will into a Yank. It is hard to imagine that the Virginia Company did not continue playing *The Purse* as an "American" play, although as elsewhere managers could be damned for making changes and damned for not. In any event, *The Purse*, with John William Green in a signature role as Will Steady, entertained the city in many seasons, sometimes more than once a year, from 1797 to 1810. The loyalty of the tar was matched by Green's own loyalty to the Virginia Company and to Norfolk, even after the retirement of Margaretta West and Green's reorganization of the company in 1809 with Alexander Placide. Sailors and others may have seen in Will not only an emblem of seagoing virtues but also a sign of Green's commitment to their entertainment. With the destruction of the Richmond theatre in 1811 and Green's grief over the loss of his daughter in that fire contributing to his retirement, even Will Steady had to abandon ship Norfolk.

As has been suggested, a number of the British plays performed in Virginia had resonance with local audiences, based either on nationality or ancestral ethnic identification, or occupation, as with the tars. On a few known occasions, the managers of the company made efforts to localize even further by putting on plays written in the United States or about American subjects, or else altering a well-known British play to meet local circumstances. In the latter case, for instance, one finds the aforementioned 1796 *The Purse* or two 1802 *Inkle and Yarico* productions with titles adjusted to encourage national identification; in the latter, Colman's comic opera was billed as '*or, American Heroine*' in its first performance, then titled *The American Heroine; or Ingratitude Punished* in the second.[62] In one of the more interesting such alterations, Thomas West made a few small changes to convert Elizabeth Inchbald's *The Mogul Tale* into *The Norfolk Cobler*, as performed on July 10, 1797. In the original, Johnny Atkins, an English shoemaker, his wife Fanny, and a hare-brained academic 'doctor' take a balloon from their homeland to Muslim-controlled India, have various adventures there, then, once the plot resolves in their favor, prepare to return. For the Norfolk production, Johnny was billed in the advertisement as '*The Norfolk Cobler*' and played by Gavin Turnbull, a poet, singer, and actor who performed in Norfolk for the 1797 and 1798 seasons as well as publishing some of his poems in the *Norfolk Herald*. Turnbull had made efforts to advertise for a subscription to a collection of his poems[63] and may have felt he could further endear himself to the Norfolk public by playing the cobbler as a local man. At the same time, as with nautical dramas, *The Norfolk Cobler* served to appeal to working-class spectators, since Johnny is a plain-speaking fellow and the main male character in the piece, while Fanny is both virtuous – she resists the Mogul's solicitations – and salt-of-the-earth. A high point in the farce occurs when a eunuch comes to take Fanny to the Mogul's seraglio; Johnny resists, '*prevents*' the eunuch from physically taking her, then says (making presumed substitutions for 'England' and 'island'):

if you was in a certain corner of the world called Old [Virginia], you would know you dog you – that if the first Prince of the Blood was to attempt the wife of a poor cobler, against her will and good liking – he had better take up the whole [country] by main force, and dash it into the sea again. (*MT* 19)

By making a few geographical alterations, the manager or an actor could transform a quintessential English artisan into a representative American one. English drama turns into American drama at the drop of a balloon, which the Virginia Company could do literally, thanks to actor James West's experience with ballooning, going back at least to his benefit with the Old American Company in New York in June of 1793.[64] Although Thomas West's decision to play Inchbald's farce as a local drama had most likely a basis in his wanting to sell tickets and aid his actor Turnbull's popularity, it demonstrated one strategy for how managers with a primarily British repertoire could address the concerns of American nationalists in their support of a Norfolk theatre.

The other, more obvious, but little-used strategy was to perform American-authored plays. In Norfolk, as in other theatre cities in the early republic, spectators were not often likely to encounter dramas by their own citizens, but to its credit, the West Company and its successor under Green did make some efforts to perform American material. Royall Tyler's *The Contrast*, for example, was produced in Norfolk on July 4, 1795, and to emphasize its nationality as well as honor the date of performance it was subtitled *The American Son of Liberty*. In the 1795 season, West also advertised Sarah Marriott's *The Chimera* and J. Kenna the Younger's *The Land of Liberty; or, A Trip to the Charleston Races*, the latter of which has not survived.[65] It should be noted that both Kenna and Mrs. Marriott were actors in the company for the 1795 season, suggesting why their plays were staged – and both died at the end of the season in Norfolk during September, suggesting further why their plays were never revived.[66] During Margaretta West's tenure as manager, in the 1802 season, *The Contrast* was revived with the same subtitle as in 1795, and *The Purse* was again subtitled *The American Tar* along with the previously mentioned use of *American Heroine* for two *Inkle and Yarico* performances. Under Green's management, other new American materials were introduced, including in 1805 the ephemeral *Easter Holidays; or, A Trip to Lindsay's Gardens*, written by a local author in celebration of a resort on the outskirts of Norfolk that often held entertainments, fireworks displays, concerts, and the like, especially during the warmer months; James Workman's *Liberty in Louisiana*, also in 1805; and James Nelson Barker's *The Indian Princess*, performed the year after its first Philadelphia performance, in 1809. Despite the three plays performed in 1795, however, it was rare for there to be more than one or two American dramas in a season; sometimes there were none.

Of the four American-created pieces that appeared in Norfolk from 1797 to 1800, one was written by a member of John Sollee's Charleston company, John Beete, who acted in a corps that included many of the actors in the West company (which no longer formally played Charleston) for the 1797 Norfolk season. Someone from the original Charleston cast probably brought a copy of *The Man of the Times* from Charleston (it had been published there) to Virginia, where Thomas Wade West produced it. Beete's farce, set in Philadelphia, combines Irish character humor, nationalist themes from *The Contrast* and *The Traveller Returned*, and concern about the buying up of soldiers' commutation notes at a fraction of their value, all situations likely to appeal to or resonate with a Norfolk audience. Major Upright tells young Charles Screwpenny that he cannot marry Upright's daughter, Lydia, until the lover forswears his father's duplicitous financial practices. Charles has been in England, and so has Lydia, each for an education, although Major Upright now regrets having sent her there. Charles, unaware and disbelieving of his father's iniquity, learns over the course of the play the truth of the accusations. Upright, like his avatar, Colonel Manly, has never left American soil; Charles, for his part, has learned not to love all things English, a la Billy Dimple, but like Murray's Rambleton to appreciate "the charms of my native country."[67] Finally, with Old Screwpenny's chicanery exposed, Charles renounces his name and ill-gotten family fortune to marry Lydia, while the sexually aggressive Irish servant, James O'Connor, marries another servant, Katy. The play denounces the effects of speculation, a major concern in the late 1790s, and affirms values created and promulgated by "republican governments" (*Man* 2). Despite its topicality and republican sentiments, however, *Man of the Times* played Norfolk only once.

The other three American dramas in Norfolk all had to do with the Revolution. The most spectacular production was that of John Daly Burk's *Bunker-Hill; or, The Death of General Warren* (1797), a play loathed by William Dunlap as nothing but fustian, but which he had to grant brought in large audiences and often saved managers when their bottom line was most threatened.[68] Given on July 4 and July 11, 1798, *Bunker-Hill* promised to be the most visually exciting performance of the year. The ad for the July 11 performance (the one for July 4 only contained the title and the author blurb) included not only the play's successful performance history "at the Theatres of Boston and New-York," but also a piece of poetry from the original prologue that nationalizes the occasion:

> A nobler theme than this, to grace the Stage;
> Where can we find in all th' Historic page?
> O! Rome and Cato's fall, the world has rung,
> Why not Columbia's rising fame be sung?[69]

Following the cast, which included Green in the hero's role as General Joseph Warren and Ann West in the female lead, Elvira, Thomas West had printed the following description of what spectators would see:

> *Scenery painted expressly for the piece.*
> The American Camp – A view of Charleston
> Burning – A view of Bunker-Hill, &c.
> *Act I, commences with confusion caused among the*
> *English troops – In Act IV, the embarkation of*
> *the British troops – Act V, opens with the*
> Battle on the Hill – *the English are*
> *obliged to* retreat three times,
> *advance, and are* again beat
> back; *when Gen.* Warren
> *addresses his Soldiers*,
> General WARREN mortally wounded.
> *The whole to conclude with*
> A GRAND FUNERAL PROCESSION,
> With an Elegy over the Bier of WARREN –
> Vocal parts by Mr. J. West & Miss Gallispie.

In staging this spectacle, West was able to bring Burk's patriotic drama, billed here as "an Historic Tragedy," to Norfolk only a few months after its opening performances in New York in September 1797 and with all the scenic extras that marked its original production. Who created the scenery is not stated, but for other productions we know that West was able to use some of the best scene painters in America, including Luke Robbins and Anthony Audin. John William Green was also a scenic painter, having been trained originally as an artist in England.[70] At any rate, it is likely that the show pleased, especially as it was offered twice only a week apart.[71]

The remaining two American plays offered in Norfolk during the seasons under review both center on the controversial subject of Major André, a figure who seems to have inspired a number of attempts to dramatize his execution at the hands of General George Washington. In Norfolk and elsewhere, André plays and pantomimes had been enacted before summer 1798 with relative frequency. Sarah Marriott had apparently written one such play, *The Land We Live In; or The Death of Major André*, sometime shortly before her death in 1795.[72] In Charleston on May 11, 1796, West's company premiered a three-act pantomime arranged by Alexander Placide called *The Death of Major André; or West Point Preserved*, while William Hill Brown had his now-lost play *West Point Preserved* performed in Boston on April 14, 1797.[73] William Dunlap produced his play of *André* three times in New York starting on March 30, 1798, and in South Carolina, on April 27, the Charleston Comedians performed a pantomime – not Placide's, apparently, although probably plagiarized from Placide, Brown, or both – with the title *The Death of Major André, and Arnold's Treachery, or West Point Preserved*, said to have been "never performed here" and "written by a citizen of the United States," as well as containing a large cast that included several American generals, a British general, and Lafayette.[74] At Lailson's Circus in Philadelphia, a grand pantomime with the same title as that produced in Charleston just a little over two weeks before was performed on May 14, 1798, and claimed to be "Composed by a Citizen of Philadelphia"; ironically, it had a nearly all-French cast. When a pantomime by the title of *The Death of Major André* was performed again in Philadelphia the following year, at the rival Ricketts' Circus, the company on February 7 used a smaller and somewhat different cast list from that at Lailson's and an even smaller list on February 9.[75] Within a three-year period, then, two plays and several pantomimes, all somewhat different from each other, enacted the André story before American audiences.[76]

Despite the comparatively large number of André-story productions in the United States through 1800, there seem to have been relatively few total performances. Therefore, from a theatre history perspective, those in Norfolk take on additional importance. Except for Dunlap's play, New York hosted no other versions of the André narrative on its boards; Norfolk put on two versions: Dunlap's and a pantomime. Of special significance is the fact that *André* was given a rare performance outside of New York in Norfolk on June 18, 1798, less than three months after its now infamous March 30 premiere in New York with John Hodgkinson as

André and Thomas Abthorpe Cooper as the young American Bland.[77] As with *Bunker-Hill* two years later, the manager took out a much longer than usual ad to trumpet the production in the *Norfolk Herald*. *André*, we are told, is a "Tragedy (never performed here)" and "Founded on the Tragic, recent and authentic story of the bold attempt, and death of Major ANDRE." Significantly, it is the only one of the four American plays performed in Norfolk in the period to carry the label that the dramatist was "*a native of the U. States*." In addition, the ad includes a long section from a prologue with these closing lines:

> Nor vainly toils our Bard for empty fame,
> But to arouse that Patriotic flame:
> Which in the deeds of your Forefathers shone,
> And bid their Sons the glorious impulse own!

A full cast list is included, down to the "Children of Mrs. Bland," and a final note announcing an element of spectacle: "In Act 5th/The Procession to the Place of Execution." Of course, spectators would leave the theatre under the spell of the Hugh Kelly farce, *Love a-la-Mode; or, the Humours of the Turf*, but that practice of following the main play with something light was no different in Norfolk from any other theatre of the time. Nevertheless, the ad copy for *André* is so long that no cast is provided for in the afterpiece, suggesting the manager intended to draw a large crowd with an American play.[78]

It is unfortunate that no commentary has come to light regarding this particular production, on which West must have exerted some additional expense. That it was not repeated in Norfolk may tell us something of audience reaction, although that can hardly be definitive. Dunlap suggests several reasons why it failed in New York, including that the events were too close to the performance, but that would be less likely to cause controversy in Norfolk than in a city where André had lived during the British occupation and where he was still remembered.[79] Of course, the best known reason for the failure of *André* in New York, from Dunlap's perspective, was the rivalry between his two lead actors and Cooper's shameful refusal to learn his lines for the opening night.[80] In Norfolk, as in New York, the best of the company engaged to play *André*. The title character was enacted by Green, by this time West's best actor in the tragic line. Margaretta West, who played Belvidera in *Venice Preserved* to acclaim,[81] took the role of Mrs. Bland, mother to the young officer – a piece of realism as Mrs. West's literal son, Thomas C. West, played

Captain Bland. Most of the other roles were taken by experienced actors most familiar at the second tier of characters: Turnbull, who had come to the United States from the Edinburgh theatre, as M'Donald, Mr. Watts[82] as Seward, Isaac Bignall as Melville, Messrs. Perkins and Matthew Sully, Sr., as an American officer and sergeant, respectively. As the General, the Washington figure, Mr. Taylor brought several years of acting experience in Boston, Philadelphia, and New York with him to Norfolk, arriving for the 1798 season in Virginia from an engagement with Wignell during the early months of that year. In the other theatres, Taylor tended to play somewhat older male characters: Sir Hubert Stanley in *Cure for a Heart-Ache* and Octavian in *Mountaineers*, for instance. Therefore, he might have had the kind of mature dignity that Dunlap's role calls for. The one other role of note is Honora, Dunlap's most poorly conceived character, as she is largely given to hysterics, but in Norfolk she was enacted by Ann West Bignall West, the best actress for female roles outside those played by her mother in the tragic lead.

In short, it is unlikely that Norfolk had much to complain about in the casting of its *André*. But what of the play itself? Dunlap describes Bland as a Virginian and thus contrasts the hotheaded southern youth with the cooler officers from the North, M'Donald (a Scottish native) and Seward. His seeming act of treachery in preferring his British friend over his country may have been disturbing to Norfolk, as it was to New York, but no doubt would have had to be played carefully so as not to offend Virginians by castigating them as potential traitors. The General, however, while never named as Washington, might well have been a point of pride for a Virginia audience, as long as Taylor played him with the kind of dignity associated with Washington by 1798 and not, as the play suggests, as a sometimes vacillating, somewhat vindictive figure. Nevertheless, there is something eerie about *André* in the South. With the recovery of the early history of Virginia in the first decade of the nineteenth century and the development of FFV ideology – First Families of Virginia – there must have been already among the wealthy Tidewater planters a growing sense of their own distinction from others – slaves and working-class whites, to be sure, but also from elites in other parts of the country. If the cockade controversy in New York had much to do with Federalist and Republican politics and a latent nostalgia among conservatives for an English past, in Virginia Bland's act of defiance, even if played in Dunlap's revision of the notorious scene, prefigures a later act of defiance, a declaration that Virginia and the South enforce allegiances that cannot be contained simply under the rubric of the United States. Norfolk, as New York did, may have felt uneasy about just what Dunlap's play was supposed to signify, but it is possible its reasons not to clamor for additional performances may have differed considerably from those of its northern neighbor.

As suggested in the earlier chapter on *André*, Dunlap also encodes a conflicted homosocial relationship between André and Bland that puts the British major – a famously attractive young man – into something of a feminized position in the play, as the nurturing and beloved "friend" whose plight inspires Bland to histrionics and despair. This androgynous reading of the character André may have inspired the other production in Norfolk, a pantomime entitled *The Death of Major André*, without a subtitle. Playing but once in Norfolk, on July 12, 1800, this production had a smaller cast than the February 7, 1799 Philadelphia list for a pantomime with the same title, and again, the characters were not the same. The major difference between the Norfolk pantomime and those in Charleston in 1798 and Philadelphia, regardless of which version in that latter city, is the elimination from the Virginia theatre of the three yeoman captors of the British spy – a significant change, given the importance William Dunlap accorded them in his revision of *André* as *The Glory of Columbia, Her Yeomanry!* Miss Corry took her benefit in the production (the afterpiece to Rowe's *Jane Shore*); and since she had been in Philadelphia at the Pantheon during the time when Lailson's mounted the original pantomime, it is possible she got her inspiration from seeing it there. It is also possible that another member of the company, Joseph Hughes, had brought ideas from the 1798 Charleston performance (he appeared in a different role in Norfolk) or that parts of Placide's original arrangement from 1796 still survived in the West Company archives.

Whatever the particular source text or performance, Miss Corry played Major André in Norfolk, one of three cross-dressed roles she had in the 1800 season, the others being Patrick in *The Poor Soldier* and Bouquet in O'Keeffe's *The Son-in-Law*. As in the first Philadelphia production, André is given a "betrothed," only in Norfolk she is called Delia (played by Miss Melford), whereas in Philadelphia in 1798 she was called Honoria, and in Dunlap and historically his mistress was named Honora. Although other pantomimes made much of having the captors in the production as part of a broad-based patriotic appeal to both elite and yeoman or working-class spectators, the Norfolk production made the cross-dressed body of Miss Corry the point of spectacle, as if to say the yeomen would be a distraction – a significant decision for a city where wealthy planters carried more clout than small farmers. Well in advance of the gender-bending displays of Adah Isaacs Menken sixty years later, and anticipating the appearance on American stages of the real-life cross-dressing soldier, Deborah Sampson Gannett, in 1802, this actress in Norfolk was aiming to appeal to audiences through a deliberate ambiguity of identification.[83] Was a woman perceived as more capable of portraying the sufferings of André than a man? Or was there an erotic component to Miss Corry's enacted death throes that brought out a latent desire for the tragic young man that had been lurking in the André story? None of the other plays or pantomimes that I have identified from this period cast a woman as a male character. Perhaps such cross-dressing also caused some problems for the Norfolk audience – or literalized their conflicted feelings about the André story. Although Miss Corry played three more years and many characters with Margaretta West's Company in Norfolk, she did not again play a male role in that city.

For a lover of the playhouse in Norfolk, the four years discussed here encompassed in microcosm the twenty years of professional theatre before 1812. There was more than theatre, of course, for entertainment. Exhibitions of animals, optical marvels, visiting acrobats, firework displays, one-man or small-ensemble performances, and concerts filled in the spaces when the Wests were not in town – and sometimes added to the mix when they were there.[84] Still, there were long stretches where almost nothing was available, as in 1799, or years where the season was truncated, as in 1797. But in the best years, including 1798 and 1800, residents and visitors to the city could experience several months of professional theatre, see many new plays and old favorites, and be entertained by music, singing, dancing, scenic spectacles, and acrobatic derring-do in the process. Rather than passively absorbing an unending retinue of British comedies, the audience seems to have influenced the choice of plays, at least to some limited degree. If the number of plays by Americans seems functionally insignificant, the choices of other plays, and the variations in playing them – turning British tars into American ones, for example – indicate desires on the part of managers to adjust their repertoire to meet perceived identifications in their particular city. The Wests did not look at Norfolk as some remote outpost, a place to make a few bucks before turning to the cities of gold elsewhere, but in fact treated their seasons there with both business acumen and professional commitment. Although much disliked by William Dunlap, the actor James Chalmers, in Norfolk for the 1800 season, was at his best a highly effective comic and tragic actor.[85] The local critic remarked that he had seen Garrick, Henderson, Smith, and Kemble in London, 'and tho' as to Garrick, it may be said, *'that we ne'er shall look upon his like again,'* yet, at the present day, Mr. Chalmers would be a good representation of him."[86] Norfolk's identity as a city was tied to its theatre, and if the critic chose to remark on peculiarities of the actors, it was done to improve what that writer took to be an already worthy company. At the same time, the Norfolk theatre reflected back to its patrons a variety of individual identities, many of which merely confirmed preexisting notions of what it meant to be Irish or Scottish, for instance, while other performances gave back more troubled readings − Benin in *Highland Reel*, Major André in Dunlap and the pantomime − of the subjecthood of blacks or a conflicted set of desires for the figure of the British spy. Given the number of plays shown, the number of different people involved in Norfolk productions − each with a history − our uncertain knowledge about the precise nature of the audience, and the current lack of knowledge about contemporary reaction, we have much more to learn not only about Norfolk but about the place of drama and theatre in figuring and reflecting identities in the early republic.

13

After The Contrast: *Tyler, civic virtue, and the Boston stage*

BY 1825, THEATRE WAS WELL ENSCONCED IN THE UNITED States. Having spread to all major seaboard cities, it was poised to move westward, and in fact had done so in part already. Cincinnati, New Orleans, Mobile, and St. Louis were but a few of the new theatre centers that would become important stops on actors' tours in the next two decades. At the end of the century's first quarter, most of the generation of actors who had brought the stage back to the former colonies after the war had retired or died; before long, American-born actors, such as Edwin Forrest and Charlotte Cushman, would rival and ultimately supplant the British stars who would continue to seek fame and gold in the New World. The success of such plays as Woodworth's *The Forest Rose* made clear to managers that American-written and set material could be lucrative and that audiences would demand more in the way of American types: the stage Yankee to be sure, but also American-honed versions of British dramatic stock characters, most especially the stage African and stage Irish. Democratic energies infused what some had tried to forge as an elite-dominated entertainment medium, and as theatres got larger, holding two or three thousand patrons, spectator demographics more accurately reflected the population as a whole.[1] If anything, 1825 would have been a good time to look back and to look forward, to see where theatre had come and where it would go.

In 1825, the year before his death, the first moderately successful American playwright for the professional stage reflected on what he called "the first theatrical representation in Boston." In his autobiographical novel, *The Bay Boy*, Royall Tyler describes a group of daring school lads in the Puritan city who mount a production of Addison's *Cato* in an empty store at night, sometime in the late 1760s or early 1770s. The scene is a humble one: a counter and empty barrels serve for stage and seating; lookouts admit the conspirators and check for the watchman. Before the final act is completed, the constables detect the breach of law and break up the performance. To his imagined nineteenth-century readers, the narrator, Updike Underhill, says that they have attended the well-lighted theatres and seen the great English actors on American boards. But they have observed nothing compared to that first amateur effort: 'Be assured that a public theatrical exhibition is in comparison stale, flat, and unprofitable. Could I once again assist at such a private theatrical I would give more for a ticket even on the steps than was ever bid at vendue for a seat in the stage box on the appearance of Cooke or Kean.'[2] This remark, coming from an author whose play *The Contrast* did much to encourage a native drama and theatre, seems odd in its evident dismissal of the institution that brought him his first bout with fame. What happened in Tyler's thinking about the stage between the premiere of his first play and his last year of life? Curiously, one of the best sources for pursuing how theatre functioned in his consciousness is his poetry, which he continued to write after he had left off producing scripts for the Old American Company. In the poems of Tyler that bridge the space between his youth and active involvement with the stage at one end, and his old age in Vermont, writing closet dramas on biblical themes, at the other, one may detect shifting attitudes toward the stage that put his *Bay Boy* reflection in context.

As the first comedy written by an Anglo-American born in North America to be produced by professional actors, *The Contrast* earned in its time, and still garners, well-deserved attention. It is probably the only American drama before 1845 (the year of Anna Cora Mowatt's *Fashion*) known widely by students of American literature. Scholars of the stage recognize in the mounting of Tyler's play the beginnings of a theatre tradition: American plays could at last compete with foreign imports on the commercial stage. Nevertheless, despite the direct line one could draw from that first production in 1787 to the present-day professional theatre in New York and elsewhere, Tyler's success with *The Contrast* was something of an aberration. It is not that he lacked talent. *The Contrast*, whatever its shortcomings, remains a readable, even actable play that takes on important themes of national identity. Tyler was a wit, wrote with a facile pen, and indeed, had he succeeded even more with stage plays, might have been allured into making drama a career. Neither is it that he shied from courting theatrical applause. Indeed, he followed his first comedy with several others, and although most of them have disappeared or only survive in fragmentary form, it is clear that he wanted to continue receiving the plaudits of the New York theatre crowd and to make something of drama in the new republic. Rather, the aberrant nature of *The Contrast* rests with Tyler's own developing sense of the proper role of the theatre in a republic. More than his plays or even his prose, Tyler's poems suggest the terms of the shift in his thinking. If there is to be republican theatre at all, he came to believe, it ought finally to be an amateur enterprise, free of the moral stain he began to see on the commercial stage.

Before 1800, in addition to his performed plays *The Contrast, May-Day in Town, The Farm House, The Doctor in Spite of Himself,* and *A Georgia Spec,* and the unperformed *The Island of Barrataria* (*Four Plays,* ed. Peach and Newbrough, pp. 1–30), Tyler wrote a few poetic prologues for theatrical productions.[3] The one attributed to him in connection with *The Contrast* is well known. There, of course, Tyler calls for native bards and "native themes," affirming that there is a place for the stage in the new republic, with a hint that the success of the theatre depends on the ability of dramatists and producers to provide substance more than wit – and the audience to watch with uncommon respect for the effort:

> Should rigid critics reprobate our play,
> At least the patriotic heart will say,
> "Glorious our fall, since in a noble cause.
> The bold *attempt alone* demands applause."[4]

Although he makes a claim for the salutary effect of satire, Tyler is at pains to stress that the drama is a pedagogical tool, "Which aims not to expose [faults], but amend" (*TC* 8). The prologue, along with the play itself, includes within it a basic assumption about theatre: it can be molded to serve the ends of republican citizenship and teach its spectators the basic virtues that constitute American identity.

A much earlier prologue, dated by Marius Péladeau as during Tyler's Harvard years (1772–1776), but perhaps also associated with the proscribed production of Joseph Addison's *Cato* depicted in *The Bay Boy,* stresses the moral dimension of drama:

> To shew the vile intentions of the mind
> To paint the real vices of mankind
> To drag out crimes conceal'd in shades of night
> To fetch the lurking mischief to the light
> To shew the effects of every baleful ill

> By black examples drawn with wondrous skill
> For this the Drama first adorned the stage
> Checking the progress of a vicious age.[5]

For Tyler, early in his career, putting on a play meant a flouting of repressive codes at the same time that it provided an instrument for the correction of society. The young patriot may have even had the same attitudes toward Boston theatrical prudery as the British general John Burgoyne, whose own staging of plays in the occupied city in 1775 represented his particular skewering of local mores. As is clear by his spoofing of Jonathan's country Puritan minister for railing against the stage ("At the play! why, did you think I went to the devil's drawing room?" [*TC* 33]), Tyler sought in *The Contrast* particularly to justify the ways of the theatre to his fellow Americans against religious prohibitions; in the words of his Harvard prologue, it was perfectly acceptable – indeed, socially necessary – to enact "black examples drawn with wondrous skill." In his *Contrast* prologue, he tries to play two sides against a middle course, rejecting on the one hand the antitheatrical rhetoric of Sam Adams and other radical whigs who saw the theatre as a corrupt, anti-republican institution of the colonizing power; and on the other, the tea-table set for whom the stage was, as for Dimple, merely an unregulated amusement that served largely as a catalyst for public display of the body.[6] In between the extremes, he argues for a nationalist theatre, one whose function is to reinforce the essential cultural ends of the Revolution without succumbing entirely to dull didacticism. In short, the theatre Tyler had in mind in the days of *The Contrast* was one both entertaining and corrective, a school not for scandal but for new American identities. In that sense, Tyler goes further than Crèvecoeur and Munford, whose satires of Revolutionary society end without a clear vision of an American future.

He develops these ideas in two later prologues. In "Occasional Prologue to The Mistake of a Night; Or, She Stoops to Conquer," prepared for a performance by the pupils of Charlestown Academy in New Hampshire in the summer of 1794, Tyler notes the production is taking place not far from a recent Mohawk raid and takes delight in the contrast between the primitive setting and the occasion for art. Conscious of the youth of the actors – itself a tacit metaphor for the youth of the country – Tyler demands a code of audience conduct. No overt signs of displeasure should be displayed, regardless of spectators' feelings about what they are seeing, lest they "nip the bud of genius." By encouraging the actors – who are, after all, putting on a British play – the audience prepares the seeds for "native lays" from the rising generation, and thus in America:

> Where our *green mountains* tower with verdant pride,
> Some future *Avon* shall meandering glide –
> Some future Shakespeare paint the poet's dreams,
> Some future Garrick act the glowing scenes;
> Till humbled Britain, aw'd by our success,
> In arts and arms, our triumph shall confess. (*Verse* 37)

For Tyler, the drama is tied to the humility of the scene and the innocence of the players, nurtured by a landscape as yet unspoiled by the social theatrics of a culturally corrupt Europe. Perhaps reading into the performance of the academy players the ideals that he felt as a schoolboy actor, he resolutely reconstructs a theatre capable of competing on the international stage as based in amateurism. By "Garrick," Tyler means not only an acclaimed actor, but a "natural" one, whose portrayals come from life rather than imitations of past traditions; by "Shakespeare," he intends to evoke the Bard's mirror. An American stage, he argues, should foster characters who draw their shape from the natural virtues enshrined in the verdant landscape and the innocence of youth – acting naturally the natural characters such a landscape produces.

Similar sentiments appear in his last prologue, "An Occasional Address," written for his brother, John Steele Tyler, the new manager of the Federal Street Theatre in Boston, and the opening of the 1795–96 season.[7] Published in *The Federal Orrery*, although for some reason never delivered, Tyler's poem again imagines the native Shakespeares and Garricks who will eclipse the British at their own game, but, more forcefully than in earlier prologues, he links the drama to American heroism and the struggle for independence. The poem appeared during contention within Boston between two political factions, the Federalists and old Antifederalists, now Democratic–Republicans, and it attempts to avoid taking sides, steering a more nationalist than partisan course. Overall, it is a rousing poem, intended to appeal to popular sentiment in the audience. Still, beyond the patriotism and apparent hearty goodwill, something else emerges from this prologue that appears more frequently in later Tyler poems: a greater consciousness of particular forms of conduct at the theatre, most notably that of women. On the one hand, that consciousness reflects the Federalism of both author and theatre, a partisanship so strong it forced Republicans to build their own theatre in Boston, the Haymarket. On the other hand, Tyler's belief in a certain decorum hints at some deeper concern than mere party politics – a concern over the social and moral instability of the theatrical world that threatened to undo the maintaining of Revolutionary virtues in a post-Revolutionary era.[8]

While Tyler was writing plays for the New York stage, he was aware of the somewhat precarious state of theatre in post-Revolutionary America, but he also knew that the home to the John Street Theatre, where *The Contrast* first played, was well disposed to support active theatrical seasons. In Boston, however, the struggle to mount plays had taken much longer; the Massachusetts capital was the last of the major seaport cities to accept theatre as a legitimate enterprise. Professional theatre had only been approved in Boston in 1793, and while it quickly became established, there remained in the city a strong cadre of antitheatrical opponents, many of whom saw theatre as corrupting the nationalist virtues identified with the generation of 1776. That opposition tended to come from the remnants of the more radical whigs, most of whom tended toward Democratic–Republicanism as a political ideology. Supporters of theatre seem first to have found a stronghold among the Federalists, and, possibly because Federalism came to dominate Massachusetts politics in the 1790s, the stage was finally ushered into Boston's hall of legitimate amusements.

As a Federalist, Tyler would have allied himself with the protheatrical forces in Massachusetts, and with his brother a theatre manager (beginning in the 1795–96 season), he had a potential outlet for his poetic and dramatic effusions. *The Contrast* played in Gloucester in February 1794, accompanied by an epilogue written by fellow Federalist and playwright Judith Sargent Murray,[9] and at the Federal Street Theatre in Boston in May 1795. However, by this time, Tyler was no longer writing original plays for the stage. Indeed, he no longer lived in Boston, having gone to Vermont to establish a law practice. Most of his belletristic writings were in the form of poetic contributions to the "Shop of Colon and Spondee" that he wrote with Joseph Dennie and published in such New England newspapers as *The Eagle*. Tyler may have wanted to stay connected to urban culture, and Boston was both the closest large city and his birthplace. Yet Tyler differed in some ways from fellow Federalists. Dennie, for one, often wrote scornfully of American culture; his pronounced Anglophilia made London the measuring stick for American literary production. Tyler, however, shared with the Republicans – at least in part – a belief that the arts would rise to a level that would rival those of any nation while preserving homespun virtues without the corruptions of urban Europe. As a consequence, his attitudes toward the stage embodied some contradictions, even as his political affiliation would have led him to be skeptical of popular sovereignty and control over the spheres of politics and art.

In the prologue mentioned above, "An Occasional Address," Tyler demonstrates a dual consciousness between support for urban, professional theatre and concern over the preservation of American innocence.[10] This he does through an attention to audience behavior and mores by addressing each audience section in its turn. To patrons in the boxes, he notes that unlike in those of English stages, where coquettes dwell, American denizens are chaste and tastefully dressed, though he feels obliged to adopt the imperative: "Be witty, cheerful, and be modest too." Comedy in America succeeds in the "hearty laugh," he tells female boxholders, not the "meretricious leer" (*Verse* 44). In the pit, where political competition between Federalists and Democratic–Republicans often produces outrageous behavior, including sharp criticism of the performances, he asks that all join in a "*Democracy of glee*" whereby differences of taste and politics are dissolved in a single accord that American arts deserve to be affirmed. And to the upper gallery, the cheap seats, he addresses a warm invitation to continue with hearty laughter in a natural vein: 'Unlac'd by fashion, unrestrain'd by art, / Your's the warm impulse of the glowing heart' (45–46). Give a shove to "good ship-Theatre" and offer the energy of your unaffected loyalty to place. Boisterousness, American good humor, modesty must take charge over covert whispers, wit struck from low jests or double entendres, and sexual display if theatre is to have a continuing place in republican culture. For Tyler, the stage and the pit should be in one accord as to what constitutes American identity, regardless of party rage in the streets.

In one sense, this prologue marks a continuation of themes enunciated in *The Contrast*. He establishes his roots in Revolutionary patriotism with references to Benjamin Franklin and the war martyrs Joseph Warren and Richard Montgomery as well as the sitting Federalist President, George Washington (43). As in the *Contrast* colloquy between Colonel Manly and Dimple on theatre behavior – Manly affirming the value of local production, Dimple despising even to look at the actors on an American stage – Tyler continues to affirm the need to patronize and champion playhouses in the United States. Manly's bow to 'THE PUBLIC' at the end of the comedy links the theatre audience with citizenship in an emerging republic (*TC* 57), and in this 1795 prologue, Tyler makes a similar appeal, albeit to more localized sentiments: 'NORTH END FOREVER!' (*Verse* 46). Despite the 'huzzas' demanded in 'An Occasional Address,' however, it should be noted that Tyler was already leaning toward some kind of control over public entertainments to prevent popular energies from breaking the decorous bounds expected in the class-consciousness of the Federalists. In other words, despite his call for a '*Democracy of glee*,' he may not have been entirely convinced that true democracy should govern the theatre. In his 1798 poem 'Vauxhall Gardens,' Tyler celebrates the recent decision in Boston to establish a public garden on the model of Vauxhall in England, where individuals of all professions and political parties can stroll, 'Like GENTLEMEN' (77).[11] More importantly, he concludes by urging that the gardens be the scene of 'CHASTEN'D PLEASURES' and adds a prose note to the purpose of desiring for the urban United States assent for the proposition '*that well-regulated amusements are* ESSENTIAL *to the prosperity of great commercial cities*' (78). Thus for Tyler, the affirmation of *theatrum* and *polis* at the end of *The Contrast* includes a caveat a decade later: the legitimacy of an American theatre requires a code of behavior that separates it from the audience traditions of European capitals, one that taps into native energies based on honest responses but that is also controlled – by whom, he does not say – for the better education of the republic in virtue.

In another sense, though, the author brings out a dimension in 'An Occasional Address' that is suppressed in *The Contrast*. As with many late eighteenth-century writers, Tyler saw the role of women in culture as largely an emblematic one. His changing view of the stage is linked to his skepticism about the ability of women to avoid succumbing to the allure of display and of men to resist their artifice. Although American theatres were already excising lines from British plays that would likely, in their view, cause virtuous women to blush, Tyler seems to have felt that such cuts were insufficient in burying the appeal to a more sardonic than satiric humor. In the 1795 prologue, Tyler gives to American women the power to condemn "the tainted manners of the times" as practiced in London, but the degree to which he lingers over concern that women in the boxes will be hearing "the coarse joke, or coxcomb rude" suggests some worry that American maidens may be unprepared for the Europeanized behavior one might encounter in an urban theatre (44). In later poems, he begins to speak a moral aversion to the theatre as a home for prostitution, or its near and all too socially acceptable cousin. In a poem like "Choice of a Wife," one of his Spondee works for *The Newhampshire and Vermont Journal* in December 1796, the voice offers advice to a would-be male lover to beware the painted woman. "Would you shun the tricking arts," he admonishes; "Be not caught with shape, nor air,/Coral lips, nor flowing hair" (*Verse* 49). In another Spondee effusion from 1798, "To Miss Flirtilla Languish," the prospective beau of the poem is smitten with a woman of artifice. She appears in the theatre of public spaces, and Tippy, her poetic admirer, coos with delight at her arch artificiality: "To see, when my charmer trips by,/Some beau point his Opera glass;/How he looks down *Cornhill*, with a sigh,/As a *shopping* Flirtilla doth pass" (81). In both poems, Tyler stresses that the made-up woman, who may be inspiring the fires of admirers, is in fact a cold fish at heart.

By contrast, the poet expresses pleasure at the woman who resists the courting of public display. In his imitation, "Horace, Ode XXII, Lib. I," Tyler praises a woman "Grac'd with a temper void of affectation" who, whether in the ball room, concert, or stage box, shows no interest in receiving the gazes of spectators, and thus, "with the blush of nature,/Looks interesting when she's sweetly smiling,/Sweetly conversing" (149). And in one other work, from 1807, the poet in "The Wolf and Wooden Beauty" urges caution to anyone who seeks a wife to avoid the woman "Who, scorning sweet domestick duty,/Sighs for the sovereignty of beauty,/And at the play house, mall, or ball,/Though bound to one, would conquer all –" (162). Whereas in *The Contrast*, the domestic woman, Maria, could be aligned with the stoic champion of a native theatre, Manly, in this poem domesticity and theatricality are put deliberately at odds. The implication is that for the Tyler of 1807, a good woman would do well to avoid the playhouse altogether.

One might argue that Tyler has not changed in the twenty years between the writing of *The Contrast* and the appearance of this last mentioned poem. It is still the Marias of the world who earn his praise and coquettes who get the satiric lash. But the persistence of this theme suggests its darkening. The coquette of *The Contrast*, Charlotte, is redeemed in the play, but for the calculating beauties in the poems, no such redemption is offered. Tyler links face paint with deadness of feeling – and the audience of a theatre. His admonition to women in the boxes – "Be witty, cheerful, and be modest too" – is precisely the dilemma faced by the protagonist of another Massachusetts writer, Eliza Wharton in Hannah Webster Foster's novel *The Coquette*.[12] Is it possible for a woman to be identified with the stage – or at least the theatre of public square or mall – and still maintain her modesty, her social standing as arbiter of virtue? Foster complicates the matter, but ultimately kills off Eliza in her failed attempt to maintain virtue and be associated with the temptations of public culture. Tyler does not develop the moral ambiguity for his female figures that Foster does for Eliza, but he creates potential contradictions for his hardening position. Although in the first decade of the nineteenth century he stopped short of being a stage abolitionist, he was growing increasingly estranged from the institution that launched his reputation as an author.

Part of this has to do with Tyler's literal exile from cultural centers. Between 1796 and 1805, while he pursued his legal and judicial career in Vermont, there is little evidence to suggest that Tyler attended the stage, except perhaps the occasional play, private theatrical, or school production. Only one of his surviving poems during this period makes any direct allusion to the theatre, and even there the reference in "Epigram" to an incident involving the stage manager John Hodgkinson could easily have been expressed with only secondhand knowledge. But for the 1805–6 Boston season, Tyler must have attended enough times to have had a good sense of the acting company's strengths and weaknesses, for he details those in two lengthy satiric poems: "Epilogue to the Theatrical Season: Or, A Review of the Thespian Corps," and "An Epistle to My Muse; Or, a Postscript to the Epilogue to the Theatrical Season," both 1806. These and three other short poems that appeared at the same time, "The Mechanick Preferred," "The Reeling Roscius," and "Love Varses to the Bucheous Daffodel," are all inspired by particular actors or individuals then in Boston.

Tyler's models for a poetic review of an acting company were likely two satires by British poets: "The Actor" (1760) by Robert Lloyd and "The Rosciad" (1761) by Charles Churchill.[13] Lloyd and Churchill were part of a group of young satirists who criticized the maintenance of older and, to their generation, artificial and outmoded styles of acting. In "The Actor," Lloyd offers a general perspective on the state of acting in London. He singles out David Garrick as his model of the natural actor, then criticizes the various techniques then in vogue that bring opprobrium to the stage. For instance, Lloyd describes the failure of players to develop proper variation to their voices:

> 'Tis not enough the Voice be sound and clear,
> 'Tis modulation that must charm the ear.

> When desperate heroines grieve with tedious moan,
> And whine their sorrows in a see-saw tone,
> The same soft sounds of unimpassioned woes
> Can only make the yawning hearers doze.¹⁴

He also wants to reserve the stage for a drama dedicated to art, not show, and attacks the eighteenth-century practice of nondramatic entertainments sharing the stage with genuine plays: "More natural uses to the stage belong/Than tumblers, monsters, pantomime, or song."¹⁵ In general, Lloyd satirizes institutional tendencies more than individuals, with an eye toward improving the stage in the trail already being blazed by Garrick. Part of the poem's appeal to Tyler could be Lloyd's attack on theatre managers who play to the lowest elements of popular taste. One reason for the split of the Boston theatres in the 1790s rested on the Haymarket's employment of pantomimes and other nontraditional dramatic forms in greater numbers than those employed by the Federal Street Theatre.¹⁶ This of course had political ramifications: as the Haymarket had been opened to appeal to Democratic–Republicans and thus to an artisan class, its populism made it an easy target for the elitist Federalists at the Federal Street Theatre.

The premise of Churchill's "The Rosciad," which builds on Lloyd's basic thesis, is that the chair of first actor, once filled by the classical-era Roscius, is now empty. A panel consisting of William Shakespeare and Ben Jonson is chosen to measure the pretenders for the throne. Unlike Lloyd's broader approach, Churchill gets very particular and alludes in unmistakable ways (to his contemporaries, anyway) to individual theatrical personalities. Of one actor, the poet remarks:

> By Nature form'd in her perversests [sic] mood,
> With no one requisite of Art endu'd,
> Next JACKSON came – Observe that settled glare,
> Which better speaks a Puppet than a Play'r;
> List to that voice – did ever DISCORD hear
> Sounds so well fitted to her untun'd ear?¹⁷

After sweeping dismissals of most of the mid-eighteenth-century London and Dublin favorites, Churchill, like Lloyd, settles on Garrick as one who best holds the mirror up to Nature. Throughout, the poet pokes, jabs, and spindles those who fail to measure up but makes clear that his purpose is to affirm the stage. In contrast to the religiously inspired attacks on the theatre by Jeremy Collier and others in the post-Restoration period, Churchill means to establish greatness for British theatrical practice and tradition. For him, although he wields a harsh rod, satire is an instrument of reform, not just of making fun.[18]

As for London in 1760, so for Boston in 1806. Like his British counterparts, Tyler in his poetic reviews of the acting corps in the Boston Theatre Company thinks little of the general level of histrionic technique then being practiced.[19] With a few English-born exceptions – the comic actor William Twaits, the tragedian Thomas Abthorpe Cooper, and the much-admired Elizabeth Harrison Powell (Judith Sargent Murray's favorite actress) – the thespian corps are fully skewered in "Epilogue to the Theatrical Season." Ellen Westray Darley, a popular player considered "charming,"[20] is handled thus for her oft-used stage tic: "Do not lov'd actress, while each heart expands,/Forever bore us with your folded hands" (*Verse* 140). An unnamed actor in "Epistle" is critiqued, in a direct echo of the passage from Lloyd quoted above, because he "See-saws the air, and swells, and struts, and brags,/And kicks and tears a passion into rags" (153). Others are held up for chastening for a variety of reasons, many probably beyond their ability to do much about them. An actress finds her size depicted as "what majesty of flesh" and "Great ton of beauty, graceful by gross weight" (136); another woman, probably from the house ballet corps, is charged with dancing "all her parts," regardless of comic or tragic import (137). Perhaps the cruelest of all is Tyler's mocking of one of the supernumeraries, "that base throng, who ply beneath the stage," who, in whatever role he occupies, does so in his "*yellow shoes!*" (137). There is no sympathy here for the poverty of those lowest on the theatrical hierarchy, those jacks and jills who make costumes, build scenery, carry spears, and take the odd two-line role, in support of the main cast and stars. The mirror that Tyler holds up to the company magnifies their flaws nearly to the point of grotesquerie.

Yet it seems Tyler was having great fun in his role as playhouse skewerer. "Love Varses to the Bucheous Daffodel" attempts to recreate the tortured pronunciation of one of the actors, Gilbert Fox, and even provides a glossary to his speech.[21] "Reeling Roscius," sympathetic to the managers Snelling Powell and John Bernard, describes the efforts of a drunken patron to seek a role on stage.[22] And in the other long review poem, "An Epistle to My Muse," Tyler, despite noting the tempest his previous lengthy poem has stirred up and promising to find lines "from Flattery's beds," continues in the same earlier vein but is less explicit in naming actors. Yet if anything, the apparent anonymity of the targets of satire only frees the poet for harsher sentencing, some of it worthy of Churchill's piquant barbs:

> For still she stands, in all her tragick pride,
> Like tearful Niobe, quite petrified:
> Say, what narcotick charm has seiz'd the maid?
> Why, don't you *see? – she waits the prompter's aid*!
> Now – now she bursts the deep impassion'd pause,
> And tortures feeling with her–Hems–and–Ha–s. (153)

These poems are a far cry from Tyler's earlier kid-gloves approach to critical perspective on American productions. The gloves are off and the majority of actors given little quarter.

But it is not only the actors who feel the sting of his satire. As with his British models, so too Tyler pricks the audience for its lack of discrimination. An actress may get "the thundering clap, the gallery's roar,/The cheering whistle, or the loud encore," but without private virtue in the individual thus acclaimed, the applause is so much hot wind (139). On the other hand, many in the audience may not even be cognizant of truly good acting when it occurs before them. To actress Elizabeth Powell, he warns, "What though thy scenick pencil oft portrays/Fine strokes of nature lost to common gaze?" Instead of meeting the public favor, your best efforts may be missed, the cries of approval fewer, "And the house slumbers when it should applaud" (141). The establishment of a theatre of taste requires an audience sensible and virtuous enough to demand and reward it. Whatever virtue Tyler might have expected from the 'PUBLIC' that Colonel Manly addressed in 1787, he seems to think much less would be forthcoming in 1806. In other words, the kind of social control he imagined to be exercised by a coterie of virtuous (and probably Federalist) patrons has given way, during the administration of Jefferson, to an unfortunate democratization of taste. Without surveillance – the kind provided by the satirist – the stage indulges the basest of tastes among the lowest citizens, and thus its role as instructor to the nation diminishes. This is more democracy of the lash than one of glee.

Among Tyler's best occasional poems as poems, the two long satiric reviews raise a number of questions about Tyler's vision of the stage. From the perspective of theatre history, the Boston Theatre Company in 1805–6 had a relatively strong corps. Beset by managerial problems and destructive competition from the Haymarket Theatre in its early years, after 1802 the Federal Street house had efficient and profitable management and featured a number of good and respected players, even though it continued to have its highs and lows. Given his earlier calls in the prologues to *The Contrast* and the Charlestown Academy mounting of *She Stoops to Conquer* for the audience to be gentle on American productions, his satiric jabs at the professionals then in Boston can be taken either as a demand for international standards of excellence – or a sign that theatre, and in particular, professional theatre, no longer satisfied Tyler's changing cultural taste or his concerns over what identities would be rendered by such patently artificial forms of acting as he witnessed in Boston.

The difficulty of discerning Tyler's position can be gleaned from a short poem, "The Mechanick Preferred," which appeared in April 1806. Several women at a tea-table argue about who would make the best husband. Sally prefers a physician, Sophy a lawyer, and Nancy a parson. Another woman, more arch than the rest, gives her preference in a pun:

> I am not so high-minded, says sly little Mary,
> As to raise my ambition to men literary;
> Those wise learned husbands to you I resign,
> But give me, O give me, a COOPER for mine. (*Verse* 133)

Thus "sly" Mary gets away with seeming to be content with a barrel maker when in fact she wants the handsome actor who has just played in Boston, Thomas Cooper.[23] As a poem, "Mechanick" is full of verbal cleverness – "colloquialisms ... feminine rhymes ... risque metaphor"[24] – but as a statement on the theatre, it is ambiguous. Cooper had played in Boston for six weeks in spring of 1805, and, based on the success of that run, was hired on for much of the next season, from October 5, 1805, to February 28, 1806. Cooper's return was trumpeted in the press as the arrival of "The American Roscius," and in *Polyanthos*, the Boston monthly edited by Joseph Buckingham where Tyler's poems were appearing at this time, his acting was praised as "preeminent."[25] In his epigram, however, Tyler compromises Mary's choice by having her be "sly," as if both mocking the adulation and romantic fanfare for actors on the one hand and suggesting that Mary is not all that she seems on the other.

In "Epilogue," Tyler joins the chorus of approval for Cooper, but only in the last four lines, after spending most of the poem enumerating the flaws of the others. Cooper would seem to occupy the role in this poem that Garrick does in those by Lloyd and Churchill:

> But last of all, see COOPER grace the stage –
> COOPER – "the pride, the wonder of our age!"
> Here place the laurel, crown him with thy bays,
> Nor aim to praise him WHO'S BEYOND ALL PRAISE. (*Verse* 141)

Cooper's exceptionality nearly proves the rule. As the leading Shakespearean actor of his time in America, with experience in the London theatres behind him, he brought a no doubt needed professionalism to American acting. But Tyler does offer praise elsewhere, if with an edge to it. The company's leading male singer, John Darley, is identified as "That mighty master of the powers of the song" and is declared to be "unrivall'd in song-singing fame." When he steps outside comic love and singing roles, however, he falls into Tyler's snare:

> 'Tis false ambition thy desire awaits,
> To copy COOPER or to mimick TWAITS;
> Believe me, DARLEY, that I tell you true,
> To sing and love is all that you can do. (*Verse* 138)

William Twaits, the English-born actor whose specialty was low comedy, seems especially to catch Tyler's fancy in "Epilogue." The poet sees his analogue in the actor, who seeks "With squint-eyed satire, a bad age reclaim,/And vice and folly laugh to open shame" (*Verse* 139). Though the Muse (Thalia) might be reluctant to bestow a crown of laurel on "*a zany actor's noodle*," Tyler begs she give Twaits "one little sprig!" (139). The basic thrust of this criticism is to keep all actors in their proper places. Acts of transgression – the comic who stumbles over the line into tragedy or the singer who tries to act – become only lamentable *playing* and destroy any integrity the *play* may have had.[26] There is something quite Puritan in Tyler's attitude; he demands that actors play true to type, as if their identities are not put on or off but somehow real: one is comic or tragic, a star or a secondary figure, with no transgression of role permitted.

In the April 1806 edition of *Polyanthos*, along with works by Tyler, there appeared an account of the life of John Bernard, a noted comic actor and one of the managers of the Federal Street Theatre. The writer in his laudatory remarks about Bernard suggests some of what is driving Tyler, namely, that the American theatre needs improvement in the direction of Bernard's taste and artistry. "It is to be lamented," says the author, that the proper excitation of compassion in tragedy and ridicule of folly for the purpose of correction in comedy have:

not always been kept in view; and the American theatre, in many respects, has been highly censurable. But we hope the time is not very distant, when some of its excrescences will be lopped off, and the stage be respected, as *the imitation of life – the mirror of manners – the representation of truth.*[27]

Thus one of the impulses behind Tyler's satires may be that very correction alluded to, with the ultimate aim of producing a theatre on the model suggested by Bernard's *Polyanthos* biographer. What American theatre needs is a rigorous representation of truth – whatever that may mean – but what it receives is nothing of the sort. Whatever the biographer had in mind by "excrescences," for Tyler they seem to have meant more than a few correctable flaws. One wonders if in fact Tyler was already leaning toward lopping off the whole professional stage altogether.

The key for a successful theatre and the light that will properly illuminate truth is also the key to American identity: virtue. In the sketch of Bernard, for instance, the writer comments that only "Such as have attained this distinction by professional talents, and virtuous private character, are justly entitled to publick respect."[28] The language of virtue appears in Tyler as well. His praise of Ellen Darley and Elizabeth Powell depends upon their reputations as domestically fit for their roles in life more, perhaps, than for their effective stage representations:

> But see, two females every grace impart,
> The fair associates of the scenick art;
> Pride of the stage and pride of private life,
> Whether beheld as actress, mother, wife . . .
> 'Tis private virtue gives their palm of fame. (*Verse* 139)

Although Tyler calls the Muse "prudish" for her reluctance to give honor to the comic Twaits, he himself waxes prudish on the subject of female virtue and the stage. What distinguishes Tyler from his British predecessors in theatrical satire, Lloyd and Churchill, is essentially this insistence that acting must come from someone whose private character gives no lie to represented chastity. Lloyd and Churchill wanted better acting for the sheer glory of the British stage; Tyler wants better acting accompanied by better morals, for the social integrity of the American republic. The upholders of stage morality must be women, he in essence argues, resorting to the old double standard of his era. This is the point where the theatre is most vulnerable, for the representation of women on stage goes beyond mere gender typing to an iconography tied to Tyler's understanding of America's promise as that imaged in female innocence:

> Oh could those "frail impures," who heedless make
> Their pearls the banquet of the swinish rake,
> Once know the pain that men of sense endure
> When virtuous speeches flow from lips impure;
> Or the deep interest which we all possess;
> When real virtue acts the feign'd distress;
> They'd seek the homage to your virtues due,
> Reform their manners and soon copy you. (*Verse* 140)

Women whose private deportment brings criticism do more than damage their reputations as actors; they defile the entire process of "scenick art" and destroy the necessary illusion that what is in the glass of Nature is both appearance and reality. But even to make such statements, Tyler must accept the common prejudice of the time, that actresses were more likely than not to be morally compromised. Thus Powell and Darley are singled out as distinctive for maintaining (publicly) a virtuous private character. The default position for a woman in the theatre, Tyler suggests, is the stain of profligacy.

Without an equivalent belief to Churchill's that his theatre was a worthy successor to that of the ancients, Tyler's tepid endorsement of the stage in his own country is a measure of his distance from the playhouses of urban America. Even so, his increasingly minority position as a critic not just of actors but of the whole theatrical enterprise suggests that within the country as a whole, the playhouse, whatever its popularity, called forth among old-style republicans a deep skepticism of its worth in the United States. Whereas Tyler worked hard in *The Contrast* to justify a kind of drama and theatre that Americans could embrace without compromise to classical republican notions of the virtuous individual as the bedrock of society, in his poetry he grows increasingly skeptical that such persons can be found either on the stage or in the pit. Tyler's later plays – largely religious dramas – seem not to have been written for the professional stage at all but more with an idealized amateur troupe in mind, playing before an audience of the virtuous. Nevertheless, after 1806, Tyler appears to have had little to do with any literal stage.

Tyler's last poem of consequence, "The Chestnut Tree," written in 1824 when he was seriously ill with cancer, lacks the outrageousness of the 1806 attacks, but finishes out a long-time criticism of the theatre. The poem purports to be a prophecy of America in the twentieth century, and as such has some interest for readers today. The tone is somber; change and death are the themes. From under the chestnut tree that begins in the poet's time as a "misshapen seed," the future of the country can be observed: "For underneath thy spreading shade/All casts of characters are seen,/As if some theatre display'd/Life's varied, shifting empty scene" (*Verse* 197). Much of the poem is an attack on industrialization and what Tyler foresees as the creation of vast differences of wealth and poverty. Again, the devoted domestic woman is praised while the future coquette is rebuked for her preference for pleasure: "Can the assemblies' bounding train?/Cards, rout, or ball, or Thespian play?/Or Oratorio's lofty strain?/Such solace to the heart convey?" (211). He does not imagine theatre disappearing in the twentieth century, but he hears it will remain a seductive force that will lure the American fair into the realms of vice.

With this last poem, written at nearly the same time as *The Bay Boy*, Tyler repudiates the public, commercial stage entirely. Republican virtue, his poems argue, if acted out, can only be maintained in the private theatrical of the domestic sphere, safe from the entrapping gaze of the sexual marketplace that he saw as the American theatre. Thus the irony of the professionally produced *The Contrast* is that it gave Tyler a platform – a stage – from which to catch the attention of the public that he might, in later years, lecture them in poems on the seductions and dangers of a commercial theatre. By 1824 or 1825, however, such a message could not be heard for all the wild applause being showered on American theatres for just about any drama, including the racist vehicles for the stage Yankee descendants of Tyler's Jonathan, that could be fit upon the boards. In 1787, Tyler imagined that the theatre could be shaped by American themes to serve the ends of civic virtue in the fostering of republican identity. In 1825, the dying poet understood that the power of playhouse traditions to overwhelm such themes was too great for the stage to serve as a school-house for such an identity. He had over time become Jonathan's minister in condemning the stage as the devil's drawing room, where British vice would corrupt American manners. And as he affirmed amusingly, if ironically, in *The Contrast*, so he now recognized bitterly: the devil had won.

Like Charles Brockden Brown and other critics of the American stage, Tyler could not stop the proliferation of theatre in America. Citizens of relatively small cities like Norfolk showed themselves ready to embrace actors and plays that had been imported from their recent wartime enemy, even if they sometimes demanded a change or two in a line or role to meet local politics and taste. As people moved west, and new cities embraced the stage, even citizens in the remotest corners of the republic might expect at least a few strolling players to appear with some truncated version of *Richard III* or a vernacular or dialect comedy. Tyler had fought a rear-guard action to prevent the spread of commercial theatre and its encouragement of the "meretricious leer" – and by 1825, the year before his death, he had lost.

Yet the poems of Tyler, like the newspapers of Norfolk or novels by Brown and Foster, remind us that the theatre was a presence in the new United States, a part of its texture, a spot on the landscape, a refuge, an eyesore – a physical place that became part of the cultural consciousness of numerous individuals and groups. African Americans might have found that whites liked to "imitate" them, but in a way that distorted their language, their bodies, and their true experience, even as the stage reflected back to the audience, white and black, an understanding that comic abuse and violence in the theatre still revealed the agony of broken bodies and spirits outside the entrance door. Almost anyone with an ethnic or national identity, a sense of being majority or minority, in control or not, male or female, even a little queer, could go to an American theatre and find in its distorted mirror some dimension of American attitudes toward her or him represented, even if the drama were set in London and the characters all British types one had seen before.

Despite efforts by playwrights like John Murdock, Judith Sargent Murray, James Nelson Barker, and others to set plays in the United States and dwell on themes of citizenship and national character, most spectators saw something else, on the surface at least – a procrustean bed of plots and characters imported and recycled in which one strained to hear a syllable spoken on things American. Perhaps, as Brown suggests, the stage has nothing to do with nationality anyway, that its very presence in the United States dissolves nationality into a supranational cesspool of uncertainty, social disguise, and individual conniving that leaves one without any faith that a man on the street is any more recognizable as himself than a man on the stage in an obvious costume. But managers were conscious of the national question, and even though they stubbornly insisted on playing Reynolds over Tyler or Cumberland instead of Murray, they nevertheless found themselves still tweaking British farces into performances of American identities. *The Contrast*, often the only play in modern anthologies from before 1825 (or 1845), tells us a lot about the new republic and the position of playwright, but American theatre is so much more than that. It is Shakespeare, sure, as scholars have noted, but it is more often *The Mogul Tale*, *The Poor Soldier*, *The Dramatist*, *Thomas and Sally*, and *The Purse* than anything scribed by the Bard or Susanna Rowson. Brown and Tyler knew in deeper, darker ways than the Norfolk critics that theatre appealed to sensibilities other than those of self-conscious, virtuous citizenship, and they were afraid of it; but like the Norfolk critics, they could not ignore it. American muses may have been confused by who or what they were supposed to be, how much British, how much the Others of the British stage, how much themselves; but it is almost impossible to talk about identity in the new republic without slipping in the door of one of those long extinct playhouses for a look at the lookers and their stages.

Notes

Introduction

1. Information, if not point of view, in this paragraph from standard drama and theatre histories, notably Arthur Hobson Quinn, *A History of the American Drama from the Beginning to the Civil War* (New York: Appleton-Century-Crofts, 1943); Hugh F. Rankin, *The Theater in Colonial America* (Chapel Hill: University of North Carolina Press, 1965); Walter J. Meserve, *An Emerging Entertainment: the Drama of the American People to 1828* (Bloomington: University of Indiana Press, 1977). More extensive notes and references to other histories and critical studies will be found in subsequent chapters. Fortunately, some recent studies have focused more serious attention on the early dramatic and theatrical history of the United States, including Jared Brown, *The Theatre in America During the Revolution* (Cambridge: Cambridge University Press, 1995); Don B. Wilmeth and Christopher Bigsby, eds., *The Cambridge History of American Theatre*, 3 vols. (Cambridge: Cambridge University Press, 1998–2000), vol. I: *Beginnings to 1870*; S. E. Wilmer, *Theatre, Society, and Nation: Staging American Identities* (Cambridge: Cambridge University Press, 2002); and Heather S. Nathans, *Early American Theatre from the Revolution to Thomas Jefferson: Into the Hands of the People* (Cambridge: Cambridge University Press, 2003).
2. On the scarcity of production of American plays in the early republic, see Nathans, *Early American Theatre*, pp. 85–88.
3. William Ioor, *Independence; or Which Do You Like Best, The Peer, or the Farmer?* (Charleston: Bounetheau, 1805). The novel on which it is based is Andrew McDonald, *The Independent*, 2 vols. (London: Cadell, 1784). Essential information on Ioor and this play can be found in Charles S. Watson, 'Jeffersonian Republicanism in William Ioor's *Independence*, the First Play of South Carolina,' *South Carolina Historical Magazine* 69 (1968), 194–203, and Watson, *The History of Southern Drama* (Lexington: University Press of Kentucky, 1997), pp. 32–37. The first review of the play in the April 1, 1805 Charleston *Courier*, by S. C. Carpenter, identified the author by name. Ioor's other play, also acted in Charleston, is *The Battle of the Eutaw Springs* (Charleston: Hoff, 1807). Nathans, *Early American Theatre*, pp. 87–88.
4. For a discussion of *Slaves in Algiers* as one of several literary works dealing with the captivity of Americans in North Africa, see Paul Baepler, Introduction, in Baepler,

ed., *White Slaves, African Masters: An Anthology of American Barbary Captivity Narratives* (Chicago: University of Chicago Press, 1999), pp. 1–58.
5. Benedict Anderson, *Imagined Communities: Reflections on the Origin and Spread of Nationalism*, rev. edn. (London: Verso, 1991); David Waldstreicher, *In the Midst of Perpetual Fetes: The Making of American Nationalism, 1776–1820* (Chapel Hill: University of North Carolina Press, 1997).
6. On the constitution of ethnicity, see Paul R. Brass, *Ethnicity and Nationalism: Theory and Comparison* (New Delhi: Sage, 1991), pp. 19–20; Waldstreicher, *In the Midst of Perpetual Fetes*, p. 78.
7. Jean-Christophe Agnew, *Worlds Apart: The Market and Theater in Anglo-American Thought, 1550–1750* (Cambridge: Cambridge University Press, 1986); Jeffrey H. Richards, *Theater Enough: American Culture and the Metaphor of the World Stage, 1607–1789* (Durham, N.C.: Duke University Press, 1991).
8. John Howe, *Language and Political Meaning in Revolutionary America* (Amherst: University of Massachusetts Press, 2004), p. 124.
9. The Cherokee visit to John Street took place on December 14; George C. D. Odell, *Annals of the New York Stage*, 15 vols. (New York: Columbia University Press, 1927–1949), vol. I, pp. 118–19.
10. Tucker's plays, all in manuscript, rest in the Special Collections department of the Swem Library, College of William and Mary, Williamsburg, Virginia. His War of 1812 plays are "The Times; or The patriot rous'd," completed in December 1811, and "The Patriot cool'd," completed in 1815. On his attempts to interest theatre managers, see letters from Tucker to William Wirt on Aug. 21, 1812, April 4, 1813, and Aug. 7, 1813, William Wirt Papers, Maryland Historical Society, copies in Special Collections, Swem Library, College of William and Mary. Ginger Strand, "The Many Deaths of General Montgomery: Audiences and Pamphlet Plays of the Revolution," *American Literary History* 9 (1997), 1–20.
11. Warren's plays include *The Adulateur* (1772), *The Defeat* (1773), *The Group* (1775), and the two historical verse dramas, *The Ladies of Castile* and *The Sack of Rome*, both published in her *Poems, Dramatic and Miscellaneous* (Boston: Thomas and Andrews, 1790). All of the plays can be accessed in Mercy Otis Warren, *The Plays and Poems*, ed. Benjamin Franklin V (Delmar, N.Y.: Scholars Facsimiles, 1980). Information on publishing history, the attempt to have her plays performed, and relationship of playwriting to her overall career is found in Jeffrey H. Richards, *Mercy Otis Warren* (New York: Twayne, 1995), pp. 84–120. A number of scholars have attempted to argue that *The Blockheads*, *The Motley Assembly*, and *Sans Souci* are by Warren, but as I tried to make clear – and should have made clearer – there is nothing to support her authorship of any play beyond the five for which there is significant documentary evidence.

1 American identities and the transatlantic stage

1. Mary Rowlandson, *The Soveraignty & Goodness of God ... Being a Narrative of the Captivity and Restauration of Mrs. Mary Rowlandson*, 2nd edn (Cambridge, Mass.: Green, 1682), and reprinted in numerous anthologies, including Alden T. Vaughan and Edward W. Clark, eds., *Puritans among the Indians: Accounts of Captivity and*

Redemption, 1676–1724 (Cambridge, Mass.: Belknap/Harvard University Press, 1981), pp. 29–75.
2. There is now a substantial secondary literature on Rowlandson, too vast to recapitulate here. Some of the identity complications of her text are probed by Mitchell Robert Breitwieser, *American Puritanism and the Defense of Mourning: Religion, Grief, and Ethnology in Mary White Rowlandson's Captivity Narrative* (Madison: University of Wisconsin Press, 1990); Michelle Burnham, "The Journey Between: Liminality and Dialogism in Mary White Rowlandson's Captivity Narrative," *Early American Literature* 28 (1993), 60–75; Lisa Logan, "Mary Rowlandson's Captivity and the 'Place' of the Woman Subject," *Early American Literature* 28 (1993), 255–77; June Namias, *White Captives: Gender and Ethnicity on the American Frontier* (Chapel Hill: University of North Carolina Press, 1993), pp. 21–48; and Tiffany Potter, "Writing Indigenous Femininity: Mary Rowlandson's Captivity Narrative," *Eighteenth-Century Studies* 36 (2003), 153–67.
3. Michael Wigglesworth, *The Day of Doom*, in Harrison T. Meserole, ed., *Seventeenth-Century American Poetry* (New York: Anchor, 1968), pp. 55–113; Edward Taylor, *God's Determinations*, in *The Poems of Edward Taylor*, ed. Donald E. Stanford (New Haven: Yale University Press, 1960), pp. 387–459.
4. Some of the early political plays include Robert Hunter, *Androboros* (New York: Bradford, 1714); an untitled work in the Massachusetts Historical Society from 1732 on "the debate over gubernatorial salaries," entitled by its editor, Robert E. Moody, as "Boston's First Play," and printed in the Society's *Proceedings* 92 (1980), 117–39; *The Paxton Boys* (Philadelphia: Armbruster, 1764); and *A Dialogue Containing Some Reflections* (Philadelphia: Steuart, 1764). For a discussion of the first and last two, see Wilmer, *Theatre, Society and Nation*, pp. 20–24.
5. Peter A. Davis, "Puritan Mercantilism and Anti-Theatrical Legislation," in Ron Engle and Tice L. Miller, eds., *The American Stage: Social and Economic Issues from the Colonial Period to the Present* (Cambridge: Cambridge University Press, 1993), pp. 18–29.
6. John Smith, *The Complete Works of Captain John Smith*, ed. Philip L. Barbour, 3 vols. (Chapel Hill: University of North Carolina Press, 1986), vol. 1, pp. 235–36; Odai Johnson and William J. Burling, eds., *The Colonial American Stage, 1665–1774: A Documentary Calendar* (Madison, N.J.: Fairleigh Dickinson University Press, 2001), pp. 92–94, 96–97, 99–132. Byrd's knowledge of, writing for, and participation in theatrical activities is explored in Carl R. Dolmetsch, "William Byrd II: Comic Dramatist," *Early American Literature* 6 (1971), 18–30.
7. Richards, *Theater Enough*, pp. 61–84.
8. Eve Kornfeld, "Women in Post-Revolutionary American Culture: Susanna Haswell Rowson's American Career, 1793–1824," *Journal of American Culture* 6/4 (1983), 56–62.
9. Information on Green's appearances from Thomas Clark Pollock, *The Philadelphia Theatre in the Eighteenth Century* (1933; rpt. New York: Greenwood, 1968). Green's popularity was graded by 'Philo-Theatricus,' *Gazette of the United States*, Dec. 16, 1796, and cited by Pollock, *Philadelphia Theatre*, pp. 60–61. The top-rated performer was Mrs. Merry with 15; the bottom-rated ones were Mrs. L'Estrange and Susanna Rowson, with 3 each. It should be noted, however, that Green did not simply disappear, as so many lesser actors in the United States seemed to. For his later career, see Chapter 12.

10. *The Downfall of Justice and the Farmer Just Return'd from Meeting on Thanksgiving Day. A comedy lately acted in Connecticut*, "2nd ed." (Danvers, [Mass.], 1777), hereafter *DJ*.
11. Jack's sympathetic position is noticed by Meserve, *Emerging Entertainment*, pp. 84–85.
12. Mercy Otis Warren, *The Adulateur* (1772) and *The Group* (1775), in Warren, *Plays and Poems*; Edmund M. Hayes, ed., "Mercy Otis Warren: *The Defeat* [1773]," *New England Quarterly* 49 (1976), 440–58; John Leacock, *The Fall of British Tyranny; or American Liberty Triumphant* (Philadelphia: Styner and Cist, 1776); *The Battle of Brooklyn. A Farce of Two Acts* (New York: Rivington, 1776); Jonathan Sewall, *A Cure for the Spleen, or Amusement for a Winter's Evening* (Boston: n.p., 1775). For a recent discussion on this literature, from the perspective of an American "refashioning" of identity from loyal Brit to independent Yank, see Wilmer, *Theatre, Society and the Nation*, pp. 34–52.
13. Isaac Bickerstaff, *The Padlock: A Comic Opera* (London: W. Griffin, 1768). The story by Cervantes is "The Jealous Husband." *The Padlock* appeared in New York as early as 1769.
14. Shane White, *Somewhat More Independent: The End of Slavery in New York City, 1770–1810* (Athens: University of Georgia Press, 1991); Waldstreicher, *In the Midst of Perpetual Fetes*, pp. 294–352.
15. Originally published in 1790, Royall Tyler's *The Contrast* is available in a number of modern editions; citations here from Tyler, *The Contrast*, in Jeffrey H. Richards, ed., *Early American Drama* (New York: Penguin, 1997), pp. 6–57; hereafter *TC*.
16. Among the many studies of Tyler's comedy that raise the question of identity, see especially Roger B. Stein, "Royall Tyler and the Question of Our Speech," *New England Quarterly* 38 (1965), 454–74; G. Thomas Tanselle, *Royall Tyler* (Cambridge, Mass.: Harvard University Press, 1967), pp. 49–81; Daniel F. Havens, *The Columbian Muse of Comedy: The Development of a Native Tradition in Early American Social Comedy, 1787–1845* (Carbondale: Southern Illinois University Press, 1973), pp. 8–51; Donald T. Siebert, Jr., "Royall Tyler's 'Bold Example': *The Contrast* and the English Comedy of Manners," *Early American Literature* 13 (1978), 3–11; Lucy Rinehart, "A Nation's 'Noble Spectacle': Royall Tyler's *The Contrast* as Metatheatrical Commentary," *American Drama* 3/2 (1994), 29–52; John Evelev, "*The Contrast*: The Problem of Theatricality and Political and Social Crisis in Postrevolutionary America," *Early American Literature* 31 (1996), 74–97; Jennifer Jordan Baker, "A Speculative Language: Finance and Literary Imagination in Early America," Ph.D. dissertation, University of Pennsylvania (2000), pp. 137–71.
17. See the Epilogue to *Fashion*, in Richards, ed., *Early American Drama*, pp. 366–67.
18. Henry David Thoreau, *Walden and Civil Disobedience*, ed. Owen Thomas (New York: Norton, 1966), p. 140.
19. Anna Cora Mowatt, *Autobiography of an Actress; or, Eight Years on the Stage* (Boston: Ticknor, Reed, and Fields, 1854); cited in Eric Wollencott Barnes, *The Lady of Fashion: The Life and Theatre of Anna Cora Mowatt* (New York: Scribner's, 1954), pp. 15–17.
20. Moncure Daniel Conway, *The Theater: A Discourse* (Cincinnati: Truman & Spofford, 1857); Conway, *Autobiography: Memories and Experiences*, 2 vols. (Boston: Houghton Mifflin, 1904), vol. I, pp. 257–59.

21. Saint John Chrysostom, *Commentary on Saint John the Apostle and Evangelist*, trans. Sister Thomas Aquinas Goggin, vol. I, *Homilies 1–47* (Washington: Catholic University of America Press, 1957), esp. homilies 1, 2, 3, 42.
22. William Henry Smith, *The Drunkard; or the Fallen Saved*, in Richards, ed., *Early American Drama*, pp. 252–303.
23. John Beete, *The Man of the Times; or, A Scarcity of Cash* (Charleston, S.C.: Young, [1797]). Parenthetical references, *Man*, are to this edition. Beete was an actor with the Charleston company.
24. Montrose Moses, ed., *Representative Plays by American Dramatists from 1763 to the Present Day*, 3 vols. (New York: Dutton, 1925), vol. II, pp. 606, 610.
25. Elihu Hubbard Smith, *The Diary of Elihu Hubbard Smith (1771–1798)*, ed. James E. Cronin (Philadelphia: American Philosophical Society, 1973).
26. Mrs. [Sarah] Marriott, *The Chimera; or, Effusions of Fancy* (New York: Swords, 1795), p. 3.
27. Passage quoted in Odell, *Annals*, vol. I, p. 380.
28. Sarah Marriott's acting in Norfolk and death date in Lucy Blandford Pilkinton, "Theatre in Norfolk, Virginia, 1788–1812," Ph.D. dissertation, University of Michigan (1993), pp. 511–12.
29. Washington Irving, writing as Jonathan Oldstyle, complains about this mixture of costume features in a letter to the New York *Morning Chronicle*, Dec. 11, 1802, reprinted in Irving, *History, Tales, and Sketches* (New York: Library of America, 1983), pp. 20–21.

2   Revolution and unnatural identity in Crèvecoeur's 'Landscapes'

1. Hugh Henry Brackenridge, *The Death of General Montgomery* (Norwich, Conn.: Trumbull, 1777), and Brackenridge, *The Battle of Bunkers-Hill* (Philadelphia: Bell, 1776).
2. Originally published under his adopted American name, J. Hector St. John, *Letters from an American Farmer* (London: Davies, 1782; 2nd edn, 1783). Most modern editions are based on the 1783 edition, which includes largely nonsubstantive corrections whose authority is difficult to identify. Editions in French, published as *Lettres d'un Cultivateur Américain* (Paris: Cuchet, 1784; 1787), include material not in the 1783 English edition, but in some cases the French essays differ from the equivalent pieces in the long unpublished manuscripts in English.
3. 'Landscapes' first appeared in J. Hector St. John de Crèvecoeur, *Sketches of an Eighteenth Century American: More Letters from an American Farmer*, ed. Henri Bourdin, Ralph Gabriel, and Stanley Williams (New Haven: Yale University Press, 1925). J. Hector St. John de Crèvecoeur, *Letters from an American Farmer and Sketches of Eighteenth-Century America*, ed. Albert E. Stone (New York: Penguin, 1981), reprints the 1925 version (pp. 424–89) and for the purposes of readability is the source of all quotations from Crèvecoeur cited parenthetically, hereafter L. Dennis Moore, ed., *More Letters from the American Farmer: An Edition of the Essays in English Left Unpublished by Crèvecoeur* (Athens: University of Georgia Press, 1995), pp. 230–93, reproduces the literal text of the manuscript (as 'Landskapes') in modern typography. Moore includes a more complete version of

Crèvecoeur's introduction to the play and prints a few other prose pieces (separate from "Landskapes") not found in the 1925 or 1981 versions. All passages from Stone have been checked against the text established by Moore, and significant differences are so noted.

4. One of the first critics to take the *Sketches* seriously was John Brooks Moore in "The Rehabilitation of Crèvecoeur," *Sewanee Review* 35 (1927), 216–30, but few others have followed up. See, however, Everett Emerson, "Hector St. John de Crèvecoeur and the Promise of America," in Winfried Fluck, Jürgen Peper, and Willi Paul Adams, eds., *Forms and Functions of History in American Literature: Essays in Honor of Ursula Brumm* (Berlin: Schmidt, 1981), pp. 44–55; John Hales, "The Landscape of Tragedy: Crèvecoeur's 'Susquehanna,'" *Early American Literature* 20 (1985), 39–63; and David M. Robinson, "Community and Utopia in Crèvecoeur's *Sketches,*" *American Literature* 62 (1990), 17–31. "Landscapes" is discussed in the context of other works by Crèvecoeur in Thomas Philbrick, *St. John de Crèvecoeur* (New York: Twayne, 1970), pp. 126–27; Manfred Putz, "Dramatic Elements and the Problem of Literary Mediation in the Works of Hector St. John de Crèvecoeur," *REAL: The Yearbook of Research in English and American Literature* 3 (1985), 111–30; Norman S. Grabo, "Crèvecoeur's American: Beginning the World Anew," *William and Mary Quarterly* 48 (1991), 164–65; and Dennis Moore, introduction, *More Letters from the American Farmer*, pp. xviii, xxi, xxii, xxiv, xxv, xxvii, xxxvii, xxxviii, xl, xlii–xlvii. There is almost nothing on "Landscapes" in studies of American drama.

5. The use of familial language in the works of other writers has been documented by Edwin G. Burrows and Michael Wallace, "The American Revolution: The Ideology and Psychology of National Liberation," *Perspectives in American History* 6 (1972), 167–306; and Jay Fliegelman, *Prodigals and Pilgrims: The American Revolution against Patriarchal Authority, 1750–1800* (Cambridge: Cambridge University Press, 1982). For Crèvecoeur, the literal family's fortunes become symbolic of the national fate.

6. David J. Carlson, "Farmer versus Lawyer: Crèvecoeur's *Letters* and the Liberal Subject," *Early American Literature* 38 (2003), 259.

7. Philbrick, *St. John de Crèvecoeur*, p. 119, thinks the voice of "Landscapes" is "inappropriate" for Farmer James. Dennis Moore, ed., *More Letters*, p. xli, implicitly distinguishes the "narrator" of "Landskapes" from Farmer James. Compare, however, Grantland Rice, "Crèvecoeur and the Politics of Authorship in Republican America," *Early American Literature* 28 (1993), 91–119.

8. As Moore's edition of the manuscript shows, Crèvecoeur inconsistently labels each part as either a "landskape" or a "scene." Stone's edition, following the 1925 transcription, labels each part a "landscape."

9. For an intriguing discussion of the act of writing letters and the consequent tensions between public and private, see Elizabeth Heckendorn Cook, *Epistolary Bodies: Gender and Genre in the Eighteenth-Century Republic of Letters* (Stanford: Stanford University Press, 1996), pp. 140–72.

10. The tendency in earlier Crèvecoeur criticism has been to see him as a hopeful, if not utopian, writer on America. See, for example, Russel B. Nye, "Aristocrat in the Forest," in *American Literary History 1607–1830* (New York: Knopf, 1970), pp. 154–59; James C. Mohr, "Calculated Disillusionment: Crèvecoeur's *Letters* Reconsidered," *South Atlantic Quarterly* 69 (1970), 354–63; Emerson, "Hector St. John de

Crèvecoeur"; Grabo, "Crèvecoeur's American"; and Joseph Fichtelberg, "Utopic Distresses: Crèvecoeur's *Letters* and Revolution," *Studies in the Literary Imagination* 27 (1994), 85–101. The problem of anthologizing Crèvecoeur is succinctly analyzed by Cathy Davidson, *Revolution and the Word: The Rise of the Novel in America* (New York: Oxford University Press, 1986), 257; see also Carlson, "Farmer versus Lawyer."

11. Biographical information on Crèvecoeur drawn from Albert Stone's Introduction, Crèvecoeur, *Letters*, ed. Stone, 7–25; Gay Wilson Allen and Roger Asselineau, *St. John de Crèvecoeur: The Life of an American Farmer* (New York: Viking, 1987); and Everett Emerson and Katherine Emerson, "Crèvecoeur, J. Hector St. John de," *American National Biography*, vol. v, pp. 729–32.

12. Stephen Carl Arch makes use of the quoted passage to indicate the wholeness of *Letters* in "The 'Progressive Steps' of the Narrator in Crèvecoeur's *Letters from an American Farmer*," *Studies in American Fiction* 18 (1990), 145–58. By reading 'Landscapes' and other pieces that were not included in *Letters*, however, one can see that the attempts to find unity in *Letters* do not fully account for Crèvecoeur's thoughts on Revolutionary America.

13. Mary E. Rucker, "Crèvecoeur's *Letters* and Enlightenment Doctrine," *Early American Literature* 13 (1978), 203.

14. Sung Bok Kim, "Impact of Class Relations and Warfare in the American Revolution: The New York Experience," *Journal of American History* 69 (1982), 326–46.

15. Owen S. Ireland, "The Crux of Politics: Religion and Party in Pennsylvania, 1778–1789," *William and Mary Quarterly* 42 (1985), 471; see also Ireland, "The Ethnic-Religious Dimension of Pennsylvania Politics, 1778–1779," *William and Mary Quarterly* 30 (1973), 423–48.

16. Allen and Asselineau, *St. John de Crèvecoeur*, pp. 21–22, 35. In addition to his knowledge of French and other European painting, Crèvecoeur may also have seen engravings of works by the American Benjamin West, who had set up in London. See Dorinda Evans, *Benjamin West and His American Students* (Washington, D.C.: Smithsonian Institution Press, 1980), and James Thomas Flexner, *American Painting: First Flowers of Our Wilderness* (Cambridge, Mass.: Harvard University Press, 1947), pp. 194–243. The painted landscape of Pine Hill is reproduced in the frontispiece of Howard Rice, *Le Cultivateur Américain: Etude sur l'oeuvre de Saint John de Crèvecoeur* (Paris: Champion, 1933).

17. The relation between painting and theatre for these works is discussed fully in Michael Fried, *Absorption and Theatricality: Painting and Beholder in the Age of Diderot* (Berkeley: University of California Press, 1980).

18. Crèvecoeur anticipates Washington Irving's *The Sketch-Book of Geoffrey Crayon, Esq.* (1819) in this preference for the humble over the grand. In explaining his depiction of "nooks, and corners, and by-places" rather than "the great objects studied by every regular traveler," Irving's narrator tells us that "His sketch-book was accordingly crowded with cottages, and landscapes, and obscure ruins; but he had neglected to paint St. Peter's, or the Coliseum; the cascade of Terni, or the bay of Naples; and had not a single glacier or volcano in his whole collection." Irving, *Sketch-Book*, ed. Susan Manning (New York: Oxford University Press, 1996), p. 13.

19. Fried, *Absorption*, pp. 7–70; Peter Brooks, *The Melodramatic Imagination: Balzac, Henry James, Melodrama and the Mode of Excess* (1976; New Haven: Yale University Press, 1995), pp. 82–93.
20. Moore, ed., *More Letters*, p. xlv. On the matter of Farmer James's wife in view of other comments by Crèvecoeur, literal and metaphorical, on women, see Anna Carew-Miller, "The Language of Domesticity in Crèvecoeur's *Letters from an American Farmer*," *Early American Literature* 28 (1993), 242–54. D. H. Lawrence typified James's wife as the "Amiable Spouse" in his *Studies in Classic American Literature* (1923; New York: Viking, 1964), p. 24.
21. Murray, "On the Domestic Education of Children" (1790), in Paul Lauter *et al.*, eds., *Heath Anthology of American Literature*, 2 vols. (Lexington, Mass.: Heath, 1990), vol. I, p. 1030. A number of works have looked at the iconographic representation of females in the Revolutionary era, among them Linda K. Kerber, *Women of the Republic: Intellect and Ideology in Revolutionary America* (Chapel Hill: University of North Carolina Press, 1980), and Lester Olson, *Emblems of American Community in the Revolutionary Era: A Study in Rhetorical Iconology* (Washington, D.C.: Smithsonian Institution Press, 1991), and for the use of the abused, mutilated, violated, and fetishized body in late eighteenth-century images, Shirley Samuels in *Romances of the Republic: Women, the Family, and Violence in the Literature of the Early American Nation* (New York: Oxford University Press, 1996), pp. 3–22.
22. A. W. Plumstead, "Hector St. John de Crèvecoeur," in Everett Emerson, ed., *American Literature, 1764–1789: The Revolutionary Years* (Madison: University of Wisconsin Press, 1977), p. 223.
23. On McCrea, see Namias, *White Captives*, pp. 117–44.
24. Two earlier contenders for the honor of first do not hold up under scrutiny. Both Thomas Forrest, *The Disappointment* (1767), and Robert Munford, *The Candidates* (1770 or 1771), have characters who are referred to in the literature as black but in fact are likely not. See David Mays, Introduction, in Forrest, *The Disappointment; or, The Force of Credulity*, ed. Mays (Gainesville: University Press of Florida, 1976), and Rodney M. Baine, *Robert Munford: America's First Comic Dramatist* (Athens: University of Georgia Press, 1967), pp. 64–65. A better candidate for first is Leacock's *The Fall of British Tyranny* (1776).
25. Doreen Alvarez Saar, "The Heritage of American Ethnicity in Crèvecoeur's *Letters from an American Farmer*," in Frank Shuffelton, ed., *A Mixed Race: Ethnicity in Early America* (New York: Oxford University Press, 1993), p. 245.
26. Crèvecoeur clearly intends much to pivot on slavery and its place amidst the felicity he describes earlier. For an argument on the primacy of another unpublished letter, "Sketches of Jamaica and Bermudas and Other Subjects," first penned in 1773, in asserting that "the very notion of stable and discrete cultural identities is untenable in an interconnected and volatile Atlantic" – one that includes West Indian plantation slavery – see Christopher Iannini, "'The Itinerant Man': Crèvecoeur's Caribbean, Raynal's Revolution, and Fate of Atlantic Cosmopolitanism," *William and Mary Quarterly* 61 (2004), 210–34.
27. This use of the slave issue to attack patriot interests can be seen in another episode from 1776. In Westmoreland County, Virginia, a resident, Henry Glass, was complained against to the local committee of safety for maintaining that slaves owned by patriots

were 'ill used,' an act that led to Glass's 'Censure.' See Richard Barksdale Harwell, ed., *The Committees of Safety of Westmoreland and Fincastle: Proceedings from the County Committees, 1774–1776* (Richmond: Virginia State Library, 1956), pp. 52–53.

28. The precise status of blacks in the play, as servants or slaves, is not entirely clear. However, in *Letters*, blacks routinely appear as slaves unless Crèvecoeur is trying to make a point, as in the account of John Bartram's farm. Without evidence to the contrary, and given Eltha's threat to sell Nero, I assume that Tom and Nero are slaves.
29. See, however, Cook, *Epistolary Bodies*, pp. 164–67, and Iannini, "'Itinerant Man,'" 230, who argue for a measure of black agency in Crèvecoeur's depictions of Africans.
30. That is, William Alexander (1726–1783), an American Revolutionary officer, sometimes referred to as Lord Stirling.
31. Words in brackets indicate the actual words, if not spelling, of Crèvecoeur's original, replacing incorrect transcription from 1925 text. Moore, ed., *More Letters*, p. 236.
32. Crèvecoeur's narrator also inveighs against the disruptive, and finally anti-domestic ardor of true believers in 'Liberty of Worship,' one of the essays omitted in 1782. *L* 321–36.
33. Douglas Jerrold, *Black-Ey'd Susan; or, 'All in the Downs.' A Nautical and Domestic Drama*, in George Rowell, ed., *Nineteenth-Century Plays* (London: Oxford University Press, 1953), pp. 1–43; George Aiken, *Uncle Tom's Cabin; or, Life Among the Lowly, a Domestic Drama* (1853), in Richards, ed., *Early American Drama*, pp. 373–443; Augustin Daly, *Under the Gaslight; or, Life and Love in These Times* (1867), in Daniel C. Gerould, ed., *American Melodrama* (New York: Performing Arts Journal Publications, 1983), pp. 135–81.
34. Because he only refers to violence in speeches, never showing it on stage, I do not think Crèvecoeur really intended to write the rape into the play itself. But see the note to this passage in Moore, ed., *More Letters*, p. 375.
35. For other slight variants from the Penguin edition, compare Moore, ed., *More Letters*, p. 293.

3 British author, American text

1. There were, of course, a number of amateur productions of British plays before the Revolution; one of the most popular was *Cato*, especially among college students, that play having been acted in British America as early as 1732. The standard work on colonial performance of Addison's play is Fredric M. Litto, 'Addison's *Cato* in the Colonies,' *William and Mary Quarterly* 23 (1966), 431–49. For a more in-depth look at collegiate productions, with special attention to Nathan Hale and Yale, see Jason Shaffer, "Great Cato's Descendants': A Genealogy of Colonial Performance," *Theatre Survey* 44/1 (2003), 5–28.
2. Randall Fuller, 'Theaters of the American Revolution: The Valley Forge *Cato* and the *Meschianza* in Their Transcultural Contexts,' *Early American Literature* 34 (1999), 126–46.
3. Richards, *Theater Enough*, pp. 265–72.
4. Odell, *Annals*, vol. 1, p. 239.
5. Tyler, *The Contrast*, p. 35, hereafter *TC*.

6. Frederick M. Link, *John O'Keeffe: A Bibliography* (Lincoln: University of Nebraska Press, 1983), p. 88.
7. Oscar G. Sonneck, *Early Opera in America* (1943; New York: Blom, 1963), p. 74; Pollock, *Philadelphia Theatre*, pp. 137–39. On the appearance of puppets in early American theatres, see Julian Mates, *The American Musical Stage before 1800* (New Brunswick, N.J.: Rutgers University Press, 1962), p. 35.
8. Odell, *Annals*, vol. I, pp. 246ff.
9. Quoted in "Trivia," *William and Mary Quarterly* 5 (1948), 396.
10. Susan Porter, *With an Air Debonair: Musical Theater in America, 1785–1815* (Washington, D.C.: Smithsonian Institution Press, 1991), p. 413. Not all locations were hooked on *The Poor Soldier*. In Norfolk, O'Keeffe's musical played only three times in the three seasons of professional theatre during the period 1797–1800. Even so, two of those occurred in the 1800 season, suggesting that it was still something that audiences expected to see, if not as often as before. *Norfolk Herald* June 6, 1798; Feb. 13, 1800; March 29, 1800.
11. William Brasmer and William Osborne, Preface, in Brasmer and Osborne, eds., *The Poor Soldier (1783)* by John O'Keeffe and William Shield (Madison: A-R Editions, 1978), p. viii.
12. Joseph Roach, *Cities of the Dead: Circum-Atlantic Performance* (New York: Columbia University Press, 1996).
13. Porter, *With an Air Debonair*, p. 192.
14. June C. Ottenberg, "Popularity of Two Operas in Philadelphia in the 1790s," *International Review of the Aesthetics and Sociology of Music* 18 (1987), 205–10.
15. Frederick M. Link, "John O'Keeffe," *Dictionary of Literary Biography*, vol. LXXXIX, p. 287.
16. The second most popular new afterpiece on the late eighteenth-century American stage was O'Keeffe's *The Highland Reel*, with 175 performances between 1786 and 1815. Porter, *With an Air Debonair*, p. 413.
17. John O'Keeffe, *Recollections of the Life of John O'Keeffe*, 2 vols. (1826; New York: Blom, 1969), vol II, p. 73; O'Keeffe, *The Poor Soldier* (Dublin: n.p., 1786); O'Keeffe, *The Poor Soldier* (Philadelphia: Seddon and Spotswood, 1787), p. 3. Quotations from the Philadelphia edition, hereafter *PS*. In Air XII (as designated in the Philadelphia printing), Carton is named.
18. Karen J. Harvey and Kevin B. Pry, "John O'Keeffe as an Irish Playwright within the Theatrical, Social and Economic Context of His Time," *Eire-Ireland* 22 (1987), 19–43; Heinz Kosok, "'George my belov'd King, and Ireland my honour'd country': John O'Keeffe and Ireland," *Irish University Review* 22 (1992), 40–54.
19. O'Keeffe, *Recollections*, vol. II, pp. 59–60.
20. O'Keeffe, *Recollections*, vol. I, p. 295; Brasmer and Osborne, eds., *The Poor Soldier*, p. 60; O'Keeffe, *Poor Soldier* (Dublin), p. 16.
21. George F. Scheer and Hugh F. Rankin, *Rebels and Redcoats* (New York: World, 1957), pp. 435–38; Robert Middlekauff, *The Glorious Cause: The American Revolution, 1763–1789* (New York: Oxford University Press, 1982), pp. 476–77; Lawrence E. Babits, *A Devil of a Whipping: The Battle of Cowpens* (Chapel Hill: University of North Carolina Press, 1998), pp. 144–45.
22. Susan L. Porter, "English-American Interaction in American Musical Theater at the Turn of the Nineteenth Century," *American Music* 4 (1986), 13.

23. One possible clue to O'Keeffe's choice of battle comes from a remark in his memoirs. A Dublin friend, Colonel MacMahon, a veteran of the American campaign, reportedly liked *Poor Soldier* best of all O'Keeffe's plays "as he had himself been fighting in America at Beattie's Ford, where my soldier Patrick saves the life of Captain Fitzroy" (O'Keeffe, *Recollections*, vol. I, p. 295). One wonders whether it was O'Keeffe's knowledge of MacMahon's experience that inspired the choice initially.
24. O'Keeffe, *Recollections*, vol. II, pp. 70–71; *PS* II.
25. Odell, *Annals*, vol. I, p. 245; Pollock, *Philadelphia Theatre*, pp. 137–38; William Dunlap, *History of the American Theatre*, 2 vols. (London: Bentley, 1833), vol. I, p. 248.
26. Dunlap, *History*, vol. I, p. 140.
27. Odell, *Annals*, vol. I, pp. 253, 254.
28. Susan Branson, *These Fiery Frenchified Dames: Women and Political Culture in Early National Philadelphia* (Philadelphia: University of Pennsylvania Press, 2001), p. 109.
29. American-authored plays caused stirs as well, but even in the case of Dunlap's *André*, for example, the turmoil was limited by the paucity of productions. See Chapter 6.
30. Wilmer, *Theatre, Society and Nation*, p. 57. As Wilmer explains, the Boston managers eventually cut the character of Bagatelle altogether to avoid further controversy.
31. Sonneck, *Early Opera*, p. 145; Porter, *With an Air Debonair*, p. 79. The Federal Street Theatre in Boston, the original, had in its ownership and patronage Federalist leanings, but in its first two years of operation had to take into account the broad range of political views of the spectators. That changed with the opening of the Haymarket at the end of December 1796, when that theatre made clear it was "even more decidedly Republican." Strand, "Theater and the Republic," p. 21. Sonneck misinterprets the political affiliation of the two theatres. For a related problem at the Federal Street Theatre, the singing of a French revolutionary song, see Nathans, *Early American Theatre*, pp. 79–81.
32. O'Keeffe, *Recollections*, vol. II, pp. 56, 55.
33. George A. Thompson, Jr., *A Documentary History of the African Theatre* (Evanston: Northwestern University Press, 1998); Shane White, *Stories of Freedom in Black New York* (Cambridge, Mass.: Harvard University Press, 2002).
34. Simon Snipe, *Sports of New York* (New York, 1823); printed in Thompson, *Documentary*, p. 116.
35. On the attack on the Mercer Street theatre on August 10, 1822, see Thompson, *Documentary*, pp. 99–112; White, *Stories*, pp. 92–96.
36. *National Advocate* (N.Y.), August 9, 1822; printed in Thompson, *Documentary*, p. 93.
37. Twaites, "Theatricals Extraordinary," *Commercial Advertiser*, August 10, 1822; printed in Thompson, *Documentary*, pp. 94–96.
38. Twaites in Thompson, *Documentary*, p. 95; White, *Stories*, pp. 111–12.
39. As White remarks, "Snipe and Twaites demonstrate an almost perverse refusal to hear or appreciate what was going on"; *Stories*, p. 99. On racism in New York, see also White, *Somewhat More Independent*.
40. Pollock, *Philadelphia Theatre*, pp. 172, 182, 293; Porter, *With an Air Debonair*, p. 259. For more on cross-dressed performances of *Poor Soldier*, see Chapter 12.
41. The presentation of Deborah Sampson as the subject of Herman Mann's sensationalized biography, *The Female Review* (1797), as well as her exhibition of herself,

using a text by Mann, five years later, is discussed by Judith Hiltner, "'She Bled in Secret': Deborah Sampson, Herman Mann, and *The Female Review*," *Early American Literature* 34 (1999), 190–220; Judith R. Hiltner, "'Like a Bewildered Star': Deborah Sampson, Herman, and *Address, Delivered with Applause*," *Rhetoric Society Quarterly* 29.2 (1999), 3–24; Sandra M. Gustafson, "The Genders of Nationalism: Patriotic Violence, Patriotic Sentiment in the Performances of Deborah Sampson Gannett," in Robert Blair St. George, ed., *Possible Pasts: Becoming Colonial in Early America* (Ithaca, N.Y.: Cornell University Press, 2000), pp. 380–99; and in the exhaustive biographical study by Alfred F. Young, *Masquerade: The Life and Times of Deborah Sampson, Continental Soldier* (New York: Knopf, 2004). See also Chapter 11.

42. John Daly Burk, *Female Patriotism; or, The Death of Joan D'Arc* (New York: Hurtin, 1798).
43. Branson, *These Fiery Frenchified Dames*, p. 110.
44. Pollock, *Philadelphia Theatre*, p. 207.
45. O'Keeffe, *Recollections*, vol. 1, pp. 380–81.
46. John O'Keeffe, *Patrick in Prussia, or, Love in a Camp* (Dublin: Davis, 1786).
47. For the specific tunes used by Dunlap, see Patricia Virga, *The American Opera to 1790* (Ann Arbor: UMI Research Press, 1982), pp. 287–88.
48. William Dunlap, *Darby's Return* (New York: Hodge, Allen, and Campbell, 1789), p. 9; hereafter *DR*.
49. Dunlap, *History*, vol. 1, pp. 160–61.
50. Dunlap, *History*, vol. 1, pp. 162, 161.
51. Dunlap, *History*, vol. 1, p. 162.
52. Smith, *The Diary*, ed. Cronin, p. 223 (entry for September 26, 1798); Dennie, quoted in Porter, *With an Air Debonair*, p. 179.

4 American author, British source

1. Sarah J. Purcell, *Sealed with Blood: War, Sacrifice, and Memory in Revolutionary America* (Philadelphia: University of Pennsylvania Press, 2002), pp. 1, 118–26.
2. John Daly Burk, *Bunker-Hill, or The Death of General Warren*, in Richard Moody, ed., *Dramas from the American Theatre, 1762–1909* (Cleveland: World, 1966), pp. 70–86, hereafter *BH*. For Dunlap's attitude and some of the house receipts for the play, see Moody's introduction, pp. 61–69.
3. Richards, *Theater Enough*, pp. 215–17.
4. Branson, *These Fiery Frenchified Dames*, pp. 118–19. Branson unfortunately misspells the names of both playwright and lead female character.
5. Nathans, *Early American Theatre*, p. 115.
6. The assertion of an American identity in the play from a Democratic Republican perspective is explored by Wilmer, *Theatre, Society and Nation*, pp. 53–65.
7. Judith Sargent Murray, *The Traveller Returned*, in Sharon M. Harris, ed., *Selected Writings of Judith Sargent Murray* (New York: Oxford University Press, 1995), pp. 103–52, hereafter *TR*. The play is also reprinted in Amelia Howe Kritzer, ed., *Plays by Early American Women, 1775–1850* (Ann Arbor: University of Michigan Press, 1995), pp. 97–136.

8. Janet Rider, "Creating American Womanhood: The Social and Cultural World of Judith Sargent Murray," Ph.D. dissertation, University of Connecticut (2004), chap. 5.
9. Judith Sargent Murray, *Virtue Triumphant*, in *The Gleaner*, 3 vols. (Boston: Andrews, 1798), vol. IV, pp. 15–87, hereafter *VT* and *The Gleaner* as *G*. The play had one performance, but was withdrawn by Murray after unfavorable critical response. Sheila L. Skemp, *Judith Sargent Murray: A Brief Biography with Documents* (Boston: Bedford, 1998), p. 102.
10. This is not to say that one could not look at *VT* further through an American lens; indeed, the play is well worth analysis. My point here is that of her two plays, *TR* is more overtly about American identity in the context of the Revolution. For brief discussions of *VT* see Meserve, *Emerging Entertainment*, pp. 154–55; Kritzer, ed., introduction, *Plays by Early American Women*, p. 14; Peter A. Davis, "Poets and Playwrights to 1800," in Wilmeth and Bigsby, eds., *Cambridge History*, vol. I, p. 246; and Branson, *These Fiery Frenchified Dames*, pp. 120–21.
11. Nathans, *Early American Theatre*, pp. 86–87.
12. Branson, *These Fiery Frenchified Dames*, pp. 104–5; Murray, "Occasional Epilogue to *The Contrast*, a Comedy, Written by Royal [*sic*] Tyler, Esq.," *Massachusetts Magazine*, March 1794; reprinted in Lauter, *et al.*, eds., *Heath Anthology*, vol. I, pp. 1039–42.
13. There has been relatively little criticism on the play, although it has been increasingly recognized for what it raises about female authorship and the portrayal of female characters. In addition to sources cited below, see the brief discussion in Mary Anne Schofield, "The Happy Revolution: Colonial Women and the Eighteenth-Century Theater," in June Schlueter, ed., *Modern American Drama: The Female Canon* (Rutherford, N.J.: Fairleigh Dickinson University Press, 1990), pp. 31–32.
14. Meserve, *Emerging Entertainment*, pp. 153–55.
15. For comments by Paine, see Vera Bernadette Field, *Constantia: A Study of the Life and Works of Judith Sargent Murray, 1751–1820* (Orono: University of Maine Press, 1931), pp. 38–40; for additional context, see Kritzer, ed., *Plays by Early American Women*, pp. 14–15; and Skemp, *Murray*, pp. 102–3.
16. Richard Cumberland, *The West Indian: A Comedy* (London: Dilly, 1792); hereafter *WI*.
17. As mentioned earlier, Warren had written two verse dramas, *The Ladies of Castile* and *The Sack of Rome*, and was curious about their chances on the London stage. Cumberland told Adams, apparently, that the taste of the time and prejudice against American authors would not admit them to the theatre: Richards, *Mercy Otis Warren*, p. 108. It is either an ironic accident or a testament to Adams's thoroughness that he asked both Cumberland and Murphy, rivals and combatants over the use of sentiment in drama; see Oliver Ferguson, "Sir Fretful Plagiary and Goldsmith's 'An Essay on the Theatre': The Background of Richard Cumberland's 'Dedication to Detraction,'" in Larry S. Champion, ed., *Quick Springs of Sense: Studies in the Eighteenth Century* (Athens: University of Georgia Press, 1974), p. 116.
18. Performance history from Johnson and Burling, *Colonial American Stage*, pp. 395–96, *passim*; Pollock, *The Philadelphia Theatre*, p. 144, *passim*; Jared Brown, *Theatre in America during the Revolution*, pp. 88–89, *passim*; Errol Hill, *The Jamaican Stage*,

1655–1900: Profile of a Colonial Theatre (Amherst: University of Massachusetts Press, 1992), pp. 79–80; Martin Staples Shockley, *The Richmond Stage, 1784–1812* (Charlottesville: University Press of Virginia, 1977), pp. 13, 20, *passim*. In his discussions of *WI*, Kenneth Silverman claims more American printed editions and American Company performances for the play than I can confirm but rightly notes its importance: *A Cultural History of the American Revolution* (1976; New York: Columbia University Press, 1987), pp. 220, 237.

19. Dunlap, *History*, vol. I, p. 135. See also his comment on seeing the first military performance in New York on January 15, 1778 in *History*, vol. I, p. 100.

20. Richard Cumberland, *The West Indian* ([Boston]: West and West, [1794]). The play was advertised in the *Columbian Centinel* for April 2, 1794, and the print version claims the text is 'As performed at the theatre in Boston.' On Carey's edition, see Nathans, *Early American Theatre*, p. 87.

21. Cumberland claimed to be rescuing a maligned group, West Indian planters, from savage portrayals on stage, but as Elizabeth M. Yearling notes, few plays with island planters as characters had made it to the London theatre before Cumberland's: 'Cumberland, Foote, and the Stage Creole,' *Notes and Queries* (UK) 25 (1978), 59–60. However, Cumberland may have had in mind the introduction of Sir Peter Pepperpot from Samuel Foote's *The Patron* (1764). When Sir Peter enters with 'two blacks,' he abuses them and threatens violence against them: Foote, *The Patron*, in *Dramatic Works of Samuel Foote*, 2 vols. (1809; New York: Blom, 1969), vol. I, pp. 10–17. When the African servants enter in *West Indian*, they appear with a sailor who speaks well of Belcour's benevolence. On Cumberland's problems in rewriting a stereotype, see also Yearling, 'Victims of Society in Three Plays by Cumberland,' *Durham University Journal* 43 (1981), 23–26.

22. For some of the problems faced by theatre professionals, most especially that of confronting the anti-playhouse sentiment of revolutionary republicanism, see Bruce McConachie, 'American Theatre in Context, from the Beginnings to 1870,' in Wilmeth and Bigsby, eds., *Cambridge History*, vol. I, pp. 126–30.

23. There is some irony in Murray's borrowing, for Cumberland was accused of being a plagiarist, most notoriously in his alleged use of Thomas Shadwell's *The Squire of Alsatia* for his play *The Choleric Man* (1774). See Oliver Ferguson and Eugene M. Waith, 'Richard Cumberland, Comic Force, and Misanthropy,' *Comparative Drama* 17 (1978), 283–99, for contrasting views on Cumberland's reputation as a 'plagiary.'

24. Cumberland *Memoirs of Richard Cumberland* (New York: Brisban and Brannan, 1806), p. 137.

25. Robert J. Detisch, 'The Synthesis of Laughing and Sentimental Comedy in *The West Indian*,' *Educational Theatre Journal* 22 (1970), 294n.6, 297n.8.

26. On Murray's decision to use the more conventional stereotype, see Chapter 9.

27. Elizabeth Yearling, 'The Good-Natured Heroes of Cumberland, Goldsmith, and Sheridan,' *Modern Language Review* 67 (1972), 495.

28. Olver Goldsmith, *The Good Natur'd Man*, in Goldsmith, *The Comedies*, ed. Joseph Jacobs (New York: Stokes, [1899]), pp. 159–310.

29. Susan Lamb, 'The Popular Theater of Samuel Foote and British National Identity,' *Comparative Drama* 30 (1996), 250–51.

30. Sharon M. Harris, Introduction, in Harris, ed., *Selected Writings*, pp. xxxviii–xxxix.
31. Susanna Rowson, *Slaves in Algiers*, in Kritzer, ed., *Plays by Early American Women*, p. 62.
32. Susanna Rowson moved from Philadelphia to Boston and played with the Federal Street company in the fall 1796 season, but too late for her personally to have any direct influence on *Traveller Returned*, which had opened on March 9. It is still possible, however, that Murray had read the text of *Slaves* before she completed *TR*.
33. Harris, ed., *Selected Writings*, p. xxxix.
34. Louisa Montague's status as Republican Mother who has been allowed to err is explored by Amelia Howe Kritzer, 'Playing with Republican Motherhood: Self-Representation in Plays by Susanna Haswell Rowson and Judith Sargent Murray,' *Early American Literature* 31 (1996), 154–56.
35. Yearling, "Good-Natured," 497–500.
36. Although Goldsmith includes "low" characters in *The Good-Natured Man*, the practice of striking humor from them was condemned by critics of the time – including Cumberland (Yearling, "Good-Natured," 496).
37. Killmallock, of course, is also the name of the Irish character in George Colman the Younger, *The Mountaineers*, a musical play that opened in Boston on April 4, 1795, and quite possibly known by Murray.
38. Murray's play called *The African* has not been found; it was never printed, and she asked for all manuscript copies after its stage failure (Kritzer, ed., *Plays by Early American Women*, p. 15; Skemp, *Murray*, p. 103).
39. Richard Dircks, *Richard Cumberland* (Boston: Twayne, 1976), p. 150.
40. At the time of production, the Federal Street Theatre was the only one in Boston, accommodating both Federalists and Democratic Republicans, the latter of whom tended to include more of the artisanal class. By December, the Haymarket Theatre had been built, appealing to Democratic–Republicans and thus, to some degree, changing the class mix at the Federal Street.
41. Judith Sargent Murray, 'Reverence Thy Self,' printed in Karen L. Schiff, "Objects of Speculation: Early Manuscripts on Women and Education by Judith Sargent (Stevens) Murray," *Legacy* 17 (2000), 221–22.

5 Patriotic interrogations

1. Middlekauff, *Glorious Cause*, pp. 216–18; Catherine S. Crary, *The Price of Loyalty: Tory Writings from the Revolutionary Era* (New York: McGraw-Hill, 1973), pp. 55–56; Harwell, ed., *Committees*.
2. In the Cape Fear region of North Carolina, the local committee largely worried about contraband, not political leanings. Leora H. McEachern and Isabel M. Williams, eds., *Wilmington–New Hanover Safety Committee Minutes, 1774–1776* (Wilmington, N.C.: Wilmington–New Hanover County American Revolution Bi-centennial Association, 1974). For complaints about committee justice, see Ronald Lettieri and Charles Wetheell, 'The New Hampshire Committees of Safety and Revolutionary Republicanism, 1775–1784,' *Historical New Hampshire* 35 (1980), 271–75.
3. Historians and biographers of the loyalist experience, however, tend to discuss the committees more often than those affirming the patriot conclusion, as the notes below indicate.

4. Mercy Otis Warren, *History of the Rise, Progress and Termination of the American Revolution*, ed. Lester H. Cohen, 2 vols. (Indianapolis: Liberty Classics, 1988), vol. II, p. 112; see also Cohen's source note to the episode, p. 113, and James F. Vivian and Jean H. Vivian, "'A Jurisdiction Competent to the Occasion': A Benjamin Rumsey Letter, June, 1776," *Maryland Historical Magazine* 67/2 (1972), 144–55.
5. The most authoritative article on the play, and one to which I will refer again below, is Michael A. McDonnell, "A World Turned 'Topsy Turvy': Robert Munford, *The Patriots*, and the Crisis of the Revolution in Virginia," *William and Mary Quarterly* 61 (2004), 235–70. As McDonnell rightly notes, the play has rarely received any serious attention either from literary scholars or historians. For earlier overviews of this play, see Canby, "Robert Munford's 'The Patriots,'" *William and Mary Quarterly* 6 (1949), 437–47; Baine, *Robert Munford*, pp. 73–92; Meserve, *Emerging Entertainment*, pp. 86, 88–89; and Davis, "Plays and Playwrights to 1800," p. 241. The date of the play is uncertain, but it has to be later than 1776, the date Davis assigns. As Baine and Meserve note, Munford alludes to events as late as May 1777, but their composition date of 1779 – based on tone – strikes me as unlikely. Given the references to Trenton and Princeton, battles from Dec. 1776 and Jan. 1777 (and none later), and the trials of Scots merchants in April, it seems most likely that Munford wrote the play over a period stretching from late winter to summer 1777 – sometime before the battle of Saratoga in October. For concurring information on a 1777 composition date, with an emphasis on 1775 as being the date dramatized, see McDonnell, "World Turned," 244.
6. Quoted in Richard Maxwell Brown, "Violence and the American Revolution," in Stephen G. Kurtz and James H. Hutson, eds., *Essays on the American Revolution* (Chapel Hill: University of North Carolina Press, 1973), p. 111.
7. Culpeper County minutes, as printed in William J. Van Schreeven and Robert L. Scribner, eds., *Revolutionary Virginia: The Road to Independence*, 7 vols. (Charlottesville: University Press of Virginia, 1978), vol. IV, p. 29.
8. Samuel Ludlow Frey, ed., *The Minute Book of the Committee of Safety of Tryon County, the Old New York Frontier* (New York: Dodd, Mead, 1905), pp. 55–56; hereafter *MB*. I wish to thank Hugh MacDougall for making this text available to me.
9. Harwell, *Committees*, pp. 32–36.
10. Robert McCluer Calhoon, *The Loyalists in Revolutionary America, 1760–1781* (New York: Harcourt Brace Jovanovich, 1973), p. 304.
11. Harwell, *Committees*, pp. 90, 92.
12. Peter Oliver, *Peter Oliver's Origin and Progress of the American Rebellion: A Tory View*, ed. Douglass Adair and John A. Schutz (San Marino: Huntington Library, 1961), p. 157; see also R. M. Brown, "Violence," p. 104.
13. Oliver, *Origin*, p. 143.
14. Crary, *Price of Loyalty*, pp. 58–60; R. M. Brown, "Violence," p. 112.
15. For a good summary of whig persecution of tories, see Wallace Brown, *The Good Americans: The Loyalists in the American Revolution* (New York: Morrow, 1969), pp. 126–46. Brown is careful to point out, however, that where it was feasible, as in New York and Georgia, there were equivalent abuses of whigs by tories.
16. Crèvecoeur, "Landscapes," p. 429; hereafter *L*. On the text of "Landscapes," see the notes to Chapter 2.

17. In one of several such examples, Wallace Brown, *Good Americans*, p. 137, records what one contemporary said of a pregnant Massachusetts loyalist wife: that there was "a guard of Rebels always in her room, who treated her with great rudeness and indecency, exposing her to the view of their banditti, as a sight "See a tory woman' and striped [*sic*] her and her Children of all their Linen and Cloths."
18. Thomas Jones, *History of New York during the Revolutionary War*, ed. Edward Floyd DeLancey, 2 vols. (New York: New York Historical Society, 1879), vol. I, pp. 76–77; see also Crary, *Price of Loyalty*, p. 79. It should be noted that Mary Johnson, after being held in Albany for six months, removed to an area near Orange County, Crèvecoeur's home, in early 1777; therefore, it is possible that the author of 'Landscapes' had some first- or near-hand knowledge of her situation. See DeLancey's notes to this episode, Jones, *History*, vol. I, pp. 583–93.
19. Page Smith, *A New Age Now Begins: A People's History of the American Revolution*, 2 vols. (New York: McGraw-Hill, 1976), vol. I, p. 664.
20. McDonnell, 'World Turned,' 240. McDonnell explains how Munford's position as a rising patriot was cut short in 1774 by his inability to support fully resolves in Virginia that had been urged by Patrick Henry. When voters met in Mecklenburg to elect a committee to enforce the Continental Association, Munford, a prominent landholder, was not chosen.
21. Baine, *Robert Munford*, pp. 82–92, details a number of possible parallels of persons known to Munford in Mecklenburg County and characters or situations in the play.
22. Munford, *The Patriots*, text in Canby, 'Robert Munford's 'The Patriots,'" 462; other page references to this edition, cited as *TP*. *The Patriots* first appeared in a posthumous edition of his works, published by his son William Munford, in 1798.
23. McDonnell, 'World Turned,' 245.
24. David Garrick, *Miss in Her Teens; or, The Medley of Lovers* (London: Tonson and Draper, 1747).
25. Woody Holton, *Forced Founders: Indians, Debtors, Slaves, and the Making of the American Revolution in Virginia* (Chapel Hill: University of North Carolina Press, 1999).
26. George Villiers, 2nd Duke of Buckingham, *The Rehearsal* (London: Thomas Dring, 1672); George Farquhar, *The Recruiting Officer*, ed. Michael Shugrue (Lincoln: University of Nebraska Press, 1966). For a discussion of Farquhar's influence on Munford, see McDonnell, 'World Turned,' 239 n.8 and 259 n.43.
27. Although Williamsburg had supported a number of theatrical seasons between 1750 and 1775, few playbills survive; however, both the Farquhar and Garrick plays were among the most popular plays in the repertoire of the companies that came to Williamsburg during the period.
28. Behn's play can be found, for instance, in Myra Jehlen and Michael Warner, eds., *The English Literatures of America, 1500–1800* (New York: Routledge, 1997), pp. 233–91.
29. Johnson and Burling, *Colonial American Stage*.
30. The connections between the play and seventeenth-century Virginia are most thoroughly pursued by Jenny Hale Pulsipher, '*The Widow Ranter* and Royalist Culture in Virginia," *Early American Literature* 39 (2004), 41–66.
31. Baine, *Robert Munford*, pp. 74–76 suggests that Munford may have been satirizing a real-life model, Col. Bennett Goode, in this episode, but acknowledges as well a

number of possible literary influences in the mock battle. As for Isabella, McDonnell suggests that her sword-wielding fanaticism "only reinforces this unmanly patriotism" as that performed by members of the committee, while Mira, a much less colorful character, is Munford's ideal of the patriotic woman who leaves it to men of cool reason to handle politics. McDonnell, "World Turned," 250, 251.

32. Munford himself, after a brief recovery of his position in Mecklenburg, fell out again at the end of the war, took up heavy drinking, and died in 1783, only in his mid-forties. See McDonnell, "World Turned," 265.
33. Murray, *Traveller Returned*, p. 127; hereafter *TR*.
34. Charles F. Adams, ed., *Correspondence between John Adams and Mercy Warren* (1878; New York: Arno, 1972); Richards, *Mercy Otis Warren*, pp. 22–23, 40–41.
35. David S. Shields, *Civil Tongues and Polite Letters in British America* (Chapel Hill: University of North Carolina Press, 1997).

6 Dunlap's queer *André*

1. On the basic problem of putting André in the hero's position, see Norman Philbrick, "The Spy as Hero: An Examination of *André* by William Dunlap," in Oscar G. Brockett, ed., *Studies in Theatre and Drama: Essays in Honor of Hubert C. Heffner* (The Hague: Mouton, 1972), pp. 97–119.
2. William Dunlap, Preface, *André*, in Richards, ed., *Early American Drama*, p. 64; hereinafter *A*. See also Dunlap, *History*, vol. II, pp. 20–21.
3. Elihu Hubbard Smith, *Diary*, pp. 434, 436.
4. The transformation of *André* to *Glory of Columbia* is described in the introduction to the latter in Richard Moody, ed., *Dramas from the American Theatre*, pp. 87–93; it is also addressed in the context of other nineteenth-century plays on the subject of André and Arnold in Miriam J. Shillingsburg, "The West Point Treason in American Drama, 1798–1891," *Educational Theatre Journal* 30 (1978), 73–89.
5. Robert H. Canary, *William Dunlap* (New York: Twayne, 1970), pp. 91–101; Fliegelman, *Prodigals and Pilgrims*, pp. 216–19.
6. François Jost, "German and French Themes in Early American Drama," *JGE: The Journal of General Education* 28/3 (1976), 190–222; Jack Zipes, "Dunlap, Kotzebue, and the Shaping of American Theatre: A Re-evaluation from a Marxist Perspective," *Early American Literature* 8 (1974), 272–89.
7. Gary A. Richardson, "Nationalizing the American Stage: The Drama of Royall Tyler and William Dunlap as Post-Colonial Phenomena," in A. Robert Lee and W. M. Verhoeven, eds., *Making America/Making American Literature* (Amsterdam: Rodopi, 1996), p. 234.
8. On the cultural barrier against staging American plays in the new republic, see Harold J. Nicholls, "The Prejudice against Native American Drama from 1778 to 1830," *Quarterly Journal of Speech* 60 (1975), 279–88.
9. Robert E. Cray, Jr., "Major John André and the Three Captors: Class Dynamics and Revolutionary Memory Wars in the Early Republic, 1780–1831," *Journal of the Early Republic* 17 (1997), 371–97; Andy Trees, "Benedict Arnold, John André, and His Three Yeoman Captors: A Sentimental Journey or American Virtue Defined," *Early American Literature* 35 (2000), 246–73.

10. For a variety of readings of *André* compare Gerald Argetsinger, 'Dunlap's *André*: Beginning of American Tragedy,' *Players* 49 (1974), 62–64; Meserve, *Emerging Entertainment*, pp. 107–9; Benjamin Franklin Fisher IV, 'William Dunlap's Transformations of the Gothic in *André*,' *Publications of the Mississippi Philological Association* (1990), 196–206; Gary Richardson, *American Drama from the Colonial Period through World War I: A Critical History* (New York: Twayne, 1993), pp. 52–60; Jeffrey H. Richards, Introduction to *André*, in Richards (ed), *Early American Drama*, pp. 58–61; Lucy Rinehart, '"Manly Exercises': Post-Revolutionary Performances of Authority in the Theatrical Career of William Dunlap,' *Early American Literature* 36 (2001), 273–80; Wilmer, *Theatre, Society and the Nation*, pp. 65–69.
11. Gary A. Richardson, 'In the Shadow of the Bard: Republican Drama and the Shakespearean Legacy,' in Judith L. Fisher and Stephen Watt, eds., *When They Weren't Doing Shakespeare: Essays on Nineteenth-Century British and American Theatre* (Athens: University of Georgia Press, 1989), p. 242.
12. John Loftis, *The Politics of Drama in Augustan England* (Oxford: Oxford University Press, 1963), pp. 15–19, 56–61; Loftis, Introduction, in Nathaniel Lee, *Lucius Junius Brutus*, ed. Loftis (Lincoln: University of Nebraska Press, 1967), pp. xi–xxiv. There is a vast literature on *Cato* in America, which need not be rehearsed here. The three British plays are discussed by Julie Ellison, *Cato's Tears and the Making of Anglo-American Emotion* (Chicago: University of Chicago Press, 1999), pp. 23–47, in ways that have some impact here, particularly in her understanding of the expression of feeling in a homosocial context.
13. As, for example, Rinehart, 'Manly Exercises,' 276.
14. Production information from Odell, *Annals*, vols. I and II, *passim*; Pollock, *Philadelphia Theatre*; Jared Brown, *Theatre in America During the Revolution*, pp. 173–87.
15. Canary, *William Dunlap*, p. 94.
16. Meserve, *Emerging Entertainment*, p. 148. On other contemporary stage versions of the André story, see Chapter 12.
17. For American politics in the 1797–1799 period, including the Alien and Sedition Acts and XYZ affair, see John Ferling, *A Leap in the Dark: The Struggle to Create the American Republic* (New York: Oxford University Press, 2003), pp. 405–49. Even among Federalists, Ferling notes, fears or charges of conspiracy were rife, particularly in President John Adams's concern over Alexander Hamilton.
18. John Parke, *Virginia: A Pastoral Drama, on the Birth-day of an illustrious Personage and the Return of Peace, February 11th, 1784*, in Parke, *Lyric Works of Horace Translated into English Verse: To Which Are Added, a Number of Original Poems. By a Native of America* (Philadelphia: Oswald, 1786), pp. 321–34.
19. Odell, *Annals*, vol. I, p. 451. Although most theatre histories only note the New York production, *André* played elsewhere in 1798; Susanne K. Sherman, *Comedies Useful: Southern Theatre History, 1775–1812* (Williamsburg, Va.: Celest Press, 1998), p. 250, without elaboration or documentation, identifies Norfolk and Alexandria as two other cities where Dunlap's play was performed. On the Norfolk production, see Chapter 12.
20. Smith, *Diary*, p. 414.
21. Dunlap, *History*, vol. II, pp. 21–22; Smith, *Diary*, p. 434.

22. Thomas Otway, *Venice Preserved; or A Plot Discovered* [1682], in Robert G. Lawrence, ed., *Restoration Plays* (London: J. M. Dent, 1992), p. 328; hereafter *VP*.
23. Ellison, *Cato's Tears*, p. 9. A recent study of masculinity in the United States, Michael Kimmel, *Manhood in America: A Cultural History* (New York: Free Press, 1996), p. 16, begins with Tyler's *The Contrast*, but Kimmel's analysis seems so peculiar – naming Col. Manly as the type of the 'Heroic Artisan,' for instance – that it would be difficult to find analogues for his types in Dunlap.
24. Anthony Ashley Cooper, third earl of Shaftesbury, "*Sensus Communis*': An Essay on the Freedom of Wit and Humour," *Characteristicks of Men, Manners, Opinions, Times*, 3 vols. (Indianapolis: Liberty Fund, 2001), vol. I, pp. 37–93; see also Shields, *Civil Tongues*, pp. 44–45; and Ellison, *Cato's Tears*, pp. 25–28.
25. Caleb Crain, *American Sympathy: Men, Friendship, and the Literature of the New Nation* (New Haven: Yale University Press, 2001), p. 14.
26. Jessica Munns, *Restoration Politics and Drama: The Plays of Thomas Otway, 1675–1683* (Newark: University of Delaware Press, 1995), p. 190.
27. Dunlap, *History*, vol. I, pp. 381–82.
28. For examination of this passage, I am indebted to an unpublished paper by Cheryl Oreovicz, 'Contextualizing *André*,' delivered at the Society of Early Americanists convention, Charleston, South Carolina, April 1999. Along with other scholars of early American drama, I regret the sudden death of Professor Oreovicz in 2003.
29. Rinehart, 'Manly Exercises,' 278.
30. The issues of performed masculinity as both a theatrical and social category are nicely summarized by Carla J. McDonough, *Staging Masculinity: Male Identity in Contemporary American Drama* (Jefferson, N.C.: McFarland, 1997), pp. 5–17.
31. I take my cue here from a comment by Robert Brustein at a talk at Yale in the late 1960s who claimed that, in periods when drama had few overt gay characters, gay actors enjoyed the freedom from traditional constraints on masculine behavior offered by Restoration plays.
32. Crain, *American Sympathy*; Stephen Shapiro, "Dread and Curious Alteration': Republican Panic and Personal Intimation in Early American Fiction," Ph.D. dissertation, Yale University, 1995.
33. Rinehart. 'Manly Exercises,' 276, 275.
34. Dana Nelson, *National Manhood: Capitalist Citizenship and the Imagined Fraternity of White Men* (Durham, N.C.: Duke University Press, 1998), pp. 29–60.
35. John Hodgkinson, *Narrative of His Connection with the Old American Company from the Fifth of September, 1792, to the Thirty-First of March, 1797* (New York: Oram, 1797).
36. Richardson, 'Shadow,' p. 246.

7 Susanna Rowson and the dramatized Muslim

1. *Slaves in Algiers* played twice in Philadelphia in 1794, on June 30 and December 22, and twice in Baltimore, November 20, 1794 and November 26, 1795; it seems also to have appeared once in New York, on May 9, 1796. Rowson contributed something to the libretto of *The Highland Reel* by John O'Keeffe, at least in one of its American versions, and wrote at least two other plays immediately after *Slaves, The Female Patriot* and *The Volunteers*, both 1795 and both apparently lost.

2. See, for example, Kornfeld, 'Women in Post-Revolutionary American Culture,' 58; Benilde Montgomery, 'White Captives, African Slaves: A Drama of Abolition,' *Eighteenth-Century Studies* 27 (1994), 618–22; Baepler, Introduction, *White Slaves, African Masters*, p. 47.
3. For a somewhat different reading of the Islamic context for *Slaves*, see Robert J. Allison, *The Crescent Obscured: The United States and the Muslim World, 1776–1815* (New York: Oxford University Press, 1995), esp. pp. 67–68, 74–77.
4. Pollock, *Philadelphia Theatre*, p. 259.
5. Irving, *History, Tales, and Sketches*, pp. 11–12. This play shows another instance of American conversion, beginning its life as *The Veteran Tar* at Drury Lane in 1801 (by Samuel James Arnold and music by his father Samuel), then crossing the Atlantic to become *The Tripolitan Prize; or American Tars on an English Shore* when Oldstyle saw it. Porter, 'English–American Interaction,' 15–16.
6. Odell, *Annals*, vol. II, pp. 228–30.
7. Susanna Rowson, *Slaves in Algiers*; hereafter *SA*.
8. Dorothy Brewster, *Aaron Hill: Poet, Dramatist, Projector* (1913; rpt. New York: AMS Press, 1966), p. 141.
9. James J. Lynch, *Box, Pit, and Gallery: Stage and Society in Johnson's London* (Berkeley: University of California Press, 1953), pp. 17, 20, 38, 39.
10. Norman Housley, *The Later Crusades from Lyons to Alcazar, 1274–1580* (Oxford: Oxford University Press, 1992), p. 64.
11. Joshua Prawer, *The Latin Kingdom of Jerusalem: European Colonialism in the Middle Ages* (London: Weidenfeld and Nicolson, 1972), pp. 108–9, *et passim*.
12. Nicholas Rowe, *Tamerlane, a Tragedy*, 2nd edn (London: Tonson, 1703).
13. Aaron Hill, *Tragedy of Zara* (London: J. Watts, 1736), p. 5; hereafter *Z*.
14. The Louis referred to here is probably Louis IX, the great crusader who fought Muslims in Egypt, lived in Syria, and captured Tunis, where he died in 1270. At the time of Voltaire's composition, the French king was Louis XV.
15. Brewster, *Aaron Hill*, p. 145.
16. Pollock, *Philadelphia Theatre*, p. 105; Odell, *Annals*, vol. I, p. 147.
17. Middlekauff, *Glorious Cause*, p. 232.
18. 'On Saturday next will be perform'd, by a society of ladies and gentlemen, at Faneuil-Hall, the tragedy of Zara' (Boston, 1775).
19. Quoted in Jared Brown, *Theatre in America*, p. 25.
20. Aphra Behn, *The Round-heads, or, The Good Old Cause* (London: D. Brown, 1682).
21. Brown, *Theatre in America*, p. 25.
22. Scheer and Rankin, *Rebels and Redcoats*, p. 497.
23. Edward W. Said, *Orientalism* (New York: Vintage, 1978).
24. Samuel Low, *The Politician Out-witted* (New York: Ross, 1789), p. 12; hereafter *PO*.
25. Anthony Gerard Barthelemy, *Black Face, Maligned Race: The Representation of Blacks in English Drama from Shakespeare to Southerne* (Baton Rouge: Louisiana State University Press, 1987), pp. 1–17.
26. Isaac Bickerstaff, *The Sultan, or A Peep into the Seraglio*, 2nd edn (London: Dilly, 1787). By 1796, the New York theatre advertised this play as *The American Captive* (not to be confused with James Ellison's 1812 play of Tripolitan captivity by the same title), probably simply making Roxalana a native of the United States rather than England, but as in other

such cases, the modified British play outlasted the original American one. See Porter, *With an Air Debonair*, pp. 430, 490; and Allison, *Crescent Obscured*, pp. 69–71.

27. James Miller, *Mahomet the Imposter* (Edinburgh: Apollo Press, 1782). For an analysis of this play and its American reception (it opened in British occupied New York, then was performed in the mid-1790s, after Rowson's premiere), see Allison, *Crescent Obscured*, 43–46.
28. Jonathan Burton, 'Anglo-Ottoman Relations and the Image of the Turk in *Tamburlaine*,' *Journal of Medieval and Early Modern Studies* 30/1 (2000), 125–56.
29. Housley, *Later Crusades*, pp. 144–45.
30. For a survey history on this topic, see Samuel C. Chew, 'Moslems on the London Stage,' in Chew, *The Crescent and the Rose: Islam and England during the Renaissance* (New York: Oxford University Press, 1937), pp. 469–540.
31. E. W. Bovill, *The Battle of Alcazar: An Account of the Defeat of Don Sebastian of Portugal at El-Ksar el-Kebir* (London: Batchworth Press, 1952), pp. 43–52; Nabil I. Matar, *Turks, Moors, and Englishmen in the Age of Discovery* (New York: Columbia University Press, 1999), p. 46. On the Battle of Alcazar, however, Matar argues that England supported Sebastian, an unlikely conclusion, despite the presence of English adventurer Thomas Stukeley, given the negotiations with the Saadians over arms shipments. See pp. 46–47.
32. George Peele, *The Battle of Alcazar*, ed. John Yoklavich, in *The Life and Works of George Peele*, ed. Charles Tyler Prouty, 3 vols. (New Haven: Yale University Press, 1952–1970), vol. II, p. 296; hereafter *BA*.
33. John Yoklavich, editorial introduction, *The Battle of Alcazar* by George Peele, *Life and Works*, vol. II, p. 222.
34. *The Famous Historye of the life and death of Captaine Thomas Stukeley* (London: Pavyer, 1605). There is no certain authorship. Although it has been ascribed to Thomas Heywood, the chaotic structure seems to belong to an author relatively unused to writing for the stage.
35. Barthelemy, *Black Face*, p. 88.
36. Montaigne's essay was published in English in 1603 as 'Against Idleness'; in Michel de Montaigne, *The Essays*, trans. John Florio, 3 vols. (New York: AMS Press, 1967), vol. II, pp. 412–16. The matter of identity in Heywood's drama has never been satisfactorily explained. One suggestion, by the name, is Mulai Mohammed ech-Sheik, the son of Ahmed and a contender for the succession after his father died in 1603. However, the evidence suggests for Part I a composition date somewhat earlier, c. 1600. I am inclined to believe that Heywood's grasp of the particulars in Morocco, unlike Peele's, was not precise. He could have used the name of ech-Sheik, applied rumored characteristics of the still-living king, Ahmed, and created a character who would live by type in other personations of Islamic potentates in English drama. In any event, given the fame of the battle of El-Ksar and the fairly widespread and sympathetic understanding of Abd el-Malik, one that Heywood must have known at least in part, Mullisheg is *de facto* the author's commentary on the possibility of a noble Moroccan king. Because Part II was apparently written nearly thirty years after the original composition of Part I, Heywood seems more influenced by his own type from earlier than anything historical having to do with the Saadian kings. Thomas Heywood, *The Fair Maid of the West, Parts I and II*, ed. Robert K. Turner (London: Arnold, 1968).

37. On Heywood's depiction of the lusting Moor, see Barthelemy, *Black Face*, pp. 163–64, 166–67.
38. Dryden uses the name Abdelmelech, a variant of the same name that informs Muley-Moluch, in *The Conquest of Granada*, but that has less immediate relevance to Rowson than does the figure in *Don Sebastian*.
39. John Dryden, *Don Sebastian, King of Portugal*, ed. Earl Miner, George R. Guffey, and Franklin B. Zimmerman (1976), in *The Works of John Dryden*, ed. Edward Niles Hooker, H. T. Swedenberg, and Vinton A. Dearing, 20 vols. (Berkeley: University of California Press, 1956–2000), vol. XV, p. 70. For the editors' discussion of Dryden's sources and of the play itself, see Earl Miner, George R. Guffey, and Franklin B. Zimmerman, Commentary, *Works*, vol. XV, pp. 382–408.
40. Lynch, *Box, Pit*, p. 41.
41. O'Keeffe, *Recollections*, vol. II, p. 396.
42. Kritzer, 'Playing with Republican Motherhood,' 150–66.
43. N. I. Matar, 'The Renegade in English Seventeenth-Century Imagination,' *Studies in English Literature 1500–1900* 33 (1993), 489–505; Matar, 'Turning Turk: Conversion to Islam in English Renaissance Thought,' *Durham University Journal* 86.1 (1994), 33–41.
44. Ben Hassan also resembles, to some degree, the stage Muslim character The Cadi in Isaac Bickerstaff's comic opera *The Captive* (London: Griffin, 1769), a play based loosely on scenes from *Don Sebastian*; there are also parallels between garden scenes in both plays. However, *The Captive* did not play in Philadelphia any time before Rowson's comedy.
45. I do not mean to suggest that these are the only parallels to Dryden in Rowson's play – for example, she too has a character named Sebastian, although Spanish and a slave rather than Portuguese and a king – but only to focus on those directly related to the presentation of Islam. By the same token, there are many other Islamic subject plays that appeared in American theatres on which Rowson might have drawn; for a discussion of some not mentioned here, see Chapter 12.
46. Ironically, the Turks themselves, at least in the late sixteenth century, had a remarkably tolerant society in which 'Jews, Christians, and Muslims [could] live peacefully within the same community'; Rowson substitutes republicanism for absolutism, but the end result is the same. Daniel J. Vitkus, 'Turning Turk in *Othello*: The Conversion and Damnation of the Moor,' *Shakespeare Quarterly* 48/2 (1997), 161.

8 James Nelson Barker and the stage American Native

1. Eve Kornfeld, 'Encountering 'the Other': American Intellectuals and Indians in the 1790s,' *William and Mary Quarterly* 52 (1995), 287–97. The lyrics to *Tammany* are found in Ann Julia Hatton, *The Songs of Tammany; or, The Indian Chief* (New York: Harrison, 1794).
2. As happened when the Cherokee leaders came to New York in 1767 and attended the new John Street Theatre; see Hugh F. Rankin, *The Theater in Colonial America*, pp. 124–25; also David Grimsted, *Melodrama Unveiled: American Theater and Culture, 1800–1850* (Chicago: University of Chicago Press, 1968), pp. 61–62. On visits by Native chiefs to Philadelphia, see Eliana Crestani, 'James Nelson Barker's

Pocahontas: The Theatre and the Indian Question," *Nineteenth Century Theatre* 23/1–2 (1995), 13–14.
3. David Humphreys, *The Widow of Malabar; or, The Tyranny of Custom*, in *Miscellaneous Works* (New York: Hodge, Allen, and Campbell, 1790), pp. 115–76; A.-M. Le Mierre, *La veuve du Malabar, ou L'Empire des Coutumes* (Paris: Duchesne, 1780). For composition history of Humphreys's play, see Edward Cifelli, *David Humphreys* (New York: Twayne, 1982), pp. 72–73. Cifelli takes no note, however, of the publishing and theatrical curiosity discussed below; see Chapter 11. Mariana Starke, *The Widow of Malabar* (London: William Lane, 1791); and Starke, *The Widow of Malabar* (Philadelphia: E. Story, 1792).
4. On the European condemnation of *sati* and the Hindu nationalist response, see Partha Chatterjee, "The Nation and Its Women," in Ranajit Guha, ed., *A Subaltern Studies Reader, 1986–1995* (Minneapolis: University of Minnesota Press, 1997), p. 252.
5. Humphreys, *Widow*, p. 175. Part of the appeal of the play, which also had productions in New York, Baltimore, and Richmond, was "a representation of the Funeral Pile [*sic*] in Flames" (Humphreys, *Widow*, p. 120).
6. Matar, *Turks, Moors and Englishmen*, pp. 3–18, 83–107. I am indebted to Matar's book for some of the details and for lines of thought that inform this paragraph.
7. Meserve, *Emerging Entertainment*, p. 181. Other plays with Native characters had been written in America or by American writers but not acted, including Robert Rogers, *Ponteach* (1766) and Joseph Croswell, *A New World Planted* (1802), the latter of which features a New England Indian named Pocahonte. For a discussion of Croswell's play, see John Seelye, *Memory's Nation: The Place of Plymouth Rock* (Chapel Hill: University of North Carolina Press, 1998), pp. 47–50. This accounting does not take into consideration the many British plays with Native American characters or references, some of which will be discussed below.
8. For the play's use of mood and other interstitial music, see Anne Dhu Shapiro, "Action Music in American Pantomime and Melodrama, 1730–1913," *American Music* 2/4 (1984), 49–72.
9. Moses, "James Nelson Barker," in *Representative Plays*, vol. I, p. 569; Meserve, *Emerging Entertainment*, p. 177. The only modern full-length study of Barker's life and work is Paul H. Musser, *James Nelson Barker* (Philadelphia: University of Pennsylvania Press, 1929), who also provides some background to *Indian Princess*, pp. 19–26. Other overviews of Barker's career include Meserve, *Emerging Entertainment*, pp. 177–84, 259–64, and Gary A. Richardson, *American Drama from the Colonial Period through World War I: A Critical History* (New York: Twayne, 1993), pp. 60–68, although the latter does not discuss the play in question.
10. Dunlap, *History*, vol. II, pp. 313–14.
11. Porter, *With an Air Debonair*, p. 519; Shockley, *Richmond Stage*, p. 295.
12. John W. Crowley, "James Nelson Barker in Perspective," *Educational Theatre Journal* 24 (1972), 366.
13. Joyce Flynn, "Melting Plots: Patterns of Racial and Ethnic Amalgamation in American Drama before Eugene O'Neill," *American Quarterly* 38 (1986), 412–38; Eugene H. Jones, *Native Americans as Shown on the Stage, 1753–1916* (Metuchen, N.J.: Scarecrow Press, 1988), pp. 50–53; Priscilla Sears, *A Pillar of Fire to Follow:*

American Indian Dramas, 1808–1859 (Bowling Green: Bowling Green University Popular Press, 1982), pp. 38–42.

14. Robert S. Tilton, *Pocahontas: The Evolution of an American Narrative* (New York: Cambridge University Press, 1994), pp. 26, 48, 55, 59, 74.
15. Susan Scheckel, 'Domesticating the Drama of Conquest: Barker's Pocahontas on the Popular Stage,' *American Transcendental Quarterly* 10 (1996), 235.
16. James Nelson Barker, *The Indian Princess*, in Richards, ed., *Early American Drama*, p. 117; hereafter *IP*.
17. Smith in his own life was the subject of theatrical renderings in Jacobean playhouses, perhaps inspiring plays by his own use of theatrical metaphors. See Philip L. Barbour, "Captain John Smith and the London Theatre," *Virginia Magazine of History and Biography* 83 (1975), 277–79; Richards, *Theater Enough*, pp. 85–98. Smith's experiences as "performances" are covered by Joseph Fichtelberg, "Colonial Stage: Risk and Promise in John Smith's Virginia," *Early American Literature* 39 (2004), 11–40.
18. In addition to the female characters that Barker added to Smith's Virginia account, the play also mentions Smith's putative female protectors from his European adventures as recorded in his autobiography, *The True Travels, Adventures, and Observations of Captaine John Smith* (1630), ed. Barbour, vol. III, pp. 137–241. See also Scheckel, 'Domesticating," 233.
19. The Walt Disney animated feature *Pocahontas* (1995), in addition to following the mythologized love relationship between the Native woman (not girl) and Smith, preserves the female friend aspect of Barker's play, but for different ends.
20. The best studies of American theatre audiences of the period include Bruce McConachie, *Melodramatic Formations: American Theatre and Society, 1820–1870* (Iowa City: University of Iowa Press, 1992), esp., for the period under review, pp. 1–63; and McConachie, "American Theatre in Context," esp. pp. 126–47. Of course, the theatres were already attracting prostitutes, who became a fixture in American urban playhouses until the 1850s. Claudia D. Johnson, 'That Guilty Third Tier: Prostitution in the Nineteenth-Century American Theater,' in Daniel Walker Howe, ed., *Victorian America* (Philadelphia: University of Pennsylvania Press, 1976), pp. 111–20.
21. Lydia –, letter to Elizabeth D. Whiton, 13 Feb. 1839, ALS William L. Clements Library, University of Michigan.
22. Patricia C. Click, *The Spirit of the Times: Amusements in Nineteenth-Century Baltimore, Norfolk and Richmond* (Charlottesville: University Press of Virginia, 1989), p. 37.
23. As William C. Spengemann has argued, the Americanness of texts in the early period is worth questioning. His inquiry into Smith's first American text, *True Relation*, serves as a lens through which one can question how someone like Barker, writing in the period of independence, can be said to be an "American" playwright. Spengemann, *A New World of Words: Redefining Early American Literature* (New Haven: Yale University Press, 1994), pp. 51–93.
24. Peter Hulme, *Colonial Encounters: Europe and the Native Caribbean, 1492–1797* (London: Methuen, 1986), p. 227, observes the resemblance of the *Inkle and Yarico* story to that of Pocahontas, without specifically mentioning Barker.

25. There is, of course, a tradition of New World settings in English drama, but compared to the total number of plays between, say, 1600 and 1800, the number is quite small. On the linkages between seventeenth-century British plays and the American colonial experience, particularly in the portrayal of Native women, consult Heidi Hutner, *Colonial Women: Race and Culture in Stuart Drama* (New York: Oxford University Press, 2001).
26. *Inkle and Yarico* opened in New York on July 6, 1789, and remained a favorite in American theatres for the next twenty years. Not only did it play multiple times in all the big venues, including Boston, but it appeared in such moderate or small theatres as Norfolk and Edenton, North Carolina. Although not as often acted as *The Poor Soldier*, Colman's comedic opera would have been nearly as well known, both through frequency of acting and American editions of the text. A few playbills survive from the eighteenth century. See, for example, "Mr. Jones's Benefit. Boston Theatre. Friday Evening, November 4, 1796" (Boston, 1796), a performance that included among its cast Susanna Rowson as Patty and her daughter as Narcissa; and "The Last Night of Performance at Edenton, this Season. On Thursday evening, the 20th of July, 1797" (Edenton, N. C., 1797), a production by a very small company led by the redoubtable Thomas Wall. In arguing that Susanna Rowson must have observed two other performances of *IY* in Boston (November 7 and December 2, 1796) while a cast member in the afterpiece to Colman's opera, Steven Epley overlooks her role in *IY* itself. See his otherwise convincing account of Rowson's appropriations of *IY* in her novels: "Alienated, Betrayed, and Powerless: A Possible Connection between *Charlotte Temple* and the Legend of Inkle and Yarico," *Papers on Language and Literature* 38 (2002), 200–22.
27. Texts of many of these and a chronology of versions appear in Lawrence Marsden Price, *Inkle and Yarico Album* (Berkeley: University of California Press, 1937). A somewhat different cluster of texts on the same theme can be found in Frank Felsenstein, ed., *English Trader, Indian Maid: Representing Gender, Race, and Slavery in the New World. An Inkle and Yarico Reader* (Baltimore: Johns Hopkins University Press, 1999).
28. The Native element in the history of the Inkle and Yarico narrative is explored most fully by Hulme, *Colonial Encounters*, pp. 225–63.
29. Price, *Inkle and Yarico Album*, pp. 10, 35–43, 23–24; [Mrs. Weddell?], *Incle and Yarico, a Tragedy* (London, 1742); Edward Jerningham, *Yarico to Inkle, an Epistle* (London: J. Dodsley, 1766), p. 6.
30. George Colman, Jr., *Inkle and Yarico*, p. 8; hereafter *IY*.
31. The color of a Wedgwood teapot is *rosso antico*, or "antique red," something that the practiced connoisseur George Colman, Jr., would have known quite well. Nandini Bhattacharya, "Family Jewels: George Colman's *Inkle and Yarico* and Connoisseurship," *Eighteenth-Century Studies* 34.2 (2001), 207–26.
32. For Daniel O'Quinn, the makeup humor "emphasizes that the sexual exchange between Trudge and Wowski is between two white subjects, one of whom appears before the audience in blackface. Interracial contact, therefore, is staged in the narrative but ultimately contained in performance." "Mercantile Deformities: George Colman's *Inkle and Yarico* and the Racialization of Class Relations," *Theatre Journal* 54 (2002), 405.

33. As discussed in later chapters, the same gender qualification can be found in dramas featuring Irish characters, where a thick brogue is the marker of the male, and in plays featuring African American characters, where a mulatta sometimes plays off darker, male characters as a sign of her accessibility to whites.
34. The complex matter of English and American depiction of Native color, including the eighteenth-century use of "tawny," is pursued by Alden T. Vaughan, 'From White Man to Redskin: Changing Anglo-American Perceptions of the American Indian,' *American Historical Review* 87 (1982), 917–53.
35. Hill, *Jamaican Stage*, p. 80; O'Quinn, 'Mercantile,' 391–92.
36. Jean-Jacques Rousseau, *The Confessions* (New York: Modern Library, [1945]), pp. 13–16.
37. McConachie, *Melodramatic Formations*, p. 1.
38. John Seelye, *Prophetic Waters: The River in Early American Life and Literature* (New York: Oxford University Press, 1977), p. 76.
39. Smith, *Complete Works*, vol. II, p. 151.
40. Paula Gunn Allen, *Pocahontas: Medicine Woman, Spy, Entrepreneur, Diplomat* (San Francisco: HarperSanFrancisco, 2003), pp. 48–50; J. A. Leo Lemay, *The American Dream of Captain John Smith* (Charlottesville: University Press of Virginia, 1991), p. 8.
41. Rebecca Blevins Faery, *Cartographies of Desire: Captivity, Race, and Sex in the Shaping of an American Nation* (Norman: University of Oklahoma Press, 1999), p. 163, notes Davis's erotic predilection.
42. Jeffrey D. Mason, *Melodrama and the Myth of America* (Bloomington: University of Indiana Press, 1993), pp. 23–59.
43. Nelson, *National Manhood*, pp. 61–101.
44. Smith, *Complete Works*, vol. I, pp. 149–50; Lemay, *American Dream*, pp. 73–75.
45. Wiley Sword, *President Washington's Indian War: The Struggle for the Old Northwest, 1790–1795* (Norman: University of Oklahoma Press, 1985), pp. 171–91.
46. Smith, *Generall Historie*, in *Complete Works*, vol. II, pp. 258–62.
47. In 'Virginias Verger,' Purchas says, for instance, that 'Virginia was violently ravished by her owne ruder Natives, yea her Virgin cheekes dyed with the bloud of three Colonies,' and, calling the white settlers 'Christian suters' for Virginia, describes the land as 'like a modest Virgin she is now vailed with wild Coverts and shadie Woods, expecting rather ravishment then Mariage from her Native Savages,' Samuel Purchas, *Hakluytus Posthumus, or Purchas His Pilgrimes*, 20 vols. (Glasgow: McLehose, 1906), vol. XIX, pp. 229, 232, 242.
48. As Roy Harvey Pearce points out, there is little in the way of direct representation of 'savage' behavior in the play, but I would contend that the love talk makes imperialism a subversive, not a confrontational mode of subjugation. That is, Barker shows that Indian bloodthirstiness, while threatening rape, is essentially impotent, powerless against European Eros. Pearce, *The Savages of America: A Study of the Indians and the Idea of Civilization*, rev. edn (Baltimore: Johns Hopkins University Press, 1965), pp. 173–74. For an interesting transhistorical essay on the place of love in world diplomacy as a substitute for war, see Thomas A. Breslin, *Beyond Pain: The Role of Pleasure and Culture in the Making of Foreign Affairs* (Westport, Conn.: Praeger, 2001).

49. Annette Kolodny, *The Lay of the Land: Metaphor as Experience and History in American Life and Letters* (Chapel Hill: University of North Carolina Press, 1975).
50. Faery, *Cartographies*, p. 88.
51. Lemay, *American Dream*, p. 72.
52. Smith, *Complete Works*, vol. II, p. 183.
53. O'Quinn, 'Mercantile,' 395.
54. Smith, *True Travels*, in *Complete Works*, vol. III, pp. 204–6. He describes the king as 'not blacke, as many suppose, but Molata, or tawnie' (p. 205).
55. Matar, *Turks, Moors, and Englishmen*, pp. 109–28.
56. Jones, *Native Americans*, pp. 52–53.

9 American stage Irish in the early republic

1. J. O. Bartley charts frequency of Irish, Scottish, and Welsh characters over two centuries of British drama and notes a steep rise in Irish characters in the period 1760–1800. See the chart preceding the title page and pp. 166–205 of Bartley, *Teague, Shenkin and Sawney: Being an Historical Study of the Earliest Irish, Welsh and Scottish Characters in English Plays* (Cork: Cork University Press, 1954).
2. Carl Wittke discusses the later nineteenth-century history of the type, including the repudiation of the stage Irishman in the early twentieth century, in *The Irish in America* (Baton Rouge: Louisiana State University Press, 1956), pp. 253–63.
3. The best general survey of Irish characters in early American plays remains Kent G. Gallagher, *The Foreigner in Early American Drama: A Study in Attitudes* (The Hague: Mouton, 1966), pp. 115–34. For the period after 1820, see the quantitative analysis of the type by Dale T. Knobel, 'A Vocabulary of Ethnic Perception: Content Analysis of the American Stage Irishman, 1820–1860,' *American Studies* (UK) 15 (1987): 45–71; and a discussion of alterations of the type around mid-century in Gary A. Richardson, 'Poets and Playwrights: 1800–1865,' in Wilmeth and Bigsby, eds., *Cambridge History*, pp. 279–82. Some of the material in this chapter was originally given at the American Society for Eighteenth-Century Studies conference at Notre Dame, April 1998, on a panel organized by Dennis Moore devoted to 'Historicizing the Stage-Irish Figure in America'; other papers included Gary A. Richardson, 'Domesticating the Irish: Brogues, Stage History, and National Identity,' and Amelia Howe Kritzer, 'Irish-Americans in Early Working Class Dramas by Mary Carr Clarke, Charles S. Talbot, and John Minshull.' I am indebted to that panel experience for encouraging my thinking on this topic.
4. R. B. Graves, 'The Stage Irishman among the Irish,' *Theatre History Studies* 1 (1981), 30.
5. Quoted in Maureen Waters, *The Comic Irishman* (Albany: State University of New York Press, 1984), p. 41.
6. Waters, *Comic Irishman*, p. 11; see also Bartley, *Teague*, pp. 206–11.
7. On the history of Irish characters in British theatres, see G. C. Duggan, *The Stage Irishman: A History of the Irish Play and Stage Characters from the Earliest Times* (1937; New York: Blom, 1969); Bartley, *Teague*; Annelise Truniger, *Paddy and the Paycock: A Study of the Stage Irishman from Shakespeare to O'Casey* (Bern: Francke, 1976); and Waters, *Comic Irishman*.

8. For further discussion of British Irish-character plays in the American theatre, see Chapter 12.
9. Robert K. Dodge, 'The Irish Comic Stereotype in the Almanacs of the Early Republic,' *Eire-Ireland* 19 (1984), 111–20.
10. William H. A. Williams, *'Twas Only an Irishman's Dream: The Image of Ireland and the Irish in American Popular Song Lyrics, 1800–1920* (Urbana: University of Illinois Press, 1996), p. 59.
11. For a review of Irish motifs and characters in many of the plays mentioned here, see Duggan, *Stage Irishman*, *passim*; and Bartley, *Teague*, pp. 166–205. For plays on American stages, see listings in such comprehensive works as Odell, *Annals*; Pollack, *Philadelphia Theatre*; Porter, *With an Air Debonair*; Shockley, *Richmond Stage*; and Silverman, *Cultural History*.
12. Michael Ragussis, 'Jews and Other "Outlandish Englishmen": Ethnic Performance and the Invention of British Identity under the Georges,' *Critical Inquiry* 26 (2000), 778, 780.
13. Paul Goring, '"John Bull, pit, box, and gallery, said No!": Charles Macklin and the Limits of Ethnic Resistance on the Eighteenth-Century London Stage,' *Representations* no. 79 (Summer 2002), 62.
14. References are to Forrest, *The Disappointment*, which is based on the 1767 version; hereafter *TD*. In addition to David Mays's introduction, the best and most extended discussion of the play and its music is Virga, *American Opera to 1790*, pp. 17–148.
15. Both Mays and Virga dispute earlier attempts to identify Raccoon as black; see Virga, *American Opera*, pp. 35–36. Each suggests Swedish as the most likely ethnicity for the character.
16. Ragussis, 'Jews,' 778.
17. Pollack, *Philadelphia Theatre*, p. 94.
18. Thomas Sheridan, *The Brave Irishman* (Edinburgh: n.p., 1755).
19. Dunlap, *Darby's Return*. A modern reprint of *The Glory* is found in Moody, ed., *Dramas from the American Theatre*, pp. 94–114. See also Moody's introduction, pages 87–93, and Meserve, *Emerging Entertainment*, p. 240.
20. Nathans, *Early American Theatre*, pp. 92–101.
21. John Murdock, *The Triumphs of Love; or Happy Reconciliation* (Philadelphia: Folwell, 1795): pp. 21, 26, hereafter *TL*.
22. Nathans, *Early American Theatre*, p. 98.
23. Murray, *Traveller Returned*, pp. 103–41; Barker, *Indian Princess*, pp. 109–65. Intratextual references to *Traveller Returned* (*TR*) and *Indian Princess* (*IP*) will be to the editions cited here. See also Kritzer, ed., *Plays by Early American Women*, pp. 12–15. My point is not to say that plays discussed here are the only American ones worth looking at for Irish characters or motifs – Mary Carr's *The Fair Americans* is another in the period that deserves attention – but that, as in other chapters, they represent the divergent aspects of such portrayals in the new republic.
24. Leith Davis argues that the appearance of Thomas Moore's *Irish Melodies* in 1808 (the same year as Barker's play) marks a negotiation between the reality of English bookselling practices and taste and the Anglo-Irish writer Moore's own allegiance to Ireland, with the result that the 'products of a colonized country' become co-opted into British culture ('Irish Bards and English Consumers: Thomas Moore's "Irish Melodies" and the Colonized Nation,' *Ariel* 24/2 (1993), 7). Moore's lyrics became

25. Crèvecoeur, *Letters*, pp. 86–105.
26. Williams, *'Twas Only*, p. 63. Among Federalists especially was a parallel fear of Irish immigration, as expressed by Harrison Gray Otis in 1797, who hoped to prevent the arrival of "hordes of wild Irishmen ... to come here with a view to disturb our tranquillity." Quoted in David A. Wilson, *United Irishmen, United States : Immigrant Radicals in the Early Republic* (Ithaca: Cornell University Press, 1998), p. 48.
27. Cumberland, *Memoirs*, pp. 136–37.
28. Richard J. Dircks, ed., *The Letters of Richard Cumberland* (New York: AMS Press, 1986), p. 64.
29. Charles Macklin, *Love a-la-Mode* (Philadelphia: Taylor, 1791).
30. Graves, "Stage Irishman," 30–31, discusses the derivation of Irish types from classical models.
31. Williams, *'Twas Only*, p. 15.
32. David Garrick, *The Irish Widow*, in *Plays of David Garrick*, ed. Harry William Pedicord and Fredrick Louis Bergmann, 7 vols. (Carbondale: Southern Illinois University Press, 1956–1980), vol. II, pp. 151–84.
33. Gallagher, *Foreigner*, pp. 117–19.
34. Murray does not number scenes; I do it here for convenience.
35. On other relationships among these types, see Grimsted, *Melodrama Unveiled*, pp. 186–92.
36. For a contrast between Murdock's Patrick and Royall Tyler's Jonathan in *The Contrast*, see Nathans, *Early American Theatre*, p. 98.
37. Harris, ed., *Selected Writings*, p. xxxvii.
38. For this discussion, I am relying on Wilson, *United Irishmen*, and the chapter "Irish Radicals" in Michael Durey, *Transatlantic Radicals and the Early American Republic* (Lawrence: University Press of Kansas, 1997), pp. 80–133. Data from Wilson, *United Irishmen*, p. 2.
39. Wilson, *United Irishmen*, p. 104.
40. John Minshull, *Rural Felicity* (New York: n. p., 1801), p. 14; hereafter *RF*. On production, see Odell, *Annals*, vol. II, p. 217. For some reason Odell loathed Minshull's role in New York theatrical history; Meserve, *Emerging Entertainment*, pp. 217–20, attempts to defend him.
41. The texts by Smith mentioned here can be found in John Smith, *Complete Works*.
42. Richards, ed., *Early American Drama*, p. 110. For American productions, see previous chapter.
43. Burk, *The History of Virginia, from its First Settlement to the Present Day*, 4 vols. (Petersburg, Va.: Dickson and Pescud, 1804–16); see also Wilson, *United Irishmen*, pp. 100–3.
44. If Barker did have Burk in mind, then the play, which opened in Philadelphia on April 6, 1808, served as an unintended and perhaps unfortunate epitaph: Burk died in a duel only a few days later, on April 11.
45. For a social history of the place, see Henry Glassie, *Passing the Time in Ballymenone: Culture and History of an Ulster Community* (Philadelphia: University of Pennsylvania Press, 1982).

46. For a summary of the English dramatic version of this type, see Truniger, *Paddy*, pp. 26–32.
47. David Garrick, *The Jubilee*, in Pedicord and Bergmann (eds.), *Plays of David Garrick*, vol. II, pp. 97–126.
48. Porter, *With an Air Debonair*, p. 463.
49. Although Barker's play is not discussed explicitly in her article, Joyce Flynn's term 'racial and ethnic amalgamation' fits the situation in *Indian Princess* ('Melting Pots,' 417).
50. Charles Macklin, *The True-Born Irishman, or Irish Fine Lady* (Philadelphia: Spotswood, 1784).
51. That said, however, it should be pointed out that later cartoon depictions of Irish people often gave them apelike features, forcing Anglo-Americans to perceive them as not quite white and human.

10 Black theatre, white theatre, and the stage African

1. Helen M. Morgan, ed., *A Season in New York 1801: Letters of Harriet and Maria Trumbull* (Pittsburgh: University of Pittsburgh Press, 1969), p. 132.
2. The books by two scholars supersede all previous attempts to account for the African Theatre: Thompson, *Documentary*; and White, *Stories*.
3. Thompson, *Documentary*, pp. 26, 29; White, *Stories*, pp. 68–125.
4. White, *Stories*, pp. 127–84.
5. White, *Stories*, p. 215.
6. Thompson, *Documentary*, pp. 125–52; White, *Stories*, pp. 127–66.
7. White, *Stories*, pp. 200–2.
8. Moody, ed., *Dramas from the American Theatre*, p. 147.
9. Oral Sumner Coad, 'The Plays of Samuel Woodworth,' *Sewanee Review* 27 (1919), 168–69; Moody, ed., *Dramas from the American Theatre*, pp. 149–51. For a sample of contemporary response in London to Silsbee's Jonathan, see Portia Kernodle, 'Yankee Types on the London Stage, 1824–1880,' *Speech Monographs* 14 (1947), 141–42.
10. Richard M. Dorson, 'The Yankee on the Stage – A Folk Hero of American Drama,' *New England Quarterly* 13 (1940), 467–93.
11. Grimsted, *Melodrama Unveiled*, p. 187.
12. Grimsted, *Melodrama Unveiled*, p. 188.
13. Thompson, *Documentary*, p. 147.
14. On minstrelsy, see, for example, Carl Wittke, *Tambo and Bones – A History of the American Minstrel Stage* (Durham, N.C.: Duke University Press, 1930); Constance Rourke, 'Traditions for a Negro Literature,' *The Roots of American Culture* (New York: Harcourt, Brace, 1942), 262–74; Alan W. C. Green, "Jim Crow,' 'Zip Coon': The Northern Origins of Negro Minstrelsy," *Massachusetts Review* 11 (1970), 385–97; Robert C. Toll, *Blacking Up: The Minstrel Show in Nineteenth-Century America* (New York: Oxford University Press, 1974); and Dale Cockrell, *Demons of Disorder: Early Blackface Minstrels and Their World* (Cambridge: Cambridge University Press, 1997).
15. For a survey of black characters in nineteenth-century plays, see Richard Moody, *America Takes the Stage: Romanticism in American Drama and Theatre, 1750–1900*

(Bloomington: Indiana University Press, 1955), pp. 60–78. Grimsted rightly identifies the stage Negro as a "low comedy" type, akin to the Yankee and the Irishman (*Melodrama Unveiled*, pp. 190–92), but plot resolutions more often favor the latter two while denying to the black on stage much in the way of "success."

16. Toni Morrison, *Playing in the Dark: Whiteness and Literary Imagination* (New York: Vintage, 1993), p. 52.
17. Mark Twain, *Pudd'nhead Wilson and Those Extraordinary Twins*, ed. Malcolm Bradbury (New York: Penguin, 1969), p. 303. The eponymous twins are conjoined, Luigi and Angelo, one a dark Italian, the other light. On the way in which the Italian characters register the racial politics of the book, see Joseph P. Cosco, *Imagining Italians: The Clash of Romance and Race in American Perceptions, 1880–1910* (Albany: State University of New York Press, 2003), pp. 143–70.
18. In a traditional formulation of the identity issue in *Forest Rose* and similar plays, Winifred Morgan remarks, "The Jonathan character and the genteel American hero together represented American virtue repulsing the dangers of European moral decay embodied in the villian [sic]" (Winifred Morgan, *An American Icon: Brother Jonathan and American Identity* (Newark: University of Delaware Press, 1988), p. 47). The point here is that such surface readings – no doubt intended by the play's author – mask other, more confusing messages sent by the signs of Yankee virtue in a language of dishonesty and abuse.
19. On the appeal to, if not outright portrayal of, yeomanry in the roles played by Edwin Forrest in the years immediately following *The Forest Rose*, see McConachie, *Melodramatic Formations*, pp. 104–7. For a brief discussion of the play in terms of the use of typed characters as figures of non-European identity on the American stage, see Jürgen Wolter, "Die Helden der Nation: Yankee, Pionier und Indianer als nationale Stereotypen im amerikanischen Drama vor dem Bürgerkrieg," *Amerikastudien* 24 (1979), 250.
20. On Jonathan's use of a "tag," although not the one cited here, see Morgan, *American Icon*, pp. 43–44; additional commentary on *Forest Rose*, pp. 46–49.
21. George Samuel Schuyler, "Our Greatest Gift to America," in Lauter *et al.*, eds., *Heath Anthology*, vol. II, pp. 1611–15.
22. Francis Hodge, *Yankee Theatre: The Image of America on the Stage, 1825–1850* (Austin: University of Texas Press, 1964), p. 58.
23. Hodge, *Yankee Theatre*, p. 77.
24. Clifford Ashby, however, has found one small piece of evidence to suggest that on rare occasions, an African American may have appeared in person with a white company in a non-speaking role. See Ashby, "A Black Actor on the Eighteenth-Century Boston Stage?" *Theatre Survey* 28/2 (1987), 101–2.
25. S. Foster Damon, "The Negro in Early American Songsters," *Papers of the Bibliographical Society of America* 28 (1934), 132–63.
26. This list of musical plays only, like the list of American plays to follow, is not meant to be exhaustive for dramas with Africanist characters. Of the British plays mentioned, *Inkle and Yarico* is discussed in Chapter 8; *The Romp* (an abridged version of Bickerstaff's *Love in the City*) and *Irishman in London* are dealt with in Chapter 12.
27. Of course, as a number of scholars have recently pointed out, British playwrights from Shakespeare forward may have had firsthand experience with Anglo-Africans

living in England. See, for example, Imtiaz Habib, *Shakespeare and Race: Postcolonial Praxis in the Early Modern Period* (Lanham, Md.: University Press of America, 2000).
28. Tyler, *The Contrast*, p. 12; hereafter *TC*.
29. Imtiaz Habib, "Hel's Perfect Character' or The Blackamoor Maid in Early Modern English Drama: The Postcolonial Cultural History of a Dramatic Type," *LIT* 11 (2000), 283.
30. Katherine Schall Jarvis, 'Royall Tyler's Lyrics for *May Day in Town*," *Harvard Library Bulletin* 23 (1969), 191.
31. Since *surdus* in Latin means 'deaf,' Tyler is having his little joke.
32. Jarvis, 'Royall Tyler's Lyrics," 193.
33. Jarvis, 'Royall Tyler's Lyrics," 196.
34. Jarvis, 'Royall Tyler's Lyrics," 198.
35. J. Robinson, *The Yorker's Stratagem; or, Banana's Wedding* (New York: Swords, 1792), p. 9.
36. Rarely discussed in the historical or critical literature, Robinson's play is examined for its reflection of Hamiltonian economics in Sean X. Goudie, 'The West Indies, Commerce, and a *Play* for U. S. Empire: Recovering J. Robinson's *The Yorker's Stratagem*," *Early American Literature*, 40 (2005), 1–35.
37. Murdock, *Triumphs of Love*, p. 19; hereafter *TL*.
38. On the politics behind the George–Sambo relationship, see Nathans, *Early American Theatre*, p. 98.
39. John Murdock, *The Politicians; or, A State of Things* (Philadelphia: "for the author," 1798), p. 21.
40. William Milns, *All in a Bustle; or The New House* (New York: Literary Printing Office, 1798), p. 15.
41. Susan E. Klepp, "Seasoning and Society: Racial Differences in Mortality in Eighteenth-Century Philadelphia," *William and Mary Quarterly* 51 (1994), 473–506.
42. Ann Kellan, 'Bones Reveal Little-Known Tale of New York Slaves," CNN, Feb. 12, 1998, www.cnn.com/TECH/9082/12t_t/burial.ground/; Harry Brunius, 'African Burial Ground under New York Streets," *Christian Science Monitor*, June 17, 1999, csmweb2.emcweb.com/durable/1999/06/17/p16s1.htm; Andrea Frohne, 'Commemorating the African Ground in New York City: Spirituality of Space in Contemporary Art Works,' *Ijele: Art eJournal of the African World* 1.1 (2000), www.ijele.com/ijele/vol1.1/frohne.html; 'Do the Dead Tell Tales After All?:" National Library of Medicine *Newsline* 56.1–2 (2001), www.nlm.nih.gov/pubs/nlmnews/janjun01/jj01_dead.html. The head conservator of the dig has co-authored a young adult title with a chapter on the conditions the bones reflect. See Joyce Hansen and Gary McGowan, *Breaking Ground, Breaking Silence: The Story of New York's African Burial Ground* (New York: Holt, 1998), pp. 75–80.
43. For the situation facing blacks in northern areas in the early nineteenth century, see the summary discussion in James Oliver Horton and Lois E. Horton, *In Hope of Liberty: Culture, Community, and Protest among Northern Free Blacks, 1700–1860* (New York: Oxford University Press, 1997), pp. 77–124; for the situation specifically in New York, including abuse and resistance to it, as well as the ending of slavery, consult White, *Somewhat More Independent*.

44. Shane White and Graham White, *Stylin': African American Expressive Culture from its Beginnings to the Zoot Suit* (Ithaca: Cornell University Press, 1998), p. 122.
45. Samuel Woodworth, *The Forest Rose*, in Moody, ed., *Dramas from the American Theatre*, p. 159; hereafter *FR*.
46. Moody, *America Takes the Stage*, p. 120.
47. Meserve, *Emerging Entertainment*, p. 239.
48. White, *Somewhat More Independent*, p. 71. White suggests, however, that whereas Irish in almanacs are always under attack, blacks are sometimes portrayed sympathetically (pp. 72–73).
49. John Saillant, "Before Douglass: Race and 'the Nation of Nantucket,'" an essay presented at the James Bradford Ames Symposium on African American History, Nantucket, Massachusetts, June 20, 1998, and supported by an Ames Fellowship for Research on Black Life and History on Nantucket. The author wishes to thank Professor Saillant for permission to quote from his manuscript.
50. Coad, "Plays of Samuel Woodworth," 175.
51. Rosemarie Bank, *Theatre Culture in America, 1825–1860* (Cambridge: Cambridge University Press, 1997), pp. 36–37, briefly and cogently discusses the play for its transcendental pastoralism, for example, but omits any discussion of race.
52. Quoted by Grimsted, *Melodrama Unveiled*, p. 188.
53. Moody, ed., *Dramas from the American Theatre*, p. 147.
54. Mason, *Melodrama and the Myth of America*, p. 90.
55. *The Forest Rose* is not the first play in American theatre to use the device of the disguised black female in the lover's role. Damon, "Negro in Early American Songsters," 135, quotes British General John Burgoyne's *The Blockade of Boston* (1775), whose African American character, Fan Fan, sings in the finale, "Tho' in Public you scoff, I see many a Spark/Would tink me a sweet pretty Girl in the Dark."
56. Given some of the 'racy' badinage in the play, 'glove' here may suggest 'condom' (made from sheep intestine) and thus once more link interracial love to sexual perversion.
57. Anna Cora Mowatt, *Fashion*, in Richards, ed., *Early American Drama*, p. 323.
58. Lawrence La Bree [sic], *Ebenezer Venture; or, Advertising for a Wife* (New York: Samuel French, n.d.), p. 7; Dorson, "Yankee on the Stage," 469. Venture also refers to a black servant as "Mr. Blackball" (La Bree, *Venture*, p. 3).
59. I do not mean to say that this is all that *Fashion* says; indeed, Zeke shows signs of a more complex characterization, where his own awareness of the Tiffanys' pretense enters into his performance as a man in livery. But Trueman, as voice of the play's moral and the one who restores the Tiffanys to virtue, despite his own antipathies to the treatment of Zeke, still speaks what the audience thinks; such a reductionism as "grinning nigger," even if meant sympathetically, must be considered in the overall assessment of the play's racial vocabulary.
60. Dion Boucicault, *The Octoroon*, in Richards, ed., *Early American Drama*, p. 491.
61. Saillant, "Before Douglass"; Joanne Pope Melish, *Disowning Slavery: Gradual Emancipation and 'Race' in New England, 1780–1860* (Ithaca, N.Y.: Cornell University Press, 1998). See especially Melish's chapter on "racial" humor and broadsides in New England in the 1820s, pp. 163–209.

62. On Garrison's learning curve and the resistance to racial equality among many abolitionist groups, see the otherwise sympathetic biography by Henry Mayer, *All on Fire: William Lloyd Garrison and the Abolition of Slavery* (New York: St. Martin's, 1998).
63. Aiken, *Uncle Tom's Cabin*, p. 388.
64. Tyler, *The Contrast*, p. 25.
65. Davy Crockett, *The Crockett Almanacs*, in Lauter *et al.*, eds., *Heath Anthology*, vol. I, pp. 1434, 1433.
66. Harriet E. Wilson, *Our Nig; or, Sketches from the Life of a Free Black*, ed. Henry Louis Gates, Jr. (New York: Vintage, 1983), p. 129. Many of the novel's details have been verified with regard to the family that employed author Harriet Wilson as a servant. Barbara A. White, "'Our Nig' and the She-Devil: New Information about Harriet Wilson and the 'Bellmont' Family," *American Literature* 65 (1993), 19–52.
67. Melish, *Disowning Slavery*, p. 284.

Part III Theatre, culture, and reflected identity

1. Quoted in George C. Rogers, Jr., *Charleston in the Age of the Pinckneys* (Norman: University of Oklahoma Press, 1969), pp. 109–10.

11 Tales of the Philadelphia Theatre

1. Brooks McNamara, *The American Playhouse in the Eighteenth Century* (Cambridge, Mass.: Harvard University Press, 1969); Tom Goyens, "Theater in Williamsburg: A Summary Report on the Second and Third Playhouse (1751–1787)," unpublished report (Williamsburg, Va.: Colonial Williamsburg Foundation Research Division, October 2001); Lisa E. Fischer and Tom Goyens, *The Search for the 'old Theatre, near the Capitol': Archaeological Investigations of the Douglass Theater, Williamsburg, Virginia* (Williamsburg, Va.: Department of Archaeological Research, Colonial Williamsburg, 2005), forthcoming.
2. Odai Johnson, "(Im)Material Witness and Narrativity in the Colonial American Theatre," unpublished manuscript.
3. Anna Cora Mowatt, *Mimic Life; or, Before and Behind the Curtain*, ed. Jeffrey H. Richards (Acton, Mass.: Copley, 2000).
4. Among numerous studies in this regard, see Ray B. Browne, "Popular Theater in *Moby Dick*," in Browne *et al.* (eds.), *New Voices in American Studies* (Lafayette, Ind.: Purdue Studies, 1966), pp. 89–100; Jeffrey Hamilton Richards, "Hawthorne and the Metaphor of Theatre" (Ph.D. dissertation, University of North Carolina, 1982); Don Loftis Latham, "Hawthorne's 'Coup de Théâtre': Theatricality and Self-Performance in the American Romances" (Ph.D. dissertation, University of Georgia, 1995); Alan L. Ackerman, Jr., *The Portable Theater: American Literature and the Nineteenth-Century Stage* (Baltimore: Johns Hopkins University Press, 1999).
5. Hannah Webster Foster, *The Coquette*, ed. Cathy N. Davidson (New York: Oxford University Press, 1986); Julia Stern, *The Plight of Feeling: Sympathy and Dissent in the Early American Novel* (University of Chicago Press, 1997), pp. 113–30; Jeffrey H. Richards, "The Politics of Seduction: Theater, Sexuality, and National Virtue in

the Novels of Hannah Foster," in Della Pollock (ed.), *Exceptional Spaces: Essays in Performance and History* (Chapel Hill: University of North Carolina Press, 1998), pp. 238–57; C. Leiren Mower, "Bodies in Labor: Sole Proprietorship and the Labor of Conduct in *The Coquette*," *American Literature* 74 (2002), 315–44.

6. J. H. Powell, *Bring Out Your Dead: The Great Plague of Yellow Fever in Philadelphia in 1793* (Philadelphia: University of Pennsylvania Press, 1949); Philip Gould, "Race, Commerce, and the Literature of Yellow Fever in Early National Philadelphia," *Early American Literature* 35.2 (2000), 157–86.

7. On *Ormond* and identity, contrast Roland Hagenbüchle, "American Literature and the Nineteenth-Century Crisis in Epistemology: The Example of Charles Brockden Brown," *Early American Literature* 23.2 (1988), 138, but see also W. M. Verhoeven, "Displacing the Discontinuous; Or, The Labyrinths of Reason: Fictional Design and Eighteenth-Century Thought in Charles Brockden Brown's *Ormond*," *Rewriting the Dream: Reflections on the Changing American Literary Canon*, ed. W. M. Verhoeven (Amsterdam: Rodopi, 1992), pp. 202–29.

8. Peter Kafer, "Charles Brockden Brown and Revolutionary Philadelphia: An Imagination in Context," *Pennsylvania Magazine of History and Biography* 116 (1992), 467–98.

9. Brown apparently wrote *Ormond* in one six-weeks period of intense activity, from mid-November to the end of December. Steven Watts, *The Romance of Real Life: Charles Brockden Brown and the Origins of American Culture* (Baltimore: Johns Hopkins University Press, 1994), p. 72. The issues engendered by such rapid composition are taken up by Paul C. Rodgers, Jr., "Brown's *Ormond*: The Fruits of Improvisation," *American Quarterly* 26 (1974), 4–22.

10. Rosenthal, Introduction, in Bernard Rosenthal, ed., *Critical Essays on Charles Brockden Brown* (Boston: G. K. Hall, 1981), pp. 2, 10. See also the review from the *European Magazine* (1824) reprinted in Rosenthal, ed., *Critical Essays*, pp. 41–47.

11. For example, William Hedges claims that Brown's novels in general are about "the loss of identity, or, even more, the inability to find or create one": "Charles Brockden Brown and the Culture of Contradictions," *Early American Literature* 9 (1974), 107.

12. Shortly after he completed *Ormond*, Brown "took a geographic turn" in periodical essays: Martin Brückner, "Geography, Reading, and the World of Novels in the Early Republic," in Klaus H. Schmidt and Fritz Fleischmann, eds., *Early America Re-Explored: New Readings in Colonial, Early National, and Antebellum Culture* (New York: Lang, 2000), p. 387.

13. W. M. Verhoeven, "'This blissful period of intellectual liberty': Transatlantic Radicalism and Enlightened Conservatism in Brown's Early Writings," in Philip Barnard, Mark L. Kamrath, and Stephen Shapiro, eds., *Revising Charles Brockden Brown: Culture, Politics, and Sexuality in the Early Republic* (Knoxville: University of Tennessee Press, 2004), p. 24.

14. Stephen Burroughs, *Memoirs* (Hanover, N. H.: Benjamin True, 1798). Other editions followed, including one in 1811. On the problematic aspects of identity raised by Burroughs, see Daniel E. Williams, "In Defense of Self: Author and Authority in the *Memoirs of Stephen Burroughs*," *Early American Literature* 25 (1990), 96–122; Stephen Carl Arch, *After Franklin: The Emergence of Autobiography in Post-Revolutionary America, 1780–1830* (Hanover, N. H.: University Press of New England, 2001),

pp. 113–36; Larry Cebula, 'A Counterfeit Identity: The Notorious Life of Stephen Burroughs,' *The Historian* 64 (2002), 317–33; and Stephen Mihm, 'The Alchemy of Self: Stephen Burroughs and the Counterfeit Economy of the Early Republic,' *Early American Studies* 2 (2004), 123–59.
15. As in, for example, Henry Carey, *The Honest Yorkshire-Man* (London: Gilliver, 1736).
16. Verhoeven, 'Displacing the Discontinuous,' p. 212.
17. Watts, *Romance*, p. 95.
18. William J. Scheick sees the problem as one of uncertain origins, both in the epistemological sense and in the way, for instance, that Brown establishes such motifs as that of the orphan in the novel: Scheick, 'The Problem of Origination in Brown's *Ormond*,' in Rosenthal, ed., *Critical Essays*, pp. 126–41.
19. On anti-Scottish feelings, see Peter Ross, *The Scot in America* (New York: Raeburn, 1896), pp. 103–5; William M. Dabney, 'Letters from Norfolk: Scottish Merchants View the Revolutionary Crisis,' in Darrett B. Rutman, ed., *The Old Dominion: Essays for Thomas Perkins Abernethy* (Charlottesville: University Press of Virginia, 1964), pp. 109–21; Rogers, *Charleston*, pp. 89–90; Robert M. Weir, *Colonial South Carolina: A History* (Millwood, N.Y.: KTO Press, 1983), p. 286.
20. William Lee, quoted in J. H. Soltow, 'Scottish Traders in Virginia, 1750–1775,' *Economic History Review* 12 (1959), 83.
21. The identity problems faced by one immigrant Scot to colonial America tell much of this tale. Klaus H. Schmidt, 'A Scotsman in British America; or, Up against Provincialism: The Construction of Individual and Collective Identities in Dr. Alexander Hamilton's *Itinerarium*,' in Schmidt and Fleischmann, eds., *Early America Re-Explored*, pp. 151–81.
22. Stern, *Plight of Feeling*, pp. 165ff. On the matter of observation in the novel, see also Bill Christophersen, 'Charles Brockden Brown's *Ormond*: The Secret Witness as Ironic Motif,' *Modern Language Studies* 10/2 (1980), 37–41.
23. On their alleged 'delight' in violence, see Arthur G. Kimball, 'Savages and Savagism: Brockden Brown's Dramatic Irony,' *Studies in Romanticism* 6 (1967), 217–19.
24. The most concise discussion of this connection is that of Robert S. Levine, 'Villainy and the Fear of Conspiracy in Charles Brockden Brown's *Ormond*,' *Early American Literature* 15 (1980), 124–40.
25. Julia Stern, 'The State of 'Women' in *Ormond*; or, Patricide in the New Nation,' in Barnard, Kamrath, and Shapiro, eds., *Revising Charles Brockden Brown*, p. 195.
26. Paul A. Gilje and Howard B. Rock, '"Sweep O! Sweep O!": African American Chimney Sweeps and Citizenship in the New Nation,' *William and Mary Quarterly* 51 (1994), 507–38.
27. Elizabeth Jane Wall Hinds, *Private Property: Charles Brockden Brown's Gendered Economics of Virtue* (Newark: University of Delaware Press, 1997), p. 67.
28. Charles Brockden Brown, *Ormond; or The Secret Witness*, ed. Mary Chapman (Peterborough, Ontario: Broadview, 1999), p. 94, hereafter *O*. The plays performed on opening night, Feb. 17, 1794, were John O'Keeffe's comic opera, *The Castle of Andalusia*, and Elizabeth Cowley's farce, *Who's the Dupe?* – works as far from referring to the horrors of the yellow fever epidemic in Philadelphia as one could imagine.

29. In addition to the numerous observations in Stern on theatricality in the text, see Heather Smyth, "Imperfect Disclosures: Cross-Dressing and Containment in Charles Brockden Brown's *Ormond*," in Merril D. Smith, ed., *Sex and Sexuality in Early America* (New York: New York University Press, 1998), pp. 253–54.
30. On the heterosocial conversation world of the Friendly Club circle, see Fredrika J. Teute, "A 'Republic of Intellect': Conversation and Criticism among the Sexes in 1790s New York," in Barnard, Kamrath, and Shapiro, eds., *Revising Charles Brockden Brown*, pp. 149–81.
31. Pollock, *Philadelphia Theatre*, p. 221, lists the performance without noting it is by Starke, but prints the cast list, which is Starke's, not Humphreys's. The reasons for switching to Starke may go beyond simply the preference of an English over an American version of a French play. In Humphreys, the lead Europeans are French; in Starke, English. Given the backlash against France at the height of the Terror, Wignell no doubt felt it prudent to play to English rather than French sympathies. See also Chapter 8. On the problems faced by Philadelphia and Boston in staging plays in the context of split American attitudes toward the French Revolution, see Nathans, *Early American Theatre*, pp. 77–83.
32. Statistics have been generated from the chronological lists of advertised performances in Pollock. All further references to Philadelphia performances come from this source.
33. Nicholas Rowe, *The Fair Penitent*, ed. Goldstein, p. 48.
34. One other tragedy featuring a woman as the central figure, Thomas Southerne's *Isabella*, also appeared twice in the 1794 season, although in altered form via Garrick and Hopkins, the Drury Lane prompter. Ruth Harsha McKenzie, "Organization, Production, and Management at the Chestnut Street Theatre, Philadelphia from 1791 to 1820" (Ph.D. dissertation, Stanford University, 1952), p. 89.
35. Henry Brooke, *Gustavus Vasa, The Deliverer of His Country* (London: Dodsley, 1739).
36. Joseph Addison, *Cato*, in *The Miscellaneous Works*, ed. A. C. Guthkelch, 2 vols. (London: Bell, 1914), vol. I, pp. 335–420.
37. Otway, *Venice Preserved*, pp. 315–94.
38. Branson, *These Fiery Frenchified Dames*, pp. 55–99.
39. The connection between Martinette and Gannett is noticed by Gustafson, "Genders of Nationalism," pp. 393–95. For a more feminist reading of this and the other rape scenes than I provide, see Hana Layson, "Rape and Revolution: Feminism, Antijacobinism, and the Politics of Injured Innocence in Brockden Brown's *Ormond*," *Early American Studies* 2 (2004), 160–91.
40. For Heather Smyth, "Imperfect Disclosures," 255, the costuming of such characters as Martinette and Ormond is "frightening in [its] implications of social chaos."
41. Stern, "State of 'Women,'" p. 206.

12 A British or an American tar?

1. Among the standard theatre histories, there is little to no accurate information on the professional theatre in Norfolk. Only a few writers have attempted to correct the record. A brief but serviceable overview of Norfolk theatre after the

Revolution can be found in George Holbert Tucker, *Norfolk Highlights 1584–1881* (Norfolk: Norfolk Historical Society, 1972), pp. 52–54; for the 1790s, see also Thomas C. Parramore, Peter C. Stewart, and Tommy L. Bogger, *Norfolk: The First Four Centuries* (Charlottesville: University Press of Virginia, 1994), pp. 108–9. The pioneer scholar of the eighteenth-century Norfolk theatre is Susanne Ketchum Sherman, who published two articles in the early 1950s, then began assembling a history of early Southern theatre with a focus on the West Company circuit. Sherman prepared a partial manuscript before she died in 1966, published later by her family as *Comedies Useful: Southern Theatre History, 1775–1812*, a copy of which led me to inquire further into the particular conditions in Norfolk. The other key text is Lucy Blandford Pilkinton, "Theatre in Norfolk, Virginia, 1788–1812." Inspired herself by Sherman – indeed, she helped the Sherman family pull together *Comedies Useful* – Pilkinton prepared for her dissertation an extraordinary document, including in her vast appendices every piece of contemporary printed material she could find having to do with the theatre in post-Revolutionary Norfolk before the War of 1812. In the body of her dissertation, Pilkinton takes earlier scholars to task for either ignoring or, even worse, misrepresenting the importance of Norfolk. Unfortunately, Pilkinton also died (1994) before she could see any of her dissertation into print. Although my work is different from either hers or Sherman's, which are true theatre histories whereas this chapter is something of a hybrid of history and literary and cultural criticism, I wish to express my debt to both scholars for their heretofore largely unacknowledged labors.

On Norfolk after the war, Thomas J. Wertenbaker, *Norfolk: Historic Southern Port* (Durham, N.C.: Duke University Press, 1931), pp. 81–95; and Parramore, Stewart, and Bogger, *Norfolk*, pp. 119–31. On the Norfolk theatre building, Pilkinton, "Theatre in Norfolk," pp. 127–29.

2. The 1790 population of the city was 2,957, which included 1,294 slaves and 61 free blacks; the 1800 census showed a total population of 6,816, with 2,614 slaves and 352 free persons of color. Tommy L. Bogger, *Free Blacks in Norfolk, Virginia, 1790–1860: The Darker Side of Freedom* (Charlottesville: University Press of Virginia, 1997), p. 8.
3. Pilkinton, "Theatre in Norfolk," pp. 30–31.
4. The partisan plights of New York, Boston, and Philadelphia theatres for the late 1790s are examined by Nathans, *Early American Theatre*, pp. 150–69.
5. Citations to Norfolk newspapers, unless cited otherwise, are from my own photocopies; where legibility in the original was a problem, I have checked them against transcripts in Pilkinton, "Theatre in Norfolk."
6. Although tracing the activities of stage orchestra musicians is even more difficult than those of seemingly phantom actors, there is enough information in the record to show that Mr. Decker, a leader of the orchestra, was capable of composing original music (Pilkinton, "Theatre in Norfolk," p. 470).
7. Philip H. Highfill, Jr., Kalman A. Burnim, and Edward A. Langhans, *A Biographical Dictionary of Actors, Actresses, Musicians, Dancers, Managers and Other Stage Personnel in London, 1660–1800*, 16 vols. (Carbondale: Southern Illinois University Press, 1973–1993), vol. XV, pp. 373–75.

8. Pilkinton, "Theatre in Norfolk," pp. 7–9, 187, includes comments by contemporaries in praise of Ann West Bignall's ability including letters by the Virginia justice and historian John Marshall.
9. My information on actors comes from a gleaning of theatre histories as well as the information assembled by Pilkinton related to their Norfolk roles, with as much cross-checking as possible in order to weed out obvious errors. The ones most frequently used include Odell, *Annals*, vols. I and II; Pollock, *Philadelphia Theatre*; David Ritchey, *A Guide to the Baltimore Stage in the Eighteenth Century* (Westport, Conn.: Greenwood, 1982); Eola Willis, *The Charleston Stage in the XVIII Century* (1933; New York: Blom, 1968). Others are identified where necessary.

   Otherwise, there is no convenient or reliable set of biographical notices for the actors who appeared on American stages before 1800. Reference works like Gerald Bordman, *The Oxford Companion to American Theatre*, 2nd edn (New York: Oxford University Press, 1992), or Weldon Durham, ed., *American Theatre Companies, 1749–1887* (New York: Greenwood, 1986), while useful, have incomplete, inaccurate, or more likely, no information on the performers in the Southern theatres. The most authoritative reference source to date is Highfill, Burnim, and Langhans, *Biographical Dictionary*, which does include some information on British actors who later emigrated to the United States, but that source does not include appearances in Norfolk.
10. As Pilkinton notes, the chief historian of theatre in Virginia, Martin Staples Shockley, *Richmond Stage*, sees the West company almost entirely through the lens of the capital, as if it were the Richmond company. Not only did West and Bignall, and then West alone, play longer seasons in Charleston than in Richmond, but as Pilkinton notes, West built his permanent home in Norfolk, and when he played Norfolk, often did so for longer seasons than those in Richmond. However, although Shockley also has errors in his identification of personnel among the Wests, his book still remains an essential source for studying early national theatre in Virginia.

    As for the Wests' involvement with Charleston, in addition to relevant chapters in Willis, see Mary Julia Curtis, "The Early Charleston Stage, 1703–1798" (Ph.D. dissertation, University of Indiana, 1968); however, it should be noted that Pilkinton identifies a number of errors in Curtis connected with the Wests, especially in regard to Norfolk.
11. On West's death, see Sherman, *Comedies Useful*, pp. 149–51.
12. After 1806, the company ceased to function as the Virginia Company. Margaretta West remained "proprietress" of the Norfolk Theatre until her death in 1810, but probably left the daily decisions for the acting company to Green after 1804. Green meanwhile joined forces with Alexander Placide in 1809 to create the Charleston and Virginia Company, which then played in Norfolk, among its other venues, until the company's demise after the tragic Richmond fire of 1811.
13. Sherman, *Comedies Useful*, pp. 153–71; Pilkinton, "Theatre in Norfolk," pp. 241–79; Jane Kathleen Curry, *Nineteenth-Century American Women Theatre Managers* (Westport, Conn.: Greenwood, 1994), p. 12.
14. Dunlap, *History*, vol. I, pp. 174–77.
15. Pilkinton, "Theatre in Norfolk," pp. 222–23.

16. Johnson, '(Im)Material Witness,' provides the kind of reading of the scanty material record that will be necessary to make better sense of the role physical properties played in the production and choice of plays in the colonial and early national periods.
17. The West Company put on *The Purse* four times; one other performance in 1800 was put on by a small troupe led by Marlborough Hamilton, a one-time player with West.
18. Burk's play was written on board ship from Ireland to his adopted country, so its Americanness is by virtue of its subject matter and the intent of the author to emigrate. One other piece, the pantomime *The Siege of Quebec; or The Death of General Wolfe*, while dealing with a North American subject, was created for the English stage by Giles Barrett and premiered in London in 1784.
19. Samuel Foote, *The Lyar*, in *Dramatic Works*, 2 vols. (1809; New York: Blom, 1969), vol. 1.
20. The Norfolk critic remarked of M'Kenzie that he 'spoke the Scottish language with the accent so well, that we forgot the distance across the Atlantic, and fancied ourselves (for the time) in the Highlands of Scotland.' *Norfolk Herald and Public Advertiser* June 28, 1800, hereafter called *Norfolk Herald* and abbreviated *NH*. The newspaper has several similar names during the period, but I refer to all as *NH*.
21. Highfill, Burnim, and Langhans, *Biographical Dictionary*, vol. XIV, pp. 338–40; Willis, *Charleston Stage*, pp. 187–92.
22. *NH* July 1, 1800.
23. A writer for the *Norfolk Herald* complained about 'reservoirs of putrid substances,' 'piles of dirty and foetid substances,' and 'poisonous exhalations' in the city. June 17, 1797. See also Parramore, Stewart, and Bogger, *Norfolk*, pp. 106–8.
24. George Colman, Jr., *The Mountaineers* (Dublin: M'Donnel, 1794), p. 8.
25. Elizabeth Inchbald, *The Mogul Tale; or, The Descent of the Balloon* (London: Powell, 1796), pp. 19, 21; hereafter *MT*.
26. Joseph Mosier (curator of Myers Papers), 'Myers Family Scorecard,' unpublished document (Norfolk: Chrysler Museum of Art, 2004).
27. Tucker, *Norfolk Highlights*, pp. 82, 101; Moses Jacob Barak, 'Moses Myers of Norfolk' (M.A. thesis, University of Richmond, 1954), p. 62.
28. Sherman, *Comedies Useful*, pp. 283–84 n.262; Pilkinton, 'Theatre in Norfolk,' pp. 36–37.
29. Another Dibdin portrayal of the stage Jew, *Family Quarrels*, prompted London Jews to protest in 1803. Ragussis, 'Jews and Other 'Outlandish Englishmen,'' 777.
30. Dibdin denies having created his character based on Cumberland's but does claim to have submitted the manuscript to the more prominent author for revisions so as to minimize the likeness. Thomas Dibdin, Advertisement, *The Jew and the Doctor* (London: Longman and Rees, 1800), n.p.; hereafter *JD*.
31. *NH* March 15, 1803, quoted in Pilkinton, 'Theatre in Norfolk,' p. 49. See also Heather Nathans, 'A Much Maligned People: Jews on and off the Stage in the Early American Republic,' *Early American Studies* 2/2 (2004), 310–42.
32. Bogger, *Free Blacks in Norfolk*, p. 8.
33. The lives of black sailors at this time are best covered in W. Jeffrey Bolster, *Black Jacks: African American Seamen in the Age of Sail* (Cambridge, Mass.: Harvard University Press, 1997).

34. In Norfolk's pleasure gardens, where its actors sometimes performed as singers or in small performances, blacks and prostitutes were routinely excluded, but no public notice regarding African Americans in the theatre appeared until Green inserted this statement in newspaper playbills: "Persons of colour will find their seats within the division of the upper boxes" (*Norfolk Gazette and Publick Ledger*, March 18, 1805, quoted in Pilkinton, "Theatre in Norfolk," p. 43). On the life of free blacks in the 1790s, see Bogger, *Free Blacks*, pp. 7–31. The period of the 1790s and early 1800s was one of increasing vigilance of and restrictions on blacks, both slave and free (Parramore, Stewart, and Bogger, *Norfolk*, pp. 127–28).
35. White and White, *Stylin'*, pp. 5–62. White and White reprint a watercolor by Benjamin Latrobe showing young black men doing each other's hair in preparation for socializing in Norfolk in the late 1790s. See Edward C. Carter II, John C. Van Horne, and Charles E. Brownell, eds., *Latrobe's View of America, 1795–1800: Selections from the Watercolors and Sketches* (New Haven: Yale University Press, 1985), pp. 102–3.
36. Shockley, *Richmond Stage*, p. 241.
37. It is possible one or more of these productions was a pantomime in which the Africanist element is less apparent in the play; see below.
38. Thomas Morton, *A Cure for the Heart-Ache* (London: Longman, 1797), p. 11; hereafter *CHA*. Although "black" is the term used in the stage directions, we have to assume that Morton means South Asian Indian, since Vortex has recently returned from India and named his English country house Bangalore Hall. See the discussion of *Cure* below.
39. [Isaac Bickerstaff], *The Romp* (London: Lowndes, 1786), p. 8.
40. John O'Keeffe, *The Highland Reel* (New York: Harrisson, 1794), p. 52; hereafter *HR*.
41. *NH* July 10, 1798.
42. See, for example, the comment at the end of the playbill for James Chalmers's benefit: "Mr. Chalmers thinks it necessary to observe, that the Pieces given after the Play, notwithstanding their variety, will not occupy more time (if so much) as is usual with a common Entertainment." *NH* July 12, 1800.
43. William Macready, *The Irishman in London*, p. 18; hereafter *IL*.
44. The plot of *IL* might well have been drawn from Henry Carey's *The Honest Yorkshire-Man*, a comedy of the 1730s, in which the dialect-speaking Sapscull, like Colloony, comes to London with his servant in order to marry a woman whose love interests lie elsewhere. But Macready's addition of a racially marked character to the British dialect figure (where Yorkshireman can easily be exchanged for Irishman) creates a situation that has more resonance in the United States of the 1790s.
45. Aside from mentions of his appearances in New York by Odell, there is little secondary information on this well-traveled entertainer; Falconi gets a brief mention in Paul McPharlin, *The Puppet Theatre in America: A History, 1524–1948* (Boston: Plays, 1969), p. 62.
46. On French migration from St. Domingue to Norfolk, see Parramore, Stewart, and Bogger, *Norfolk*, pp. 102–6.
47. McKenzie, "Organization," p. 321.
48. *NH* July 17, 1800.
49. *NH* July 26, 1800. The *Herald* writer, in noting the poor attendance, prefaces his observation by saying, "There are some actors, who are certainly of the *first rate*, and

others whose skill is not so eminent; but when it is recollected that they all labour alike, it seems to be confessed as common Justice, to requite, as well, the exertions of the one as the other.' Presumably, Bignall is one of those 'not so eminent.'
50. *NH* June 26, 1800.
51. John O'Keeffe, *The Farmer* (London: Longman and Rees, 1800).
52. Porter, *With an Air Debonair*, p. 413; Frances Brooke, *Rosina* (London: Cadell, 1783), p. 5, hereafter *R*.
53. McKenzie, 'Organization,' p. 300.
54. Prince Hoare, *No Song, No Supper*, 4th edn (London: n.p., 1796), p. 18; hereafter *NS*.
55. Isaac Bickerstaff, *Thomas and Sally; or The Sailor's Return* (London: Griffin, n.d.), p. 19; hereafter *TS*.
56. *NH* June 7, 1800.
57. *NH* July 12, 1800 and April 16, 1801. See Pilkinton, 'Theatre in Norfolk,' pp. 32–33, 49. Seamen had since before the Revolution been a vocal force against impressment and tyranny, including organizing for mob actions in Norfolk and other cities against British officials and officers. As a group, American sailors remained demonstrably patriotic, even when held in notorious British prison ships; given that history, there would be no surprise in sailors in 1800 being assertive in the theatre – or theatre managers doing their best to keep them happy. Jesse Lemisch, 'Jack Tar in the Streets: Merchant Seamen in the Politics of Revolutionary America,' *William and Mary Quarterly* 25 (1968), 371–407.
58. *NH* June 24, 1800.
59. *NH* June 17, 1800.
60. John C. Cross, *The Purse; or Benevolent Tar* (Dublin: n.p., 1794), p. 23; hereafter *TP*.
61. Porter, 'English-American Interaction,' 12–13.
62. In the second case, the performance may have been a pantomime rather than the play. Jean-François Arnould produced and published a pantomime in Paris called *L'héroïne américane: Pantomime en trois actes* (1786) that was translated by Samuel Chandler as *The American Heroine: A Pantomime in Three Acts* and printed in Philadelphia in 1797. Five years previous, however, at Drury Lane an afterpiece was advertised with the title *The American Heroine; or Ingratitude Punished*, a version that does not seem to have been printed. The text of the Chandler translation is reprinted with an introductory note in Felsenstein, ed., *English Trader*, pp. 234–46. It seems most likely that the second 1802 Norfolk production (and possibly the first as well) used the Chandler translation of Arnould's published text as the basis of the performance, but borrowed the Drury Lane subtitle. In any event, the theme story in all productions is that of Inkle and Yarico.
63. *NH* March 23, 1797.
64. Odell, *Annals*, vol. I, pp. 329–30.
65. *NH* July 4, 1795; August 12, 1795; August 8, 1795.
66. Death information in Pilkinton, 'Theatre in Norfolk,' pp. 505, 512.
67. Beete, *Man of the Times*, p. 15; hereafter *Man*.
68. Dunlap, *History*, vol. I, pp. 312–16.
69. *NH* July 11, 1798. The prologue is reprinted in Burk, *Bunker-Hill*, in Moody, ed., *Dramas from the American Theatre*, pp. 70–71.

70. Although Margaretta West's nephew Lawrence Sully was a professional miniaturist and had a business in Norfolk, and thus might have contributed to scene painting, he did not advertise in the city between 1796 and 1799. The other Sullys, including the fifteen-year-old future painter, Thomas, do not make much of an appearance in Norfolk in 1798, except for Matthew, Sr., who appeared in *Bunker-Hill* but is not known to have worked as a scenic artist.
71. For further commentary on Burk's extravaganza, see Chapter 4.
72. Pilkinton, "Theatre in Norfolk," p. 511; there does not appear to be an extant text.
73. Porter, *With an Air Debonair*, p. 443; Meserve, *Emerging Entertainment*, p. 148.
74. Willis, *Charleston Stage*, pp. 407–8.
75. Pollock, *Philadelphia Theatre*, pp. 372, 377–78.
76. Shillingsburg, "West Point Treason," 73–89, lists some of the plays on André that appeared in the United States but ignores the pantomimes.
77. It may also have been played by the West Company in Alexandria; see Sherman, *Comedies Useful*, p. 250.
78. *NH* June 16, 1798.
79. Dunlap, Preface, *André*, p. 64.
80. Dunlap, *History*, vol. II, pp. 21–22.
81. On West's Belvidera, see the positive commentary in *NH* June 26, 1800.
82. Watts had apparently been in Boston at the start of its professional theatre, and with his wife had toured with the West Company in 1796 and from 1798 to 1800, playing a broad array of minor roles. The Wattses must have been in difficult financial straits, however, because patronage for their benefit for July 29, 1800 was encouraged in order to lift them "above despondency" (Pilkinton, "Theatre in Norfolk," p. 71).
83. From a theatrical point of view, cross-dressing served as a novelty enticement, as in Sarah Marriott's appearance as young Norval in a 1795 Norfolk benefit production of *Douglas*. But that does not mean that other messages were not sent and received in individual performances. For the best study of Menken's career, particularly her Mazeppa, see Renée M. Sentilles, *Performing Menken: Adah Isaacs Menken and the Birth of American Celebrity* (Cambridge: Cambridge University Press, 2003), pp. 166–99; on Sampson Gannett's theatrical tour, Young, *Masquerade*, pp. 197–224.
84. As gleaned from *NH* through 1800. For the diversity of entertainments in Norfolk for the post-1800 period, see Click, *Spirit of the Times*.
85. Dunlap, *History*, vol. II, pp. 19–20; Highfill, Burnim, and Langhans, *Biographical Dictionary*, vol. III, pp. 137–40. The authors of the latter, however, do not have any information on Chalmers's Norfolk experience.
86. *NH* June 17, 1800.

13 After *The Contrast*

1. Moody, *America Takes the Stage*; Grimsted, *Melodrama Unveiled*; McConachie, *Melodramatic Formations*; Bank, *Theatre Culture in America*; Richards, ed., *Early American Drama*, pp. ix–xxxvi.

2. Royall Tyler, *The Bay Boy*, in Marius B. Péladeau, ed., *The Prose of Royall Tyler* (Rutland, Vt.: Tuttle, 1972), p. 149.
3. Of the plays listed after *The Contrast*, only *The Island of Barrataria* exists in a complete script, available in Tyler, *Four Plays*, ed. Arthur Wallace Peach and George Floyd Newbrough, America's Lost Plays series, vol. XV (Bloomington: Indiana University Press, 1965), pp. 1–30. Tyler's biblical dramas – *The Origin of the Feast of Purim, Joseph and His Brethren*, and *The Judgement of Solomon* – are also printed in the same volume. The remnants of one other play are reprinted with commentary in Jarvis, "Royall Tyler's Lyrics," 186–98.
4. Tyler, *The Contrast*, p. 8; hereafter *TC*. There is a considerable secondary bibliography on *The Contrast*, some of which is listed in the Penguin text, but commentators rarely connect his play to the poems that follow.
5. Royall Tyler, "A Prologue to Be Spoken by Mr. Frankley," in Marius B. Péladeau, ed., *The Verse of Royall Tyler* (Charlottesville: University Press of Virginia, 1968), pp. 5–6; hereafter *Verse*.
6. On the post-Revolutionary debate on theatre, see William W. Clapp, Jr., *A Record of the Boston Stage* (1853; New York: Greenwood, 1969), pp. 1–18; Richards, *Theater Enough*, pp. 265–79; and Nathans, *Early American Theatre*, pp. 35–70. On tea-table culture in general, consult Shields, *Civil Tongues*.
7. The opening play of the season was Irish writer Arthur Murphy's *Know Your Own Mind* (1777).
8. On the conflicts in the 1790s in Boston, see Ginger Strand, "The Theater and the Republic: Defining Party on Early Boston's Rival Stages," in Jeffrey D. Mason and J. Ellen Gainor, eds., *Performing America: Cultural Nationalism in American Theater* (Ann Arbor: University of Michaigan Press, 1999), pp. 19–36; and Nathans, *Early American Theatre*, pp. 71–72, 106–21, *passim*.
9. Murray, "Occasional Epilogue," pp. 1039–42.
10. Tyler, "An Occasional Address, Intended to have been spoken by Colonel J. S. Tyler, at the opening of The Boston Theater, this season, By a Gentleman of Vermont," *The Federal Orrery*, 9 November 1795; reprinted in *Verse* 42–46.
11. According to Clapp, *Boston Stage*, p. 60, the park was to be located in Cambridge, just across the Charles River bridge, "but the project fell through." There was also a theatre in the Bowery section of New York called Vauxhall Gardens at this same time.
12. See Chapter 11, note 5.
13. Tanselle, *Royall Tyler*, p. 131.
14. Robert Lloyd, *The Poetical Works*, 2 vols. (London: Evans, 1774), vol. II, p. 16.
15. Lloyd, *Poetical Works*, vol. II, p. 21.
16. Strand, "Theater and the Republic," p. 25.
17. Charles Churchill, "The Rosciad," in *English Poetry 1700–1780: Contemporaries of Swift and Johnson*, ed. David W. Lindsay (London: Dent, 1974), p. 134. The reference is to actor John Jackson.
18. Lloyd's and Churchill's satires elicited hostile responses, leading to a variety of charges and counter-charges. See, for example, Lloyd's defense of Churchill in "An Epistle to C. Churchill, Author of The Rosciad," *Poetical Works*, vol. II, pp. 84–95.

19. For an overview of the company, in addition to other sources noted below, see Weldon B. Durham, "The Boston ['Federal Street'] Theatre Company," in Durham, ed., *American Theatre Companies*, pp. 75–93.
20. Clapp, *Boston Stage*, p. 79.
21. "Mr. Fox was originally an engraver in Philadelphia. He had a great impediment in his speech, and stuttered so badly, that when he first made application for an engagement he was laughed at. [The managers] gave him a trial, however, and on the stage there was not the least hesitation or peculiarity. He was a versatile, pleasant actor, good in tragedy, comedy, or comic opera" (Clapp, *Boston Stage*, p. 82). In 1809, Fox appeared in Norfolk with the Charleston and Virginia Company, the successor to the Wests' Virginia Company, and played over thirty roles there, including Miami in Barker's *Indian Princess*. He died in Charleston on April 15, 1810. Pilkinton, "Theatre in Norfolk," pp. 477–78. For his career as an engraver, see the entry on him in George C. Groce and David H. Wallace, eds., *The New-York Historical Society's Dictionary of Artists in America, 1564–1860* (New Haven: Yale University Press, 1957), p. 237.
22. Péladeau names the "P*****" in the poem as Charles Stuart Powell, Snelling Powell's brother, but the publication date of the poem – June 1806 – and the fact that Charles did not rejoin the Boston Company until the 1806–7 season, after several years in Canada, work against that identification. Snelling Powell, who had been manager of the Federal Street Theatre from 1802, enlisted John Bernard and his brother-in-law J. H. Dickson as co-managers in early 1806, and remained as a manager (in various combinations) for most of the rest of his life (he died in 1821) (Durham, *American Theatre Companies*, p. 77). For Snelling Powell, see *Dictionary of American Biography* (New York: Scribner's, 1958–1964), vol. VIII, pp. 150–51; and Clapp, *Boston Stage*, pp. 78–79. For Charles Powell, see *Dictionary of Canadian Biography* (Toronto: University of Toronto Press, 1966–), vol. V, pp. 688–90; and Clapp, *Boston Stage*, p. 89.
23. Cooper's appearances in Boston in 1805 and 1806 are discussed in Geddeth Smith, *Thomas Abthorpe Cooper, America's Premier Tragedian* (Madison, N.J.: Fairleigh Dickinson University Press, 1996), pp. 106–14.
24. Tanselle, *Royall Tyler*, p. 120.
25. Smith, *Cooper*, pp. 112, 113.
26. Clapp, *Boston Stage*, p. 90, in an otherwise laudatory account of Twaits in Boston notes the actor's overestimation of his abilities in the tragic line. Joseph Ireland, *Records of the New York Stage from 1750–1860* (New York: Morell, 1866), p. 235, mentions Twaits's 'ridiculous representation of *Richard III*, though he redeemed his reputation by the great merit of his *Caleb Quotem*, in the afterpiece' in a May 1806 appearance in New York.
27. "Sketch of the Life of Mr. John Bernard," quoted in William C. Young, *Famous Actors and Actresses: Documents of American Theater History*, 2 vols. (New York: Bowker, 1975), vol. I, p. 95.
28. Young, *Famous Actors*, vol. I, p. 95.

Bibliography

Ackerman, Alan L., Jr. *The Portable Theater: American Literature and the Nineteenth-Century Stage*. Baltimore: Johns Hopkins University Press, 1999.
Adams, Charles F., ed. *Correspondence between John Adams and Mercy Warren*. 1878; New York: Arno, 1972.
Addison, Joseph. *Cato*, in Joseph Addison, *The Miscellaneous Works*, ed. A. C. Guthkelch, 2 vols. London: Bell, 1914.
Agnew, Jean-Christophe. *Worlds Apart: The Market and Theater in Anglo-American Thought, 1550–1750*. Cambridge: Cambridge University Press, 1986.
Aiken, George. *Uncle Tom's Cabin; or, Life Among the Lowly, a Domestic Drama*, in Richards, ed. *Early American Drama*.
Allen, Gay Wilson, and Roger Asselineau. *St. John de Crèvecoeur: The Life of an American Farmer*. New York: Viking, 1987.
Allen, Paula Gunn. *Pocahontas: Medicine Woman, Spy, Entrepreneur, Diplomat*. San Francisco: HarperSanFrancisco, 2003.
Allison, Robert J. *The Crescent Obscured: The United States and the Muslim World, 1776–1815*. New York: Oxford University Press, 1995.
Anderson, Benedict. *Imagined Communities: Reflections on the Origin and Spread of Nationalism*, rev. edn. London: Verso, 1991.
Arch, Stephen Carl. *After Franklin: The Emergence of Autobiography in Post-Revolutionary America, 1780–1830*. Hanover, N.H.: University Press of New England, 2001.
  "The 'Progressive Steps' of the Narrator in Crèvecoeur's *Letters from an American Farmer*." *Studies in American Fiction* 18 (1990), 145–58.
Argetsinger, Gerald. "Dunlap's *André*: Beginning of American Tragedy." *Players* 49 (1974), 62–64.
Ashby, Clifford. "A Black Actor on the Eighteenth Century Boston Stage?" *Theatre Survey* 28/2 (1987), 101–2.
Babits, Lawrence E. *A Devil of a Whipping: The Battle of Cowpens*. Chapel Hill: University of North Carolina Press, 1998.
Baepler, Paul, ed. *White Slaves, African Masters: An Anthology of American Barbary Captivity Narratives*. Chicago: University of Chicago Press, 1999.
Baine, Rodney M. *Robert Munford: America's First Comic Dramatist*. Athens: University of Georgia Press, 1967.

Baker, Jennifer Jordan. "A Speculative Language: Finance and Literary Imagination in Early America." Ph.D. dissertation, University of Pennsylvania, 2000.
Bank, Rosemarie. *Theatre Culture in America, 1825–1860*. Cambridge: Cambridge University Press, 1997.
Barak, Moses Jacob. "Moses Myers of Norfolk." M.A. thesis, University of Richmond, 1954.
Barbour, Philip L. "Captain John Smith and the London Theatre." *Virginia Magazine of History and Biography* 83 (1975), 277–79.
Barker, James Nelson. *The Indian Princess*, in Richards, ed. *Early American Drama*.
Barnard, Philip, Mark L. Kamrath, and Stephen Shapiro, eds. *Revising Charles Brockden Brown: Culture, Politics, and Sexuality in the Early Republic*. Knoxville: University of Tennessee Press, 2004.
Barnes, Eric Wollencott. *The Lady of Fashion: The Life and Theatre of Anna Cora Mowatt*. New York: Scribner's, 1954.
Barthelemy, Anthony Gerard. *Black Face, Maligned Race: The Representation of Blacks in English Drama from Shakespeare to Southerne*. Baton Rouge: Louisiana State University Press, 1987.
Bartley, J. O. *Teague, Shenkin and Sawney: Being an Historical Study of the Earliest Irish, Welsh and Scottish Characters in English Plays*. Cork: Cork University Press, 1954.
The Battle of Brooklyn. A Farce of Two Acts. New York: Rivington, 1776.
Beete, John. *The Man of the Times; or, A Scarcity of Cash*. Charleston, S.C.: Young, [1797].
Behn, Aphra. *The Round-heads, or, The Good Old Cause*. London: D. Brown, 1682.
  The Widow Ranter, in Jehlen and Warner, eds. *English Literatures*.
Bhattacharya, Nandini. "Family Jewels: George Colman's *Inkle and Yarico* and Connoisseurship." *Eighteenth-Century Studies* 34 (2001), 207–26.
Bickerstaff, Isaac. *The Captive*. London: Griffin, 1769.
  The Padlock: A Comic Opera. London: Griffin, 1768.
  The Romp. London: Lowndes, 1786.
  The Sultan, or A Peep into the Seraglio, 2nd edn. London: Dilly, 1787.
  Thomas and Sally; or The Sailor's Return. London: Griffin, n.d.
Bogger, Tommy L. *Free Blacks in Norfolk, Virginia, 1790–1860: The Darker Side of Freedom*. Charlottesville: University Press of Virginia, 1997.
Bolster, W. Jeffrey. *Black Jacks: African American Seamen in the Age of Sail*. Cambridge, Mass.: Harvard University Press, 1997.
Bordman, Gerald. *The Oxford Companion to American Theatre*, 2nd edn. New York: Oxford University Press, 1992.
Boucicault, Dion. *The Octoroon*, in Richards, ed. *Early American Drama*.
Bovill, E. W. *The Battle of Alcazar: An Account of the Defeat of Don Sebastian of Portugal at El-Ksar el-Kebir*. London: Batchworth Press, 1952.
Brackenridge, Hugh Henry. *The Battle of Bunkers-Hill*. Philadelphia: Bell, 1776.
  The Death of General Montgomery. Norwich, Conn.: Trumbull, 1777.
Branson, Susan. *These Fiery Frenchified Dames: Women and Political Culture in Early National Philadelphia*. Philadelphia: University of Pennsylvania Press, 2001.
Brasmer, William, and William Osborne, eds. *The Poor Soldier (1783) by John O'Keeffe and William Shield*. Madison: A-R Editions, 1978.

Brass, Paul R. *Ethnicity and Nationalism: Theory and Comparison.* New Delhi: Sage, 1991.
Breitwieser, Mitchell Robert. *American Puritanism and the Defense of Mourning: Religion, Grief, and Ethnology in Mary White Rowlandson's Captivity Narrative.* Madison: University of Wisconsin Press, 1990.
Breslin, Thomas A. *Beyond Pain: The Role of Pleasure and Culture in the Making of Foreign Affairs.* Westport, Conn.: Praeger, 2001.
Brewster, Dorothy. *Aaron Hill: Poet, Dramatist, Projector.* 1913; New York: AMS Press, 1966.
Brooke, Frances. *Rosina.* London: Cadell, 1783.
Brooke, Henry. *Gustavus Vasa, The Deliverer of His Country.* London: Dodsley, 1739.
Brooks, Peter. *The Melodramatic Imagination: Balzac, Henry James, Melodrama and the Mode of Excess.* 1976; New Haven: Yale University Press, 1995.
Brown, Charles Brockden. *Ormond; or The Secret Witness,* ed. Mary Chapman. Peterborough, Ontario: Broadview, 1999.
Brown, Jared. *The Theatre in America during the Revolution.* Cambridge: Cambridge University Press, 1995.
Brown, Richard Maxwell. "Violence and the American Revolution," in Stephen G. Kurtz and James H. Hutson, eds. *Essays on the American Revolution.* Chapel Hill: University of North Carolina Press, 1973.
Brown, Wallace. *The Good Americans: The Loyalists in the American Revolution.* New York: Morrow, 1969.
Browne, Ray B. "Popular Theater in *Moby Dick,*" in Ray B. Browne, Donald M. Winkelman, and Allen Hayman, eds. *New Voices in American Studies.* Lafayette, Ind.: Purdue Studies, 1966.
Brückner, Martin. "Geography, Reading, and the World of Novels in the Early Republic," in Schmidt and Fleischmann, eds. *Early America Re-Explored.*
Brunius, Harry. "African Burial Ground under New York Streets." *Christian Science Monitor,* June 17, 1999, csmweb2.emcweb.com/durable/1999/06/17/p16s1.htm.
Burk, John Daly. *Bunker-Hill, or The Death of General Warren,* in Moody, ed. *Dramas from the American Theatre.*
  Female Patriotism; or, The Death of Joan D'Arc. New York: Hurtin, 1798.
  The History of Virginia, from its First Settlement to the Present Day. 4 vols. Petersburg, Va.: Dickson and Pescud, 1804–16.
Burnham, Michelle. "The Journey Between: Liminality and Dialogism in Mary White Rowlandson's Captivity Narrative." *Early American Literature* 28 (1993), 60–75.
Burroughs, Stephen. *Memoirs.* Hanover, N.H.: Benjamin True, 1798.
Burrows, Edwin G., and Michael Wallace. "The American Revolution: The Ideology and Psychology of National Liberation." *Perspectives in American History* 6 (1972), 167–306.
Burton, Jonathan. "Anglo-Ottoman Relations and the Image of the Turk in *Tamburlaine.*" *Journal of Medieval and Early Modern Studies* 30/1 (2000), 125–56.
Calhoon, Robert McCluer. *The Loyalists in Revolutionary America, 1760–1781.* New York: Harcourt Brace Jovanovich, 1973.
Canary, Robert H. *William Dunlap.* New York: Twayne, 1970.
Canby, Courtlandt. "Robert Munford's 'The Patriots.'" *William and Mary Quarterly* 6 (1949), 437–503.
Carew-Miller, Anna. "The Language of Domesticity in Crèvecoeur's *Letters from an American Farmer.*" *Early American Literature* 28 (1993), 242–54.

Carey, Henry. *The Honest Yorkshire-Man*. London: Gilliver, 1736.
Carlson, David J. "Farmer versus Lawyer: Crèvecoeur's *Letters* and the Liberal Subject." *Early American Literature* 38 (2003), 257–79.
Carter, Edward C., II, John C. Van Horne, and Charles E. Brownell, eds. *Latrobe's View of America, 1795–1800: Selections from the Watercolors and Sketches*. New Haven: Yale University Press, 1985.
Cebula, Larry. "A Counterfeit Identity: The Notorious Life of Stephen Burroughs." *The Historian* 64 (2002), 317–33.
Chatterjee, Partha. "The Nation and Its Women," in Ranajit Guha, ed. *A Subaltern Studies Reader, 1986–1995*. Minneapolis: University of Minnesota Press, 1997.
Chew, Samuel C. *The Crescent and the Rose: Islam and England during the Renaissance*. New York: Oxford University Press, 1937.
Christophersen, Bill. "Charles Brockden Brown's *Ormond*: The Secret Witness as Ironic Motif." *Modern Language Studies* 10/2 (1980), 37–41.
Chrysostom, Saint John. *Commentary on Saint John the Apostle and Evangelist*, trans. Sister Thomas Aquinas Goggin, vol. I, *Homilies 1–47*. Washington: Catholic University of America Press, 1957.
Churchill, Charles. "The Rosciad," in *English Poetry 1700–1780: Contemporaries of Swift and Johnson*, ed. David W. Lindsay. London: Dent, 1974.
Cifelli, Edward. *David Humphreys*. New York: Twayne, 1982.
Clapp, William W., Jr. *A Record of the Boston Stage*. 1853; New York: Greenwood, 1969.
Click, Patricia C. *The Spirit of the Times: Amusements in Nineteenth-Century Baltimore, Norfolk and Richmond*. Charlottesville: University Press of Virginia, 1989.
Coad, Oral Sumner. "The Plays of Samuel Woodworth." *Sewanee Review* 27 (1919), 153–73.
Cockrell, Dale. *Demons of Disorder: Early Blackface Minstrels and Their World*. Cambridge: Cambridge University Press, 1997.
Colman, George, Jr. *Inkle and Yarico*. London: Robinson, 1787.
  The Mountaineers. Dublin: M'Donnel, 1794.
Conway, Moncure Daniel. *The Theater: A Discourse*. Cincinnati: Truman & Spofford, 1857.
  Autobiography: Memories and Experiences, 2 vols. Boston: Houghton Mifflin, 1904.
Cook, Elizabeth Heckendorn. *Epistolary Bodies: Gender and Genre in the Eighteenth-Century Republic of Letters*. Stanford: Stanford University Press, 1996.
Cooper, Anthony Ashley, third earl of Shaftesbury. *Characteristicks of Men, Manners, Opinions, Times*. 3 vols. Indianapolis: Liberty Fund, 2001.
Cosco, Joseph P. *Imagining Italians: The Clash of Romance and Race in American Perceptions, 1880–1910*. Albany: State University of New York Press, 2003.
Crain, Caleb. *American Sympathy: Men, Friendship, and the Literature of the New Nation*. New Haven: Yale University Press, 2001.
Crary, Catherine S. *The Price of Loyalty: Tory Writings from the Revolutionary Era*. New York: McGraw-Hill, 1973.
Cray, Robert E., Jr, "Major John André and the Three Captors: Class Dynamics and Revolutionary Memory Wars in the Early Republic, 1780–1831." *Journal of the Early Republic* 17 (1997), 371–97.
Crestani, Eliana. "James Nelson Barker's Pocahontas: The Theatre and the Indian Question." *Nineteenth Century Theatre* 23/1–2 (1995), 5–32.

Crèvecoeur, J. Hector St. John de. *Letters from an American Farmer and Sketches of Eighteenth-Century America*, ed. Albert E. Stone. New York: Penguin, 1981.
Crockett, Davy. *The Crockett Almanacs*, in Lauter et al., eds. *Heath Anthology of American Literature*, vol. I.
Cross, John C. *The Purse; or Benevolent Tar*. Dublin: n.p., 1794.
Crowley, John W. "James Nelson Barker in Perspective." *Educational Theatre Journal* 24 (1972), 363–69.
Cumberland, Richard. *The Jew*. New York: Campbell, 1795.
   Memoirs of Richard Cumberland. New York: Brisban and Brannan, 1806.
   The West Indian. [Boston]: West and West, [1794].
   The West Indian: A Comedy. London: Dilly, 1792.
Curry, Jane Kathleen. *Nineteenth-Century American Women Theatre Managers*. Westport, Conn.: Greenwood, 1994.
Curtis, Mary Julia. "The Early Charleston Stage, 1703–1798." Ph.D. dissertation, University of Indiana, 1968.
Dabney, William M. "Letters from Norfolk: Scottish Merchants View the Revolutionary Crisis," in Darrett B. Rutman, ed. *The Old Dominion: Essays for Thomas Perkins Abernethy*. Charlottesville: University Press of Virginia, 1964.
Daly, Augustin. *Under the Gaslight; or, Life and Love in These Times*, in Daniel C. Gerould, ed., *American Melodrama*. New York: Performing Arts Journal Publications, 1983.
Damon, S. Foster. "The Negro in Early American Songsters." *Papers of the Bibliographical Society of America* 28 (1934), 132–63.
Davidson, Cathy. *Revolution and the Word: The Rise of the Novel in America*. New York: Oxford University Press, 1986.
Davis, John. *Captain Smith and Princess Pocahontas*. New York: Plowman, 1805.
   The First Settlers of Virginia. New York: Southwick and Hardcastle, 1805.
Davis, Leith. "Irish Bards and English Consumers: Thomas Moore's 'Irish Melodies' and the Colonized Nation." *Ariel* 24/2 (1993), 7–25.
Davis, Peter A. "Plays and Playwrights to 1800," in Wilmeth and Bigsby, eds. *Cambridge History*, vol. I.
   "Puritan Mercantilism and Anti-Theatrical Legislation," in Ron Engle and Tice L. Miller, eds., *The American Stage: Social and Economic Issues from the Colonial Period to the Present*. Cambridge: Cambridge University Press, 1993.
Detisch, Robert J. "The Synthesis of Laughing and Sentimental Comedy in *The West Indian*." *Educational Theatre Journal* 22 (1970), 291–300.
A Dialogue Containing Some Reflections. Philadelphia: Steuart, 1764.
Dibdin, Thomas. *The Jew and the Doctor*. London: Longman and Rees, 1800.
Dictionary of American Biography. 10 vols. New York: Scribner's, 1958–1964.
Dictionary of Canadian Biography. 14 vols. Toronto: University of Toronto Press, 1966–.
Dircks, Richard. *Richard Cumberland*. Boston: Twayne, 1976.
Dircks, Richard J., ed. *The Letters of Richard Cumberland*. New York: AMS Press, 1986.
"Do the Dead Tell Tales After All?" National Library of Medicine *Newsline* 56.1–2 (2001), www.nlm.nih.gov/pubs/nlmnews/janjun01/jj01_dead.html.
Dodge, Robert K. "The Irish Comic Stereotype in the Almanacs of the Early Republic." *Eire-Ireland* 19 (1984), 111–20.

Dolmetsch, Carl R. "William Byrd II: Comic Dramatist." *Early American Literature* 6 (1971), 18–30.
Dorson, Richard M. "The Yankee on the Stage – A Folk Hero of American Drama." *New England Quarterly* 13 (1940), 467–93.
The Downfall of Justice and the Farmer Just Return'd from Meeting on Thanksgiving Day. A comedy lately acted in Connecticut. "2nd ed." Danvers, [Mass.], 1777.
Dryden, John. *Don Sebastian, King of Portugal*, in Hooker, Swedenberg, and Dearing, eds. *The Works of John Dryden*, vol. XV.
Duggan, G. C. *The Stage Irishman: A History of the Irish Play and Stage Characters from the Earliest Times*. 1937; New York: Blom, 1969.
Dunlap, William. *André*, in Richards, ed. *Early American Drama*.
  Darby's Return. New York: Hodge, Allen, and Campbell, 1789.
  The Glory of Columbia, Her Yeomanry! In *Dramas from the American Theatre, 1762–1909*. Cleveland: World, 1966, pp. 94–114.
  History of the American Theatre, 2 vols. London: Bentley, 1833.
Durey, Michael. *Transatlantic Radicals and the Early American Republic*. Lawrence: University Press of Kansas, 1997.
Durham, Weldon, ed. *American Theatre Companies, 1749–1887*. New York: Greenwood, 1986.
Ellison, Julie. *Cato's Tears and the Making of Anglo-American Emotion*. Chicago: University of Chicago Press, 1999.
Emerson, Everett. 'Hector St. John de Crèvecoeur and the Promise of America,' in Winfried Fluck, Jürgen Peper, and Willi Paul Adams, eds. *Forms and Functions of History in American Literature: Essays in Honor of Ursula Brumm*. Berlin: Schmidt, 1981.
Emerson, Everett, and Katherine Emerson. 'Crèvecoeur, J. Hector St. John de.' *American National Biography*, vol. V, pp. 729–32.
Epley, Steven. 'Alienated, Betrayed, and Powerless: A Possible Connection between *Charlotte Temple* and the Legend of Inkle and Yarico." *Papers on Language and Literature* 38 (2002), 200–22.
Evans, Dorinda. *Benjamin West and His American Students*. Washington, D.C.: Smithsonian Institution Press, 1980.
Evelev, John. "*The Contrast*: The Problem of Theatricality and Political and Social Crisis in Postrevolutionary America." *Early American Literature* 31 (1996), 74–97.
Faery, Rebecca Blevins. *Cartographies of Desire: Captivity, Race, and Sex in the Shaping of an American Nation*. Norman: University of Oklahoma Press, 1999.
The Famous Historye of the life and death of Captaine Thomas Stukeley. London: Pavyer, 1605.
Farquhar, George. *The Recruiting Officer*, ed. Michael Shugrue. Lincoln: University of Nebraska Press, 1966.
Felsenstein, Frank, ed. *English Trader, Indian Maid: Representing Gender, Race, and Slavery in the New World. An Inkle and Yarico Reader*. Baltimore: Johns Hopkins University Press, 1999.
Ferguson, Oliver. 'Sir Fretful Plagiary and Goldsmith's 'An Essay on the Theatre': The Background of Richard Cumberland's 'Dedication to Detraction,'" in Larry S. Champion, ed. *Quick Springs of Sense: Studies in the Eighteenth Century*. Athens: University of Georgia Press, 1974.

Ferguson, Oliver, and Eugene M. Waith. "Richard Cumberland, Comic Force, and Misanthropy." *Comparative Drama* 17 (1978), 283–99.

Ferling, John. *A Leap in the Dark: The Struggle to Create the American Republic.* New York: Oxford University Press, 2003.

Fichtelberg, Joseph. "Colonial Stage: Risk and Promise in John Smith's Virginia." *Early American Literature* 39 (2004), 11–40.

"Utopic Distresses: Crèvecoeur's *Letters* and Revolution." *Studies in the Literary Imagination* 27 (1994), 85–101.

Field, Vera Bernadette. *Constantia: A Study of the Life and Works of Judith Sargent Murray, 1751–1820.* Orono: University of Maine Press, 1931.

Fischer, Lisa E., and Tom Goyens. *The Search for the 'old Theatre, near the Capitol': Archaeological Investigations of the Douglass Theater, Williamsburg, Virginia.* Williamsburg, Va.: Department of Archaeological Research, Colonial Williamsburg, 2005, forthcoming.

Fisher, Benjamin Franklin IV. "William Dunlap's Transformations of the Gothic in *André*." *Publications of the Mississippi Philological Association* (1990), 196–206.

Flexner, James Thomas. *American Painting: First Flowers of Our Wilderness.* Cambridge, Mass.: Harvard University Press, 1947.

Fliegelman, Jay. *Prodigals and Pilgrims: The American Revolution against Patriarchal Authority, 1750–1800.* Cambridge: Cambridge University Press, 1982.

Flynn, Joyce. "Melting Plots: Patterns of Racial and Ethnic Amalgamation in American Drama before Eugene O'Neill." *American Quarterly* 38 (1986), 412–38.

Foote, Samuel. *Dramatic Works of Samuel Foote*, 2 vols. 1809; New York: Blom, 1969.

The Patron, in *Dramatic Works of Samuel Foote*, vol. I.

Forrest, Thomas. *The Disappointment; or, The Force of Credulity*, ed. David Mays. Gainesville: University Press of Florida, 1976.

Foster, Hannah Webster. *The Coquette*, ed. Cathy N. Davidson. New York: Oxford University Press, 1986.

Frey, Samuel Ludlow, ed. *The Minute Book of the Committee of Safety of Tryon County, the Old New York Frontier.* New York: Dodd, Mead, 1905.

Fried, Michael. *Absorption and Theatricality: Painting and Beholder in the Age of Diderot.* Berkeley: University of California Press, 1980.

Frohne, Andrea. "Commemorating the African Ground in New York City: Spirituality of Space in Contemporary Art Works." *Ijele: Art eJournal of the African World* 1.1 (2000), www.ijele.com/ijele/vol1.1/frohne.html.

Fuller, Randall. "Theaters of the American Revolution: The Valley Forge *Cato* and the Meschianza in Their Transcultural Contexts." *Early American Literature* 34 (1999), 126–46.

Gallagher, Kent G. *The Foreigner in Early American Drama: A Study in Attitudes.* The Hague: Mouton, 1966.

Garrick, David. *The Irish Widow*, in *Plays of David Garrick*, ed. Pedicord and Bergmann, vol. II.

The Jubilee, in *Plays of David Garrick*, ed. Pedicord and Bergmann, vol. II.

Miss in Her Teens; or, The Medley of Lovers. London: Tonson and Draper, 1747.

Plays of David Garrick, ed. Harry William Pedicord and Fredrick Louis Bergmann, 7 vols. Carbondale: Southern Illinois University Press, 1956–1980.

Gilje, Paul A., and Howard B. Rock. "Sweep O! Sweep O!': African-American Chimney Sweeps and Citizenship in the New Nation." *William and Mary Quarterly* 51 (1994), 507–38.
Glassie, Henry. *Passing the Time in Ballymenone: Culture and History of an Ulster Community*. Philadelphia: University of Pennsylvania Press, 1982.
Goldsmith, Oliver. *The Good Natur'd Man*, in *The Comedies*, ed. Joseph Jacobs. New York: Stokes, [1899], pp. 159–310.
Goring, Paul. "'John Bull, pit, box, and gallery, said No!': Charles Macklin and the Limits of Ethnic Resistance on the Eighteenth-Century London Stage." *Representations* no. 79 (Summer 2002), 61–81.
Goudie, Sean X. 'The West Indies, Commerce, and a Play for U. S. Empire: Recovering J. Robinson's *The Yorker's Stratagem* (1792)." *Early American Literature* 40 (2005), 1–35.
Gould, Philip. "Race, Commerce, and the Literature of Yellow Fever in Early National Philadelphia." *Early American Literature* 35/2 (2000), 157–86.
Goyens, Tom. 'Theater in Williamsburg: A Summary Report on the Second and Third Playhouse (1751–1787)." Unpublished report. Williamsburg, Va.: Colonial Williamsburg Foundation Research Division, October 2001.
Grabo, Norman S. 'Crèvecoeur's American: Beginning the World Anew." *William and Mary Quarterly* 48 (1991), 159–72.
Graves, R. B. 'The Stage Irishman among the Irish." *Theatre History Studies* 1 (1981), 29–38.
Green, Alan W. C. "'Jim Crow,' 'Zip Coon': The Northern Origins of Negro Minstrelsy." *Massachusetts Review* 11 (1970), 385–97.
Grimsted, David. *Melodrama Unveiled: American Theater and Culture, 1800–1850*. Chicago: University of Chicago Press, 1968.
Groce, George C., and David H. Wallace, eds. *The New-York Historical Society's Dictionary of Artists in America, 1564–1860*. New Haven: Yale University Press, 1957.
Gustafson, Sandra M. 'The Genders of Nationalism: Patriotic Violence, Patriotic Sentiment in the Performances of Deborah Sampson Gannett,' in Robert Blair St. George, ed., *Possible Pasts: Becoming Colonial in Early America*, Ithaca, N.Y.: Cornell University Press, 2000.
Habib, Imtiaz. "'Hel's Perfect Character' or The Blackamoor Maid in Early Modern English Drama: The Postcolonial Cultural History of a Dramatic Type." *LIT* 11 (2000), 277–304.
  Shakespeare and Race: Postcolonial Praxis in the Early Modern Period. Lanham, Md.: University Press of America, 2000.
Hagenbüchle, Roland. 'American Literature and the Nineteenth-Century Crisis in Epistemology: The Example of Charles Brockden Brown." *Early American Literature* 23 (1988), 121–51.
Hales, John. 'The Landscape of Tragedy: Crèvecoeur's 'Susquehanna.'" *Early American Literature* 20 (1985), 39–63.
Hansen, Joyce, and Gary McGowan. *Breaking Ground, Breaking Silence: The Story of New York's African Burial Ground*. New York: Holt, 1998.
Harris, Sharon M., ed. *Selected Writings of Judith Sargent Murray*. New York: Oxford University Press, 1995.

Harvey, Karen J., and Kevin B. Pry. 'John O'Keeffe as an Irish Playwright within the Theatrical, Social and Economic Context of His Time.' *Eire-Ireland* 22 (1987), 19–43.

Harwell, Richard Barksdale, ed. *The Committees of Safety of Westmoreland and Fincastle: Proceedings from the County Committees, 1774–1776*. Richmond: Virginia State Library, 1956.

Hatton, Ann Julia. *The Songs of Tammany; or, The Indian Chief*. New York: Harrison, 1794.

Havens, Daniel F. *The Columbian Muse of Comedy: The Development of a Native Tradition in Early American Social Comedy, 1787–1845*. Carbondale: Southern Illinois University Press, 1973.

Hayes, Edmund M., ed. 'Mercy Otis Warren: *The Defeat* [1773].' *New England Quarterly* 49 (1976), 440–58.

Hedges, William. "Charles Brockden Brown and the Culture of Contradictions." *Early American Literature* 9 (1974), 107–42.

Heywood, Thomas. *The Fair Maid of the West, Parts I and II*, ed. Robert K. Turner. London: Arnold, 1968.

Highfill, Jr., Philip H., Kalman A. Burnim, and Edward A. Langhans. *A Biographical Dictionary of Actors, Actresses, Musicians, Dancers, Managers and Other Stage Personnel in London, 1660–1800*, 16 vols. Carbondale: Southern Illinois University Press, 1973–1993.

Hill, Aaron. *The Tragedy of Zara*. London: J. Watts, 1736.

Hill, Errol. *The Jamaican Stage, 1655–1900: Profile of a Colonial Theatre*. Amherst: University of Massachusetts Press, 1992.

Hiltner, Judith R. "'Like a Bewildered Star': Deborah Sampson, Herman Mann, and *Address, Delivered with Applause*." *Rhetoric Society Quarterly* 29/2 (1999), 3–24.

 "'She Bled in Secret': Deborah Sampson, Herman Mann, and *The Female Review*." *Early American Literature* 34 (1999), 190–220.

Hinds, Elizabeth Jane Wall. *Private Property: Charles Brockden Brown's Gendered Economics of Virtue*. Newark: University of Delaware Press, 1997.

Hoare, Prince. *No Song, No Supper*, 4th edn. London: n.p., 1796.

Hodge, Francis. *Yankee Theatre: The Image of America on the Stage, 1825–1850*. Austin: University of Texas Press, 1964.

Hodgkinson, John. *Narrative of His Connection with the Old American Company from the Fifth of September, 1792, to the Thirty-First of March, 1797*. New York: Oram, 1797.

Holton, Woody. *Forced Founders: Indians, Debtors, Slaves, and the Making of the American Revolution in Virginia*. Chapel Hill: University of North Carolina Press, 1999.

Hooker, Edward Niles, H. T. Swedenberg, and Vinton A. Dearing, eds. *The Works of John Dryden*, 20 vols. Berkeley: University of California Press, 1956–2000.

Horton, James Oliver, and Lois E. Horton. *In Hope of Liberty: Culture, Community, and Protest among Northern Free Blacks, 1700–1860*. New York: Oxford University Press, 1997.

Housley, Norman. *The Later Crusades from Lyons to Alcazar, 1274–1580*. Oxford: Oxford University Press, 1992.

Howe, John. *Language and Political Meaning in Revolutionary America*. Amherst: University of Massachusetts Press, 2004.

Hulme, Peter. *Colonial Encounters: Europe and the Native Caribbean, 1492–1797*. London: Methuen, 1986.
Humphreys, David. *Miscellaneous Works*. New York: Hodge, Allen, and Campbell, 1790.
The Widow of Malabar; or, The Tyranny of Custom, in Humphreys, *Miscellaneous Works*.
Hunter, Robert. *Androboros*. New York: Bradford, 1714.
Hutner, Heidi. *Colonial Women: Race and Culture in Stuart Drama*. New York: Oxford University Press, 2001.
Iannini, Christopher. "'The Itinerant Man': Crèvecoeur's Caribbean, Raynal's Revolution, and the Fate of Atlantic Cosmopolitanism." *William and Mary Quarterly* 61 (2004), 210–34.
Inchbald, Elizabeth. *Animal Magnetism*. Dublin: P. Byron, n.d.
The Mogul Tale; or, The Descent of the Balloon. London: Powell, 1796.
Ioor, William. *The Battle of the Eutaw Springs*. Charleston: Hoff, 1807.
Independence; or Which Do You Like Best, The Peer, or the Farmer? Charleston: Bounetheau, 1805.
Ireland, Joseph. *Records of the New York Stage from 1750–1860*. New York: Morell, 1866.
Ireland, Owen S. "The Crux of Politics: Religion and Party in Pennsylvania, 1778–1789." *William and Mary Quarterly* 42 (1985), 453–75.
"The Ethnic-Religious Dimension of Pennsylvania Politics, 1778–1779," *William and Mary Quarterly* 30 (1973), 423–48.
Irving, Washington. *History, Tales, and Sketches*. New York: Library of America, 1983.
The Sketch-Book of Geoffrey Crayon, Esq., ed. Susan Manning. New York: Oxford University Press, 1996.
Jarvis, Katherine Schall. "Royall Tyler's Lyrics for *May Day in Town*." *Harvard Library Bulletin* 23 (1969), 186–98.
Jehlen, Myra, and Michael Warner, eds. *The English Literatures of America, 1500–1800*. New York: Routledge, 1997.
Jerningham, Edward. *Yarico to Inkle, an Epistle*. London: J. Dodsley, 1766.
Jerrold, Douglas. *Black-Ey'd Susan; or, "All in the Downs." A Nautical and Domestic Drama*, in George Rowell, ed. *Nineteenth-Century Plays*. London: Oxford University Press, 1953.
Johnson, Claudia D. "That Guilty Third Tier: Prostitution in the Nineteenth-Century American Theater," in Daniel Walker Howe, ed. *Victorian America*. Philadelphia: University of Pennsylvania Press, 1976.
Johnson, Odai. "(Im)Material Witness and Narrativity in the Colonial American Theatre." *Theatre Survey* 46/1 (2005), forthcoming.
Johnson, Odai, and William J. Burling, eds. *The Colonial American Stage, 1665–1774: A Documentary Calendar*. Madison, N.J.: Fairleigh Dickinson University Press, 2001.
Jones, Eugene H. *Native Americans as Shown on the Stage, 1753–1916*. Metuchen, N.J.: Scarecrow Press, 1988.
Jones, Thomas. *History of New York during the Revolutionary War*, ed. Edward Floyd DeLancey, 2 vols. New York: New York Historical Society, 1879.

Jost, François. "German and French Themes in Early American Drama." *JGE: The Journal of General Education* 28/3 (1976), 190–222.
Kafer, Peter. "Charles Brockden Brown and Revolutionary Philadelphia: An Imagination in Context." *Pennsylvania Magazine of History and Biography* 116 (1992), 467–98.
Kellan, Ann. "Bones Reveal Little-Known Tale of New York Slaves," CNN, Feb. 12, 1998, www.cnn.com/TECH/9082/12t_t/burial.ground/.
Kerber, Linda K. *Women of the Republic: Intellect and Ideology in Revolutionary America*. Chapel Hill: University of North Carolina Press, 1980.
Kernodle, Portia. "Yankee Types on the London Stage, 1824–1880." *Speech Monographs* 14 (1947), 139–47.
Kim, Sung Bok. "Impact of Class Relations and Warfare in the American Revolution: The New York Experience." *Journal of American History* 69 (1982), 326–46.
Kimball, Arthur G. "Savages and Savagism: Brockden Brown's Dramatic Irony." *Studies in Romanticism* 6 (1967), 217–19.
Kimmel, Michael. *Manhood in America: A Cultural History*. New York: Free Press, 1996.
Klepp, Susan E. "Seasoning and Society: Racial Differences in Mortality in Eighteenth-Century Philadelphia." *William and Mary Quarterly* 51 (1994), 473–506.
Knobel, Dale T. "A Vocabulary of Ethnic Perception: Content Analysis of the American Stage Irishman, 1820–1860." *American Studies* (UK) 15 (1987): 45–71.
Kolodny, Annette. *The Lay of the Land: Metaphor as Experience and History in American Life and Letters*. Chapel Hill: University of North Carolina Press, 1975.
Kornfeld, Eve. "Encountering 'the Other': American Intellectuals and Indians in the 1790s." *William and Mary Quarterly* 52 (1995), 287–97.
"Women in Post-Revolutionary American Culture: Susanna Haswell Rowson's American Career, 1793–1824." *Journal of American Culture* 6/4 (1983), 56–62.
Kosok, Heinz. "'George my belov'd King, and Ireland my honour'd country': John O'Keeffe and Ireland." *Irish University Review* 22 (1992), 40–54.
Kritzer, Amelia Howe. "Irish-Americans in Early Working Class Dramas by Mary Carr Clarke, Charles S. Talbot, and John Minshull." Unpublished paper delivered at the American Society for Eighteenth-Century Studies conference, South Bend, Ind., April 1998.
"Playing with Republican Motherhood: Self-Representation in Plays by Susanna Haswell Rowson and Judith Sargent Murray," *Early American Literature* 31 (1996), 150–66.
Kritzer, Amelia Howe, ed. *Plays by Early American Women, 1775–1850*. Ann Arbor: University of Michigan Press, 1995.
La Bree, Lawrence. *Ebenezer Venture; or, Advertising for a Wife*. New York: Samuel French, [1841].
Lamb, Susan. "The Popular Theater of Samuel Foote and British National Identity." *Comparative Drama* 30 (1996), 250–51.
"The Last Night of Performance at Edenton, this Season. On Thursday evening, the 20th of July, 1797." Edenton, N.C., 1797.
Latham, Don Loftis. "Hawthorne's 'Coup de Théâtre': Theatricality and Self-Performance in the American Romances." Ph.D. dissertation, University of Georgia, 1995.

Lauter, Paul H., *et al.*, eds. *Heath Anthology of American Literature*. 2 vols. Lexington, Mass.: Heath, 1990.
Lawrence D. H., *Studies in Classic American Literature*. 1923; New York: Viking, 1964.
Layson, Hana. "Rape and Revolution: Feminism, Antijacobinism, and the Politics of Injured Innocence in Brockden Brown's *Ormond*." *Early American Studies* 2 (2004), 160–91.
Leacock, John. *The Fall of British Tyranny; or American Liberty Triumphant*. Philadelphia: Styner and Cist, 1776.
Lee, Nathaniel. *Lucius Junius Brutus*, ed. John Loftis. Lincoln: University of Nebraska Press, 1967.
Lemay, J. A. Leo. *The American Dream of Captain John Smith*. Charlottesville: University Press of Virginia, 1991.
Le Mierre, A. -M. *La veuve du Malabar, ou L'Empire des Coutumes*. Paris: Duchesne, 1780.
Lemisch, Jesse. "Jack Tar in the Streets: Merchant Seamen in the Politics of Revolutionary America." *William and Mary Quarterly* 25 (1968), 371–407.
Lettieri, Ronald, and Charles Wetheell. "The New Hampshire Committees of Safety and Revolutionary Republicanism, 1775–1784." *Historical New Hampshire* 35 (1980), 271–75.
Levine, Robert S. "Villainy and the Fear of Conspiracy in Charles Brockden Brown's *Ormond*." *Early American Literature* 15 (1980), 124–40.
Link, Frederick M. "John O'Keeffe," *Dictionary of Literary Biography*, vol. LXXXIX.
  John O'Keeffe: A Bibliography. Lincoln: University of Nebraska Press, 1983.
  "Addison's *Cato* in the Colonies." *William and Mary Quarterly* 23 (1966), 431–49.
Lloyd, Robert. *The Poetical Works*, 2 vols. London: Evans, 1774.
Loftis, John. *The Politics of Drama in Augustan England*. Oxford: Oxford University Press, 1963.
Logan, Lisa. "Mary Rowlandson's Captivity and the 'Place' of the Woman Subject." *Early American Literature* 28 (1993), 255–77.
Low, Samuel. *The Politician Out-witted*. New York: Ross, 1789.
Lydia – . Letter to Elizabeth D. Whiton, 13 Feb. 1839, William L. Clements Library, University of Michigan.
Lynch, James J. *Box, Pit, and Gallery: Stage and Society in Johnson's London*. Berkeley: University of California Press, 1953.
Macklin, Charles. *Love a-la-Mode*. Philadelphia: Taylor, 1791.
  The True-Born Irishman, or Irish Fine Lady. Philadelphia: Spotswood, 1784.
Macready, William. *The Irishman in London; or, The Happy African*. London: Woodfall, 1793.
Marriott, Mrs. [Sarah]. *The Chimera; or, Effusions of Fancy*. New York: Swords, 1795.
Mason, Jeffrey D. *Melodrama and the Myth of America*. Bloomington: University of Indiana Press, 1993.
Matar, Nabil I. "The Renegade in English Seventeenth-Century Imagination." *Studies in English Literature 1500–1900* 33 (1993), 489–505.
  Turks, Moors, and Englishmen in the Age of Discovery. New York: Columbia University Press, 1999.
  "Turning Turk: Conversion to Islam in English Renaissance Thought." *Durham University Journal* 86.1 (1994), 33–41.

Mates, Julian. *The American Musical Stage before 1800.* New Brunswick, N.J.: Rutgers University Press, 1962.
Mayer, Henry. *All on Fire: William Lloyd Garrison and the Abolition of Slavery.* New York: St. Martin's, 1998.
McConachie, Bruce. "American Theatre in Context, from the Beginnings to 1870," in Wilmeth and Bigsby, eds., *Cambridge History,* vol. 1.
— *Melodramatic Formations: American Theatre and Society, 1820–1870.* Iowa City: University of Iowa Press, 1992.
McDonald, Andrew. *The Independent,* 2 vols. London: Cadell, 1784.
McDonnell, Michael A. "'A World Turned 'Topsy Turvy'': Robert Munford, *The Patriots,* and the Crisis of the Revolution in Virginia." *William and Mary Quarterly* 61 (2004), 235–70.
McDonough, Carla J. *Staging Masculinity: Male Identity in Contemporary American Drama.* Jefferson, N.C.: McFarland, 1997.
McEachern, Leora H., and Isabel M. Williams, eds. *Wilmington-New Hanover Safety Committee Minutes, 1774–1776.* Wilmington, N.C.: Wilmington-New Hanover County American Revolution Bi-centennial Association, 1974.
McKenzie, Ruth Harsha. "Organization, Production, and Management at the Chestnut Street Theatre, Philadelphia from 1791 to 1820." Ph.D. dissertation, Stanford University, 1952.
McNamara, Brooks. *The American Playhouse in the Eighteenth Century.* Cambridge, Mass.: Harvard University Press, 1969.
McPharlin, Paul. *The Puppet Theatre in America: A History, 1524–1948.* Boston: Plays, 1969.
Melish, Joanne Pope. *Disowning Slavery: Gradual Emancipation and 'Race' in New England, 1780–1860.* Ithaca, N.Y.: Cornell University Press, 1998.
Meserve, Walter J. *An Emerging Entertainment: The Drama of the American People to 1828.* Bloomington: Indiana University Press, 1977.
Middlekauff, Robert. *The Glorious Cause: The American Revolution, 1763–1789.* New York: Oxford University Press, 1982.
Mihm, Stephen. "The Alchemy of Self: Stephen Burroughs and the Counterfeit Economy of the Early Republic." *Early American Studies* 2 (2004), 123–59.
Miller, James. *Mahomet the Imposter.* Edinburgh: Apollo Press, 1782.
Milns, William. *All in a Bustle; or The New House.* New York: Literary Printing Office, 1798.
Miner, Earl, George R. Guffey, and Franklin B. Zimmerman. Commentary on *Don Sebastian,* in Hooker, Swedenberg, and Dearing, eds. *The Works of John Dryden,* vol. XV.
Minshull, John. *Rural Felicity.* New York: n. p., 1801.
Mohr, James C. "Calculated Disillusionment: Crèvecoeur's *Letters* Reconsidered." *South Atlantic Quarterly* 69 (1970), 354–63.
Montaigne, Michel de. *The Essays,* trans. John Florio, 3 vols. New York: AMS Press, 1967.
Montgomery, Benilde. "White Captives, African Slaves: A Drama of Abolition." *Eighteenth-Century Studies* 27 (1994), 615–30.
Moody, Richard. *America Takes the Stage: Romanticism in American Drama and Theatre, 1750–1900.* Bloomington: Indiana University Press, 1955.

ed. *Dramas from the American Theatre, 1762–1909*. Cleveland: World, 1966.
Moody, Robert E., ed. 'Boston's First Play." *Massachusetts Historical Society Proceedings* 92 (1980), 117–39.
Moore, Dennis, ed. *More Letters from the American Farmer: An Edition of the Essays in English Left Unpublished by Crèvecoeur*. Athens: University of Georgia Press, 1995.
Moore, Edward. *The Gamester*. London: R. Franklin, 1753.
Moore, John Brooks. 'The Rehabilitation of Crèvecoeur." *Sewanee Review* 35 (1927), 216–30.
Morgan, Helen M., ed. *A Season in New York 1801: Letters of Harriet and Maria Trumbull*. Pittsburgh: University of Pittsburgh Press, 1969.
Morgan, Winifred. *An American Icon: Brother Jonathan and American Identity*. Newark: University of Delaware Press, 1988.
Morrison, Toni. *Playing in the Dark: Whiteness and Literary Imagination*. New York: Vintage, 1993.
Morton, Thomas. *A Cure for the Heart-Ache*. London: Longman, 1797.
Moses, Montrose, ed. *Representative Plays by American Dramatists from 1763 to the Present Day*, 3 vols. 1925; New York: Blom, 1964.
Mosier, Joseph. "Myers Family Scorecard." Unpublished document. Norfolk: Chrysler Museum of Art, 2004.
Mowatt, Anna Cora. *Fashion*, in Richards, ed. *Early American Drama*.
　Mimic Life; or, Before and Behind the Curtain, ed. Jeffrey H. Richards. Acton, Mass.: Copley, 2000.
Mower, C. Leiren. "Bodies in Labor: Sole Proprietorship and the Labor of Conduct in *The Coquette*." *American Literature* 74 (2002), 315–44.
'Mr. Jones's Benefit. Boston Theatre. Friday Evening, November 4, 1796.' Boston, 1796.
Munns, Jessica. *Restoration Politics and Drama: The Plays of Thomas Otway, 1675–1683*. Newark: University of Delaware Press, 1995.
Murdock, John. *The Politicians; or, A State of Things*. Philadelphia: 'for the author,' 1798.
　The Triumphs of Love; or Happy Reconciliation. Philadelphia: Folwell, 1795.
Murray, Judith Sargent. *The Gleaner*, 3 vols. Boston: Andrews, 1798.
　'Occasional Epilogue to *The Contrast*, a Comedy, Written by Royal [sic] Tyler, Esq.,' in Lauter, *et al.*, eds., *Heath Anthology*, vol. I.
　'On the Domestic Education of Children,' in Lauter, *et al.*, eds. *Heath Anthology*, vol. I.
　The Traveller Returned, in Harris, ed., *Selected Writings*.
　Virtue Triumphant, in Murray, *The Gleaner*, vol. III.
Musser, Paul H. *James Nelson Barker*. Philadelphia: University of Pennsylvania Press, 1929.
Namias, June. *White Captives: Gender and Ethnicity on the American Frontier*. Chapel Hill: University of North Carolina Press, 1993.
Nathans, Heather S. *Early American Theatre from the Revolution to Thomas Jefferson: Into the Hands of the People*. Cambridge: Cambridge University Press, 2003.
Nathans, Heather. "A Much Maligned People: Jews on and off the Stage in the Early American Republic," *Early American Studies* 2/2 (2004), 310–42.
Nelson, Dana. *National Manhood: Capitalist Citizenship and the Imagined Fraternity of White Men*. Durham, N.C.: Duke University Press, 1998.

Nicholls, Harold J. "The Prejudice against Native American Drama from 1778 to 1830." *Quarterly Journal of Speech* 60 (1975), 279–88.
Norfolk Herald and Public Advertiser, 1797–1800.
Nye, Russel B. *American Literary History 1607–1830*. New York: Knopf, 1970.
Odell, George C. D. *Annals of the New York Stage*, 15 vols. New York: Columbia University Press, 1927–1949.
O'Keeffe, John. *The Farmer*. London: Longman and Rees, 1800.
  The Highland Reel. New York: Harrisson, 1794.
  Patrick in Prussia, or, Love in a Camp. Dublin: Davis, 1786.
  The Poor Soldier. Dublin: n.p., 1786.
  The Poor Soldier. Philadelphia: Seddon and Spotswood, 1787.
  Recollections of the Life, 2 vols. 1826; New York: Blom, 1969.
  The Young Quaker. Dublin: P. Wogan, 1784.
Oliver, Peter. *Peter Oliver's Origin and Progress of the American Rebellion: A Tory View*, ed. Douglass Adair and John A. Schutz. San Marino: Huntington Library, 1961.
Olson, Lester. *Emblems of American Community in the Revolutionary Era: A Study in Rhetorical Iconology*. Washington, D.C.: Smithsonian Institution Press, 1991.
"On Saturday next will be perform'd, by a society of ladies and gentlemen, at Faneuil-Hall, the tragedy of Zara." Boston, 1775.
O'Quinn, Daniel. "Mercantile Deformities: George Colman's *Inkle and Yarico* and the Racialization of Class Relations." *Theatre Journal* 54 (2002), 389–409.
Oreovicz, Cheryl. "Contextualizing *André*." Unpublished paper, delivered at the Society of Early Americanists convention, Charleston, South Carolina, April 1999.
Ottenberg, June C. "Popularity of Two Operas in Philadelphia in the 1790s." *International Review of the Aesthetics and Sociology of Music* 18 (1987), 205–10.
Otway, Thomas. *Venice Preserved; or A Plot Discovered*, in Robert G. Lawrence, ed., *Restoration Plays*. London: J. M. Dent, 1992.
Parke, John. *Virginia: A Pastoral Drama, on the Birth-day of an illustrious Personage and the Return of Peace, February 11th, 1784*, in John Parke, *Lyric Works of Horace Translated into English Verse: To Which Are Added, a Number of Original Poems. By a Native of America*. Philadelphia: Oswald, 1786.
Parramore, Thomas C., Peter C. Stewart, and Tommy L. Bogger. *Norfolk: The First Four Centuries*. Charlottesville: University Press of Virginia, 1994.
The Paxton Boys. Philadelphia: Armbruster, 1764.
Pearce, Roy Harvey. *The Savages of America: A Study of the Indians and the Idea of Civilization*, rev. edn. Baltimore: Johns Hopkins University Press, 1965.
Peele, George. *The Battle of Alcazar*, ed. John Yoklavich, in Prouty, *et al.*, eds. *Life and Works*, vol. II.
Péladeau, Marius B., ed. *The Prose of Royall Tyler*. Rutland, Vt.: Tuttle, 1972.
  ed. *The Verse of Royall Tyler*. Charlottesville: University Press of Virginia, 1968.
Philbrick, Norman. "The Spy as Hero: An Examination of *André* by William Dunlap," in Oscar G. Brockett, ed. *Studies in Theatre and Drama: Essays in Honor of Hubert C. Heffner*. The Hague: Mouton, 1972.
Philbrick, Thomas. *St. John de Crèvecoeur*. New York: Twayne, 1970.
Pilkinton, Lucy Blandford. "Theatre in Norfolk, Virginia, 1788–1812." Ph.D. dissertation, University of Michigan, 1993.

Plumstead, A. W. "Hector St. John de Crèvecoeur," in Everett Emerson, ed. *American Literature, 1764–1789: The Revolutionary Years*. Madison: University of Wisconsin Press, 1977.
Pollock, Thomas Clark. *The Philadelphia Theatre in the Eighteenth Century*. 1933; rpt. New York: Greenwood, 1968.
Porter, Susan L. "English-American Interaction in American Musical Theater at the Turn of the Nineteenth Century." *American Music* 4 (1986), 6–19.
  With an Air Debonair: Musical Theater in America, 1785–1815. Washington, D.C.: Smithsonian Institution Press, 1991.
Potter, Tiffany. "Writing Indigenous Femininity: Mary Rowlandson's Captivity Narrative." *Eighteenth-Century Studies* 36 (2003), 153–67.
Powell, J. H. *Bring Out Your Dead: The Great Plague of Yellow Fever in Philadelphia in 1793*. Philadelphia: University of Pennsylvania Press, 1949.
Prawer, Joshua. *The Latin Kingdom of Jerusalem: European Colonialism in the Middle Ages*. London: Weidenfeld and Nicolson, 1972.
Price, Lawrence Marsden. *Inkle and Yarico Album*. Berkeley: University of California Press, 1937.
Prouty, Charles Tyler, *et al.*, eds. *The Life and Works of George Peele*, 3 vols. New Haven: Yale University Press, 1952–1970.
Pulsipher, Jenny Hale. "*The Widow Ranter* and Royalist Culture in Virginia." *Early American Literature* 39 (2004), 41–66.
Purcell, Sarah J. *Sealed with Blood: War, Sacrifice, and Memory in Revolutionary America*. Philadelphia: University of Pennsylvania Press, 2002.
Purchas, Samuel. *Hakluytus Posthumus, or Purchas His Pilgrimes*, 20 vols. Glasgow: McLehose, 1906.
Putz, Manfred. "Dramatic Elements and the Problem of Literary Mediation in the Works of Hector St. John de Crèvecoeur." *REAL: The Yearbook of Research in English and American Literature* 3 (1985), 111–30.
Quinn, Arthur Hobson. *A History of the American Drama from the Beginning to the Civil War*. New York: Appleton-Century-Crofts, 1943.
Ragussis, Michael. 'Jews and Other 'Outlandish Englishmen': Ethnic Performance and the Invention of British Identity under the Georges.' *Critical Inquiry* 26 (2000), 773–97.
Rankin, Hugh F. *The Theater in Colonial America*. Chapel Hill: University of North Carolina Press, 1965.
Rice, Grantland. "Crèvecoeur and the Politics of Authorship in Republican America." *Early American Literature* 28 (1993), 91–119.
Rice, Howard. *Le Cultivateur Américain: Etude sur l'oeuvre de Saint John de Crèvecoeur*. Paris: Champion, 1933.
Richards, Jeffrey H. "Hawthorne and the Metaphor of Theatre." Ph.D. dissertation, University of North Carolina, 1982.
  Mercy Otis Warren. New York: Twayne, 1995.
  "The Politics of Seduction: Theater, Sexuality, and National Virtue in the Novels of Hannah Foster," in Della Pollock, ed. *Exceptional Spaces: Essays in Performance and History*. Chapel Hill: University of North Carolina Press, 1998.
  Theater Enough: American Culture and the Metaphor of the World Stage, 1607–1789. Durham, N.C.: Duke University Press, 1991.

Richards, Jeffrey H., ed. *Early American Drama*. New York: Penguin, 1997.
Richardson, Gary A. *American Drama from the Colonial Period through World War I: A Critical History*. New York: Twayne, 1993.
   "Domesticating the Irish: Brogues, Stage History, and National Identity." Unpublished paper delivered at the American Society for Eighteenth-Century Studies conference, South Bend, Ind., April 1998.
   "In the Shadow of the Bard: Republican Drama and the Shakespearean Legacy," in Judith L. Fisher and Stephen Watt, eds. *When They Weren't Doing Shakespeare: Essays on Nineteenth-Century British and American Theatre*. Athens: University of Georgia Press, 1989.
   "Nationalizing the American Stage: The Drama of Royall Tyler and William Dunlap as Post-Colonial Phenomena," in A. Robert Lee and W. M. Verhoeven, eds. *Making America/Making American Literature*. Amsterdam: Rodopi, 1996.
   "Poets and Playwrights: 1800–1865," in Wilmeth and Bigsby, eds. *Cambridge History*.
Rider, Janet. "Creating American Womanhood: The Social and Cultural World of Judith Sargent Murray." Ph.D. dissertation, University of Connecticut, 2004.
Rinehart, Lucy. "'Manly Exercises': Post-Revolutionary Performances of Authority in the Theatrical Career of William Dunlap." *Early American Literature* 36 (2001), 273–80.
   "A Nation's 'Noble Spectacle': Royall Tyler's *The Contrast* as Metatheatrical Commentary." *American Drama* 3/2 (1994), 29–52.
Ritchey, David. *A Guide to the Baltimore Stage in the Eighteenth Century*. Westport, Conn.: Greenwood, 1982.
Roach, Joseph. *Cities of the Dead: Circum-Atlantic Performance*. New York: Columbia University Press, 1996.
Robinson, David M. "Community and Utopia in Crèvecoeur's *Sketches*." *American Literature* 62 (1990), 17–31.
Robinson, J. *The Yorker's Stratagem; or, Banana's Wedding*. New York: Swords, 1792.
Rodgers, Paul C., Jr. "Brown's *Ormond*: The Fruits of Improvisation." *American Quarterly* 26 (1974), 4–22.
Rogers, George C., Jr. *Charleston in the Age of the Pinckneys*. Norman: University of Oklahoma Press, 1969.
Rosenthal, Bernard, ed. *Critical Essays on Charles Brockden Brown*. Boston: G. K. Hall, 1981.
Ross, Peter. *The Scot in America*. New York: Raeburn, 1896.
Rourke, Constance. *The Roots of American Culture*. New York: Harcourt, Brace, 1942.
Rousseau, Jean-Jacques. *The Confessions*. New York: Modern Library, [1945].
Rowe, Nicholas. *The Fair Penitent*, ed. Malcolm Goldstein. Lincoln: University of Nebraska Press, 1969.
   Tamerlane, a Tragedy, 2nd edn. London: Tonson, 1703.
Rowlandson, Mary. *The Soveraignty & Goodness of God ... Being a Narrative of the Captivity and Restauration of Mrs. Rowlandson*, 2nd edn (Cambridge, Mass.: Green, 1682); rpt. in *Puritans among the Indians: Accounts of Captivity and Redemption, 1676–1724*, ed. Alden T. Vaughan and Edward W. Clark. Cambridge, Mass.: Belknap/Harvard University Press, 1981, pp. 29–75.

Rowson, Susanna. *Slaves in Algiers*, in Kritzer, ed. *Plays by Early American Women*.
Rucker, Mary E. "Crèvecoeur's *Letters* and Enlightenment Doctrine." *Early American Literature* 13 (1978), 193–212.
Saar, Doreen Alvarez. "The Heritage of American Ethnicity in Crèvecoeur's *Letters from an American Farmer*," in Frank Shuffelton, ed. *A Mixed Race: Ethnicity in Early America*. New York: Oxford University Press, 1993.
Said, Edward W. *Orientalism*. New York: Vintage, 1978.
Saillant, John. "Before Douglass: Race and 'the Nation of Nantucket.'" Unpublished paper delivered at the James Bradford Ames Symposium on African American History, Nantucket, Massachusetts, June 20, 1998.
Samuels, Shirley. *Romances of the Republic: Women, the Family, and Violence in the Literature of the Early American Nation*. New York: Oxford University Press, 1996.
Scheckel, Susan. "Domesticating the Drama of Conquest: Barker's Pocahontas on the Popular Stage." *American Transcendental Quarterly* 10 (1996), 231–43.
Scheer, George F., and Hugh F. Rankin, *Rebels and Redcoats*. New York: World, 1957.
Scheick, William J. "The Problem of Origination in Brown's *Ormond*," in Rosenthal, ed. *Critical Essays*.
Schiff, Karen L. "Objects of Speculation: Early Manuscripts on Women and Education by Judith Sargent (Stevens) Murray." *Legacy* 17 (2000), 213–28.
Schmidt, Klaus H. "A Scotsman in British America; or, Up against Provincialism: The Construction of Individual and Collective Identities in Dr. Alexander Hamilton's *Itinerarium*," in Schmidt and Fleischmann, eds. *Early America Re-Explored*.
Schmidt, Klaus H. and Fritz Fleischmann, eds. *Early America Re-Explored: New Readings in Colonial, Early National, and Antebellum Culture*. New York: Lang, 2000.
Schofield, Mary Anne. "The Happy Revolution: Colonial Women and the Eighteenth-Century Theater," in June Schlueter, ed. *Modern American Drama: The Female Canon*. Rutherford, N.J.: Fairleigh Dickinson University Press, 1990.
Schuyler, George Samuel. "Our Greatest Gift to America," in Lauter, *et al.*, eds. *Heath Anthology of American Literature*, vol. II.
Sears, Priscilla. *A Pillar of Fire to Follow: American Indian Dramas, 1808–1859*. Bowling Green: Bowling Green University Popular Press, 1982.
Seelye, John. *Memory's Nation: The Place of Plymouth Rock*. Chapel Hill: University of North Carolina Press, 1998.
  Prophetic Waters: The River in Early American Life and Literature. New York: Oxford University Press, 1977.
Sentilles, Renée M. *Performing Menken: Adah Isaacs Menken and the Birth of American Celebrity*. Cambridge: Cambridge University Press, 2003.
Sewall, Jonathan. *A Cure for the Spleen, or Amusement for a Winter's Evening*. Boston: n.p., 1775.
Shaffer, Jason. "'Great Cato's Descendants': A Genealogy of Colonial Performance." *Theatre Survey* 44 (2003), 5–28.
Shapiro, Anne Dhu. "Action Music in American Pantomime and Melodrama, 1730–1913." *American Music* 2/4 (1984), 49–72.

Shapiro, Stephen. "'Dread and Curious Alteration': Republican Panic and Personal Intimation in Early American Fiction." Ph.D. dissertation, Yale University, 1995.
Sheridan, Richard Brinsley. *The School for Scandal*. New York: Gaine, 1786.
Sheridan, Thomas. *The Brave Irishman; or Captain O'Blunder*, Edinburgh: n.p., 1755.
Sherman, Susanne K. *Comedies Useful: Southern Theatre History, 1775–1812*. Williamsburg, Va.: Celest Press, 1998.
Shields, David S. *Civil Tongues and Polite Letters in British America*. Chapel Hill: University of North Carolina Press, 1997.
Shillingsburg, Miriam J. "The West Point Treason in American Drama, 1798–1891." *Educational Theatre Journal* 30 (1978), 73–89.
Shockley, Martin Staples. *The Richmond Stage, 1784–1812*. Charlottesville: University Press of Virginia, 1977.
Siebert, Donald T., Jr. "Royall Tyler's 'Bold Example': *The Contrast* and the English Comedy of Manners." *Early American Literature* 13 (1978), 3–11.
Silverman, Kenneth. *A Cultural History of the American Revolution*. 1976; New York: Columbia University Press, 1987.
Skemp, Sheila L. *Judith Sargent Murray: A Brief Biography with Documents*. Boston: Bedford, 1998.
Smith, Elihu Hubbard. *The Diary of Elihu Hubbard Smith (1771–1798)*, ed. James E. Cronin. Philadelphia: American Philosophical Society, 1973.
Smith, Geddeth. *Thomas Abthorpe Cooper, America's Premier Tragedian*. Madison, N.J.: Fairleigh Dickinson University Press, 1996.
Smith, John. *The Complete Works of Captain John Smith*, ed. Philip L. Barbour, 3 vols. Chapel Hill: University of North Carolina Press, 1986.
Smith, Page. *A New Age Now Begins: A People's History of the American Revolution*, 2 vols. New York: McGraw-Hill, 1976.
Smith, William Henry. *The Drunkard; or the Fallen Saved*, in Richards, ed. *Early American Drama*.
Smyth, Heather. "Imperfect Disclosures: Cross-Dressing and Containment in Charles Brockden Brown's *Ormond*," in Merril D. Smith, ed. *Sex and Sexuality in Early America*. New York: New York University Press, 1998.
Soltow, J. H. "Scottish Traders in Virginia, 1750–1775." *Economic History Review* 12 (1959), 83–98.
Sonneck, Oscar G. *Early Opera in America*. 1943; New York: Blom, 1963.
Spengemann, William. C. *A New World of Words: Redefining Early American Literature*. New Haven: Yale University Press, 1994.
Starke, Mariana. *The Widow of Malabar*. London: William Lane, 1791.
The Widow of Malabar. Philadelphia: E. Story, 1792.
Stein, Roger B. "Royall Tyler and the Question of Our Speech." *New England Quarterly* 38 (1965), 454–74.
Stern, Julia. *The Plight of Feeling: Sympathy and Dissent in the Early American Novel*. University of Chicago Press, 1997.
"The State of 'Women' in *Ormond*; or, Patricide in the New Nation," in Barnard, Kamrath, and Shapiro, eds. *Revising Charles Brockden Brown*.
Strand, Ginger. "The Many Deaths of General Montgomery: Audiences and Pamphlet Plays of the Revolution." *American Literary History* 9 (1997), 1–20.

"The Theater and the Republic: Defining Party on Early Boston's Rival Stages," in Jeffrey D. Mason and J. Ellen Gainor, eds. *Performing America: Cultural Nationalism in American Theater*. Ann Arbor: University of Michigan Press, 1999.

Sword, Wiley. *President Washington's Indian War: The Struggle for the Old Northwest, 1790–1795*. Norman: University of Oklahoma Press, 1985.

Tanselle, G. Thomas. *Royall Tyler*. Cambridge, Mass.: Harvard University Press, 1967.

Taylor, Edward. *God's Determinations*, in *The Poems*, ed. Donald E. Stanford. New Haven: Yale University Press, 1960.

Teute, Fredrika J. "A 'Republic of Intellect': Conversation and Criticism among the Sexes in 1790s New York," in Barnard, Kamrath, and Shapiro, eds. *Revising Charles Brockden Brown*.

Thompson, George A., Jr. *A Documentary History of the African Theatre*. Evanston: Northwestern University Press, 1998.

Thoreau, Henry David. *Walden and Civil Disobedience*, ed. Owen Thomas. New York: Norton, 1966.

Tilton, Robert S. *Pocahontas: The Evolution of an American Narrative*. New York: Cambridge University Press, 1994.

Toll, Robert C. *Blacking Up: The Minstrel Show in Nineteenth-Century America*. New York: Oxford University Press, 1974.

Trees, Andy. "Benedict Arnold, John André, and His Three Yeoman Captors: A Sentimental Journey or American Virtue Defined." *Early American Literature* 35 (2000), 246–73.

"Trivia." *William and Mary Quarterly* 5 (1948), 396–97.

Truniger, Annelise. *Paddy and the Paycock: A Study of the Stage Irishman from Shakespeare to O'Casey*. Bern: Francke, 1976.

Tucker, George Holbert. *Norfolk Highlights 1584–1881*. Norfolk: Norfolk Historical Society, 1972.

Tucker, St. George. Papers. Special Collections, Swem Library, College of William and Mary.

Twain, Mark. *Pudd'nhead Wilson and Those Extraordinary Twins*, ed. Malcolm Bradbury. New York: Penguin, 1969.

Tyler, Royall. *The Contrast*, in Richards, ed. *Early American Drama*.

Four Plays, ed. Arthur Wallace Peach and George Floyd Newbrough. Bloomington: Indiana University Press, 1965.

Van Schreeven, William J., and Robert L. Scribner, eds. *Revolutionary Virginia, the Road to Independence*. 7 vols. Charlottesville: University Press of Virginia, 1973.

Vaughan, Alden T. "From White Man to Redskin: Changing Anglo-American Perceptions of the American Indian." *American Historical Review* 87 (1982), 917–53.

Vaughan, Alden T. and Edward W. Clark, eds. *Puritans among the Indians: Accounts of Captivity and Redemption, 1676–1724*. Cambridge, Mass.: Belknap/Harvard University Press, 1981.

Verhoeven, W. M. "Displacing the Discontinuous; Or, The Labyrinths of Reason: Fictional Design and Eighteenth-Century Thought in Charles Brockden Brown's *Ormond*," in W. M. Verhoeven, ed. *Rewriting the Dream: Reflections on the Changing American Literary Canon*. Amsterdam: Rodopi, 1992.

"'This blissful period of intellectual liberty': Transatlantic Radicalism and Enlightened Conservatism in Brown's Early Writings," in Barnard, Kamrath, and Shapiro, eds. *Revising Charles Brockden Brown*.

Villiers, George, second Duke of Buckingham. *The Rehearsal*. London: Thomas Dring, 1672.

Virga, Patricia. *The American Opera to 1790*. Ann Arbor: UMI Research Press, 1982.

Vitkus, Daniel J. "Turning Turk in *Othello*: The Conversion and Damnation of the Moor." *Shakespeare Quarterly* 48/2 (1997), 145–76.

Vivian, James F., and Jean H. Vivian. "'A Jurisdiction Competent to the Occasion': A Benjamin Rumsey Letter, June, 1776." *Maryland Historical Magazine* 67/2 (1972), 144–55.

Waldstreicher, David. *In the Midst of Perpetual Fetes: The Making of American Nationalism, 1776–1820*. Chapel Hill: University of North Carolina Press, 1997.

Warren, Mercy Otis. *The Plays and Poems of Mercy Otis Warren*, ed. Benjamin Franklin V. Delmar, N.Y.: Scholars Facsimiles, 1980.

History of the Rise, Progress and Termination of the American Revolution, ed. Lester H. Cohen, 2 vols. Indianapolis: Liberty Classics, 1988.

Waters, Maureen. *The Comic Irishman*. Albany: State University of New York Press, 1984.

Watson, Charles S. *The History of Southern Drama*. Lexington: University Press of Kentucky, 1997.

"Jeffersonian Republicanism in William Ioor's *Independence*, the First Play of South Carolina." *South Carolina Historical Magazine* 69 (1968), 194–203.

Watts, Steven. *The Romance of Real Life: Charles Brockden Brown and the Origins of American Culture*. Baltimore: Johns Hopkins University Press, 1994.

[Weddell, Mrs.?]. *Incle and Yarico, a Tragedy*. London, 1742.

Weir, Robert M. *Colonial South Carolina: A History*. Millwood, N.Y.: KTO Press, 1983.

Wertenbaker, Thomas J. *Norfolk: Historic Southern Port*. Durham, N.C.: Duke University Press, 1931.

White, Barbara A. "'Our Nig' and the She-Devil: New Information about Harriet Wilson and the 'Bellmont' Family." *American Literature* 65 (1993), 19–52.

White, Shane. *Somewhat More Independent: The End of Slavery in New York City, 1770–1810*. Athens: University of Georgia Press, 1991.

Stories of Freedom in Black New York. Cambridge, Mass.: Harvard University Press, 2002.

White, Shane, and Graham White. *Stylin': African American Expressive Culture from its Beginnings to the Zoot Suit*. Ithaca: Cornell University Press, 1998.

Wigglesworth, Michael. *The Day of Doom*, in Harrison T. Meserole, ed. *Seventeenth-Century American Poetry*. New York: Anchor, 1968.

Williams, Daniel E. "In Defense of Self: Author and Authority in the *Memoirs of Stephen Burroughs*." *Early American Literature* 25 (1990), 96–122.

Williams, William H. A. *'Twas Only an Irishman's Dream: The Image of Ireland and the Irish in American Popular Song Lyrics, 1800–1920*. Urbana: University of Illinois Press, 1996.

Willis, Eola. *The Charleston Stage in the XVIII Century*. 1933; New York: Blom, 1968.

Wilmer, S. E. *Theatre, Society and the Nation: Staging American Identities*. Cambridge: Cambridge University Press, 2002.
Wilmeth, Don B., and Christopher Bigsby, eds. *The Cambridge History of American Theatre*, 3 vols. Cambridge: Cambridge University Press, 1998–2000.
Wilson, David A. *United Irishmen, United States: Immigrant Radicals in the Early Republic*. Ithaca: Cornell University Press, 1998.
Wilson, Harriet E. *Our Nig; or, Sketches from the Life of a Free Black*, ed. Henry Louis Gates, Jr. New York: Vintage, 1983.
Wirt, William. Papers. Maryland Historical Society.
Wittke, Carl. *The Irish in America*. Baton Rouge: Louisiana State University Press, 1956.
  Tambo and Bones – A History of the American Minstrel Stage. Durham, N.C.: Duke University Press, 1930.
Wolter, Jürgen. 'Die Helden der Nation: Yankee, Pionier und Indianer als nationale Stereotypen im amerikanischen Drama vor dem Bürgerkrieg." *Amerika-studien* 24 (1979), 246–63.
Woodworth, Samuel. *The Forest Rose; or, American Farmers*, in Moody, ed. *Dramas from the American Theatre*.
Yearling, Elizabeth M. 'Cumberland, Foote, and the Stage Creole." *Notes and Queries* (UK) 25 (1978), 59–60.
  'The Good-Natured Heroes of Cumberland, Goldsmith, and Sheridan." *Modern Language Review* 67 (1972), 490–500.
  'Victims of Society in Three Plays by Cumberland." *Durham University Journal* 43 (1981), 23–26.
Yoklavich, John. Editorial introduction, *The Battle of Alcazar* by George Peele, in Prouty, *et al.*, eds. *Life and Works*, vol. II.
Young, Alfred F. *Masquerade: The Life and Times of Deborah Sampson, Continental Soldier*. New York: Knopf, 2004.
Young, William C. *Famous Actors and Actresses: Documents of American Theater History*, 2 vols. New York: Bowker, 1975.
Zipes, Jack. 'Dunlap, Kotzebue, and the Shaping of American Theater: A Re-evaluation from a Marxist Perspective.' *Early American Literature* 8 (1974), 272–89.

Index

Abd el-Malik, 155–57, 161, 186
Adams, John, 89, 121
Adams, Samuel, 105
Addison, Joseph,
   Cato, 14, 60, 86, 127, 151, 253, 254, 270, 296
African, stage type, 8, 9, 24–25, 25–27, 49,
   50–51, 70–71, 100, 176, 198, 214, 215, 218–25,
   227–28, 235, 249, 270–75
African Americans, 26–27, 71–74, 225–26, 249,
   269–70, 314
   In theatre, 217, 224, 236, 265. *See also* African
      Theatre; Hewlett, James
African Burial Ground, 225
African Company. *See* African Theatre
African Theatre (N.Y., founded *c*. 1801), 211–12,
   236
African Theatre (N.Y., founded 1821), 71–74,
   76, 82, 212–13, 236
Africanism, 214, 216, 230
Ahmed el-Mansur, 155, 156, 157
Aickin, Francis, 158
Aiken, George
   Uncle Tom's Cabin, 31, 229
Alexandria (Va.) theatre, 262
Alien and Sedition Acts, 128, 135
American Company of Comedians, 89, 148, 192.
   See also Old American Company
American Heroine, The (various productions),
   286
American identity, 16, 244, 246, 257
Anderson, Benedict, 5
André, John, 100, 124, 290
Arnold, Benedict, 124, 126, 134
Arnould, Jean-François
   Death of Captain Cook, The, 266
   Fôret Noire, La, 275, 278

Audin, Anthony, 289

Bacon's Rebellion, 118
Barker, James Nelson, 169, 203, 314
   Indian Princess, The, 9, 169–73, 176, 194–95,
   203–8, 236, 267, 277, 288
Barker, John, 169
Barthelemy, Anthony, 154
Barton, Andrew. *See* Forrest, Thomas
Bastille, fall of, 81
Battle of Brooklyn, The, 25, 37, 56
Bayezid I, 146
Bear and the Cub, The, 20
Beattie's Ford, N. C., 67
Beaumont, Francis
   Rule a Wife and Have a Wife, 279
Beebe, Abner, 111
Beete, John, 288
   Man of the Times, The, 30, 264, 288
Behn, Aphra, 40
   Round-heads, The, 149
   Rover, The, 118
   Widow Ranter, The, 75, 118, 173
Bernard, John, 307, 310
Bickerstaff, Isaac, 252, 263
   Love in a Village, 279
   Love in the City. See Romp, The
   Padlock, The, 9, 26, 70, 71, 217, 270
   Romp, The, 217, 227, 271, 274
   Spoiled Child, The, 74, 271
   Sultan, The, 154, 267
   Thomas and Sally, 279, 283, 315
Bignall, Ann West, 261, 262, 289, 292
Bignall, Harriet West, 274
Bignall, Isaac, 262, 274, 278, 284, 292
Bignall, John, 259, 261

INDEX

Blakey, Michael, 225
Blockheads, The, 13
Boston Theatre Company, 307, 308
Boucicault, Dion, 93, 188
  Octoroon, The, 232
Bourgeois, Maurice, 189
Brackenridge, Hugh Henry, 10, 37, 58, 129
  Death of Montgomery, The, 124
Bradshaw, Mrs., 74
Bray, John, 169
British, stage types, 279. *See also* Scot, stage type
British identity, 18, 189
British military theatre, 148
Brooke, Frances
  Rosina, 29, 173, 190, 215, 276, 278, 279, 280–81
Brooke, Henry
  Gustavus Vasa, 253–54
Brown, Charles Brockden, 136, 243
  Edgar Huntly, 166
  Ormond, 11, 242–43, 243–58, 314
Brown, John
  Barbarossa; or, The Fall of the Tyrant of Algiers, 266
Brown, Richard Maxwell, 111
Brown, William Alexander, 212
  King Shotaway, 212
Brown, William Hill
  West Point Preserved, 128, 290
Burgoyne, John, 148, 149–50, 299
Burk, John Daly, 201, 202
  Bunker-Hill, or The Death of General Warren, 85–86, 88, 99, 104, 124, 264, 288–89
  Female Patriotism, 75
Burroughs, Stephen, 7, 245
Burton, Jonathan, 156
Byrd, William, II, 20

Calhoon, Robert, 110
Calvinism, in drama, 20, 52, 53
Canary, Robert, 125
Carey, Henry
  Honest Yorkshire Man, The, 247
Carey, Mathew, 89, 202
Carlson, David, 39
Centlivre, Susanna, 21, 252
Cervantes, Miguel de, 26
Chalmers, James, 294
Chardin, Jean-Baptiste-Siméon, 45
Charlestown Academy (N.H.), 299

Cheer, Margaret, 148
Chestnut Street Theatre (Philadelphia), 250, 251
Chrysostom, John, 30
Churchill, Charles
  "The Rosciad,", 306–7, 311
Cibber, Colley, 252
  Provoked Husband, The, 279
Coad, Oral, 228
Colman, George, Jr., 252
  Africans, The, 217
  Blue-Beard, 145
  Inkle and Yarico, 8, 9, 173–77, 180, 182, 184, 217, 227, 236, 252, 271, 275, 286
  Mountaineers, The, 264, 266–67, 276, 278
Colman, George, Sr., 188, 252
committees of safety, 45, 105–23, 243
Constitution, American, celebration of, 80
Continental Association, 105, 108
Continental Congress, 19, 105, 113, 114, 148, 150
Conway, Moncure, 30
Cooper, Anthony Ashley, Earl of Shaftesbury, 132
Cooper, Thomas Abthorpe, 129, 212, 291, 307, 309–10
Copeland, Mr., 273
Cornwallis, Charles, Lord, 67
Corry, Miss, 293–94
Covent Garden (Theatre Royal, London), 74, 75
Cowpens (S. C.), Battle of, 67
Crain, Caleb, 133
Crèvecoeur, Michel Guillaume Jean de (J. Hector St. John de), 9, 10, 38, 55, 105, 109, 138
  "History of Mrs. B., The," 48
  "Landscapes," 38–40, 40–41, 43–59, 50–51, 64, 71, 106, 111, 112–14, 120, 122–23, 235
  Letters from an American Farmer, 38–39, 41–43, 45, 49, 54, 55, 58, 95, 107, 114, 196
Crockett, Davy, 234
Cromwell, Oliver, 149
Cross, John C.
  Death of Captain Cook, The, 266
  Purse, The, 11, 264, 284–86, 315
cross-dressing, 75, 163, 164, 173, 184, 293–94
Cumberland, Richard, 3, 89, 93, 102, 197
  Jew, The, 162, 268
  West Indian, The, 3, 29, 75, 89–90, 92–99, 100–1, 102, 104, 105, 197, 201, 217, 252, 271, 276, 278

Darley, Ellen Westray, 307, 311, 312
Darley, John, 310
Davis, John, 171, 180
  Captain Smith and Princess Pocahontas, 170
  First Settlers of Virginia, The, 170
Davis, Peter, 19
Dawes, Rufus, 174
Death of Major André, The (various pantomimes), 264, 293
Death of Major André, and Arnold's Treachery, or West Point Preserved, The, 290
Delpini, Carlo
  Don Juan, 71
Dennie, Joseph, 78, 83, 301
Dermot and Kathleen, 74
Dibdin, Charles
  Wapping Landlady, The, 284
  Waterman, The, 284
Dibdin, Thomas John
  Jew and the Doctor, The, 268, 269
Diderot, Denis, 45
Dimond, William
  Aethiop, The, 217
Dircks, Richard, 102
Dixon, Miss, 72
Douglass, David, 20, 148, 191, 192
Douglass, Frederick, 232
Downfall of Justice, The, 24–28, 48, 49, 51, 59, 71, 218, 220, 235
Dryden, John
  Don Sebastian, 155, 157–59, 162
  Indian Queen, The, 173
Dunlap, William, 3, 31, 78, 82, 85, 89, 128, 136, 138, 169, 172, 244, 251, 264, 294
  André, 10, 124–27, 128–38, 264, 290
  Darby's Return, 63, 78–82, 83, 87, 126, 193
  Father, or American Shandyism, The, 78
  Glory of Columbia, Her Yeomanry!, The, 10, 125, 138, 193, 293
  History of the American Theatre, 81, 96
  Trip to Niagara, A, 193
  Yankee Chronology, 193
Durang, John, 63, 273

Easter Holidays; or, A Trip to Lindsay's Gardens, 288
Elizabeth I, 155, 156, 168
El-Ksar el-Kebir, Battle of, 155, 157
Ellison, Julie, 132
erotics of power, 168, 180–87

ethnicity on stage, 8–11, 22–28, 70, 101, 190, 236, 265
  See also under separate stage types (e.g., Irish)
Eyre, Edmund John
  Maid of Normandy, The, 275

Faery, Rebecca, 184
Falconi, Signior Joseph, 275
Famous Historye of the life and death of Captaine Thomas Stukeley, 157, 160
Farquhar, George, 21, 87
  Beaux' Stratagem, The, 87, 279
  Recruiting Officer, The, 117
Fawcett, John
  Obi, or Three Fingered Jack, 212, 217
Federal Orrery, The, 285
Federal Street Theatre (Boston), 70, 86, 89, 102, 107, 300, 301, 308, 310
Fletcher, John
  Rule a Wife and Have a Wife, 279
Fliegelman, Jay, 126
Foote, Samuel, 40
  Lyar, The, 264
Forrest, Thomas
  Disappointment, The, 191–93, 247
Foster, Hannah Webster
  Coquette, The, 242, 304
Fox, Gilbert, 307
Foxe, John, 20
Francis, William, 74
Franklin, Benjamin, 7, 31, 246, 302
French, stage type, 33, 71, 275–76
Fried, Michael, 45
Friendly Club, 133, 135, 251

Gage, Thomas, 149
Gallagher, Kent, 198
Gannett, Deborah Sampson, 75, 256, 294
Garrick, David, 87, 89, 279, 300, 305, 306
  Catherine and Petruchio, 263
  Irish Widow, The, 190, 198, 207, 276
  Jubilee, The, 204
  Miss in Her Teens: or, the Medley of Lovers, 116, 117
Garrison, William Lloyd, 232
George III, 151, 247
Godwin, William
  Caleb Williams, 244
Goethe, Johann Wolfgang von, 174
Goldsmith, Oliver, 98
  Good-Natur'd Man, The, 94

Goring, Paul, 191, 209
Green, Frances Willems, 262
Green, John William, 23–24, 67, 249, 262, 285, 287, 289, 291
Greuze, Jean-Baptiste, 45
Grimsted, David, 214
Grove Theatre (N.Y.), 202
Guilford Court House, N.C., 67

Habib, Imtiaz, 219
Hallam, W. Tuke, 137
Hallam, Lewis, Jr., 9, 33, 81, 89, 137, 148, 217, 220
Hallam, Lewis, Sr., 20
Hamilton, Marlborough, 278
Harris, Sharon, 96
Harris, Thomas, 66
Harvey, Karen, 66
Hatton, Ann Julia Kemble
    Tammany; or, The Indian Chief, 166
Hawthorne, Nathaniel, 233
    Blithedale Romance, The, 242
    Scarlet Letter, The, 242
Haymarket Theatre (Boston), 86, 301, 306, 308
Henry, Ann Storer, 148, 167
Henry, John, 33, 61, 74, 81, 89, 148
Henslowe, Philip, 157
Hewlett, James, 72, 74, 76, 212–13, 235
Heywood, Thomas
    Faire Maid of the West, Part I, 157, 159, 160, 161
    Faire Maid of the West, Part II, 157, 160
Hill, Aaron
    Zara, 145–53, 161
Hill, George Handel, 229
Hoare, Prince
    No Song, No Supper, 264, 279, 281, 283
Hodge, Francis, 216–17, 229
Hodgkinson, John, 129, 137, 285, 290, 305
Holcroft, Thomas
    Deserted Daughter, 279
Home, John
    Douglas, 69, 279
homosociality, 130, 132, 134, 137, 171, 293
Howe, John, 7
Howe, William, 149
Hughes, Joseph, 293
Humphreys, David
    Widow of Malabar, The, 166–68, 172, 175, 181, 182, 251
Hutchinson, Thomas, 13, 37, 110, 111, 149

identity, 4, 6–8, 17–33, 74, 134, 138, 161
imitation, 21, 31, 91, 103–4, 246, 252, 258
imperialism, 184
Inchbald, Elizabeth, 252, 263
    Animal Magnetism, 264, 275
    Every One Has His Fault, 76
    Mogul Tale, The, 266, 267, 286, 315. See also *Norfolk Cobler, The*
Indians, 166. See also Native Americans and South Asians
Ioor, William, 4
    Independence, 4
Ireland, Owen, 44
Irish, stage type, 8, 33, 62, 65–66, 70, 71, 80, 93, 100–1, 186, 188–210, 275, 276–79, 280, 288
Irving, Washington, 144
    "Rip Van Winkle," 21, 181
Islamic character. See Muslim, stage type
Italian, stage type, 275

Jean De Saintré, 275
Jefferson, Thomas, 211, 279
Jerningham, Edward, 174
Jew, stage type, 5, 8, 163, 191, 268–69
John Street Theatre (N.Y.), 29, 60, 62, 64, 148, 152, 301
Johnson, John, 113
Johnson, Mary Watts, 113
Jones, Eugene, 187
Jones, Thomas, 113

Kafer, Peter, 243
Kean, Edmund, 212
Kelly, Hugh
    Love-a-la-Mode; or, the Humours of the Turf, 291
Kemble, John Philip
    Farm House, The, 280
Kenna, J., 287
    Land of Liberty; or, A Trip to the Charleston Races, 287
Kenna, Mrs., 74
Kolodny, Annette, 184
Kosok, Heinz, 66
Kotzebue, August von, 4, 126
    Stranger, The, 4, 264, 266

La Bree, Lawrence
    Ebenezer Venture, 231
Lailson's Circus (Philadelphia), 290

Leacock, John
   Fall of British Tyranny, The, 25, 37, 40, 50
Lee, Nathaniel
   Lucius Junius Brutus, 128
Lemay, J. A. Leo, 184
Le Mierre, A.-M.
   Veuve du Malabar, La, 167
liberty, 253–56
Liberty, representation of, 76, 151
Ligon, Richard, 174, 175
Lillo, George
   London Merchant, The, 252
Lloyd, Robert,
   "The Actor," 305–6, 311
Low, Samuel
   Politician Out-witted, The, 152–53
Lusignan, King Henri II, 146

Macklin, Charles, 191
   Irish Fine Lady, The. See *True Born Irishman, The*
   Love a-la-Mode, 190, 191, 197, 247, 276
   True Born Irishman, The, 190, 208
McCartey, John, 110
McConachie, Bruce, 178
McCrea, Jane, 48
Macready, William
   Irishman in London, The, 190, 217, 227, 274–75, 276
   Village Lawyer, The, 280
Mann, Herman, 256
Marble, Danforth, 229
Marlowe, Christopher
   Tamburlaine, Parts I and II, 155
Marriott, Sarah, 32, 287
   Chimera, The, 31–32, 264, 287
   Land We Live In; or The Death of Major André, The, 290
Maryland Council of Safety, 106
masculinity, 132, 134, 181
Mason, Jeffrey, 181
Massinger, Philip, 144
   New Way to Pay Old Debts, A, 279
Matar, Nabil, 162, 168, 176
Mathews, Charles, 212, 214
Mays, David, 192
Melford, Miss, 293
Melville, Herman
   Confidence Man, The, 242
   Moby-Dick, 242

Menken, Adah Isaacs, 294
Meschianza, 60
Meserve, Walter, 227, 229
miles gloriosus, 204
Miller, James
   Mahomet the Imposter, 155
Milns, William, 224
Minshull, John
   Rural Felicity, 202–3, 208
M'Kenzie, Daniel, 264, 269
Mohammed, Prince of Morocco, 155, 156
Moncrieff, William Thomas
   Tom and Jerry; or Life in London, 212
Montaigne, Michel de, 157
Montgomery, Richard, 124, 302
Moody, John, 93
Moody, Richard, 213, 226
Moor, stage type, 23, 160, 168, 267, 270. See also Muslim, stage type, and Turk, stage type
Moore, Dennis, 46
Moore, Edward
   Gamester, The, 40, 68, 252
Moreton, John Pollard, 129
Morgan, Daniel, 67
Morris, Shadrick, 110
Morrison, Toni
   Playing in the Dark, 214–15, 230
Morton, Thomas, 263
   Cure for the Heart-Ache, A, 271, 279, 282–83
   Zorinski, 266, 278
Motley Assembly, The, 13
Mowatt, Anna Cora, 30
   Fashion, 29, 231
   Mimic Life, 242
Muly Molocco, 157
Munford, Robert, 10, 107
   Candidates, The, 107
   Patriots, The, 106, 107, 114–19, 120, 122–23, 247
Murad III, 156
Murdock, John, 12, 193, 314
   Beau Metamorphized, 224
   Politicians, The, 217, 224
   Triumphs of Love, The, 195, 198, 201, 207, 208, 217, 222–24, 235
Murphy, Arthur, 89
   Citizen, The, 23
Murray, Judith Sargent, 3, 10, 14, 46, 90, 105, 137, 138, 172, 190, 301, 307, 314
   African, The, 88

"Desultory Thoughts upon the Utility of encouraging a degree of Self-Complacency, especially in Female Bosoms," 103
Gleaner, The, 89, 90–91, 96
Medium; or Happy Tea Party, The. See *Virtue Triumphant*
"Reverence Thy Self," 103
Traveller Returned, The, 3, 86, 87–88, 92, 106, 107, 119–23, 124, 154, 194–95, 197–201, 202, 208
Virtue Triumphant, 87, 96
Muslim, stage type, 5, 8, 79, 143–45, 150, 151, 154, 164, 165, 182, 236, 266–68
Myers, Eliza Judah Chapman, 268
Myers, Moses, 268, 269

Nathans, Heather, 4, 85, 193
national character, 244–48, 265, 285, 314
Native American, stage type, 8, 9, 166, 176, 205, 236
Native Americans, 6, 27–28, 166, 168, 175, 182, 186
nautical drama, 283–86
Nelson, Dana, 137
New Theatre (Philadelphia). See Chestnut Street Theatre
Newhampshire and Vermont Journal, The, 304
Norfolk Cobler, The, 286–87
Norfolk Herald, The, 261, 277, 286, 291
Norfolk theatre, 259–95

O'Keeffe, John, 2, 61, 83, 158, 173, 252
  Agreeable Surprise, The, 63
  Basket Maker, The, 71
  "Darby & Patrick," 69
  'Definitive Treaty, A," 66–67, 79
  Farmer, The, 280
  Highland Reel, The, 13, 264, 272–74, 279
  Patrick in Prussia, or, Love in a Camp, 63, 77, 79, 190, 198
  Peeping Tom of Coventry, 63
  Poor Soldier, The, 2, 61–65, 65–66, 67–78, 87, 93, 105, 138, 190, 193, 198, 264, 276, 279, 293, 315
  Son-in-Law, The, 63, 293
  Young Quaker, The, 71, 272
Old American Company, 61, 74, 89, 125, 137, 152, 167, 250, 251, 273
Oliver, Peter, 111

O'Neill, Eugene, 209
Ottoman Empire, 146, 155, 186
Otway, Thomas
  Venice Preserved, 4, 127–31, 132, 133, 134, 136, 138, 253, 254–55, 279

"Paddy Bull's Expedition," 190
"Paddy O'Blarney," 190
Paine, Robert Treat, 88
Park Theatre (N.Y.), 71, 73, 126, 145, 224, 236
Parke, John, 129
Peele, George
  Battle of Alcazar, The, 155, 156, 157, 160, 164
Péladeau, Marius, 298
Perkins, Mr., 292
Petersburg theatre, 262
Philip II, 155
Pilon, Frederick
  Fair American, The, 95
Placide, Alexander
  Death of Major André; or West Point Preserved, The, 290
Pocahontas, 168, 169, 179. See also Barker, James, *Indian Princess, The*
Polyanthos, 310
Powell, Elizabeth Harrison, 307, 308, 312
Powell, Snelling, 307
Presbyterians, 43
providential stage, 7
Pry, Kevin, 66
Purchas, Samuel, 183

Quakers, 243
  in drama, 54–55

race, 180, 249
racism, 214, 228, 234
Ragussis, Michael, 190
Rawdon, Francis, Lord, 149
Reed, Richard, 110
Reinagle, Alexander, 251, 276
renegade, stage type, 162–63, 164
Republican Mother, 98, 137
Republicanism, 165
resistance, 91
Restoration drama, 135
Revolution, American, 37, 40, 44, 60, 63, 76, 80, 85, 87, 88, 92, 108, 114, 121, 122, 124, 126, 138, 288, 302
Revolution, French, 121, 255

Reynolds, Frederick, 252, 263
   Dramatist, The, 276, 315
   Fortune's Fool, 279
Richardson, Gary, 126
Ricketts' Circus (Philadelphia), 290
Riffets, Mr., 273
Rinehart, Lucy, 136
Roach, Joseph, 63
Robbins, Luke, 289
Robinson, J.
   Yorker's Stratagem, The, 217, 221–22, 230, 251
Rosenthal, Bernard, 244
Rousseau, Jean-Jacques, 177
   Confessions, 178
Rowe, Nicholas, 21
   Fair Penitent, The, 40, 253
   Jane Shore, 253
   Tamerlane, 146, 147, 162, 182
Rowlandson, Mary, 18
Rowson, Susanna, 22, 33, 143, 148, 172
   Female Patriot, The, 144
   Reuben and Rachel, 166
   Slaves in Algiers, 5, 22, 23, 75, 97, 143–45, 153–54, 158, 159–65, 166, 167, 182, 251, 267, 268

Saad, House of, 155, 186
Saar, Doreen, 49
Said, Edward, 151, 155
Saillant, John, 227
Sans Souci, 13
Santo Domingo, 70
sati, 167
Scheckel, Susan, 170
Schuyler, George, 216
Scot, as stage type, 115–16, 191, 247
Sebastian, King of Portugal, 155, 161
Seeber, Jacob, 109
Seelye, John, 183
Sewall, Jonathan, 25, 42
Shadwell, Thomas
   Woman Captain, The, 75
Shakespeare, William, 125, 264, 300, 306
   As You Like It, 178, 263
   Hamlet, 252
   Macbeth, 252, 263
   Merchant of Venice, The, 162
   Othello, 71, 252, 270
   Richard III, 265
   Romeo and Juliet, 266
   Taming of the Shrew, The, 206. *See also* Garrick, David, *Catherine and Petruchio*
   Tempest, The, 173, 184
   Titus Andronicus, 154
Sheridan, Richard Brinsley, 2, 87, 98, 126
   Critic, The, 89, 263, 275
   Robinson Crusoe, 217
   School for Scandal, The, 2, 29, 87, 94, 263
Sheridan, Thomas
   Brave Irishman; or Captain O'Blunder, The, 192, 197
Shield, William, 61, 79
Shields, David, 122
Siege of Quebec, The, 275
Silsbee, Joshua, 229
slavery, 22, 165, 283
Smith, Captain John, 168, 170, 171. *See also* Barker, James Nelson, *Indian Princess, The*
   Generall Historie of Virginia, The, 169, 171, 181, 182
   True Travels, The, 186, 205
Smith, Elihu Hubbard, 31, 83, 125, 136, 251
Smith, William Henry
   Drunkard, The, 30
Snipe, Simon (pseud.), 72, 74
social class, 102, 122, 123
Sollee, John, 288
South Asian, stage character, 167, 168, 175
Southwark Theatre (Philadelphia), 250, 251
Spoiled Child, The, 74
stage as community, 6
Stanhope, Philip, Lord Chesterfield, 99
Starke, Mariana
   Widow of Malabar, The, 167, 175, 252
Steele, Richard, 174
Stern, Julia, 248, 249, 257
Stone, John Augustus
   Metamora, 181
Stowe, Harriet Beecher, 31
Strand, Ginger, 12
Stuart, John, Earl of Bute, 247
Stukeley, Thomas, 157
Sully, Chester, 284
Sully, Matthew, Jr., 284
Sully, Matthew, Sr., 262, 265, 284, 292
supranationality, 248, 250, 254, 256, 314

Tarleton, Banastre, 67
tavern, as scene, 66
Taylor, Edward, 19

Taylor, Mr., 292
textual alterations, 69, 78, 81
theatre as metaphor, 7, 20
theatricality in novel, 241–42
Thompson, George, 71
Thoreau, Henry David, 29
Tilton, Robert, 170, 179, 183
tories, 111, 112, 113, 117
transatlanticism, 4, 90, 95, 104, 245
transnationality, in theatre, 67
Treaty of Paris, 151
Tripolitan Prize, The, 144
Tripolitan War, 145
Trumbull, Harriet, 211
Trumbull, Maria, 211
Tucker, St. George, 11–12, 62
Turk, stage type, 79, 151, 168, 186, 205, 236
Turks, 146
Turnbull, Gavin, 286, 287, 292
Twain, Mark
  Pudd'nhead Wilson, 215, 236
Twaites (pseud.), 72–73, 74
Twaits, William, 72, 307, 310, 311
Tyler, John Steele, 300
Tyler, Royall, 1, 14, 87, 129, 172, 305
  Bay Boy, The, 296
  Contrast, The, 1, 2, 3, 28–29, 30, 31, 33, 60, 61, 63, 63–64, 66, 68, 69, 70, 77–78, 79, 81, 82, 83, 85, 87, 92, 98, 101, 102, 105, 126, 152, 208, 213, 215, 218–19, 231, 264, 287, 297–99, 301, 302, 303, 304, 308, 312, 315
  May Day in Town, 9, 71, 219–21, 235
  Poems, 297–314

Valley Forge, 60
Verhoeven, Wil, 246
Villiers, George, Duke of Buckingham
  Rehearsal, The, 117
Virginia Company, 261–94
Voltaire, 146
  Mahomet, 155
  Zaïre, 145, 147

Waldstreicher, David, 5, 6
Wall, Thomas, 148, 150, 151
Wall–Ryan Company, 89
Wardrobe, David, 110
Warrell, Mrs., 74
Warren, Joseph, 124, 139, 302

Warren, Mercy Otis, 10, 13–14, 16, 25, 40, 58, 89, 121, 129
  Adulateur, The, 37
  Defeat, The, 37
  Group, The, 14, 37, 47, 124
  Ladies of Castile, The, 14
  History of the Rise, Progress, and Termination of the American Revolution, 106
Warwick, Anthony, 111
Washington, George, 79, 80, 81, 87, 88, 95, 99, 103, 119, 124, 138, 151, 156, 167, 290, 292, 302
Watts, Mr., 292
Watts, Steven, 246
Weddell, Mrs., 175
West, Ann West Bignall. *See* Bignall, Ann West
West, James, 262, 273, 287
West, Margaretta Sully, 259, 261, 262, 265, 274, 286, 287, 291
West, Thomas C., 262, 291
West, Thomas Wade, 259, 261, 262, 268, 273, 286, 287, 289
West Indian, stage type, 96
West Indies, 252
whigs, 48, 111, 113, 117, 151
White, Alexander, 109
White, Shane, 71, 73, 74, 227
Whitefield, George, 52
Whiteness, 214, 235. *See also* Woodworth, Samuel, *Forest Rose, The*
Whittier, John Greenleaf, 232
Wigglesworth, Michael, 19
Wignell, Thomas, 33, 61, 77, 79, 250, 251, 262
Williams, Mrs., 72, 73
Williams, William, 196
Williamsburg (Va.) theatre, 241
Williamson, Mrs., 74
Wilson, David, 202
Wilson, Harriet
  Our Nig; or Sketches from the Life of a Free Black, 234
Winstanley, John, 174
woman, identity as, 47–49, 51, 74–76, 96, 97, 136, 164, 171–72, 187, 294, 303–5, 311–12
Woodham, Mrs., 74
Woodworth, Samuel
  The Forest Rose, or, American Farmers, 9, 10, 27, 209, 213–14, 215–17, 226–29, 230–33

Woodworth, Samuel (cont.)
   Widow's Son; or, Which Is the Traitor?, The, 217
Workman, James
   Liberty in Louisiana, 288

Yale College, 89

Yankee, stage type, 33, 64, 82, 101, 198, 208, 216–17, 227, 227–29, 231, 232, 233, 234, 235, 284
Yearling, Elizabeth, 94
Yorkshireman, stage type, 33
Yorktown, Battle of, 151

argument 2, 4, 7, 11, 33, 144,
method 15
melodrama 46